CODES+ISSS 2003

First IEEE/ACM/IFIP International Conference on Hardware/Software Codesign & System Synthesis

Photo credit: Copyright © 2003 Newport Beach Conference & Visitors Bureau. For educational purpose only.

Newport Beach, California, USA • October 1-3, 2003

Co-Sponsored by

SIGBED SIGSOFT IEEE Computer Society SIGDA

Supported by

SYNOPSYS CONEXANT IBM Allied Telesyn CoWare XILINX

The Association for Computing Machinery
1515 Broadway
New York, New York 10036

Notice to Past Authors of ACM-Published Articles

ACM intends to create a complete electronic archive of all articles and/or other material previously published by ACM. If you have written a work that has been previously published by ACM in any journal or conference proceedings prior to 1978, or any SIG Newsletter at any time, and you do NOT want this work to appear in the ACM Digital Library, please inform permissions@acm.org, stating the title of the work, the author(s), and where and when published.

ISBN: 1-58113-742-7

IEEE Catalog Number: 03TH8721

Additional copies may be ordered prepaid from:

ACM Order Department
PO Box 11405
New York, NY 10286-1405

Phone: 1-800-342-6626
(US and Canada)
+1-212-626-0500
(all other countries)
Fax: +1-212-944-1318
E-mail: acmhelp@acm.org

ACM Order Number 477039
Printed in the USA

Message from the Chairs

Welcome to CODES+ISSS 2003!

After over a year of preparation and hard work on the part of the organizing committee and the program committee, it is our great pleasure to introduce you the technical program of the *First International IEEE/ACM/IFIP Conference on Hardware/Software Co-design and System Synthesis.* This conference represents the unification of the erstwhile CODES and ISSS communities. Both the International Symposium on Hardware/Software Codesign (CODES) and the International Symposium on System Synthesis (ISSS) have been active forums with over a decade of continuous community participation and technical community building in all aspects of embedded systems hardware and software. During this period, the community also saw the emergence of a number of new forums examining specific related areas: from compilers/architectures (CASES), software (EMSOFT) to validation and testing (HLDVT). These forums are a living testament to a growing thriving community in embedded systems.

Being the oldest forums, CODES and ISSS represented the greatest momentum as reflected by the number of submissions and attendee participation. There was also a great sense of camaraderie between the two communities: over one-third of technical program committee members in one forum could also be found in the other one. As an acknowledgment of this relationship between the two forums, we started an email discussion in May 2002 on the possibility of co-locating the two events. What followed the initial email was a torrential discussion on various possibilities including the merger of two events into creating *the* primary event in embedded systems design. This discussion led to a thorough examination of the effectiveness of each of the two forums and the possibility of leveraging these into creating a single forum that would reflect the best and brightest of the technical advances in the broad areas of embedded systems and system-level design. This forum – it was envisioned – would provide the greatest meeting point for industry and academia looking to make a direct impact on the industry practice in system design. Following open meetings at DAC and ISSS in 2002, we converged on the guidelines and organizing committee for the new forum. A "transition committee" of the CODES and ISSS volunteers was set up to guide the merger process and the formation of the new community. Two separate polls were conducted to gather detailed community feedback on substantive issues, such as the scope of the meeting, the structure of the meeting and, of course, the naming for the new event. We reached consensus on almost all items, though we decided to postpone the invention of a new name for the meeting in favor of the more straightforward CODES+ISSS.

As you attend the conference program and read through these proceedings, we are confident that one thing would be abundantly clear: the new combined event is much greater than the sum of the parts. This is reflected in many ways from the breadth of the program, and the depth of presentations to the diversity of the conference attendees and its sponsors. The CODES+ISSS call for papers received 143 full submissions. The TPC led by TPC Co-Chairs, Alex Orailoglu and Pai Chou, organized the massive review process where on an average each paper received 5 *substantial* reviews (on an average 3-4 pages of reviews for each paper). Each of the submitted papers went through a close scrutiny of the reviews received and the overall reviewer opinion. A subset of the papers – composed of the papers that were evaluated to be marginal and/or exhibiting excessive divergence in reviewer opinions – was selected for a newly introduced rebuttal process. The authors were invited to read the reviews and respond to specific questions prior to the program committee meeting. An *ad hoc* subcommittee with program committee members outside the original reviewers subsequently examined the reviews and the rebuttal to make a recommendation to the whole Program Committee for each such paper. Following a marathon 11-hour TPC meeting in early June 2003, held under the strictest code of conduct on conflict of interest rules, the committee identified, based on the perceived strength of the technical contribution, 30 regular papers. Four more papers that were perceived to be highly innovative were additionally selected for presentation in an "innovative work-in-progress" session. We are convinced that the collection of papers selected represents substantial advances in theory or in practice in the area of embedded systems, and hope that you would agree with our assessment.

The CODES+ISSS conference this year also features a workshop, named ESTIMedia or the First Workshop on Embedded Systems for Real-Time Multimedia. This workshop is a result of our efforts to enhance the academia-industry participation by providing opportunities for discussions on specific application areas. The ESTIMedia workshop will provide a venue for bringing together experts in multimedia systems design, theory and practice. Under the leadership of ESTIMedia general chair, Hiroto Yasuura and technical program chairs Gerhard Fohler and Radu Marculescu, the response to ESTIMedia call for papers has been tremendous. This first workshop received 38 submissions, many of very high quality. This is clearly a testament to the importance of this emerging topic area. We thank Petru Eles for driving the process of workshop selection and its organization. We hope to welcome additional workshops and synergistic events like ESTIMedia, in the future.

An ambitious conference such as CODES+ISSS'03 could not have come about without the help and support from a large number of volunteers and supporters. Foremost among them are the transition committee members (listed on a separate page) who generously gave their time and worked with the conference organizers in providing timely and measured guidance that allowed us to keep the conference charter broad and in step with the exciting developments in the area. We thank our corporate supporters for their participation and financial support that makes various elements of the conference social program, awards and student participation possible. We sincerely thank our conference managers MP Associates for their help with conference logistics, Adrienne Griscti at ACM, Lisa Tolles at Sheridan Printing, and Kathy Preas at ACM/SIGDA for their support in putting together the conference proceedings and CD-ROMs. Our special thanks to Melanie Sanders for organizing the weekly committee meetings of the conference organizers and providing timely meeting minutes to a large number of volunteers. Finally, but most importantly, our sincere thanks to you, the conference attendee, for your participation and in making all this effort worthwhile.

As we close, we would like to express our wishes that you will all find CODES+ISSS not only highly informative and valuable but also enjoyable. We hope that you will have a chance to enjoy the beautiful Newport Beach area and its weather this October. We look forward to welcoming you to Newport Beach this year and also hope to see you in Sweden in 2004!

Rajesh Gupta
Yukihiro Nakamura
General Co-Chairs

Pai Chou
Alex Orailoglu
Technical Program Co-Chairs

Table of Contents

Keynote Talk

Chair: R. Gupta *(University of California, San Diego)*

Invited Session A: Industry Best Practices and Upcoming Challenges in Embedded Software and Hardware

Chair: R. Camposano *(Synopsys)*

Invited Session B: Challenges and New Directions in On-Chip Communication

Chairs: S. Hu *(University of Notre Dame)*, J. Henkel *(NEC)*

Panel 1

Organizers: R. Bergamaschi *(IBM T. J. Watson Research Center)*, G. Martin *(Cadence Berkeley Labs)*

Invited Talk

Chair: D. Gajski *(University of California. Irvine)*

Panel 2

Organizer: N. Dutt *(University of California. Irvine)*

Session 3A: System Modeling

Chairs: L. Lavagno *(Politecnico di Torino)*, R. Marculescu *(Carnegie Mellon University)*

CODES+ISSS'03 Organization

General Co-chair
Rajesh Gupta,
University of California, San Diego, USA

General Co-chair
Yukihiro Nakamura,
Kyoto University, Japan

Program Co-chair
Alex Orailoglu,
University of California, San Diego, USA

Program Co-chair
Pai H. Chou,
University of California, Irvine, USA

Past Chair
(ISSS) Mostapha Aboulhamid,
University of Montreal, Canada

Past Chair
(CODES) Sharon Hu,
University of Notre Dame, USA

Past Chair
(CODES) Joerg Henkel,
NEC, USA

Finance & Local Arrangements Chair
Tony Givargis,
University of California, Irvine, USA

New Topics Chair
JoAnn Paul,
Carnegie Mellon University, USA

Panels Chair
Reinaldo Bergamaschi,
IBM TJ Watson Research Center, USA

Publications Chair
Ali Dasdan,
Synopsys, USA

Publicity Chair
Frank Vahid,
University of California, Riverside, USA

Registration Chair
Harry Hsieh,
University of California, Riverside, USA

Special Sessions Chair
Luciano Lavagno,
Politecnico Torino, Italy

Workshops Chair
Petru Eles,
Linkoping University, Sweden

Electronic Media Chair
Ismet Bayraktaroglu,
Sun Microsystems, USA

Administrative Support
Melanie Sanders,
University of California, Irvine, USA

Awards Chair
Raul Camposano,
Synopsys, USA

Liaisons:

Industry Liaison
Grant Martin,
Cadence Design Systems, USA

ACM SIGDA Liaison
Robert Walker,
Kent State University, USA

ACM SIGSOFT
Mary Jean Harrold,
Georgia Tech, USA

Computer Society Liaison
Wayne Wolf,
Princeton University, USA

European Connection
Axel Jantsch,
Royal Institute of Technology, Sweden

CASS Liaison
Giovanni De Micheli,
Stanford University, USA

ACM SIGBED
Janos Sztipanovits,
Vanderbilt University, USA

IFIP Liaison
Nikil Dutt,
University of California, Irvine, USA

Latin Connection
Ricardo Reis,
Universidade Federal do Rio Grande do Sul, Brazil

Asian Liaison
Hiroto Yasuura,
Kyushu University, Japan

Technical Program Committee:

Guido Araujo, *State Univ Campinas, Brazil*
M. Balakrishnan, *Indian Institute of Technology, Delhi, India*
Luca Benini, *University of Bologna, Italy*
Joe Buck, *Synopsys, USA*
Sujit Dey, *University of California, San Diego, USA*
Rolf Ernst, *Technical University of Braunschweig, Germany*
Daniel Gajski, *University of California, Irvine, USA*
Cathy Gebotys, *University of Waterloo, Canada*
Soonhoi Ha, *Seoul National University, Korea*
Roman Hermida, *Universidad Complutense de Madrid, Spain*
Margarida F. Jacome, *University of Texas, Austin, USA*
Fadi J. Kurdahi, *University of California, Irvine, USA*
Juan Carlos Lopez, *University of Castilla-La Mancha, Spain*
Jan Madsen, *Technical University of Denmark, Denmark*
Lev Markov, *Sun Microsystems, USA*
Peter Marwedel, *University of Dortmund & ICD, Germany*
Anne Mignotte, *INSA Lyon, France*
Miguel Miranda, *IMEC, Belgium*
Vincent Mooney, *Georgia Tech, USA*
Kazuaki Murakami, *Kyushu University, Japan*
Walid Najjar, *University of California, Riverside, USA*
Sanjiv Narayan, *Cadence Design Systems, USA*
Sri Parameswaran, *University of South Wales, Australia*
Wolfgang Rosenstiel, *University of Tuebingen, Germany*
Alberto Sangiovanni-Vincentelli, *University of California, Berkeley, USA*
Majid Sarrafzadeh, *University of California, Los Angeles, USA*
Donatella Sciuto, *Politecnico di Milano, Italy*
Edwin Sha, *University of Texas at Dallas, USA*
Juergen Teich, *Universitat Erlangen-Nuremberg, Germany*
Don Thomas, *Carnegie Mellon University, USA*
Stamatis Vassiliadis, *Technical University of Delft, Germany*
Kees A. Vissers, *University of California, Berkeley, USA*
Kazutoshi Wakabayashi, *NEC, Japan*
Albert van der Werf, *Philips, the Netherlands*
Allen C.-H. Wu, *National Tsinghua University, Taiwan*

Additional Reviewers

Javed Absar, *IMEC, Belgium*
Bilge Akgul, *Georgia Tech, USA*
Tankut Akgul, *Georgia Tech, USA*
Iosif Antochi, *Delft University of Technology, The Netherlands*
Tetsuya Aoyama, *NEC, Japan*
Baris Arslan, *University of California, San Diego, USA*
Isabelle Augé-Blum, *INSA Lyon, France*
Rodolfo Azevedo, *University of Campinas, Brazil*
Jean-Philippe Babau, *INSA Lyon, France*
Xiaoliang Bai, *University of California, San Diego, USA*
Marco Bekooij, *Philips Research Eindhoven, The Netherlands*
Etienne Bergeron, *University of Montreal, Canada*
Erik Brockmeyer, *IMEC, Belgium*
Humberto Calderón, *University of California, Irvine, USA*
Jeremy Chan, *University of South Wales, Australia*
Naehyuck Chang, *Seoul National University, Korea*
Luc Charest, *University of Montreal, Canada*
Li Chen, *University of California, San Diego, USA*
Dmitry Cheresiz, *Delft University of Technology, The Netherlands*
Newton Cheung, *University of South Wales, Australia*
Kiyoung Choi, *Seoul National University, Korea*
Susan Cotterell, *University of California, Riverside, USA*
Dan Crisu, *Delft University of Technology, The Netherlands*
Kristof Denolf, *IMEC, Belgium*
Dirk Desmet, *IMEC, Belgium*
Marc Duranton, *Philips Research Eindhoven, The Netherlands*
Nur Engin, *Philips Research Eindhoven, The Netherlands*
Heiko Falk, *University of Dortmund, Germany*
Sune Fallegaard, *Nielsen Technical University of Denmark, Denmark*
Milagros Fernandez, *Universidad Complutense, Spain*
Antoine Fraboulet, *INSA Lyon, France*
Paolo Gai, *The Sant'Anna School of University Studies and Doctoral Research, Italy*
Om Prakash Gangwal, *Philips Research Eindhoven, The Netherlands*
Oscar Garnica, *Universidad Complutense, Spain*
Georgi Gaydadjiev, *Delft University of Technology, The Netherlands*
Arijit Ghosh, *University of California, Irvine, USA*
John Glossner, *University of California, Irvine, USA*
Kees Goossens, *Philips Research Eindhoven, The Netherlands*
Ann Gordon-Ross, *University of California, Riverside, USA*
Hui Guo, *University of South Wales, Australia*
Masachika Hamabe, *NEC, Japan*
Gerald Heim, *University of Tuebingen, Germany*
Ignacio Hidalgo, *Universidad Complutense, Spain*
Hans Holten-Lund, *Technical University of Denmark, Denmark*
Pao-Ann Hsiung, *National Chung Cheng University, Taiwan, ROC*
Chih-Tsun Huang, *National Tsing Hua University, Taiwan, ROC*
I.-J. Huang, *National Sun Yet-sen University, Taiwan, ROC*
Raynald Huaulme, *INSA Lyon, France*
Andhi Janapsatya, *University of South Wales, Australia*
Murali Jayapala, *Katholieke Universiteit Leuven, Belgium*
Jer-Min Jou, *National Cheng Kung University, Taiwan, ROC*
Igor Katchan, *University of Tuebingen, Germany*
Arun Kejariwal, *University of California, Irvine, USA*
Jihong Kim, *Seoul National University, Korea*
Pramote Kuacharoen, *Georgia Tech, USA*
Casper Lageweg, *Delft University of Technology, The Netherlands*
Kanishka Lahiri, *University of California, San Diego, USA*
Walter Lange, *University of Tuebingen, Germany*
Dong-Gi Lee, *University of California, San Diego, USA*
Jaehwan Lee, *Georgia Tech, USA*
Kasia Leijten-Nowak, *Philips Research Eindhoven, The Netherlands*
Rainer Leupers, *RWTH Aachen, Germany*
Donglin Liu, *University of Notre Dame, USA*
Marisa López-Vallejo, *University of Madrid, Spain*
Markus Lorenz, *University of Dortmund, Germany*
Ivan Lu, *University of South Wales, Australia*
Tiehan Lv, *Princeton University, USA*
Roman Lysecky, *University of California, Riverside, USA*
Zhe Ma, *IMEC, Belgium*
Shankar Mahadevan, *Technical University of Denmark, Denmark*
Theodore Marescaux, *IMEC, Belgium*
Sean Patrick Mccarthy, *University of California, Irvine, USA*
Bingfeng Mei, *IMEC, Belgium*
Jose M. Mendias, *Universidad Complutense, Spain*

Additional Reviewers (continued)

Carsten Menn, *FZI, Germany*
Bart Mesman, *Philips Research Eindhoven, The Netherlands*
Maria Michael, *University of Notre Dame, USA*
Maria C. Molina, *Universidad Complutense, Spain*
Nahri Moreano, *UFMS, Brazil*
Francisco Moya, *University of Castilla-La Mancha, Spain*
José Manuel Moya, *University of Madrid, Spain*
Akira Mukaiyama, *NEC, Japan*
Shoubhik Mukhopadhyay, *University of California, San Diego, USA*
Richard Murphy, *University of Notre Dame, USA*
Andre Costi Nacul, *University of California, Irvine, USA*
Masayuki Nakajima, *NEC, Japan*
Noritsugu Nakamura, *NEC, Japan*
Rick Nas, *Philips Research Eindhoven, The Netherlands*
Edna Natividade, *UFPE, Brazil*
Gabriela Nicolescu, *University of Montreal, Canada*
Shinichi Noda, *NEC, Japan*
Tobias Oppold, *University of Tuebingen, Germany*
Elena Moscu Panainte, *Delft University of Technology, The Netherlands*
Debashis Panigrahi, *University of California, San Diego, USA*
Antonis Papanikolaou, *IMEC, Belgium*
Jun Cheol Park, *Georgia Tech, USA*
Jorgen Peddersen, *University of South Wales, Australia*
Prakash Peranandam, *University of Tuebingen, Germany*
Peter Petrov, *University of California, San Diego, USA*
Luis Pinuel, *Universidad Complutense, Spain*
Manuel Prieto, *Universidad Complutense, Spain*
Gang Quan, *University of South Carolina, USA*
Andrei Radulescu, *Philips Research Eindhoven, The Netherlands*
Naomi Ramos, *University of California, San Diego, USA*
Wenjing Rao, *University of California, San Diego, USA*
Edwin Rijpkema, *Philips Research Eindhoven, The Netherlands*
Fernando Rincón, *University of Castilla-La Mancha, Spain*
Tanguy Risset, *INSA Lyon, France*
Jürgen Ruf, *University of Tuebingen, Germany*
Kyeong Keol Ryu, *Georgia Tech, USA*
Marcos Sanchez-Elez, *Universidad Complutense, Spain*
Stephen Schmitt, *University of Tuebingen, Germany*
Jürgen Schnerr, *FZI, Germany*
Carsten Schulz-Key, *University of Tuebingen, Germany*
Thomas Schweizer, *University of Tuebingen, Germany*
Krishna Sekar, *University of California, San Diego, USA*
Mohamed Shalan, *Georgia Tech, USA*
Zili Shao, *University of Texas at Dallas, USA*
Eung Shin, *Georgia Tech, USA*
Axel Siebenborn, *University of Tuebingen, Germany*
Mihai Sima, *Delft University of Technology, The Netherlands*
Ozgur Sinanoglu, *University of California, San Diego, USA*
Martin Stark, *Robert Bosch, Germany*
Joergen Steensgaard-Madsen, *Technical University of Denmark, Denmark*
Stefan Steinke, *University of Dortmund, Germany*
Greg Stitt, *University of California, Riverside, USA*
Katsuharu Suzuki, *NEC, Japan*
Klass Tack, *IMEC, Belgium*
Wataru Takahashi, *NEC, Japan*
Takashi Takenaka, *NEC, Japan*
Yudong Tan, *Georgia Tech, USA*
Clark Taylor, *University of California, San Diego, USA*
Bo Tian, *University of California, Irvine, USA*
Takao Toi, *NEC, Japan*
Minoru Tomobe, *NEC, Japan*
Rasit Topaloglu, *University of California, San Diego, USA*
Daniel Tracy, *University of California, San Diego, USA*
Albert van der Werf, *Philips Research Eindhoven, The Netherlands*
Karel Van Oudheusden, *IMEC, Belgium*
Tom Vander Aa, *Katholieke Universiteit Leuven, Belgium*
Andreas Vörg, *FZI, Germany*
Flavio Rech Wagner, *Universidade Federal do Rio Grande do Sul, Brazil*
Jens Wagner, *University of Dortmund, Germany*
Eduardo Wanderley, *CEFET-RN, Brazil*
Zhong Wang, *University of Notre Dame, USA*
Lars Wehmeyer, *University of Dortmund, Germany*
Markus Winterholer, *University of Tuebingen, Germany*
Stephan Wong, *Delft University of Technology, The Netherlands*
Jiang Xu, *Princeton University, USA*
Tsukasa Yamauchi, *NEC, Japan*
Peng Yang, *IMEC, Belgium*
Shengqi Yang, *Princeton University, USA*
Chuanjun Zhang, *University of California, Riverside, USA*
Yumin Zhang, *Synopsys, USA*
Yi Zhao, *University of California, San Diego, USA*
Qingfeng Zhuge, *University of Texas at Dallas, USA*

Virtual Synchronization Technique with OS Modeling for Fast and Time-accurate Cosimulation

Youngmin Yi   Dohyung Kim   Soonhoi Ha

CAP Laboratory
Department of Computer Science and Engineering
Seoul National Univ., Seoul, Korea
+82 2 8807292
{ymyi, dhkim, sha}@iris.snu.ac.kr

ABSTRACT
Hardware/Software cosimulation is the key process to shorten the design turn around time. We have proposed a novel technique, called virtual synchronization, for fast and time accurate cosimulation that involves interacting component simulators. In this paper, we further extend the virtual synchronization technique with OS modeling for the case where multiple software tasks are executed under the supervision of a real-time operating system. The OS modeler models the RTOS overheads of context switching and tick interrupt handling as well as preemption behavior. While maintaining the timing accuracy to an acceptable level below a few percents, we could reduce the simulation time drastically compared with existent conservative approach by removing the need of time synchronization between simulators. It is confirmed with a preliminary experiment with a multimedia example that consists of four real-life tasks.

Categories and Subject Descriptors
B.7.2 [**Design Aids**]: Simulation and Verification

General Terms
Performance, Verification.

Keywords
Cosimulation, virtual synchronization, OS modeling

1. INTRODUCTION
Software modules are taking more and more roles in embedded systems and it is crucial to enable software development concurrently with the hardware development to reduce the design time. This can be achieved by hardware/software cosimulation in the hardware/ software codesign methodology that uses a virtual prototype.

Cosimulation can be used to evaluate several candidate architectures in the architecture selection stage of which the goal is to find out an optimal architecture for a given application. A popular cosimulation technique in this stage is to use host code execution with delay annotation. A task is not cross-compiled to target code but compiled and executed as host code and its timing information is estimated a priori and annotated. Data exchange between processing components is modeled and performed at the transaction level. Since static timing estimation cannot take into account any run-time variation of performance, timing accuracy of cosimulation is limited. Recently, there have appeared many research results ([3][4][6]) and commercial tools([14][15]) that are considering this level of abstraction.

Cosimulation can also be used for coverification of designed system where timing accuracy is the key requirement. In this stage, time-accurate instruction set simulator (ISS) and RTL simulator are usually used for software component and for hardware component respectively[1][14][15]. As a result, cosimulation involves multiple component simulators running concurrently and interacting with each other. It is known that time-accurate cosimulation is much slower than delay-annotated transaction level cosimulation by some orders of magnitude. Since a time-accurate cosimulation may also be used for the last stage of design space exploration such as fine-tuning of communication architecture and memory systems, it is desirable to speed up the cosimulation speed, which is the main concern of this paper.

There are two main causes for low performance of time accurate cosimuation: one is slow simulation speed of each component simulator, and the other is time synchronization overhead between component simulators. There have been several efforts to speed up time-accurate cosimulation. Compiled ISS[2] was proposed to boost the simulation speed of software simulator. It achieves high simulation speed by removing the overhead of instruction decoding at run time. Instead, it translates each target instruction directly to one or more host instructions at compile time. But it has a drawback that it lacks of adaptability to the modification of the architecture or the compiler. Also, it is difficult to apply this approach to the dynamic program such as OS model. Moreover, time synchronization overhead remains between component simulators.

Recently, we have proposed the virtual synchronization technique for distributed time-accurate cosimulation to reduce the simulation time and the time synchronization overhead simultaneously[7]. The virtual synchronization technique eliminates the need for time synchronization between component simulators at all: synchronization appears accomplished only when events are exchanged. Also it improves the performance of an individual simulator by removing the overhead of redundant local clock advancement.

However, there is a critical constraint on the simulated tasks to apply the virtual synchronization technique. The task execution

CODES+ISSS '03, October 1-3, 2003, Newport Beach, California, USA model that virtual synchronization assumes is that the execution results of the task do not depend on the arrival times of input events but only on the arrival order of them. Once a task is executed with a given set of input samples, it assumes completed without interruption.

In this paper, we extend the virtual synchronization technique to the case where multiple software tasks are executed under the supervision of a real-time operating system (RTOS) in a processor. Virtual synchronization cannot be directly applied in this case since an RTOS does not satisfy the execution model that virtual synchronization assumes: if the input samples for a task with higher priority arrives at the processor, the RTOS preempts the current task execution in the middle. On the other hand, it is a big burden to run the RTOS itself on the processor ISS. The proposed approach runs only application tasks on the ISS and models the RTOS in the cosimulation backplane to achieve faster cosimulation still preserving the timing accuracy to an acceptable level below a few percents.

In the next section, we explain the time synchronization problem between component simulators and the virtual synchronization technique our work is based on. Section 3 presents motivation and section 4 describes the proposed technique with RTOS modeling. In section 5, we formulate the expected performance improvement when the modeling is used. Experimental results are shown in section 6. Related work and conclusions follow in section 7 and 8 respectively.

2. TIME SYNCHRONIZATION PROBLEM AND VIRTUAL SYNCHRONIZATION

A time-accurate cosimulation environment consists of a set of component simulators. Figure 1(a) illustrates a simple example that involves a HW simulator and a SW simulator. The source block models an environment and generates the triggering events to the SW task periodically with period of 8 time units. The number denoted inside a block indicates the simulated time duration of event processing: for example, the SW task takes 4 time units for event processing. And we assume for simple illustration that the SW simulator is twice faster than the HW simulator to advance its local clock one time unit.

When multiple simulators are involved, the main difficulty is to synchronize the simulators to avoid the causality error. A simple but most popular scheme for time synchronization between component simulators is conservative approach[11]. In this approach, the local clock advancement is marshaled at every time unit as illustrated in Figure 1(b). Then, the cosimulation speed is bounded by the performance of the slowest simulator further degraded by synchronization overhead. And the component simulator takes simulation time for clock advancement without doing any useful work during the idle time. To reduce the synchronization overhead, some advanced techniques have been developed: optimized approach[13] and optimistic approach[12]. Unfortunately, they usually assume special features of component simulators so their applicability is severely restricted. Virtual synchronization technique, on the other hand, does not assume such special features of simulators. Instead, it assumes the execution model of simulated tasks: they are functional and monotonic meaning that the output results of the tasks depend only on the arrival order not on the arrival times of input events.

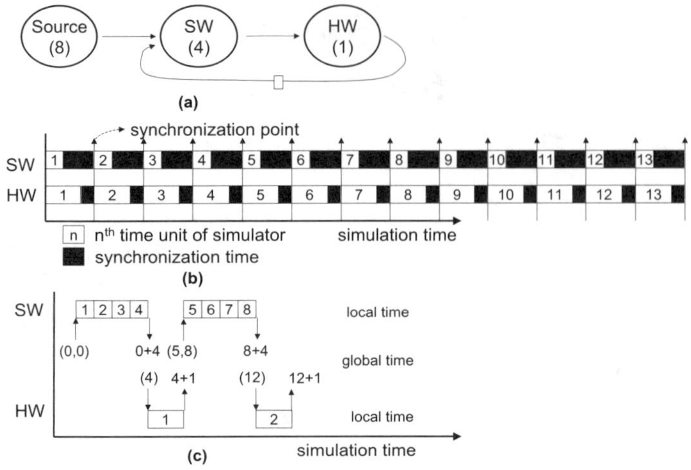

Figure 1. (a) A simple cosimulation example, (b) cosimulation scenario of a conservative approach, (c) that of the virtual synchronization approach.

A typical software function meets this requirement. Suppose a software task is a function call with two arguments of which one is supplied by the source block and the other by the hardware block in Figure 1(a). Then, the execution of this task waits until two arguments arrive at the input ports. At the second invocation of the software block, one event arrives at time 8 from the source block and the other at time 5 from the hardware block. Then, the software block starts execution at time 8 and produces an output event at time 12. It means that the software block does no useful work from simulated time 4 to time 8.

In virtual synchronization, the local clock of a component simulator is not synchronized with the system-wide global clock. Instead, a wrapper is inserted at the interface between the component simulator and the cosimulation backplane as shown in Figure 2(a). When a data sample d1 is delivered from the backplane to the simulator at simulated time t1, the wrapper translates the time stamp of the event to the current time of the component simulator. When it receives an output event from the simulator, it computes the elapsed time $\Delta(d1)$ and reconstructs the correct time stamp of the output event with $t1 + \Delta(d1)$.

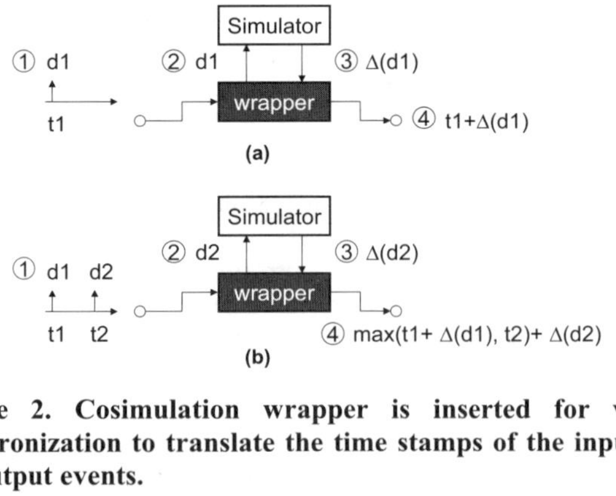

Figure 2. Cosimulation wrapper is inserted for virtual synchronization to translate the time stamps of the input and the output events.

Figure 2(b) illustrates how the wrapper adjusts the time stamp of the next event assuming that input events d1 and d2 arrive at t1 and t2 respectively. If t2 is larger than $t1+\Delta(d1)$, the output event for d2 simply has the time stamp $t2+\Delta(d2)$. Special care should be taken when t2 is smaller than t1+Δ(d1) meaning that the next input event arrives while the component processes the current event. Since a software simulator may accept the input event after completion of the current execution. Then, the time stamp of the output event would be t1+Δ(d1) + Δ(d2).

Thus, time synchronization is accomplished when data samples are exchanged. It means that virtual synchronization removes all time synchronization overheads except the time stamp translation overhead of the wrapper, which is negligible. Figure 1(c) illustrates the scenario when the virtual synchronization technique is used for the cosimulation of Figure 1(a). The software simulator clock stops advancement at time 4 after sending an output event to the hardware simulator. The hardware simulator receives the input event at local time 0 and advances 1 time unit to produce an output. Therefore, the wrapper of the hardware simulator translates the time stamp of the input event from 4 to 0 and reconstructs the time stamp of the output event from 1 to 5. The software simulator resumes the second invocation after it receives an event from the source block at simulated time 8.

Note that virtual synchronization not only removes the synchronization overhead but also reduces the active duration of component simulators. A simulator does not need to increase the local clock until it receives a new input data after processing the last data samples. Thus, the virtual synchronization technique boosts the performance of the simulator itself.

3. MOTIVATION AND OS MODELER

While the virtual synchronization technique requires that a software task runs to completion once invoked, it is not the case if the task runs under the supervision of an operating system. A real time operating system (RTOS) usually services a periodic tick interrupt for real-time scheduling based on accurate time duration in terms of real-time clock ticks. It may preempt the current task execution with later arrived input samples if they trigger a task with a higher priority. If there are multiple runnable tasks at the same time, which task would be executed depends on the scheduling policy of the RTOS.

Figure 3 illustrates an example case where a G.723 decoder task and an H.263 decoder task are executed in the same software component. Figure 3(a) shows the desired simulation behavior when the G.723 decoder has a higher priority than the H.263 decoder and an input stream to the G.723 decoder arrives later. Since virtual synchronization executes the H.263 decoder first without interruption as shown in Figure 3(b), it fails to simulate the preemption behavior.

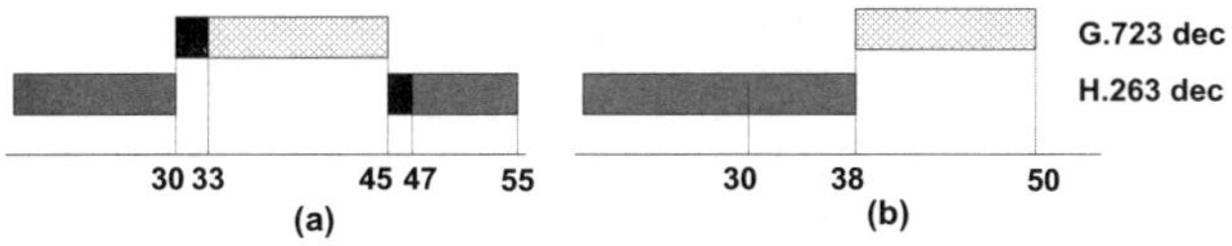

Figure 3. Executing multiple tasks on a simulator: G.723 decoder has higher priority than H.263 decoder. (a) Correct execution scenario, and (b) execution scenarios with virtual synchronization of the previous section.

On the other hand, it is a big burden to run the RTOS itself on the processor ISS, which we want to avoid for faster cosimulation. Executing the applications with an RTOS involves execution of RTOS kernel codes such as scheduler codes as well as context switching routines. In addition, it also involves the execution of idle tasks when CPU is in the idle state. In fact, during an idle period, an RTOS generally runs an idle task that is merely a loop without doing any meaningful work.

Another disadvantage of running the RTOS on the processor ISS is that tick interrupt modeling is required to advance the global OS tick for task scheduling. Most simulators supply the means to model the periodic exception generator. However, we observe that the use of this kind of simulation API degrades the overall simulator performance. This is because the simulator must check at every simulated cycle whether the scheduled (booked) exception generator should be invoked or not.

Therefore, for fast cosimulation, we want to avoid running the RTOS itself but run only the application tasks on the ISS. The question is how to reconstruct the correct time stamp of the output events from the software simulator considering the effects of the RTOS supervision. The proposed solution is to model the effect of the RTOS on the task execution time in the wrapper: we define "OS modeler" to perform this job. An OS modeler that resides in the wrapper of the software component simulator plays the role of adjusting the time stamps considering the RTOS scheduling policy.

In the proposed technique, we execute a software task ignoring the preemption possibility using the virtual synchronization technique. As shown in Figure 3(b), H.263 decoder ends the execution at time unit 38 and returns the output data to the associated OS modeler. The OS modeler waits until it receives the next input data from the backplane that will be sent to the simulator. When it receives the input data for the G.723 decoder at time 30, it compares the time stamp with that of the H.263 decoder output data. Since the G.723 decoder has a higher priority and the time stamp of its input data is earlier than that of the H.263 decoder output, the OS modeler postpones setting the time stamp of the output data until the G.723 decoder completes. After it completes, the OS modeler marks the time stamp of the output data considering the effect of preemption and the OS overhead. The time stamp of the output data of the H.263 decoder is finally set to be 55 as shown in Figure 3(a). Such adjustment mimics the preemption behavior successfully without preemption in reality. This approach achieves faster cosimulation, still preserving timing accuracy to an acceptable level below a few percents. Detailed OS modeling is the theme of the next section.

4. PROPOSED RTOS MODELING

An OS modeler models not only the preemption behavior but also the RTOS overhead during task execution. Two main ingredients of the RTOS overhead are the context switch overhead and the tick interrupt handling overhead. Whenever a tick interrupt (timer interrupt) occurs, the current task is preempted and the tick interrupt handler is called. The handler clears the interrupt and calls the scheduler. The scheduler of RTOS examines whether there exists any ready (runnable) task that has a higher priority than the current task. If this is the case, it calls the subsequent context switching routine that saves the context of the current task and restores the context of the newly scheduled task. Otherwise, no further routine is called and the RTOS yields the control to make the current task resume its execution. We assume that other interrupt handling tasks are modeled as separate software tasks that have higher priority than application tasks. To model the RTOS scheduler accurately, therefore, the OS modeler should be informed of the accurate context switch overhead and the execution time of the tick interrupt handler. With a given frequency of tick interrupt, the OS modeler can accurately calculate how many interrupts occurs during task execution.

The OS modeler determines the response time, R_i, of a software task by the following formula for the priority-based preemptive scheduler:

$$\overline{E}_i = f(E_i)\cdot E_t + E_i \quad , \quad R_i = \overline{E}_i + \sum_{\forall j, \pi_j > \pi_i, S_i \le S_j \le S_i + R_i} (\overline{E}_j + C)$$

where, $f(x) = \left\lfloor \frac{x}{tick\ size - E_t} \right\rfloor$ is the number of tick interrupt occurrences during x. Tick size is the time duration between the consecutive timer interrupts. E_t is the execution time of the tick interrupt handler. E_i is the execution time, s_i is the start time, and π_i is the priority of task i. C is the context switch overhead. The second term of the formula is the total preemption time and the resultant context switch overhead that task i suffers by those tasks with higher priority. The accuracy of the proposed OS modeling approach depends on the accuracy of the estimated overheads of context switch and tick interrupt handling. To guarantee predictable timing behavior, an RTOS usually has the constant overheads or at least bounded overheads. Therefore, the proposed formula provides very accurate results as demonstrated in the experiments.

A major source of inaccuracy is cache. If cache is used, the estimated response time of a task from the proposed approach might be different from the real one. Consider a situation illustrated in Figure 4. Figure 4(a) and 4(b) describes the actual task execution order and a possible task execution order in the proposed scheme respectively. If the G.723 decoder is executed consecutively as in Figure 4(b), it experiences smaller cache misses than the real situation. It can shorten the estimated execution time of the second instance of G.723. Moreover, the G.723 decoder pollutes the cache states of the H.263 decoder task, which cannot be modeled in the proposed approach.

Although the OS modeler approach cannot model these types of cache misses, experiments show that the resultant inaccuracy is negligible for most of the multimedia applications, which is the main target application of our concern. Since multimedia applications tend to have large size data of stream type, temporal locality is less significant than spatial locality. The proposed scheme fails to model accurately the effect of temporal locality.

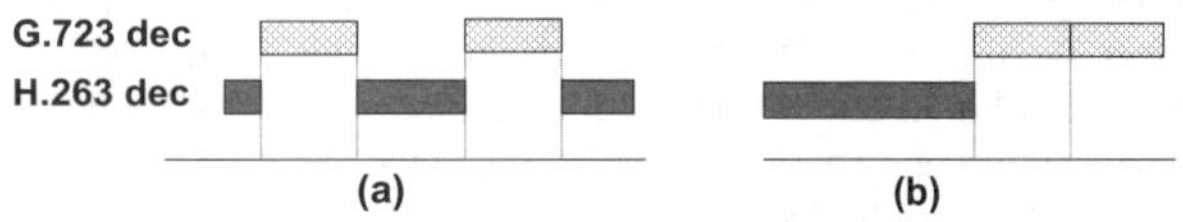

Figure 4. Task execution order (a) in reality and (b) in the proposed approach before time adjustment

Finally, the proposed OS modeler enables us to choose an optimal RTOS and its scheduling policy as well as task priorities without modifying the real RTOS. Therefore, fast and time accurate cosimulation with OS modeling can be effectively used for the last stage of design space exploration: OS selection and optimization.

5. EXPECTED PERFORMANCE IMPROVEMENT

In this section, we compute the expected performance improvement from the proposed technique of RTOS modeling against running the RTOS code directly on the ISS. The overheads of running the RTOS code are three-folds. First, there is a run-time overhead of kernel mode associated with tick interrupt handling and context switching. We denote r as the ratio of this overhead to the total simulation time. If the tick interrupt overhead dominates the context switch overhead, as usually is the case, this overhead is nearly equal to the ratio of the execution time of the tick interrupt handler to the tick size. Second, the RTOS runs a default idle task when there is no useful work to do. Therefore, there is no visible idling duration during the simulation. On the other hand, we can save this idle duration if we use the virtual synchronization technique only to the application code. We denote i as the ratio of the CPU idle duration to the total simulation time. Third, we have to call a specific API provided in the simulator to schedule (or book) the exception generator periodically inside the simulator. We denote s as the degradation ratio of the simulation time to advance one simulated time unit.

Now, we further define the following notations to establish a formula of the expected performance improvement:

ST_{RTOS} : the total simulation time in case we run the RTOS on the ISS

ST_{model} : the total simulation time in case we execute the application tasks only through the proposed scheme

T : the simulation time of the application tasks

R : the simulation time for the RTOS overheads

I : the simulation time for the idle task execution

Then, the performance improvement would be $1 - \frac{ST_{model}}{ST_{RTOS}}$.

Since $ST_{RTOS} = T + R + I$ and $ST_{model} = \frac{T}{(1+s)}$, the performance improvement can be expressed as

$$1 - \frac{ST_{model}}{ST_{RTOS}} = 1 - \frac{\frac{T}{(1+s)}}{T + R + I} \qquad (5.1)$$

Since $R = (T + R + I)\cdot r$ and $I = (T + R + I)\cdot i$, equation (5.1) is reduced to

$$1 - \frac{ST_{model}}{ST_{RTOS}} = 1 - \frac{1-(r+i)}{1+s} = \frac{s+r+i}{1+s} \qquad (5.2)$$

Equation (5.2) indicates the expected performance gain we can get from the proposed approach without taking the synchronization overhead into account. If we consider the synchronization overhead, the expected performance is further multiplied by the gain due to the removal of the synchronization overhead.

In (5.2), and are constant once a specific RTOS and the simulator are given. Therefore, if CPU idle ratio can be obtained before simulation, designers can easily estimate the performance gain of the proposed approach against the case when RTOS is actually executed on the ISS.

6. EXPERIMENTS

In this section, we show some preliminary experimental results on the performance improvement and on the accuracy. We consider a real-life multimedia application, a video phone, which consists of four tasks; an H.263 encoder, an H.263 decoder, a G.723 encoder and a G.723 decoder. They are assumed to be mapped to an ARM720T processor with 8KB unified cache. The RTOSes we used in the experiments are eCOS[9] and uCOS-ii[10]. We used ARMulator[8] for the processor simulator that runs on the dual Xeon 1.8GHz machine.

Depending on which RTOS is used and whether cache is used or not, different sets of task deadlines are used as shown in Table 1. Also, the priorities of the tasks are assigned as shown in Table 1. We assume that the period of a task equals to its deadline. The tick size is set to 10 ms for both eCOS and uCOS.

Even though the OS modeling technique is proposed for hardware/software cosimulation, we used the software simulator only for experiments to focus on the performance improvement due to the OS modeling. Thus we could ignore the effect of the hardware simulator performance on the experiments.

Table 1. Timing constraints of the example task group; 1tick is 368,640 cycles (=10ms)

Deadline	G.723 dec	G.723 enc	H.263 dec	H.263 enc
eCOS, cache ON	30 ticks	30 ticks	300 ticks	300 ticks
uCOS, cache ON	20 ticks	20 ticks	200 ticks	200 ticks
eCOS, cache OFF	400 ticks	400 ticks	4000 ticks	4000 ticks
uCOS, cache OFF	300 ticks	300 ticks	3000 ticks	3000 ticks
Priority	1	2	3	4

6.1 Performance Result

In the performance experiments, we classified the performance improvement into two factors. The first one is the improvement due to OS modeling itself (apart from synchronization overheads) and the second one is due to the removal of the time synchronization overheads.

Table 2 shows the performance improvement due to OS modeling itself. Simulation was performed with cache enabled and with the corresponding timing constraints defined in Table 1. For eCOS simulation, using the equation (5.2), the expected gain is 19.7% while the measured improvement in Table 2 is 18.2%. For uCOS simulation, we can obtain the expected gain similarly. It is 37.4% and the measured value is 38.0%. Recall that is the degradation ratio, the idle ratio and the RTOS ratio to the total simulation time.

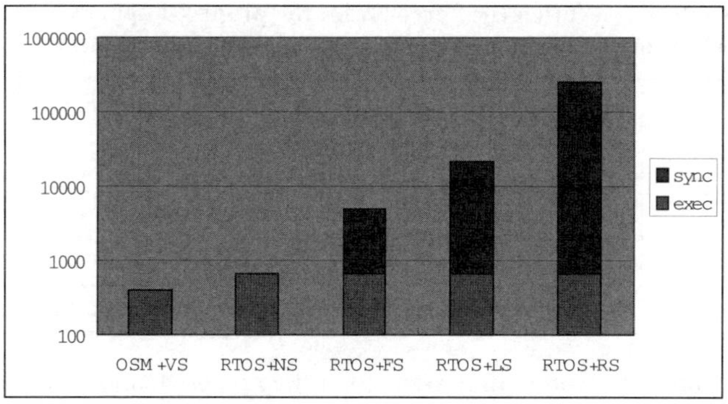

Figure 5. The time consumed to simulate uCOS-ii with cache enabled. The processor utilization is 73.0%

Table 2. Performance improvement due to OS modeling

	Estimated				Measured		
	s (%)	i (%)	r (%)	$1-\frac{ST_{model}}{ST_{RTOS}}$	ST_{RTOS} (sec)	ST_{model} (sec)	$1-\frac{ST_{model}}{ST_{RTOS}}$
eCOS	15	4.2	3.4	19.7%	905	740	18.2%
uCOS	15	27.0	1.0	37.4%	668	414	38.0%

Figure 5 illustrates the gain we can obtain from the removal of time synchronization. The first bar shows the simulation time from the proposed virtual synchronization approach with OS modeler. The time synchronization takes less than 1 second. It confirms that the virtual synchronization technique has nearly zero overhead of time synchronization. The second one shows the case when we simulate the tasks with RTOS without any synchronization. The third one is the case when we run RTOS with conservative approach, where time synchronization is performed every cycle with function call overhead of approximately 5.0 usec per simulated cycle. The fourth and fifth ones are the cases when we perform synchronization through TCP/IP socket call locally and remotely respectively. The measured the socket call overheads are 27.9 and 336.7 usec per simulated cycle respectively. Compared with the conservative approach where RTOS is run on the ISS, the proposed approach gives significant performance improvement due to the removal of time synchronization between component simulators

6.2 Accuracy Result

As the metric of time accuracy, we compute the error between the proposed RTOS modeling and RTOS simulation in terms of simulated times of task completion. Table 3 shows the results with eCOS and uCOS assuming that the cache memory is disabled. Since the RTOS overhead is accurately measured and almost constant at run time, the error is quite low. The execution cycles for the same task in two RTOSes are different because different compilers are used for each RTOS and these compilers use different library for floating-point arithmetic.

Since the proposed approach does not accurately model the cache affects, the error grows as demonstrated in Table 4. The error comes from the fact that the proposed approach underestimates the cold miss rate when a task starts or resumes as explained in section 4.

Table 3. Execution time error from the proposed approach for eCOS and uCOS-ii with cache disabled (time unit: cycles)

	Instances	eCOS	uCOS	exec. time (eCOS)	exec. Time (uCOS)
G.723 dec	100	0.06 %	-0.02 %	26,948,018	15,649,829
G.723 enc	100	-0.02 %	-0.05 %	31,101,618	17,629,837
H.263 dec	10	-0.03 %	-0.03 %	125,734,905	76,448,526
H.263 enc	10	-0.08 %	0.01 %	713,685,303	395,145,693

Table 4. Execution time error from the proposed approach for eCOS and uCOS-ii with cache enabled (time unit: cycles)

	Instances	eCOS	uCOS	exec. time (eCOS)	exec. Time (uCOS)
G.723 dec	100	-1.4 %	-7.3 %	1,765,217	921,301
G.723 enc	100	-1.5 %	-1.0 %	2,209,160	966,276
H.263 dec	10	-0.9 %	-1.3 %	11,610,644	6,707,270
H.263 enc	10	-0.6 %	-0.7 %	55,996,252	19,920,577

7. RELATED WORK

There has been no work on RTOS modeling for time accurate cosimulation with the ISS of a processor, to our best knowledge. On the other hand, there are some research results on the RTOS modeling for the transaction-level cosimulation with delay-annotated C-level software simulation. The RTOS modeling is addressed in Pia codesign environment[5]. In Pia, a software simulator blocks and synchronizes whenever it meets a receive operation. If an interrupt occurs, Pia preempts the current task execution and performs roll-back if necessary. Although interrupt handling is modeled with roll-back mechanism, preemptive scheduler modeling was not mentioned. No timing accuracy is reported in their work.

POLIS[3] also adapted RTOS scheduler modeling where a software task is synthesized to a timing annotated C code. A software task is executed atomically to produce the output results. If it is detected later that an interrupt or an input event for higher priority task arrives during task execution, the timing of the output events produced by the current task is delayed by the execution time of interrupt handler or higher priority task, which is similar to the proposed idea of time translation. They report that the accuracy was within 20% and this is due to the limit of host code execution with delay annotation approach. Cockx[4] also proposed a similar way of modeling of preemption. In his codesign environment, TIPSY, to reduce the context switch between software threads due to preemption, out-of-order execution of software threads is allowed. And timing adjustment is performed later for reconstruct the correct ordering of thread executions.

Yoo et al[6] proposed a fast timed simulation method by annotating delay in systemC simulation model. Instead of modeling the OS, they annotate the execution time to the OS code itself. The rationale is to make the simulation code and the synthesis code as much similar as possible. Since time adjustment is not used in this approach, synchronization should be performed either conservatively or optimistically.

8. CONCLUSIONS

In this paper, we extend the virtual synchronization technique with OS modeling for the case where multiple software tasks are executed under the supervision of a real-time operating system. The OS modeler models the RTOS overheads of context switching and tick interrupt handling as well as preemption behavior.

While maintaining the timing accuracy to an acceptable level below a few percents, we could reduce the simulation time drastically compared with existent conservative approaches by removing the need of time synchronization between simulators. It remains as a future work to model OS more accurately when cache is enabled

9. ACKNOWLEDGEMENTS

This work was supported by National Research Laboratory Program (number M1-0104-00-0015) and Brain Korea 21 Project. The ICT at Seoul National University provided the research facilities for this study.

REFERENCES

[1] Seamless CVE, http://www.mentorg.com/seamless/

[2] V. Zivojnovic and H. Meyr, "Compiled HW/SW co-Simulation", *In Proc. 33rd DAC.*, June 1996

[3] C. Passerone, "Fast hardware/software co-simulation for virtual prototyping and trade-off analysis", *In Proc. 34th Design Automation Conf.*, 1997

[4] J. Cockx, "Efficient modeling of preemption in a virtual prototype", *In Proc. 11th RSP*, 2000, pp 14 –19

[5] K. Hines, "Pia: a framework for embedded system co-simulation with dynamic communication support", *Technical Report UW-CSE-96-11-04*, 1997

[6] S. Yoo et al. "Automatic generation of fast timed simulation models for operating systems in SoC design", *In Proc. Design Automation and Test in Europe*, Mar. 2002

[7] D. Kim et al. "Virtual synchronization for fast distributed Cosimulation of dataflow task graphs", *In Proc. 15th International Symposium on System Synthesis*, Jun. 2002

[8] ARMulator, http://www.arm.comr

[9] eCOS, http://sources.redhat.com/ecos

[10] uCOS, http://www.ucos-ii.com

[11] K. Hagen and H. Meyer, "Timed and Untimed hardware software co-simulation: application and efficient implementation", *In Proc. CODES*, Oct. 1993

[12] S. Yoo and K. Choi, "Optimistic Distributed Timed Cosimulation Based on Thread Simulation Model", *In Proc. 6th CODES*, Mar. 1998

[13] W. Sung and S. Ha, "Efficient and Flexible Cosimulation Environment for DSP Applications", *IEICE Transactions on Fundamentals of Electronics, Communications and Computer Sciences, Special Issue on VLSI Design and CAD algorithms*, Vol.E81-A, No. 12, pp. 2605-2611, Dec. 1998

[14] CoCentric System Studio, http://www.synopsys.com /products/cocentric_studio

[15] CoWare N2C, http://www.coware.com/cowareN2C.html

A Modular Simulation Framework for Architectural Exploration of On-Chip Interconnection Networks

Tim Kogel, Malte Doerper, Andreas Wieferink, Rainer Leupers, Gerd Ascheid, Heinrich Meyr
Integrated Signal Processing Systems
Aachen University of Technology, Germany
http://www.iss.rwth-aachen.de
Tim.Kogel@iss.rwth-aachen.de

Serge Goossens
CoWare, Inc.
Interleuvenlaan 15A
B-3001 Leuven, Belgium
http://www.CoWare.com
Serge.Goossens@CoWare.com

ABSTRACT

Ever increasing complexity and heterogeneity of SoC platforms require diversified on-chip communication schemes beyond the currently omnipresent shared bus architectures. To prevent time consuming design changes late in the design flow, we propose the early exploration of the on-chip communication architecture to meet performance and cost requirements. Based on SystemC 2.0.1 we have defined a modular exploration framework, which is able to capture the effect on performance for different on-chip networks like dedicated point-to-point, shared bus, and crossbar topologies. Monitoring of performance parameters like utilization, latency and throughput drives the mapping of the inter-module traffic to an efficient communication architecture. The effectiveness of our approach is demonstrated by the exemplary design of a high performance Network Processing Unit (NPU), which is compared against a commercial NPU device.

Categories and Subject Descriptors

B.8.2 [**Performance And Reliability**]: Performance Analysis and Design Aids; C.2.1 [**Computer-Communication Networks**]: Network Architecture and Design—*Network topology*; I.6.7 [**Simulation And Modelling**]: Simulation Support Systems—*Environments*

General Terms

Performance, Design, Measurement

Keywords

Network-on-Chip, Architecture Exploration, SystemC, Simulation

1. INTRODUCTION

IP reuse has been long identified as a key technology to cope with ever increasing System-on-Chip (SoC) complexity along with ever shrinking time-to-market constraints. However, the problem of dealing with the interconnection of tens or even hundreds of IP blocks has only recently entered into the focus of researchers.

Current design practice for on-chip communication is predominantly based on shared bus architectures, which are available from core vendors [1, 2] or industry partnerships [3]. Due to the easy programming model, high flexibility and IP availability, this concept is clearly advantageous for today's small and medium scale embedded systems, where a small number of blocks exchange moderate amount of data. However, shared busses are not eligible for high throughput requirements and chip-wide interconnect, because of the limited scalability with respect to performance, number of connected blocks and range of coverage as well as limited support for QoS requirements.

Consequently, researchers in academia and industry have conceived alternative topologies to cope with the limitations of shared bus architectures. These efforts have recently been subsumed under the *Networks on Chip* (NoC) design paradigm. NoC advocates to replace current ad-hoc wiring of IP blocks with a disciplined approach, where full-fledged on-chip networks provide communication services according to the ISO/OSI reference model [4, 5]. By that the manifold problems in on-chip communication like signal integrity issues, link reliability, or Quality of Service (QoS) are separately resolved on the respective OSI layer. Depending on the intended application domain, recent proposals for NoC architectures differ significantly in terms of cost, performance, QoS and ISO/OSI compliance [6], [7], [8].

This kind of on-chip networks will probably not replace but complement bus based and point-to-point communication schemes, such that predominantly self-contained IP islands using local communication are connected via the global NoC. Hence, one of the most challenging tasks in future System-on-Chip design projects is to *conceive an on-chip communication infrastructure for heterogeneous platform architectures* in adherence to the specified flexibility, performance and cost requirements.

In this context we propose a modular NoC exploration framework, which addresses the system level design of the SoC communication architecture. Data exchange is modeled on the high abstraction level of packet transfers, which hides low-level implementation details but captures the effect on performance introduced by the network type. Thus the designer can partition the system communication into global network(s) and local interconnect and parameterize the selected communication architecture.

The unique contribution and major benefit of our approach is the ability to *capture the impact of on-chip communication on the system performance in a unified way*. By providing a library of different network modules with configurable topologies and arbitration protocols, our approach enables the rapid exploration and coherent comparison of architectural alternatives. Additionally, the high abstraction level of packet based communication yields *highest achievable simulation speed* together with *excellent modeling efficiency*.

The accuracy of the simulation results is of course affected by the coarse granularity of packet based communication. The proposed exploration framework is therefore not adequate to measure with full cycle accuracy the communication in small-scale embedded systems employing just a single bus. Especially particularities of certain bus architectures, like e.g. explicit insertion of busy or idle cycles of the AMBA high performance bus, cannot be captured in our generalized communication models. Instead, we address the early exploration and profiling driven partitioning of large-scale systems with complex and heterogeneous communication schemes.

The following section discusses related work in the area of exploration of system level communication architectures. After that the projected design flow followed by the technical details of our NoC exploration framework are presented. Section 5 contains our experiences from an industry cooperation, where the framework has been deployed in the design of a NPU platform. Finally we conclude our approach and give an outlook on future research topics.

2. RELATED WORK

System Level Design is considered the appropriate way to deal with the ever increasing complexity and heterogeneity of SoC architectures [9]. Various frameworks are proposed addressing design space exploration and the partitioning/mapping of an abstract functional model to the target architecture [10, 11, 12]. Complementary to this general approach, our focus is on the conceptualization and performance analysis of the on-chip communication architecture.

Recent work on system level exploration of the communication architecture can be subdivided into static analysis [13, 14] and simulation based techniques [15, 16]. Lahiri et al. [17] have proposed a hybrid procedure combining simulation with analytical post-processing to achieve higher accuracy of the performance estimation.

However, current approaches do not cope with the requirements introduced by the system level design of full-fledged on-chip networks. In order to apply analytical estimation, enhanced algorithms are necessary to analyze the performance of complex network topologies with sophisticated arbitration mechanisms. Equally, current simulation environments fall short to provide efficient support for exploration of on-chip networks.

On the other hand, traditional networking design environments like OPNET [18] are not suited for SoC design, since only the abstract communication structure can be captured without any support for chip-level architecture modeling.

The SystemC Open Core Protocol (SOCP) communication channel in the StepNP simulation platform [19] addresses the exploration of the communication infrastructure based on the OCP semantics. In a more general approach, we further abstract from architecture specific communication primitives to establish a unified framework for the investigation of heterogeneous on-chip networks.

3. SYSTEM LEVEL DESIGN FLOW

The NoC exploration framework is implemented on top of the SystemC library [20], which provides the underlying event-driven simulation engine and is considered as the emerging EDA standard for System Level Design. In this section we briefly introduce the basic concepts SystemC 2.0.1 based System Level Design and highlight the relation to our work. Please refer to Groetker et al. [21] for a thorough representation of this topic area.

As illustrated in figure 1, SystemC 2.0.1 follows the *Interface Method Call (IMC)* principle to achieve high modularity in communication modeling. Processes are wrapped into modules and access communication services through ports. The available methods are declared in the interface specification and implemented by the channel. Graphically a port is represented as a square containing two diametrical arrows and an interface is represented as a circle containing a u-turn arrow. A channel implementing an interface shows a rhombic shape.

The IMC scheme has been conceived to realize a *Transaction-Level Modeling (TLM)* style, where communication is abstracted from the low-level implementation details of the Register Transfer Level. The resulting improvement in terms of simulation speed and modeling efficiency enables the system architect to create an executable specification of the complete platform architecture.

As depicted in table 1, the TLM paradigm can be further subdivided by applying abstraction w.r.t. data and timing accuracy. By that the manifold design problems during the definition of the system level architecture can be resolved in the appropriate design step. Note that not all steps are necessarily performed for all platform designs: e.g. cycle- and bit-accurate TLM is usually sufficient for the design of small and medium scale embedded systems.

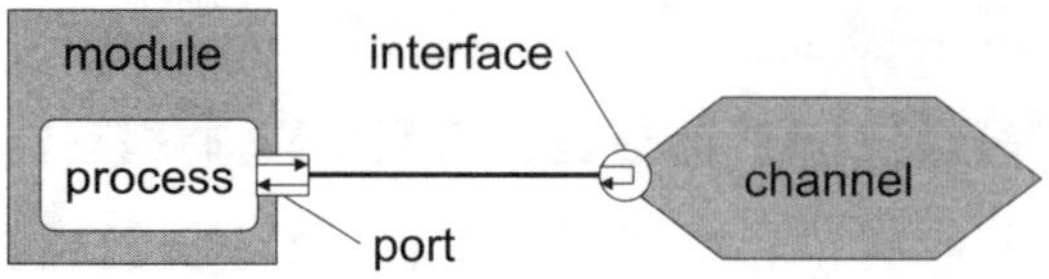

Figure 1: Interface Method Call Principle

Timing Accuracy	Data Accuracy	Addressed Design Problems
untimed-functional	Abstract Data Type	functional specification
timed-functional	Abstract Data Type	architecture exploration
cycle true	bit true	finalize architecture, SW development

Table 1: TLM Abstraction Levels

This paper addresses the conceptualization of large scale heterogenous systems, which need a customized communication infrastructure to meet performance and cost requirements. Hence, the proposed NoC exploration environment is situated on the untimed- and timed functional level. In analogy with traditional network design environments, we advocate to design the on-chip network on the packet level, i.e. the considered data granularity are sets of functionally associated data, which are combined to Abstract Data Types (ADTs).

Quantitative numbers on the simulation speed are highly dependent on the complexity of the considered application and are thus not well comparable. However, experiments show, that a medium scale embedded system modeled on the cycle- and bit-accurate transaction level runs at about 200k cycles per second on a 2.4 GHz Linux PC, which is about two orders of magnitude faster than the corresponding RTL model without loss of accuracy [22]. In our framework an *additional* order of magnitude is achieved by abstracting the data representation to the ADT level. Migrating from the untimed to the timed functional level is realized by adding execution delays in terms of timing annotations, which has no significant impact on the simulation speed.

4. NOC EXPLORATION FRAMEWORK

This section introduces the proposed simulation framework for system level exploration of the communication architecture. We first present our unified approach to the modeling of on-chip communication and the associated NoC architecture exploration methodology. Afterwards we elaborate on the internal structure of the framework and the algorithms, which capture the performance characteristics of the distinctive on-chip networks.

4.1 Unified Modeling of On-Chip Communication

In general two different kinds of modules can participate in a communication event or *transaction*: While master modules actively initiate transactions, the slave modules can only react passively. Typical masters are processors, DMA controllers or autonomous ASIC blocks, whereas typical slaves are memories or co-processors. Of course peer-to-peer communication between two masters is also possible.

This general master-slave communication scheme is reflected in the overall organization of the NoC evaluation framework depicted in figure 2.

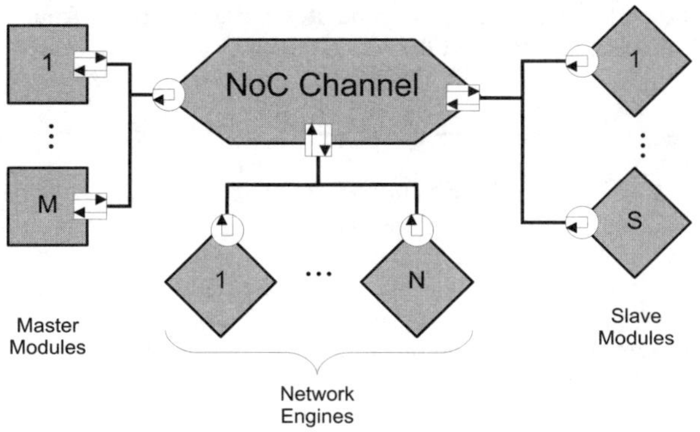

Figure 2: NoC Channel Overview

On-chip communication services are offered through a generalized master interface. In concordance with the *Interface Based Design* principle [23] [24], master modules initially not compliant to this interface can be attached by means of adapters.

The processing of communication is handled by the NoC Channel, which constitutes the central module of the simulation framework. The attached *network engines* are responsible for modeling the traffic characteristics and the impact on performance related to the the on-chip network.

4.2 NoC Exploration Methodology

Our framework enables the systematic design space exploration of most complex on-chip communication networks. During the simulation, the evaluation modules connected to the network engines collect statistical information like resource utilization, latency, and throughput. Based on these data, the system architect designs the communication infrastructure according to the following successive refinement steps:

- During the *initial throughput measurement*, the overall on-chip traffic is functionally captured by means of an unconstrained point-to-point network engine. The resulting communication profile identifies interacting partners and rough throughput requirements.
- The *coarse network partitioning* is dedicated to the identification of the optimum mix of network types. The system architect maps the point-to-point communication to an appropriate set of network types by configuring the NoC Channel with the corresponding set of network-specific engines.
- By iterative *parameter calibration*, the selected communication architecture is fine-tuned to the traffic requirements. Parameters refer to e.g. the bandwidth of a bus system or the queue-length of a crossbar architecture.

Of course the network partitioning has superior impact on the final quality of results. Here our unified approach enables a rapid exploration of totally different network architectures by simply exchanging the network engines. By that the system architect can optimize the communication in an iterative exploration cycle. In case of very complex applications, the simulation driven approach can be complemented with statistical post-processing techniques like regression analysis to reduce the overall design space.

4.3 The NoC Channel

The network independent master interface provides a symmetric request-response communication scheme, that follows the generic TLM channel proposal [25]. The interface implementation inside the NoC Channel translates master requests into an internal Transaction Data Structure (TDS), which contains all relevant information related to the transaction, like e.g. source- and destination address, the actual data packet, and an engine identifier. As illustrated in figure 3, the TDS is then forwarded to the selected network engine.

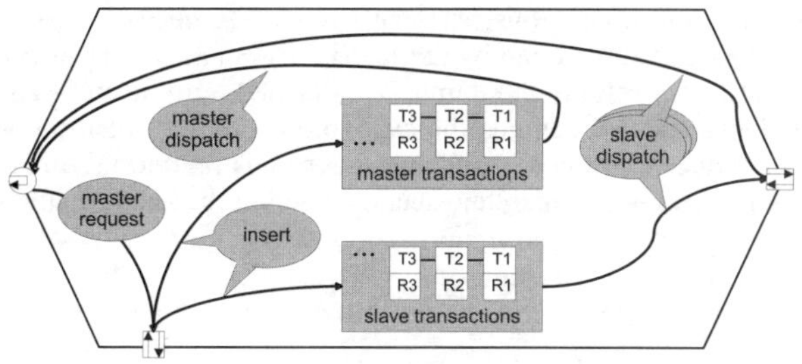

Figure 3: Internal NoC Channel Structure

After the transactions are processed by the network engine, the respective TDS is passed back to the NoC Channel with an attached tag. This tag denotes the calculated arrival time of the transaction. According to this arrival tags T_i, three types of processes inside the NoC Channel deliver the transactions R_i to the destination module. The processes work on two separated list data structures for master and slave transactions, where transactions are sorted according to the arrival tag.

The *insert* process is sensitive to the routed transactions from the network engines and inserts them into the appropriate list structure according to the forward tag and the type of the destination module.

The two types of *dispatch* processes are sensitive to the arrival tags of the head-of-line transaction stored in the list. When simulation time reaches this arrival tag, transactions are dequeued and processed according to their destination module and transaction type. For illustration purposes this processes are presented in a condensed C/C++-like pseudo-syntax.

```
master_dispatch() {
  tds = dequeue_transaction();
  notify_master(tds.id);
}

slave_dispatch() {
 tds = dequeue_transaction();
 if (tds.type == WRITE) {
  slaves[tds.dest]->write(tds.addr, tds.data);
 }
 else {
  slaves[tds.dest]->read(tds.addr, data);
  tds.data = data;
  notify_master(tds.id);
 }
}
```

In case the destination module is one of the attached master modules, this master is notified and subsequently can read the data via the response channel of the master interface. If otherwise the destination is a slave module, the respective slave method is called: write transactions are simply mapped to the `write()` method of the addressed slave, instead for read transactions the slave `read()` method returns the data via a call-by-reference parameter. Thus the TDS is updated and the master is notified on the completion of the read transaction to read the data method via the master response channel.

Since the slave methods are blocking, one dispatch process per attached slave is instantiated. Thus we are able to account for the (potentially significant) execution delays introduced by the attached slaves on this high level of abstraction.

4.4 Network Engine Algorithms

In the following we will elaborate on the algorithms for selected network engines, i.e. basically the calculation of the arrival tag. The selection is by far not complete, but the modular structure enables easy integration of further network topologies and routing algorithms.

The mechanism to notify the NoC Channel of a finished transaction is common for all network engines listed below and implemented by the `notify()` method. Upon calling the latter, the `insert()` process in the NoC Channel is activated to get the TDS together with the corresponding tag from the network engine.

The *point-to-point engine* models transactions between source and destination module over exclusive link connections. This engine is configured by a bandwidth-matrix $B = (M \times (M + S))$, where M and S refer to the number of attached masters and slaves respectively and b_{ij} denotes the available bandwidth of the connection between producer i and consumer j. A second tag-matrix $T = (M \times (M + S))$ maintains per connection the last arrival tag.

```
add_request(tds) {
 if (b[tds.id][tds.dest] > 0) {
  last_tag = maximum(now(), t[tds.id][tds.dest]);
  arrival_tag = last_tag + tds.size / b[tds.id][tds.dest];
  t[tds.id,tds.dest] = arrival_tag ;
  notify(tds,arrival_tag);
 }
 else { error("no connection"); }
}
```

The point-to-point engine processes incoming requests immediately, whereas the following engines model shared communication resources. For this purpose the requests are stored temporarily until they are handed back to the NoC Channel by an additional `arbitrate()` process.

The *bus engine* models data exchange over a shared bus medium. Internally this engine maintains a list, where pending requests are queued until the bus is granted by the arbitration process. This engine can be specialized towards priority or TDMA like bus arbitration schemes by different implementations of the `select()` algorithm, which determines the grant from the list of pending requests. The priority based bus arbiter simply selects the request with highest priority, whereas the TDMA arbiter is based on a static allocation table. The bus engine is configured by the `bandwidth` parameter to determine the duration of the transaction.

```
add_request(tds) {
 if (list.is_empty()) { wake_up_arbiter() }
 list.enqueue(tds);
}

arbitrate() {
 do {
   tds = select(list);
   arrival_tag = tds.size / bus_bandwidth;
   notify(tds, arrival_tag);
   wait( arrival_tag );
   if( list.is_empty() ) { wait(); }
 } while( true );
}
```

A refined version of the bus engine provides additional configurability with respect to the calculation of the arrival tag. Accounting for detailed timing characteristics of the bus architecture like number of pipeline stages, the re-arbitration latency or consideration of split-transactions significantly improves the simulation accuracy. During our refinement flow we have compared the accuracy for different versions of the bus engine against a fully cycle accurate reference bus model. Whereas the coarse calculation based on the bandwidth is up to 50% inaccurate, configuration with the correct bus specific parameter settings improves the accuracy of the bus engine towards a negligible 3% deviation.

The *crossbar engine* models on-chip network architectures, that perform more than one transaction at the same time. Since crossbar networks differ significantly, it is not possible to capture all possible incarnations with a single engine. The engine elaborated below models Virtual Output Queued (VOQ) [26] architectures for equal-size data packets with a non-blocking, buffer-less $((M + S) \times P)$ crossbar matrix, where P denotes the number of supported priorities. According to the VOQ principle, incoming packets are stored separately per output before they pass through the crossbar matrix. This technique prevents from head-of-line blocking in case of asymmetric traffic or partially blocked outputs and hence improves overall throughput and fairness.

In analogy to the bus engine, the crossbar engine can be specialized to static, weighted and un-weighted arbitration algorithms by different implementations of the `select()` method. The engine maintains an internal VOQ data structure, which queues requests per destination module and per priority. For every arbitration interval, the `select()` algorithm generates a grant matrix G from the head-of-line snapshot S of the VOQ queues.

```
add_request(tds) {
 if (queue[tds.dest][tds.prio].is_empty()) {
  s[tds.dest][tds.prio] = tds.prio;
 }
 queue[tds.dest][tds.prio].append(tds);
}

arbitrate() {
 do {
  g = select(s);
  for (i=0; i<M+S; i++) for (j=0; j<P; j++)
   if (g[i][j] == true) {
    tds =  queue[i][j].dequeue();
    notify(tds,arbitration_interval);
    if (queue[i][j].is_empty()) s[i][j] = -1;
    else s[i][j] = queue[i][j].first().prio;
   }
  wait(arbitration_interval);
 } while(true);
}
```

The implementation of network engines is of course not restricted to the algorithmic modeling style outline above, instead the designer has the full expressiveness of C++ and SystemC to extend the engine library. In particular complex network topologies can be composed from elementary engines by recursively instantiating the NoC Channel inside *hierarchical engines*. For example

- an engine modeling a homogenous multi-hob topology contains an NoC Channel along with master modules representing the network nodes, which are connected using the point-to-point engine.
- an engine modeling a complex multi-layered bus network contains an NoC Channel along with master modules representing the bridges, which are connected using several bus engines.

5. NPU CASE STUDY

In this section we present the results of a design project, where the proposed NoC exploration methodology has been applied to the design of Network Processing Unit (NPU) for IP forwarding. After a brief introduction of the application, we illustrate the benefits of a) a custom optimized communication architecture and b) the proposed exploration framework by comparing our application specific NPU against the commercial IXP2400 NPU from Intel [27].

5.1 IP Forwarding with QoS Support

IP forwarding is a central part of the IP network infrastructure. This challenging application domain combines sophisticated functionality for QoS support with highest performance requirements: at OC-48 wire speed (corresponds to 2.5Gbit/s) the timing budget in the NPU for the processing of a minimum size 48Byte packet is as short as 147ns.

IP Forwarding with QoS Support according to the DiffServ proposal [28] requires the following functional blocks: The *Parser* performs sanity checks on the incoming packet and provides the following units with a unique packet descriptor (PD), which holds all the relevant header information of the respective IP packet. The *Route Lookup Unit* (RLU) performs forwarding of IP Packets based on the longest match table search algorithm. The forwarding decision is based upon destination IP address and the routing table. The *Classifier* classifies incoming packets into Classes of Service (CoS), so the packets are processed according to their negotiated Quality of Service parameters by the following blocks. The *Meter* measures the IP packet rate and drops packets exceeding the negotiated traffic characteristics to protect the succeeding queuer unit from greedy traffic streams. The *WRED* unit drops additional packets employing

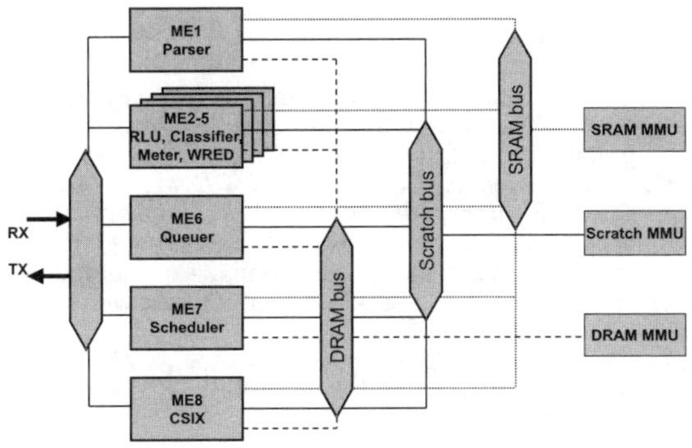

Figure 4: a) Intel IXP2400 Mapping

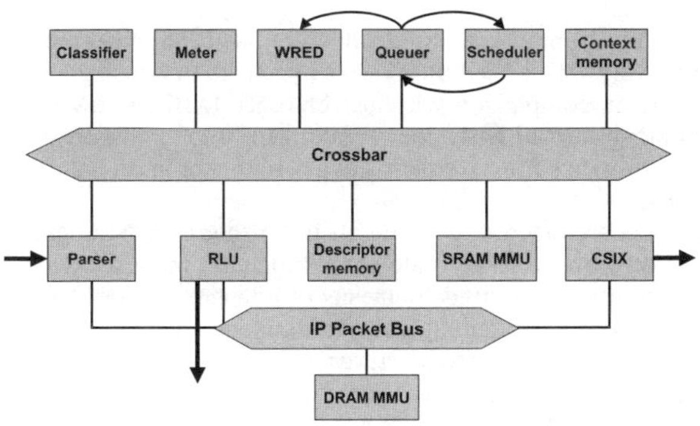

Figure 4: b) NPU Final Architecture View

the weighted RED algorithm [29] to avoid throughput degradation in a TCP friendly manner due to congestion. The *Queuer* stores IP packets according to their CoS until they can be forwarded to the CSIX unit. The *Scheduler* decides on the basis of the priority and the actual fill status of the packet queues in the queuer unit. Finally the *CSIX* unit segments IP packets into fixed size packets in compliance with the standardized CSIX bus protocol [30] to interface the switch fabric. The *Memory Management Unit (MMU)* performs the memory allocation and deallocation of the IP- and PD-memory.

5.2 Exploration of the Communication Architecture

Figure 4 displays the mapping of the IP forwarding application onto two different platforms: 4 a) shows the realization on the IXP2400 reference NPU and 4 b) depicts the final version of the custom optimized communication architecture. To achieve a fair comparison between both NPU platforms, the processing and communication requirements of all functional units as well as the IXP-2400 mapping are taken from the original Intel documentation [31].

According to the general design flow described in section 3, first an untimed functional SystemC model is created from the functional specification document [28, 31]. This functional model is already based on the NoC Channel, but employs only the point-to-point network engine. This model is well suited to validate completeness and functional correctness, but does not yet impose any assumptions on the architectural realization.

This initial setup of the NoC exploration framework was created and validated within 2 months by a team of two experienced engineers. The functional model comprises 6,800 Lines of SystemC code and simulates about 20,000 IP packets per second on a 1.0GHz Pentium III having 256KB L2 cache running Linux 2.4.18.

line	engine descriptor	engine config.	utilization	trn. delay in cycles	IP latency in cycles
1	p2p	unconstr.	0%	0	910
2	p2p	32bit	8%	22	1526
3	ixp2400	32bit_bus	83%	143	4910
4	custom	mix	68%	73	3470
5	sram_p2p	32bit	4%	17	408
6	sram_dual_bus	32bit	78%	125	3000
7	sram_dual_bus	64bit	39%	107	2568
8	sram_tripel_bus	32bit	67%	65	1488
9	sram_crossbar	32bit	39%	65	1560

Table 3: NoC Exploration Results

After annotating the estimated execution delay to each of the functional blocks in conformity with [31], the SystemC model is prepared for the exploration of the communication architecture. An excerpt of the NoC exploration results is printed in table 3. Besides the engine-descriptor and -configuration we list the resource utilization and the mean delay per transaction of the respective NoC setup. The right column contains the overall packet latency introduced by the IP processing chain. Since the timing annotations of the functional units are constant during all our experiments, the measured packet latency clearly unveils the impact of the selected NoC configuration on the system level performance.

According to the exploration methodology described in section 4.2, the point-to-point (p2p) engine is employed to generate an initial traffic profile. The unconstrained p2p engine performs all communication with zero overhead, so the IP latency in line 1 reflects only the timing annotations of the functional units. The 32 bit wide p2p engine in line 2 serves as a 'lower-bound' reference configuration and not as a realistic design option, because - among other unrealistic assumptions - this would implicate a packet descriptor memory with 6 read and 6 write ports.

Besides an insignificant amount of local communication between the buffer and its neighboring units, the statistics generated by the p2p engine admits the classification of the on-chip traffic into two domains: (a) Parser, RLU and CSIX unit regularly access the IP memory (DRAM) to store and forward the arriving IP Packets and (b) all master blocks heavily access the SRAM and scratch memory, where the packet descriptor, routing information, traffic parameters and per flow statistics are stored.

Line 3 in table 3 shows the performance of the engine configuration, which corresponds to figure 4 a) and emulates the mapping to the IXP2400 NPU as proposed in [31]. The huge communication overhead of 4000 cycles is caused by the expensive access of external memories via shared busses. To keep up OC-48 wire-speed processing, the IXP2400 hides the memory latency by exploiting the potential for packet-level parallelism: the application is executed on a functional pipeline formed by 8 micro-engines, each supporting up to 8 parallel processing threads.

The second section in table 3 is dedicated to the exploration of a customized communication architecture for the access to the SRAM and scratch memories, which together account for 3000 cycles in the IXP2400 architecture.

The complete p2p mesh in line 5 is way too expensive and inefficient, while line 6 corresponds to the suboptimal dual bus configuration of the IXP2400 NPU. Duplicating the bandwidth effectively halves the bus utilization, however the sequential access to the 32 bit memories still mark the actual bottleneck. A closer analysis of the simulation results shows, that the scratch memory is best exclusively allocated for the packet descriptor and that the the context information used by the Classifier and Queuer units can be efficiently stored in an additional on-chip context memory. As shown in line 8, the transaction delay is significantly improved as soon as the context memory is accessed through an additional third bus.

Replacing the three separate busses with a dedicated crossbar network introduces a minor performance penalty due to increased arbitration complexity. However this option was selected as the final communication network, because a switched NoC yields several architectural advantages like e.g. improved scalability, simplified block interface and potential for physical optimization.

Based on the proposed NoC exploration framework, the specification of the communication architecture has been performed and quantitatively verified within 2 weeks by a team of two experienced designers. In comparison with the reference IXP2400 Intel NPU, the resulting custom NPU configuration in line 4 gains an overall 30% performance improvement along with major architectural optimizations.

After the architecture exploration is finished, the NoC channel is replaced with cycle-accurate communication models, while the functional units are reused by means of adapters bridging the different levels of abstraction. The comparison of packet-based and cycle accurate communication revealed, that the simulation accuracy depends on the type of the network engine: The point-to-point engine as well as the crossbar engine produce 100% correct results, since the "packet nature" of the communication events is preserved at the cycle accurate level. The accuracy of the bus engine is already discussed in section 4.4.

6. CONCLUSION

In the near future, SoC platforms will integrate tens or even hundreds of IP blocks. The resulting demand of on-chip data exchange can only be accomplished by a sophisticated communication infrastructure, which employs local shared bus systems as well as chip-wide network architectures.

This paper presents a unified approach to the conceptualization of heterogeneous on-chip networks. The proposed Network-on-Chip Exploration Framework combines concepts from the traditional networking design environments with recent System Level Design methodologies to enable a rapid exploration of architectural alternatives.

The presented approach has been successfully applied to the system architecture design of an application specific Network Processing Unit, which performs IP forwarding with Quality of Service support. The high simulation speed, modeling efficiency and support in performance monitoring enabled the specification and quantitative evaluation of a sophisticated communication architecture within two weeks by a team of two experienced designers. Comparison aginst the commercial state-of-the-art IXP2400 NPU from Intel clearly demonstrates the value of a) customized communication architectures and b) the proposed exploration framework to rapidly explore and benchmark competing design options. For the considered case-study, the loss of accuracy caused by the packet-based communication paradigm proved to be negligible.

Our future work will focus on the modeling of further network engines and the additional deployment of analytical analysis- and optimization-techniques.

7. REFERENCES

[1] D. Flynn. Amba: enabling reusable on-chip designs. *IEEE Micro*, 17(4):20–27, July-Aug 1997.

[2] IBM CoreConnect. *http://www.chips.ibm.com/products/powerpc/cores*.

[3] Open Core Protocol International Partnership (OCP-IP). *OCP datasheet, http://www.ocpip.org*.

[4] L. Benini, G. De Micheli. Networks on Chips: A New SoC Paradigm. *IEEE Computer*, pages 70–78, January 2002.

[5] Marco Sgroi, M. Sheets, A. Mihal, Kurt Keutzer, Sharad Malik, Jan M. Rabaey, and Alberto L. Sangiovanni-Vincentelli. Addressing the system-on-a-chip interconnect woes through communication-based design. In *Design Automation Conference*, pages 667–672, 2001.

[6] F. Karim, A. Nguyen, S. Dey, R. Rao. On-Chip Communication Architecture for OC-768 Network Processors. In *Proceedings of the Design Automation Conference (DAC)*, 2001.

[7] P. Guerrier, A. Greiner. A Generic Architecture for On-Chip Packet-Switched Interconnections. In *"Proc. Int. Conf. on Design, Automation and Test in Europe(DATE)"*, 2000.

[8] E. Rijpkema, K.G.W. Goossens, A. Radulescu, J. Dielissen, J. van Meerbergen, P. Wielage, and E. Waterlander. Trade Offs in the Design of a Router with Both Guaranteed and Best-Effort Services for Networks on Chip. In *"Proc. Int. Conf. on Design, Automation and Test in Europe(DATE)"*, 2003.

[9] K. Keutzer, S. Malik, A.R. Newton, J.M. Rabaey, A. Sangiovanni-Vincentelli. System-level design: Orthogonalization of concerns and platform-based design. *IEEE Transactions on Computer-Aided Desig of Integrated Circuits and Systems*, 19(12):1523–1543, December 2000.

[10] F. Balarin, Y. Watanabe, H. Hsieh, L. Lavagno, C. Passerone, A. Sangiovanni-Vincentelli. Metropolis: An integrated electronic system design environment. *IEEE Computer*, 36(4):45–52, April 2003.

[11] D. Gajski, J. Zhu, R. Dömer, A.Gerstlauer, S. Zhao. *SpecC: Specification Language and Methodology*. Kluwer Academic Publishers, 2000.

[12] Vladimir D. Zivkovic, Ed Deprettere, Erwin de Kock, Pieter van der Wolf. Fast and Accurate Multiprocessor Architecture Exploration with Symbolic Programs. In *"Proc. Int. Conf. on Design, Automation and Test in Europe(DATE)"*, 2003.

[13] M. Gasteiner and M. Glessner. Bus-based communication synthesis on system level. *AM Trans. Design Automation Electronic Systems*, pages 1–11, January 1999.

[14] Peter Voigt Knudsen and Jan Madsen. Integrating communication protocol selection with partitioning in hardware/software codesign. In *Proc. Int. Symp. on System Synthesis*, 1998.

[15] K. Hines, G. Borriello. Dynamic communication models in embedded system co-simulation. In *Proceedings of the Design Automation Conference (DAC)*, 1997.

[16] A. Baghdadi, D. Lyonnard, N.-E. Zergainoh, A. Jerraya. An Efficient Architecture Model for Systematic Design of Application-Specific Multiprocessor SoC. In *"Proc. Int. Conf. on Design, Automation and Test in Europe(DATE)"*, 2001.

[17] K. Lahiri, A. Raghunathan S. Dey. Performance analysis of systems with multi-channel communication architectures. In *"Proc. Int. Conf. VLSI Design"*, pages 530–537, 2000.

[18] OPNET. *http://www.opnet.com*.

[19] Pierre G. Paulin, Chuck Pilkington, and Essaid Bensoudane. StepNP: A System-Level Exploration Platform for Network Processors. *IEEE Design & Test of Computers*, 19(6):17–26, Dev-Dec 2002.

[20] SystemC initiative. *http://www.systemc.org*.

[21] T. Grötker, S. Liao, G. Martin, S. Swan. *System Design with SystemC*. Kluwer Academic Publishers, 2002.

[22] O. Ogawa, K. Shinohara, Y. Watanabe, H. Niizuma, T. Sasaki, Y. Takai, S. Bayon de Noyer and P. Chauvet. A Practical Approach for Bus Architecture Optimization at Transaction Level. In *"Proc. Designers' Forum, Int. Conf. on Design, Automation and Test in Europe(DATE)"*, 2003.

[23] J.A. Rowson and A. Sangiovanni-Vincentelli. Interface-Based Design. In *Proceedings of the Design Automation Conference (DAC)*, 1997.

[24] W. Cesario, A. Baghdadi, L. Gauthier, D. Lyonnard, G. Nicolescu, Y. Paviot, S. Yoo, A. Jerraya, M. Diaz-Nava. Component-Based Design Approach for Multicore SoCs. In *Proceedings of the Design Automation Conference (DAC)*, 2002.

[25] Norman Weyrich, Anssi Haverinen. *A SystemC Generic Transaction Level Communication Channel, http://www.systemc.org*, 2003.

[26] Y. Tamir, G. Frazier. High performance multi-queue buffers for VLSI communication Switches. In *Proc. Of 15th Ann. Symp. On Comp. Arch.*, 1988.

[27] Intel Network Processors. *http://developer.intel.com/design/network/products/npfamily/*.

[28] An Architecture for Differentiated Services. *http://www.ietf.org/rfc/rfc2475.txt*.

[29] S. Floyd, and V. Jacobson. Random early detection gateways for congestion avoidance. *IEEE/ACM Transactions on Networking*, 1(4):379–413, August 1993.

[30] The Network Processor Forum. *founded by CSIX/CPIX members in 2001 http://www.npforum.org*.

[31] S. Lakshmanamurthy, K.-Y. Liu, Y. Pun, L. Huston, U. Naik. Network Processor Performance Analysis Methodology. *Intel Technology Journal*, August 2002.

An Efficient Retargetable Framework for Instruction-Set Simulation

Mehrdad Reshadi, Nikhil Bansal, Prabhat Mishra, Nikil Dutt
Center for Embedded Computer Systems, University of California, Irvine.
{reshadi, nbansal, pmishra, dutt}@cecs.uci.edu

ABSTRACT

Instruction-set architecture (ISA) simulators are an integral part of today's processor and software design process. While increasing complexity of the architectures demands high performance simulation, the increasing variety of available architectures makes retargetability a critical feature of an instruction-set simulator. Retargetability requires generic models while high performance demands target specific customizations. To address these contradictory requirements, we have developed a generic instruction model and a generic decode algorithm that facilitates easy and efficient retargetability of the ISA-simulator for a wide range of processor architectures such as RISC, CISC, VLIW and variable length instruction set processors. The instruction model is used to generate compact and easy to debug instruction descriptions that are very similar to that of architecture manual. These descriptions are used to generate high performance simulators. The generation of the simulator is completely separate from the simulation engine. Hence, we can incorporate any fast simulation technique in our retargetable framework without loosing performance. We illustrate the retargetability of our approach using two popular, yet different realistic architectures: the Sparc and the ARM.

Categories and Subject Descriptors

I.6.5 [Simulation And Modeling]: Model Development;
I.6.7 [Simulation And Modeling]: Simulation Support Systems

General Terms: Design, Language, Performance

Keywords: Retargetable Instruction-Set Simulation, Generic Instruction Model, Instruction Binary Encoding, Decode Algorithm, Architecture Description Language.

1. INTRODUCTION

Instruction-set architecture (ISA) simulators are indispensable tools in the development of new architectures. They are used to validate an architecture design, a compiler design as well as to evaluate architectural design decisions during design space exploration. Running on a *host* machine, these tools mimic the behavior of an application program on a *target* machine. These simulators should be fast to handle the increasing complexity of processors, flexible to handle all features of applications and processors, e.g. runtime self modifying codes, multi mode processors; and retargetable to support a wide spectrum of architectures. Although in the past years, performance has been the most important quality measure for the ISA simulators, retargetability is now an important concern, particularly in the area of the embedded systems and SoC design.

A retargetable ISA simulator requires a generic model, supported by a language, to describe the architecture and its instruction set. The simulator uses the architecture description to decode instructions of the input program and execute them. The challenge is to have a model that is efficient in terms of both quality of the description and performance of the simulator. To have a high quality description, the model must easily capture the architectural information in a natural, compact and manageable form for a wide range of architectures. On the other hand, to generate a high performance simulator and to reduce the operations that the simulator must do dynamically at run time, the model should provide as much static information as possible about the architecture and its instruction set.

Designing an efficient model that captures a wide range of architectures is a hard problem because such architectures have different instruction-set format complexities. There is a tradeoff between speed and retargetability in ISA simulators. Some of the retargetable simulators use a very general processor model and support a wide range of architectures but are slow, while others use some architectural or domain specific performance improvements but support only a limited range of processors. Also in some description languages, deriving a fast simulator requires lengthy descriptions of all possible formats of instructions.

In this paper, we present a retargetable simulation framework that supports many variations of architectures with any instruction-set complexity while generating high performance ISA simulators. To achieve maximum retargetability, we have developed a generic instruction model coupled with a decoding technique that flexibly supports variations of instruction formats for widely differing contemporary processors. This model can also be used to exploit all possible instruction formats to generate optimized code for them. We use this generic model to capture the behavior and binary encoding of the instructions. The EXPRESSION Architecture Description Language (ADL) [1] is used to capture the structure of the architecture. The instruction descriptions, based on our generic model, are very compact and easy to debug and verify. In our framework, we have used the Instruction-Set Compiled Simulation (IS-CS) technique [2] to generate fast and flexible simulators by automatically generating the instruction templates from the descriptions. Our retargetable framework is generic enough to incorporate any other simulation optimization technique as well.

The rest of the paper is organized as follows. Section 2 presents related work addressing ISA simulator generation techniques and distinguishes our approach. Section 3 outlines the retargetable simulation framework. It describes three key components of the framework: a generic instruction model, a decoding algorithm, and the simulation code generation. Section 0 compares the efficiency of the instruction model with other architecture description languages and presents simulation performance results

CODES+ISSS'03, October 1–3, 2003, Newport Beach, California, USA.

using two contemporary processor architectures: ARM7 and SPARC. Section 5 concludes the paper.

2. RELATED WORK

An extensive body of recent work has addressed instruction-set architecture simulation. A fast and retargetable simulation technique is presented in [3]. It improves traditional static compiled simulation by mapping the target machine registers to the host machine registers through a low level code generation interface. Retargetable simulators based on an ADL have been proposed within the framework of FACILE [4], Sim-nML [5], ISDL [6], and MIMOLA [7]. The proposed ADL in ISDL is mainly suitable for assembly/binary code generation. FACILE is optimized for out-of-order processor simulation; Sim-nML only supports DSP processors. FLEXWARE Simulator [8] uses a VHDL model of a generic parameterizable model. SimC [9] is based on a machine description in ANSI C. It uses compiled simulation and has limited retargetability. Babel [10] was originally designed for retargeting the binary tools and has been recently used for retargeting the SimpleScalar simulator [11].

The just-in-time cache compiled simulation (JIT-CCS) [12] technique, the closest to our approach, combines some retargetability, flexibility and high simulation performance. It uses the LISA machine description and its performance improvement is gained by caching the decoded instruction information. LISA supports simple RISC like instruction formats and efficient support of complex instruction formats requires extensive coding in this language.

In contrast, our simulation framework efficiently supports a wide variety of instruction formats supported by contemporary processor architectures as well as architectures with complex hybrid instruction sets. Our generic instruction model results in very compact and easy to debug descriptions and the proposed decode algorithm can extract the required information for any simulator generation technique.

3. RETARGETABLE SIMULATION FRAMEWORK

In a retargetable ISA simulation framework, the range of architectures that can be captured and the performance of the generated simulators depend on three issues: first, the model based on which the instructions are described; second, the decoding algorithm that uses the instruction model to decode the input binary program; and third, the execution method of decoded instructions. These issues are equally important and ignoring any of them results in a simulator that is either very general but slow or very fast but restricted to some architecture domain. However, the instruction model significantly affects the complexity of decode and the quality of execution. We have developed a generic instruction model coupled with a simple decoding algorithm that lead to an efficient and flexible execution of decoded instructions.

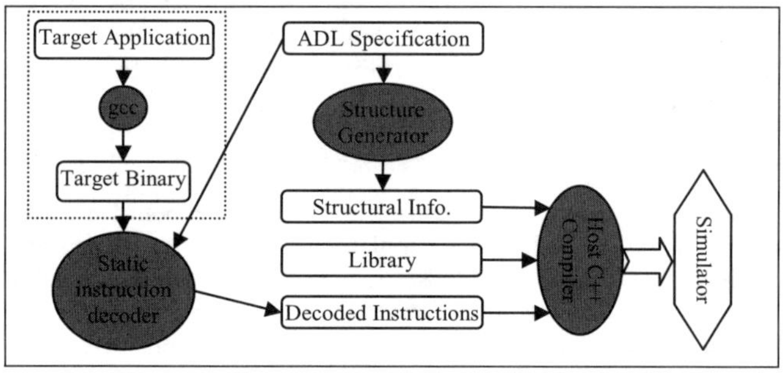

Figure 1- Generating the simulator from ADL

Figure 1 shows our retargetable simulation framework that uses the ADL specification of the architecture and the application program binary (compiled by *gcc*) to generate the simulator. The ADL captures behavior and structure of the target architecture. We describe the binary encoding and behavior of instructions, based on our generic instruction model, as described in Section 3.1. Using the instruction specifications from ADL, the *Static Instruction Decoder* decodes the target program one instruction at a time, as described in Section 3.2. It then generates the optimized source code of the decoded instructions (Section 3.3), that is loaded in the instruction memory.

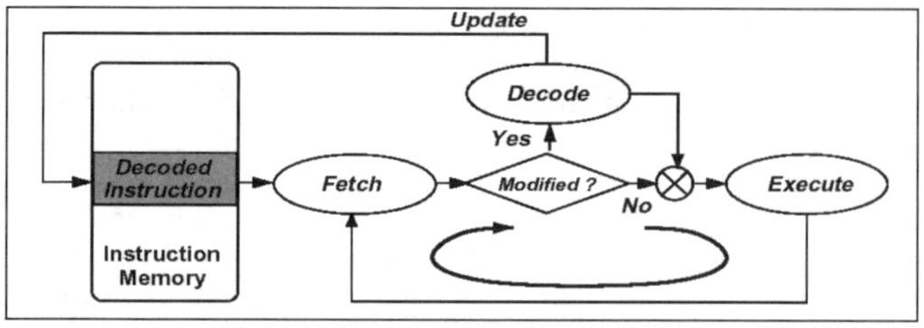

Figure 2- Simulation Engine Flow

The *Structure Generator* compiles the structural information of the ADL into components and objects that keep track of the state of the simulated processor. It generates proper source code for instantiating these components at run time.

The target independent components are described in the *Library*. This library is finally combined with the *Structural Information* and the *Decoded Instructions* and is compiled on the host machine to get the final ISA simulator. Figure 2 shows the flow of the simulation engine. This engine fetches the decoded instructions from the instruction memory and executes them. If the simulator detects that the program code of a previously executed address has changed it initiates a re-decoding and then updates the instruction memory. The simulation engine is specified by the *Library* component. Therefore, by modifying this component, we can integrate other simulation techniques and optimizations in our retargetable framework.

In the remainder of this section, we describe the generic instruction model used in the ADL for capturing the binary encoding and behavior of instruction set. Then, we explain how the decoding algorithm decodes the program binary using the description of instructions in the ADL. Finally, we show how we can generate fast and optimized code for simulation.

3.1 Generic Instruction Model

A major challenge in retargetable simulation is the ability to capture a wide variety of instructions. We propose an instruction model that is generic enough to capture variations of instruction formats of contemporary processors. The focus of this model is on the complexities of different instruction binary formats in different architectures. As an illustrative example, we model the integer arithmetic instructions of the Sparc V7 processor. The completer description is shown in Figure 3.

Example 1: Sparc V7 [15] is a single-issue processor with 32-bit instruction. The integer-arithmetic instructions, *IntegerOps* (as shown below), perform certain arithmetic operation on two source operands and write the result to the destination operand. This subset of instructions is distinguished from the others by the following bit mask:

Bitmask:	10xxxxx0	xxxxxxxx	xxxxxxxx	xxxxxxxx
IntergerOps: <opcode dest src1 src2>				

A bit mask is a string of '1', '0' and 'x' symbols and it matches the bit pattern of a binary instruction if and only if for each '1' or

'0' in the mask, the binary instruction has a 1 or a 0 value in the corresponding position respectively. The 'x' symbol matches with both 1 and 0 values.

In this model, an *instruction* of a processor is composed of a series of *slots*, $I=<sl_0, sl_1,\ldots>$, and each slot contains only one *operation* from a subset of operations. All the operations in an instruction execute in parallel. Each operation is distinguished by a mask pattern. Therefore, each slot (sl_i) contains a set of operation-mask pairs (op_i, m_i) and is defined in the following format. The length of an operation is equal to the length of mask pattern.

$$sl_i=<(op_i^0, m_i^0) \mid (op_i^1, m_i^1) \mid \ldots>$$

An *operation class* refers to a set of similar operations in the instruction set that can appear in the same instruction slot and have similar format. The previous slot description can be rewritten using an operation class *clops*: $sl_i=<(clOps_i, m_i)>$. For example, integer arithmetic instructions in Sparc V7 can be grouped in a class (IntegerOps) as shown below:

I_{SPARC}= <(*IntegerOps*, 10xx-xxx0 xxxx-xxxx xxxx-xxxx xxxx-xxxx)| … >

An operation class is composed of a set of *symbols* and an *expression* that describes the behavior of the operation class in terms of the values of its symbols. For example, the operation class in Example 1 has four symbols: *opcode*, *dest*, *src1* and *src2*. The *expression* for this example will be: $dest = f_{opcode}(src1, src2)$. Each symbol may have a different *type* depending on the bit pattern of the operation instance in the program. For example, the possible types for src2 symbol in Example 1 are register and immediate integer. The value of a symbol depends on its type and can be static or dynamic. For example, the value of a register symbol is dynamic and is known only at run time, whereas the value of an immediate integer symbol is static and is known at compile time. Each symbol in an operation has a possible set of types. A general operation class is then defined as:

$$clOps=<(s_0, T_0), (s_1, T_1), \ldots \mid exp(s_0, s_1, \ldots)>$$

where (s_i, T_i) are *(symbol, type)* pairs and $exp(s_0,s_1,\ldots)$ is the behavior of the operations based on the values of the symbols.

The type of a symbol can be defined as a register (∈ *Registers*) or an immediate constant (∈ *Constants*) or can be based on certain *micro-operations* (∈ *Operations*). For example, a data processing instruction in ARM (e.g., add) uses shift (micro-operation) to compute the second source operand, known as ShifterOperand. Each possible type of a symbol is coupled with a mask pattern that determines what bits in that operation must be checked to find out the actual type of the corresponding symbol. Possible types of a symbol are defined as:

$$T = \{(t, m) \mid t \in \text{Operations} \cup \text{Registers} \cup \text{Constants},\ m \in (1 \mid 0 \mid x)^*\}$$

For example, the opcode symbol in Example 1 can be any of valid integer arithmetic operations and can be described as:

```
OpTypes = {
    (Add, xxxx-xxxx 0000-xxxx xxxx-xxxx xxxx-xxxx),
    (Sub, xxxx-xxxx 0100-xxxx xxxx-xxxx xxxx-xxxx),
    ...}
```

Note that this provides more freedom for describing the operations because here the symbols are not directly mapped to some contiguous bits in the instruction and a symbol can correspond to multiple bit positions in the instruction binary.

The actual register in a processor is defined by its class and its index. The index of a register in an instruction is defined by extracting a slice of the instruction bit pattern and interpreting it as an unsigned integer. An instruction can also use a specific register with a fixed index, as in a branch instruction that update the program counter. A register is defined by:

$$r= [regClass, i, j] \mid [regClass, index]$$

where i and j define the boundary of index bit slice in the instruction. For example, the *dest* symbol (in Example 1) is from 25th to 29th bits in the instruction, and is an integer register. Its type can be described as:

$$DestType = [IntegerRegClass, 29, 25].$$

Similarly a portion of an instruction may be considered as a constant. For example, one bit in an instruction can be equivalent to a Boolean type or a set of bits can make an integer immediate. It is also possible to have constants with fixed values in the instructions. A constant type is defined by c =# type, i, j# | # type, value# where i and j show the bit positions of the constant and *type* is a scalar type such as integer, Boolean, float, etc.

```
SPARCInst = $
    (InegerOps, 10xx-xxx0 xxxx-xxxx xxxx-xxxx xxxx-xxxx) | …
$;
IntegerOp = <
    (opcode, OpTypes), (dest, DestType), (src1, Src1Type), (src2, Src2Type)
    | { dest = opcode(src1, src2); }
>;
OpTypes = {
    (Add, xxxx-xxxx 0000-xxxx xxxx-xxxx xxxx-xxxx),
    (Sub, xxxx-xxxx 0100-xxxx xxxx-xxxx xxxx-xxxx),
    (Or , xxxx-xxxx 0010-xxxx xxxx-xxxx xxxx-xxxx),
    (And, xxxx-xxxx 0001-xxxx xxxx-xxxx xxxx-xxxx),
    (Xor, xxxx-xxxx 0011-xxxx xxxx-xxxx xxxx-xxxx),
    …
};
DestType = [IntegerRegClass, 29, 25];
Src1Type = [IntegerRegClass, 18, 14];
Src2Type = {
    ([IntegerRegClass,4,0], xxxx-xxxx xxxx-xxxx xx0x-xxxx xxxx-xxxx),
    (#int,12,0#, xxxx-xxxx xxxx-xxxx xx1x-xxxx xxxx-xxxx)
};
```

Figure 3- Integer arithmetic instcutions in SPARC

Figure 3 shows the complete description of integer-arithmetic instructions in SPARC processor (Example 1). Figure 4 describes how to capture data-processing instructions of the ARM processor using our instruction model. ARM has complex 32-bit instruction formats that are all conditional. In data-processing operations (DPOperation), if the condition (16 possibilities) is true, some arithmetic operation (16 possibilities) is performed on the two source operands and the result is written in the destination operand. The destination and the first source operand are always registers. The second source operand, called ShifterOperand, has three fields: shift operand (register/immediate), shift operation (5 types) and shift value (register/immediate). The shift value shows the number of shifts that must be performed on the shift operand by the specified shift operation. For example, the "*ADD r1, r2, r3 sl #10*" is equivalent to "*r1=r2+(r3 << 10)*" expression. If indicated in the instruction opcode, the flag bits (Z, N, C, and V) are updated. Therefore, 16x16x(2x5x2)x2=10240 formats of instructions binaries are possible in this class of instructions. All these formats are covered by the description of Figure 4. In the next sections, we show how all these possibilities are explored for generating an optimized code for each type of instruction.

We defined a set of macros that can be used for compact description. For example *mask(8, 2, "10")* macro generates an 8 bit mask that has a '10' at position 2 i.e. xxxx-x10x.

In this model, instructions that have similar format are grouped together into one class. Most of the time this information is readily available from the instruction set architecture manual. For example, we defined six instruction classes for the ARM processor viz., Data Processing, Branch, LoadStore, Multiply, Multiple LoadStore, Software Interrupt, and Swap.

In this section, we have demonstrated two key features of our instruction model: first, it is generic enough to capture architectures with complex instruction sets; second, it captures the instructions efficiently by allowing instruction grouping.

```
ARMInst = $
   (DPOperation, xxxx-001x xxxx-xxxx xxxx-xxxx xxxx-xxxx) |
   (DPOperation, xxxx-000x xxxx-xxxx xxxx-xxxx xxx0-xxxx) |
   (DPOperation, xxxx-000x xxxx-xxxx xxxx-xxxx 0xx1-xxxx) |
   ...
$;
DPOperation = <
   (cond, Conditions), (opcode, Operations), (dest, [intReg,15,12]),
   (src1, [intReg,19,16]), (src2, ShifterOperand),
   (updateFlag, {(true, mask(32, 20, "1"), (false, mask(32, 20, "0")})
   | {
      if (cond()) {
         dest = opcode( src1, src2);
         if (updateFlags) {/*Update flags*/}
      }
   }
>;
Conditions = {
   (Equal, mask(32, 31, "0000"), (NotEqual, mask(32, 31, "0001"),
   (CarrySet, mask(32, 31, "0010"), (CarryClear, mask(32, 31, "0011"),
   ..., (Always, mask(32, 31, "1110"), (Never, mask(32, 31, "1111")
};
Operations = {
   (And, mask(32, 24, "0000"), (XOr, mask(32, 24, "0001"),
   (Sub, mask(32, 24, "0010"), (Add, mask(32, 24, "0100"), ...
};
ShifterOperand = <
   (op, {([intReg,11,8], mask(32,4,"0")), (#int,11,7#, mask(32,7,"0xx1"))}),
   (sh, {(ShiftLeft, mask(32,6,"00)), (ShiftRight, mask(32,6,"01)), ...}),
   (val, {([intReg,3,0], mask(32,25,"0")), (#int,7,0#, mask(32,25,"1"))})
   | { sh(op, val) }
>;
```

Figure 4- Data processing instructions in ARM

3.2 Generic Instruction Decoder

A key requirement in a retargetable simulation framework is the ability to automatically decode application binaries of different processors architectures. This necessitates a generic decoding technique that can decode the application binaries based on instruction specifications. In this section we propose a generic instruction decoding technique that is customizable depending on the instruction specifications captured through our generic instruction model.

```
Algorithm 1: StaticInstructionDecoder
Input: Target Program Binary Appl, Instruction Specifications InstSpec;
Output: Decoded Program DecodedOperations;
Begin
      Addr = Address of first instruction in App;   DecodedOperations={};
   While (Appl not processed completely)
      BinStream = Binary stream in Appl starting at Addr;
      (Exp, AddrIncrement) = DecodeOperation (BinStream, InstSpec);
      DecodedOperations = DecodedOperations U <Exp, Addr>;
      Addr = Addr + AddrIncrement;
   EndWhile;
   return DecodedOperations ;
End;
```

Algorithm 1 describes how *Static Instruction Decoder* of Figure 1 works. This algorithm accepts the target program binary and the instruction specification as inputs and generates a source file containing decoded instructions as output. Iterating on the input binary stream, it finds an operation, decodes it using Algorithm 2, and adds the decoded operation to the output source file. Algorithm 2 also returns the length of the current operation that is used to determine the beginning of the next operation.

Algorithm 2 gets a binary stream and a set of specifications containing operation or micro-operation classes. The binary stream is compared with the elements of the specification to find the specification-mask pair that matches with the beginning of the stream. The length of the matched mask defines the length of the operation that must be decoded. The types of symbols are determined by comparing their masks with the binary stream. Finally, using the symbol types, all symbols are replaced with their values in the expression part of the corresponding specification. The resulting expression is the behavior of the operation. This behavior and the length of the decoded operation are produced as outputs.

```
Algorithm 2: DecodeOperation
Input: Binary Stream BinStream, Specifications Spec;
Output: Decoded Expression Exp, Integer DecodedStreamSize;
Begin
   (OpDesc, OpMask) = findMatchingPair(Spec, BinStream);
   OpBinary = initial part of BinStream whose length is equal to OpMask;
   Exp = the expression part of OpDesc;
   ForEach pair of (s, T) in the OpDesc
      Find t in T whose mask matches the OpBinary;
      v = ValueOf(t, OpBinary);
      Replace s with v in Exp;
   EndFor
   return (Exp , size(OpBinary));
End;
```

Consider the following SPARC Add operation example and its binary pattern:

Add g1, #10, g2	31 1000-0100	23 0000-0000	15 0110-0000	7 0000-1010

Using the specifications of Figure 3, in the first line of Algorithm 2, the (InegerOps, 10xx-xxx0 xxxx-xxxx xxxx-xxxx xxxx-xxxx) pair matches with the instruction binary. This means that the *IntegerOps* operation class matches this operation. It calls Algorithm 3 to decode the symbols of *IntegerOps* viz. *opcode, dest, src1, src2.*

```
Algorithm 3: ValueOf
Input: Type t, Operation Binary OpBinary;
Output: Extracted Value extValue;
Begin
   Switch (t)
      case #type, value#: extValue = (type) value; endcase
      case #type, i, j#: extValue = (type) OpBinary[i:j]; endcase
      case [regClass, index]: extValue = REGS[regClass][index]; endcase
      case [regClass, i, j]: extValue = REGS[regClass][ OpBinary[i:j]]; endcase
      case Operation Spec: (extValue, tmp) = DecodeOperation(OpBinary, t);
      endcase
   EndSwitch;
   return extValue;
End;
```

Algorithm 3 gets a symbol type and an operation binary (*OpBinary*), and returns the actual value of the corresponding symbol. If the type itself is a micro-operation specification, the decode algorithm (Algorithm 2) is called again and the result is returned. If the type is not a fixed constant (register), the value is calculated by interpreting the proper portion of the operation binary (*OpBinary[i:j]*) as a constant (register index).

In the previous example, the four symbols (*opcode, dest, src1, src2*) are decoded using Algorithm 3. Symbol *opcode*'s type is *OpTypes* in which the mask pattern of *Add* matches the operation pattern. So the value of *opcode* is *Add* function. Symbol *dest*'s type is *DestType* which is a register type. It is an integer register whose index is bits 25th to 29th (00010), i.e. 2. Similarly, the values for the symbols *src1* and *src2* can be computed. By replacing these values in the expression part of the *IntegerOps* the final behavior of the operation would be: g2 = Add(g1, 10); which means g2 = g1 + 10.

The complexity of the decoding algorithm is $O(n{*}m{*}log_2m)$, where n is the number of operations in the input binary program and m is the number of operations in the instruction set.

3.3 Generating Fast Code for Simulators

Typically in simulators, for each instruction of the simulated architecture instruction set, there is a general piece of code (in form of a function or switch-case statements) that simulates the behavior of the instances of that instruction. However, these instances may have a constant value for a particular field that can be used for further optimizations. For example, a majority of the ARM instructions execute unconditionally (condition field has value always) and hence it is a waste of time to check the condition for such instructions every time they are executed. By considering these constant (static) values and applying the partial evaluation technique [14], it is possible to generate a customized code for different formats of instructions. To take advantage of such situations we need separate functions (or *case* statements) for each and every possible format of instructions so that the function can be optimized by the compiler at compile time and produce the best performance at run time. In our instruction model, all of these formats and their corresponding functions can be constructed by generating all of the permutations of the symbol values in an operation class. The number of generated formats (functions) can be controlled by excluding some of the symbols or iterating only on a subset of symbol values. Controlling the level of optimizations and number of generated formats using the same small description is one of the unique features of our model.

However, generating all of the instruction formats of an instruction set may not be feasible in practice. For example, as discussed in section 3.1, there are 10240 possible formats for the data processing instructions of the ARM processor and generating all these formats, imposes a huge overhead on the compiler. To solve this problem in our framework, we generate the customized code only for the instruction instances of the simulated program. Furthermore, instead of generating distinct functions, we use C++ templates and customize them during decode. We generate a template for each operation or micro-operation class specification. For each symbol in the operation class the corresponding template has a parameter in its parameter list. During the decode phase, these parameters are replaced with the values of the symbols. Finally during the compilation on host machine, these customized templates are optimized by the compiler. After *extracting* the templates in this way, we can use IS-CS technique for generating a high performance simulator. The details of *using* and optimizing these templates in IS-CS technique are described in [2]. Figure 5 shows the extracted template and its parameters for data-processing instructions in ARM, described in Figure 4.

```
/* extracted template for data processing operations of ARM*/
template<class Conditions, class Operations, class ShifterOperand, bool
updateFlag >
class DPOperations {
   intReg dest, src1;        ShifterOperand src2;
public:
   ...
   virtual void execute() {
      if (Conditions::f()){
         dest = Operations::f(src1, src2);
         if (updateFlag){ Z = (dest == 0); N= (dest < 0); ...}
      }
   }
};
```

Figure 5- Code generation for an ARM instruction

Note that the decode algorithm, described in Section 3.2, relies only on the descriptions of instructions to extracts the values of symbols corresponding to an instruction instance. These values can be used either dynamically in some conditional statements or statically to generated the source code of proper functions. Therefore the generic instruction model and the proposed decode algorithm can be used in any simulation technique and does not depend on IS-CS technique.

4. EXPERIMENTS

In order to evaluate the applicability of our framework, we modeled two contemporary, yet very different, processors: ARM7[16] and SPARC [15] to demonstrate the usefulness of our approach. The ARM7 processor is a RISC machine with fairly complex instruction set. We used *arm-linux-gcc* for generating target binaries for ARM7 and validated the generated simulator by comparing traces with Simplescalar-arm [11] simulator. The Sparc V7 is a high performance RISC processor with 32-bit instructions. We used *gcc3.1* to generate the target binaries for Sparc and validated the generated simulator by comparing traces with *Shade* [13] simulator. We have used benchmarks from SPEC 95 and DSP domains. In this section we show the results using three application programs: *adpcm*, *099.go* and *129.compress*.

4.1 Efficiency of description

It took us one man-month for each processor to study the manual and generate the corresponding simulator. This very short generation time was mainly because of the three following reasons. First, the description of instructions in our model is very similar to their representation in the architecture manual and therefore we needed a simple mapping between manual and the language. Second, the descriptions are very compact and efficient. For example by adding a very small code for an operation and its mask to the *Operations* class in the Figure 4, we can add a new instruction and reuse the rest of the description. Third, since all of the operations in an operation class share the same expression, it is very easy to debug and verify the descriptions. For example, in Figure 4 if the expression of *DPOperations* class works correctly for *Add*, it will also work well for *Sub* and other operations that can be replaced with symbol *opcode*.

```
01:  RESOURCE {
02:     PROGRAM_MEMORY byte8 prog_mem[0x0..0x1000];
03:     REGISTER word32 R[1..15];
04:  }
05:  OPERATION ADD {
06:     DECLARE { GROUP dst,src1,src2 = {Register}}
07:     CODING { 0b01011 0b0000 src1 src2 dst}
08:     SYNTAX { "ADD" dst "," src1 "," src2 }
09:     BEHAVIOR{ dst = src1 + src2}
10:  }
11:  OPERATION Register {
12:     DECLARE { LABEL index; }
13:     CODING { index=0bx[4]}
14:     SYNTAX { "R" index }
15:     EXPRESSION { R[index]}}
```

Figure 6- LISA sample code for Add operation

Figure 6 shows a sample code in LISA language taken from a recent publication [12]. In this figure an operation *Add* with register parameters is described. To describe an *Add* operation with immediate integer operands the 'OPERATION ADD' section (lines 5-10) must be repeated again with slight modification. In other words, for every possible addressing mode in the architecture, a separate section for an operation is needed in LISA description. In LISA, a C function is generated in the simulator for the behavior section of each operation. Therefore to exploit different instruction formats and generate faster simulation, the formats must be explicitly included in the description. For example consider the data processing instructions in ARM (Section 3.1). In these operations since one of the sources can be a ShifterOperand addressing mode, each instruction needs at least five OPERATION sections. Now consider the optimizations discussed in Section 3.3. Since all ARM instructions are predicated but majority of them execute unconditionally in a program, we can generate two formats for each instructions: the conditional version that checks the proper condition, and the unconditional one that executes faster. This is only one of the possible optimizations. Considering five formats for the ShifterOperand addressing mode and only two formats for the optimization, each instruction needs ten OPERATION sections similar to the one presented in lines 5-10 in Figure 6. Finally for sixteen instructions in this group we need at least 16x10x5=800 lines in the LISA description. As shown in Figure 4, in our mode, this group of instructions is represented by only three operation classes (*DPOperation, Conditions,* and *Operations*) in less than 50 lines.

A similar approach to LISA is used in Babel [10]. In Babel, a separate section is needed to describe each individual format of an instruction. For example Sparc description in Babel is more than 2300 lines long while its description with our model contains less than 400 lines of code.

Additionally, in these languages, the instruction can contain only contiguous fields. Therefore dummy or multiple fields are needed to describe non-contiguous opcodes (as in Sparc). These extra fields not only increase the size of description but also make the decoder inefficient. On the other hand, since in our model we use bit masks, the descriptions are more natural and does not require such tricks in similar cases.

4.2 Performance of the simulator

The IS-CS performance results presented in [2] are based on generating the instruction templates manually. We extracted similar instruction templates automatically from our instruction model and generated the simulator. Typically retargetable approaches slow down the simulation. In our framework, since the generation of the simulator and extraction of the templates is completely separate from the simulation engine itself, there are no negative effects imposed on the performance.

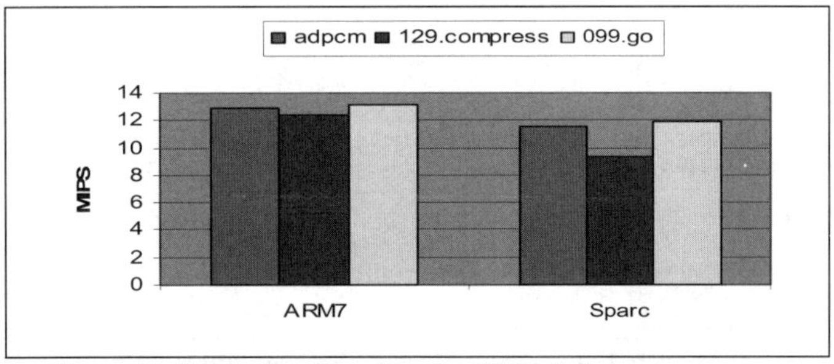

Figure 7- Simulation Results of ARM7 & Sparc processors

Figure 7 shows the simulation performance of our technique on both ARM7 and Sparc processor models. The performance results of the retargetable framework are exactly similar to that of IS-CS. We achieved 30%-50% performance improvement compared to best published results in this category of simulators. Note that, the overall performance of ARM simulator is slightly better than that of Sparc. ARM instructions are more complex and in most cases are equivalent to more than one Sparc instruction. Therefore optimizing one ARM instruction is equivalent to optimizing multiple instructions in Sparc. Also simulating Sparc model on a Pentium host machine requires a data encoding translation (Big-Endian to Little-Endian).

5. SUMMARY

In this paper, we presented a retargetable framework for generating fast and flexible ISA simulator. We proposed a generic instruction model as well as a generic decode algorithm that can specify and decode many variations of instruction binary formats with any complexity. We demonstrated the applicability of the approach on two radically different architectures, viz. ARM and Sparc processors. Use of symbols in the generic instruction model enables maximum reuse of descriptions among operations and results in very compact descriptions. It also simplifies the debug and verification of the whole description. Furthermore, describing instructions in our generic model is very simple due to its similarity with the architecture manual. The ISA described using our generic instruction model is an order of magnitude smaller in size than other languages such as LISA and Babel. To achieve high performance simulation, we have integrated the IS-CS simulation technique in our retargetable framework by automatically extracting the required templates for simulating the instructions. Since the generation of the simulator is completely separate from the simulation engine, we can incorporate any other fast simulation technique without loosing performance. Future work will concentrate on using this framework for cycle accurate simulation of complex architectures including reconfigurable platforms.

6. ACKNOWLEDGMENTS

This work was partially supported by NSF grants CCR-0203813 and CCR-0205712.

7. REFERENCE

[1] A.Halambi et al. EXPRESSION: A Language for Architecture Exploration through Compiler/Simulator Retargetability. DATE, 1999.

[2] M.Reshadi et al, Instruction-Set Compiled Simulation: A Technique for Fast and Flexible Instruction Set Simulation, DAC, 2003.

[3] J.Zhu et al. A Retargetable, Ultra-fast Instruction Set Simulator. DATE, 1999.

[4] E.Schnarr et al. Facile: A language and compiler for high-performance processor simulators. PLDI, Jun. 2001.

[5] M.Hartoog et al. Generation of Software Tools from Processor Descriptions for Hardware/Software Codesign. DAC, 1997.

[6] G.Hadjiyiannis et al. ISDL: An instruction set description language for retargetability. In Proc. DAC, 1997.

[7] R.Leupers et al. Generation of Interpretive and Compiled Instruction Set Simulators. DAC, 1999.

[8] P.Paulin et al. FlexWare: A flexible firmware development environment for embedded systems. In Proc. Dagstuhl Code GenerationWorkshop, 1994.

[9] F.Engel et al. A generic tool set for application specific processor architectures. (CODES), May 2000.

[10] W.S.Mong et al, A Retargetable Micro-architecure Simulator. DAC, 2003.

[11] Simplescalar Home page: http://www.simplescalar.com

[12] A.Nohl et al. A Universal Technique for Fast and Flexible Instruction-Set Architecture Simulation. DAC, 2002.

[13] R.F.Cmelik et al. Shade: A fast instruction set simulator for execution profiling. ACM SIGMETTRICS Conference on Measurment and Modeling of computer systems, Philadelphia, 1996.

[14] Y. Futamura. Partial Evaluation of Computation Process: an Approach to a Compiler-Compiler. Systems, Computers, Controls, 1971.

[15] Sparc Version 7 Instruction set manual: http://www.sun.com

[16] The ARM7 User Manual, http://www.arm.com

Transaction Level Modeling: An Overview

Lukai Cai and Daniel Gajski
Center for Embedded Computer Systems
University of California, Irvine
Irvine, CA 92697, USA
{lcai,gajski}@cecs.uci.edu

ABSTRACT

Recently, the transaction-level modeling has been widely referred to in system-level design community. However, the transaction-level models(TLMs) are not well defined and the usage of TLMs in the existing design domains, namely modeling, validation, refinement, exploration, and synthesis, is not well coordinated. This paper introduces a TLM taxonomy and compares the benefits of TLMs' use.

Categories and Subject Descriptors

C.0 [**Computer Systems Organization**]: General

General Terms

Design

Keywords

Transaction level model, modeling, validation, refinement, exploration, synthesis

1. INTRODUCTION

In order to handle the ever increasing complexity of system-on-chips (SoCs) and time-to-market pressures, the design abstraction has been raised to the system level in order to increase design productivity. This higher level of abstraction generated large interest in transaction-level modeling, synthesis, and verification [10][12].

In a transaction-level model (TLM), the details of communication among computation components are separated from the details of computation components. Communication is modeled by channels, while transaction requests take place by calling interface functions of these channel models. Unnecessary details of communication and computation are hidden in a TLM and may be added later. TLMs speed up simulation and allow exploring and validating design alternatives at the higher level of abstraction.

However, the definition of TLMs is not well understood. Without clear definition of TLMs, not only the predefined

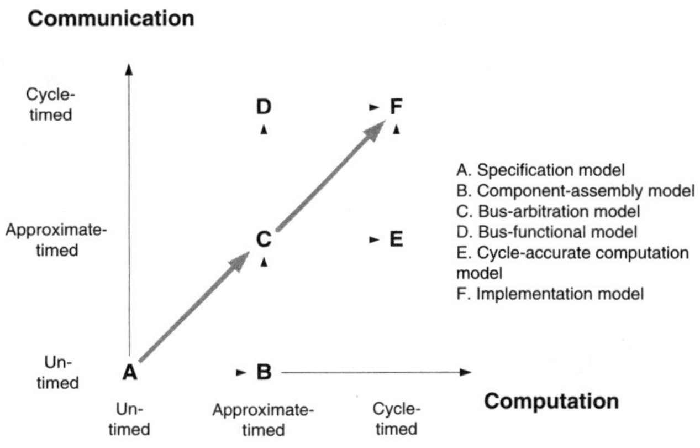

Figure 1: System modeling graph

TLMs cannot be easily reused, but also the usage of TLMs in the existing design domains, namely modeling, validation, refinement, exploration, and synthesis, cannot be systematically developed. Consequently, the inherent advantages of TLMs don't effectively benefit designers. In order to eliminate some ambiguity of TLMs, this paper attempts to explicitly define several transaction-level models, each of which is adopted for different design purpose. It also explores the usage of defined TLMs under a general design flow and analyzes how the TLMs are used in the design domains.

This paper is organized as follows: Section 2 reviews the related work; Section 3 defines four TLMs; Section 4 introduces the usage of TLMs in different design domains; Finally, the conclusion is given in section 5.

2. RELATED WORK

The concept of TLM first appears in system level language and modeling domain. [10] defines the concept of a **channel**, which enables separating communication from computation. It proposes four well-defined models at different abstraction levels in a top-down design flow. Some of these models can be classified as TLMs. However, the capabilities of TLMs are not explicitly emphasized. [12] broadly describes the TLM features based on the channel concept and presents some design examples. However, the TLMs are not well defined and the usage of TLMs in the existing design domains is not addressed. [10] [12] also demonstrate that both SpecC [3] and SystemC [2] support transaction level modeling using the channel concept.

The TLMs can be used in top-down approaches such as

CODES+ISSS'03, October 1–3, 2003, Newport Beach, California, USA.

proposed by SCE [6] that starts design from the system behavior representing the design's functionality, generates a system architecture from the behavior, and gradually reaches the implementation model by adding implementation details. In comparison to the top-down approaches, meet-in-the-middle approaches [13] map the system behavior to the predefined system architecture, rather than generating the architecture from the behavior. An example of meet-in-the-middle approach is VCC [5] for architecture estimation/exploration and N2C [1] for interface synthesis. Unlike above two approaches, bottom-up approaches assemble the existing computation components by inserting wrappers among them. Bottom-up approaches, such as proposed in [9], focus on component reuse and wrapper generation. All of above three design practices fully or partly cover the design from the system behavior to the detailed system implementation, which exhibits great potential of employing TLMs.

Some other research groups have applied TLMs in the design. [14] adopts TLMs to ease the development of embedded software. [15] defines a TLM with certain protocol details in a platform-based design, and uses it to integrate components at the transaction level. [11] implements co-simulation across-abstraction level using channels, which implies the usage of TLM. Each of above research addresses only one limited aspect of TLMs.

3. TRANSACTION LEVEL MODELS

In order to simplify the design process, designers generally use a number of intermediate models. The intermediate models slice the entire design into several smaller design stages, each of which has a specific design objective. Since the models can be simulated and estimated, the result of each of these design stages can be independently validated.

In order to relate different models, we introduce the system modeling graph (shown in Figure 1) [8]. X-axis in the graph represents computation and y-axis represents communication. On each axis, we have three degrees of time accuracy: un-timed, approximate-timed, and cycle-timed. Un-timed computation/communication represents the pure functionality of the design without any implementation details. Approximate-timed computation/communication contains system-level implementation details, such as the selected system architecture, the mapping relations between processes of the system specification and the processing elements of the system architecture. The execution time for approximate-timed computation/communication is usually estimated at the system level without cycle-accurate RTL (register transfer level) /ISS (instruction set simulation) level evaluation [5]. Cycle-timed computation/communication contains implementation details at both system level and the RTL/ISS level, such that cycle-accurate estimation can be obtained.

Inspired by [10] [12], we define six abstraction models in the system modeling graph, which are indicated by circles. Among them, component-assembly model, bus-arbitration model, bus-functional model, and cycle-accurate computation model are TLMs, which are indicated by shaded circles.

Specification model. It describes the system functionality and is free of any implementation details. This model is similar to the *specification model* in [10] and *untimed functional model* in [12]. It can model the data transfer between processes through variable accessing without using

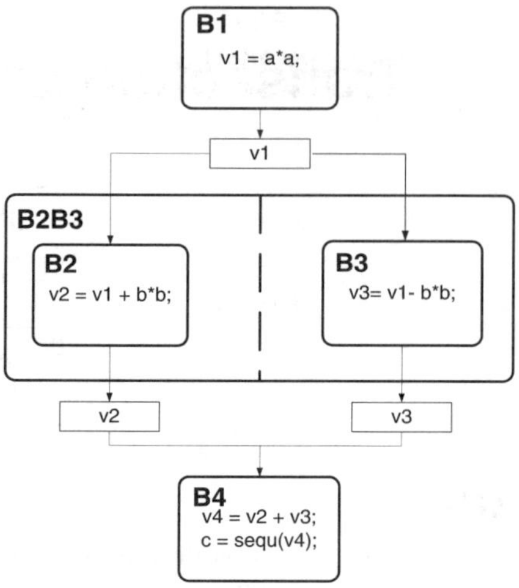

Figure 2: The example of specification model

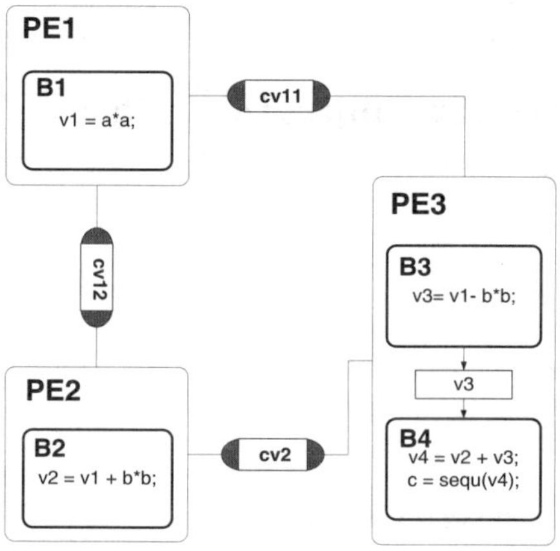

Figure 3: The example of component-assembly model

channel concept, which eases to convert C/C++ language to SystemC/SpecC language. Specification model is an untimed model. Figure 2 displays an example of specification model. Processes *B1, B2B3, and B4* execute sequentially. *B2B3* is a parallel composition of *B2* and *B3*. Variables *v1, v2* and *v3* are used to transfer data among processes.

Component-assembly model. The entities at the top level of the model represent concurrently executing processing elements (PEs) and global memories, which communicate through channels. A PE can be a custom hardware, a general-purpose processor, a DSP, or an IP. The channels are message passing channels, which only represent data transfer or process synchronization between PEs without any bus/protocol implementation. The communication part of the model (channel) is un-timed, while computation part of the model (PE) is timed by approximately estimating the execution on specific PE. The estimated time of computation is computed by system-level estimator such as [5]. The estimated time is annotated into the code by inserting *wait* statements. Component-assembly model is the same as *architecture model* defined in [10] and belongs

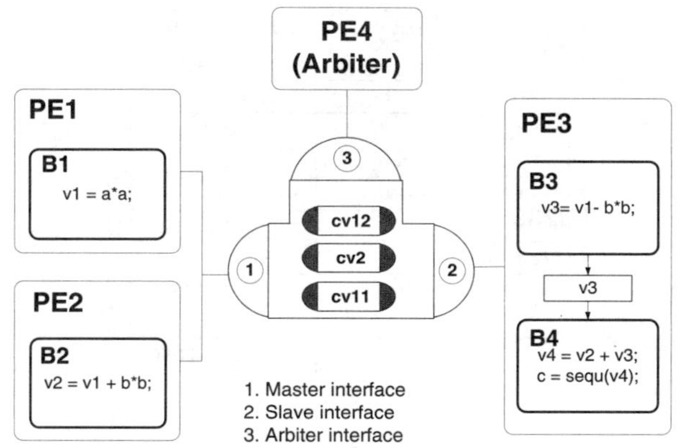

Figure 4: The example of bus-arbitration model

to *timed functional model* defined in [12]. In comparison to specification model, component-assembly model explicitly specifies the allocated PEs in the system architecture and process-to-PE mapping decision. The example of component-assembly model is displayed in Figure 3. *PE1, PE2* and *PE3* are three allocated PEs. *cv11, cv12, cv2* are the message-passing channels.

Bus-arbitration model. In comparison to component-assembly model, channels between PEs in bus-arbitration model represent buses, which are called abstract bus channels. The channels still implement data transfer through message passing, while bus protocols can be simplified as blocking and nonblocking I/O. No cycle-accurate and pin-accurate protocol details are specified. The abstract bus channels have estimated approximate time, which is specified in the channels by one *wait* statement per transaction. Because several channels may be grouped to one abstract bus channel, two parameters are added to the interface functions of channels: logical address and bus priority. Logical address distinguishes interface function calls of different PEs or processes; bus priority determines the bus access sequence when bus conflict happens. Furthermore, a bus arbiter is inserted into the system architecture as a new PE to arbitrate the bus conflict. Master PEs, slave PEs, and the arbiter call the functions of different interfaces of the same abstract bus channels.

Figure 4 illustrates an example of bus-arbitration model refined from component-assembly model in Figure 3. The three channels in component-assembly model are encapsulated into an abstract bus channel representing a system bus. In order to access the new channel, the bus masters (*PE1* and *PE2*), the bus slave (*PE3*), and the inserted arbiter (*PE4*) use different channel interfaces.

Bus-functional model. It contains time/cycle accurate communication and approximate-timed computation. Two types of bus-functional model are specified: time-accurate model and cycle-accurate model. Time-accurate model specifies the time constraint of communication, which is determined by the time diagram of component's protocol. For example, in Figure 5(a), the time is limited in the time range between 25 and 75. Cycle-accurate model can specify the time in terms of the bus master's clock cycles, as displayed in Figure 5(b). The task of refining a time-accurate model to a cycle-accurate model is called protocol refinement.

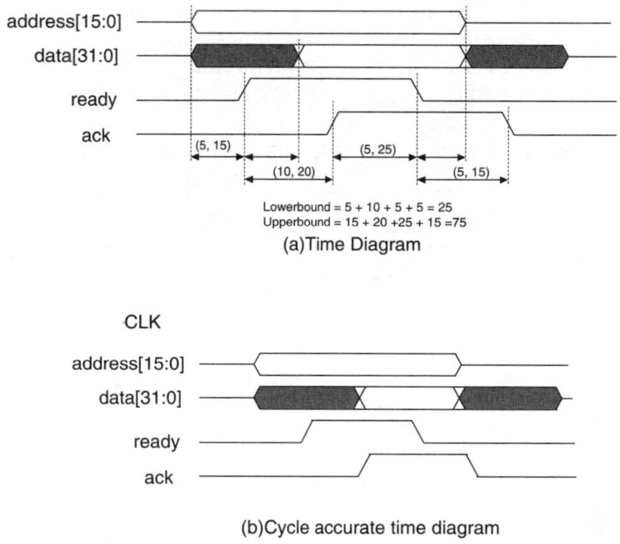

Figure 5: Time/cycle accurate diagram

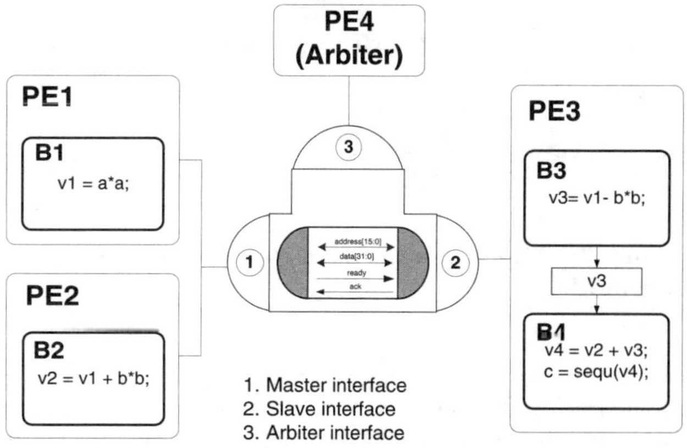

Figure 6: The example of bus-functional model

In bus-functional model, the message-passing channels are replaced by protocol channels. A protocol channel is time/cycle accurate and pin-accurate. Inside a protocol channel, wires of the bus are represented by instantiating corresponding variables/signals. Data is transferred following the time/cycle accurate protocol sequence. At its interface, a protocol channel provides functions for all abstraction bus transaction. A protocol channel is the same as a protocol channel of [10]. We call an abstract bus channel containing a protocol channel a detailed bus channel. It should be noted that in the bus-functional model, it is not necessary to refine all the abstract bus channels into detailed bus channels. Some abstract bus channels can be refined while others are untouched. The refinement process from bus-arbitration model to the bus-functional model is similar to the *protocol insertion* introduced in [10]. Figure 6 illustrates our bus-functional model.

Cycle-accurate computation model. It contains cycle-accurate computation and approximate-timed communication. This model can be generated from the bus-arbitration

Models	Communication time	Computation time	Communication scheme	PE interface
Specification model	no	no	variable/channel	(no PE)
Component-assembly model	no	approximate	message-passing channel	abstract
Bus-transaction model	approximate	approximate	abstract bus channel	abstract
Bus-functional model	time/cycle accurate	approximate	detailed bus channel	abstract
Cycle-accurate computation model	approximate	cycle-accurate	abstract bus channel	pin-accurate
Implementation model	cycle-accurate	cycle-accurate	wire	pin-accurate

Table 1: Characteristics of different abstraction models

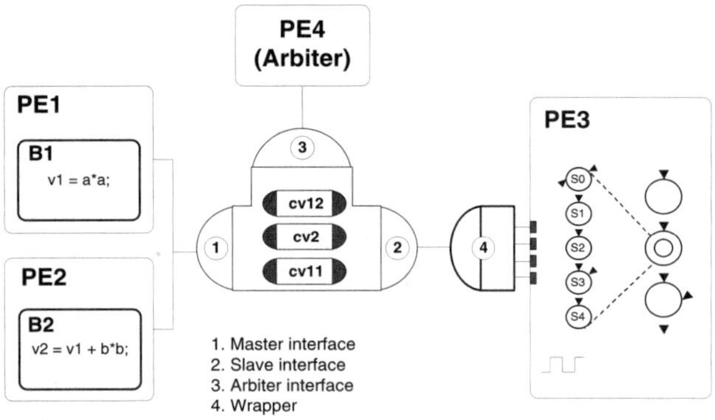

Figure 7: The example of cycle-accurate computation model

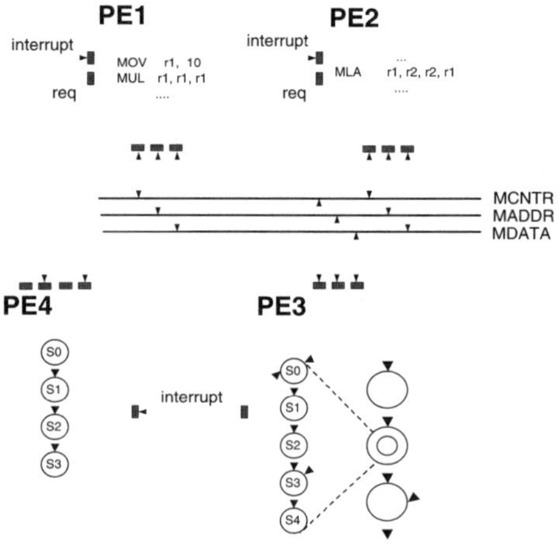

Figure 8: The example of implementation model

model. In this model, computation components (PEs) are pin accurate and execute cycle-accurately. The custom hardware components are modeled at register-transfer level, and general-purpose processors and DSPs are modeled in terms of cycle-accurate instruction set architecture. To enable communication between cycle-accurate PEs and abstract level interfaces of abstract bus channels, wrappers which convert data transfer from higher level of abstraction to lower level abstraction are inserted to bridge the PEs and the bus interfaces. Similar to the bus-functional model, it is not necessary to refine all the PEs to the cycle-accurate level. Some PEs can be refined while others are untouched. Figure 7 illustrates a cycle-accurate computation model, in which only *PE3* is refined to a time-accurate and pin-accurate model.

Implementation model. It has both cycle-accurate communication and cycle-accurate computation. The components are defined in terms of their register-transfer or instruction-set architecture. The implementation model can be obtained from the bus-functional model or the cycle-accurate computation model. The implementation model is the same as the implementation model in [10] and register-transfer level model in [12]. Figure 8 displays an example of the implementation model. *PE1* and *PE2* are microprocessors while *PE3* and *PE4* are custom-hardwares.

Table 1 summaries the characteristics of different abstraction models. Although models indicated by × in Figure 1 can also be specified, they will not be discussed in this paper because they are not commonly used.

4. SYSTEM DESIGN WITH TLMS

4.1 Design Flow

The gray solid arrow in Figure 1 represents a well-accepted design flow. It goes through models *A, C,* and *F*, which represents system functionality, abstract system architecture, and cycle-accurate system implementation respectively. Among them, bus-arbitration model divides the system flow into two stages: system design stage and component design stage. System design stage selects/generates system architecture and maps the system behavior to that architecture. Component design stage refines/systhezises computation and communication components to the cycle accurate level. In general, different design flows include different models. For example, [10] goes through models *A, B, D* and *F*, [9] goes through models *A, C, E* and *F*, while [12] goes through models *A, B, C, D* and *F*.

4.2 Design Domain Definition

In Figure 1, we use arrows to represent a set of tasks that generate one abstraction model from the previous one. Figure 9 shows a general design flow with five design domains for generating *model B* from *model A*.

1. **Modeling domain**. It deals with languages and styles of writing models. In other words, it deals with seman-

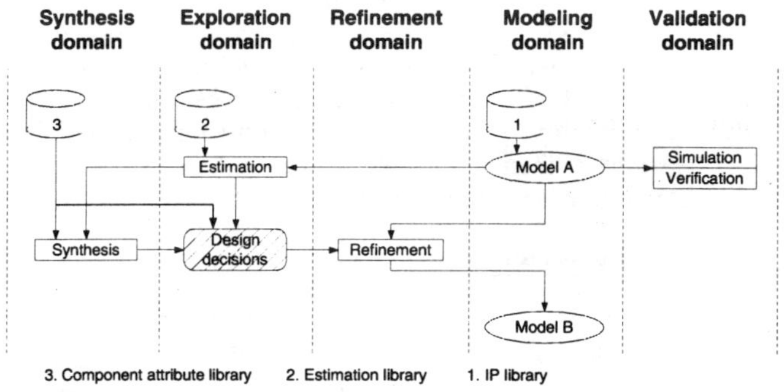

Figure 9: A general design flow with five domains

tics of different models used for different design tasks, such as verification, refinement, and synthesis. System modeling task can be simplified if the part of model has been predefined as IP and saved in *IP library*. An example of modeling is that designers can specify the *Model A* using system level design languages such as SpecC and SystemC.

The modeling styles of TLMs have been briefly discussed in section 3. Especially, because communication is completed separated from computation in TLM, designers can specify different components of one model at different abstraction levels. Such a model is called multi-level model. Both SpecC and SystemC support TLM modeling. The difference of modeling TLMs using SpecC and SystemC is discussed in [8].

2. **Validation domain**. Validation asserts that the model represents the system properties faithfully. The correctness of the model can be validated by different methods such as simulation and formal verification.

   Validating TLMs can be performed by simulation. For example, SystemC provides a Verification Standard [4] to improve the validation capability with standard APIs for transaction-based verification tasks. On the other hand, [7] proposes a formal verification approach that proves the equivalence of models generated through automatic refinement.

   Furthermore, validating components through simulating multi-level model can dramatically speed up the validation time. If we model the component which we want to validate at the cycle-accurate level, and model the rest of components at the approximate-timed level, then simulation time can be dramatically shorter than the time needed for simulating the pure cycle-accurate model. Both [14] and [15] work in this direction.

3. **Refinement domain**. Every time a new design detail is added, the original model must be rewritten or refined in order to include the new design detail. These design decisions made by the designers or an automatical synthesis tool can be incorporated into the new model manually or automatically. An automatic refinement for the flow which goes through models A, B, D, and F in Figure 1 can be founded in [10], which defines four abstraction models and proposes refining guidelines. In comparison to our defined models, it has a bus-functional model (called communication model) which has cycle/pin accurate communication and abstract computation. The same strategy can be easily applied to the sequence *A, B, C, D* and *F*.

   The refinement tasks for the flow which goes through models C, E, and F can be founded in [9], which refines model C to E by producing software and co-simulation wrappers for microprocessors and refines model E to F by producing hardware wrappers among microprocessors.

4. **Exploration domain**. In order to aid designers to make better decisions, the different metrics for potential design decisions should be estimated, based on the *Model A* and the availability of buses, channels, RTOS, ISS, drivers, arbiters, and other SW/HW components in the *estimation library*.

   Different TLMs require different estimation supports. We need to estimate approximate computation time for PEs in model B, approximate communication time for abstract bus channels in model C, cycle-accurate communication time for detailed bus channels in model D, and cycle-accurate computation time for PEs in model E. For example, [16] proposes an simulation-based estimation approach.

   Furthermore, in order to speed up the simulation and enlarge the exploration space, we can perform architecture exploration at bus-arbitration model, which has both approximate-timed computation and approximate-timed communication. In order to estimate components at such an approximate-timed level more accurately, we can first refine the components to the cycle-accurate level and achieve cycle-accurate estimation by simulation or some other methods. Then we annotate back this estimation to the component models at approximate-timed level. Back annotation ensures very fast simulation with cycle-accurate estimation.

5. **Synthesis domain**. Synthesis algorithms perform automatical exploration and produce optimal solution for given constraints and optimization metrics. Synthesis algorithms relieve designers from making decision decision. However, designers always can override the algorithms and make their own decision since new model generation is separated from decision making.

   Synthesis algorithms can be divided into several groups where each group contains algorithms for transformation of one model to another.

   Component assembly (A->B) contains algorithms for selecting PEs from PE libraries, mapping of processes in the specification model to the selected PEs, and selecting real time operating systems (RTOS) for general-purpose processors or DSPs.

   Communication exploration (B->C) contains algorithms for producing the bus-topology, determining abstract bus protocols, mapping channels to the buses, assigning bus-accessing priorities to the processes in PEs, and determining bus arbitration mechanism.

   Protocol refinement (C->D) contains algorithms that determine the pin-accurate and time-accurate bus protocols, and refine time-accurate bus protocols to cycle-accurate bus protocols if required.

PE refinement (D->F) contains algorithms that synthesize the processes mapped to cycle-accurate custom hardware to register transfer models, convert the processes mapped to general-purpose processors or DSPs to ANSI-C code which is ready to be compiled and ready to be linked to the corresponding cycle-accurate instruction set models.

PE replacement (C->E) contains algorithms that select lower level PE models which have pin-accurate interface to replace the higher level PE models, and vice versa, and insert across level wrappers to bridge the lower level PE models and bus-abstraction channels.

Communication synthesis (E->F) contains algorithms that determine the pin-accurate and time-accurate bus protocols and synthesize channels and across-level wrappers to cycle-accurate communication coprocessors.

4.3 Design Flow Styles

The style of design flows may depend on the companies and system design tools. In any case, it becomes easier with the usage of well-defined aforementioned TLMs with intermixed application of the three design practices mentioned in section 2.

The initial version of the design can be designed using top-down approach. During the implementation process, all the generated models at different levels are stored in the IP library. After this step we have a predefined platform which can be used further.

The changes in the design can be inserted by rewriting of the specification model. At this stage we have a predefined platform which allows us to apply meet-in-the-middle approach. Furthermore, we have an accurate estimation of the system behavior obtained from the initial version of the design. Now, the designers only need to estimate the new additions of the system behavior. Hence, the component assembly and communication exploration for the new design can be easily made using the generated platform.

After generating the bus-arbitration model for the new version, designers can perform computation or communication component implementation at the component design stage. For the components that are not updated, designers can reuse the pre-designed bus-functional model and implementation model, instead of carrying out refinement from bus-arbitration model again. Only the updated components need to be refined.

On the other hand, if designers want to replace an old IP by an new IP for the designed system, bottom-up design can be exploited. Starting from cycle-accurate computation model of the design, designers can replace an old IP and its wrapper with the new IP and its wrapper in the cycle-accurate computation model. Then communication synthesis is performed again for the new IP and its wrapper. Starting with cycle-accurate computation model saves us several synthesis tasks.

5. CONCLUSION

In order to eliminate the some ambiguity with the transaction level model, this paper attempts to define several TLMs and present the system level design flow and major design tasks for generation of each model. The major challenge in front of us is to define the semantics of each model in detail and formally so that algorithms and tools for modeling, verification, refinement, exploration, and synthesis can be developed and deployed in industry.

6. REFERENCES

[1] CoWare home page (www.coware.com).

[2] OSCI home page (www.systemc.org).

[3] STOC home page (www.specc.org).

[4] The SystemC Verification Standard, version 1.0 (www.systemc.org).

[5] VCC home page (www.cadence.com/products/vcc.html).

[6] S. Abdi et al. System-On-Chip Environment (SCE): Tutorial. Technical Report CECS-TR-02-28, UCI, Sept 2002.

[7] S. Abdi et al. Formal Verification of Specification Partitioning. Technical Report CECS-TR-03-06, UCI, Mar 2003.

[8] L. Cai et al. Comparison of SpecC and SystemC Languages for System Design. Technical Report CECS-TR-03-11, UCI, May 2003.

[9] W. Cesario et al. Multiprocessor SoC Platforms: a Component-Based Design Approach. In *IEEE Trans. on Design and Test*, Nov-Dec 2002.

[10] D. Gajski et al. *SpecC: Specification Language and Methodology.* Kluwer, Jan 2000.

[11] P. Gerin et al. Scalable and Flexible Cosimulation of SoC Designs with Heterogeneous Multi-Processor Target Architectures. In *ASPDAC*, 2001.

[12] T. Grotker et al. *System Design with SystemC.* Kluwer, 2002.

[13] K. Keutzer et al. System Level Design: Orthogonalization of Concerns and Platform-Based Design. *IEEE Trans. on CAD*, Dec 2000.

[14] S. Pasricha. Transaction Level Modelling of SoC with SystemC 2.0. In *Synopsys User Group Conference*, 2002.

[15] P. Paulin et al. StepNP: A System-Level Exploration Platform for Network Processors. In *IEEE Trans. on Design and Test*, Nov-Dec 2002.

[16] N. Pazos et al. System Level Performance Estimation. *In SystemC Methodologies and Applications. Kluwer*, 2003.

Extending the SystemC Synthesis Subset by Object-Oriented Features

Eike Grimpe
OFFIS Research Institute
Escherweg 2
26121 Oldenburg, Germany
grimpe@offis.de

Frank Oppenheimer
OFFIS Research Institute
Escherweg 2
26121 Oldenburg, Germany
oppenheimer@offis.de

ABSTRACT

In this article we present an approach to object-oriented hardware design and synthesis based on SystemC. We will give an introduction to an extended SystemC synthesis subset which we propose, and, in particular, its object-oriented features. We will also briefly outline our basic synthesis concepts for object-oriented hardware specifications. Finally we will present some examples for the application of the extended synthesis subset, which are directly processable by a first synthesis tool prototype which we have developed for this purpose.

Categories and Subject Descriptors

B.6.3 [**Logic Design**]: Design Aids—*Automatic synthesis, Hardware description languages*; B.7.1 [**Integrated Circuits**]: Types and Design Styles—*VLSI*; C.0 [**General**]: *System specification methodology*; C.3 [**Special-Purpose and Application-Based Systems**]: *Real-time and embedded systems*

General Terms

Design, Languages

Keywords

SystemC, C/C++ based design, hardware description language, hardware synthesis, system level design, object-orientation, high-level synthesis

1. INTRODUCTION

One of the most serious challenges in embedded system design today is the growing design productivity gap. Driven by the enormous technological advances in semiconductor manufacturing and by ever increasing demands for extended functionality the complexity of embedded systems is rapidly growing. Unfortunately the designer's productivity does not grow at the same rate causing a growing gap between what can be technically realized on a single chip, and what can be effectively mastered by a design staff of reasonable size, in reasonable time.

Most probably, there will not be a sole solution to this problem, but rather a combination of different ones, including, for example, IP-centric modelling, application specific processor synthesis, a growing portion of software, and so on. However, we believe that increasing the level of abstraction which can be directly applied to hardware design is another important building block. A lesson which can be learned from software engineering is that the object-oriented modelling paradigm can help a lot in successfully handling systems of great complexity. Additionally, a convergence between hardware and software modelling paradigms is quite desirable for making a further step towards real system level design. Most embedded systems today consist of hardware as well as of software, and a unified modelling approach would allow one to make the decision on hardware/software partitioning later in the design process, maybe even automatically.

For this reason the goal of our research work is the development of design methodologies, languages, and tools which support hardware synthesis from object-oriented specifications. Existing hardware design languages, such as VHDL and Verilog, do not support object-oriented modelling, and lack respective language concepts. The still emerging system level design language SystemC™ [2, 7] would principally allow for applying object-oriented modelling, since it is in fact a C++ class library which provides the possibility of modelling and simulating hardware based on C/C++. But existing synthesis tools which are able to process SystemC specifications, such as the CoCentric™SystemC Compiler[1] [13, 14], only support a synthesis subset that is widely equivalent to common RT/Behavioral level VHDL and Verilog synthesis subsets, excluding almost all object-oriented C++ features. We try to overcome these limitations with new synthesis techniques, and also with some additions to SystemC which provide some object-oriented concepts in a way which better suits the requirements from hardware synthesis.

The remainder of this article will first give a short overview of related work. Section 3 will very briefly define the terms structural and data type based object-orientation in order to allow for a better classification of the approach presented in

[1]In fact this is the only working synthesis tool at the moment, the authors of this paper are aware of, which is able to process SystemC

CODES+ISSS'03, October 1–3, 2003, Newport Beach, California, USA.

this work. Section 4 will introduce and discuss our proposed extended SystemC synthesis subset. Section 5 outlines our basics synthesis concepts for object-oriented language constructs, and section 6 will present some examples illustrating the application of the extended subset. The article will close with the conclusions, and an outlook on future work.

2. RELATED WORK

Over the last years there have already been several approaches on object-oriented hardware design. Some of these approaches are based on object-oriented programming languages and augment them by capabilities for hardware modelling [4, 3, 15], whilst other approaches are based on existing hardware description languages and augment them by object-oriented language features [12, 11, 1]. None of these approaches reached a general breakthrough so far, because they either primarily focus on simulation rather than on synthesis, lack sufficient tool support, or, like SystemC, make only use of an object-oriented programming language in order to add hardware modelling capabilities, but basically do not allow for object-oriented modelling. However, especially the VHDL based approaches [9, 11, 1] have strongly motivated and influenced our work.

3. STRUCTURAL VS. DATA TYPE BASED OBJECT-ORIENTATION

We distinguish basically two principle approaches to object-oriented hardware design. Structural approaches model whole hardware components/entities as concurrent objects. That means, for instance, that components like multiplexer, arithmetic logical units (ALU), decoders, registers, and register files are modelled as self-contained objects. Although this modelling style seems to be quite natural at first sight, it raises various problems. The combination of parallelism and object-oriented modelling poses some fundamental problems that are well known and discussed in object-oriented concurrent programming, for several years now. For example, the fundamental object-oriented concept of inheritance can only be hardly combined with the concept of concurrent, objects, i.e., objects with an own thread of control. This problem is known as so called *inheritance anomaly* [5]. Up to now, the authors of this article are not aware of a general solution to this problem.

Data type based approaches make use of object-orientation as a way to create new user defined data types, but not structural objects, as used from programming languages, such as C++ and Java. Objects in this sense do not have an own thread of control, and they are not going to be independent entities as discussed above. First class objects are user defined data objects, such as data packages, data containers, computational elements, like complex numbers, vectors, matrices or filters, etcetera. These elements are used within a sequential context, usually a process, and may move from place to place in a design, but do not determine the structure of a system.

Our approach focuses on data type based object-oriented modelling for mainly two reasons; first, because of the problems of the structural approaches as mentioned above, and second, because it can be applied relatively easy, and in a straightforward way, for extending the limited SystemC/C++ subset which is supported for synthesis by existing tools. The application of a kind of structural object-orientation is also possible, based on so called global objects (refer to section 4.3), but only in a very limited way, thus avoiding most of the problems of object-oriented concurrent programming.

4. EXTENDING THE SYSTEMC SYNTHESIS SUBSET

The modelling language SystemC is gaining increasing importance as system level design language for several reasons. First of all it allows one to model hardware based on C/C++, since it is in fact a C++ class library comprising hardware modelling and simulation features. C/C++ is presumably the most widespread and known programming language most designers are familiar with even more likely than with any hardware description language, such as VHDL or Verilog. And C/C++ is supported by a wide range of established tools and development environments, a lot of them even available as freeware. A SystemC design can just be compiled with most common C++ compilers, and then be simulated by running the resulting executable without requiring an external simulator. Starting the design process with a 'golden model' written in C/C++ is a common practice in embedded system design. SystemC allows one to keep this language whilst refining a design down to a cycle accurate or even synthesizable level. Moreover modelling at different levels of abstraction and new design methodologies, such as *transaction level modelling*, provide for the possibility of a quick and flexible design space exploration.

Although SystemC does not limit the use of C++ in principle, existing synthesis tools for SystemC do not support object-oriented features, as mentioned in the introduction. But by applying some additional synthesis techniques, as being outlined in section 5, this restricted synthesis subset can be extended by a wide range of object-oriented C++ features which are discussed in the following.

4.1 Classes and Co.

The basic language feature of C++ that allows for object-oriented modelling is its class concept in combination with inheritance. Therefore our extended synthesis subset includes most of the class related language constructs provided by C++. In particular, this means the ability to:

- declare classes;
- create new classes by means of inheritance from already existing classes;
- derive classes from multiple and virtual parent classes;
- declare data members of scalar and complex type, including class types and array types;
- declare member functions and operators;
- redefine member functions and data members in derived classes;
- declare constructor methods;
- declare class templates with scalar and type parameters.

As being common practice in C++, classes can be used as types for objects in a design, for instance, as type for a variable, a signal, or port, as a return type for a function, or as a type for a formal parameter. A class type can just be used wherever another type can be used. Data members and member functions can also be used and accessed in the same way as in C++.

Supporting these features should provide for the possibility of declaring and using classes and objects in basically the same way as usual in C++, but there are, of course, also some restrictions and limitations with respect to hardware modelling and synthesis. For instance, dynamic object creation, and destruction by means of the `new` and `delete` operators are excluded from the synthesis subset for obvious reasons. Pointer variables, or, more precisely, pointer arithmetic, is also excluded. We believe that pointer synthesis, although possible in principle, tends towards producing inefficient hardware, in terms of area and speed, but, at the same time, offers only very little modelling benefit in the absence of dynamic memory allocation.

4.2 Polymorphism

Polymorphism is a modelling concept which, simply speaking, allows one to handle objects, or references to objects, of different classes but with common features uniformly. Objects of different classes may provide the same abstraction of an operation—which means with the same signature—but with different implementations. An operation that is requested on a reference that may refer to objects of different classes is dynamically bound[2] to a concrete implementation at runtime, dependent on the class of the object actually being referenced. Whoever requests this operation does not have to explicitly take care about that. A classical example from software engineering for the application of polymorphism is a class hierarchy of geometrical objects, like `Circle` and `Square`, being derived from a common base class, all providing a `draw()`-method. If an instance of a geometrical object should be drawn to a screen just this `draw()`-method has to be invoked without having to know the concrete type of the geometrical object. A runtime system will automatically bind the correct method implementation to the call.

There is also a wide range of potential applications for polymorphism in hardware. For instance, different formats of data packages, or datagrams, may differ in several aspects but may share the same address format. A hardware component with the purpose to route data packages could handle packages of different formats, even dynamically at runtime, since it only would have to deal with the address, whose format is always the same. Another example are different kinds of filters which could be dynamically exchanged at runtime dependent on actual needs, e.g., for best fitting varying kinds of data streams. Further examples include instructions and operations that could be grouped according to common features. For instance, a store instruction usually has a source and a destination, no matter, if it operates on registers or memory addresses, and whether it includes immediate operands or not. Likewise, binary arithmetical operations, as illustrated by Figure 1, always have two operands and return a result on execution. A concrete example for the application of these operations is given in section 6.

[2]Regarding runtime, or dynamic, polymorphism.

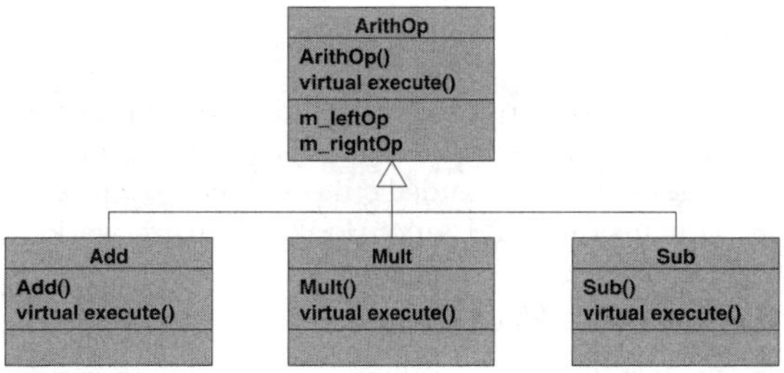

Figure 1: Class hierarchy of arithmetic operations

The polymorphism mechanism provided by C++, and therefore by SystemC, too, is based on the use of pointers. A pointer may reference instances of different classes at runtime, and thus methods invoked on a pointer are dynamically dispatched. As explained in the previous section, pointers are excluded from our synthesis subset, making an alternative polymorphism realization necessary.

What we propose as alternative, and what is also supported by our synthesis tool prototype, is a *tagged object* approach. A tagged object—we call this also a polymorphic object—is a self-contained object, with an own state space, which means it is not just a reference to an object, like a pointer. This makes reference resolution for a polymorphic object at runtime obsolete. Only its actual class must be determinable at runtime. In the synthesised hardware the actual class of a polymorphic object is tracked by an artificial attribute, called *tag*. More details on this are given in section 5. The important point for modelling is, that a polymorphic object provides for dynamic binding of operations, and that it behaves widely similar to a pointer in C++, for instance, in respect of assignment rules. Making use of polymorphic objects requires for including an additional C++ class library, called 'OOHWLib', which is freely available. An application example is given in section 6.

4.3 Global Objects

Communication modelling is one of the key aspects in the design of complex embedded systems. Methodologies and techniques that would help to improve the modelling of communication between subcomponents could also significantly improve the whole design process. For this reason SystemC provides the concept of channels for communication. A channel can be used to abstract from the details of a certain form of communication—for instance, a certain protocol—, and allows processes to communicate and exchange data with each other, based on method calls instead of signals. This concept already has led to a new kind of design methodology, called *transaction level*, or *transaction based*, modelling, actually being intensively discussed in the SystemC community [10].

Indeed the channel concept provides for modelling communication at a higher level of abstraction, and to separate communication and behavior more cleanly. But unfortunately, channels do not generally possess a clear synthesis semantics. And, although being intended for communication between concurrent components, they do not posses built-in mechanisms for handling concurrent accesses. This makes channels quite useful for creating un-timed models and for simulation but not for synthesis.

For this reason we offer an alternative concept to SystemC channels, based on so called global objects. A global object is, in principle, an object which is declared as member of a SystemC module, like a port or signal. Therefore it is visible and accessible by all processes declared in the same module. Like any other object a global object may specify a set of methods which forms its interface. This allows processes to communicate and exchange data via global objects based on method calls, as illustrated in Figure 2, similar to SystemC's channels. Like ports and signals, global objects which are located in different modules can be bound to each other, thus making communication throughout a hierarchy of modules possible.

Figure 2: Method based communication via global object

In contrast to channels, a global object possesses built-in mechanisms for handling concurrent accesses, a clear synthesis semantics, and it exhibits a timed behavior during simulation. Handling concurrent accesses is basically realised by means of a scheduler which has to be specified for each global object by the user. The scheduler determines which client process is granted to access the global object in the case of concurrent requests. All other requesting clients are blocked meanwhile. As a consequence accesses to a global object are mutual exclusive. In addition this is supported by a guard mechanism which allows one to associate a Boolean expression—the so called *guard*—with a member function. Clients requesting an operation whose guard is 'false' at that moment are ignored for scheduling and are blocked. The timed behavior of global objects gives the designer an early and realistic impression on the temporal behavior of the modelled system during simulation even before preforming synthesis.

In order to declare and to use global objects in a design, the user has to include the same additional class library, that also provides the polymorphic objects discussed in the previous section.

5. SYNTHESIS BASICS

In this section we will give a very brief overview of our basic synthesis concepts. More details can be found in [8] which builds the foundation of our work.

The key of the synthesis concept we apply to object-oriented hardware specifications forms a mapping of objects to bit vectors. Data members of an object are represented by slices of the generated bit vector. Therefore, the width of a bit vector representing an object is given by the sum of the bit widths of all individual data members of the object. For instance, for a Boolean member 1 bit is added, and for an arbitrary sized integer (`sc_bigint<>`) the respective number of bits which were used for its declaration. If a data member is itself an object, it is transformed into a bit vector first and then contributes to the size of its super object. Wherever a class type was used before, it is replaced by a bit vector of appropriate size during synthesis. Access to data members of an object is replaced with access to the appropriate slice of the bit vector representing the original object. Member functions, also including constructors and overloaded operators, are transformed into ordinary non-member functions which operate on the synthesised bit vectors instead of the original objects.

Bit vectors representing polymorphic objects are chosen big enough to store objects of different classes, which basically means as big as the biggest object ever being assigned. Additionally, an artificial attribute—the tag mention in section 4.2—is added to the state space of a polymorphic object allowing for tracking its actual class. With the ability to dynamically determine the class of a polymorphic object by means of the tag, dynamic binding of operations can be easily realised, for instance, by means of a set of 'if statements', or a 'switch statement', which select from different implementations dependent on the current value of the tag.

From a global object a set of synchronous and asynchronous processes is generated which implement the scheduling of concurrent accesses, the evaluation of the guard conditions, the operations provided by a global object, and all the necessary multiplexing. The communication between a global object and its client processes is mapped to a signal based communication with a fixed handshake protocol.

5.1 The ODETTE Synthesizer

The ODETTE synthesizer is a synthesis tool prototype which was developed—and which is still under development—in the course of the European project ODETTE [6]. It is able to process the extended SystemC/C++ subset which is described in the previous section. Starting from a SystemC description, which is based on this subset, the synthesis tool generates behavioral equivalent SystemC or VHDL code that can be further processed with existing tools and technologies. As shown in Figure 3 the tool is settled on top of existing tool chains and does neither perform behavioral synthesis nor logic synthesis at the moment. It just maps object-oriented language elements in the input specification to behavioral equivalent lower lever constructs, according to the basic synthesis concepts outlined in the previous section.

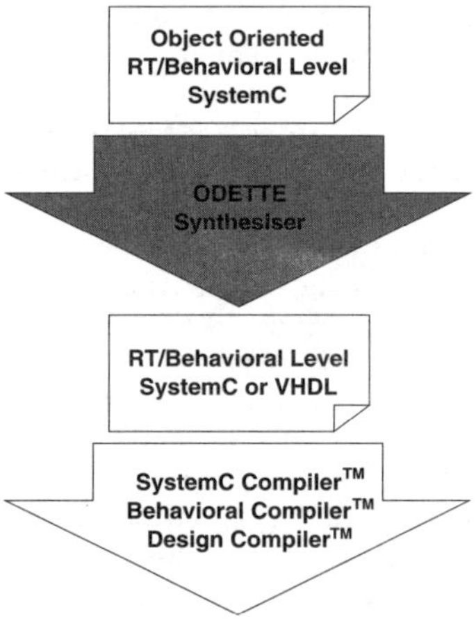

Figure 3: Synthesis flow

The synthesis tool prototype has now reached a state where it provides for the possibility of performing concrete modelling and synthesis experiments. That means that it effectively supports all the features that are listed in section 4, and that it allows one to start the automated synthesis flow from a higher level of abstraction. But it is still a prototype offering a high potential for improvements. In particular, more sophisticated optimization techniques could be integrated which aim at producing better results in terms of circuit area and speed.

6. EXAMPLES

The following code excerpts will demonstrate the application of some higher level language concepts, namely global objects and polymorphic objects, included in our extended SystemC synthesis subset. The presented code is directly processable with the ODETTE synthesis tool prototype without any need for further manual refinement. The generated output is a SystemC or VHDL specification which can be fed into off-the-shelf synthesis tools, such as the CoCentric SystemC Compiler, or the Synopsys Design Compiler^{TM}.

In the first example a classical producer/consumer system is modelled which is also often used as an example for demonstrating the benefits of channels in SystemC. Producer and consumer are exchanging data via a bounded buffer, which represents a shared resource (see also Figure 2). In 'plain' SystemC the bounded buffer would be modelled as a channel. According to our approach it is implemented as a global object now combining high level modelling with automated synthesis.

```
#include "systemc.h"
#include "oohwlib.h"

SC_MODULE(ProdCons) {
  sc_in< bool > clock;
  sc_in< bool > reset;
  sc_out< ElementType > output;

  // Declaration of a global object with scheduler 'RoundRobin'
  // and user defined class template 'FIFO<>':
  GlobalObject< RoundRobin, FIFO< int, 12 > >
    sharedBuffer;

  void producerOdd() {
    int val;
    sharedBuffer.reset ();
    sharedBuffer.subscribe ();
    val = 1;
    wait ();
    while( true ) {
      // Blocking global method call to 'sharedBuffer':
      GLOBAL_PROCEDURE_CALL( sharedBuffer, put( val ) );
      val += 2;
      wait ();
    }
  }

  void producerEven() {...}

  void consumer() {...}

  SC_CTOR(top)
  {
    SC_CTHREAD( producerOdd, clock.pos() );
    watching( reset.delayed() == true );

    SC_CTHREAD( producerEven, clock.pos() );
    watching( reset.delayed() == true );

    SC_CTHREAD( consumer, clock.pos() );
    watching( reset.delayed() == true );
  }
};
```

Figure 4: Using a global object

Three client processes are connected to the global object `sharedBuffer`; two producers, one producing odd numbers, the other producing even numbers, and a consumer which reads elements from the buffer and writes them to an output port. In the same way any further client process could be connected. In a real world application instead of numbers any kind of data could be exchanged via the buffer, e.g., data packages, frames, or samples.

The following code shows an excerpt from the implementation of class template `FIFO` that was used in the above example. In principle it is an ordinary C++ class declaring some data members and member functions. Modelling it as a template which is parameterized with the element type and the size of the buffer makes it possible to use it very flexible. What makes the implementation different from an implementation in plain C++ is the declaration of some methods as guarded methods. But this does not prevent the class from being used like any other class, since the guard mechanism is only invoked on global objects (cf. 4.3).

```
#include "oohwlib.h"

template< class Type, unsigned int SIZE >
class FIFO {

public:
  FIFO() {
    reset ();
  }

  GUARDED_METHOD( void,                    // return type
                  put( const Type &t ), // signatue
                  ! isFull () ) {          // guard
    m_buffer[m_bottom] = t;
    m_bottom = nextIndex( m_bottom );
    m_empty = false;
    m_full = ( m_bottom == m_top );
    m_numberOfEntries = m_numberOfEntries + 1;
  }

  GUARDED_METHOD( void, reset(), true ) {...}
  GUARDED_METHOD( Type, get(), !isEmpty() ) {...}
  GUARDED_METHOD( void, remove(), !isEmpty() ) {...}
  GUARDED_METHOD( bool, isFull() const, true ) {...}
  GUARDED_METHOD( bool, isEmpty() const, true ) {...}

protected:
  ... // further member declarations
};
```

Figure 5: Declaration of class FIFO

The next example picks up the polymorphic arithmetic operations illustrated in Figure 1. The `execute` method is dynamically dispatched which means that one does not have to take care about the concrete type of an operation being sent via input port `operation`, as demonstrated in process `behavior`. Dependent on the actual type of the operation always the correct implementation of `execute` will be invoked. Like the previous example, the presented code can be directly processed by the ODETTE synthesiser. Note, that this is a very simplified example due to spacial limitations in this article.

```
#include "systemc.h"
#include "oohwlib.h"

class ArithOp {
  // 'tag' the class for polymorphic usage:
  POLYMORPHIC( ArithOp )
public:
  ArithOp( const int leftOp, const int rightOp ) :
        m_leftOp( leftOp ), m_rightOp ( rightOp ) {
```

```
    }

    virtual void execute( int &result ) {
      // nothing to do here. Will be implemented in derived classes.
    }

  protected:
    int m_leftOp;
    int m_rightOp;
};

class Mult : public ArithOp {
  // 'tag' the class:
  POLYMORPHIC( Mult )
public:
  virtual void execute( int &result ) {
    return( m_leftOp * m_rightOp );
  }
};

class Add : public ArithOp {
  // 'tag' the class:
  POLYMORPHIC( Add )
public:
  virtual void execute( int &result ) {
    return( m_leftOp + m_rightOp );
  }
};

SC_MODULE( PolyALU ) {
  sc_in< bool > clock;
  sc_in< bool > reset;
  sc_out< int > acc;
  // Declaration of a 'polymorphic' port:
  sc_in< PolyObject< ArithOp > > operation;

  void behavior() {
    PolyObject< ArithOp > localOp;
    int result;
    wait();
    while( true ) {
      localOp = operation.read();
      opResult = acc.read();
      // The following function call is dynamically dispatched
      localOp->execute( result );
      acc.write( result );
      wait();
    }
  }

  SC_CTOR( PolyALU ) {
    SC_CTHREAD( behavior, clock.pos() );
    watching( reset.delayed() == true );
  }
};
```

Figure 6: Applying polymorphism

7. CONCLUSIONS AND OUTLOOK

In this paper we have illustrated how the limited SystemC synthesis subset which is supported by existing synthesis tools can be simply extended by most object-oriented C++ features, and we have proposed an appropriate synthesis technique for this purpose. We have also discussed how hardware design can benefit from the application of object-orientation modelling techniques. We have further presented a tool prototype which is able to process the proposed extended synthesis subset by performing the illustrated synthesis techniques, and which generates SystemC or VHDL specifications that are further processable with existing off-the-shelf tools.

Future work will mainly consist in improving the synthesis tool prototype. One major focus will be the integration of more sophisticated optimisation techniques and strategies in order to produce better results in terms of circuit area and speed. Another focus will be the further extension of the supported synthesis subset, and, in the mid- or long-term, the integration of concepts from behavioral synthesis.

8. REFERENCES

[1] P. Ashenden, P. Wilsey, and D. Martin. Suave: Object-oriented and genericity extensions to vhdl for high-level modeling. In *Proceedings of Forum on Design Languages (FDL98)*, pages 109–118, September 1998.

[2] T. Grötker, S. Liao, G. Martin, and S. Swan. *System Design with SystemC*. Kluwer Academic Publishers, 2002.

[3] T. Kuhn, T. Oppold, C. Schulz-Key, M. Winterholer, W. Rosenstiel, M. Edwards, and Y. Kashai. Object oriented hardware synthesis and verification. In *ISSS'01*, pages 189–194, October 2001.

[4] T. Kuhn, W. Rosenstiel, and U. Kebschull. Object oriented hardware modeling and simulation based on java. In *International Workshop on IP Based Synthesis and System Design, Grenoble, France*, 1998.

[5] S. Matsuoka and A. Yonezawa. Analysis of inheritance anomaly in object-oriented concurrent programming languages. In G. Agha, P. Wegner, and A. Yonezawa, editors, *Research Directions in Concurrent Object-Oriented Programming*, pages 107–150. MIT Press, 1993.

[6] ODETTE. *Object-oriented co-DEsign and functional Test TEchniques.* http://odette.offis.de.

[7] Open SystemC Initiative. *SystemC Version 2.0 User's Guide. Update for SystemC 2.0.1*, 2002.

[8] M. Radetzki. *Synthesis of Digital Circuits from Object-Oriented Specifications.* PhD thesis, University of Oldenburg, 2000.

[9] M. Radetzki, W. Putzke-Röming, and W. Nebel. Objective vhdl: The object-oriented approach to hardware reuse. In J.-Y. Roger, B. Stanford-Smith, and P. T. Kidd, editors, *Advances in Information Technologies: The Business Challenge*, 1998.

[10] H.-J. Schlebusch, G. Smith, D. Sciuto, D. Gajski, C. Mielenz, C. K. Lennard, F. Ghenassia, S. Swan, and J. Kunkel. Transaction based design: Another buzzword or the solution to a design problem? In *Proceedings of DATE'03*, 2003.

[11] G. Schumacher. *Object-Oriented Hardware Specification and Design with a Language Extension to VHDL.* PhD thesis, University of Oldenburg, 1999.

[12] S. Swamy, A. Molin, and B. Covnot. Oo-vhdl object-oriented extensions to vhdl. *IEEE Computer*, 28(10):18–26, October 1995.

[13] Synopsys, Inc. *CoCentric(R) SystemC Compiler Behavioral Modeling Guide*, 2002.

[14] Synopsys, Inc. *CoCentric(R) SystemC Compiler RTL User and Modeling Guide*, 2002.

[15] S. Vernalde, P. Schaumont, and I. Bolsens. An object oriented programming approach for hardware design. In *IEEE Computer Society Workshop on VLSI'99*, Orlando, April 1998.

RTOS Scheduling in Transaction Level Models

Haobo Yu, Andreas Gerstlauer, Daniel Gajski
Center for Embedded Computer Systems
University of California, Irvine
Irvine, CA 92697, USA
{haoboy,gerstl,gajksi}@cecs.uci.edu

ABSTRACT

Raising the level of abstraction in system design promises to enable faster exploration of the design space at early stages. While scheduling decision for embedded software has great impact on system performance, it's much desired that the designer can select the right scheduling algorithm at high abstraction levels so as to save him from the error-prone and time consuming task of tuning code delays or task priority assignments at the final stage of system design. In this paper we tackle this problem by introducing a RTOS model and an approach to refine any unscheduled transaction level model (TLM) to a TLM with RTOS scheduling support. The refinement process provides a useful tool to the system designer to quickly evaluate different dynamic scheduling algorithms and make the optimal choice at the early stage of system design.

Categories and Subject Descriptors

D.4.m [**Operating Systems**]: Miscellaneous; B.7.2 [**Design Aids**]: Simulation

General Terms

System Design, Specification Languages

Keywords

RTOS, SpecC, System Design, Model

1. INTRODUCTION

Real time systems differs fundamentally from other systems in that both *computation result* and *time* affect the correctness of the whole system. These two aspects are addressed separately in system design. The computation correctness is usually determined at the early stage of system design by a high level model,whereas the actual timing properties are checked at run time through target specific binary code implementation. Wether a piece of computation can be finished on time or not largely depends on both the scheduling scheme and the system architecture. Since the scheduling behavior is hard to capture through high level model simulation, the timing properties of a system design usually change from high level model to implementation. As a result, the designer has to tune code delays or task priority assignments at final stage of system design which is both error prone and time consuming. However, this situation can be avoided if we provide a way to abstract the dynamic scheduling behavior and adjust the scheduling algorithm at higher abstraction levels.

Transaction level modeling is a high level approach to model digital systems where communication among system components is separated from the implementation of the processing elements (PE) [11]. This allows to abstract the communication between PEs independently from the implementation of the PEs. A high level of communication abstraction achieves high simulation speeds, hence enabling early architecture exploration and speeding embedded software development.

Many designers use preemptive, priority-driven and task-based real time operating systems (RTOS) [1, 3] to support the dynamic real-time behavior of the the system. To capture the dynamic scheduling behavior at higher level, we need techniques to abstract the RTOS scheduling because using a real RTOS implementation would negate the purpose of a high level model. Furthermore, at higher levels, not enough information might be available to target a specific RTOS.

In this paper, we address this design challenge by introducing a high level RTOS model and a set of refinement steps to create a TLM with RTOS scheduling support from any unscheduled TLM. We make a scheduling refinement tool implementing these refinement steps. The output model generated by our tool provides simulation result close to the final implementation (in terms of RTOS timing) and the tool can be easily integrated into the existing system level design flows to accurately evaluate a potential system design (e.g. in respect to timing constraints) for early and rapid design space exploration.

The rest of this paper is organized as follows: Section 2 gives an insight into the related work on software modeling and synthesis. Section 3 describes how the scheduling refinement process is integrated with the system level design flow. Section 4 provides information of the RTOS model used to model dynamic scheduling, Section 5 gives the detailed information of the RTOS scheduling refinement process. Experimental results are shown in Section 6 and

CODES+ISSS'03, October 1–3, 2003, Newport Beach, California, USA.

Section 7 concludes this paper with a brief summary and an outlook on future work.

2. RELATED WORK

A lot of work recently has been focusing on automatic RTOS and code generation for embedded software. In [6], a method for automatic generation of application-specific operating systems and corresponding application software for a target processor is given. In [4], a way of combining static task scheduling and dynamic scheduling in software synthesis is proposed. While both approaches mainly focus on software synthesis issues, their papers do not provide any information regarding high level model of dynamic scheduling integrated into the whole system.

In [12], a technique for modeling fixed-priority preemptive multi-tasking systems based on concurrency and exception handling mechanisms provided by SpecC is shown. However, their model is limited in its support for different scheduling algorithms and inter-task communication, and its complex structure makes it hard to use.

In [5], a high-level model of OS called SoCOS is introduced as a high level RTOS model supporting software generation. The main difference between our approach and theirs is that SoCOS requires its own proprietary simulation engine while our RTOS model is build on top of existing system level design language (SLDL) and can be directly integrated into any system model and design flow supported by the chosen SLDL. Besides, we generate RTOS based dynamic scheduling TLM automatically while the SoCOS based system model is created manually.

3. DESIGN FLOW

Figure 1 shows a typical system level design flow [9]. The system design process starts with the specification model written by the designer to specify the desired system functionality. During system design, the specification functionality is partitioned onto multiple processing elements (PEs). The result is a TLM in which each PE executes a specific behavior in parallel with other PEs and communication between PEs takes place through abstract channels. After that, the communication synthesis step generates the bus functional model in which a communication architecture consisting of busses and bus interfaces is synthesized to implement communication between PEs.

Due to the inherently sequential nature of PEs, processes inside the same PE need to be serialized. Depending on the nature of the PE and the data inter-dependencies, processes are scheduled statically or dynamically. In case of dynamic scheduling, a RTOS is required for the final implementation. Usually, the scheduling process takes place after the bus functional model has been generated. In our approach, we move the scheduling into higher level of abstraction, i.e. perform scheduling at TLM level. Since a detailed communication architecture is not required to evaluate scheduling results, using a TLM can improve the simulation speed and result in faster design space exploration.

Current definition of TLM is general and ambiguous. Depending on the abstraction of transaction, there are different kind of TLMs. In the higher abstraction level, transaction between the PEs is represented by the message passing channels. On the other hand,abstracting only low level bus protocol primitives (i.e. *send*, *receive*) between the PEs results

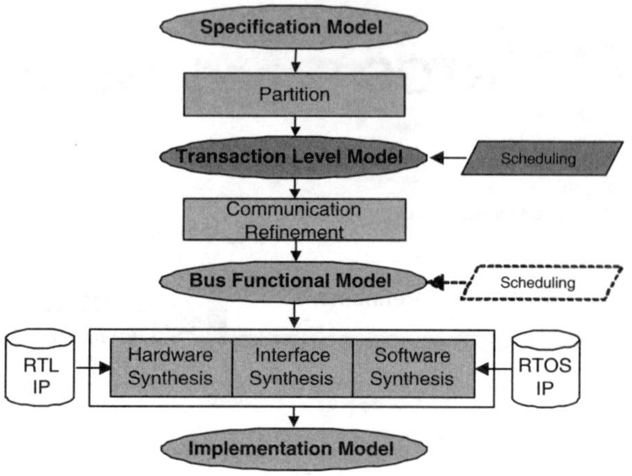

Figure 1: Design flow

in a different TLM where the bus drivers are used inside each PE to drive the protocol channels. Note that interrupt handlers are used as part of the bus drivers. Our scheduling refinement tool can be used in both of the TLMs. However, in order to demonstrate the effect of the interrupt scheduling, we use the latter TLM in our example.

In order to validate the scheduling in TLM, a representation of the dynamic scheduling implementation, which is usually handled by a RTOS in the real system, is required. Therefore, a high level model of the underlying RTOS is needed for inclusion into TLMs during system design. The RTOS model provides an abstraction of the key features that define a dynamic scheduling behavior independent of any specific RTOS implementation.

The scheduling refinement tool (Figure 2) refines the unscheduled TLM into a scheduled TLM based on the refinement decisions from the designer. In general, for each PE in the system a RTOS model corresponding to the selected scheduling strategy is imported from the library and instantiated in the PE. Processes inside the PEs are converted into tasks with assigned priorities. Synchronization as part of communication between processes is refined into OS-based task synchronization. In the scheduled output TLM, each PE runs multiple tasks on top of its local RTOS model instance. Therefore, the output model can be validated through simulation or verification to evaluate different dynamic scheduling approaches (e.g. in terms of timing) as part of system design space exploration.

As the last step of the design flow, each PE in the bus functional model is then implemented separately. Custom hardware PEs are synthesized into a RTL description. Communication interfaces are synthesized in hardware and software. Finally, embedded software is generated from the scheduled output TLM of the schedule refinement tool. In this process, services of the RTOS model are mapped onto the API of a specific standard or custom RTOS. The code is then compiled into the processor's instruction set and linked against the RTOS libraries to produce the final executable.

4. THE RTOS MODEL

As mentioned previously, the RTOS model is a very import component of the scheduling refinement tool. We implemented the RTOS model on top of the SpecC SLDL [8].

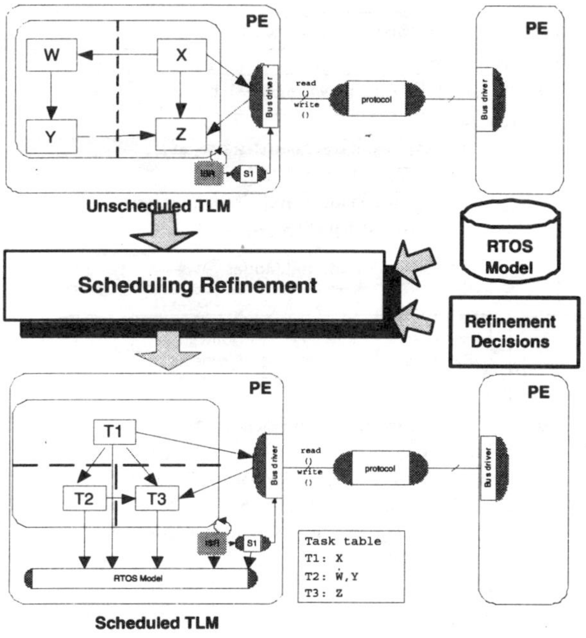

Figure 2: Scheduling refinement tool

It is incorporated into the RTOS model library of the refinement tool. The library provides RTOS models with different scheduling algorithms typically found in RTOS implementations, e.g. round-robin or priority-based scheduling. In addition, the models are parameterizable in terms of task parameters, preemption, and so on. The detailed information about the RTOS model can be found in [10].

Figure 3 shows the interface of the RTOS model. The RTOS model provides four categories of services: operating system management, task management, event handling, and time modeling.

Operating system management mainly deals with initialization of the RTOS during system start where *init* initializes the relevant kernel data structures while *start* starts the multi-task scheduling.

Task management is the most important function in the RTOS model. It includes various standard routines such as task creation (*task_create*), task termination (*task_terminate*, *task_kill*), and task suspension and activation (*task_sleep*, *task_activate*). Two special routines are introduced to model dynamic task forking and joining: *fork* suspends the calling task and waits for the child tasks to finish after which *join* resumes the calling task's execution. Our RTOS model supports both periodic hard real time tasks with a critical deadline and non-periodic real time tasks with a fixed priority. In modeling of periodic tasks, *task_endcycle* notifies the kernel that a periodic task has finished its execution in the current cycle.

Event handling in the RTOS model sits on top of the basic SLDL synchronization events. Two system calls, *enter_wait* and *wakeup_wait*, are wrapped around each SpecC wait primitive. This allows the RTOS model to update its internal task states (and to reschedule) whenever a task is about to get blocked on and later released from a SpecC event.

During simulation of high level system models, the logical

```
interface RTOS
{ /* OS management */
  void init();
  void start(int sched_alg);
  /* Task management */
  Task task_create(const char *name,
           int type,sim_time period);
  void task_terminate();
  void task_sleep();
  void task_activate(Task t);
  void task_endcycle();
  void task_kill(Task t);
  Task fork();
  void join(Task t);
  /* Event handling */
  Task enter_wait();
  void wakeup_wait(Task t);
  /* Delay modeling */
  void time_wait(sim_time nsec);
};
```

Figure 3: Interface of the RTOS model

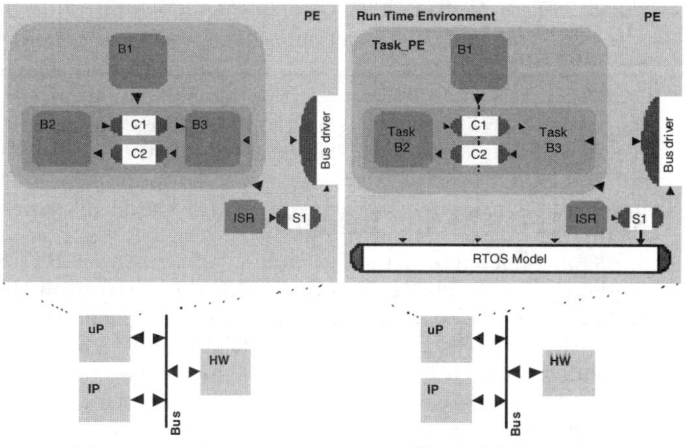

(a) unscheduled model (b) scheduled model

Figure 4: Refinement example

time advances in discrete steps. SLDL primitives (such as `waitfor` in SpecC) are used to model delays. For the RTOS model, those delay primitives are replaced by *time_wait* calls which model task delays in the RTOS while enabling support for modeling of task preemption.

The RTOS model interface introduced in this section will be later implemented by using the real RTOS APIs during software synthesis. Generally, this means that each routine of the RTOS model interface will be mapped to 1 or N target RTOS APIs.

5. SCHEDULING REFINEMENT

The scheduling refinement tool refines the input unscheduled model into a RTOS based multi-task model. In this section, we illustrate the scheduling refinement process through a simple yet typical example (Figure 4). The unscheduled model (Figure 4(a)) executes behavior *B1* followed by the parallel composition of behaviors *B2* and *B3*. Behaviors *B2* and *B3* communicate via two channels *C1* and *C2* while *B3* communicates with other PEs through a bus driver. As part of the bus interface implementation, the interrupt handler

Algorithm 1 TaskCreate(IR_{Design}, B_{PE})

```
1: for all Behavior B ∈ IR_Design do
2:   if IsChildBehavior(B,B_PE) then
3:     BInst = FindInstance(B);
4:     while BInst ≠ NULL do
5:       if IsParallel(BInst,B_PE) then
6:         GenTaskFromBehavior(B,BInst);
7:       end if
8:       BInst = FindNextInstance(B,BInst);
9:     end while
10:  end if
11: end for
12: for all Function F ∈ IR_Design do
13:   if IsMemberFunction(F,B_PE) then
14:     Stmnt = GetFirstStatement(B);
15:     while Stmnt ≠ NULL do
16:       if IsParStatment(Stmnt) then
17:         GenDynamicTasks(Stmnt);
18:       end if
19:       Stmnt = GetNextStatment(B,Stmnt);
20:     end while
21:   end if
22: end for
```

Algorithm 2 SyncRefine(IR_{Design}, B_{PE})

```
1: for all Channel C ∈ IR_Design do
2:   if IsUsedInBehavior(C,B_PE) then
3:     for all Function F ∈ C do
4:       Stmnt=GetFirstStatement(B);
5:       while Stmnt ≠ NULL do
6:         if IsWaitStatment(Stmnt) then
7:           RefineWait(Stmnt);
8:         end if
9:         Stmnt = GetNextStatment(B,Stmnt);
10:      end while
11:    end for
12:  end if
13: end for
14: for all Function F ∈ IR_Design do
15:   if IsMemberFunction(F,B_PE) then
16:     Stmnt = GetFirstStatement(B);
17:     while Stmnt ≠ NULL do
18:       if IsWaitStatment(Stmnt) then
19:         RefineWait(Stmnt);
20:       end if
21:       Stmnt = GetNextStatment(B,Stmnt);
22:     end while
23:   end if
24: end for
```

ISR for external events signals the main bus driver through a semaphore channel *S1*.

5.1 RTOS Model Instantiation

As the first step of the scheduling refinement, a RTOS model implementing `interface` *RTOS* is selected from the RTOS library and a run time environment which coordinates the interaction between the RTOS model and tasks is created for each PE. The run time environment is implemented as a behavior which wrappers around the top-level PE behavior. The RTOS model gets instantiated in the run time environment and the initial values of the internal data structures for the RTOS model are set. At the same time, a main task (*task_PE*) for the PE is created which is the only task available for the RTOS model to schedule at system start time.

5.2 Task Creation

The task creation step converts parallel processes/behaviors in the specification into RTOS-based tasks. This is by far the most important and time consuming part of the scheduling refinement process. The task creation process is shown in Algorithm1. The input to Algorithm1 is the internal representation for the whole design IR_{Design} and the top level behavior for the PE B_{PE}.

Task creation is carried out in a two-step process. In the first step (line 1-11), each behavior instance *BInst* inside B_{PE} are checked to see if they are running in parallel with other behavior instance inside B_{PE}. If such a behavior instance is found (line 5), a task definition for this behavior instance is created (line 6).

In our example, since `behavior` *B2* and *B3* are running in parallel (Figure 4(a)), function *GenTaskFromBehavior* create the task definition *Task_B2* (Figure 5(b)) for `behavior` *B2* (Figure 5(a)). The task is modeled as a `behavior`[2] and there's an method *os_task_create* inserted into to the behavior for construction of the task. Finally, the main body of the task (method *main*) is enclosed in a pair of *task_activate* / *task_terminate* calls so that the RTOS model can control the task activation and termination.

The second step (line 12-22) involves dynamic creation of child tasks in a parent task. The tool goes through each statement of the member functions of `behavior` B_{PE} or any of it's child behaviors. If a parallel statement (`par` statement in SpecC) is found (line 16), a dynamic task instances are created for this statement (line 17).

This step is illustrated by our example in Figure 6. The `par` statement in the input model (line 9-12 in Figure 6(a)) is converted to dynamically fork and join child tasks as part of the parent's execution (line 6-13 in Figure 6(b)). During this refinement process, the *init* methods of the children are called to create the child tasks (line 6,7 in Figure 6(b)). Then, *fork* is inserted before the *par* statement to suspend the calling parent task by the RTOS model before the children are actually executed in the `par` statement. After the two child tasks finish execution and the `par` exits, *join* is inserted to resume the execution of the parent task by the RTOS model.

5.3 Synchronization Re£nement

Replacing SLDL synchronization primitives with RTOS calls is necessary to keep the internal task state of the RTOS model updated. This is achieved by synchronization refinement which wraps event wait primitives in the input model with the RTOS model interface routines *enter_wait* and *wakeup_wait*. The two routines make sure that the RTOS model can intercept event wait primitives thus takes care of task switching.

Algorithm 2 shows how the synchronization refinement works. It is also a two step process: the first step (line 1-13) refines all the `wait` statements inside the channels used in the selected PE while the second step (line 14-23) refines the `wait` statements inside all the member functions of behavior B_{PE} and its child behaviors.

```
1  behavior B2()
2  {void main(void)
3   { ...
4     waitfor(BLOCK1_DELAY);/*model delay*/
5     ...
6     waitfor(BLOCK2_DELAY);/*model delay*/
7     ...
8   }
9  };
```

(a) unscheduled model

```
1  behavior task_B2(RTOS os) implements Init
2  {Task h;
3   void init(void) {
4     h = os.task_create("B2", APERIODIC, 0);
5   }
6   void main(void) {
7     os.task_activate(h);
8     ...
9     os.time_wait(BLOCK1_DELAY);/*model delay*/
10    ...
11    os.time_wait(BLOCK2_DELAY);/*model delay*/
12    ...
13    os.task_terminate(h);
14   }
15 };
```

(b) scheduled model

Figure 5: Task modeling

```
behavior B2B3()
{B2 b2();
 B3 b3();
void main(void)
{



  par
  { b2.main();
    b3.main();
  }

}
```

(a) before

```
behavior B2B3(RTOS os)
{Task_B2 task_b2(os);
 Task_B3 task_b3(os);
 void main(void)
{Task t;
 task_b2.init();
 task_b3.init();
 t = os.fork();
 par  {
   b2.main();
   b3.main();
 }
 os.join(t);
}
```

(b) after

Figure 6: Task creation

```
1  channel C1()
2  {event eRdy;
3   event eAck;
4   void send(...)
5   {
6     ...
7     notify eRdy;
8     ...
9
10    wait(eAck);
11
12    ...
13    }
14 };
```

(a) before

```
1  channel C1(RTOS os)
2  {event eRdy;
3   event eAck;
4   void send(...)
5   { Task t;
6     ...
7     notify eRdy;
8     ...
9     t = os.enter_wait();
10    wait(eAck);
11    os.wakeup_wait(t);
12    ...
13    }
14 };
```

(b) after

Figure 7: Synchronization refinement

Figure 7 shows the synchronization refinement for our example: the `wait` statement inside `channel` $C1$ in the input model (line 10 in Figure 7(a)) is refined into three lines of code in the output model (line 9-11 in Figure 7(b)).

5.4 Preemption Point Creation

In high level system models, simulation time advances in discrete steps based on the granularity of `waitfor` statements used to model delays (e.g. at behavior or basic block level) (line 4,6 in Figure 5(a)). The time-sharing implementation in the RTOS model makes sure that delays of concurrent task are accumulative as required by any model of serialized task execution.

Usually the task switch happens when a task calls the RTOS routine (e.g. `wait` *event*), however, additionally replacing `waitfor` statements with corresponding RTOS time modeling calls is necessary to accurately model preemption. The *time_wait* method (line 9,11 in Figure 5(b)) allows the RTOS kernel to reschedule and switch tasks whenever time increases, i.e. in between regular RTOS system calls. Normally, this would not be an issue since task state changes can not happen outside of RTOS system calls. However, external interrupts can asynchronously trigger task changes in between system calls of the current task in which case proper modeling of preemption is important for the accuracy of the model (e.g. response time results). For example, an interrupt handler can release a semaphore on which a high priority task for processing of the external event is blocked.

5.5 Scheduling Re£nement Example

Figure 8 illustrates the simulation result of the output model generated from our refinement tool for the example from Figure 4. Figure 8(a) shows the simulation trace of the unscheduled model. Behaviors *B2* and *B3* are executing truly in parallel, i.e. their simulated delays overlap.

After executing for time d_1, *B3* waits until it receives a message from *B2* through the channel *c1*. Then it continues executing for time d_2 and waits for data from another PE. *B2* continues for time $(d_6 + d_7)$ and then waits for data from *B3*. At time t_4, an interrupt happens and *B3* receives its data through the bus driver. *B3* executes until it finishes. At time t_5, *B3* sends a message to *B2* through the channel *c2* which wakes up *B2* and both behaviors continue until they finish execution.

Figure 8(b) shows the simulation result of the scheduled model for a priority based scheduling. It demonstrates that in the refined model *task_B2* and *task_B3* execute in an interleaved way. Since *task_B3* has the higher priority, it executes unless it is blocked on receiving or sending a message from/to *task_B2* (t_1 through t_2 and t_5 through t_6), waiting for an interrupt (t_3 through t_4), or it finishes (t_7) at which points execution switches to *task_B2*. Note that at time t_4, the interrupt wakes up *task_B3* and *task_B2* is preempted by *task_B3*. However, the actual task switch is delayed until the end of the discrete time step d_6 in *task_B2* based on the granularity of the task's delay model. In summary, as required by priority based dynamic scheduling, at any time only one task, the ready task with the highest priority, is executing.

	Lines of code	Sim. time	Context switches	Transcoding delay
Unsched.	11,313	27.3s	0	9.7ms
Roundrobin	13,343	28.6s	3262	10.29ms
Encod>decod	13,356	28.9s	980	11.34ms
Decod>encod	13,356	28.5s	327	10.30ms
Impl.	79,096	5h	327	11.7ms

Table 1: Vocoder experimental results.

6. EXPERIMENTAL RESULTS

We used the scheduling refinement tool in the design of a voice codec for mobile phone applications.The vocoder contains two tasks for encoding and decoding in software, assisted by a custom hardware co-processor. For the implementation, the Vocoder was compiled into assembly code for the Motorola DSP56600 processor and linked against a small custom RTOS kernel that uses a scheduling algorithm where the decoder has higher priority than the encoder[7].

Table 1 shows the results for the vocoder model. The vocoder models were exercised by a testbench that feeds a stream of 163 speech frames corresponding to 3.26 s of speech into encoder and decoder. The transcoding delay is the latency when running encoder and decoder in back-to-back mode and is related to response time in switching between encoding and decoding tasks.

Experimental results show that the simulation overhead introduced by the scheduling refinement tool is negligible while providing accurate results. As explained by the fact that both tasks alternate with every time slice, round-robin scheduling causes by far the largest number of context switches while providing the lowest response times. Note that context switch delays in the RTOS were not modeled in this example, i.e. the large number of context switches would introduce additional delays that would offset the slight response time advantage of round-robin scheduling in a final implementation. The simulation result shows that in priority-based scheduling, it is of advantage to give the decoder the higher relative priority. Since the encoder execution time dominates the decoder execution time this is equivalent to a shortest-job-first scheduling which minimizes wait times and hence overall response time. Furthermore, the number of context switches is lower since the RTOS does not have to switch back and forth between encoder and decoder whenever the encoder waits for results from the hardware co-processor. Therefore, priority-based scheduling with a high-priority decoder was chosen for the final implementation. Note that the final delay in the implementation is higher due to inaccuracies of execution time estimates in the high-level model. In summary, compared to the huge complexity required for the implementation model, the scheduling refinement tool enables early and efficient evaluation of dynamic scheduling implementations.

7. SUMMARY AND CONCLUSIONS

In this paper,we presented a RTOS model and the refinement steps for transforming an unscheduled TLM into TLM with RTOS scheduling support. In the design flow, our contribution is primarily the automation of the scheduling refinement process that facilitates rapid evaluation of scheduling algorithms in the early stage of system design using TLM. We developed a tool to automate the refinement process. Experiments are performed to show the usefulness of the tool in system design. Currently the tool is written for SpecC SLDL because of its simplicity. However, the concepts can be applied to any SLDL (SystemC, Superlog) with support for event handling and modeling of time.

Future work includes the development of tools for software synthesis from the scheduled TLM down to target-specific application code linked against the target RTOS libraries.

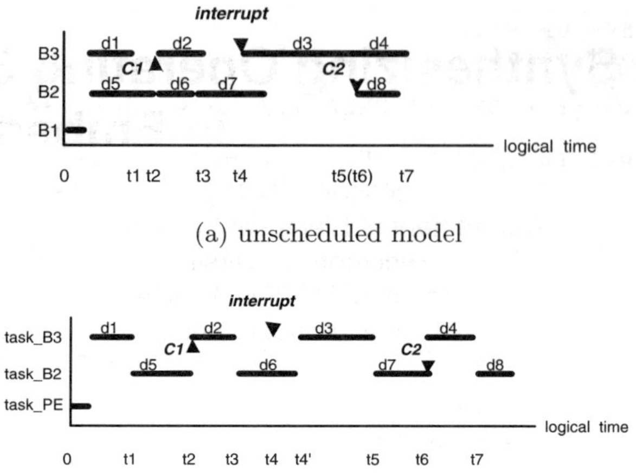

(a) unscheduled model

(b) scheduled model

Figure 8: Simulation trace for model example.

8. REFERENCES

[1] QNX. Available: http://www.qnx.com/.

[2] SpecC. Available: http://www.specc.org/.

[3] VxWorks. Available: http://www.vxworks.com/.

[4] J. Cortadella. Task generation and compile time scheduling for mixed data-control embedded software. In *IEEE Design Automation Conference*, Jun. 2000.

[5] D. Desmet, D. Verkest, and H. D. Man. Operating system based software generation for system-on-chip. In *IEEE Design Automation Conference*, Jun. 2000.

[6] L. Gauthier, S. Yoo, and A. A. Jerraya. Automatic generation and targeting of application-specific operating systems and embedded systems software. *IEEE Trans. on CAD*, Nov. 2001.

[7] A. Gerstlauer et al. Design of a GSM Vocoder using SpecC Methodology. Technical Report ICS-TR-99-11, UCI, Feb. 1999.

[8] A. Gerstlauer and D. Gajski. Specc language reference manual. In *SpecC Technology Open Consortium*, Dec. 2002.

[9] A. Gerstlauer and D. Gajski. System-level abstraction semantics. In *ISSS*, Oct. 2002.

[10] A. Gerstlauer, H. Yu, and D. Gajski. RTOS modeling for system level design. In *DATE*, Mar. 2003.

[11] T. Grötker, S. Liao, G. Martin, and S. Swan. *System Design with SystemC*. Kluwer Academic Pub, 2002.

[12] H. Tomiyama, Y. Cao, and K. Murakami. Modeling fixed-priority preemptive multi-task systems in SpecC. In *SASIMI*, October 2001.

Synthesizing Operating System Based Device Drivers in Embedded Systems

Shaojie Wang
Department of Electrical Engineering
Princeton University
Princeton, NJ 08544, USA
wsj@ee.princeton.edu

Sharad Malik
Department of Electrical Engineering
Princeton University
Princeton, NJ 08544, USA
sharad@ee.princeton.edu

ABSTRACT

This paper presents a correct-by-construction synthesis method for generating operating system based device drivers from a formally specified device behavior model. Existing driver development is largely manual using an ad-hoc design methodology. Consequently, this task is error prone and becomes a bottleneck in embedded system design methodology.

Our solution to this problem starts by accurately specifying device access behavior with a formal model, *viz.* extended event driven finite state machines. We state easy to check soundness conditions on the model that subsequently guarantee properties such as bounded execution time and deadlock-free behavior. We design a deadlock-free resource accessing scheme for our device access model. Finally, we synthesize an operating system (OS) based event processing mechanism, which is the core of the device driver, using a disciplined methodology that assures the correctness of the resulting driver.

We validate our synthesis method using two case studies: an infrared port and the USB device controller for an SA1100 based handheld. Besides assuring a correct-by -construction driver, the size of the specification is 70% smaller than a manually written driver, which is a strong indicator of improved design productivity.

Categories and Subject Descriptors

D.2.4 [**Software Engineering**]: Software/Program verification – *Formal method*; D.1.2 [**Programming Techniques**]: Automatic Programming – Program synthesis; D.2.1 [**Software Engineering**]: Requirements/Specifications – *Methodologies*; D.2.2 [**Software Engineering**]: Design Tools and Techniques – *computer aided software engineering*.

General Terms: Algorithms, Design, Experimentation, Verification.

Keywords: Correct-by-construction, device driver, operating system based software synthesis, embedded system software.

1. INTRODUCTION

Device drivers are the glue software providing the bridge between peripheral devices on one side and the upper layers of the operating system and the application software on the other. They are critical software elements that significantly affect the quality and productivity of system development tasks. They are also notoriously hard to design and debug. Complex hardware behaviors and complicated system synchronization requests and mechanisms are the two main contributors to driver errors. Most modern operating systems are multi-tasking. As part of the kernel, the driver software must handle concurrent accesses from multiple tasks, which is difficult to design and debug. This, coupled with the complexity of hardware-software interactions makes the development and design of drivers laborious and error-prone.

The low productivity and unreliability of manual driver development provides a strong motivation for the correct-by-construction methodology proposed in this paper. This methodology is based on a formal specification of a device access model with easy to specify semantics. The correctness of the driver generation algorithm is then easy to demonstrate.

The remainder of this paper is organized as follows: Section 2 reviews related work; Section 3 explains general concepts of device drivers; Section 4 presents issues related to choosing appropriate preemption prevention mechanisms; Section 5 provides an overview of the device driver synthesis framework; Section 6 presents the formal device access model essential to the proof to the correctness of the code synthesized; Section 7 discusses the synthesis procedure in detail and the correctness proof; Section 8 describes our case studies; and finally Section 9 provides some concluding remarks.

2. RELATED WORK

We briefly discuss related research work in the area of device driver development methodology and operating system based software generation methodology. As part of the methodology described in our earlier publication [1], our effort distinguishes itself by the formal specification of device access behavior, the design of the resource sharing scheme and the synthesis of an event processing mechanism based on OS primitives which is provably correct according to our formal model specification. In this paper we provide the details of this specification and methodology.

Early device driver synthesis techniques, as part of hardware/software co-design efforts, focus on generating simple interrupt handlers synchronizing the software and the device [5, 6]. Recently, attempts have also been made to generate operating system based device drivers [1, 2]. These methodologies propose a high-level abstract model and synthesize operating system based device drivers. By using a library for each supported OS and an automatic selection mechanism, they generate device drivers for a range of operating systems. O'Nil [2] proposes a Yacc-like language ProGram [8] to model the communication protocol between the device and the software. Finite state machines are extracted from the specification to enable code synthesis. Iris [1] proposes to separate the device programming interface, device control and data path accesses to provide a higher level abstraction which enables cleaner specification and more efficient checking. While our earlier publication [1] gives an overview of the overall methodology, this paper focuses on the synthesis technique of correct-by-construction OS based device drivers.

Traditional system level design languages are based on hardware description languages, and tend to describe static architectures. More recently, researchers have realized the importance of dynamic behavior and propose to include it in system level design models. Such dynamic features are essentially services provided by an OS. SoCOS [3] proposes a concurrency model including asynchronous, reactive and synchronous communications and generates embedded system software based on a real-time operating system (RTOS) through several refinement steps. Gerstlauer [4] adopts a similar approach. They propose an RTOS model, which is effectively a set of commonly used RTOS services, to extend the original specC language's ability to handle the interleaved execution behavior of dynamic schedulers.

3. BACKGROUND

Device drivers are a collection of functions and data structures, used to set up and initialize the device, transfer data between the device and the software, configure the device, monitor and trace the status of the device, reset the device, and shut down the device as requested. These functions are called *entry* functions, which are usually part of the kernel. User space programs access device drivers through the OS input-output (I/O) system calls, which are file system calls in the case of the UNIX operating system. The OS is responsible for routing user space requests contained in system calls to appropriate entry functions.

Operating systems provide device driver models reflecting device-processor data transfer patterns and data processing patterns. For example, UNIX [7] provides four basic device driver models: character (for byte-stream low volume data), terminal (a special type of character driver for terminal functions including tab expansions), block (high volume data such as storage devices), and stream (for packet based network data).

4. OPERATING SYSTEM EXECUTION LEVELS AND PREEMPTION PREVENTION MECHANISMS

Operating systems typically define multiple execution levels. The code executing at a higher execution level preempts the code executing at a lower level by default. For example, the execution level of interrupt handlers is higher than that of a normal piece of code and interrupts preempt those codes by default. However, preemption can corrupt the integrity of the data (critical sections) shared between the code and the interrupt handler. Thus, a preemption prevention mechanism is required to ensure the correct execution of the program. Operating systems define preemption prevention primitives. Concurrent programs must select appropriate preemption prevention mechanisms to protect their critical sections. For example, Linux defines interrupt disable/enable mechanisms to prevent interrupt intrusion. Locking mechanisms are used to protect critical sections shared by the kernel parts of user processes. For the older version of the Linux kernel, timer handlers are executed by timer interrupt handlers, the executions of normal interrupt handlers and timer handlers do not interleave. This is not true for the newer kernel in which timer handlers are executed by *tasklet*, an execution entity managed by the kernel and interruptible by the interrupts. Clearly, the correct preemption mechanism needs to be selected based on the execution levels of the codes sharing the critical section and functionality range of the primitives provided by the OS. We provide a formal mechanism to specify the preemption prevention primitives. With limited space we choose to omit its description in favor of the main driver synthesis framework.

5. OVERVIEW OF DEVICE DRIVER SYNTHESIS FRAMEWORK

An overview of our device driver synthesis framework is provided in our earlier publication on this [1]. We briefly review it here. Device driver entry functions are partitioned into three parts: core functions, platform functions, and registry functions. The core functions are the platform (processor and OS) independent part of the driver. The others are the platform dependent part of the driver. The core functions are synthesized from a device specification, which is based on a device access model. The platform functions and registry functions are implemented as libraries and templates. They are mapped to a particular operating system automatically according to the driver configuration. To demonstrate the correct-by-construction code synthesis technique, we describe the specification of the device access model in this section.

Figure 1 shows an overview of the device access model. We partition a device into multiple sub-devices according to the function they implement. Sub-devices may share a physical interface (ITF). The access of each sub-device is modeled in two

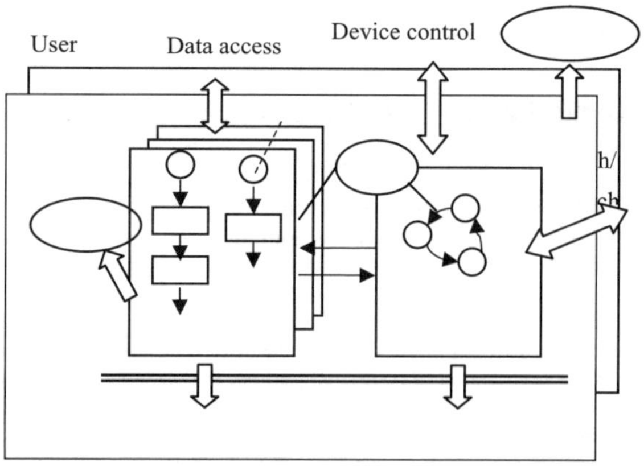

layers. The first layer is the device programming interface model. In this layer, the device memory and register accesses are modeled through aggregating data structures and access functions. For example, a UART has 12 interface registers controlling its communication with the processor. The read-only register, Receive Buffer Register (RBR), is the read-point of the UART receiving FIFO. The FIFO is modeled at the device programming interface layer and the access function of the FIFO is automatically synthesized from the model. The second layer is the device behavior model. The device behavior model has two parts: device control and data channels.

- Device control models the logical states and state transitions of a device with an extended event driven finite state machine.
- Data channels model the physical data exchange channels of the device with an event driven finite state machine that conforms to one of a small set of templates. This is sufficient since these behaviors tend to be limited to a small set of possibilities. A sub-device may possess multiple parallel data channels competing for system resources such as DMA channels. A data channel has at most two ports: *read* and *write*. Each port access is modeled as a series of data unit accesses. A *data unit* access is a series of hardware data transfer operations performed without any intervening synchronization. Because they have multiple data unit accesses, data port accesses (read and write) of a single channel are concurrent. The data channel is shared at the granularity of a data unit. Three data port access modes are defined: *blocked*, *buffered*, and *asynchronous*. Blocked and buffered mode accesses are initiated by the user while the asynchronous mode accesses are initiated by the device. For blocked mode accesses, the data accumulation buffer is provided by the caller. For the other access modes, the buffer is managed by the driver.

A data port is available only when the device controller is in certain states. A data port may share data (SH_{data}) with event handlers of the device controller.

The device controller and data port accesses communicate synchronously or asynchronously. A data port pushing data to the device controller communicates with the controller

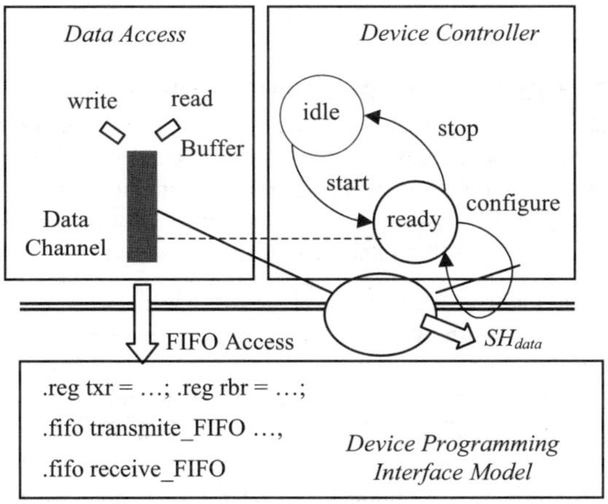

asynchronously. The controller accessing a blocking data port communicates with the data port synchronously.

Figure 2 illustrates the device access model of a half-duplex UART. It has only one sub-device. The first layer models the register accesses of the UART including a transmit FIFO and a receive FIFO. The second layer models UART behavior.

- The device controller state machine has two states: *idle* and *ready*. State *idle* is the start state. A UART in the *idle* state is not initialized by any software and is not operating. It moves to *ready* state after being initialized, and returns to *idle* state when the software issues the *stop* event and shuts down the device. The initialization is triggered by event *start*. Software can configure a UART in *ready* state.
- The UART has one data channel with two ports: read and write. The data unit of the read port reads from the receive FIFO until it is empty. The data unit of the write port writes to the transmit FIFO until it is full (or there is no more data).

The data port accesses are available only when the device is in *ready* state. Configuration data, baud rate setting, is shared between the *configure* event handler and the channel. The half-duplex feature of the UART is modeled elegantly by our data channel sharing model.

6. FORMAL MODELING OF THE DEVICE BEHAVIOR

The device access behavior model we propose is based on a formal model: extended event driven finite state machine. This section describes the extended event driven state machine model, the control function model, the synchronization and communication model of the state machines, and the timing model formally. The correctness of the implementation of the model and the soundness of the model are also defined.

6.1 Extended Event Driven Finite State Ma-chine Model

The extended event driven state machine is defined as a 5-tuple (S, S_0, E, Δ, C). S represents the state set. S_0 represents the initial state set. E is the event set. Each event is a pair, (e_t, e_d), where e_t represents the type of the event and e_d represents the data associated with it. C is a set of event handlers, invariant to state and event space of the state machine, i.e. the code in the event handler does not influence the state transition or the output events emitted. Δ is the set of transitions satisfying $\Delta : S \times E \rightarrow S \times 2^E \times C$, where 2^E is the power set of E.

A transition, $\delta_1 : s_1 \times e_0 \rightarrow s_2 \times E_{out} \times c_{\delta_1}$ is enabled if the state machine is in state s_1 and event e_0 (enabling event of the transition) appears. E_{out} is the set of output events. c_{δ_1} is the event handler, which is a piece of executable code not synchronized with any events. The firing of an enabled transition has three steps: (1) e`xecute the event handler, (2) emit the output events, E_{out}, and (3) change the state of the state machine from s_1 to s_2. The enabling event of a transition is consumed when it is fired. The firing of a transition is atomic.

Each event has a priority. A transition inherits the priority from its enabling event. An enabled transition of the highest priority is fired. If there are multiple instances of the same event, the one that arrived the earliest is consumed. If multiple instances appear simultaneously, a random one is picked. Because the firing of a transition is atomic, new events are blocked. Besides priority, an event has the additional attributes of *stickiness*, *reliability*, and *recognition type*. An event is either *sticky* or *non-sticky*. Assume the events visible to a state machine before the firing of transition δ_1 are E_1, after the firing are E_2. Obviously, $E_{out} \subseteq E_2$. An event e is *sticky* iff $\forall \delta_1, e \in E_1, e \neq e_0 \Rightarrow e \in E_2$, that is, a sticky event remains visible unless it is consumed. An *unreliable* event may not be captured by the state machine even if it occurs, while a *reliable* event is guaranteed to be captured. Event reliability models the features of a hardware signal. Recognition type has two possibilities. We can define an event to be recognized by polling. By default, an event notifies its appearance by itself.

Input events are sticky. An output event is *internal* if it is invisible outside the state machine; otherwise it is *external*. An output event is always reliable. Internal output events are non-sticky because they represent execution status rather than synchronization states. External output events are sent to a particular state machine.

6.2 Control Function Model

A control function is defined as a series of state transitions of a single state machine. Because events being exchanged between different state machines enable state transitions, an execution of a control function might involve several state machines. We define two forms of control functions.

F1) A pair of an event and a set of destination states. The control function is issued when the event is emitted to the state machine and completes when the state machine reaches a state in the destination state set.

F2) A pair of events. The first event enables the request. It can be empty. The second event is an output event. When the state machine emits the output event, the control function ends.

A control function is referred to as a *request* in the following sections as it models a request from the device by the software. Request functions can overlap because a request function takes several transitions to complete and events are visible at the states. Five policies to coordinate two requests of the different types, and different instances of the same type, are defined. They are declaratively specified for the control functions.

P1) Coexist.

P2) Block the new request until the previous one finishes.

P3) Abort the previous request and execute the new request from the current state.

P4) Abort the previous request and execute the new request from the state where the previous request starts.

P5) Suspend the previous request and resume it after the new one completes its execution.

Assume requests A and B coexist. Request C is blocked by A and aborts B. When C appears while A and B are executing, a dilemma occurs: whether to execute or to block B.

- Consider A and C first. C is blocked while A executes. Then consider B. Because A and B coexist, the result is that A and B execute and C is blocked.
- Consider B and C first. B is blocked and C executes. Then consider A. Because C is blocked by A, the result is A executes, B and C are blocked.

We say coordination policies are *incompatible* when there is an inconsistency in deciding whether to execute a request, or transition to the next state of the state machine. Compatibility can be checked by the synthesizer.

6.3 Synchronization and Communication Model of the State Machines

Two message-passing based communication modes, asynchronous and synchronous, are defined.

- A state machine M_1 communicates *asynchronously* with a state machine M_2 if it calls a request of M_2 and does not block for the end of the request. Such requests are typically F2 type requests.
- A state machine M_1 communicates *synchronously* with state machine M_2 if its event handler calls a request of M_2 and blocks for the end of the request. Such requests are typically F1 type requests.

To call a request, an output event is emitted and the state machine accepts an input event at a certain point. The original event handler is defined to be invariant of state and event space of the state machine. To simplify the description, we say an event handler calls a request by putting output event emission (and blocking for the end of request, for synchronous communication) in the handler. We say a request f is *nested* in a request r if an event handler of r calls f. The communication between event-driven finite state machines may enforce an execution order between them. When two state machines are not ordered, their execution order is arbitrary. Clearly, the execution order changes as the execution progresses.

The event driven finite state machines are synchronized when they share resources. Resources are shared between event handlers of different state machines. Each resource is managed by a state machine. The resource users communicate with the resource management state machines.

6.4 Timing Model of Event Handlers

Because of the complexity and speed of software execution, we cannot ignore the execution time of event handlers. We capture the timing behavior of event handlers by its worst case execution time (WCET) because our main concern is the relationship between atomic event handler execution and event occurrence.

We define chained execution of event handlers as executing several handlers without processing other events. For example, an event handler h may call a request r synchronously. If we execute r after h without processing a new event when h ends, we say we chain h and r. Chaining happens only when request nesting occurs. Let $W_H(h)$ denote the WCET of chained event handles started by h. $T_{WCET}(c)$ denotes the WCET of a piece of code c. Because of chaining,, $W_H(h)$ is not simply $T_{WCET}(h)$. When the state machine is in different states, the handler enabled by an event e differs. For an event e, define H(e) as the set of event handlers enabled by event e, and define W_E as

$$W_E(e) = \underset{\forall h \in H(e)}{MAX}(W_H(h)) .$$

The timing model of chained event handlers, started by h, $W_H(h)$, is defined as:

$$W_H(h) = \begin{cases} W_E(e), & h = sync(e,S) \\ T_{WCET}(h) + W_E(e), & h = async(e) \\ T_{WCET}(h), & Otherwise. \end{cases}$$

When the event handler contains a synchronous request (type F1), the time cost is estimated as the maximum WCET of all the event handlers enabled by the request event. If the event handler generates an output event, the WCET of the event handler is sum of the WCET of the handler code itself and the maximum time cost of all the event handlers enabled by the output events. Otherwise, the time cost of an event handler without synchronization is defined as the WCET of the code. Clearly, if the chaining has a loop, $W_H(h) = \infty$.

6.5 Modeling Device Access Behavior with Extended Event Driven Finite State machines

As illustrated in Section 5, device access behavior has two parts: data channel and device control. Both of these parts are modeled by extended event driven finite state machines, though a data port access function conforms to one of a set of templates.

We define five types of input events according to their appearance and functionality: *interrupt*, *timer*, *task request*, *interrupt request*, and *asynchronous input*. A *timer* event occurs when the timer expires. An *interrupt request* event occurs when an interrupt needs to be serviced. A *task request* event is emitted when a task, user (or kernel) process (or thread), issues a service request. Other interrupts are grouped together as *interrupt* events. An *asynchronous input* is the output of a type F2 request of a state machine. A timer event is *obsolete* if the state machine no longer waits for it. The obsoleteness of the timer event models event occurrence timeout. Moreover, a state has at most one up-to-date timer event.

To assign priorities to the input events, we classify the input events according to their appearances. An asynchronous input inherits the priority of the event enabling the transition which emits it. The interrupt related events, including interrupt and interrupt request events, have the highest priorities. The task request events have the lowest priority. The timer events have a priority in the middle. Because of the obsoleteness of the timer event, all the timer events share the same priority. The task requests share the same priority though we can prioritize them. Interrupt events may have multiple priority levels. This event priority assignment scheme agrees with the execution level definition of operating systems. Because most operating systems define similar execution levels for interrupts, timer and system calls, this scheme is compatible with a range of operating systems.

An event could be unreliable. It explains the mysterious behavior of a line printer driver as highlighted in [7]: the driver hangs although the program is logically perfect and the printer works fine. The line printer model has a channel with a write port. The synchronization event of the write port data unit is an interrupt indicating that the buffered data are printed. Unfortunately, the interrupt is easily lost, i.e., not captured by the processor. The data access state machine is stuck in a state blocking for the interrupt. To avoid this situation, we associate a time out value with an unstable event indicating its latest arrival time if it appears.

6.6 Composition of Extended Event Driven Finite State Machines

We define a *sub-device* as a set of device controller state machines and data port access state machines. Each state machine belongs to exactly one sub-device. According to our experience with device drivers, we define four types of resources shared by the device controller and data port access state machines. The shared resources defined are the interface (ITF) shared between sub-devices, data (SH_{data}) shared by data channels and device controller requests, system resources such as dynamically allocated DMA shared by data channels, and physical data channel (P_{CH}) shared by the two port accesses of the same channel. The communication between the state machines is also constrained because M_{data} is responsible for transfering data while M_{ctrl} is responsible for assigning the data transfer task and coordinating the entire device processor interaction process. The communication and synchronization between the device controller state machine (M_{ctrl}) and data port access state machine (M_{data}) complies with the following rules.

- Cmp1) Requests defined in M_{data} do not nest in each other.
- Cmp2) An M_{data} (including its nested requests) only communicates with a M_{ctrl} in the same sub-device.
- Cmp3) M_{data} share DMA. An M_{data} requires at most 1 DMA.
- Cmp4) Each state machine requires one ITF.
- Cmp5) SH_{data} are shared between M_{ctrl} requests and M_{data} requests.
- Cmp6) Two M_{data} (read, write) of the same channel share a P_{CH}. A M_{data} requires one P_{CH}.

6.7 Correct Implementation Model

The correct-by-construction code synthesis technique requires a proof of the correctness of the implementation of the event processing mechanism. We say an event processing mechanism is correct if it satisfies the following conditions. The event processing mechanism designer (synthesis technique) should guarantee that the conditions are satisfied.

- E1) The sticky events are queued.
- E2) The enabled transition, the enabling event of which is at the highest priority, is fired.
- E3) A state machine with an enabled transition is executed at most *T* time units after the transition is enabled (the time the enabling event occurs, not the time it is checked). T is a constant for the state machines. However, the transition that fires is not required to be the first transition enabled.

E3 guarantees the fairness of the implementation, i.e., a state machine with an enabled transition is executed in bounded time. E3 also limits the highest frequency of the events of high priority.

6.8 Model Soundness

To guarantee the deterministic behavior and finite request execution time, we impose certain conditions on the model. A model is *sound* if and only if it satisfies the following:

S1) Request nesting is not conditional.
S2) Request coordination policies are compatible.
S3) The request terminates in finite time assuming all the events are stable and the input events occur eventually.
S4) Composition rule (Section 6.6) of event driven finite state machine is satisfied.
S5) No circular shared resource requirements.
S6) The execution result is not affected by the execution order of the state machines.

Rule S1 constrains our synthesis method to a statically defined communication of the state machines. Rule S2 is necessary to guarantee deterministic behavior of the model. Rule S3 is necessary to guarantee finite request execution time. Rule S4 constrains the network of event driven finite state machines to one suitable to device modeling. Rule S5 is necessary to ensure deadlock free. The soundness constraint S6 avoids the following dilemma. The state machine M_1 is in state S_1 and event e_1 occurs at t_1. However, M_1 is not executed until event e_2 occurs at time t_2. The priority of e_2 is higher than e_1. If M_1 executes between t_1 and t_2, e_1 is consumed. After t_2, e_2 is consumed. If the correctness is dependent on which event is consumed, the model is not sound. Given a correct implementation scheme and a model which does not satisfy soundness constraint S6, we either restructure the state machine or require $t_2 - t_1 > T$ to make it sound.

Rule S1 and S2 are checked statically. S3 is reducible to the reachability problem and can be checked by tools for state space traversal such as SMV [9]. Rule S4 items are either enforced by the specification or checked statically. The checking of rule S5 is discussed in Section 7.1. S6 reduces to equivalence under asynchronous communication. Formally this can be checked using formal verification techniques. However, informally the designer may be able to convince themselves of this based on explicit use of synchronization when needed, much as is done in parallel programming. We assume the latter case for now.

7. OPERATING SYSTEM BASED DEVICE DRIVER SYNTHESIS

The device driver synthesis procedure generates data structures and functions for a sound model. As part of the methodology mentioned in [1], we focus on synthesizing core functions modeled by event driven finite state machines. It contains three parts: handling unstable events, implementing the request coordination policy, and designing event processing mechanisms and resource sharing schemes. The unreliable events of the original finite state machines are switched to reliable ones by inserting new transitions, (S_1, S_{err}), enabled by time out events, where S_{err} is an error state. The time out value is the maximum time out value of the unstable events on the out edges of the state S_1. The coordination policy implementation includes request state definition and processing specific to each coordination rule. Because of the lack of space, we omit the details of the algorithms.

7.1 Resource Sharing Scheme

According to Section 6.6, four types of shared resources, ITF, SH_{data}, DMA, and P_{CH}, are defined. The resource acquiring and releasing operations follow the following rules.

R1) An ITF is acquired right before a transition fires. The current ITF is released and a new ITF is acquired when we execute a transition in another state machine with a different ITF.
R2) If a request requires a SH_{data}, it acquires SH_{data} after the ITF of the first transition is obtained and holds SH_{data} until the request ends. If SH_{data} is not obtained, the ITF is released.
R3) Dynamically allocated DMA is acquired when data unit executes (after SH_{data} is acquired). It is held until data unit execution finishes.
R4) A P_{CH} is required at the start of the data unit execution. If DMA is used, it is required after DMA is obtained. It is held until the data unit execution ends.

Given the resource sharing scheme and soundness rule S4, we conclude that the soundness rule S5 is guaranteed.

Proof:
Assume we have a circular resource requirement, (A_1, A_2, …, A_K, A_1), where A_i (i=1, …, K) is a shared resource.

- A P_{CH} is not in the circle. Data unit operations are essentially event handlers of data port access state machines. According to Cmp1 and Cmp2, a M_{data} never requires an ITF after SH_{data} is acquired. Given this fact, according to R3, a request never requires an ITF or SH_{data} after a DMA is held. Hence, according to Cmp6 and R4, P_{CH} is always the last resource to be acquired.
- A DMA is not in the circle. According to R3, R4 and Cmp3, the only possible resource required while holding a DMA is P_{CH}. Because a P_{CH} is not in the circle, DMA is not in the circle.
- According to Cmp1, a request never requires a SH_{data} while holding one. According to Cmp2, a request never requires a SH_{data} while holding an ITF. Because of the previous 2 items, SH_{data} is not in the circle.
- According to R1, there is not an ITF circle.

Hence the circular resource requirement cannot exist.

7.2 Event Processing Mechanism

Because the device behavior is modeled as multiple communicating event-driven finite state machines, our main objective is to design the event processing mechanism. Each state machine is a schedulable entity managed by the event processing kernel. A traditional event processing kernel queues the events and executes the schedulable entities. Figure 3 shows the sketch of the code. It has a background kernel thread dedicated to event processing. The events in the event queue are ordered according to their priorities. A key feature of our solution is to take advantage of the services provided by the operating system and remove the explicit central event manager and the event queue. The code sketch is shown in Figure 4. It is based on the observation that a lower level event has no chance to be issued when a higher level transition fires on a single CPU because the event priority assignment agrees with the operating system

```
Interrupt (Timer) handler, User request: {
  Enqueue the event to the dest FSM atomically;
  Block for the end of the request if it is a request;
}

Event process kernel (a kernel thread):
For each state machine {
      For each event {
            if (enabled transitions exist)
                  Fire it;
                  Enqueue the output events;
                  Delete the enabling event;
                  Unblock a request ends;
            else
                  if (event is non-sticky) remove it;
      }
}
```

Figure 3. Traditional event processing kernel

execution level definition. Sticky events are simulated by registering a timer handler simulating the occurrence of the event repeatedly, that is, we poll for the consumption of the event. For the multiple CPU case, primitives such as spin locks are used. The preemption mechanism is calculated according to the discussion in Section 4.

The scheme shown in Figure 4 has lower cost and predictable execution time. Besides the saving of the queue management operations, we do not maintain a background thread and save context switches. Moreover, the gap between when a background thread becomes ready and it executes is not predictable for a non-real-time operating system. This is hazardous for a device driver. For example, the USB device controller receives a command from the host. If the command is not processed in time, a protocol error occurs. Figure 4 shows an extreme case of zero synchronization time and NULL queue maintenance which is useful for a class of drivers (such as devices in our case studies). We prove that for a model satisfying soundness rule S1, the scheme (Figure 4) is a correct implementation scheme when the following constraints are satisfied. These constraints should be checked by the synthesizer.

C1) There are no internal output events.

C2) Let f_p denote the highest frequency of the events of priority p. Define W_p as the longest execution time of the code executing at priority p without processing a new event, that is,

$$W_P(p) = \max_{\forall e, P(e)=p}(W_E(e)) \ .$$

The input event sequence satisfies the following condition. If two events can overwrite each other, they have the same priority, say P_0. Their occurrence interval, T_{inter}, satisfies

$$T_{inter} > \max_{\forall p, p<P_0}(W_P(p)) \Big/ \Big(1 - \sum_{\forall p, p \geq p_0}(W_P(p) \times f_p)\Big)$$

when preemption can be disabled.

C3) The caller of an F2 type request always blocks for the end of it.

C4) When an F1 type request of a state machine is called, the machine is always ready to receive the request.

C5) $1 > \sum_{\forall p}(W_P(p) \times f_P)$ is satisfied.

Proof:

C1 guarantees E1 for internal events. Because the event priority definition agrees with operating system code execution level definition, S1, C3 and C4 guarantee E2 and E1 for the algorithm shown in Figure 4.

```
Execute FSM with event e: {
   Fire the enabled transition of highest priority;
   if (F2 typed request (r) ends)
         execute FSM(r's caller) with the output event;
   else if (F1 types request (r) is activated)
         execute the FSM the request resides
         with the request evt;
}

Interrupt (Timer) Handler: {
  Require shared resources if necessary;
  Disable preemption;
  Execute FSM with interrupt (or timer) events;
  Enable preemption;
  Release shared resources if necessary;
}

User request: {
  Request coordination and start a request;
  Require shared resources if necessary;
  Disable preemption;
  Execute FSM with event (user request);
  Block for destination & Enable preemption;
  Release interface and data shared if necessary;
  Request coordination (cleanup operations);
}
```

Figure 4. OS based event processing

Assume the minimum interval between two over-writable events is T_{inter}. In this period, there are at most (T_{inter}*f_p) instances of events of priority p. Two types of code may block the execution of the event handlers of event with priority p: event handlers of higher (or the same) priority events and lower priority event with preemption disabled. Because an event handler with a higher priority is selected each time a handler finishes, the event handler of higher priority is blocked by at most one event handler of lower priority. Hence, we have

$$T_{inter} > \max_{\forall p<p_0}(W_P(p)) + \sum_{\forall p, p \geq p_0}(T_{inter} \times f_P \times W_P(p)) \ ,$$

which results in C2 guaranteeing E1 for input events, that is, input events are not lost.

Similarly, in time period T mentioned in E3, there are at most (T*f_p) instances of events of priority p. The WCET of the event handlers satisfies $T > \sum_{\forall p}(T \times f_p \times W_P(p))$, i.e., C5 guarantees E3.

8. CASE STUDIES

We demonstrate our device driver synthesis techniques with two case studies: the infrared port (IRDA) for the Intel Pentium III mobile processor and the USB device controller (UDC) for an Intel StrongArm SA1100 based handheld. These peripherals are among the most popular peripherals for SoC embedded processors.

IRDA An infrared port is modeled as a single sub-device consisting of a data channel and a device controller. The channel has two ports, read and write, which are asynchronous and blocking respectively. The device controller has three control functions: *start*, *stop*, and *configure*. Besides the request events, *start*, *stop*, and *configure*, a poll event (recognition type) representing the emptiness of the transmitting buffer is defined. The baud rate setting data is shared between the device controller and the port access state machines. Line discipline (a special terminal interface) and network interface are defined for the driver. Because the infrared port matches the model of the line discipline model perfectly, low level access functions such as register FIFO accesses are already included in the line discipline library functions. Hence the device programming interface is not necessary.

To test the correctness of the driver, we bind the IRDA protocol stack on top of the driver and setup the PPP connection between an IBM T23 (Redhat 8 with linux kernel 2.4.18) and a DELL Inspiron 5000 (RedHat 9.0 with linux kernel 2.4.20). The correctness of driver is verified successfully by executing the *scp* command correctly.

UDC The USB device controller of SA1100 is modeled as a single sub-device consisting of a device controller and 3 data channels, ep0, ep1, and ep2. Channel ep0 has two ports, read and write, which are asynchronous and blocking respectively. Channel ep1 has only an asynchronous read port. Channel ep2 has only a blocking write port. Channel ep1 and ep2 have pre-allocated DMA channels. The device controller includes the specification of the USB device controller setup protocol. The read port access of ep0 communicates asynchronously with the device controller. The device controller communicates synchronously with the write port access of ep0. A network interface is defined for it.

To test the correctness of the driver, we bind the IP socket layer on top of the driver and set up the USB connection between the HP iPaq3600 handheld (Familiar v0.5.3 with linux kernel 2.4.17) and a 686 based desktop (Redhat 7.2 with linux kernel 2.4.9). The correctness of the driver is tested successfully by executing the standard TCP/IP command *ping* correctly.

Table 1 Line count of IRDA and UDC drivers

Device	Iris Specification	Linux source code	Synthesized (library excluded)
IRDA	30	775	283
UDC	620	2002	971

We use the reduction of line count as a metric to evaluate our methodology's ability to increase productivity. Although line count is not a perfect measure of software complexity, it is a first order estimate of how much effort is required to develop the software. Table 1 shows the line count comparison of the specification, the original Linux driver (may include several files), and the synthesized code (library and templates are excluded). From Table 1 we see a significant reduction in the size of the specification compared to the original Linux driver which is a strong indication of increased productivity. Moreover, our specification style helps the developer to understand the device behavior and thus is more suitable to driver development compared with a general language such as C. Further, the structure of the driver is provably correct because both the models are sound and satisfy implementation correctness constraints (C1 to C5).

9. CONCLUSIONS

This paper addresses the issue of modeling device access behavior with a formal model, *viz.* extended event driven finite state machines, and using it to synthesize a correct-by-construction operating system based device driver. We apply this methodology to develop device drivers for two devices: an infrared port and the USB device controller of a SA110 based handheld. The experiments show a 70% reduction of specification size which is an indication of increased productivity.

10. REFERENCES

[1] Shaojie Wang, Sharad Malik, and Reinaldo A. Bergamaschi, Modeling and Integration of Peripheral Devices in Embedded Systems, DATE 2003.

[2] Mattias O'Nil, and Axel Jantsch, Device Driver and DMA Controller Synthesis from HW/SW Communication protocol specifications, Design Automation for Embedded Systems, Vol 6, 2001. pp 177-205.

[3] Dirk Desmet, D. Verkest, and Hugo De Man, Operating system based software generation for system-on-chip, DAC 2000.

[4] Andreas Gerstlauer, Haobo Yu, and Daniel D. Gajski, RTOS Modeling for System Level Design, DATE 2003.

[5] F. Balarin, M. Chiodo, P. Giusto, H. Hsieh, A. Jurecska, L. Lavagno, C. Passerone, A. Sangiovanni-Vincentelli, E. Sentovich, K. Suzuki, and B. Tabbara, Hardware-Software Co-Design of Embedded Systems: The Polis Approach, Kluwer Academic Press, 1997.

[6] I. Bolsen, H. J. De Man, B. Lin, K. van Rompaey, S. Vercauteren, and D. Verkest, Hardware/software co-design of digital telecommunication systems, Proceeding of the IEEE, Vol 85, 1997. pp391-418.

[7] George Pajari, Writing UNIX Device Drivers, Addison-Wesley Publishing Company, Inc., 1992.

[8] Johnny Oberg, Anshul Kumar, and Ahmed Hemani, "Grammar-based Hardware Synthesis of Data Communication Protocols", In Proc. of the 9th ISSS, Nov. 1996, pp14-19

[9] K. L. McMillan, Symbolic Model Checking: An approach to the state explosion problem, CMU Tech Rpt. CMU-CS-92-131.

Hardware Support for Real-time Operating Systems

Paul Kohout[1]
EVI Technology , LLC.
7138 Columbia Gateway Dr.
Columbia Maryland 21046
pkohout@evitechnology.com

Brinda Ganesh and Bruce Jacob
Department of Electrical and Computer Engineering
University of Maryland, College Park
Maryland 20742
{brinda,blj}@eng.umd.edu

[1] Work done when Paul was at UMD.

ABSTRACT

The growing complexity of embedded applications and pressure on time-to-market has resulted in the increasing use of embedded real-time operating systems. Unfortunately, RTOSes can introduce a significant performance degradation. This paper presents the Real-Time Task Manager (RTM)—a processor extension that minimizes the performance drawbacks associated with RTOSes. The RTM accomplishes this by supporting, in hardware, a few of the common RTOS operations that are performance bottlenecks: task scheduling, time management, and event management. By exploiting the inherent parallelism of these operations, the RTM completes them in constant time, thereby significantly reducing RTOS overhead. It decreases both the processor time used by the RTOS and the maximum response time by an order of magnitude.

Categories and Subject Descriptors

A.0 [General]: Conference Proceedings

General Terms

Performance, Design, Experimentation.

Keywords

RTOS, Hardware-Software Codesign.

1. MOTIVATION

RTOSes have become extremely important to the development of real-time systems as reflected by the growing market for RTOSes; half a billion dollars in shipments of RTOSes will be sold in 2002 [5]. RTOSes provide services for better hardware abstraction multitasking, task synchronization etc. However, the benefits that RTOSes provide do not come for free. The use of RTOSes has several important effects on various performance parameters of real-time systems.

Processor Utilization: The fraction of processing power that an application is able to use. In order to provide services like multitasking, preemption, and numerous others, the RTOS introduces an overhead which lowers the processing power available to the application.

Response Time: The time it takes for a real-time system to response to external stimuli. This delay is highly dependent on several factors, including whether or not the RTOS is preemptive and whether polling or interrupts are used to sense the stimulus. The effects of RTOSes on response time vary widely, but, in general, RTOSes increase response time to varying degrees.

Much of the performance degradation caused by RTOSes can be traced to their core operations, namely task scheduling, time management, and event management. Analysis of these functions reveals that they are executed frequently, that they perform inter-related actions, and that these actions exhibit parallelism. That parallelism cannot be exploited by software-based implementations; however, hardware-based solutions can exploit this parallelism and lower the performance degradation. Also, the rapidly dropping cost of logic [7] has made it possible to put custom hardware for enhancing frequently executing operations on embedded processors, without increasing costs significantly.

These factors suggest that RTOSes would greatly benefit from a custom hardware solution. This is the motivation for the Real-Time Task Manager (RTM), a memory-mapped on-chip peripheral designed to optimize task scheduling, time management, and event management that is compatible with a wide range of RTOSes. Measurements have been taken of the performance impact of the RTM on models of realistic real time systems. These measurements show that processor utilization and maximum response time are both reduced by an order of magnitude.

2. BACKGROUND

To better understand that the commonly seen bottlenecks in RTOSes, we present some of the details regarding their nature — what they are, how they are implemented and how often they are invoked.

Task Scheduling: Process of determining which task should be running at any given time. The most commonly implemented approach to scheduling in commercial RTOSes is based on task priorities [8]. Priority-driven schedulers assign each task a priority and execute the task with the highest priority that is ready.

Time Management: The RTOS gets its sense of time by a periodic interrupt generated every clock tick by a hardware timer. The rate of the generation of this clock tick is the system clock frequency which is not to be confused with the CPU clock frequency. Typically the system clock frequency is on

Table 1. RTOS Function Details

	Implementation / Overhead	Performed When
Scheduling	• Unsorted Ready List - Task Selection has Linear Overhead • Sorted Ready List -Task Selection has Constant small overhead, Task Insertion on Ready Queue has Linear Overhead • Bit-Vectors[6] - Constant Overhead implementation for systems with unique and static priorities.	• System calls which change task status e.g. Priority Change. Scales with workload size. • Preemptive System- After Timer Interrupt. Scales with system clock frequency. • Non Preemptive System - Task Completion Points, After Timer Interrupt if System is Idling. Scales with workload size.
Time Management	• Each task has individual delay counter containing its absolute delay. Timer Update requires updating each counter and has a linear overhead • UNIX Callout Table[2]. Delay counters hold delays relative to that of previous element. Updates have variable overhead. Task Insertions has linear overhead.	• Preemptive System - After Timer Interrupt. Scales linearly with system clock frequency. • Non Preemptive System - Task Completion Points, After Timer Interrupt if System is Idling. Scales with workload size.
Event Management	Similar to Task Scheduling with each event having its own Blocked Queue.	• Tasks use IPC. Dependent on extent to which workload uses IPC.

the order of kHz while the CPU clock is on the order of MHz. *Time management* refers to the RTOS's ability to allow tasks to use this mechanism to be scheduled at specific times i.e. have the tasks block for a specific time before becoming ready.

Event Management: Most real-time operating systems provide services for communication and synchronization between tasks—known as *interprocess communication (IPC)*. Examples are semaphores, message queues etc. Event management involves keeping track of which tasks are blocked i.e. waiting for IPC and which tasks should be released i.e. have to receive IPC on resource availability.

Note that as shown in Table 1, the overhead of the RTOS due to these operations is proportional to the product of frequency and complexity. Since both of these components may increase linearly with the number of tasks, there may be a quadratic relationship between the number of tasks in the system and the RTOS overhead due to them. In addition the overhead of task scheduling and time management increases linearly with the system clock frequency.

The longest time that it takes to perform any critical section of code (including task scheduling, event or time management) adds to the maximum response time in preemptive systems. However, in non-preemptive systems where interrupts are polled, a response task is delayed more by executing workloads than by RTOS operations. This is because workloads execute for longer periods than RTOS operations and thus disable interrupt response for longer periods.

3. RELATED WORK

Dick, Lakshminarayana, Raghunathan, and Jha first published a study of the power consumption of RTOSes in embedded systems [4] on an instruction-level simulator of the Fujitsu SPARClite processor, using embedded applications running on µC/OS. They suggested ways in which to design application software so that the power consumption is minimized.

Adomat, Furunäs, Lindh, and Stärner described the Real-Time Unit (RTU)—an external hardware module designed to perform RTOS functions [1]. The RTM-based RTOS lies at an intermediate point in the design spectrum whose two extremities are represented by a purely software based RTOS and the RTU — an exclusively hardware-based design. The RTU improves performance, but it does not allow for existing RTOSes to easily take advantage of its offerings.

Mooney and his co-authors [12,13] have explored hardware implementations of lock synchronization, deadlock detection, dynamic memory management in a multi processor system. These schemes effectively solve problems seen in a multi-processor system namely atomic access of data, potential resource conflicts. Our scheme is orthogonal to their scheme because it explores hardware acceleration for basic RTOS operations. In addition Mooney et al [14] have looked at building a cyclic scheduler in hardware. Unlike our design it is application specific and does not investigate support for alternate scheduling mechanisms like EDF etc.

4. REAL-TIME TASK MANAGER

The RTM is a hardware module that implements a task database and thus supports the key RTOS operations: task scheduling, time management, and event management. It is an on-chip peripheral that communicates with the core via a memory-mapped interface.

Figure 1. Reference RTM Data Structure

The reference RTM architecture has 64 records. The status, priority and event ID fields are each 8 bits wide and the delay field is 16 bits wide. Each record uses 40 bits of storage but is mapped into the I/O space at even-word (64 bit) boundaries to simplify and speed up addressing.

The RTM is pictured in Figure 1; where each record contains information about a single task. The RTM is accessed through the global address space and each record can be read from or written to as if it were any other array of structures.

A record is composed of four individually addressable fields. Each record contains a *status field*, containing several bits that describe the status of the corresponding record. The *valid bit* is necessary to indicate if that the record is used by a task. The *delayed bit* indicates that the task is waiting for the amount of clock ticks specified by the *delay field* before being ready-to-run. The *event bit* indicates that the task is pending on the event with the identifier specified by the *event ID field.* The *suspended bit* indicates that the task has been suspended. If the valid bit is set, but the delayed, event, and suspended bits are clear, then the task is ready-to-run. Finally, the *priority field* indicates the task's priority. Also, the maximum number of records is some fixed constant, such as 64 or 256. The RTOS can issue instructions to or retrieve certain information from the RTM via a set of memory mapped registers.

The RTM can be queried for the highest priority ready task and thus supports static-priority scheduling. The RTM does time management by decrementing the delay fields of all records by the number of clock ticks specified by the RTOS and updating the delay bit if this value reaches zero. Event management is

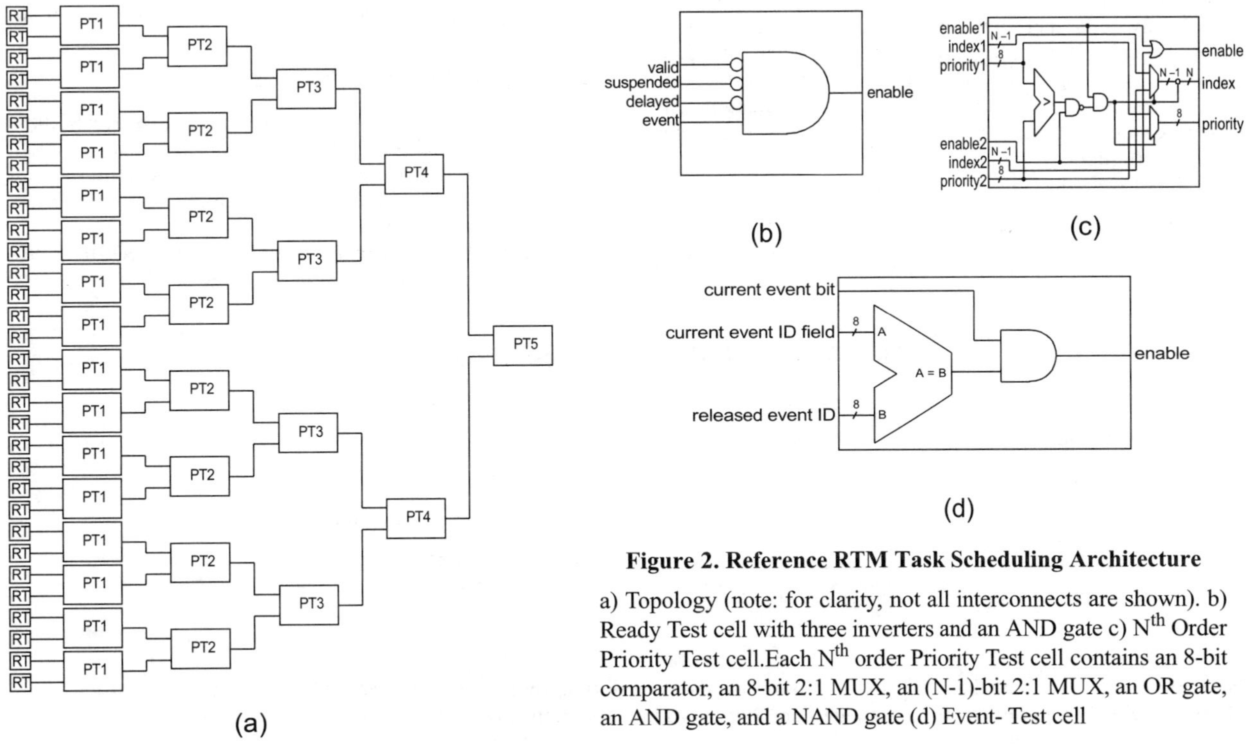

Figure 2. Reference RTM Task Scheduling Architecture

a) Topology (note: for clarity, not all interconnects are shown). b) Ready Test cell with three inverters and an AND gate c) Nth Order Priority Test cell.Each Nth order Priority Test cell contains an 8-bit comparator, an 8-bit 2:1 MUX, an (N-1)-bit 2:1 MUX, an OR gate, an AND gate, and a NAND gate (d) Event- Test cell very similar to static-priority scheduling. The RTM queries for the highest priority task that is pending on a given event identifier, instead of querying its data structure for the highest priority ready task.

5. ARCHITECTURE

A reference architecture is presented here to illustrate the complexity and scalability of implementing the hardware architecture of the RTM. For a 64 record RTM with entries as shown in the figure the total number of flip-flops required is 2304, which is small enough to easily be implemented. These parameters are based on common limits and are sufficient for the majority of real-time applications.

Task scheduling is performed using 64 Ready Test cells and a binary tree of 63 Priority Test cells. Owing to space considerations we show this for a 32 entry case in Figure 2. The Ready Test cells simply determine which tasks are ready-to-run. Each Priority Test cell takes in as input two task priorities and ready bits. It then outputs which of these is the highest priority ready task. These priority values propagate down the comparator tree until the single sixth order cell where the index of the overall highest priority ready task is output. Each Nth order Priority Test cell contains an 8-bit comparator, an 8-bit 2:1 MUX, an (N-1)-bit 2:1 MUX, an OR gate, an AND gate, and a NAND gate. The logic required task scheduling scales linearly with the number of records in the RTM (n RTM records requires n RT cells plus n-1 PT cells). The computational delay is proportional to the logarithm of the number of records. For a reasonable number of records i.e. the numbers typically used in production RTOSes, this implementation of task scheduling will be sufficiently fast and small.

In order to implement time management, 64 delay decrement cells are all that is required, as shown in Figure 3. Delay decrement cells consists of a simplified 16-bit adder and an AND gate. Delay cells decrement the delay field and perform a comparison to clear the delay bit when necessary. In this implementation, the logic scales linearly with the number of records; however, the computational delay is a constant. In designs where the CPU clock frequency is lower than the system clock frequency, the delay decrement cells can be reused and thus lower the number of delay cells required.

The event management is almost exactly the same as task scheduling. The only difference is that instead of Ready Test cells, it has Event Test cells, as seen in Figure 2. This allows the binary tree of Priority Test cells to be used for both scheduling and event management. The Event Test cells just check if the event bit is set and if the event ID of the resource being released matches the event ID in a specific record. They each use an 8-bit comparator and an AND gate. The combinational logic required for event management scales linearly, except that the majority can be shared with the task scheduler. Also, the computational delay is O(log(n)), as it is with scheduling.

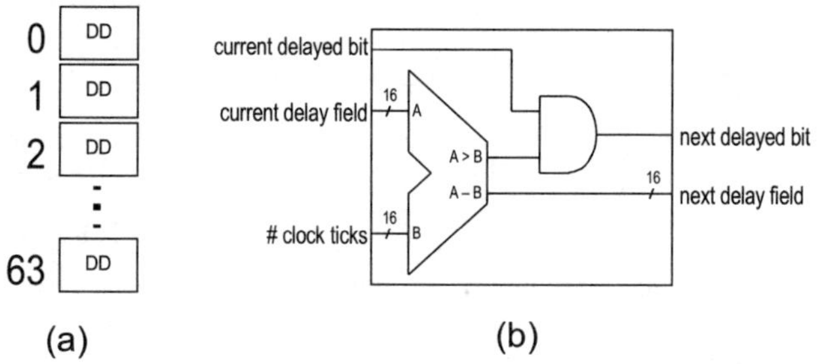

Figure 3. Reference RTM Event and Time Management Architecture

a) Topology (note: for clarity, not all interconnects are shown). b) Delay Decrement Cell.

The die area that the RTM needs is important in determining its feasibility. Based on existing area models for register files and caches [9], the RTM reference architecture requires approximately 2600 register-bit equivalents (RBEs). This is roughly equivalent to the die area used by a 32-bit by 64-word register file making it feasible to implement the RTM in hardware. This number is large compared to a simple core but is small compared to the whole chip. This is because a typical embedded processor consists of the core and other on-chip devices like memory and various I/O devices.

6. EXPERIMENTS

In order to formally justify the use of the Real-Time Task Manager in actual real-time systems, an accurate quantification of the effects that it has on performance is done by analyzing models of real-time systems that use RTOSes. All measurements are made on a inhouse cycle-accurate C-based simulator of the Texas Instruments TMS320C6201. The

Table 2. Details of RTOSes used in study

	µC/OS-II	**NOS**
Preemptive	Yes	No
IPC?	Yes	No
Task Scheduling	Constant -Bit Vector	Linear - Sorted Ready Queue
Time Management	Linear - Unsorted Queue	Linear - UNIX Callout Queue
Event Management	Constant - Bit Vector	n/a

The table gives details of the RTOSes used in the study. The details regarding the overhead of the implementation of the RTOS functions (scheduling, time management and event management) are given along with the method employed.

processor is a high-performance 32-bit VLIW fixed-point DSP with a 200 MHz clock that can issue eight 32-bit instructions per cycle [11]. The simulator is capable of loading the same executable binary files that run in actual systems and executing them exactly as they would on a real processor.

Two differing RTOSes have been used in this study: µC/OS-II, a popular commercial preemptive RTOS [6]; and NOS, a "homegrown" non-preemptive RTOS, that is representative of over 25% of RTOSes which are merely subsets of complete RTOSes [5]. More details are given in table below.

Several applications from the MediaBench suite [7] are used in this analysis including workloads like GSM decompress, ADPCM encode and decode and the encryption and decryption benchmark Pegwit. The benchmarks are modified so that they are separated into two periodic tasks, an input processing task and an output task, with periods of 20 ms. In µC/OS, semaphores are used to synchronize the access of the data channel by the two tasks. An additional noise task (with a period of 32 ms) purpose is to insert the type of background noise commonly present in real-time applications, e.g., many systems have LCD displays which have to be periodically refreshed. Aperiodic tasks which respond to external stimuli, such as I/O events are simulated as a polling task in NOS or by interrupts in µC/OS systems. The I/O events arrival times are geometrically distributed with an average arrival rate of 10 milliseconds.

7. RESULTS

The goal of the Real-Time Task Manager is to reduce the performance loss problem associated with RTOSes. In order to validate the success of the RTM, we characterize its effects on processor utilization, response time.

7.1 RTOS Overhead

For purposes of brevity we present the average processor utilization across 5 benchmarks for different workloads. For all benchmarks the performance was reasonably close to the average and for no benchmark did the configurations with the RTM perform worse than those without.

µC/OS-II: The RTOS processor utilization has been divided into five categories for system configurations that use µC/OS. These five categories include Scheduling, Interprocess Communication i.e. Event Management, Timer Interrupts, Processing Clock Ticks i.e. Time Management or updating the timer queue and a Miscellaneous category which includes task Creation etc.

As seen in the graph in fig. 4, the RTOS processor utilization without the RTM can be quite significant. The bulk of the reduction comes from converting the overhead of time management operations that ready tasks that reach their release times at every clock tick from a linear one to a constant one. The gains in event management and scheduling are lower, 14% and 30% respectively, because of the effectiveness of the software-based bit vector scheme employed in µC/OS. The timer interrupt overhead and miscellaneous category which are not optimized account for a constant less than 1% of the processor utilization, both with and without the RTM. The basic RTOS operations that the RTM implements result in the processing overhead required by µC/OS to be reduced by 60% to 90%.

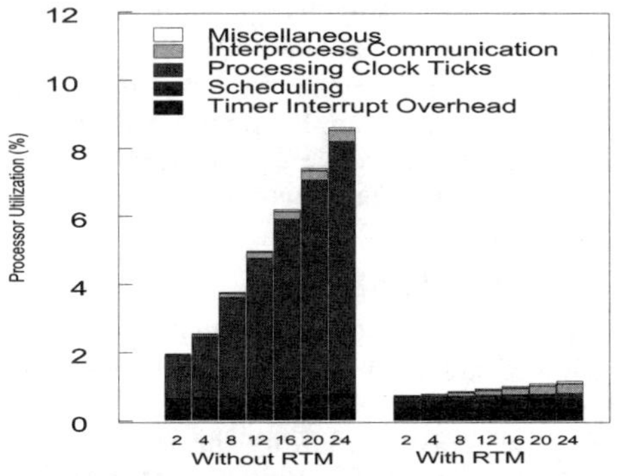

Table 3. µC/OS-II

Function	% Reduction
Scheduling	31
Processing Time	83 (average)
Event Management	14

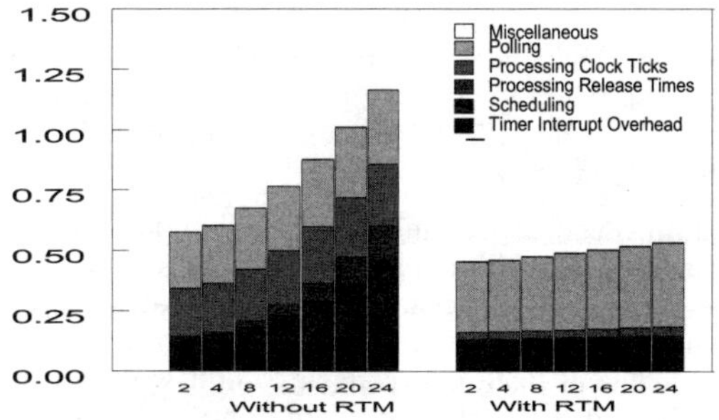

Table 3. NOS

Function	% Reduction
Scheduling	98
Processing Time	85 (average)
Event Management	14
Polling	Increase 25%
Release Times	95%

Figure 4. Processor Utilization Using µC/OS-II and NOS

The percent of the total processing time spent executing the operations in each of these categories and how they vary with system load, for every benchmark tested, both with and without using the RTM. System load refers to the amount of processing power used by the application, which, in this case, is determined by the number of data channels processed in the application

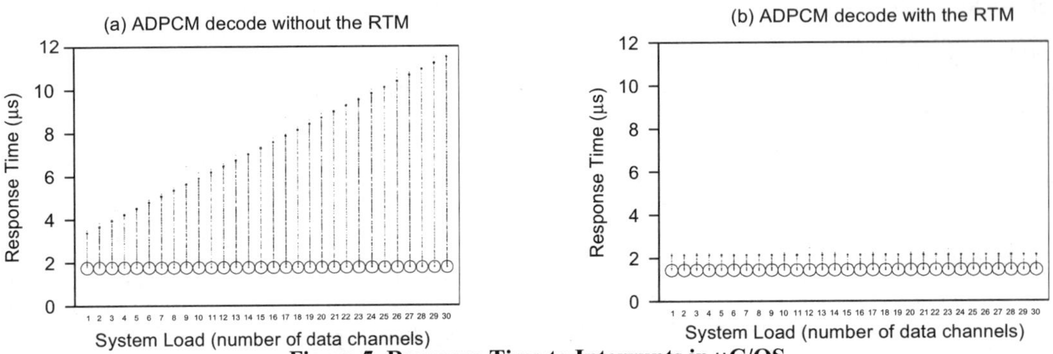

Figure 5. Response Time to Interrupts in µC/OS

The distribution of aperiodic interrupt response time for different workload sizes for µC/OS configurations for the benchmark ADPCM decode is shown. Each data point is represented as a circle whose area is proportional to the probability of the response occurring at that point.

NOS: For NOS, the processor utilization has been divided into six categories. These categories include Scheduling, Processing Release Times i.e. inserting a task onto the pause queue or timeout queue, Polling i.e. selecting a task to run while idling, Timer Interrupt Overhead, Processing Clock Ticks and Miscellaneous. As seen in the graphs, the RTOS processor utilization is not quite as large as it is for µC/OS, however, it is still significant enough to be worth optimizing.

Polling is the processing done to call the highest priority task's function, if any or to enter idling otherwise. It occurs after a task completes and when the processor is idle, after every timer interrupt. Unfortunately, the RTM can increase the processing time consumed by the polling operations by up to 25%. This is because without the RTM, polling is as simple as looking at the head of the ready queue. The RTM-based approach has an additional overhead associated with communicating the request to the RTM. The category of processing clock ticks execute at the same instances as polling. But in this case, the RTM reduces the magnitude of the overhead by around 85%.

Both scheduling and processing the release times utilizations increase quadratically with the system load for systems that do not use the RTM. This is because of the linear dependence of their computational complexity and frequency of invocation on the workload. The utilization is constant and trivial for systems with the RTM and it is not even visible on some graphs. The bulk of the lowering of the overhead comes from the nearly 98% reduction in scheduling overhead. The basic RTOS operations that the RTM implements result in the processing overhead required by NOS to be reduced by 20% to 65%.

7.2 Response Time

µC/OS-II: As seen in the graphs, the majority of the response time measurements are a constant value of 1.8 microseconds without the RTM and 1.4 microseconds with the RTM. This is because µC/OS is a preemptive RTOS and it responds to interrupts right away. Deviations from the main value are due to the effects of disabling interrupts while responding to timer interrupts and aperiodic interrupts. When the RTM is not used, the execution time of the timer interrupt ISR is dominated by the time management operation, which scales linearly with the number of tasks. The effect on the response time, as seen in the graphs, is a uniform distribution of values, ranging from the common 1.8 microsecond value to an upper limit, that increases with system load, (up to 11.8 microseconds for the loads studied). However, by using the RTM, the time management operation is always performed in trivial time. The effect of the timer interrupt on response time when using the RTM is a uniform distribution of measurements, ranging from 1.4 microseconds to 2.2 microseconds, an 83% decrease on average.

NOS: Unlike with µC/OS, the response time with NOS has little to do with the effects of the RTOS. Instead, the biggest determining factor has to do with the application code. During the execution of a task, responses to interrupts cannot occur until that task completes. Thus the response time numbers are a uniform distribution of values from the minimum idling response time of 1.4 microseconds to some limit that is only dependent upon the benchmark.

For most applications NOS, being a non-preemptive OS, has virtually no effect on the response time. It is the duration of the processing task and the system load that dictate the response time. However, for small applications whose task invocations finish quickly, NOS does have an effect on response time, and the RTM is able to eliminate this increase.

8. CONCLUSIONS

In this paper we presented the Real-Time Task Manager (RTM)—a hardware module that implements a few common RTOS operations: task scheduling, time management, and event management. By exploiting the inherent parallelism of these operations, the RTM is able to complete them in trivial time, thereby minimizing RTOS overhead. It decreases the processing time used by the RTOS by up to 90% and decreases the maximum response time by up to 81%.

9. ACKNOWLEDGEMENTS

The work of Brinda Ganesh and Paul Kohout was supported in part by NSF grant EIA-9806645 and NSF grant EIA-0000439. The work of Bruce Jacob was supported in part by NSF CAREER Award CCR-9983618, NSF grant EIA-9806645, NSF grant EIA-0000439, DOD award AFOSR-F496200110374, and by Compaq and IBM.

10. REFERENCES

[1] J. Adomat, J. Furunäs, L. Lindh, and J. Stärner. "Real-Time Kernel in Hardware RTU: A step towards deterministic and high performance real-time systems." In *Proceedings of*

Eighth Euromicro Workshop on Real-Time Systems, L'Aquila, Italy, June 1996, pp. 164-168.

[2] M. Bach. *The Design of the UNIX Operating System*. Prentice-Hall, Englewood Cliffs, NJ, 1986.

[3] K. Baynes, C. Collins, E. Fiterman, B. Ganesh, P. Kohout, C. Smit, T. Zhang, and B. Jacob. "The Performance and ENergy Consumption of Three Embedded Real-Time Operating Systems." In *Proceedings of the 2001 International Conference on Compilers, Architecture, and Synthesis for Embedded Systems (CASES '01)*, Atlanta, GA, November 2001, pp. 203-210.

[4] R. Dick, G. Lakshminarayana, A. Raghunathan, and N. Jha. "Power Analysis of Embedded Operating Systems." In *Proceedings of the 37th Design Automation Conference*, Los Angeles, CA, June 2000.

[5] International Technology Working Group. *International Technology Roadmap for Semiconductors 2001 Edition: Executive Summary*. Semiconductor Industry Association, 2001.

[6] J. Labrosse. *MicroC/OS-II: The Real-Time Kernel*. R & D Books, Lawrence, KS, 1999.

[7] C. Lee, M. Potkonjak, and W. Mangione-Smith. "MediaBench: A Tool for Evaluating and Synthesizing Multimedia and Communications Systems." In *Proceedings of the 30th Annual International Symposium on Microarchitecture (MICRO '97)*, Research Triangle Park, NC, December 1997.

[8] J. Liu. *Real-Time Systems*. Prentice Hall, Upper Saddle River, NJ, 2000.

[9] J. Mulder, N. Quach, and M. Flynn. "An Area Model for On-Chip Memories and its Application." *IEEE Journal of SOLID-STATE Circuits*, Vol. 26, No. 2, February 1991, pp. 98-106.

[10] Texas Instruments. *Code Composer Studio User's Guide*. February 2000.

[11] J. Turley and H. Hakkarainen. "TI's New 'C6x DSP Screams at 1,600 MIPS." *The Microprocessor Report*, Vol. 11, 1997, pp. 14-17.

[12] V. J. Mooney and D. M. Blough, "A Hardware-Software Real-Time Operating System Framework for SOCs," IEEE Design and Test of Computers, pp. 44-51, November-December 2002.

[13] B. E. S. Akgul and V. J. Mooney, "The System-on-a-Chip Lock Cache," International Journal of Design Automation for Embedded Systems, 7(1-2) pp. 139-174, September 2002.

[14] V. Mooney and G. De Micheli, "Hardware/Software Codesign of Run-Time Schedulers for Real-Time Systems,"*Design Automation of Embedded Systems*, 6(1), pp. 89-144, September 2000.

[15] T. Coopee. "Embedded Intelligence." *InfoWorld*, November 17, 2000.

Invited Talk

Programming Embedded Networked Sensor Systems

Feng Zhao, Jie Liu, Jim Reich, Maurice Chu, and Juan Liu
Embedded Collaborative Computing Area
Palo Alto Research Center (PARC)
3333 Coyote Hill Road
Palo Alto, California 94304, USA

Abstract

This talk describes a state-centric abstraction for application users to interact with sensor networks. Just as in data-centric routing and storage where physical nodes are less important than the data itself, state-centric abstraction introduces "states" as a natural vocabulary to describe spatio-temporal physical phenomena that the sensor networks are typically designed for. Application programmers specify the computation as creation, sharing, and transformation of states, which naturally map to descriptions in signal processing and control applications. We argue that due to the dynamic nature of sensor networks, programs written in state-centric abstractions are more invariant to constant changes in data stream configurations and make the resulting software more portable across multiple sensor network platforms. With help of models of sensor collaboration, sensing, and estimation, the state-centric specifications are mapped into collaborative processing tasks at compile time, and further maintained at run time, leveraging the data-centric caching and routing services. We use a multi-target tracking system as an example to show how state-centric programming models can raise the abstraction level for users to interact with sensor networks and help modularize the design.

Biography of Feng Zhao

F. Zhao

Feng Zhao is a Principal Scientist and manages the Embedded Collaborative Computing Area in the Systems and Practices Laboratory at PARC (formerly known as Xerox PARC). He is also Consulting Associate Professor of Computer Science at Stanford. The two main projects in his group, Collaborative Sensing and Smart Matter Diagnostics, investigate how MEMS sensor and networking technology can change the way we build and interact with physical devices and environments. His research interest includes distributed sensor data analysis, diagnostics, qualitative reasoning, and control of dynamical systems.

Dr. Zhao received his PhD in Electrical Engineering and Computer Science from MIT in 1992, where he developed one of the first algorithms for fast N-body computation in three spatial dimensions and phase-space nonlinear control synthesis. From 1992 to 1999, he was Assistant and Associate Professor of Computer and Information Science at Ohio State University. His INSIGHT Group developed the SAL software tool for rapid prototyping of spatio-temporal data analysis applications; the tool is currently used by a number of other research groups.

Dr. Zhao received the ONR Young Investigator Award and the NSF Young Investigator Award, and was an Alfred P. Sloan Research Fellow in Computer Science. He serves on the editorial boards of IEEE Transaction on Signal Processing, IEEE Transaction on Control Systems Technology, AI Magazine, New Generation Computing, and guest co-edited an IEEE Signal Processing Magazine special issue on collaborative signal and information processing (CSIP) in microsensor networks. He co-chaired the 1st and 2nd International Workshop on Information Processing in Sensor Networks (IPSN: www.parc.com/events/ipsn03). He has authored or co-authored over 90 technical papers in the areas of networked embedded systems, artificial intelligence, nonlinear control, and programming tools, and is a co-inventor of three US Patents and five pending patent applications.

CODES+ISSS'03, October 1-3, 2003, Newport Beach, California, USA.
ACM 1-58113-742-7/03/0010.

Design Space Exploration of a Hardware-Software Co-designed $GF(2^m)$ Galois Field Processor for Forward Error Correction and Cryptography

Wei-Ming Lim[1], M. Benaissa[2]
University of Sheffield
Department of Electronic and Electrical Engineering,
Mappin Street, Sheffield, S1 3JD, United Kingdom
[1]elp00wml@sheffield.ac.uk [2]m.benaissa@sheffield.ac.uk

ABSTRACT
This paper describes a hardware-software co-design approach for flexible programmable Galois Field Processing for applications which require operations over $GF(2^m)$, such as RS and BCH codes, Elliptic Curve Cryptography and the AES. Complexities of flexible implementations of different applications on a same computation architecture can be migrated to software during design time. However, the underlying $GF(2^m)$ arithmetic architecture needs to be designed with software programmability (or reconfigurability) in mind. We describe novel reconfigurable subword parallel $GF(2^m)$ arithmetic architectures designed with an associated instruction set architecture for different applications over $GF(2^m)$ and same applications with differing parameters. Design space exploration is carried out with two simple parameters P and Q which can be changed at design time and will affect the performance of different applications and flexibility of the final implementation. We show implementation results given for an FPGA prototype of the processor and programmed for RS and BCH coding, AES and elliptic curve cryptography with differing parameters. Complexity figures and configuration overheads for subword parallel $GF(2^m)$ arithmetic architectures are also estimated and discussed.

Categories and Subject Descriptors
C.3 [Special-Purpose And Application-Based Systems]: Real-time and embedded systems; B.2 [Arithmetic And Logic Structures]: Design Styles---Parallel

General Terms:
Design, Algorithm, Performance

Keywords
Galois Field Processor, $GF(2^m)$ Arithmetic, Forward Error Control Coding, Reed-Solomon Code, BCH Code, Cryptography, Elliptic Curve Cryptography, Advanced Encryption Standard, Hardware-Software Co-design, Design Space Exploration

1. INTRODUCTION
$GF(2^m)$ arithmetic has been used extensively in the domains of Forward Error Correction (FEC) Codes and Cryptography. Well known examples include Reed Solomon and BCH Codes for FEC [1], Elliptic Curve Cryptography (ECC) [2] for Public Key Cryptography and lately, the Advanced Encryption Standard [3] (AES) using the Rijndael Algorithm for Private Key Cryptography.

As systems get increasingly complex, more and more effort has being channelled into re-usable implementations, particularly software controlled architectures, by allowing design re-use simply through re-programming. Some examples are described in [4-7]. Here, we define two parameters P and Q: P is the number of parallel arithmetic computation units (multiplication, division and Addition) and Q is the bit size of each unit. This paper will concentrate on the design space exploration of a software driven hardware architecture for applications over $GF(2^m)$ with P and Q as the central design parameters.

A hardware-software co-design approach is described for hardware architectures over $GF(2^m)$ whereby software allows the same hardware to be re-used for different applications. This entails a design space exploration where the requirements of different applications over $GF(2^m)$ are systematically explored, and also the formulation of a hardware architecture to facilitate these applications. This design space can be broadly define into three levels of abstraction as shown in Table 1. The top level determines the global requirements of the specific applications. For example, application area (cryptography or FEC), code rate and error correction capability of a RS or BCH code (N,K), key size of the AES and the curve parameters of ECC.. etc.

The bottom level consists of the basic arithmetic circuits that form the basis of the applications. Choices here include the size and type of the arithmetic for example in terms of field size, irreducible polynomial and basis representation. These are of course influenced by the global requirements. The middle level provides the "bridge" between the top and bottom levels. Usually, this middle level determines the overall structure of a derived architecture and is determined by the primitive operations of an application. For each application, we identify these primitive operations, and this is an important first step towards designing efficient hardware/software architectures. Table 2 shows the requirements of various different operations.

There has been a trend towards using parallel arithmetic computation units driven by software for FEC algorithms as evident in [5, 6], since there is substantial inherent parallelism in these algorithms. The same principle can be applied directly to the

AES. Due to the large field size, parallel arithmetic computations are not considered for ECC as these need multiple arithmetic units. Obviously a simplistic implementation of ECC would be achieved by setting: P = 1 and Q equals the field size over which the ECC is defined. To bridge the gap of an architecture flexible enough for RS codes, BCH codes and the AES is relatively simple, however, the same cannot be said if ECC is to be included with other applications. Although a $GF(2^{163})$ processor designed for ECC can be used directly for $GF(2^8)$ computations for the AES (or RS/BCH codes), it will be highly inefficient as only 8 out of a possible 163 bits are used at any one time. (Assuming the underlying arithmetic units can support variable field sizes and irreducible polynomials). This is one main obstacle towards developing efficient processor architectures for the domain of $GF(2^m)$.

Table 1 : Abstraction Levels

Abstraction Levels	Application	
Algorithm Level	Cryptography	FEC
	AES Diff Key Lengths ECC Diff Curve sizes	RS(N, K) codec BCH (N,K) codec
Primitive Operations	Point Additions/ Doubling over Projective or Affine Co-ordinates	Key Equation Solving Using BMA or Euclidean Algorithm, Systematic Non Systematic Encoding
		Different Polynomial Operations
Arithmetic Level	Variable Field Size, Variety of Bases, Variable Irreducible Polynomials	

Table 2 : Requirements Analysis of Applications over $GF(2^m)$

Application	RS Codes	BCH	AES	ECC
Ranges	3-8 Bits	3-16 Bits	8 Bits	>100 Bits
Primitive Operations	Polynomial		Matrix and Polynomial like	Quadratic Equations

Subword parallelism (SWP) is a concept from computer architecture first introduced by Lee in [8]. Multiple subwords are packed into a word and processed with a single instruction, which can be seen as a form of SIMD (Single instruction Multiple Data). This concept can be extended to the domain of $GF(2^m)$ as well. It can provide the flexibility without loss of efficiency required for a $GF(2^m)$ processor and solves the problem of large data size mismatch for different applications. A SWP $GF(2^m)$ processor is defined as an entity with a data path of m = PxQ bits and can operate in two modes : Single Instruction Single Data (SISD) and Single Instruction Multiple Data (SIMD) mode. A SWP $GF(2^m)$ arithmetic circuit allows the processor to compute P $GF(2^n)$ arithmetic operations ($n \leq Q$) or one $GF(2^n)$ arithmetic operation ($Q < n \leq PxQ$) per instruction. This means by suitable selection of P and Q, it is possible to define a structure that can be utilized efficiently for both large and small field size operations. For e.g, if P = 21 and Q = 8, m = 168. The processor can be used for one large $GF(2^n)$ computation ($n \leq 168$) or 21 parallel smaller $GF(2^n)$ computations ($n \leq 8$), the former useful for ECC and the latter useful for AES, RS and BCH codecs.

The process of design space exploration is very much top down/bottom up. In the very first pass, the top down approach will attempt to identify the requirements of each application at each level as given in table 1. The bottom up approach will attempt to formulate suitable architectures to suit these requirements at each level, and this may take several iterations before a compromise is reached for a given cost function in terms of speed versus area versus power for example. To reach a compromise on all of these requirements plus considerations for flexibility is not a trivial task and further work are needed here. In this paper, we will be concentrating primarily on the requirements issues for the domain of $GF(2^m)$ which is not a common subject in the published literature.

The SWP type architectural structure of the arithmetic circuits of the $GF(2^m)$ processor forms the middle abstraction level in Table 1 in this paper. An Instruction Set Architecture can then be defined over this architecture which allows the processor to compute the primitive operations for different applications.

2. SUBWORD PARALLEL ARCHITECTURES

This section describes the architecture of a Subword Parallel $GF(2^m)$ processor which consists of the SWP $GF(2^m)$ arithmetic circuits.

2.1. SWP $GF(2^m)$ Arithmetic Circuits

We briefly describe how a subword parallel $GF(2^m)$ multiplier can be designed using a simple example for m = 4. The GF multiplication algorithm used here is based on the well known MSB first algorithm operating over a polynomial basis which is outlined in [9] and reproduced briefly below. We need to compute C(y) = A(y).B(y) mod G(y).

Multiplication Algorithm [9]

```
1  C'(y) = all zeros
2  for i = 0 to m-1
3       C'(y) = C'(y) + G(y).c'm + A(y).bm-1
4       B(y) = y.B(y) mod (y^m)
5       C'(y) = y.C'(y) mod (y^m+1)
6 end loop;
```

We can break line 3 of the algorithm into bit slices, ($0 \leq k \leq m$):

$$c'_k = c'_k \oplus (g_k \bullet c'_m) \oplus (a_k \bullet b_{m-1})$$

Figure 1 shows a 4-bit bit slices cascaded together. This performs one iteration of the multiplication algorithm. By feeding the intermediate result back into the same structure m times, a m-bit $GF(2^m)$ multiplication can be performed. Notice that as long as the data are MSB justified, the same m-bit structure can be used for $GF(2^n)$ multiplications ($n \leq m$) by varying the number of iterations n. From the algorithm, we can see that at every iteration, b_{m-1} and c'_m are used to determine whether C'(y) is added with A(y) and G(y). We call these global signals.

B(y) is loaded into a shift register and is MSB shifted n times during the course of the algorithm. At the ith iteration, the most significant bit of the shift register will be the ith bit of B(y), b_i. Line 4 and 5 of the algorithm is simply the mathematical representation of logical shift with the MSB discarded. Shifting of Line 5 can be hardwired as shown in Figure 1. Suppose the structure in Figure 1 is cut into two parts of 2-bits each, and additional configuration circuitry (basically multiplexers and basic gates) are added to each 2-bits parts called Logic Units (LU). The configuration circuitry of each LU is controlled by a set of control signals MSBlock and LSBlock. Setting both MSBlock and LSBlock of a LU to '1' "isolates" that particular LU such that all global signals are derived from the same LU, and shifting signals do not cross into other LUs. In fact, both LUs in this situation can be seen as independent 2-bit multipliers. Similarly, setting LSBlock[2] and MSBlock[1] to '0', and setting LSBlock[1] and MSBlock[2] to '1' configures the structure in Figure 2 to behave as if it is a 4-bit multiplier, as the global signals are now multiplexed from the MSB LU (LU 2) and shifting signals are allowed to pass between LUs. In general, we can thus break-up a large M-bits GF(2^m) multiplier into P smaller Q-bits LUs, which essentially are Q-bits GF(2^Q) multipliers. In practice, it will be easier to design a LU of a specific size (Q-bits) and couple as many of them together to achieve the required large field size.

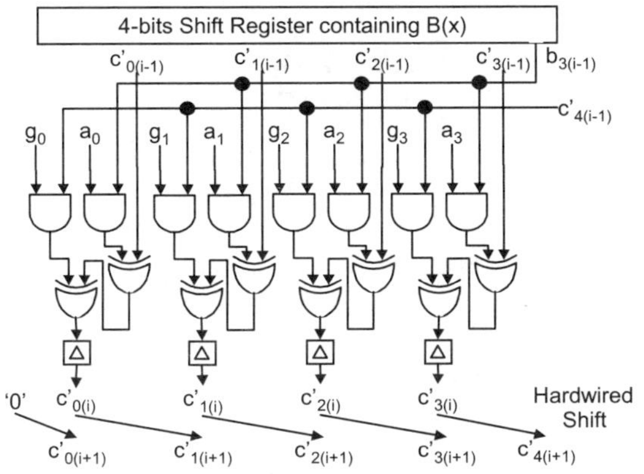

Figure 1: 4-bit GF(2^m) Multiplier

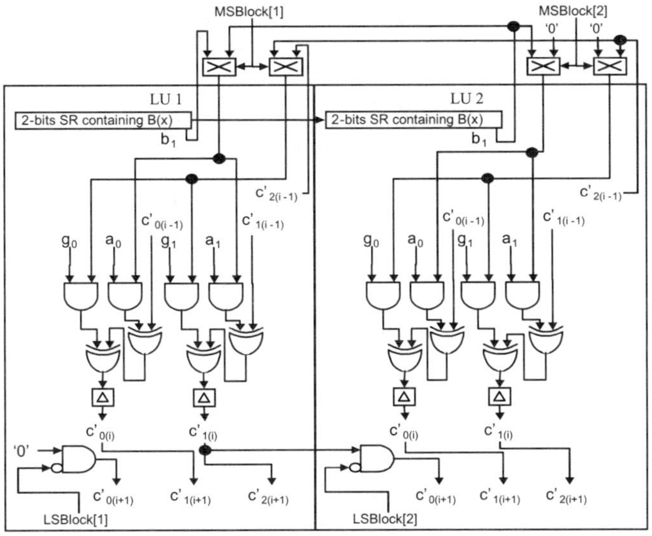

Figure 2: Modified GF(2^m) multiplier with 2 LUs.

The same procedure can be applied to a GF(2^m) division algorithm, although this is not described here it due to length constraints. In particular, Brunner in [10] described a polynomial basis GF(2^m) division algorithm which can be used for modification into the SWP structure as it is regular in structure and computation cycles. This regularity is important as it makes modifications easier. GF(2^m) addition needs no modifications as it only involves bit-wise XOR operations.

2.1.1. *Complexity Analysis*

Table 3 shows the complexity figures of the SWP GF(2^m) arithmetic circuits in terms of P and Q. The size of the arithmetic circuits without modification are comparable to that outlined in [9, 10], which is expected since they use the same algorithm. Due to the configuration circuitry, the overall area and time complexity incurs a penalty. For reasonable choices of P and Q, this added complexity represents a small percentage overall. For example, if P = 21 and Q = 8 giving M = 168, the percentage overhead due to the configuration circuitry will be 4.01% for the multiplier and 5.81% for the divider circuit. The added propagation delay due to the configuration circuits for multiplication and division corresponds to T_{MUX2} and to $T_{MUX2} + T_{MUXQ}$ respectively. (Note: T_{MUXi} is the propagation delay through an i-input multiplexor.)

Table 3 : Complexity Figures of SISD/SIMD ALU

	Gates for P, Q-bits Logic Unit without Control		Gates for Config. Cct.		Overall Propagation Delay
Multiplier	2PQ 2PQ 2PQ PQ	XOR AND F/F MUX_2	2P 2P	MUX_2 AND	$T_{MUX2} + 2\,T_{XOR} + T_{AND}$
Divider	P(4Q + 1) P(3Q + 1) P(5Q + 2) P(Q + 1) P(16Q + 7)	XOR AND F/F NOT MUX_2	5P P 4P	MUX_2 MUX_Q AND	$T_{XOR} + T_{AND} + 2\,T_{MUX2} + T_{MUXQ}$

2.2. SWP GF(2^m) Processor Architecture

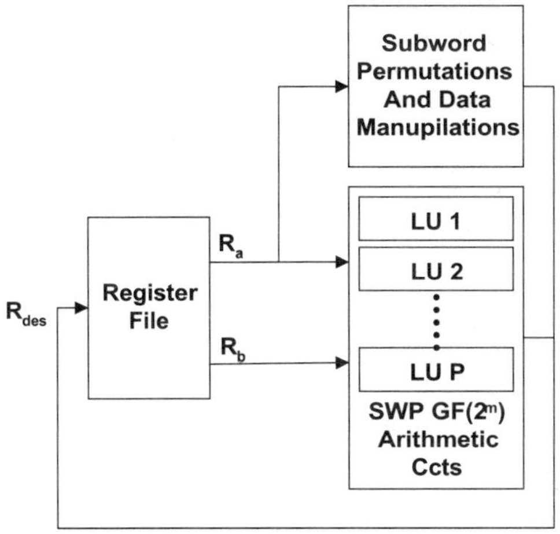

Figure 3 : Processor Datapath Block Diagram

A simplified processor datapath block diagram is shown in Figure 3. It consists of the SWP arithmetic circuits (multiplication, division and addition over GF(2^m) and subword permutation circuits which are necessary to handle subword manipulations. The register file is made up of many Register Locations each with a word size of M bits wide and each Register Location (a word) can be seen as P number of Coefficient Locations (subwords), each Q bits wide (i.e. m=PxQ). In SIMD mode, the data in each Register location can be viewed as a polynomial of degree P-1, with coefficients as elements of a Galois Field up to a size of

$GF(2^Q)$ (i.e. the name coefficient locations). A polynomial with degree larger than P can be stored in two or more Register Locations. In SISD mode, each Register Location will only have one data element in it. See Figure 4.

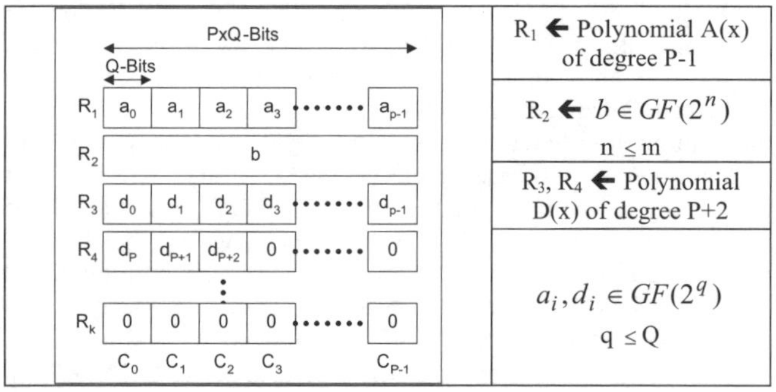

Figure 4 : Register File Structure with different contents

2.3. Core Instruction Set Architecture

For each different sets of applications, the instruction set architecture maybe different. This is because for different applications, additional specialized instructions maybe included to improve significantly the performance of the processor running these applications. However, it is possible to identify a core set of instructions that will be applicable for a majority of applications, and these are usually present regardless of the applications the processor is designed for.

2.3.1. Core Instructions

We denote R_j (C_i) as the ith Coefficient Location of the jth Register Location. In SIMD Mode, MULT, DIVI and ADDP instructions operate on p parallel data pairs in a pair of Register Locations. In SISD Mode, they will operate on only one data pair per pair of Register Locations. The other instructions are required for subword re-arrangement, data alignment and movement (shifting, copying, Subword copying etc).

Table 4: Core Arithmetic Instructions

$ADDP_{SIMD}$	$R_{des}(C_i) \leftarrow [R_a(C_i) + R_b(C_i)] \bmod G(y)$	for i = 0 to P-1
$ADDP_{SISD}$	$R_{des} \leftarrow [R_a + R_b] \bmod G(y)$	
$SUMA_{SIMD}$	$R_{des}(C_a) \leftarrow \sum_{i=0}^{P-1} R_a(C_i)$	
$MULT_{SIMD}$	$R_{des}(C_i) \leftarrow [R_a(C_i) \times R_b(C_i)] \bmod G(y)$	for i = 0 to P-1
$MULT_{SISD}$	$R_{des} \leftarrow R_a \times R_b \bmod G(y)$	
$DIVI_{SIMD}$	$R_{des}(C_i) \leftarrow [R_a(C_i) / R_b(C_i)] \bmod G(y)$	for i = 0 to P-1
$DIVI_{SISD}$	$R_{des} \leftarrow [R_a / R_b] \bmod G(y)$	
$REPA_{SIMD}$	$[R_{des}(C_i)] \leftarrow R_a(C_a)$	for i = 0 to P-1
$REPO_{SIMD}$	$R_{des}(C_{des}) \leftarrow R_a(C_a)$	
SHPX	R_{des} ← LSB/MSB Bit Shift R_a by x-bits. Pad with Zeros	
COPY	$R_{des} \leftarrow R_a$	
SETC	Setup Instruction for SIMD/SISD mode, Irreducible Polynomial etc	

3. PRIMITIVE OPERATIONS

In this section, we show that almost all of the primitive operations for different applications over $GF(2^m)$ can be synthesized from the core ISA.

3.1. Reed Solomon and BCH codes

All of the primitive operations required in RS and BCH codec can be broken down into polynomial operations over $GF(2^m)$ of one form or another. They are: Polynomial Multiplications (PM), Polynomial Divisions (PD) and Polynomial Evaluations (PE). Non-Systematic RS encoding is basically a PM whereas systematic RS Encoding is a PD. Syndrome Computation and Chien Search of the decoding stage are PEs. Key Equation Solving using Extended Euclidean Algorithm is a combination of PDs and PMs. Therefore, deriving efficient ways of computing these polynomial operations are crucial. This section will briefly describe some ways these polynomial operations can be synthesized simply by the core ISA described before and are by no means definitive. It will be straightforward to extend the techniques presented here to more general polynomial operations.

3.1.1. Polynomial Multiplication

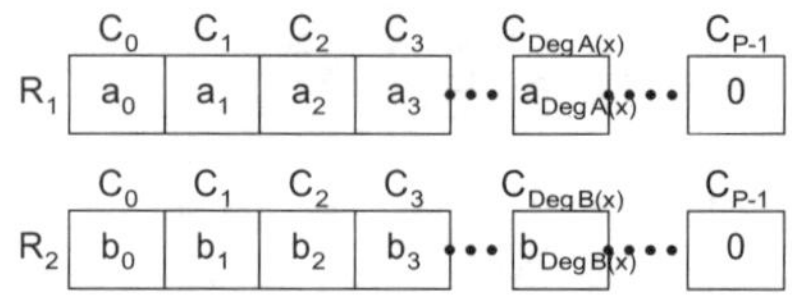

Figure 5 : Data Orientation of A(x) and B(x) for PM

Let $A(x) = \sum_{i=0}^{\deg(A(x))} a_i x^i$, $B(x) = \sum_{i=0}^{\deg(B(x))} b_i x^i$, $a_i, b_i \in GF(2^m)$. The polynomial multiplication of $D(x) = A(x) \times B(x)$ is given by:

$$D(x) = \sum_{i=0}^{\deg(A(x))} \sum_{j=0}^{\deg(B(x))} a_i b_j x^{i+j}$$

Assuming the degrees of A(x) and B(x) is less than P-1, then each of the polynomial can be fitted into a single Register Location LSB justified as shown in Figure 5. Using the core Arithmetic Instructions, a PM can thus be synthesised:

- R_1 ← A(x); R_2 ← B(x); R_{Temp1} ← Zero Polynomial
- For i = 0 to deg (A(x)) Loop
- R_{Temp2} ← REPA $R_1(C_i)$
- R_{Temp3} ← MULT R_{Temp2}, R_2
- R_{Temp1} ← ADDP R_{Temp3}, R_{Temp1}
- $R_{Result}(C_i)$ ← REPO $R_{Temp1}(C_i)$
- R_{Temp1} ← SHPX LSB, R_{Temp1}, Q-Bits
- End Loop;
- For j = 0 to deg(B(x)) – 1 Loop
- $R_{Result}(C_{deg(A(x))+j})$ ← REPO $R_{Temp1}(C_j)$
- End Loop;

This is basically a multiply-add-shift operation of A(x) and B(x). The result D(x) will be stored in R_{Result}. Note that if deg(A(x) + deg(B(x)) > P-1, the result D(x) maybe exceed the size of one Register Location and have to be stored accordingly. Since the degrees of A(x), B(x) and D(x) of all PMs present in RS and BCH codes can be predetermined, it is relatively easy determine the storage required.

3.1.2. Polynomial Division

Again, let A(x) and B(x) follows the same notation as before. Given A(x) and B(x), calculate find D(x) and E(x) which satisfies the expression:

$$D(x) \times B(x) + E(x) = A(x)$$

In other words, we want to calculate A(x)/B(x) and get the quotient D(x) and the remainder which is E(x). Assuming the deg(A(x)) = deg(B(x)) + 1, then deg(E(x)) = 1 and deg(D(x)) = deg(B(x)) – 1. For simplicity, here we assume that each A(x) and B(x) can be fitted into a single Register Location MSB justified. The steps involved in the polynomial division (also commonly known as Polynomial Long Division) are:

1.	R_1 ← A(x); R_2 ← B(x);		
2.	R_{Temp1}	← REPA	$R_1(C_{P-1})$
3.	R_{Temp2}	← MULT	R_{Temp1}, R_2
4.	R_{Temp1}	← REPA	$R_2(C_{P-1})$
5.	R_{Temp2}	← DIVI	R_{Temp2}, R_{Temp1}
6.	$R_{Quotient}(C_1)$	← REPO	$R_{Temp2}(C_{P-1})$
7.	R_{Temp3}	← ADDP	R_{Temp2}, R_1
8.	R_{Temp1}	← REPA	$R_{Temp3}(C_{P-2})$
9.	R_{Temp2}	← MULT	R_{Temp1}, R_2
10.	R_{Temp1}	← REPA	$R_2(C_{P-1})$
11.	R_{Temp2}	← DIVI	R_{Temp2}, R_{Temp1}
12.	$R_{Quotient}(C_0)$	← REPO	$R_{Temp2}(C_{P-2})$
13.	$R_{Remainder}$	← ADDP	R_{Temp3}, R_{Temp2}
14.	$R_{Quotient}$ = D(x), $R_{Remainder}$ = E(x)		

The number of instructions needed to compute a polynomial division will be minimum when A(x) and B(x) can be fitted into a single register. Polynomial division is the fundamental primitive operation in Key Equation Solving using the Euclidean Algorithm and it can be concluded that as long as P ≥ 2t, where t is the error correcting capability of a BCH or RS code, the number of instructions needed for the Euclidean Algorithm will be at a minimum.

3.1.3. Polynomial Evaluation

	C_0	C_1	C_2	C_3		C_{P-1}
R_1	a_0	a_1	a_2	a_3	......	a_{p-1}
R_2	a_P	a_{P+1}	a_{P+2}	0	......	0
R_3	1	α	α^2	α^3	......	α^{p-1}
R_4	α^p	α^{p+1}	α^{p+2}	0	......	0

Figure 6 :Data Orientation for Polynomial Evaluation

Compute $A(\alpha) = \sum_{i=0}^{\deg(A(x))} a_i\alpha^i$ where $\alpha \in GF(2^m)$. As an example, we assume that A(x) in this case spans two Register Locations as shown in Figure 6. To save on computation cycles, P-1 multiple powers of α are pre-computed and stored in multiple Register Locations as well. To evaluate $A(\alpha)$;

1.	R_1, R_2 ← A(x); R_3, R_4 ← Pre-computed Powers of α ;		
2.	R_{Temp1}	← MULT	R_1, R_3
3.	R_{Temp2}	← MULT	R_2, R_4
4.	R_{Temp1}	← ADDP	R_{Temp1}, R_{Temp2}
5.	$R_{Result}(C_0)$	← SUMA	R_{Temp1}
6.	$A(\alpha) = R_{Result}(C_0)$;		

3.2. Advanced Encryption Standard

In general, the basic operations of the AES can be synthesized using the core ISA (with the exception of the Affine Transform required in the SubWord Transformation). We can easily modify the DIVI instruction so that an Forward Affine Transform (FAT) or Inverse Affine Transform (IAT) is computed after and before an inversion is computed respectively (See Table 5). There is substantial parallelism in the AES algorithm, which makes its implementation in a SWP architecture very attractive. An AES State is stored in the register file in the way as shown in Figure 7, where a 128-bit Block (or a state) is stored across 4 Registers Locations. If P > 4, multiple blocks of data can be stored in the same 4 Register Locations. In the example of Figure 7, P = 8, hence we can store 2 AES states every 4 register locations. This also means that multiple AES encryptions or decryptions can be computed at the same time. On closer examination, it is evident that the ShiftRow Operation of the AES is the bottleneck of the system if it is implemented with just the core ISA. A new instruction SHPW is created specifically for the ShiftRow Operation in AES.

Table 5 : Extended Instructions for AES

DIVI (SIMD-AES)	$R_{des}(C_i)$ ← FAT[1/$R_b(C_i)$] mod G(y) $R_{des}(C_i)$ ← 1/ IAT[$R_b(C_i)$] mod G(y)	for i = 0 to P-1
SHRW	R_{des} ← Shift-Row-Index, R_a	

	C1	C2	C3	C4	C5	C6	C7	C8
R1	$S_{0,0}$	$S_{0,1}$	$S_{0,2}$	$S_{0,3}$	$S_{0,0}$	$S_{0,1}$	$S_{0,2}$	$S_{0,3}$
R2	$S_{1,0}$	$S_{1,1}$	$S_{1,2}$	$S_{1,3}$	$S_{1,0}$	$S_{1,1}$	$S_{1,2}$	$S_{1,3}$
R3	$S_{2,0}$	$S_{2,1}$	$S_{2,2}$	$S_{2,3}$	$S_{2,0}$	$S_{2,1}$	$S_{2,2}$	$S_{2,3}$
R4	$S_{3,0}$	$S_{3,1}$	$S_{3,2}$	$S_{3,3}$	$S_{3,0}$	$S_{3,1}$	$S_{3,2}$	$S_{3,3}$
	1st AES State				2nd AES State			

Figure 7 : Storage of AES state in Register File

3.3. Elliptic Curve Cryptography

The primitive operations of the Elliptic Curve Cryptography can be broken down simply into Point Additions and Point Doubling. A Non-Supersingular Elliptic Curve [2] is defined over Affine Co-ordinates as:

$$y^2 + xy = x^3 + a_2x^2 + a_6 \quad \text{where } a_2 \text{ and } a_6 \in GF(2^m)$$

Given that two points A = (x_1,y_1) and B = (x_2,y_2) lie on an Elliptic Curve, point addition D = A + B is defined as below, where D = (x_3,y_3). If A ≠ B then

$$\theta = \frac{y_2 - y_1}{x_2 - x_1},\ x_3 = \theta^2 + \theta + x_2 + x_1 + a_2,\ y_3 = \theta(x_3 + x_1) - y_1$$

If A=B then $\theta = x_1 + \frac{y_1}{x_1}$ or $\theta = x_2 + \frac{y_2}{x_2}$

and, $x_3 = \theta^2 + \theta + a_2$, $y_3 = x^2 + (\theta + 1)x_3$.

These operate over quadratic equations defined over GF(2^m). and can be synthesized using the core ISA, primarily ADDP, MULT and DIVI operating in SISD mode

4. RESULTS & CONCLUSIONS

It is evident that once the requirements of the primitive operations are determined and a processor architecture is designed to meet these requirements, a stable platform is available that can be tailored for different applications or different groups of applications by changing P and Q at design time. We show an example where P and Q are fixed and determine the range of applications this processor can be used for without re-design. This is to show the inherent flexibility of the processor architecture for different applications and does not represent a practical design flow, where applications usually determine the values of P and Q.

4.1. P = 8, Q = 8 for RS, BCH, AES and ECC

The largest small field size the processor can compute in parallel is constrained by Q. For a BCH or RS (N,K) codes, this will constrain the maximum value of N. Table 6 shows the ranges of (N,K) codecs that can be computed without re-design for Q = 8. For the AES, the only variable is the different key schedule computation and P/4 denotes the number of parallel AES blocks that can be computed at the same time for a specific value of P. The largest field size the processor can operate on in this case is $GF(2^{64})$ (m = PxQ. In practical applications, P can be chosen to be large enough for secure elliptic curve cryptography. A proof of concept prototype GF Processor has been implemented on Field Programmable Gate Arrays (Xilinx Virtex XCV-800) using the concepts outlined in this paper for the parameters of P=8 and Q=8 and Table 7 shows the throughput of a few applications from Table 6. The processor was designed using VHDL on Xilinx Foundation 3.1e and occupies 2505 Slices with an equivalent gate count of 43,251 gates. Through analysis, it can be determined that the size of the processor scales more or less linearly with m (i..e. PxQ).

Table 6: Ranges of Applications for P= 8 and Q=8

Application	Variables for Q = 8	
RS, BCH codec	(255,K) (127,K) (63,K)	(31,K) (15,K) (7,K)
AES	128, 192, 256 Bits Key size. P/4 Parallel Blocks Computations	
ECC	Up to $GF(2^{64})$	

Table 7 : Throughput of $GF(2^{64})$ Processor for P = 8, Q = 8

Results for m = 64 P = 8, Q = 8	Speed 40MHz Clock
RS(255,247) Decoder	11 Mbps
RS(31,25) Decoder	6.6Mbps
BCH(31,16) Decoder*	1.33Mbps
128-Bit Key AES (10 Rounds) without key Expansion. 2 Parallel Computations	3.8 Mbps
128-but Key Schedule Computation	42.5 µs
Elliptic Curve Point Addition Affine Coordinates $GF(2^{61})$	7.125 µs
Elliptic Curve Point Doubling Affine Coordinates $GF(2^{61})$	8.425 µs
*Uses the same program as RS(31,25) Codec. i.e. not optimised for BCH Codec.	

4.2. Conclusions

Flexibility of a given architecture cannot be measured easily in quantifiable terms. Yet, as systems get increasingly complex, issues of design re-use makes a flexible architecture with programmable parameters over a large range of applications increasingly important. There has been a general trend to migrate complexity of traditionally application specific implementations towards software controlled architectures, where flexibility of software automatically allows the maximum flexibility over different applications. However, not all such migrations can be achieved easily, with problems ranging from designing flexible arithmetic circuits to supporting flexible software controlled architectures. This paper has outlined a design space exploration for domain applications based on Galois Fields. The applications are broken down into their primitive operations and a flexible software programmable processor has been designed to handle these primitive operations. This in turn allows the same architecture to be used for all applications that can be defined using these primitive operations. This paper focuses mainly on designing for maximum flexibility across different applications over the same domain, and further work is needed to address design issues at each abstraction level for other constraints like speed, area and power trade-offs with flexibility for a given application in the GF domain. A design methodology can then be defined for primitive based hardware/software co-design techniques.

5. Reference

[1] B. Wicker Stephen, *Error control systems for digital communication and storage*. Englewood Cliffs, N.J. ; London: Prentice Hall : Prentice-HallInternational, 1995.

[2] M. Rosing, *Implementing Elliptic Curve Cryptography*. Greenwich, CT.: Manning, 1999.

[3] J. Daemen and V. Rijmen, "AES Proposal : The Rijndael Block Cipher," *http://csrc.nist.gov/encryption/aes/rijndael/*, 2000.

[4] L. Song, K. K. Parhi, I. Kuroda, and T. Nishitani, "Hardware/software codesign of finite field datapath for low-energy Reed-Solomon codecs," *IEEE-Transactions-on-Very-Large-Scale-Integration-VLSI-Systems. April 2000; 8(2): 160-72*, 2000.

[5] H. M. Ji, "An optimized processor for fast Reed-Solomon encoding and decoding," *2002-IEEE-International-Conference-on-Acoustics,-Speech,-and-Signal-Processing.-Proceedings-Cat.-No.02CH37334. 2002: III-3097-100 vol.3*, 2002.

[6] W. Drescher, M. Mennenga, and G. Fettweis, " An architectural study of a digital signal processor for block codes," *Proceedings-of-the-1998-IEEE-International-Conference-on-Acoustics,-Speech-and-Signal-Processing,-ICASSP-'98-Cat.-No.98CH36181. 1998: 3129-32 vol.5*, 1998.

[7] M. Hasan and A. Wassal, "VLSI Algorithms, Architectures, and Implementation of a Versatile $GF(2^m)$ Processor," *IEEE Transactions On Computers*, vol. 49, pp. 1064-1073, 2000.

[8] R. B. Lee, "Subword parallelism with MAX-2," in *IEEE-Micro. Aug. 1996; 16(4): 51-9*, 1996.

[9] P. A. Scott, S. E. Tavares, and L. E. Peppard, "A Fast VLSI Multiplier for $GF(2^m)$," *IEEE Journal Selected Areas in Communications*, vol. SAC-4, pp. 62-66, 1986.

[10] H. Brunner, A. Curiger, and M. Hofstetter, "On Computing Multiplicative Inverses in GF (2^m)," *IEEE Transactions On Computers C*, vol. 42, pp. 1010, 1993.

A Fast Parallel Reed-Solomon Decoder On a Reconfigurable Architecture

Arezou Koohi,
EECS Department
University of California Irvine
949-8242481
akoohi@ece.uci.edu

Nader Bagherzadeh,
EECS Department
University of California, Irvine
949-8242481
Nader@ece.uci.edu

Chengzi Pan
EECS Department
University of California, Irvine
949-8242481
panc@uci.edu

ABSTRACT
This paper presents a software implementation of a very fast parallel Reed-Solomon decoder on the second generation of MorphoSys reconfigurable computation platform, which is targeting on streamed applications such as multimedia and DSP. Numerous modifications of the first-generation of the architecture have made a scalable computation and communication intensive architecture capable of extracting parallelisms of fine grain in instruction level. Many algorithms and the whole Digital Video Broadcasting base-band receiver as well, have been mapped onto the second architecture with impressing performance. The mapping of a Reed-Solomon decoder proposed in this paper highly parallelizes all of its sub-algorithms, including Syndrome Computation, Berlekamp Algorithm, Chein Search, and Error Value Computation, in a SIMD fashion. The mapping is tested on a cycle-accurate simulator, "Mulate", and the performance is encouragingly better than other architectures. The decoding speed of the RS (255,239,16) decoder using two different methods of GF multiplication can be 1.319Gbps and 2.534Gbps, respectively. Furthermore, since there is no functionality specifically tailored to Reed-Solomon decoder, the result has demonstrated the capability of MorphoSys architecture to extracting Instruction Level Parallelism from streamed applications.

Categories and Subject Descriptors
C.1.2 [**Computer System Organization**]: Processor Architectures, Multiple Data Stream Architectures (Multiprocessors), Single-instruction-stream, Multiple-Data - Stream Processors

General Terms
Algorithms, Performance, Design, Experimentation

Keywords: Reconfigurable Architecture, SIMD Processor, Reed_Solomon codes, Berlekamp Algorithm, Chein Search

1. INTRODUCTION
Toward a coming billion-transistor era, today's computation platform design has already foreseen the end of the road for conventional micro-architectures [4], and numerous new approaches have arisen above the horizon, such as EPIC (Itanium 2) [5], RAW [6], Imagine [7], and VIRAM [8], etc. Many of them target on stream applications, which have already been consuming more than 90% of total computing cycles nowadays [7]. The biggest challenge of architecture design is the scalability, only with which can one follow up the step of Moore's Law. The difficulty of scalability is imposed by slower decrease of wire transmission delay than that of transistor switching delay. This discrepancy requires a new philosophy on design of scalar operand network [9] and memory hierarchy. In this paper, we will introduce the 2nd-generation MorphoSys reconfigurable architecture called M2, a computation and communication intensive platform capable of extracting fine grain parallelisms at the instruction level. Many algorithms and the whole Digital Video Broadcasting base-band receiver as well, have been mapped onto M2 with impressing performance. The mapping of a Reed-Solomon decoder is proposed in this paper. RS codes are powerful block codes widely used as an error correction method in the areas such as digital communication, digital disc error correction, etc. Recently, concatenated codes made up of convolutional codes followed by RS codes have been proved as an efficient way of error correction in wireless data communication systems. We present M2 Architecture at the first section of the paper, including the architecture different parts, M2 implementation and its programming model. Section 3 introduces the RS decoding Algorithms and the mapping procedure on the M2. The section also includes the M2 architecture feasibility for different parts of the Algorithms. In section 4 we compare the result of the RS (255,239,16) decoder with the existing benchmarks including the TI64x and different Asics. The decoding speed of the RS (255,239,16) decoder using two different methods of GF multiplication can be 1.319Gbps and 2.534Gbps, respectively

2. MORPHOSYS RECONFIGURABLE ARCHITECTURE

2.1. Introduction of MorphoSys
MorphoSys is a reconfigurable computation platform targeting computation intensive data parallel applications, including streamed applications. M1 [1-2], the first prototype of MorphoSys, has been used as a platform for many applications such as multimedia, wireless communication, signal processing, and computer graphics. M2, the 2nd generation of MorphoSys, follows the basic concepts of MorphoSys; however, it is redesigned in both scalar operand network and memory hierarchy, thus greatly enhanced in performance. Feedbacks from numerous

kernel and system mappings pointed out M1's bottlenecks, which have been revisited in M2.

M2 architecture consists of three main subsystems: a core processor called TinyRISC, an array of 64 Reconfigurable Cells (RCs) organized in SIMD fashion, and a special data movement unit called Frame Buffer (FB). The programming model is simple. TinyRISC takes charge of the whole Data Control Flow (DCF); RC array and Frame Buffer are only triggered by TinyRISC and executing on their own configurations (called context) continuously for a given number of cycles specified by TinyRISC. The main difference between M1 and M2 is described in [3]. Figure 1 shows the MorphoSys diagram. Main Memory can be either on-chip or off-chip without significant difference of the connection interface, as long as Main Memory is also composed of 64 banks.

2.2. M2 implementation

The following table-1 gives out the characteristics of M2 and compares it with the other processors. Results of first order simulation using Synopsis tools show that the critical-path delay is about 1.8~2.3ns. Hence, 450 MHz is used in our simulation. Other data are either based on M1 implementation and M2 post-synthesis (current status), or projected as our design aim, which are chosen no more aggressive than commercial processors.

Though independently designed, M2 combines the structural advantages of three important architecture parameters: the overall structure of host-processor/slave-computation-fabric, the controlled size of distributed memory within each AIU clusters and the powerful sequential code, which is hard to be parallelized. Second, the modest size of distributed memory enables more AIUs to be integrated in the array and, more importantly, reduces the latency of scalar operand network, which is essential to extract to adopt wide range of optimization techniques, both coarse-grain and fine-grain, and avoids usage of hardware-specific languages as StreamC.

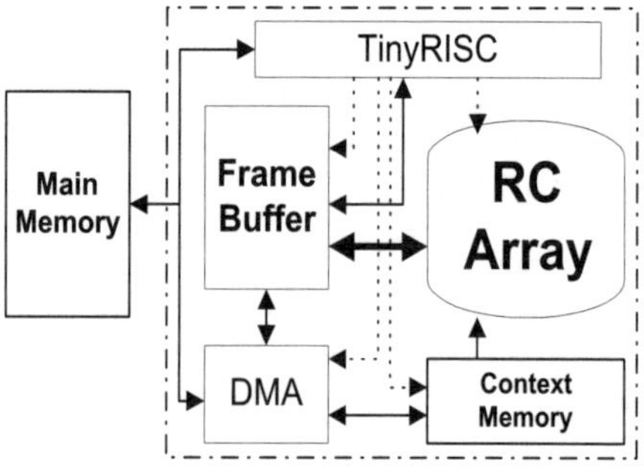

Figure 1. MorphoSys Diagram

Table 1. Comparison of M2 and other architectures* the latency is analyzed in 5-tuple <send occupancy, send latency, network hop latency, receive latency, receive occupancy> [9].

		VIRAM	Imagine	RAW	M2 (with/without on-chip memory)
Parallelism	Parallelism model	Vector	SIMD	MIMD	SIMD
Capability	Peak 16-bit OPS	6.4G	23.7G	3.6G (32-bit)	28.8G
	Clock Speed	200MHz	296MHz	225MHz	450MHz
	Chip area	$15*18mm^2$	$12*12mm^2$	$18*18mm^2$	$8*8mm^2/16*16mm^2$
	# Transistors	120M	21M	122M	20M/120M
	Power	2W(average)	4W	25W	4W(peak MAC)
	Technology	0.18μm	0.15μm	0.15μm	0.13μm
Scalar Operand Network	# Network nodes	8(Banks)	8	16	64
	Total bandwidth	51.2Gbps	75.8Gbps	922Gbps	922Gbps
	Latency*	<0,1,1,1,0>	<0,1,1,1,0>	<0,1,1~6,1,0>	<0,0,1~2,0,0>
	Full permutation	No	Yes	Yes	Yes
Memory Hierarchy	1st level size	64Kb(VRF)	96Kb(LRF)	16.4Kb(RF)	16.4Kb(RF)
	2nd level size	104Mb(DRAM)	1Mb(SRF)	16Mb(Local Mem.)	2Mb(Local Mem.)
	3rd level size	Off-chip	Off-chip	Off-chip	16Mb/off-chip
	1st level bandwidth	205Gbps	758Gbps	230Gbps	1382Gbps
	2nd level bandwidth	51.2Gbps	829Gbps**	334Gbps	461Gbps
	3rd level bandwidth	N/A	12.4Gbps	200Gbps	115Gbps/56.7Gbps

2.3. Programming Model

One potential drawback of M2 is the SIMD model of RC array. However, mapping experience on MorhpoSys, VIRAM, Imagine, and other SIMD extension of general-purpose processor like Pentium MMX, all show that SIMD is sufficient for streamed multimedia applications, not mentioning the much smaller code size than that of MIMD model. For example, mapping of DVB-T system on M2 does not need MIMD generality. Although SPMD feature might make mapping of MPEG-2 decoder easier, other subsystems are applying mostly affine array access and small portion of non-affine but static access involving random communication, which can be done efficiently by the scalar operand network. Since SIMD programming has long been a matured field in general, it is reasonable to suppose that an efficient C compiler for streamed applications is highly possible, with some previous experience already [10-11].Moreover, parallel programming in M2 can adopt domain decomposition or function decomposition, the former more straightforward, while Imagine has to stick with cumbersome function decomposition often experiencing load-unbalanced problem. The following figure illustrates a real code segment for The Berelekamp algorithm operation which also shows programming model of MorphoSys.

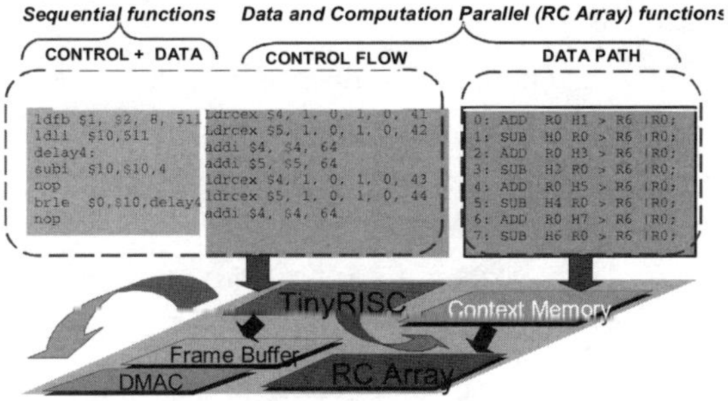

Figure 2- Programming Model in MorphoSys

2.4. Scalability

There is a misunderstanding in many places, that scalability is equal to even distribution of resources. Actually, this is not true in large scale. For example, as the tile number of RAW processor grows, the scalar operand network latency increases, and more severely, traffic load per tile increases, which will finally destroy the scalability. In order to avoid this load increase, one would expect to keep the atomic size of 8X8 basic array and instead use an incremental level of inter-array communication network accommodating this incremental load. This leads to a hierarchical scaling behavior, in each level of which there are both distributed and centralized recourses. The real billion-transistor architecture coming around year 2007 can be made up of 8 M2 together with the counterpart of TinyRISC and operand network at a high level.3 Mapping of Reed-Solomon Decoding Algorithm

3. MAPPING OF REED-SOLOMON DECODING ALGORITHM

3.1 Reed-Solomon Decoding Algorithm [14]

In the RS (n,k) code, n is the block length, k is the transmitted code word length and n-k is the minimum distance over $GF(2^n)$. Decoder is capable of correcting $t = \frac{(n-k)}{2}$ error in the received code word. RS decoder introduced in this paper is developed for the SIMD reconfigurable processor. It is necessary to find a RS decoding algorithm, which makes the parallel processing possible. Let's consider $v(x)$ is the transmitted code word and $r(x)$ is the received code word. Then the error added by channel is

$$e(x) = r(x) - v(x) \qquad (1)$$

Considering v errors are occurred in the transmitted code word the syndromes are computed as follows:

$$S_j = v(\alpha^j) = r(\alpha^j) + e(\alpha^j) = \sum_{k=0}^{n-1} e_k (\alpha^j)^k = \sum_{l=1}^{\upsilon} e_{i_l} X_l^j \qquad (2)$$

Eq (3) shows the key equation to find the error locations and error magnitudes.

$$\Lambda(x) S(x) = \Gamma(x) \bmod x^{2t} \qquad (3)$$

$\Lambda(x)$ is the error location polynomial and its roots are the inverses of the error locations. It can be presented as follows:

$$\Lambda(x) = 1 + \sigma_1 x + \ldots + \sigma_v x^{\upsilon} = \prod_{l=1}^{v} (1 - x\alpha^{i_l}) \qquad (4)$$

After calculating the error location polynomial roots the error value corresponding to each error location can be easily calculated using the Eq (5)

$$e_l = -(\alpha^{i_l})^{-1} \frac{\Gamma((\alpha^{i_l})^{-1})}{\Lambda((\alpha^{i_l})^{-1})} \qquad (5)$$

The Berlekamp algorithm [14] is used to find the error location polynomial for the SIMD implementation of this decoder.

3.2. GF Multiplication and Addition Inside Each RC

GF multiplication is the basic operation should be considered in the implementation of RS decoder. There are two ways of implementing GF multiplication inside each RC. The first method is using look up tables for converting the vector representation to the power representation. Being able to change the power representation to its vector, we can consider GF elements in the whole decoding procedure as their vector representations. The GF multiplication will be simply the addition of the two powers. After addition, Mod 255 of the result should be computed. We avoid this time consuming computation by storing two look up tables continuously instead of one for converting the power to vector. the second look up table will be the vector corresponding for the power of 255 to 512. This method works if we just have the multiplication of two GF elements and will convert the result to its vector presentation soon after that. This is the case in implementing the GF Multiplication. Total application is mainly consists of GF polynomial computation which is the GF additions after each GF multiplication. In order to make each RC the computational cell for the GF addition and multiplication, we are taking advantage of the local memory inside each RC. These memories are specially implemented for storing look up tables, which are extremely, used in the data streamed applications. The second method comes from the feasibility of implementing the GF multiplier hardware inside each RC using the fine grain block. Using this way there is no need to know about the power presentation of GF elements and all the computation will go on using the vector presentation. Using the GF multiplier instead of the look up tables will speed up total application, as now we are able to multiply two GF elements and get the result in one clock cycle.

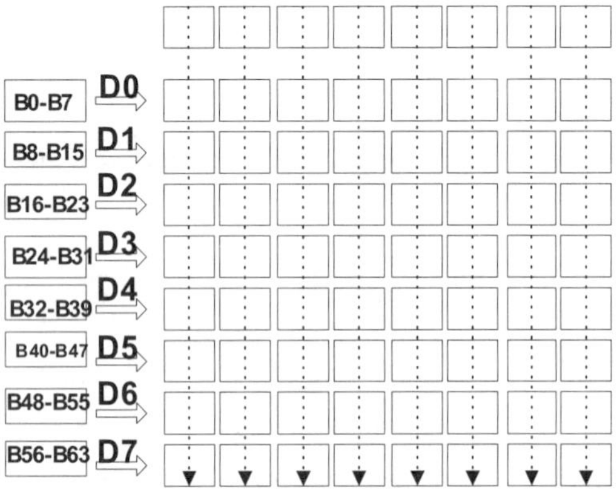

Figure 3. context broadcast to RC columns from the context memories of each column

3.3. Developing the Parallel Algorithm of the RS Decoder

In order to achieve the highest performance of the decoder implemented on the Morphosys, We should develop the introduced decoding algorithm for the SIMD processor. Fig 3 shows the parallelism exploited at the data level for the RS (255, 239,16). Each row of RC has been reconfigured for decoding one block of the data. 8 blocks of data will be decoded in parallel with each other. This will decrease the throughput to 1/8 of the total time needed for decoding 8 blocks in parallel. Fig 4 shows the task-flow diagram of the decoder. Each RC holds one coefficient of the error location polynomial, error magnitude polynomial and error correction polynomial. Each RC is the basic operational block for GF addition and multiplication. In the figure S_i Stands for the different syndromes computed during the syndrome computation. σ_i and T_i's are representing the error location and error correction polynomials coefficients respectively which are computed during the Berelekamp algorithm. In the Chein search part β_i stands for the GF (255) element, which should be substituted into the error location polynomial, to find the root of the error location polynomial. δ_i presents a coefficient of the error magnitude polynomial which is computed during the Forney's method stage and will be used to calculate the error values.

3.3.1. Syndrome Computation

The first step is the Syndrome calculation out of the received code word. Received code word is saved in the frame buffer and will be transmitted to each RC .Each RC computes two Syndromes in parallel with the other RCs of the row. This scheme is generalized depending on the number of Syndromes should be computed. This has been made easy since there is one bank of the Frame buffer corresponding to each RC. So we can easily scale the Syndrome numbers transmitting the data from frame buffer's bank to each RC.

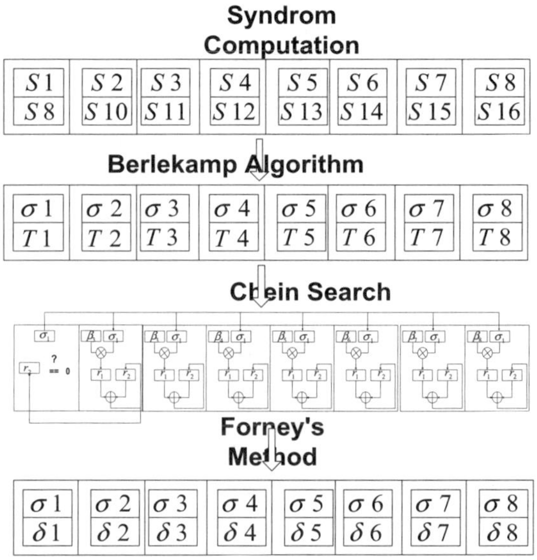

Figure 4. Task diagram of the decoding procedure in the time domain

3.3.2. Berlekamp Algorithm

Berlekamp Algorithm is consisting of three main parts. Discrepancy computation, calculation of the new error location polynomial and error correction polynomial. These calculations are basically made of addition of two polynomials together or multiplying one of them by the GF element. Addition has been made possible by storing the coefficients of the same order in the same RC. Addition of the polynomials will be adding of these two coefficients together in parallel in all RCs. In order to compute the discrepancy we need to take advantage of the data movement, between RCs. This data movement is possible in the same clock cycle as the multiplication happens using that element from the other RC. This is depicted in Fig 5.Taking advantage of the data movement between RCs is like increasing the register file of each RC to the ones from the RCs of the same row and same column. This is the strong tool to enhance the level of parallelism of the algorithm. Each RC can use the results of the other computation, as it has been stored in its register file.

3.3.3. Chein Search

Chein search can be done in parallel in the 7 RCs of the row. The first RC will check the result for the possible error detections. Each RC is responsible for trying 33 $GF(2^8)$ elements. The whole search has been done in parallel in the 7 RCs. FB will be used as a secondary memory here to store the elements of the $GF(2^8)$. Each bank will keep the necessary elements and their power, since we need up to 8 power of each element to reduce the computation time. In fact memory hierarchy is one of the important feature of the Morphosys. We can take advantage of the different parameter storage in the different levels of the memory.

3.3.4. Error Value computation

Error value calculation will be performed sequentially for the different error locations. This way we take advantage of parallel GF addition and multiplication in different RCs. Fig 6 shows different terms calculation of the error values inside each RC. Δ_k^{-1} is the discrepancy calculated during the Berlekamp algorithm part and σ_i s are the error location coefficients.

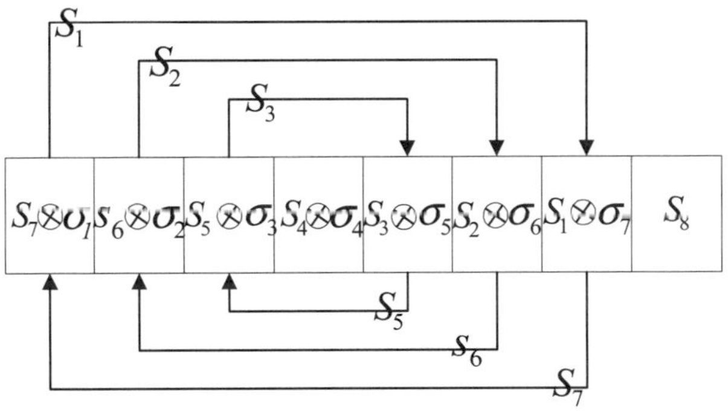

Figure 5. Data movement between RCs in order to calculate different terms of the Discrepancy in the different RC

4 CONCLUSION AND COMPARISON

MorphoSys as a reconfigurable architecture provides a very flexible platform for implementing different DSP applications. This is perfectly demonstrated through the RS decoder implementation with different error correcting length. Being able to reconfigure each RC for the different parts of the wireless communication receiver will provide the best functionality of each RC for the whole application. TI DSPs have the same approach to perform GF multiplication. In comparison Morphosys takes advantage of the higher data parallelism obtained through the SIMD characteristics of it. DSP C6400 provides the hardware support for performing the Galois Field multiplies. In the absence of hardware to effectively perform Galois field math, previous DSP implementations made use of logarithms to perform multiplication. This has decreased performance to ¼ of the present one with hardware GF multiplication. Many different Reed-Solomon ASIC Architectures are proposed in the literature [12-13]. These blocks are mostly specified and optimized for the RS decoder. They can be considered as a single chip RS decoder. In comparison Morphosys can be viewed as the programmable architecture optimized for the whole receiver Morphosys outperforms Asics, which have the smaller size. We have simulated the result on the Morphosys hardware simulator called Mulate. The result is given for the RS decoder of (255,239,16) using two different methods of GF multiplication. The decoding speed is 1.319Gbps and 2.534Gbps, respectively. Fig 7 shows the bit rate of the decoder and its comparison with the different Asics and Also TI64x

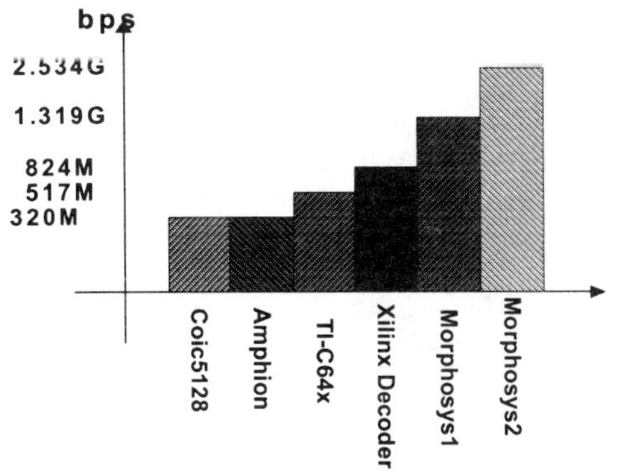

Figure7. Bit rate comparison of two decoders implemented on Morphosys with the other Asics and TIC64x

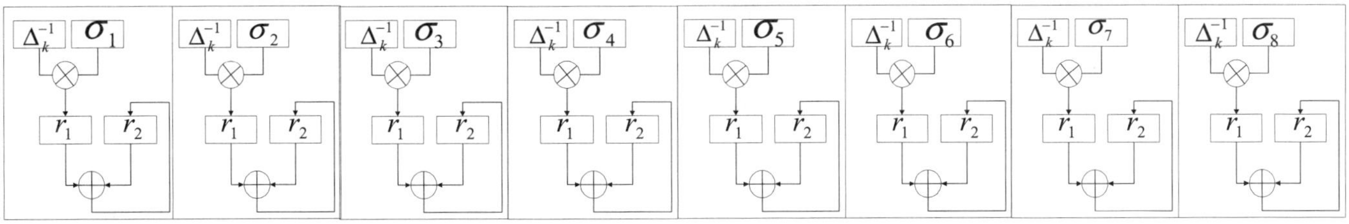

Figure 6. Different terms calculation of the error values

References:

[1] H. Singh, Lee, Lu, Bagherzadeh, Kurdahi, "MorphoSys: An Integrated Reconfigurable System for Data-Parallel and Computation –Intensive Applications," IEEE Transactions on Computers, vol. 49, No. 5, pp. 465-481, May 2000.

[2] Lee, Singh, Lu, Bagherzadeh, Kurdahi, "Design and Implementation of the MorphoSys Reconfigurable Computing Processor," Journal of VLSI Signal Processing Systems for Signal, Image, and Video Technology, vol. 24, No. 2-3, Kluwer Academic Publishers, pp. 147-164, Mar 2000.

[3] Pan, Kamalizad, Koohi, Bagherzadeh, "Design and Analysis of a Programmable Single-Chip Architecture for DVB-T Base-Band Receiver," To Appear in DATE 2003.

[4] Agarwal, Hrishikesh, Keckler, Burger, "Clock rate versus IPC: the end of the road for conventional microarchitectures," Computer Architecture, 2000. Proceedings of the 27th International Symposium on, 2000 Page(s): 248 -259

[5] Schlansker, Rau, "EPIC: Explicitly Parallel Instruction Computing," Computer, Volume: 33 Issue: 2, Feb 2000 Page(s): 37 -45

[6] Taylor, et.al. "The Raw microprocessor: a computational fabric for software circuits and general-purpose programs," Micro, IEEE , Volume: 22 Issue: 2 , Mar/Apr 2002, Page(s): 25 -35

[7] Rixner, et.al. "A bandwidth-efficient architecture for media processing," Microarchitecture, 1998. MICRO-31. Proceedings. 31st Annual ACM/IEEE International Symposium on , 30 Nov-2 Dec 1998

[8] Kozyrakis, Patterson, "Vector vs. superscalar and VLIW architectures for embedded multimedia benchmarks," Microarchitecture, 2002. (MICRO-35). Proceedings. 35th Annual IEEE/ACM International Symposium on, 2002 Page(s): 283 -293

[9] Taylor, Lee, Amarasinghe, Agarwal, "Scalar Operand Networks: On-chip Interconnect for ILP in Partitioned Architectures," HPCA 2003, February 2003.

[10] Venkataramani, Najjar, Kurdahi, Bagherzadeh, Bohm, "A Compiler Framework for Mapping Applications to a Coarse-grained Reconfigurable Computer Architecture," CASES 2001, Atlanta, GA, November 2001.

[11] Maestre, Kurdahi, Bagherzadeh, Singh, Hermida, Fernandez, "Kernel scheduling in reconfigurable computing," DATE 1999.

[12] Implementation of high speed Reed-Solomon decoder. [Conference Paper] 42nd Midwest Symposium on Circuits and Systems (Cat. No.99CH36356). IEEE. Part vol. 2, 2000, pp.808-12 vol. 2. Piscataway, NJ, USA.

[13] Martina M, Masera G, Piccinini G, Vacca F, Zamboni M. VLSI Reed Solomon decoder architecture for networked multimedia applications. [Conference Paper] *Proceedings 14th Annual IEEE International ASIC/SOC Conference (IEEE Cat. No.01TH8558). IEEE. 2001, pp.347-51. Piscataway, NJ,USASystems II-Analog & Digital Signal Processing, vol.47, no.11, Nov. 2000, pp.1254-70. Publisher: IEEE, USA.*

[14] Shu LIN/ Daniel J Costello Error Control Coding Fundamentals and applications

[15] www.amphion.com

[16] www.ti.com

[17] www.xilinx.com

The Analysis and Design of Architecture Systems for Speech Recognition on Modern Handheld-Computing Devices

Andreas Hagen
Center for Spoken Language Research, University of Colorado at Boulder
001 303 735-5227
andreash@colorado.edu

Daniel A. Connors
Department of Electrical and Computer Engineering, University of Colorado at Boulder
001 303 735-7199
dconnors@colorado.edu

Bryan L. Pellom
Center for Spoken Language Research, University of Colorado at Boulder
001 303 735-5382
bryan.pellom@colorado.edu

ABSTRACT
Growing demand for high performance in embedded systems is creating new opportunities to use speech recognition systems traditionally executed only on high performance systems. In several ways, the needs of embedded computing differ from those of more traditional general-purpose systems. Embedded systems have more stringent constraints on cost and power consumption that lead to design bottlenecks for many computationally-intensive applications. This paper characterizes the speech recognition process on hand-held mobile devices and evaluates the use of modern architecture features and compiler techniques for performing real-time speech recognition. We evaluate the University of Colorado Sonic speech recognition software on the IMPACT architectural simulator and compiler framework. Experimental results show that by using a strategic set of compiler optimization, a 500MHz processor with moderate levels of instruction-level parallelism and cache resources can meet the real-time computing and power constraints of an advanced speech recognition application.

Categories and Subject Descriptors
C.3 [Special-Purpose and Application-Based Systems]: – *Real-time and embedded systems.*

General Terms: Measurement, Performance, Design

Keywords: Speech Recognition, Embedded Systems, Performance

1. INTRODUCTION
In the recent years PDAs have become more and more powerful and affordable at the same time. It has become possible to run powerful applications such as multimedia on handheld devices. Nevertheless, PDAs have a unique interface system that differs from other general-purpose systems. Typing on PDAs is more error prone than on normal sized keyboards because of their size, also PDAs are used in situations where typing might be hard because of influences like shaking while traveling. Therefore it is very desirable to look for alternatives to typing as a user input modality on PDAs. A very natural way of controlling and giving commands to a PDA is speech since human beings are used to this kind of interaction with each other. In order to assure a comfortable speech command and control behavior a few conditions have to be given. The recognition error rate should be very small and the processing of the speech input should be possible in real time such that no delays are conceivable for the user.

The first requirement of low error rates is a task that is sufficiently solved for command and control tasks on state of the art speech recognition systems for desktop computers. By command and control task we mean a recognition task consisting between a 500 and 2000 word vocabulary and input of keywords, phrases, or small finite-state recognition grammars. The error rates for such a task are low enough for enabling a comfortable use (especially if the system is adapted to the user).

The second requirement is the necessity for real-time processing of the input speech. This requires processing of the audio as it is recorded by the PDA with recognized text strings available almost immediately after the user finishes speaking. Real-time factors less than 1.0 are desirable while factors greater than 1.0 imply that the software cannot keep up with processing the input speech. A real-time factor of 2.2, for example, would lead to processing of 5 seconds of audio during a span of 11 seconds. This would result in an unacceptable delay of 6 seconds between the time that the user finishes speaking until the time that the text string was available to the application.

In this paper we focus on system design issues for the second requirement, the real-time processing of speech on PDAs. We simulated 500-2000 word vocabulary speech recognition tasks in which each word is equally probable. Such vocabulary sizes seem to be a sufficiently large vocabulary for a set of commands that could be used to control a PDA. The recognition system works in a speaker independent manner, this means the acoustic model is trained ahead of the actual recognition and the user does not need to train the system for his or her voice.

This research was partially sponsored by Avaya Inc. via research award W0711119CWS and by NSF under award NSF/IERI 1R01HD44276-01.

In order to be useful the word error rate for such a vocabulary size should be no higher than 10% (this means about 1 in 10 words needs to be repeated). This accuracy is achievable with state of the art speech recognizers. A recognition task consisting of isolated words spoken by kids is reported in [1], where the word error rate is less then 1% for a 200-word vocabulary for 10th grade students. This task is very similar to the command and control setup mentioned earlier. Of course a noisy environment would influence the results in a negative way.

The question to be answered in this paper is if PDA architectures are fast enough to recognize the spoken utterances in real-time and what code optimizations and hardware changes could be applied to improve the performance further.

2. RELATED WORK

Speech Recognition is a very active area of research. In addition, two main problems, accuracy and running time have been analyzed in speech recognizers executing on modern general purpose hardware. Agaram et al. [2,11] have analyzed the amount of instruction level parallelism (ILP) in the SPHINX speech recognizer of CMU [3], the influence of cache sizes and other hardware specifications on the instruction per cycle (IPC) rate was simulated. They also give an estimate of the instruction throughput needed to process speech in real-time on the Alpha ISA. In [4] Vlaovic and Uhlig report cache and translation look-aside buffer (TLB) hit ratios. The cache-hit ratios are evaluated for different cache sizes. As expected the number of cache misses decreases with increasing cache size. The same behavior can be seen for different TLB sizes. The authors used the Dragon Systems NaturallySpeaking speech recognition system on an X86 ISA simulator.

In our work we evaluate the performance of the University of Colorado Sonic speech recognizer on a PDA-like architecture. Using the IMPACT architectural simulator and compiler framework [5], we provide estimates on the needed clock rate of several processors which would be required in order to process the command-and-control vocabulary in real-time. We also analyze Sonic's performance dependent on different data and instruction cache sizes. At an even higher level, the Wattch [14] power analysis tool provides accurate power estimations based on the architectural description of the simulated microprocessor.

3. THE SONIC SPEECH RECOGNIZER

3.1 Overview

The Sonic speech recognition system was developed at the University of Colorado [6,7]. The recognizer is based on decision-tree state-clustered triphone hidden Markov (CDHMM) models. In such an architecture, the basic building blocks of sounds, also known as phonemes, are characterized by 3 Markov states. The three states are used to model the statistical distribution at the beginning, middle, and end of the sound unit. Each state is modeled by a mixture of multivariate Gaussian densities. Transitions between states are modeled using a gamma probability density function.

During recognition, features are extracted every 10 ms (100 feature vectors per second) from the audio signal. The features are represented as a floating-point vector containing 12 Mel Frequency Cepstral Coefficients (MFCCs), energy, and the first and second differences of these parameters. The features encode the short-time spectrum of the audio signal. The resulting feature vector stream has a dimension of 39. Feature computation is extremely efficient consuming less than 1% of the CPU in a typical speech recognizer.

The search network in Sonic is represented using a reentrant static tree-lexicon [8]. Here, phonetic word pronunciations are expanded into sequences of context-dependent HMM states and inserted into a tree-based search structure for efficiency. In this framework, words that share similar initial phoneme sequences also share the same root node in the lexical search tree.

The recognizer implements a two-pass search strategy. The first pass consists of a frame-synchronous, beam-pruned Viterbi token-passing search [9]. Tokens are used to maintain the state of the recognizer. They encode paths (consisting of unique word sequences) that the recognizer is considering given the current feature vector of input. Tokens propagate through the tree-lexicon while consuming input frames until a leaf-node in the tree is reached. At that point, the identity of a word is known. The word-exiting token can then propogate into the root nodes of the tree allowing for continuous speech recognition.

At the transition between words, a language model probability is applied. Most state-of-the-art speech recognition systems constrain the sequence of allowable words using a fixed grammer or by using a statistical n-gram language model. N-gram language models condition the probability of transitioning to a word based on the previous N-1 words. Trigram (N=3) and bigram (N=2) language models are typical for most continuous speech recognition tasks.

The first recognition pass creates a lattice of word ends. During the second pass, the resulting word-lattice is converted into a word-graph. The word-graph is searched for the most-likely word string.

CPU requirements for the second-pass search are often negligible compared to the first-pass search.

3.2 Efficiency Issues

Speech recognition is an extremely intense task from a computational standpoint. Search within the Sonic recognizer is dominated primarily by two operations: token passing and Gaussian evaluation. Token passing refers to the maintenance of the paths (word sequences) and their relative probabilities. Gaussian evaluation is required to compute the probability of observing an input feature vector within an HMM state during search through the lexical tree.

For small to medium vocabulary tasks such as command-and-control, calculation of the Gaussian likelihoods consumes much of the CPU resources of the speech recognizer. Larger input vocabularies require more path history maintenance resulting in large CPU efforts for both token passing and Gaussian evaluation. Because our task is command and control, let's further consider the issue of Gaussian computation.

Each HMM state within Sonic is represented by a mixture of M Gaussian densities. Typical systems have between 6 and 32 Gaussian densities per HMM state. Each Gaussian density is represented by a weight (w_m), mean vector (μ_m), and covariance matrix (Σ_m). For efficiency and issues related to data sparseness, the covariance matrix is assumed to be diagonal resulting in the following likelihood calculation,

$$b(\vec{x}_t) = \sum_{m=1}^{M} \frac{w_m}{(2\pi)^{D/2}\sqrt{\prod_{d=1}^{D}\sigma_m^2[d]}} \exp\left\{-\frac{1}{2}\sum_{d=1}^{D}\frac{(x_t[d]-\mu_m[d])^2}{\sigma_m^2[d]}\right\}$$

where $b(\vec{x}_t)$ represents the probability of observing the tth frame of input (x_t). Note that the feature dimension D is 39 for most traditional speech recognition systems. We can see that evaluation of a single HMM state consisting of 6 Gaussians would require 480 floating point multiplies, 234 subtractions and 6 exp(·) operations.

The likelihood function can be computed with almost no loss using a nearest-neighbor approximation and by performing the calculations for search in the log-domain. The resulting equation for the log-likelihood becomes,

$$\log b(\vec{x}_t) \approx \arg\max_m \left\{ C_m - \frac{1}{2} \sum_{d=1}^{D} \frac{(x_t[d] - \mu_m[d])^2}{\sigma_m^2[d]} \right\}$$

where C_m is a constant that can be pre-computed prior to run-time. This implementation requires less floating-point operations in practice since the above equation can be partially computed. That is, while searching for the value of m that maximizes the equation, we can drop out of the summation loop over the D feature elements as soon as the partial sum falls below that of the best scoring mixture component. This approximation when combined with several straight-forward optimizations can improve the speed of the Gaussian computation within a speech recognizer by almost 30% with no loss in performance for most practical implementations [10].

In summary, command-and-control speech recognition tasks require many floating-point operations. This is directly related to the fact that Gaussian densities are evaluated during the recognition search process. In perspective, the recognizer receives 100 feature vectors input for one second of audio. For each frame, it is not uncommon to evaluate several hundred HMM states (each consisting of multivariate mixture Gaussians). Some speech recognition architectures, such as the older CMU Sphinx-II system, deal with this issue by using integer arithmetic and semi-continuous Gaussian densities. These improvements often come at a loss in system accuracy [8].

4. THE IMPACT COMPILER

An important requirement for evaluating Sonic's performance on different processor systems is to either have each system available in hardware or to be able to simulate Sonic's execution on a hardware simulator. A very powerful tool for doing this is the IMPACT simulator. IMPACT processes Sonic's source code and traverses various stages of optimization.

All compiler optimizations are done based on profile information. First, function inlining, which represents a compiler technique for replacing a function call with the respective function body. Next, compiler technology generates analysis of interprocedural memory dependence information maintained throughout the compilation process. After analysis, frequently executed code traces are identified using execution profiles. These traces, called Superblocks[15] are similar to extended basic blocks, except code duplication creates a single entry multiple exit region with more potential for ILP optimization. Finally, IMPACT is able to generate scheduled code, thereby adapting low-level code to a certain degree to a specific target architecture.

Furthermore IMPACT is able to simulate optimized code execution on different target architectures, these can be specified in sufficient detail in order to well approximate various architectural specifications. Some of the adjustable parameters (only a small subset) are the processor's issuing type, in our case superscalar, the issue width, the number of different functional units, cache sizes, ports, and associativities. IMPACT and detailed information about its functionality can be found in [5].

5. INTEL'S XSCALE ARCHITECTURE

Intel's XScale architecture is a special processor architecture for high performance embedded systems and is based on the ARM architecture specifications. The PXA250 processor is a highly integrated system with an XScale core. It is a 32-bit RISC microarchitecture especially designed for good performance and integration as well as low power consumption. It serves as the reference for the family of embedded systems in this work.

The PXA250 has clock frequencies from 200 to 400MHz and a 2KB mini data cache as well as an equally sized mini instruction cache. The standard caches that could be compared to L2 caches (on desktop machines) are 32KB, again one such sized for data and one for instruction caching. The processor's core represents a superscalar machine with 4 functional units. The functional units are: a memory unit, a shift and permute unit, a multiply and permute unit, and a general execution unit.

More details on the functional units are given in [11]. The branch target buffer (BTB) of the PXA250 holds 128 entries and the branch predictor is 2 bit predictor. More information on the PXA250 can be found in [12] and [13].

6. EXPERIMENTAL SETUP

In order to simulate a command and control task on handheld devices two main steps have to be taken. The first one is the setup of an appropriate speech recognition task of the necessary complexity. The other one is the setup of the hardware simulator for the target hardware and some slightly modified hardware setups.

6.1 The Recognition Task

Children's speech represents an interesting field of research because of applications in the fields of education, learning devices, and toys.

For the command and control recognition task we use the Sonic speech recognizer described in detail earlier. The vocabulary for the task consists of 500 words. The speech recognition acoustic model is trained from 1781 students from grades 1 through 10. Data from 1118 children were obtained from the OGI Kids Speech Corpus [1] while data from the remaining 663 children were collected from the Boulder Valley School district in Boulder Colorado. Data was collected from each student using a head-mounted microphone and a desktop PC. Each subject contributed 20 training word examples on average.

The models do not have to be adapted to the current user, but of course an additional adaptation step would further improve the recognition rate that is already certainly higher than 90% [1]. 10% or less word error rate seems to be sufficient for a comfortable use on a PDA. In order to evaluate the performance of this command and control task the input speech file is a 16KHz sampled instance of the spoken word 'QUIT'.

The length of the sound sample is 2.2 seconds. On a 1.7GHz Pentium 4 desktop machine the real-time factor for its processing is 0.57. In average the real-time factor for 29 different words on this machine is about 0.46 and the standard deviation results in 0.06. So the speech sample used for this task has a real-time factor slightly above average but still in the range that can be seen as representative for the set of input sound samples. This means if a system is able to process the test sound sample in real-time or even faster, it will be able to process a majority of all possible words (commands) in real-time.

6.2 Target Hardware Specifications

The simulation setup for the command and control task has to be very close to the specifications of a state of the art handheld device to give useful results and predictions. For this work we consider the following 4-wide machine:

- 2 integer units
- 2 floating point units
- 2 memory units
- 1 branch unit

Only four units out of the given seven can be active at any time. This is very similar to the PXA250 processor, which has a general execution unit and therefore about the same amount of scheduling-freedom.

Further specifications are:

- 2KB data cache
- 2KB instruction cache
- 64KB combined data and instruction cache
- 128 entry BTB w/ 2 bit branch predictor

The IMPACT simulator is adjusted to these parameters and therefore the simulation of the recognition task results in similar cycle counts as the execution of this task would require on a handheld device. This will allow us to analyze the clock frequency rates required to run the described command and control task in real-time on state of the art as well as future or extended PDAs.

7. PERFORMANCE EVALUATIONS

We compiled Sonic's code under three levels of optimization for three different architectural setups, a 2-wide issue machine, a limited 4-wide machine (described earlier, similar to the XScale architecture) and an unlimited 4-wide machine (4 floating point units, 4 integer units, 4 memory units and 1 branch unit). The three different kinds of optimized code were architecture specific scheduled O-code, which is similar to what GNU's gcc compiler would generate, superblock optimized code (S-code) which is also scheduled for the target architecture. As mentioned all codes were scheduled for each target architecture. Profiling information was also used for improved optimization, and the use of inlining/interprocedural analysis improved the base code performance by 10%.

One of the goals in this paper is to determine the lower bounds in the clock frequencies of modern handheld devices under the constraint of real-time speech recognition for the introduced command and control task. In order to do this analysis the initialization phase of Sonic needs to be subtracted from the overall cycle count of Sonic's execution cycle count, since the speech recognizer would be started once at the beginning and would not be shut down in between the recognition of multiple commands. Our simulations showed that the percentage used for Sonic's initialization compared to the overall command recognition (initialization plus recognition of one word) only takes 1.3%. Even though this means only a small impact we still took it into consideration. We found that S-code had the best performance and that the application of hyperblock formation (use of predicated execution support in the architecture) did not help but rather worsened the results.

7.1 Clock Rate Estimation

To compute the clock frequencies the cycle counts from the IMPACT simulator are normalized such that the fraction counting for the initialization part is ignored. Since the length of the input speech file is 2.2 seconds the computation of the clock frequency is simply the normalized cycle count divided by the duration of the speech input (2.2s).

7.2 Simulation Results

For the 4-wide restricted machine (comparable to the PXA250) the O-code requires a clock frequency of at least 452 MHz for the task to run in real time. The S-code improves the required clock frequency by 33 MHz to 419 MHz. This behavior can be observed for all test architectures and leads to the conclusion that superblock-optimization is beneficial. Interprocedural memory alias analysis can be safely left aside for the Sonic speech recognizer that shares many techniques with the Sphinx speech recognizer from CMU.

The estimated clock frequencies show that the command and control task for a 500-word vocabulary is almost executable on a current handheld device in real-time. The PXA250 is delivered with clock frequencies from 200 to 400 MHz. The gap of about 20 MHz is very likely to be closed in the near future. It might also be closed by an additional speaker adaptation step that would speed up the execution.

In the next section we will also show that an architectural change in cache sizes is able to close this gap already.

7.3 Cache Evaluation

We simulated different data and instruction cache sizes in order to evaluate how these changes reflect in Sonic's performance and to what extent they are beneficial. Figure 1 shows the number of cycles relative to the data cache size on the unrestricted 4-wide machine.

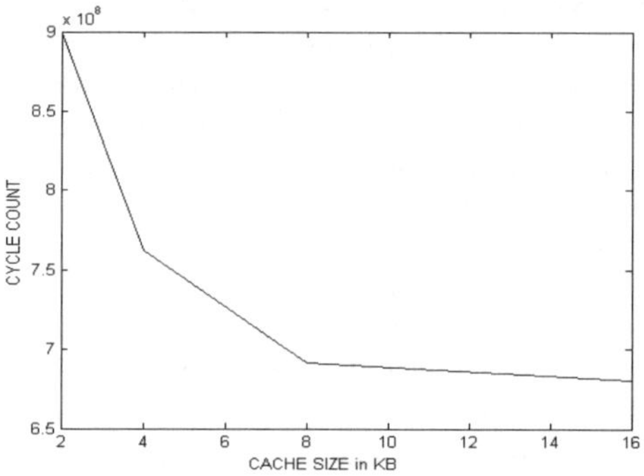

Figure 1: Cycle counts relative to data cache size

The simulation results show that a 16KB mini cache would yield in performance benefits of over 32%, an 8KB cache improves the performance by about 30%.

A 30% performance benefit due to an increased mini cache matches about a 125MHz increase in clock frequency, given the minimum required clock frequency proposed above and the fact that the whole cache and memory unit would be clocked faster by the same ratio of 30%. Therefore the consequences would be that the command and control task of 500 words would already run on a PXA250 with increased mini cache (8KB). Increasing the instruction mini cache did not result in a remarkable performance benefit that would justify the costs for expensive cache modules.

Although 500 words seem sufficient to control a PDA at this time, it might be possible that speech recognition draws increased interest in the near future, especially if the systems evolve such that more complicated commands, even small sentences are possible as control input. To give a rough estimate of the performance increase required for larger tasks, we simulated a 1000-word and a 1500-word command and control task (Table 2).

# of words	# of cycles	cycle increase
500	926278753	1.00
1000	1195492858	1.29
1500	1481844128	1.60
2000	1672314581	1.81

Table 2: Cycle counts and increases (based on the 500-word task) for variously sized command and control tasks

It turns out that the 1000-word task requires about 1.3 times the performance of the 500-word task, and the 1500-word task requires about 60% more performance compared to the 500-word vocabulary task and finally the 2000-word task needs 80% more resources than the 500-word task to run in real-time. The curve of cycle increases is expected to become more and more flat.

These tasks are expected to be executable in real-time on a PDA in the next one or two years, given the performance increase observed in the embedded systems field in the recent years.

8. POWER SIMULATION

As the issues and concerns facing power consumption grow to include high performance microprocessors as well as the pervasive hand-held and wireless computing market, novel approaches to power conservation at the architectural level are being sought. At the same time, ubiquitous computing is becoming more prevalent, and thus the performance demands made upon these devices are increasing, leading toward more complex architectures.

Although much work on energy reduction has taken place in the circuit and device technology domains [16], there has been an increasing emphasis on designing for power efficiency at the architectural level. This implies that the desired energy and power goals must be targeted early in the design cycle and that the system microarchitecture must work in concert with advances in circuit technology to reduce power demands.

To evaluate power consumption of speech recognition, we integrated the Wattch power analysis tool [14] with the IMPACT architecture simulator. Figure 2 illustrates the power consumption for the architecture studied through the duration of the sample input. During initialization, the memory system has the peak power of nearly 800mWatts, but averages 380mW, only going slightly above 400mW for the ending duration of the Sonic application.

With the studied architecture, the breakdown of architecture elements and power consumption were:

- Clock (43.3%)
- Floating-point ALUs (26.7%)
- Register file/result bus (10.2%)
- Integer ALU (7.5%)
- Mini Dcache (5.5%)
- Mini Icache (3.6%)
- Level2 Cache (3%)

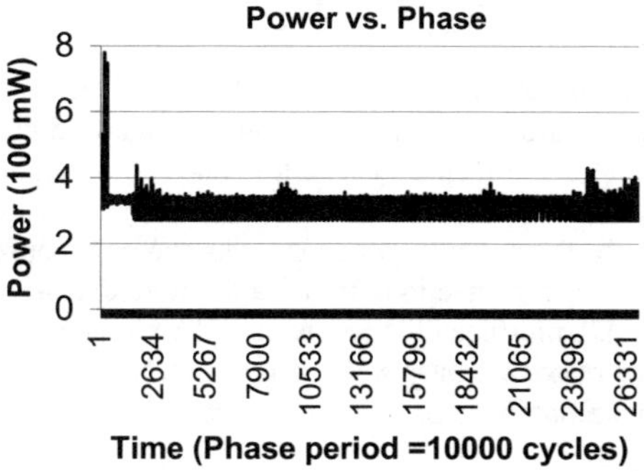

Figure 2: Power consumption timeline for Sonic

By using low-power techniques at clock distribution and clock-gating techniques for the floating-point unit, it may be possible to design a low-power system specifically designed for speech recognition. Generally all speech recognition applications require intense floating-point computations, so it is not straight forward to reduce the power spent in this unit. We are currently looking at techniques to evaluate the number of speech sentences that can be recognized and the impact on power consumption and battery lifetime.

9. SUMMARY AND FUTURE WORK

In this paper the main goal was to explore real-time speech recognition for command and control tasks on handheld devices. It was shown that real-time speech recognition is very close to being possible for optimized code. The missing 20MHz in clock frequency estimated for the PXA250 running Sonic could be filled by a larger cache size of 8KB. For non-superscalar optimized code about 50 MHz are missing for the introduced command and control task to run in real-time, this means superblock optimization is very beneficial in this application.

We gave a prediction of the required performance increases that are necessary for larger command and control tasks to still run in real-time. It could be shown that the 500-word task is at the edge of real-time executable recognition tasks on architectures similar to the PXA250.

The power simulations give an overview of the processors' by unit power consumptions. It can be seen that the dominating power consumption comes from the floating-point computations that are executed during the Gaussian mixture densities computation.

The field of speech recognition on handheld devices is an active field of research far from being sufficiently explored. Some ideas for future work that were left aside in this work are the following. We were using a language model with equal likelihood for all words, this is certainly not true for command and control tasks. Different probabilities for different commands are likely to improve performance. Another performance improving step that could be applied is speaker adaptation that also improves the recognition rate further.

Another interesting direction to further explore in the field of speech recognition systems for PDAs is a fixed-point implementation. Sonic up to this point is based on floating-point operations and all other state of the art speech recognition systems are, too. Developing a fixed-point speech recognizer is definitely an interesting project for the future.

The data used for this task are from children's speech corpus. The speech of children has a higher variability than adult speech and might therefore influence the performance in a slightly negative way. It would be interesting to use data directly recorded on PDAs. For this data the quality would be lower and as a consequence the performance is expected to drop (because more extensive search has to be done). Unfortunately there is no PDA-recorded data available as a standardized corpus, which would be of great benefit to the research community.

10. REFERENCES

[1] Khaldoun Shobaki, John-Paul Hosom, and Ronald Cole. The OGI Kids' Speech Corpus and Recognizers. In Proceedings of the International Conference on Spoken Language Processing (ICSLP), Beijing, China, October 2000.

[2] K. Agaram, S. Keckler, and D. Burger. A Characterization of Speech Recognition on Modern Computer Systems. In 4th IEEE Workshop on Workload Characterization, December 2001.

[3] Kai-Fu Lee, Hsiao-Wuen Hon, and Raj Reddy. An Overview of the SPHINX Speech Recognition System. IEEE Transactions on Acoustics, Speech and Signal Processing, 38:35--44, 1990.

[4] S. Vlaovic, R. Uhlig. Performance of Natural I/O Applications. 2nd Workshop on Workload Characterization. October 1999.

[5] http://www.crhc.uiuc.edu/Impact (link checked on 04/14/03)

[6] Pellom, B., Hacioglu, K., Recent Improvements in the Sonic ASR System for Noisy Speech: the SPINE task. Proc. IEEE International Conference on Acoustics, Speech, and Signal Processing (ICASSP), Hong Kong, April 2003.

[7] Pellom, B., Sonic: The University of Colorado Continuous Speech Recognition System. Technical Report TR-CSLR-2001-01, University of Colorado, March 2001.

[8] M. Ravishankar, Efficient Algorithms for Speech Recognition. PhD Thesis, Carnegie Mellon University, 1996.

[9] S.J. Young, N.H. Russell, J.H.S. Thornton, Token Passing: A Simple Conceptual Model for Connected Speech Recognition Systems. Cambridge University Engineering Department Technical Report CUED/F-INFENG/TR.38, 1989.

[10] Bryan Pellom, Ruhi Sarikaya, John Hansen, Fast Likelihood Computation in Nearest-Neighbor Based Search for Continuous Speech Recognition. In IEEE Signal Processing Letters, vol. 8, no. 8, pp. 221-224, August 2001.

[11] Nigel Paver. Intel XScale Micro-Architecture with Wireless MMX technology. www.intel.com/pca/developernetwork, Volume 4, Summer 2002.

[12] The Intel PXA250 Applications Processor. White Paper, Intel, February 2002.

[13] PXA250 and PXA210 Application Processors Developer's Manual, Intel, 2002.

[14] David Brooks, Vivek Tiwari, and Margaret Martonosi, *Wattch: A Framework for Architectural-Level Power Analysis and Optimizations*. 27th International Symposium on Computer Architecture (ISCA), Vancouver, British Columbia, June 2000.

[15] Hwu et al. The Superblock: An Effective Structure for {VLIW} and Superscalar Compilation. Center for Reliable and High-Performance Computing. University of Illinois, Urbana, IL. February, 1992.

[16] A. P. Chandrakasan, S. Sheng, and R. W. Brodersen. *Low-power CMOS digital design*. IEEE Journal of Solid-State Circuits, vol. 27, no. 4, pp. 473-484, April 1992

Keynote Talk

The Evolution of CDMA Wireless Devices Based on Advanced Chip Sets and BREW

Dr. Irwin Mark Jacobs
Chairman of the Board and Chief Executive Officer
Qualcomm Incorporated

I. M. Jacobs

Dr. Irwin Mark Jacobs is co-founder, chairman and CEO of QUALCOMM Incorporated, pioneer and world leader of Code Division Multiple Access (CDMA) digital wireless technology. Dr. Jacobs has led the commercialization of CDMA technology and its success as the world's fastest-growing, most advanced voice and data wireless communications technology. Now used by tens of millions of consumers worldwide, CDMA is the technology of choice for third-generation wireless communications services.

Dr. Jacobs holds several CDMA patents, contributing to QUALCOMM's extensive portfolio of more than 2,300 issued and pending U.S. patent applications. More than 100 companies have licensed CDMA for the manufacturing of wireless devices and network infrastructure equipment, integrated circuits and test equipment.

Dr. Jacobs previously served as co-founder, president, chairman and CEO of LINKABIT Corporation, directing its growth from a few part-time employees in 1969 to over 1,400 employees in 1985, and first introduction of Ku-band Very Small Aperature Earth Terminals (VSATs), commercial TDMA wireless phones, and the VideoCipher (R) satellite-to-home TV system. LINKABIT merged with M/A-COM in August 1980, at which time Dr. Jacobs served on the company's board of directors until he resigned from M/A-COM in April 1985. Over 35 San Diego communications companies trace their roots back to LINKABIT.

From 1959 to 1966, Dr. Jacobs was an assistant/associate professor of electrical engineering at Massachusetts Institute of Technology (MIT). From 1966 to 1972 he served as a professor of computer science and engineering at the University of California, San Diego (UCSD). At MIT, Dr. Jacobs co-authored a basic textbook in digital communications entitled, Principles of Communication Engineering. First published in 1965, the book remains in use today.

CODES+ISSS'03, October 1–3, 2003, Newport Beach, California, USA.
ACM 1-58113-742-7/03/0010.

Invited Session A

Industry Best Practices and Upcoming Challenges in Embedded Software and Hardware

Chair: R. Camposano
Synopsys

The growing sophistication of processors and software in embedded systems calls upon innovative techniques and tools for overcome the significant design challenges. Overcoming these challenges often requires in-depth understanding of the application domains and how these affect the system design process. This session features invited presenters from important industry segments where embedded computing has a critical role to share their experiences and the lessons learned.

PRESENTATIONS

Embedded Software Development for Wireless Handsets: Field Lessons in Extreme Programming

M. Underseth
S2Technologies

Parametric Superscalar Microprocessors

F. Karim
STMicroelectronics

A speaker from automotive industry

Invited Talk

Architectural versus Physical Solutions for On-Chip Communication Challenges

Doug Burger
Department of Computer Science,
University of Texas at Austin

Abstract:

The growing gap between transistor and global wire speeds in sub-100 nanometer technologies poses numerous challenges to computer architects and circuit designers. This challenge looks to be even more significant in far-future technologies such as molecular-scale wire transmission, whether using carbon nanotubes or quantum dots. While a fixed design scales as its area decreases with feature size reductions, future designs that use a constant area see rapidly increasing global latencies.

Two approaches to address these latencies are (1) to use signaling and design techniques to reduce the actual latencies, and (2) to use architectural innovations to reduce the distance that signals must be propagated in the common case. In this talk, after an overview of the communication latency issue, I describe current research that aims to reduce the average distance communicated for processing and memory system signals. For processor designs, I will describe the Static Placement, Dynamic Issue (SPDI) execution model, which allows the compiler to place dependent instructions near one another, and which is being implemented in the TRIPS processor. I will also describe Non-Uniform Caches Access (NUCA) designs, which attempt to reduce average signal distance for cache accesses.

CODES+ISSS'03, October 1-3, 2003, Newport Beach, California, USA.
ACM 1-58113-742-7/03/0010.

On-Chip Communication Design: Roadblocks and Avenues *

[Invited Talk - Extended Abstract]

Luca P. Carloni
EECS Dept., UC Berkeley, Berkeley, CA 94720
http://www-cad.eecs.berkeley.edu/HomePages/lcarloni

Alberto L. Sangiovanni-Vincentelli
EECS Dept., UC Berkeley, Berkeley, CA 94720
http://www-cad.eecs.berkeley.edu/HomePages/alberto

ABSTRACT

The semiconductor industry is experiencing a paradigm shift from "computation-bound design" to "communication-bound design": the number of transistors that can be reached in a clock cycle, and not those that can be integrated on a chip, will drive the design process. Interconnect latency will have a major impact on the design of on-chip communication architectures, which increasingly rely on wire pipelining to go beyond the capabilities of traditional wire buffering. The insertion of stateful repeaters *on long wires, instead of simply* stateless repeaters, *carries major consequences for the synchronous design methodology. This is the foundation of the design flows for the majority of commercial chips today, but, if left unchanged, will lead to an exacerbation of the timing closure problem for tomorrows design flows. New methodologies that regard the chip as a distributed system are necessary. Latency-insensitive design is a step in this direction.*

Categories and Subject Descriptors

B.7.1 [**Hardware**]: Integrated Circuits—*Types and Design Styles*;
B.7.2 [**Hardware**]: Integrated Circuits—*Design Aids*.

General Terms

Design

Keywords

On-Chip Networks, Latency-Insensitive Design, GALS.

1. COMMUNICATION-BOUND DESIGN

On-chip communication threatens to become a roadblock for the continuing technology progress that has been at the basis of the success of the semiconductor industry. Back in 1997, D. Matzke [13] published a study containing a gloomy forecast on Moore's Law hampered by on-chip interconnect latency (predicted to be measured soon in tens of clock cycles). This forecast has been echoed in many subsequent works studying the challenges posed by deep sub-micron design (DSM). Despite the increase in number of metal layers and in aspect ratio and the introduction of copper metallization and low-κ dielectric insulators, the resistance-capacitance (RC) delay of an average metal line with constant length is getting worse with each process generation [2, 10]. The combined increase of RC delays, chip operating frequency, die size, and average interconnect length, makes interconnect delay become the largest fraction of the clock cycle time. In particular, the relative scaling properties of wires and gates are at the center of this phenomenon. It is true that those wires that scale in length together with gate lengths present approximately a constant resistance and a falling capacitance. However, a future system-on-chip (SOC) will present many *global* wires that cannot scale in length because they need to span across multiple on-chip modules to connect distant gates [11]. In fact, the intrinsic interconnect delay of a $1mm$ length wire for a $35nm$ technology is expected to be $250ps$, i.e. two orders of magnitude larger than the corresponding minimum-geometry transistor delay [10, 14]. By studying the effects of technology scaling on traditional microprocessor architecture, Agarwal *et al.* predict that for a $35nm$ technology, the latency to transmit a signal across the chip in a top-level metal wire will vary between 12 and 32 clock cycles, depending on the frequency of the system clock. Maybe even more importantly, they confirm the expectation that the fraction of the total chip area that can be reached in a single clock cycle will be quite small, likely not higher than 2% [1]. In fact, while the number of gates reachable in a cycle will not change significantly and the on-chip bandwidth will continue to grow, the percentage of the die reachable within one cycle is constantly decreasing. Hence, a major design paradigm shift must occur because designs will be bound by the amount of state and logic that can be reached within the required number of clock cycles (communication bound) and not anymore by the number of transistors that can be integrated on a single die (computation bound) [11].

*This research was supported in part by the NSF under the project ITR (CCR-0225610), by the SRC, and by the GSRC.

CODES+ISSS'03, October 1–3, 2003, Newport Beach, California, USA.
ACM 1-58113-742-7/03/0010.

2. THE IMPACT OF WIRE LATENCY

While it has been demonstrated that interconnect impose primary limits on latency, energy dissipation, signal integrity, and design productivity for gigascale integration (GSI) [14], we focus here on the disruptive role played by interconnect latency with respect to traditional design practices [6]. The majority of today's commercial chips are realized using design flows that are based on synchronous design methodologies and are centered around the separation of two main stages: logic synthesis and physical design. In synchronous design, the chip operates under the control of a common clock signal, the system clock. This assumption, which strongly simplifies the system design and verification, translates into a main requirement: the delay of each combinational path (i.e., a signal path leaving a latch and traversing only combinational logic and wires before ending with another latch) must be smaller than the system clock period. Hence, the slowest combinational path (critical path) dictates the maximum operating frequency for the overall chip. But, since it is often the case that the operating frequency is given *a priori* as a design specification, each combinational path that presents a delay longer than the desired clock period in the final layout must be handled as a design exception that needs to be fixed. To fix these exceptions, designers use various techniques from wire buffering and transistor resizing to rerouting wires, replacing or resynthesizing modules, and even redesigning entire portions of the system. These techniques often force designers to many costly iterations between the various stages of the design flow before converging to a correct layout (*timing closure problem*). Among them, wire buffering is perhaps the most efficient but it carries precise limitations, because there is an optimal number of buffers that can be inserted on a wire of a given length to achieve a minimum transmission delay. If the required clock period is still smaller, it is necessary to go beyond wire buffering and break the long wire into smaller segments by inserting memory elements like latches or flip-flops (*wire pipelining*). This operation trades-off fixing a wire exception with increasing its latency by one or more clock cycles and allows to drive long wires with the same clock signal used to control short wires and logic gates. An alternative to wire pipelining is to drive long wires with slower clocks, thus effectively implementing the chip as a *multi-clock* system, where many isochronic regions exchange data at a speed slower than the one at which they operate. Finally, it is possible to avoid using clock mechanisms to drive long wires altogether and adopt instead *asynchronous* communication protocols to build globally-asynchronous locally-synchronous architectures (GALS). The common point among all these options is the fact that the chip must be regarded as a *distributed system* and this invalidates the main assumption of the synchronous design methodology. While this important consequence is well-understood for the case of multi-clock and GALS implementations, recent works on combining wire buffering and wire pipelining [8, 12] seem to neglect the key difference between inserting combinational buffers versus inserting latches or flip-flops. In fact, while the former are *stateless repeaters*, the latter are *stateful repeaters*, i.e. they are sequential elements that must be initialized and whose insertion modifies the latency (expressed in number of clock cycles) between the chip modules lying at the two extremes of the pipelined wire. In general, to initialize these elements and to interface them to the surrounding control logic, which was derived assumed a different communication latency, a certain amount of redesign must be performed with negative consequences on design productivity.

Finally, it must be noticed that techniques combining global placement and retiming may help avoiding the need of wire pipelining as long as the original design specification contains a sufficient number of latches that can be distributed along the interconnect paths [9]. However, retiming carries as an intrinsic limitation the fact that the number of latches on any feedback loop in the design must remain constant.

3. LATENCY-INSENSITIVE DESIGN

Latency-insensitive design [3, 5] is a methodology that guarantees the robustness of the system's functionality and performance with respect to arbitrary latency variations. The foundation of latency-insensitive design is the theory of latency-insensitive protocols [4]. A latency-insensitive protocol controls communication among components of a patient system, a synchronous system whose functionality depends only on the order of each signals events and not on their exact timing. Designers can model the chip as a synchronous system whose modules communicate by exchanging signals on a set of point-to-point channels. The protocol guarantees that the system, if composed of functionally correct modules, behaves correctly, independent from the channel delays. Consequently, it is possible to automatically synthesize a hardware implementation of the system such that its functional behavior is robust with respect to large variations in communication latency. In practice, the channel implementation does not necessarily have a point-to-point structure. Still, the methodology orthogonalizes computation and communication because it separates the module design from the choice of the communication architecture, while enabling both *ad-hoc* wire pipelining and the automatic synthesis of each component interface logic. This separation is useful in several ways:

- it simplifies the system specification thanks to the synchronous hypothesis (designers can assume that intermodule communication takes one virtual clock cycle);
- it facilitates the fixing of design exceptions due to long global wires, because any number of special stateful repeaters (*relay stations*) can be inserted on them;
- it permits the exploration of tradeoffs in deriving the communication architecture up to the design process' late stages, because the protocol guarantees that the interface logic can absorb arbitrary latency variations.

While originally conceived to ease wire pipelining in single-clock chips, latency-insensitive design can be used also as a formal framework to develop tools for the automatic deploying of synchronous designs on distributed architectures, like GALS [7].

Considering the reports on the increasing usage of wire pipelining in high-performance microprocessor design [15] and the fact that high-end microprocessor designers have traditionally anticipated the challenges that ASIC designers are going to face in working with the next process generation, we think that latency-insensitive design represents a promising avenue for on-chip communication design with DSM technologies.

4. REFERENCES

[1] V. Agarwal, M. S. Hrishikesh, S. W. Keckler, and D. Burger. Clock rate versus ipc: The end of the road for conventional microarchitectures. In *27th Annual Intl. Symposium on Computer Architecture*, pages 248–259, June 2000.

[2] M. Bohr. Interconnect Scaling - The Real Limiter to High Performance ULSI. *IEEE International Electron Devices Meeting*, pages 241–244, Dec. 1995.

[3] L. P. Carloni, K. L. McMillan, A. Saldanha, and A. L. Sangiovanni-Vincentelli. A methodology for "correct-by-construction" latency insensitive design. In *Proc. Intl. Conf. on Computer-Aided Design*, pages 309–315. IEEE, Nov. 1999.

[4] L. P. Carloni, K. L. McMillan, and A. L. Sangiovanni-Vincentelli. Latency insensitive protocols. In N. Halbwachs and D. Peled, editors, *Proc. of the 11th Intl. Conf. on Computer-Aided Verification*, volume 1633, pages 123–133, Trento, Italy, July 1999. Springer Verlag.

[5] L. P. Carloni, K. L. McMillan, and A. L. Sangiovanni-Vincentelli. Theory of latency-insensitive design. *IEEE Transactions on Computer-Aided Design of Integrated Circuits and Systems*, 20(9):1059–1076, Sept. 2001.

[6] L. P. Carloni and A. L. Sangiovanni-Vincentelli. Coping with latency in SOC design. *IEEE Micro*, 22(5):24–35, Sep-Oct 2002.

[7] L. P. Carloni and A. L. Sangiovanni-Vincentelli. A formal modeling framework for deploying synchronous designs on distributed architectures. In *FMGALS 2003: Formal Methods for Globally Asynchronous Locally Asynchronous Architecture*, Sept. 2003.

[8] P. Cocchini. Concurrent flip-flop and repeater insertion for high-performance integrated circuits. In *Proc. Intl. Conf. on Computer-Aided Design*, pages 268–273, 2002.

[9] J. Cong and X. Yuan. Multilevel global placement with retiming. In *Proc. of the Intl. Symposium on Physical Design*, pages 208–213, June 2003.

[10] J. A. Davis, R. Venkatesan, A. Kaloyeros, M. Beylansky, S. Souri, K. Banerjee, K. Saraswat, A. Rahman, R. Reif, and J. Meindl. Interconnect Limits on Gigascale Integration (GSI) in the 21st Century. *Proc. of the IEEE*, 89(3):305–324, Mar. 2001.

[11] R. Ho, K. Mai, and M. Horowitz. The Future of Wires. *Proc. of the IEEE*, 89(4):490–504, Apr. 2001.

[12] R. Lu, Z. G, C. Koh, and J. Chao. Flip-Flop and Repeater Insertion for Early Interconnect Planning. In *Proc. European Design and Test Conf.*, Mar. 2002.

[13] D. Matzke. Will Physical Scalability Sabotage Performance Gains? *IEEE Computer*, 8(9):37–39, Sept. 1997.

[14] J. D. Meindl. Interconnect opportunites for gigascale integration. *IEEE Micro*, 2003.

[15] E. Sprangle and D. Carmean. Increasing Processor Performance by Implementing Deeper Pipelines. In *29th Annual Intl. Symposium on Computer Architecture*, pages 25–36. IEEE, May 2002.

Invited Talk

Architecture and Synthesis for Multi-Cycle On-Chip Communication

Jason Cong, Yiping, Fan, Guoling Han, Xun Yang, Zhiru Zhang
Computer Science Department, University of California, Los Angeles
Los Angeles, CA 90095, USA
{cong, fanyp, leohgl, yangxun, zhiruz}@cs.ucla.edu

1. INTRODUCTION

There are two important inflection points in the development of deep sub-micron (DSM) process technologies. The first point is when the average interconnect delay exceeds the gate delay, which happened during mid 1990s and led to the so-called timing closure problem. The second point is when single-cycle full chip synchronization is no longer possible, which is about to happen soon. It can been shown that, even with the aggressive interconnect optimization techniques (e.g., buffer insertion and wire-sizing), 5 clock cycles are still needed to go from corner-to-corner for the die of 28.3mm×28.3mm in the 0.07µm technology generation, assuming a 5.63GHz clock by 2006 predicted in ITRS'01 [5].

This clearly suggests that multi-cycle on-chip communication is a necessity in multi-gigahertz synchronous designs. However, it is not supported in the current design tools and methodologies, as most of these implicitly assume that full chip synchronization in a single clock cycle is feasible.

To address the multi-cycle communication problem, one can explore the following design methodologies:

1) Asynchronous design: The state transitions of an asynchronous design are triggered by events instead of periodic clocks. This makes asynchronous designs operate correctly, regardless of the delays on gates and wires. However, due to the lack of design tools and performance overhead, it only applies to a very limited class of circuits. In general, it is unclear whether asynchronous designs can yield high performance in practice.

2) Global asynchronous locally synchronous (GALS) design: In a GALS design, all major modules are designed in accordance with proven synchronous clocking disciplines. Each module is run from its own local clock. Data exchange between any two modules strictly follows a full handshake protocol. GALS hopes to combine the advantages of synchronous and asynchronous design methodologies. However, the overhead for the "self-timed wrapper" may compromise both performance and area of the design.

3) Synchronous design with multi-cycle communication: Synchronous design is still by far the most popular design methodology. It is well understood and supported by the mature CAD toolset. However, the traditional synchronous design flow assumes that the clock signal can reach the entire chip in a single clock cycle, which is no longer true for multi-gigahertz design in nanometer technologies. In this paper, we present a new micro-architecture and a novel synthesis methodology for synchronous designs with multi-cycle communication.

Our contributions are as follows: (i) We propose a *Regular Distributed Register (RDR)* micro-architecture which offers high regularity and direct support of multi-cycle communication. (ii) We develop a set of novel architectural synthesis algorithms to efficiently synthesize behavior-level designs onto the RDR architecture.

CODES+ISSS'03, October 1–3, 2003, Newport Beach, California, USA.
ACM 1-58113-742-7/03/0010.

2. REGULAR DISTRIBUTED REGISTER ARCHITECTURE

The RDR architecture divides the entire chip into an array of islands. The registers are distributed to each island, and the island size is chosen so that all local computation and communication within an island can be performed in a single clock cycle. Figure 1 illustrates an example of RDR architecture.

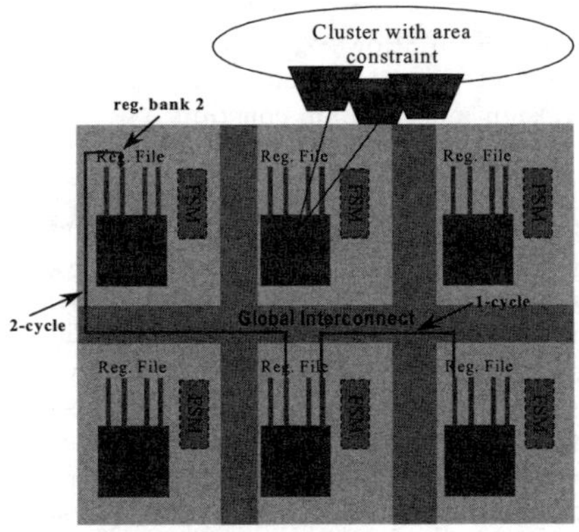

Figure 1. A 2×3 island-based RDR architecture.

Each island consists of the following components:

1) *Local Computational Cluster (LCC)*: The functional elements in an LCC provide the computational power of the circuit. They might be NAND gates, multiplexors (MUX), multipliers, or ALUs, etc. The size of the LCC is subject to a certain area constraint.

2) *Register file*: The dedicated local storages reside in the register file, which can be partitioned into *k* banks (where *k* is the maximum number of cycles needed to communicate across the chip) such that registers in bank *i* will hold the results for *i* cycles for communicating with another island that is *i* cycles away.

3) *Finite State Machine (FSM)*: Each island contains a local controller (i.e., an FSM) to control the behaviors of the computational elements and registers.

The RDR architecture is similar to recently proposed distributed-register architecture (DRA) [3] in the sense that both of these architectures distribute registers close to the local computational units, support multi-cycle communication, and allow concurrent computation and communication. However, unlike DRA, the RDR architecture is highly regular, which greatly facilitates the interconnect delay estimation. Interconnect delay can be easily estimated from the island indices of the source and the destination. Moreover, the RDR architecture has the advantage in that by varying the size of the basic island, one can easily target different clock periods and systematically explore the cycle time vs. latency tradeoff. More details of the RDR architecture are available in [1].

3. ARCHITECTURAL SYNTHESIS FOR MULTI-CYCLE COMMUNICATION

Our *architectural synthesis system for multi-cycle communication (MCAS)* is built on top of the RDR architecture. The overall design flow is shown in Figure 2.

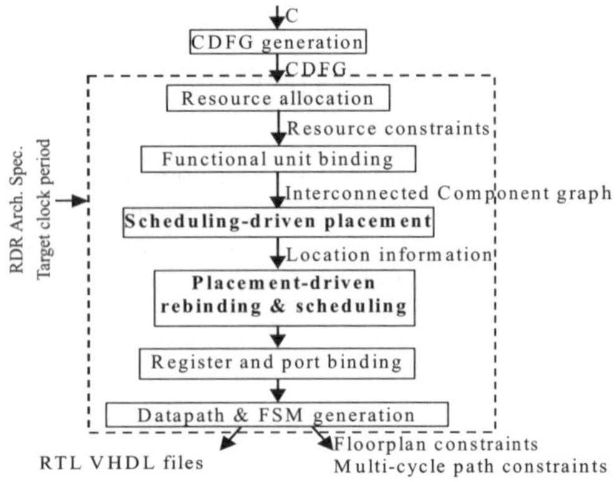

Figure 2. MCAS architectural synthesis system

Given the target clock period and the RDR architecture specification (including the island structure, functional unit library and delay table), MCAS starts with a synthesizable C description. It first generates the control data flow graph (CDFG) from the behavioral descriptions through an intermediate representation of the SUIF compiler [7].

At the front-end, MCAS performs resource allocation, followed by an initial functional unit binding. It uses the time-constrained force-directed scheduling (FDS) algorithm [4] to obtain the resource allocation. After the FDS-based resource allocation, it performs a similar algorithm in [3] to bind operation nodes to functional units for minimizing the number of potential data transfers among the components with the same types. Then an interconnected component graph (ICG) is derived from the bound CDFG.

At the core, MCAS performs the scheduling-driven placement, which takes the ICG as input, places the components in the island structure of the RDR architecture, and returns the island index of each component. After the scheduling-driven placement, both the CDFG schedule and the layout information are produced. To further minimize the schedule latency, it performs the placement-driven rescheduling-and-rebinding. The algorithm is based on the force-directed list-scheduling framework, and integrates simultaneous rebinding.

At the backend, MCAS performs register and port binding followed by datapath and distributed controllers generation. The final outputs of MCAS include the RT-level VHDL files for logic synthesis, floorplan and multi-cycle path constraints for place-and-rout. If the final design cannot meet the performance requirement, we can adjust the clock period and the basic island size by binary search and redo the synthesis.

The algorithmic details of the MCAS system are available in [2].

4. EXPERIMENTAL RESULTS

We implemented our MCAS system in C++/UNIX environments. Altera's Quartus II version 2.2 [6] is used to implement the datapath part into a real FPGA device, Stratix™ EP1S40F1508C5.

By comparing MCAS with the conventional architectural synthesis flow, which is based on the centralized register file architecture, we achieved a clock period improvement of 33% and a total latency improvement of 24% on average. We also did comparison with a commercial tool, Synopsys' Behavioral Compiler [8], and obtained the similar performance gain.

5. ACKNOWLEDGMENT

This research is partially sponsored by National Science Foundation under award CCR-0096383, MARCO/DARPA Gigascale Silicon Research Center, Semiconductor Research Center under 2001-TJ-910, and Altera Corporation under the California MICRO program.

6. REFERENCES

[1] J. Cong, Y. Fan, X. Yang and Z. Zhang, "Architecture and Synthesis for Multi-Cycle Communication," *in Proceedings of 2003 International Symposium on Physical Design*, pp. 190-196, Apr. 2003.

[2] J. Cong, Y. Fan, G. Han, X. Yang and Z. Zhang, "Architectural Synthesis Integrated with Global Placement for Multi-Cycle Communication," *to appear in Proc. of International Conference on Computer Aided Design*, Nov. 2003.

[3] D. Kim, J. Jung, S. Lee, J. Jeon and K. Choi, "Behavior-to-Placed RTL Synthesis with Performance-Driven Placement," *in Proceedings of International Conference on Computer Aided Design*, pp. 320-326, Nov. 2001.

[4] P. Paulin and J. Knight, "Force-Directed Scheduling for Behavioral Synthesis of ASICs," *in IEEE Trans. on CAD*, vol. 8(6), pp. 661-679, Jun. 1989.

[5] Semiconductor Industry Association, International Technology Roadmap for Semiconductors, 2001.

[6] Altera Web Site, http://www.altera.com.

[7] SUIF Compiler, http://suif.stanford.edu.

[8] Synopsys Web Site, http://www.synopsys.com.

Panel

System-Level Design Tools: Who Needs Them, Who Has Them, and How Much Should They Cost?

Organizer: Reinaldo Bergamaschi
IBM
T.J. Watson Research Centre
Yorktown Heights, NY 10598 USA
+1-914-945-3903
berga@us.ibm.com

Organizer & Moderator: Grant Martin
Cadence Berkeley Labs
1995 University Avenue, Suite 460
Berkeley, CA 94704 USA
+1-501-647-2804
gmartin@cadence.com

Panelists

Gary Smith
Chief Analyst, Design and Engineering, Gartner-Dataquest, USA

Pierre Paulin
Director, SoC Platform Automation, STMicroelectronics, Canada

Roger Fordham
Director, Performance Excellence, Motorola, Global Software Group, USA

Pete Hardee
Director, Product Marketing, CoWare, USA

Brian Bailey
Chief Technologist, Design Verification and Test Division, Mentor Graphics, USA

SUMMARY

CAD vendors are always faced with the question of what tools to develop and how much can they charge for them. Designers on the other hand have real problems to solve and before investing in tools they have to assess how much a given tool will actually save them. CAD vendors and designers have to estimate the savings in design time and cost that a tool may provide and compare that with the existing way of doing things, to determine if the investment in tool creation is justified. For example, if a misguided architectural decision causes weeks of delay because of missing performance targets, then a tool for early architectural analysis may be very valuable. System-level design poses exactly these types of questions because it involves optimizations and analyses across many domains, from software, to architecture, to cycle-time, and is done very early in the design cycle where it has a profound impact.

How much improvement in productivity and overall design quality (e.g., timing, area, and power) can be attained by current and future generations of system-level tools? If designers believe such improvements can be obtained, are they prepared to pay the appropriate price for the tools? Or do system-level CAD vendors still need to make believers out of designers?

This panel will bring together industry experts to review the current and future industry needs for system-level design technologies as well as discuss how much saving in design time and cost such tools can hope to achieve and whether the designers believe the price is right for the return they can get.

1. Pierre Paulin, STMicroelectronics

System-level design (SLD) tools are needed by an increasing proportion of SoC designers, both for ASIC's and ASSP's (Application-Specific Standard Products). Increasingly though, they are also needed by SoC customers to develop applications on top of increasingly programmable and/or configurable SoC platforms. Most major system houses and leading semiconductor design and manufacturing companies are actively using SLD tools. Matlab is one example that is frequently cited. The use of C++-based simulation tools (e.g SystemC coupled with in-house domain-specific extensions), is increasingly common. A significant proportion of SLD tools are developed in-house (or contracted to suppliers), in order to accelerate product design and, more frequently, to support the use and programming of complex SoC's by their customers.

This situation is reminiscent of the mid-80's, where ASIC design tools were primarily developed in-house, before the transition of this role to the current leading CAD companies. In most cases, semiconductor companies provide the tools free (or at cost), as a means to leverage higher chip volumes. This situation will continue in the short-term, but there is a need for a new business model to enable independent companies to recoup the significant R&D investment needed in SLD tools. For example, this could be a risk-sharing model where the entry cost of an SLD tool remains within current CAD budget levels, but where the tool provider participates in the upside of any product success.

2. Roger Fordham, Motorola

What Do I Need? In new product development I have two big problems; the first relates to small devices, what we call radios, terminals, phones; the second relates to large systems, what I'll call Infrastructure Systems. The two problems I have are related but of vastly different scale (several orders of magnitude) and therefore complexity, neither problem can be solved today with current technology! The problem I have with terminal devices is the rapidly changing user/consumer/market requirements and the global nature of these markets necessitates an extremely flexible, agile, and short cycle-time product and service development process. This would

CODES+ISSS '03, October 1-3, 2003, Newport Beach, California, USA.
ACM 1-58113-742-7/03/0010.

lend itself to a model-based "push-button" development process, with lots of molecular level reuse of previously developed software assets. My problem with infrastructure system development stems from not wanting to commit large amounts of financial ($100m+), human (200+ engineers), and time (2-3 years) resources to a solution only to find that it doesn't meet customer needs. Again this lends itself to model-based simulations of solution architectures against feature and performance specifications so we can have a high probability that a proposed solution will meet market needs.

What Can I Do? As you sit there reading these words, for even the simplest end-to-end terminal product, we can't build a model of requirements, simulate them, automatically transform these requirements into a design and then into code, automatically develop test cases, execute them, and feed the results back into model refinements in a closed loop manner until the product requirements model is validated, and then "print". As for the problem in the infrastructure domain . . . .

My Challenge for You: Move the system and product development business out of the stone age and into an industrial strength, fast, high quality, "correct by construction" methodology so we could all get on with using all these wonderful products we are conceiving rather than getting old worrying about yield, post-release quality, rework, cost of poor quality, and low margins and high R&D costs. As to how much these super development engines would cost I have this to say: stop pushing the technology and start pushing quantified ROI. If you can get there faster to market with a better ROI on the tool than on a human then we would use humans for what they are best suited for, coming up with and consuming new product and service ideas! Where's the Vision?

3. Gary Smith, Gartner-Dataquest

The move from RTL Design to ESL Design brings with it a new and much different design focus. RTL Design, as with Gate level Design in the 1980s, was a way to design one of the semiconductor components of an electronic system. ESL Design is the design of the entire electronic system, which constitutes the majority of an ever-increasing number of today's systems. ES Level tools are taking the lead in two major types of designs. The first is a large highly complex design dominated by the SoC. This is where the "what if analysis" of your ESL design tools becomes invaluable. Still, today many systems are architected on a white board. Tools like Matlab allow you to take a scratch pad look at your algorithmic development. Now think of tools that will set the requirements as a constraint-driven, formally provable specification and then produce multiple architectures across a broad spectrum of related requirements. Not only do you get the optimal system design, you could just find a design that falls on the periphery of your requirements that will become a new related product direction. The other type of design is a smaller, usually consumer related embedded design where the goal is not to produce a system but to produce a family of products based on variations to the major system requirements. This is being done today in markets such as cell phones. Automating this process saves a huge amount of time and money.

In the past the tools needed for the next level of design have cost five times as much as the previous level (i.e. Gate Level to RT Level). There is no reason to expect that won't happen again. Above all don't compare designing a system to designing a component. Not only is the task much larger, the ROI is at least ten times greater. Keep in mind once the ESL Design is passed to the RT Level you now have an implementation job on your hands. Modifying designs on the fly, at the RT Level, will become a thing of the past. Also, consider the significant reduction of verification effort given that you have a formally provable, constraint driven specification that has been thoroughly simulated at the ES Level. Keep in mind the entire electronic system will have been simulated - both hardware and software together. Delays due to software "integration" will also be a thing of the past.

4. Pete Hardee, CoWare

The complexity crisis is hitting the industry - finally. Complexity is highest in the Digital Convergence products driving SoCs and is driving the rise to prominence of three design problems - functional validation of the system specification, architecture design, and hardware-software verification - which are overtaking silicon implementation issues to dominate the design flow. Hence, architects, system integrators and verification specialists will lead the mass adoption of system-level design (SLD) tools, and the Transaction Level is the dominant abstraction level at which they will work.

The EDA industry is around 2% of the size of the semiconductor industry that feeds it. Research shows that the more successful semiconductor companies spend 3% of revenues on tools while the least successful spend only 1%. Research has also found that 80% of a product's unit and development costs are set in the first 20% of its development - in other words, all the value is up front. As a marketer, I believe in the link between price and value. The value of SLD tools is now demonstrably high. Expect to pay for that value, or expect to be unsuccessful.

5. Brian Bailey, Mentor Graphics

Abstraction shifts are usually expected to provide orders of magnitude productivity increases. However, accomplishing this assumes that it is attacking the bottleneck in the development process. While design is tough, it is not the biggest problem being faced by many people in the industry today - for most companies it is verification. Our ability to verify is constraining the rate at which we can consume the available silicon. We thus need to be looking at new ways to automate, accelerate and optimize the verification path.

If we look at system level tools that are gaining some success in the market, these are the ones that have a focus on the analysis and verification capabilities. If we can get an assurance that the specification is correct and that there are no significant architectural problems, then the cost to implement is fairly low. We still need better tools to perform those two functions and we need better methodologies that allow for the verification of implementations within the context of a specification. We also have no ability to measure the success or confidence levels of the verification that we have done. This requires some fundamental new research to define accurate and affordable notions of functional coverage.

Executable specifications are a must for future productivity, but I believe that this will provide an automation path for verification and not for design. The design may be an interpretation of the specification but will not, cannot, be automatically derived from it.

Invited Talk

Driving Forces Behind SOC Development

Mojy C. Chian, Ph.D.
Sr. VP, Core Technology
Mindspeed Technologies

Abstract

Over the next five years what will drive higher levels of integration, methodology, and innovation in System On Chip (SOC) development? Will there be more emphasis on application specific chips, faster migration to submicron process technologies, exotic packages, revolutionary design automation tools, and IP reuse? This will depend on the economic value they present. For instance, the fast pace of process technologies over the past several years has been a two edged sword. On one side, it has created a great opportunity to integrate many functional blocks on a die. On the other end, high mask cost and long yield maturity posed major development cost and time-to-production issues. System In a Package (SIP) might be a more viable solution than a single die SOC for a higher level of integration of systems with diverse technology requirements.

In this presentation, we will examine the vectors of cost, methodology, technology, and their interrelationship in SOC development. We will stress that now, more than ever, methodology and technology choices for SOC design and implementation have to be economically driven. If the high mortality rate of small chip companies and depressed earnings of larger ones over the past three years are any indication, we will see renewed interest in business fundamentals such as total available market (TAM) and return on investment (ROI). This is perhaps one of the most vivid changes we will all experience in the post bubble era.

Biography

M. Chian

Mojy Chian is currently Senior Vice President of Core Technology for Mindspeed Technologies. He is responsible for all common engineering and R&D activities including ASIC implementation, high performance IP and DSP core development, package engineering, and design automation.

He joined Rockwell Semiconductor Systems in 1998 and was appointed Vice President of Design Automation and IP Infrastructure for Conexant Systems. Prior to joining Rockwell he spent ten years at Intersil (Harris Semiconductor). His last position with Intesil was Director of Design Systems. He received his BS, MS, and PhD in Electrical Engineering as well as an MS in Applied Math from Florida Tech. He holds two US patents, has co-authored over 30 technical publications, and has served as adjunct professor at Florida Tech.

CODES+ISSS'03, October 1-3, 2003, Newport Beach, California, USA.
ACM 1-58113-742-7/03/0010.

Panel

Driving Agenda for Systems Research

Organizer and Moderator:
N. Dutt
University of California, Irvine

Panelists:

S. Basu
NSF

M. Hirata
STARC

D. J. Radack
DARPA

J. Sztipanovits
ACM SIGBED & Vanderbilt University

This panel will bring together members who are responsible for leading research directions in embedded systems, Systems-on-Chip (SOCs), and the attendant software and hardware, through their roles in funding research, coordinating industrial consortia, chairing professional societies, and building a community of systems researchers. The panelists will share their views on research challenges in systems, opportunities for research funding, and the role of academics, tool vendors, industry, and consortia in solving challenges for the design and development of next generation embedded systems.

CODES+ISSS'03, October 1-3, 2003, Newport Beach, California, USA.
ACM 1-58113-742-7/03/0010.

Design Optimization of Mixed Time/Event-Triggered Distributed Embedded Systems

Traian Pop, Petru Eles, Zebo Peng
Dept. of Computer and Information Science, Linköping University
{trapo, petel, zebpe}@ida.liu.se

Abstract

Distributed embedded systems implemented with mixed, event-triggered and time-triggered task sets, which communicate over bus protocols consisting of both static and dynamic phases, are emerging as the new standard in application areas such as automotive electronics. In a previous paper, we have developed a holistic timing analysis and scheduling approach for this category of systems. Based on this result, in the present paper, new design problems are solved, which we identified as characteristic for such hybrid systems: partitioning of the system functionality into time-triggered and event-triggered domains and the optimization of parameters corresponding to the communication protocol. We addressed both problems in the context of a heuristic which performs mapping and scheduling of the system functionality. We demonstrated the efficiency of the proposed technique with extensive experiments.

Categories and Subject Descriptors

B.8.2 [Performance and Reliability]: Performance Analysis and Design Aids;
C.1.4 [Processor Architectures]: Distributed Systems;
C.3 [Special-Purpose and Application-Based Systems]: Real-Time and Embedded Systems;
D.4.1 [Operating Systems]: Scheduling;
J.6 [Computer-aided Engineering]: Computer Aided Design (CAD);

General Terms

Algorithms, Performance, Design.

Keywords

Distributed embedded systems, real-time systems, time-triggered, event-triggered, mixed communication protocols, automotive applications.

1. Introduction

There are two basic approaches for handling tasks in real-time applications [7]. In the event-triggered approach (ET), activities are initiated whenever a particular event is noted. In the time-triggered (TT) approach, activities are initiated at predetermined points in time. There has been a long debate in the real-time and embedded systems communities concerning the advantages of each approach [1, 8, 12].

If we look at the communication infrastructure, message passing activities can be triggered either dynamically, in response to an event, as with the controller area network (CAN) bus [3], or statically, at predetermined moments in time, as in the case of time-division multiple access (TDMA) protocols and, in particular, the time-triggered protocol (TTP) [7].

CODES+ISSS'03, October 1-3, 2003, Newport Beach, California, USA.

In [8] the authors compare the ET and TT approaches from an industrial perspective (considering, in particular, automotive applications). Their conclusion is that one has to choose the right approach depending on the particularities of the actual tasks. This means not only that there is no single "best" approach to be used, but also that inside a certain application the two approaches can be used together, some tasks being TT and others ET.

In this context, it is not surprising that several activities have been started aiming at the development and standardization of bus protocols which support both static (ST) and dynamic (DYN) communication. Such a protocol has been suggested in [9] and [10]. Also, the first mixed protocol has been proposed by a consortium, to be used in automotive applications [6]. In [4], the authors describe the so called Universal Communication Model (UCM), a framework for modelling at a high level of abstraction the communication infrastructure in automotive applications.

New, highly sophisticated automotive applications consist of both TT and ET task sets implemented on top of complex distributed architectures based on mixed ST/DYN bus protocols. In [13] we have presented an approach to scheduling and schedulability analysis for such mixed time/event triggered systems. Such an analysis and scheduling procedure constitutes the fundament for any synthesis approach aiming at an efficient, highly optimized implementation of a distributed application which is also guaranteed to meet the timing constraints.

Starting from such a holistic scheduling and analysis, this paper is the first one to address specific design issues of hybrid ET/TT systems like those outlined above. The proposed approach solves the problems of partitioning a certain functionality into ET and TT, mapping the functionality on a distributed architecture and adjusting the parameters of the communication protocol such that the timing constraints of the final implementation are guaranteed.

The paper is organized in 7 sections. In the next section we present the architecture of the distributed systems and the application model that we are studying. Section 3 describes briefly the holistic scheduling and schedulability analysis we have developed in [13]. Some specific optimization issues are presented in Section 4. Section 5 states the design problem we intend to solve and outlines our solution, while Section 6 presents some experimental results. The last section presents our conclusions.

2. System Architecture and Application Model

2.1 Hardware Architecture and Bus Access

We consider architectures consisting of nodes connected by a unique broadcast communication channel. Each node consists of a communication controller, a CPU, memories (RAM, ROM), and an I/O interface to sensors and actuators (see Figure 1).

We model the bus access scheme using the Universal Communication Model [4]. The bus access is organized as consecutive cycles, each with the duration T_{bus}. We consider that the communication cycle is partitioned into static and dynamic phases (Figure 1). Static phases consist of time slots, and during a slot only one node is allowed to send ST messages; this is the node associated to that particular slot.

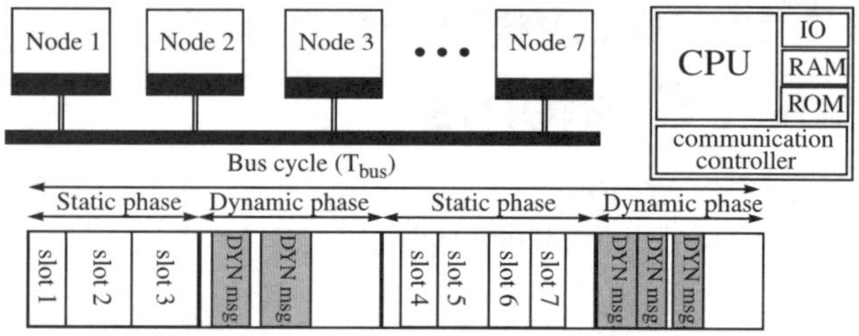

Figure 1. System Architecture

During a dynamic phase, all nodes are allowed to send DYN messages and the conflicts between nodes trying to send simultaneously are solved by an arbitration mechanism based on priorities assigned to messages. The bus access cycle has the same structure during each period T_{bus}. Every node has a communication controller that implements the static and dynamic protocol services. The controller runs independently of the node's CPU.

2.2 Software Architecture

For the systems we are studying, we have designed a software architecture which runs on the CPU of each node. The main component of the software architecture is a real-time kernel which supports both time-triggered and event-triggered activities. An activity is defined as either the execution of a task or as the transmission of a message on the bus. For the TT activities, the kernel relies on a static schedule table which contains all the information needed to take decisions on activation of TT tasks or transmission of ST messages. For the ET tasks, the kernel maintains a prioritized ready queue in which tasks are placed whenever their triggering event has occurred and they are ready for activation, or when they have been pre-empted.

The real-time kernel will always activate a TT task at the particular time fixed for that task in the schedule table. If at that moment, an ET task is running on that node, that task will be pre-empted and placed into the ready queue according to its priority. If no tasks are active, ET tasks are extracted from the ready queue and are (re)activated. ET tasks can pre-empt each other based on their priority.

The transmission of messages is handled in a similar way: for each node, the sending and receiving times of ST messages are stored in the schedule table; the DYN messages are organized in a prioritized ready queue. ST messages will be placed at predetermined time moments into a bus slot assigned to the sending node. DYN messages can be potentially sent during any dynamic phase and conflicts are solved by the communication controllers based on message priorities. Once the transmission of a DYN message has started, no other message will be sent on the bus until the current transmission finishes.

TT activities are triggered based on a local clock available in each processing node. The synchronization of local clocks throughout the system is provided by the communication protocol.

2.3 Application Model

We model an application as a set of task graphs. Nodes represent tasks and arcs represent communication (and implicitly dependency) between the connected tasks.

- A task can belong either to the TT or to the ET domain.
- Communication between tasks mapped to different nodes is performed by message passing over the bus. Such a message passing is modelled as a communication task inserted on the arc connecting the sender and the receiver tasks. The communication time between tasks mapped on the same node is considered to be part of the task execution time. Thus, such a communication activity is not modelled explicitly. For the rest of the paper, when referring to messages, we consider only the communication activity over the bus.

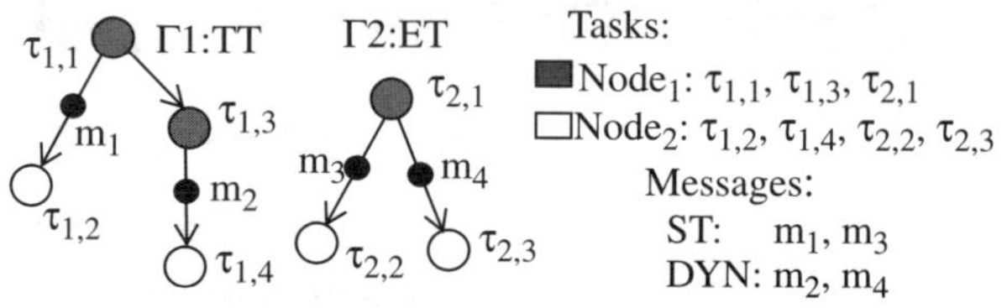

Figure 2. Application Model Example

- A message can belong either to the static (ST) or the dynamic (DYN) domain.
- All tasks in a certain task graph belong to the same domain, either ET, or TT, which is called the domain of the task graph. However, the messages belonging to a certain task graph can belong to any domain (ST or DYN). Thus, in the most general case, tasks belonging to a TT graph, for example, can communicate through both ST and DYN messages.
- Each task τ_{ij} (belonging to the task graph Γ_i), has a period T_{ij}, and a deadline D_{ij} and, when mapped on node $Proc_k$, it has a worst case execution time $C_{ij}(Proc_k)$. Each ET task also has a given priority $Prio_{ij}$.
- All tasks τ_{ij} belonging to a task graph Γ_i have the same period T_i which is the period of the task graph.
- For each message we know its size (which can be directly converted into communication time on the particular communication bus). The period of a message is identical with that of the sender task. DYN messages also have given priorities.

Figure 2 shows an application modelled as two task graphs mapped on two nodes.

In order to keep the separation between the TT and ET domains, which are based on fundamentally different triggering policies, communication between tasks in the two domains is not included in the model. Technically, such a communication is implemented by the kernel, based on asynchronous non-blocking send and receive primitives (using proxy tasks if the sender and receiver are on different nodes). Such messages are typically non-critical and are not affected by hard real-time constraints.

3. Holistic Scheduling

In [13], we introduced a scheduling and schedulability analysis approach for applications as those presented in Section 2. The algorithm constructs a correct static schedule for the TT tasks and ST messages (a schedule which meets all time constraints related to these activities) and conducts the schedulability analysis in order to check that all ET tasks meet their deadlines. Two important aspects should be noticed:

1. When performing schedulability analysis for the ET tasks and DYN messages, one has to take into consideration the interference from the statically scheduled TT tasks and ST messages.
2. Among the possible correct schedules for TT tasks and ST messages, it is important to construct one which favours, as much as possible, the schedulability of ET tasks and DYN messages.

In [13], first we developed a schedulability analysis algorithm for a set of ET tasks and DYN messages, considering a fixed given static schedule of TT tasks and ST messages. Then, we introduced a method for building a valid static schedule for the TT tasks and ST messages, which favours the schedulability of ET tasks and DYN messages. This static schedule is computed over a period T_{SS} which is equal to the least common multiplier of the periods of TT task graphs.

In order to guide the static scheduling process towards "good" solutions, we use a metric which captures the "degree of schedulability" of the ET task set. For this purpose we used a cost function similar with the one described in [15]:

$$\text{DSch} = \begin{cases} f_1 = \sum_{i=1}^{N} \sum_{j=1}^{N_i} max(0, R_{ij} - D_{ij}), \text{ if } f_1 > 0 \\ f_2 = \sum_{i=1}^{N} \sum_{j=1}^{N_i} (R_{ij} - D_{ij}), \text{ if } f_1 = 0 \end{cases}$$

• where N is the number of ET task graphs, N_i is the number of activities in the ET task graph Γ_i, and R_{ij} is the response time computed by the schedulability analysis for task τ_{ij}.

If the ET task set is not schedulable, there exists at least one task for which $R_{ij} > D_{ij}$. In this case, $f_1 > 0$ and the cost function is a metric of how far we are from achieving schedulability. If the set of ET tasks is schedulable, $f_2 \leq 0$ is used as a metric. A value $f_2 = 0$ means that the task set is "just" schedulable. A smaller value for f_2 means that the ET tasks are schedulable and a certain amount of processing capacity is still available.

4. Design Problems

Considering a hard real-time system like the one described in Section 2, several design problems emerge. There are, of course, the classical issues as selection of an architecture (e.g. number and kind of nodes), the mapping of tasks on the processing nodes, or the assignment of priorities to ET tasks and DYN messages [1, 5, 11]. However, due to the heterogeneous ET and TT nature of the application and the mixed synchronous/dynamic bus protocol, some new and very interesting problems can be identified:

- *Partitioning of the system functionality into time-triggered and event-triggered activities.* During the design process, a decision should be made on which tasks and messages will be implemented as TT/ET and ST/DYN activities, respectively. Typically, this decision is taken, based on the experience and preferences of the designer, considering aspects like the functionality implemented by the task, the hardness of the constraints, sensitivity to jitter, etc. There exists, however, a subset of tasks/messages which could be assigned to any of the domains. Decisions concerning the partitioning of this set of activities can lead to various trade-offs concerning, for example, the size of the schedule table or the schedulability properties of the system. For example, in Figure 3 we show a system with two nodes on which three tasks are mapped: τ_1 on Node_1, τ_2 and τ_3 on Node_2; τ_2 is data dependant on τ_1; worst case execution times (C_i) and deadlines (D_i) are shown in the figure. In order to keep the example simple, communication delays between τ_1 and τ_2 are ignored. When all three tasks belong to the TT domain, the system is unschedulable. In this case, either τ_2 (scheduling alternative depicted in Figure 3.a) or τ_3 (Figure 3.b) misses its deadline. If, however, τ_3 is moved into the ET domain (Figure 3.c), all tasks are schedulable (in this case, τ_2 will pre-empt the execution of τ_3).

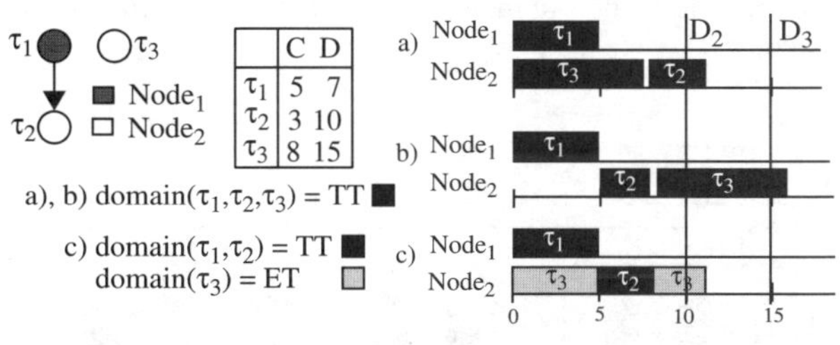

Figure 3. Partitioning into TT/ET domains

- *Determining the optimal structure of the bus access cycle.* The configuration of the bus access cycle has a strong impact on the global performance of the system. The parameters of this cycle have to be optimized such that they fit the particular application and the timing requirements. Parameters to be optimized are the number of static and dynamic phases during a communication cycle, as well as the length and order of these phases. Considering the static phases, parameters to be fixed are the order, number, and length of slots assigned to the different nodes. For example, consider the situation in Figure 4, where task τ_1 is mapped on node N_1 and sends a message m to task τ_2 which is mapped on node N_2. In case a), task τ_1 misses the start of the ST Slot_1 and, therefore, message m will be sent during the next bus cycle, causing the receiver task τ_2 to miss its deadline D_2. In case b), the order of ST slots inside the bus cycle is changed, the message m will be transmitted earlier and τ_2 will meet its deadline. The resulted situation can be further improved, as it can be seen in Figure 4.(c), where task τ_2 finishes even earlier, if the first DYN phase in the bus cycle can be eliminated without producing intolerable delays of the DYN messages (which have been ignored in this example).

The optimization problems identified above can be approached once we have solved the holistic scheduling problem outlined in Section 3 and presented in [13]. In the following section, we discuss a heuristic aiming at such a global optimization.

5. Design Heuristic

We consider a system specification and an architecture as described in Section 2. We also consider that some of the tasks are already mapped to nodes and their domain (TT or ET) is fixed. This can be the result of decisions already taken by the designer or/and because part of the functionality is inherited from previous generations of the product. However, we assume that there are tasks which are not mapped yet and some of the task graphs are not yet partitioned between the two domains. We denote with Ψ^P the set of all tasks which are not yet assigned to any of the ET or TT domains and with Ψ^M the set of all tasks which are not mapped to any node. Note that $\Psi^P \cap \Psi^M$ may be not-empty, which means that some tasks have neither a fixed domain, nor are they mapped on any node. The tasks in the set $\Psi^P \cup \Psi^M$ are those to which we refer in the rest of this paper when we discuss mapping and partitioning. None of the other tasks is affected, in terms of partitioning and mapping, by any of the design decisions. Our goal is threefold:

1. to partition the task set Ψ^P among the ET and TT domains;
2. to map the tasks in the set Ψ^M onto the nodes in the architecture;
3. to optimize the parameters of the communication protocol.

The above design tasks have to be performed with the overall goal that the timing constraints of the resulted system are satisfied. If this is achieved, we say that we have obtained a schedulable im-

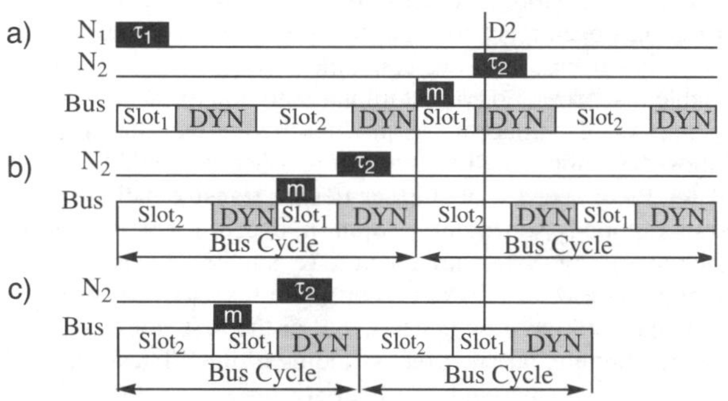

Figure 4. Optimization of Bus Access Cycle

```
01 Gen_Part, Gen_Map, Gen_Bus_Cycle
02 if TT not schedulable then
03   change partitioning (TT to ET)
04   change mapping
05   change bus cycle
06 endif
07 if TT not schedulable then stop endif
08 if ET not schedulable then
09   Mapping_and_Partitioning
10   if ET not schedulable then
11     Optimize_Bus_Access
12   endif
13 endif
```

Figure 5. Overview of the Design Heuristic

plementation of the system, which implies that the following two conditions are satisfied:

1) The tasks in the TT domain are schedulable, meaning that we were able to build a static schedule (Section 3) for all the tasks in the TT partition such that their deadlines are satisfied;

2) The tasks in the ET domain are schedulable. This means that after running the scheduling process described in Section 3, the function *DSch*, expressing the schedulability degree of the ET activities, will have a value $DSch \le 0$.

Before starting to discuss the actual heuristics, some further observations have to be made. According to the application model presented in Section 2.3, all tasks in a task graph belong to the same domain. Thus, the task set Ψ^P contains complete task graphs and, by deciding on the partitioning of a certain task, the whole task graph is assigned to either the TT or ET domain.

A similar partitioning problem, as formulated above for tasks, could be also defined at the level of messages: considering a set of messages, for each message it has to be decided if it should be transmitted in an ST phase (statically scheduled) or in a DYN phase (dynamically scheduled). In order to keep the presentation reasonably simple and given the space limitations, in this paper we consider that all messages are preassigned as ST or DYN. For the same reason, we also consider that all tasks in the set Ψ^P have a pre-assigned priority which is used if the task is assigned to the ET domain.

The design problem outlined above is a combination of subproblems, each of exponential complexity. Therefore, we have elaborated a design space exploration strategy based on the application of several heuristics in three successive steps, as shown in Figure 5:

1. The first step (lines 01-06) starts by generating an initial mapping, partitioning and bus structure, using several basic criteria (line 01). If this initial solution is not schedulable, successive transformations are applied to the partitioning, mapping, and the bus cycle, with the aim of finding a solution such that the TT tasks are schedulable. This is performed by generating configurations (in terms of partitioning, mapping and bus cycle) which are more and more favourable to the TT partition.
   The first step is stopped once a solution with a schedulable TT partition has been reached. If at the end of the first step no such solution has been found, we conclude that, given the amount of available resources, no correct implementation of the system can be generated. This decision is justified by the fact that, if under the most favorable conditions no static schedule could be generated for the TT tasks, no further design transformations could lead to a globally schedulable solution, except for modifications of the underlying system architecture (e.g adding a new node, replacing a node with a faster one or a similar replacement of the bus). If the configuration generated after the first step is not globally schedulable, but a correct schedule of the TT tasks and ST messages has been found, the heuristic moves into the second step.
2. During the second step (line 09), a partitioning and mapping algorithm tries to produce a solution such that not only the TT static schedule is correct, but also the degree of schedulability of the ET partition is as good as possible. The cost function driving the design space exploration during this step is *DSch* (see Section 3). Simultaneously with each partitioning and mapping decision, also the bus cycle is modified in order to fit the new configuration.
3. If the second step did not succeed in producing a schedulable ET partition, the third step (line 11) tries to further improve the degree of schedulability by an aggressive optimization of the bus cycle.

In the following subsections we further elaborate on the optimization steps outlined above.

5.1 The first step: Building an initial configuration

The first step starts with generating, based on a very simple and fast heuristic, a mapping and partitioning of the tasks, as well as a bus cycle (line 01 in Figure 5):

- The partitioning is performed with the only constraint to evenly distribute the load between the TT and the ET domains.
- The mapping is based on a very fast heuristic aimed at minimising inter-processor communication while keeping a balanced processor load.
- The initial bus cycle is constructed in the following two steps:
  1. The ST slots are assigned in order to the nodes such that $Node_i$ transmits during $Slot_i$ (Figure 1). The length of $Slot_i$ is set to a value which is equal to the length of the largest ST message generated by a task mapped on $Node_i$. Considering an architecture of 4 nodes, a structure like the one in Figure 6.(a) is produced after this step.
  2. Dynamic phases are introduced in order to generate a mixed ST/DYN bus cycle. We start from the rough assumption that the total length of the dynamic phases over a period T_{SS} (T_{SS} is the length of the static schedule, see Section 3) is equal to the total length of the DYN messages transmitted over the same period, which is:

$$\sum_{m_i \in DYNdomain} \frac{T_{SS}}{T_i} \cdot L_i ,$$

where T_i and L_i are the period and the length (expressed in time units) of the DYN message m_i. We set the length of a DYN phase to the length of the largest DYN message L_{DYN}^{max}. The number n of dynamic phases in each cycle can be determined from the following equation:

$$\frac{T_{SS}}{L_{ST} + n \cdot L_{DYN}^{max}} \cdot n \cdot L_{DYN}^{max} = \sum_{m_i \in DYNdomain} \frac{T_{SS}}{T_i} \cdot L_i ,$$

where L_{ST} is the total length of the static slots in a bus cycle and $L_{ST} + n\,L_{DYN}^{max}$ is the length of the bus cycle. Finally, the dynamic phases are evenly distributed inside the bus cycle. Figure 6.(b) illustrates such an initial bus configuration.

Once we have decided on the above configuration, we can run the holistic scheduling algorithm, which will lead to one of the following outcomes:

a) the system is found schedulable;

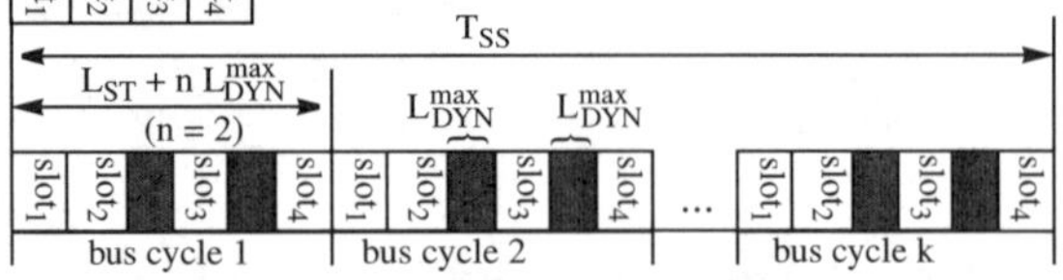

Figure 6. Initial Bus Configuration

b) the TT activities are schedulable but the ET ones are not (a valid static schedule has been built but the analysis has identified at least one ET activity for which $R_{ij} > D_{ij}$);

c) the ET activities are schedulable but the TT ones are not;

d) both ET and TT activities are not schedulable.

In the first case, the design goal has been achieved and, therefore, no further optimizations are performed. In the cases c) and d), we perform the following successive operations, aimed at achieving a schedulable TT domain (lines 03-05 in Figure 5):

1) Task graphs are moved, one by one, from the TT to the ET domain, until either the remaining TT activities are schedulable or there are no more task graphs to be moved (whole task graphs are moved and not individual tasks, because, as mentioned earlier, all tasks in a task graph belong to the same domain). The order in which task graphs are moved is based on a priority function that captures the mobility of tasks in the graph:

$$RelAvgMob(\Gamma_i) = \frac{1}{n_i} \cdot \sum_{j=1}^{n_i} \frac{D_{ij} - ASAP_{ij}}{C_{ij}}$$

where n_i is the number of tasks in the task graph Γ_i, and $ASAP_{ij}$ is the earliest possible start time for task τ_{ij}. Task graphs with a low average relative mobility are moved first, because, in principle, they are the most difficult to be scheduled statically.

2) If the TT domain still is unschedulable, TT tasks are remapped with the goal of avoiding unbalanced node utilization by TT tasks.

3) If no schedulable TT domain has been yet produced, transformations of the bus cycles are performed such that the delays produced by ST messages are reduced. In this step, a simpler and faster version of the heuristic presented in Section 5.3 is used.

If no schedulable TT domain has been produced by the above transformations, no correct implementation can be obtained with our heuristic given the available resources. If both the TT and ET domains are schedulable, we have achieved our design goal, while in the case of an unschedulable ET domain, the heuristic is continued with the second step.

5.2 The second step: Mapping and Partitioning

The mapping and partitioning step (line 09 in Figure 5) receives as an input a configuration in which the TT activities are schedulable and the ET ones are not. The algorithm is illustrated in Figure 7. It selects iteratively tasks $\tau_{ij} \in \Psi^P \cup \Psi^M$ (line 03) in order to be remapped and/or repartitioned. The order in which tasks are processed is defined by the following two rules, similar to those used in list scheduling:

1. τ_{ij} is selected only after all its predecessors in the task graph Γ_i have already been processed (these tasks are called ready).
2. Among the ready tasks, the selection is based on a priority function PF similar to the one proposed by us in [14] (line 03). This function is based on a critical path metric and it also takes into consideration the delay introduced by message passing considering the particular communication protocol, as well as the nature of the messages (ST or DYN).

Once a task τ_{ij} has been selected, its mapping and domain will be decided in a greedy fashion. If $\tau_{ij} \in \Psi^M$ (the task mapping is not fixed), it will be successively mapped to each node (lines 06-15) and for each alternative, the schedulability analysis (Section 3, [13]) returns the cost *DSch*, which captures the degree of schedulability of the produced configuration. If the domain, ET or TT, is also to be decided ($\tau_{ij} \in \Psi^P$), both alternatives are evaluated (line 08). This is performed using the function `partition` (lines 25-29). Finally, that node and domain are selected for τ_{ij} which produce the smallest value for *DSch*. If only the domain of τ_{ij} is to be decided, but the mapping is fixed, the best of the two alternatives is selected (line 19). It should be mentioned that a mapping or

```
01 while (Ψ^P∪Ψ^M ≠ ∅ and BestCost > 0) do
02    update priority function PF
03    select task τ_ij∈ Ψ^P∪Ψ^M with highest PF
04    BestCost = ∞
05    if τ_ij∈ Ψ^M then                          -- task τ_ij is not mapped
06      for (p = 1 to NrNodes)do
07        map τ_ij on Node_p and adjust bus access cycle
08        if τ_ij∈ Ψ^P then Cost,d = partition(τ_ij) -- τ_ij is not partitioned
09        else Cost = DSch; d = domain of τ_ij
10        endif
11        if BestCost > Cost then
12          BestCost = Cost; BestDomain = d;
13          BestNode = p; BestCycle = BusCycle;
14        endif
15      endfor
16    else
17      BestNode = Node on which τ_ij is mapped
18      BestCycle = BusCycle;
19      BestCost, BestDomain = partition(τ_ij);
20    endif
21    τ_ij.node = BestNode; BusCycle=BestCycle;
22    set domain(Γ_i) to BestDomain
23    Ψ^P=Ψ^P \ {τ_ij}; Ψ^M = Ψ^M \ {τ_ij}
24 end while
25 function partition(τ_ij)
26    τ_ij.domain = ET; Cost1 = DSch; d_1 = ET;
27    τ_ij.domain = TT; Cost2 = DSch; d_2 = ET;
28    return min(Cost1, Cost2) and associated d_i
29 end partition
```

Figure 7. Mapping and Partitioning algorithm

partitioning alternative is considered only if, with the resulted configuration, the TT domain is still schedulable (this aspect is not captured in Figure 7).

Whenever the mapping of a task is modified, the bus cycle has to be adjusted so that it can ensure the minimum requirements for transmitting the messages (for example, in line 07). Such an adjustment of the bus access cycle is illustrated in Figure 8, where 4 TT tasks are mapped on 3 nodes (N_1, N_2 and N_3). The number at the side of each message represents its length. Tasks mapped on different nodes communicate through ST messages and an ST slot should be able to accommodate the longest message transmitted by the associated node. The figure shows how the lengths of the slots associated with N_1 and N_2 are modified after a task has been remapped. In one case, task τ_2 is moved from N_2 to N_1 and therefore, the message $m_{1,2}$ will disappear (τ_1 and τ_2 are both mapped on N_1), while message $m_{2,4}$ will be transmitted in $Slot_1$ instead of $Slot_2$. In the second case, τ_3 is moved from N_2 to N_1, which means that $m_{1,3}$ disappears, while $m_{3,4}$ is transmitted in $Slot_1$.

5.3 The third step: Optimization of the bus cycle

It may be the case that even after the mapping and partitioning step, some ET activities are still not schedulable. In the third step (lines 10-12, Figure 5), our algorithm tries to remedy this problem by changing the parameters of the bus cycle, like ST slot lengths and order, as well as the number, length and order of the ST and DYN phases. The goal is to generate a bus access scheme which is adapt-

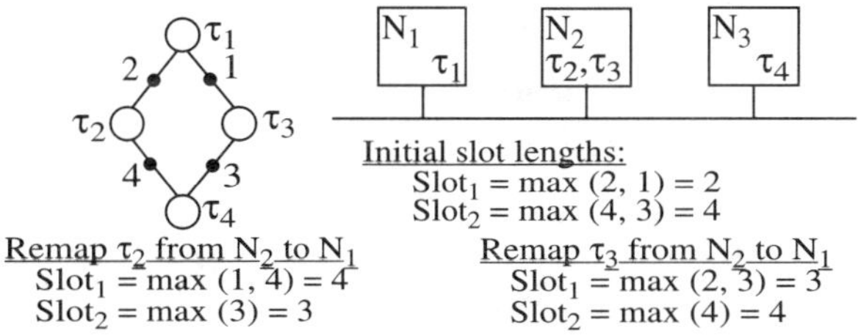

Figure 8. Adjustment of the Bus Access Cycle

ed to the particular task configuration. The heuristic is illustrated in Figure 9. The algorithm iteratively looks for the right place and size of $Slot_i$ used for transmission of ST messages from $Node_i$ (outermost two loops). $Slot_i$ is swapped with all the slots of higher order (line 03), and all alternative lengths (lines 04-05) of $Slot_i$ larger than its minimal allowed length (which is equal to the length of the largest ST message generated by a task mapped on $Node_i$) are considered. For any particular length and position of $Slot_i$, alternative lengths of the adjacent ET phase Ph_i are considered (innermost loop). For each alternative, the schedulability analysis evaluates cost *DSch*, and the solution with the lowest cost is selected. If *DSch* ≤ 0, the system is schedulable and the heuristic is stopped..

It is important to notice that the possible length π of an ET phase (line 6) includes also the value 0. Therefore, in the final bus cycle, it is not needed that each static slot is followed by a dynamic phase (see also Figure 1). Dynamic phases introduced as result of the previous steps can be eliminated by setting the length to $\pi=0$ (such a transformation is illustrated in Figure 4.c). It should be also mentioned that enlarging a slot/phase can increase the schedulability by allowing several ST/DYN messages to be transmitted quickly immediately one after another. At the same time, the following slots are delayed, which means that ST messages transmitted by nodes assigned to upcoming slots will arrive later. Therefore, the optimal schedulability will be obtained for slot and phase lengths which are not tending towards the maximum. The number of alternative slot and phase lengths to be considered by the heuristic in Figure 9 is limited by the following two factors:

1. The maximum length of a static slot or dynamic phase is fixed by the technology (e.g. 32 or 64 bits).
2. Only frames consisting of entire messages can be transmitted, which excludes several alternatives.

6. Experimental Results

In order to evaluate the proposed heuristic, we have generated a large set of applications with different characteristics. All experiments were run on an AMD Athlon 850 MHz PC. For our first experiments we considered an architecture consisting of 6 nodes. We have generated 4 sets of applications composed of 60, 75, 90, and 120 tasks respectively. Each set consists of 40 applications. The number of unmapped tasks was between 10 and the total number of tasks in the application. 10 task graphs are considered to be unassigned to any of the two domains (ET and TT). The average load on the processors is 60%. Figure 10 shows the percentage of schedulable applications obtained after the successive steps of our heuristic. By straight forward configuration we mean the mapping, partitioning and bus cycle generated at the start of step 1 (line 01 in Figure 5).This is a configuration which, in principle, could be elaborated by a careful designer without the aid of optimization tools like the one proposed in the paper. Out of the total number of applications

```
01 for i = 1 to NrNodes
02    for j = i to NrNodes
03       swap Slot_i with Slot_j
04       for all slot lengths λ > min_len(Slot_i)
05          len(Slot_i) = λ
06          for all DYN phase lengths π do
07             len(Ph_i) = π
08             if DSch ≤ 0 then stop endif
09             keep solution with smallest DSch
10          end for
11       end for
12       swap back Slot_i and Slot_j
13    end for
14    bind best position and length of Slot_i
15    bind length of Ph_i
16 end for
```

Figure 9. Bus Access Optimization

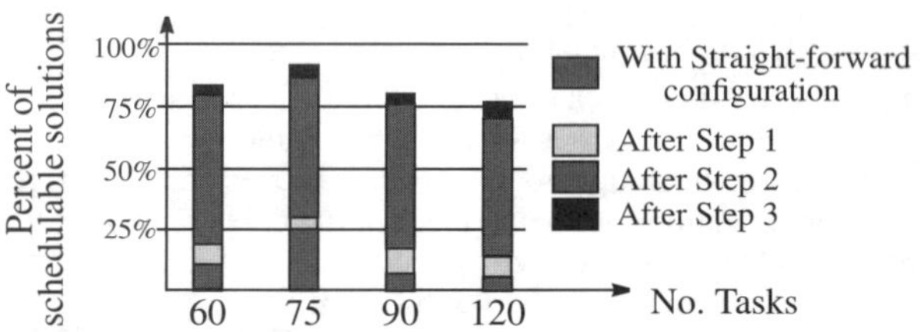

Figure 10. Percentage of Schedulable Applications

consisting of 60 tasks, for example, only 10% were schedulable with the straight-forward configuration and 90% continued the optimization process. 9% of the total number of tasks have been found schedulable with the configuration generated by step 1. As expected, the mapping, partitioning and bus cycle adjustment performed in step 2 are leading to a huge improvement, adding 61% of the total number of applications to the group of schedulable ones. An additional 4% of the total number of applications is found schedulable after performing the bus optimization in step 3. A similar trend can be followed in the experiments with 75, 90 and 120 tasks. It is easy to observe that by performing the proposed optimizations, huge improvements over the straight-forward configuration could be produced.

An interesting question is to what extent the partitioning of tasks into the ET and TT domains is contributing to the results illustrated in Figure 10. Or, ar these results mostly due to the optimized mapping? The same question can also be put relative to the bus cycle optimization. In order to answer these questions, we considered a second set of applications consisting of 60, 80 and 100 tasks grouped into 12, 15, 18 or 20 task graphs and mapped on 4 or 6 nodes. We have run our heuristic for each of these applications considering four cases. First, with a subset of tasks that have to be partitioned but no tasks to be mapped ($|\Psi^M| = 0$). Second, with the same subset of tasks open for mapping but not for partitioning ($|\Psi^P| = 0$). The third case does not allow any bus access optimization, so we switched off the optimizations in lines 5 and 11 in Figure 5 (however, we keep the bus cycle adjustment which is needed in Step 2, line 7 in Figure 7). The fourth case represents the reference, the complete heuristic. The results are presented in Figure 11, which shows the percentage of schedulable applications (relative to the total number of applications) that have been produced by each optimization step. For example, after step 2, 45% additional applications were schedulable if we only allow to perform re-mapping ($|\Psi^P| = 0$), as opposed to 74% in the case when both optimizations are performed. The same number is 40% if we only allow to perform re-partitioning ($|\Psi^M| = 0$). The percentage of unschedulable tasks after the three steps is 34% when $|\Psi^P| = 0$, 44% for $|\Psi^M| = 0$, and 24% when no bus optimization was performed, as compared to 7% in the case of the complete heuristic. The conclusions which we can draw are the following:

1. An efficient partitioning into the ET and TT domains is contributing essentially to the overall optimization, to an extent comparable to the mapping.

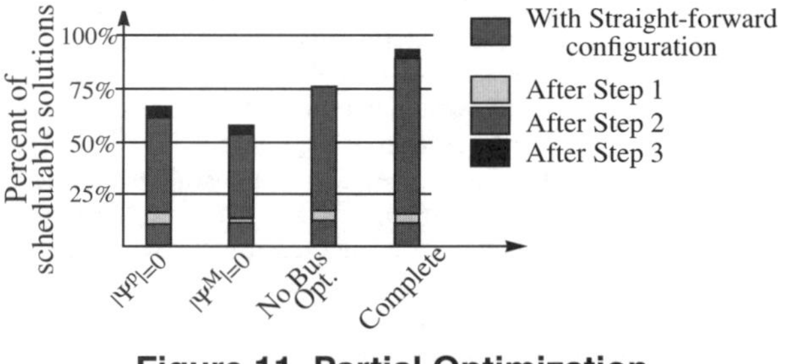

Figure 11. Partial Optimization

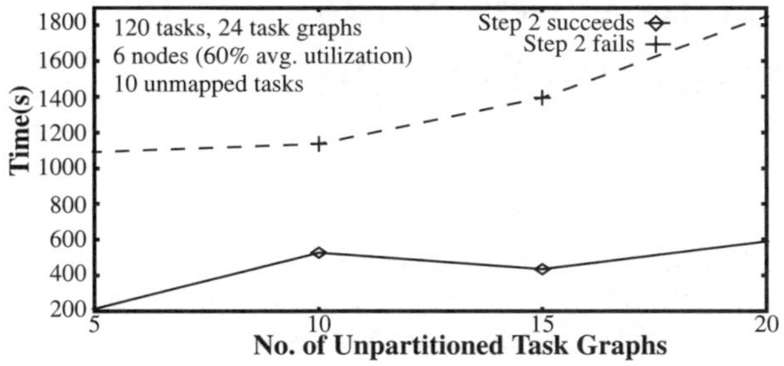

Figure 12. Runtime of step 2 function of $|\Psi^P|$

2. When applied together, the three techniques provide much better results than the ones obtained when any of the techniques is eliminated.

Concerning the runtime needed for the optimization process, we have analyzed each of the three steps separately. For the examples leading to the results in Figure 10, the average run time for step 1 was 11.7s (60 tasks), 40.1s (75 tasks), 73.2s (90 tasks), and 150s (120 tasks).

The execution time for step 2 is presented in more detail in Figure 12 and Figure 13. Figure 12 illustrates the time needed for step 2 as a function of the total number of task graphs to be partitioned (the characteristics of the applications and the number of nodes are shown in the figure). The upper curve illustrates the average execution times for those applications which are running through step 2 without reaching a system configuration which makes them schedulable. This curve can be considered as an upper bound for the execution time in step 2. The second curve in Figure 12 gives the average execution times of those applications that have been found schedulable during step 2.

In Figure 13, we show, in a similar way, the average execution times as a function of the number of unmapped tasks. The execution times needed for the third optimization step are given in Figure 14. As this step is concentrating only on the communication aspect, the average execution time is given as a function of the number of nodes.

Finally, we considered a real-life example from the automotive area, implementing a vehicle cruise controller and a control application related to the Anti Blocking System (ABS) on an architecture consisting of 5 nodes. The cruise controller consists of 42 tasks organized in 11 task graphs. One of these task graphs is fixed into the TT domain, and the other 10 are unpartitioned. 10 out of the 42 tasks are unmapped. The ABS system consists of 35 tasks already mapped over the 5 nodes and assigned to the ET domain. Running our optimization heuristic, step 1 was able to generate a correct static schedule for the TT domain, but without producing a globally schedulable system. Step 2 manages to improve the degree of schedulability of the system (function *DSch*) by two orders of magnitude without, however, producing a schedulable system. A correct

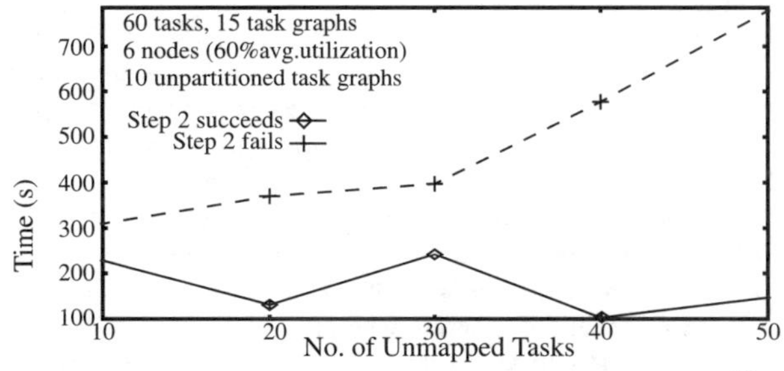

Figure 13. Runtime of step 2 function of $|\Psi^M|$

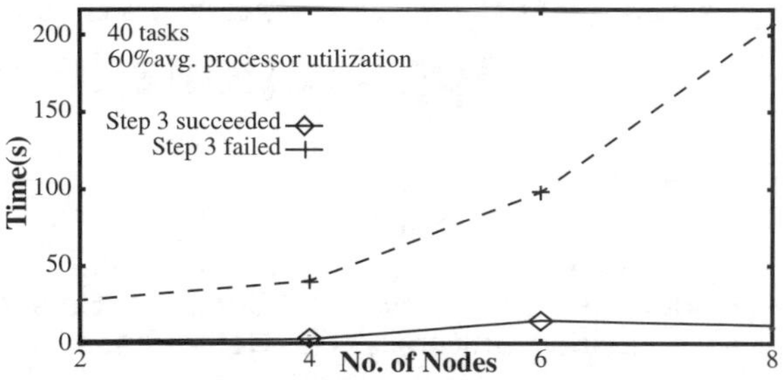

Figure 14. Runtime of step 3

implementation has been produced after the bus optimization in step 3. It is interesting to mention that for the final schedulable solution, out of the 10 unpartitioned task graphs, 2 were assigned to the ET and 8 to the TT partition. The run times for the three optimization steps were 5.3s, 708s and 164s respectively.

7. Conclusions

Distributed embedded systems based on mixed static/dynamic communication protocols are becoming the new standard for automotive applications. Such systems typically run applications consisting of both ET and TT tasks. We have identified a new class of system optimization issues typical for the heterogeneous systems considered in the paper: partitioning of the system functionality into TT and ET domains and the optimization of the bus access scheme. Both problems were considered in the context of a heuristic which performs the mapping and scheduling of the system functionality. We have shown that the quality of the system implementation can be significantly improved by the proposed optimization heuristics.

8. References

[1] N. Audsley, K. Tindell, A. et. al., "The End of Line for Static Cyclic Scheduling?", 5th Euromicro Works. on Real-Time Systems, 1993.

[2] N. Audsley, A. Burns, et. al., "Fixed Priority Preemptive Scheduling: An Historical Perspective", Real-Time Systems, 8(2/3), 1995.

[3] R. Bosch GmbH, "CAN Specification Version 2.0", 1991.

[4] T. Demmeler, P. Giusto, "A Universal Communication Model for an Automotive System Integration Platform", DATE, 2001.

[5] R. Ernst, "Codesign of Embedded Systems: Status and Trends", IEEE Design&Test of Comp., April-June, 1998.

[6] FlexRay homepage: http://www.flexray-group.com/.

[7] H. Kopetz, "Real-Time Systems - Design Principles for Distributed Embedded Applications", Kluwer Academic Publisher, 1997.

[8] H. Lönn, J. Axelsson, "A Comparison of Fixed-Priority and Static Cyclic Scheduling for Distributed Automotive Control Applications", Euromicro Conf. on Real-Time Systems, 1999.

[9] P. Pedreiras, L. Almeida, "Combining Event-Triggered and Time-Triggered Traffic in FTT-CAN: Analysis of the Asynchronous Messaging System", WFCS, 2000.

[10] P. Raja, G. Noubir, "Static and Dynamic Polling Mechanisms for Fieldbus Networks", ACM Operating Systems Review, 27(3), 1993.

[11] W. Wolf, "Hardware-Software Co-Design of Embedded Systems", *Proceedings of the IEEE*, V82, N7, 1994.

[12] J. Xu, D.L. Parnas, "On satisfying timing constraints in hard-real-time systems", IEEE Transactions on Software Engineering, 19(1), 1993.

[13] T. Pop, P. Eles, Z. Peng, "Schedulability Analysis for Distributed Heterogeneous Time/Event-Triggered Real-Time Systems", EuroMicro Conf. on Real-Time Systems, 2003.

[14] P., A. Doboli, P. Pop, Z. Peng, "Scheduling with Bus Access Optimization for Distributed Embedded Systems", IEEE Transactions on VLSI Systems, 8(5), 472-491, 2000.

[15] P. Pop, P. Eles, Z. Peng, "Bus Access Optimization for Distributed Embedded Systems based on Schedulability Analysis", DATE, 2000.

Deriving Process Networks from Weakly Dynamic Applications in System-Level Design

Todor Stefanov
Leiden Embedded Research Center
Leiden Institute of Advanced Computer Science
Leiden University, The Netherlands
stefanov@liacs.nl

Ed Deprettere
Leiden Embedded Research Center
Leiden Institute of Advanced Computer Science
Leiden University, The Netherlands
edd@liacs.nl

ABSTRACT

We present an approach to the automatic derivation of executable Process Network specifications from Weakly Dynamic Applications. We introduce the notions of Dynamic Single Assignment Code, Approximated Dependence Graph, and Linearly Bounded Sets to model and capture weakly dynamic (data-dependent) behavior of applications at the task-level of abstraction. Process Networks are simple parallel processing models that match the emerging multi-processor architectures in the sense that the mapping of Process Network specifications of applications onto multi-processor architectures can be done in a systematic and transparent way.

Categories and Subject Descriptors

I.6.3 [**Simulation and Modeling**]: Applications; J.6 [**Computer-aided Engineering**]: Computer-aided design (CAD)

General Terms

Algorithms, Design

Keywords

System-Level Design, Heterogeneous Embedded Systems, Kahn Process Networks, Weakly Dynamic Applications

1. INTRODUCTION

Single-chip embedded systems are increasingly becoming *heterogeneous systems*, i.e., systems composed of fully programmable components (microprocessors), reconfigurable components (FPGAs), and dedicated hardware blocks. Typically, these components are linked via some kind of communication structure (high-speed bus, multiple buses or programmable network) forming a multi-processor architecture. Mapping applications onto a multi-processor architecture is a key issue in the emerging system-level and platform-based design methodologies. Today, system designers experience significant difficulties because the way an application is specified by the application developer does not match the way multi-processor architectures operate. The applications are typically specified using an imperative model of computation, i.e., programming languages like C/C++. Although the imperative model of computation is a natural model for application specification it does not reveal parallelism due to its inherent sequential nature. This fact makes the mapping of an application onto a parallel multi-processor architecture very difficult. On the other hand, if the application is specified using a parallel model of computation (MoC) then the mapping will be done in a systematic and transparent way using a disciplined approach [12], but specifying an application using a parallel MoC is difficult, not well understood by application developers, and a time consuming process. That is why application developers still prefer to specify an application using the imperative model of computation, which is well understood, regardless the fact that this model is not suitable for mapping an application onto a parallel multi-processor architecture.

The facts, given above, suggest that there is a gap between the way applications are currently specified (as sequential programs in C/C++ or Matlab) and the way they should be specified (using a parallel model of computation) [12] in order to allow a systematic and transparent mapping onto parallel multi-processor architectures. Although, many parallel models of computation exist [9][10], in this paper we focus on the Process Network model of computation [7] because its operational semantics are simple, yet general enough, to specify conveniently *stream-oriented* data processing that fits nicely with the application domain we are interested in - multimedia and signal processing applications. Moreover, for this application domain a prior work described in [2][16][11] reports that indeed the Process Network (PN) model is very suitable for specifying and mapping systematically and efficiently applications onto multi-processor architectures. The PN model expresses an application in terms of distributed control (no global scheduler is present) and distributed memory that are key requirements to take advantage of the parallel resources available in multi-processor architectures.

Our previous work presented in [8] provides some techniques to bridge the gap mentioned above but these techniques are limited to automatic derivation of Process Networks only from applications described as *static* affine nested loop programs. Such programs are important in Scientific, Matrix Computation and Adaptive Signal Processing applications. In this paper, however, we focus on techniques that support automatic derivation of Process Networks from *Weakly Dynamic Applications* (WDA). We define a WDA as a **task-level** sequential program where:
A) the control structures in the program are: *for-loops* with upper and lower bounds as affine functions of iterators of other loops and parameters; *if-then-else* constructs with **no restrictions on the**

condition - the condition of the *if* may be an arbitrary function of loop iterators and/or data variables.
B) The indexing of data variables (arrays) must be an affine function of *for-loop* iterators and possible parameters.

Notice that if we constrain the condition of *if-then-else* constructs to be an affine function of loop iterators and parameters then our WDA reduces to a static affine nested loop application. Therefore, the techniques we present in this paper extend significantly the class of applications that can be handled by [8]. For example, our techniques can handle not only Scientific, Matrix Computation and Adaptive Signal Processing applications but also media applications with dynamic (data dependent) behavior such as the JPEG codecs, the MPEG codecs, etc.

As a simple example, consider the WDA shown in Figure 1. This

```
1  %parameter N 8 16;
2
3  for i = 1:1:N,
4    [x(i), t(i)] = F1(...);
5  end
6
7  for i = 1:1:N,
8    if t(i) <= 0,
9      [x(i)] = F2( x(i) );
10   end
11   [...] = F3( x(i) );
12 end
```

Figure 1: Pseudo code of simple Weakly Dynamic Application.

application consists of three function calls[1] $F1$, $F2$ and $F3$. These function calls execute tasks that communicate data via the array $x(i)$. Every element of the array can be anything from a scalar value to very complicated data structures. The execution of $F2$ depends on the condition at line 8. This condition is data dependent because of the variable $t(i)$. The values of this variable are not known at compile time, i.e., they are not known before the actual execution of the program. This fact makes the program to have dynamic behavior, unpredictable at compile time. A challenging problem is how to analyze and transform this kind of dynamic programs at compile time in order to derive automatically executable Process Network specifications. In this paper we address this problem and present a systematic solution approach.

1.1 Paper Contributions

We present a novel systematic and step-wise approach that allows automatic derivation of executable Process Network specifications from Weakly Dynamic Applications. New notions like Dynamic Single Assignment Code, Approximated Dependence Graph, and Linearly Bounded Sets have been introduced in our approach in order to capture and model weakly dynamic behaviors of an application. Most of the steps in our approach have been implemented in a prototype software framework called COMPAANPRO. The approach has been applied and validated successfully on a real-life application - Motion-JPEG encoder.

1.2 Related Work

Previous work on automatic derivation of Process Networks has been presented in [13][8]. This work focuses on deriving Kahn Process Network (KPN) specifications from applications described as static parameterized affine nested loop programs. In contrast, the work presented in this paper deals with a more general class of applications, i.e., weakly dynamic applications from which KPN specifications are derived automatically.

Kahn Process Networks are supported by the Ptolemy II framework [10] and the YAPI environment [3] for concurrent modeling and design of applications and systems. The designer has to specify manually the application as a Kahn Process Network and to give this network as an input to the Ptolemy II or YAPI simulation and verification engines. In many cases specifying manually application as a Kahn Process Network is a very time consuming and error prone process. Our work, presented in this paper, can be used as a front-end tool by Ptolemy II or YAPI. This will speedup significantly the modeling effort when Kahn Process Networks are used as well as modeling errors will be avoided because our techniques guarantee correct-by-construction generation of Kahn Process Networks.

The work presented in [2][16][11] uses Kahn Process Networks to model applications and to explore the mapping of these applications onto multi-processor architectures. This work clearly indicates that the application modeling is done manually starting from a sequential C code as well as that significant amount of time (a few weeks) is spent by designers on transforming correctly the sequential C code into Kahn Process Networks. This fact slows down the design space exploration process. The work presented in this paper gives a solution for fast automatic derivation of Kahn Process Networks from sequential C code that will contribute for faster design space exploration.

1.3 Paper Organization

In the next section, we give an overview of our step-wise approach to derive Process Networks from Weakly Dynamic Applications. In Section 3, every step in the approach is explained in detail. Section 4 presents some results we have obtained by applying our approach on a real-life application, i.e., Motion-JPEG encoder. Finally, we draw some conclusions in Section 5.

2. SOLUTION APPROACH: OVERVIEW

In this section, we present an overview of our approach to solve the problem of deriving process networks from weakly dynamic applications (WDA) as stated in Section 1. Our approach consists of three main steps shown in Figure 2.

We start with a WDA specified in Matlab or C and transform it in a *dynamic Single Assignment Code* (dSAC) representation - STEP 1 in Figure 2. There is a difference between our dSAC and the classical single assignment code (SAC) used in the compiler community and systolic array community. The classical SAC is defined as a program in which every variable is written only once whereas our dSAC has the property that: 1) every variable in the code is written *at most* once because of the dynamics in the application; 2) for some variables, it is not known whether or not they will be written or read before the actual execution of the code. The dSAC reveals all possible data-dependencies between the functions in the WDA. Some of the data dependencies in the dSAC are not exactly defined, i.e., they depend on variables having values that are not known at compile time. In Section 3.1, we give more details about the dSAC and we show a simple example.

The second step in our approach is to convert the dSAC into another representation that is a formal model. This model consists of two annotated graph structures, namely *Approximated Dependence Graph* (ADG) and *Schedule Tree* (STree). The ADG and the STree capture all the information that is present in the dSAC in a formal way. As a consequence, formal operations can be easily defined and applied on the ADG and the STree instead of the dSAC.

The ADG contains all the information that is related to the data dependencies between the functions in the dSAC. The data dependencies are approximated, i.e., the exact data dependencies are not known at compile time. Because of this, our ADG model is more general than the reduced dependence graph models that are used to represent static programs. If the data dependencies are known at compile time then the ADG is actually a polyhedral reduced de-

[1] At some places in this paper we use the word *function* instead of *function call* for the sake of brevity.

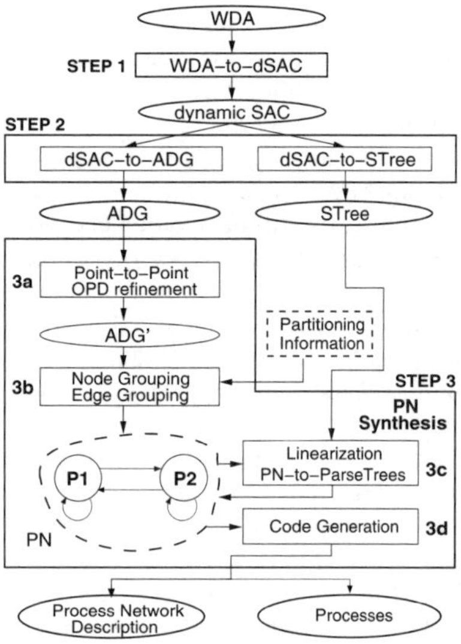

Figure 2: An approach to derive Process Networks from Weakly Dynamic Applications.

pendence graph (PRDG) [13]. In Section 3.2, we define the ADG model. Also, we briefly describe our procedure to derive the ADG from a dSAC and we give an example.

The STree contains all the information about the execution order between the functions in the dSAC. The STree represents one valid schedule between all these functions that we call global schedule. From the STree a local schedule between any arbitrary set of the functions in the dSAC can be obtained by pruning operations on the STree. In Section 3.3, we define the STree and give an example.

In the final step (STEP 3 in Figure 2) of our approach a Kahn Process Network (KPN) [7] is synthesized. A KPN consists of concurrent processes that communicate with each other over unbounded FIFO channels. Every process is specified as a sequential program. The synthesis of this program is based on information derived from the ADG and the STree. The synchronization between the processes is accomplished by blocking reads. The computational and communication workloads are distributed over the processes and the channels in accordance with some partitioning information. Such information can be given manually or delivered by the *partitioning information* box shown in Figure 2. This box implements some design space exploration procedures and/or some optimization procedures. If partitioning information is not available then we use the following partitioning by default: 1) for every node in the ADG a process is generated; 2) for every edge in the ADG a channel is generated. In Section 3.4 the process network synthesis[2] is described in details.

3. SOLUTION APPROACH: DETAILS

In this section, we explain in more details some of the models and techniques used in the approach presented in Section 2. Also, some examples are given for the sake of clarity.

3.1 Dynamic Single Assignment Code

The Dynamic Single Assignment Code (dSAC) derived from a weakly dynamic application (WDA) is a program in which every variable is written at most once. This property implies that some of the variables may be not written at all. This is because of the dynamic control structures in the application where the conditions are data-dependent, i.e., the outcome of the conditions is not known at compile time.

In order to derive a dSAC from a WDA we have to find all possible data dependencies between the functions in the WDA. Because of the dynamic control structures in the WDA an exact array dataflow analysis [5] can not be performed to find the data dependencies. The approach we follow to find the data dependencies in case of WDA is based on parametric integer programming (PIP) [4]. We use the same technique as in the exact array dataflow analysis for building a PIP system but we add to this system constraints with parameters for the dynamic control structures in the WDA. By introducing additional constraints with parameters in a PIP system we "mask" the information that is not known at compile time. Because of this, we find approximated data dependencies. Our approach to find the approximated data dependencies is based on the approach known in the literature as *Fuzzy Array Dataflow Analysis* (FADA) [6].

Using approximated data dependencies we have found a procedure to generate a dSAC that is out of the scope of this paper. As an example, in Figure 3 we show the output of this procedure for the simple program shown in Figure 1.

```
1  %parameter N 8 16;
2
3  for i = 1:1:N,
4    ctrl(i) = N+1;
5  end
6  for i = 1:1:N,
7   [out_0, out_1] = F1(...);
8   [x_1(i)] = opd(out_0);
9   [t_1(i)] = opd(out_1);
10 end
11
12 for i = 1:1:N,
13  [t_1(i)] = ipd(t_1(i));
14  if t_1(i) <= 0,
15   [in_0] = ipd(x_1(i));
16   [out_0] = F2(in_0);
17   [x_2(i)] = opd(out_0);
18   [ ctrl(i) ] = opd( i );
19  end
20
21  C = ipd( ctrl(i) );
22  if i = C,
23   [in_0] = ipd(x_2(C));
24  else
25   [in_0] = ipd(x_1(i));
26  end
27
28  [out_0] = F3(in_0);
29  [...] = opd(out_0);
30 end
```

Figure 3: Example of Dynamic Single Assignment Code.

We call the code in Figure 3 dynamic SAC because if we consider, for example, line 17 we do not know at compile time at which iteration the elements of the array $x\_2(i)$ will be written. The only thing known is that they will be written at most once. Moreover, for every execution of function $F3$ in line 28, its input is not known at compile time. The input has to be determined at run time by the code lines 22-26. Both cases described above never occur in the classical SAC cases.

Another new feature of the dSAC is the presence of parameters that originate form the data dependent control constructs in a weakly dynamic application (WDA). In order to keep the functionality of the dSAC equivalent to the functionality of the original WDA, the values of these parameters have to be changed dynamically. Our approach to accomplish the dynamic change is to introduce, for every such parameter, a control variable that stores the correct value of the parameter for every iteration. For example, C in the dSAC shown in Figure 3 is a parameter emerging form the *if*-statement in line 8 of the original program shown in Figure 1. This *if*-statement also appears in the dSAC in line 14. The dynamic change of the value of C is accomplished by the lines 18 and 21 in Figure 3. The control variable $ctrl(i)$ in line 18 stores the iterations for which the data dependent condition that introduces C is true. Also, the variable $ctrl(i)$ is used in line 21 to assign the correct value to C for the current iteration.

The dSAC we generate contains functions called **ipd** and **opd** -

[2] The process network synthesis is not limited to the generation of Kahn Process Networks only. With small modifications other process networks that have different interprocess communication and synchronization mechanisms can be generated.

see Figure 3. These functions just propagate the value of its input to its output and they play a role in the conversion of a dSAC to an approximated dependence graph presented in the next section.

3.2 Approximated Dependence Graph

In this section we give a formal definition of our Approximated Dependence Graph (ADG) model followed by a procedure to derive it from a dSAC, and an example.

Definition 3.1 (approximated dependence graph)
An Approximated Dependence Graph (ADG) is given by a tuple $ADG = (Nodes, Edges)$ where: $Nodes = \{N_{i=1..M}\}$ is a set of nodes. $Edges = \{E_{j=1..P}\}$ is a set of edges.

Definition 3.2 (node)
A node in the ADG is given by a tuple $N = (I_N, O_N, F_N, ND_N)$ where: $I_N = \{p_{k=1..K}\}$ is a set of input ports. $O_N = \{q_{l=1..L}\}$ is a set of output ports. F_N is a tuple $F_N = (F, in, out)$, where in and out are sets of variables and $F : in \rightarrow out$ is a function. ND_N is the node domain of N defined by a linearly bounded set (LBS - Definition 3.6).

Definition 3.3 (input port)
An input port is given by a tuple $p = (V_p, A_p, IPD_p)$ where: V_p is an n-dimensional variable associated with the port. A_p is a variable binding the port to the function in the node to which the port belongs if $A_p \in in \wedge A_p \neq V_p$. If $A_p = V_p$ then A_p is a variable binding the port to the node domain. A_p is a variable binding the port to IPDs of other ports if $A_p \notin in \wedge A_p \neq V_p$. IPD_p is the input port domain of p defined by a LBS (Definition 3.6).

Definition 3.4 (output port)
An output port is given by a tuple $q = (V_q, A_q, OPD_q)$ where: V_q is an m-dimensional variable associated with the port. $A_q \in out$ is a variable binding the port to the function in the node to which the port belongs. OPD_q is the output port domain of q defined by a LBS (Definition 3.6).

Definition 3.5 (edge)
An edge in the ADG is a triple $E = (q, p, M)$ where:
$q = (V_q, A_q, OPD_q)$ is an output port. $p = (V_p, A_p, IPD_p)$ is an input port. $V_p = V_q$, i.e., variables V_p and V_q have the same names and equal dimensions. $M : i_p \rightarrow i_q$ is an affine mapping where $i_p \in IPD_p$ and $i_q \in OPD_q$.

Definition 3.6 (linearly bounded set)
Let be given four sets of functions
$S1 = \{f_x^1(i) \mid x = 1..|S1|,\ i \in Z^n\}$, $S2 = \{f_x^2(i) \mid x = 1..|S2|,\ i \in Z^n\}$, $S3 = \{f_x^3(i) \mid x = 1..|S3|,\ i \in Z^n\}$, $S4 = \{f_x^4(i) \mid x = 1..|S4|,\ i \in Z^n\}$, an integral $m \times n$ matrix A and an integral n-vector b. A *linearly bounded set* (LBS) is a set of points $LBS = \{\, i \in Z^n \mid A.i \geq b,$

$$\begin{aligned} &if\ S1 \not\equiv \emptyset \Rightarrow \forall_{x=1..|S1|},\ f_x^1(i) \geq 0,\\ &if\ S2 \not\equiv \emptyset \Rightarrow \forall_{x=1..|S2|},\ f_x^2(i) \leq 0,\\ &if\ S3 \not\equiv \emptyset \Rightarrow \forall_{x=1..|S3|},\ f_x^3(i) > 0,\\ &if\ S4 \not\equiv \emptyset \Rightarrow \forall_{x=1..|S4|},\ f_x^4(i) < 0\ \}. \end{aligned}$$

The set of points $B = \{\, i \in Z^n \mid A.i \geq b \,\}$ is called *linear bound* of the LBS and the set $S = S1 \cup S2 \cup S3 \cup S4$ is called *filtering set*. Every $f_x^j(i) \in S$ can be an arbitrary function of i.

Our procedure to convert a dSAC into the ADG model defined above consists of two steps: 1) the dSAC is converted to a syntax tree [1]; 2) the syntax tree is parsed and all the elements of the ADG are created and specified in accordance with the relations given below:

1) for every function $[\ arg\ ] = \mathbf{ipd}(\ var\ )$ in the dSAC there exists a corresponding input port $p = (V_p, A_p, IPD_p)$ in the AGD, where $V_p = var$, $A_p = arg$ and IPD_p is the set of iterations in which the function **ipd** is executed.

2) for every function $[\ var\ ] = \mathbf{opd}(\ arg\ )$ in the dSAC there exists a corresponding output port $q = (V_q, A_q, IPD_q)$ in the AGD, where $V_q = var$, $A_q = arg$ and IPD_q is the set of iterations in which the function **opd** is executed.

3) for every pair $[\ arg_i\ ] = \mathbf{ipd}(\ var_i\ )$ and $[\ var_o\ ] = \mathbf{opd}(\ arg_o\ )$ in the dSAC there exists an edge $E = (q, p, M)$ in the ADG if var_i and var_o have the same name and dimension. q is the output port in the ADG corresponding to **opd** and p is the input port in the ADG corresponding to **ipd**. M is an affine mapping that gives for every iteration in which the **ipd** consumes a value, the corresponding iteration in which this value is produced by **opd**;

4) for every function $[\ oArg\ ] = \langle\mathbf{name}\rangle(\ iArg\ )$ in the dSAC with $\langle\mathbf{name}\rangle$ neither **ipd** nor **opd** there exists a corresponding node $N = (I_N, O_N, F_N, ND_N)$ in the ADG. For every function $[\ arg\ ] = \mathbf{ipd}(\ var\ )$ in the dSAC: if $arg \in iArg$ then the corresponding input port p in the ADG belongs to I_N. For every function $[\ var\ ] = \mathbf{opd}(\ arg\ )$ in the dSAC: if $arg \in oArg$ then the corresponding output port q in the ADG belongs to O_N. The elements of F_N are related to the dSAC as $F_N.F = \langle\mathbf{name}\rangle$, $F_N.in \equiv iArg$ and $F_N.out \equiv oArg$; ND_N is the set of iterations in which the function $\langle\mathbf{name}\rangle$ is executed.

As an example, consider the dSAC shown in Figure 3. Applying the procedure described above on this dSAC we obtain the ADG shown in Figure 4-a). The ADG consists of three nodes and five edges. Nodes $N1$, $N2$, and $N3$ correspond to functions $F1$, $F2$, and $F3$ of the dSAC, respectively. Edges $ED1$, $ED2$, $ED3$, $ED4$, and $ED5$ correspond to possible data dependencies between $F1$, $F2$, and $F3$ through the variables $t_1(i)$, $x_1(i)$, $x_2(i)$, and $ctrl(i)$ of the dSAC. According to Definition 3.2 node $N2$ is the tuple $N2 = (I_{N2}, O_{N2}, F_{N2}, ND_{N2})$ where: $I_{N2} = \{p1, p2\}$, $O_{N2} = \{q1, q2\}$, $F_{N2} = (F2, \{in\_0\}, \{out\_0\})$, with $F2 : \{in\_0\} \rightarrow \{out\_0\}$. ND_{N2} represents the iterations i at which function $F2$ is executed in the dSAC. The exact iterations i are not known at compile time because of the dynamic condition at line 14 in the dSAC (Figure 3). That is why we introduce the notion of linearly bounded set (LBS-Definition 3.6) by which we approximate the unknown iterations i. So, ND_{N2} is the following LBS: $ND_{N2} = \{i \in Z \mid 1 \leq i \leq N \wedge 8 \leq N \leq 16,\ t\_1(i) \leq 0\}$. The linear bound of this LBS is the polytope $B = \{1 \leq i \leq N \wedge 8 \leq N \leq 16\}$ that captures the information that we know at compile time about the bounds of the iterations i. The variable $t\_(i)$ is interpreted as an unknown function of i called filtering function whose output is determined at run time. Introducing the LBS notion in our ADG model to capture the dynamic behavior of the dSAC is to the best of our knowledge a novel approach.

Because of the semantics of the LBS, described above, we call the graph in Figure 4-a) approximated dependence graph (ADG). Another reason to call it that way is because the probability that some data dependencies exist can not be decided 100% at compile time. For example, the edge $ED3$ suggests that there might be a data dependency between $F1$ and $F3$ through the variable $x_1(i)$ but this depends on the dynamic condition at line 14 of the dSAC in Figure 3. If this condition is always true at run time the data dependency between $F1$ and $F3$ does not exist.

3.3 Schedule Tree

Definition 3.7 (schedule tree)
Let be given a syntax tree [1] $Tree = (N, E)$ derived from a dSAC. A Schedule Tree (STree) is a syntax tree $STree = (N_S, E_S)$, where node set $N_S \subset N$ and edge set $E_S \subset E$. The topology of the $STree$ represents control structure of a program that executes

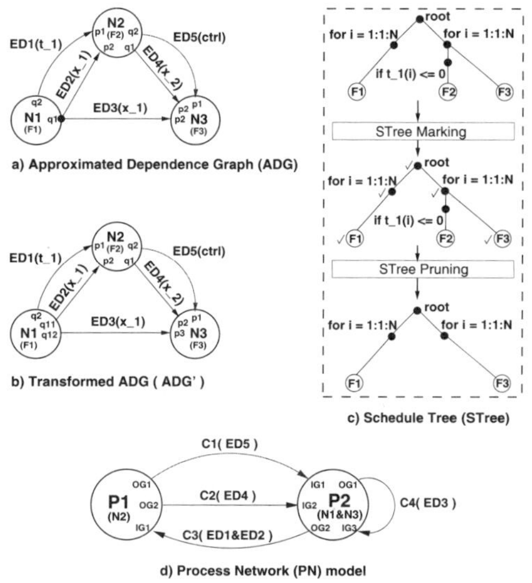

Figure 4: Examples of a) Approximated Dependence Graph (ADG) model; b) Transformed ADG; c) Schedule Tree and Transformations; d) Process Network model.

the functions $[\,] = \langle \mathbf{name} \rangle(\,)$ of the dSAC in a correct order. $\langle \mathbf{name} \rangle$ is different from **ipd** and **opd**.

Consider the dSAC shown in Figure 3. The corresponding schedule tree (STree) is depicted at the top part of Figure 4-c). If we parse this tree top-down from left to right a program can be generated that gives a valid execution order (global schedule) among the functions $F1$, $F2$ and $F3$ which is the original order given by the dSAC. The procedure to obtain the STree from the dSAC is done in two steps: 1) the dSAC is converted to a syntax tree using a standard syntax parser [1]; 2) the STree is extracted from the syntax tree by removing all the nodes and edges that are not related to nodes $F1$, $F2$ and $F3$.

3.4 Process Network Synthesis

In this section, we present the final step of our approach in which we synthesize a process network - see STEP 3 in Figure 2. Our synthesis approach is mainly a translation of the ADG model and STree model into a process network (PN) model. The structure of our PN model is defined in Section 3.4.1. Figure 2 shows that STEP 3 consists of four sub-steps. In sub-step **3a** we apply two transformations on the ADG, namely *Point-to-Point* and *OPD refinement*. This transformations have to be done because of two reasons:
1) On the one hand, our synthesis approach translates an ADG model into a PN model, where there is one-to-one correspondence between the input ports of the ADG and the input ports of the PN. The same is true for the output ports. The ADG may have several input ports connected to a single output port. On the other hand, we focus on the synthesis of a special class of process networks - Kahn Process Networks where every input port has to be connected to only one unique output port. This fact requires that we have to change the topology of the ADG such that every input port gets connected to only one unique output port - *Point-to-Point* connection. The change of the topology is always possible without changing the semantics of the ADG model. As an example, consider the ADG depicted in Figure 4-a). Two edges start from port $q1$ of node $N1$. By applying the point-to-point transformation we get the ADG shown in Figure 4-b). Now, in the transformed ADG (ADG'), node $N1$ has output ports $q11$ and $q12$ instead of port $q1$. Ports $q11$ and $q12$ are copies of port $q1$. This means that all the elements (Definition 3.4) of the ports $q11$ and $q12$ are identical with the elements of port $q1$.
2) Every output port in the PN has to send a token via the corresponding channel if the probability that the token will be needed in the process that reads this channel is not zero. This is accomplished by the transformation *OPD refinement*. This transformation is applied on every OPD that is associated with an output port in the ADG before the ADG model is translated to the PN model. The transformations *Point-to-Point* and *OPD refinement* are presented in Section 3.4.2;

In sub-steps **3b** and **3c** (Figure 2), the process network model (PN) is created gradually by creating the topology of the PN - sub-step 3b, followed by creating the behavior of the PN - sub-step 3c. The topology of the PN is created by grouping nodes and edges of the ADG into processes and channels in the PN. The grouping is based on the partitioning information delivered by the dashed box in Figure 2. In general, there is no limitation of grouping ADG nodes into PN processes. Any arbitrary grouping is possible. Grouping ADG edges into PN channels has to be performed after the PN processes are defined by the node grouping. Also, the edge grouping has to obey the following rule: All the edges that we want to group in a channel have to start form the same process, say P_i, and have to end at the same process, say P_j. An example of creating a topology of a PN by node grouping and edge grouping is given in Figure 4-d). The PN is created by grouping nodes $N1$ and $N3$ of the ADG in Figure 4-b) into process $P2$, as well as node $N2$ into process $P1$. The group of nodes of $P1$ consists of only one node $N2$. After that, edge grouping is performed where $ED1$ and $ED2$ form the channel $C3$. The channels $C1$, $C2$, and $C4$ are assigned one edge each, i.e., $ED5$, $ED4$, and $ED3$, respectively.

In sub-step **3c** in Figure 2 the behavior of the PN is created. A procedure called *Linearization* deals with the communication behavior of every process in the PN. This procedure is built depending on the target class of process networks under synthesis - in our case Kahn Process Networks (KPN) where the processes communicate with each other over 1-dimensional unbounded FIFO channels. In Section 3.4.3 we give more details about the linearization.

Internally, a process in a KPN has, by definition [7], a sequential behavior meaning that the functions that have to be executed inside the process are executed in sequential order. The procedure *PN-to-ParseTree* (Figure 2), derives this order such that the PN execution is deadlock free and expresses it as a parse tree for every process in the PN. This procedure operates on the PN model and uses the information encoded in the STree defined in Section 3.3. We illustrate part of the PN-to-ParseTree procedure by a simple example.

Consider process $P2$ of the PN shown in Figure 4-d). This process is constructed by grouping nodes $N1$ and $N3$ of the ADG shown in Figure 4-b). This means that process $P2$ has to execute in sequential order functions $F1$ and $F3$ associated with nodes $N1$ and $N3$, respectively. To find the order we use the schedule tree (STree) shown at the top in Figure 4-c). First, an operation called STree Marking finds the $F1$ and $F3$ leafs in the STree and parses the tree from these leafs to the tree root, marking all the nodes in the path - see Figure 4-c). Second, an operation called STree Pruning prunes the marked STree by removing all the unmarked nodes of this tree. The resultant tree shown at the bottom in Figure 4-c) can be converted to a program by traversing it top-down from left to right. This program gives a valid sequential order (schedule) between $F1$ and $F3$ for process $P2$ that guarantees deadlock free execution of the process network to which $P2$ belongs. Finally, the procedure *PN-to-ParseTree* adds to the tree shown at the bottom in Figure 4-c) other nodes that correspond to control structures in the program mentioned above. These control structures specify from which ports the functions $F1$ and $F3$ associated with nodes $N1$ and $N2$ get input data and to which ports they put the output data for every iteration i. For lack of space the complete tree generated by *PN-to-ParseTree* is not depicted in Figure 4-c).

The last sub-step of the PN synthesis (Figure 2-**3d**) is called *Code Generation*. In this sub-step an executable code of a Kahn process network is generated from the PN model. We use a software engineering technique called *Visitor* to visit the PN model structure and to generate the executable code. This code can be expressed in any programming language on top of which an environment to execute Kahn process networks is built. For example, the YAPI environment [3] in C++, SystemC, or the Ptolemy II framework [10] in Java.

3.4.1 Process Network Model

Definition 3.8 (process network)
A process network (PN) is given by a tuple $PN = (P, C)$ where: $P = \{P_{i=1..|P|}\}$ is a set of processes. $C = \{C_{j=1..|C|}\}$ is a set of channels.

Definition 3.9 (process)
A process in the PN is given by a tuple $P = (NP, IP, OP, ST)$ where: $NP = \{N_{m=1..M}\}$ is a set of nodes, with N_m as given in Definition 3.2. $IP = \{IG_{k=1..K}\}$ is a set of input gates. $OP = \{OG_{l=1..L}\}$ is a set of output gates. ST is a schedule tree that gives a valid execution order between the functions F associated with every N_m.

Definition 3.10 (input gate)
An input gate is given by a tuple $IG = (I_{IG}, IK_{IG})$ where: $I_{IG} = \{p_{k=1..|I_{IG}|}\}$ is a set of ports, with p_k as given in Definition 3.3. $IK_{IG} = \{InKey_{p_{k=1..|I_{IG}|}}\}$ is a set of functions, where for every $p_k \in I_{IG}$ a function $InKey_{p_k} \in IK_{IG}$ is associated, $InKey_{p_k} : IPD_{p_k} \to Z^1$ is a one-to-one mapping.

Definition 3.11 (output gate)
An output gate is given by a tuple $OG = (O_{OG}, OK_{IG})$ where: $O_{OG} = \{q_{k=1..|O_{OG}|}\}$ is a set of ports, with q_k as given in Definition 3.4. $OK_{OG} = \{OutKey_{q_{k=1..|O_{OG}|}}\}$ is a set of functions, where for every $q_k \in O_{OG}$ a function $OutKey_{q_k} \in OK_{OG}$ is associated, $OutKey_{q_k} : OPD_{q_k} \to Z^1$ is a one-to-one mapping.

Definition 3.12 (channel)
A channel is given by a tuple $C = (OG, IG, E, CM)$ where: $OG = (O_{OG}, OK_{IG})$ is an output gate. $IG = (I_{IG}, IK_{IG})$ is an input gate. $E = \{E_{m=1..|E|}\}$ is a set of edges, where E_m is given by Definition 3.5. $CM \in \{1, 2, 3, 4\}$ is the communication mode of the channel. $CM = 1$ is out-of-order communication with coloring of tokens. $CM = 2$ is out-of-order communication without coloring of tokens. $CM = 3$ is in-order communication with coloring of tokens. $CM = 4$ is in-order communication without coloring of tokens.

3.4.2 ADG transformations

Point-to-Point transformation: Let an $ADG = (Nodes, Edges)$ be given. For every edge $E_i = (q_l, p_k, M) \in Edges$ create a new port $q_{l\_i} = q_l$, add this port to the node that contains q_l and modify E_i such that $E_i = (q_{l\_i}, p_k, M)$. Finally, for every node $N \in Nodes$ remove the original output ports q_l from O_N.

OPD refinement transformation: Let an $ADG = (Nodes, Edges)$ be given. According to Definition 3.5 every edge $E \in Edges$ is given by $E = ((V_q, A_q, OPD_q), (V_p, A_p, IPD_p), M)$, where OPD_q and OPD_p are linearly bounded sets with linear bounds $B_q = \{i_q \in Z^n | A_q.i_q \geq b_q\}$ and $B_p = \{i_p \in Z^m | A_p.i_p \geq b_p\}$, respectively. The transformation *OPD refinement* derives for every $E \in Edges$ a new linearly bounded set $OPD_q^{'} = OPD_q \cap M(B_p)$, where $M(B_p)$ is the image of B_p in Z^n defined by the affine mapping M.

3.4.3 Creating the PN behavior

Formally, in a Kahn Process Network (KPN) the functions executed inside a process communicate data with functions inside other processes over channels that are 1-dimensional arrays with FIFO access. However, our approach has to derive KPNs from weakly dynamic applications (WDA) in which all these functions communicate data between each other via variables that are N-dimensional arrays with random access. In order to keep the functionality of the KPN the same as the functionality of the WDA, we apply a procedure called *Linearization* that adds to the PN model information that is necessary to realize models of communication with 1-dimensional FIFO access arrays equivalent to the communication with N-dimensional random access arrays. This procedure extends the work presented in [14]. Our PN model supports four models of communication with 1-dimensional FIFO access arrays:
1) out-of-order communication with coloring of tokens - this model is used when the order of the tokens (data) written in the FIFO channel is different than the order the tokens have to be read. Also, the number of tokens that will be written or read to/from the channel is not known at compile time. In order to keep the correct behavior of the KPN, every token is tagged by a unique number (color) that is used to reorder the tokens while reading them form the channel;
2) out-of-order communication without coloring of tokens - this model is used when the order of the tokens (data) written in the FIFO channel is different than the order the tokens have to be read. The number of tokens that will be written or read to/from the channel is known at compile time. Coloring of tokens is not necessary to do reordering;
3) in-order communication with coloring of tokens - this model is used when the order of the tokens (data) written in the FIFO channel is the same as the order the tokens have to be read. Also, the number of tokens that will be written or read to/from the channel is not known at compile time. Because of this more tokens can be written in the channel than needed at run time. Every token is tagged by a unique number (color) that is used to remove the tokens that are not needed while reading them form the channel;
4) in-order communication without coloring of tokens - this model is used when the order of the tokens (data) written in the FIFO channel is the same as the order the tokens have to be read. The number of tokens that will be written or read to/from the channel is known at compile time.

The reordering of tokens in models 1) and 2) is done by a special controller and a reordering memory located in the process that reads the tokens form the channel. The coloring of tokens in models 1) and 3) is based on the functions $InKey_{p_k}$ and $OutKey_{q_k}$ - see Definition 3.10 and Definition 3.11. The four communication models, described above, have a different cost of implementation in terms of required reordering memory and complexity of the control. The *out-of-order communication with coloring of tokens* model is the most expensive model but it is the most general model. This model can be used for every channel and the correct behavior of the PN is guaranteed. However, depending on the edges that belong to a particular channel, in some cases another less expensive communication model can be selected that still guarantees the correct behavior of the PN. We extended the work presented in [15] to find a procedure that detects at compile time the most optimal communication model for a given channel. In case the coloring of tokens is needed we derive the coloring functions $InKey_{p_k}$ and $OutKey_{q_k}$ at compile time as well.

4. RESULTS

Most of the steps in our approach, presented in Section 2 and Section 3, have been implemented in a prototype software framework called COMPAANPRO. The approach has been applied and validated successfully on a real-life application - MotionJPEG encoder (MJPEG). We started with publicly available sequential C code of the MJPEG. The code was structured by hand such that it meets the definition of a WDA given in Section 1. This took four days. After this preparation work which is a *one-time* effort only, our COMPAANPRO tool derived automatically an executable Kahn Process Network (KPN) specification from the structured MJPEG code in 30 seconds. For comparison, a KPN specification of an MJPEG encoder was derived by hand in [11] that took four weeks. The facts above show that the automated approach presented in this paper reduces significantly the time required to derive a KPN from real-life application.

COMPAANPRO generated the MJPEG network as C++ code in YAPI [3] format which allowed us to run the network and to verify its functional correctness. Without providing any partitioning information to the COMPAANPRO tool, the tool applies the partitioning strategy described at the end of Section 2. Using this strategy for the MJPEG, the computational workload was partitioned into 10 concurrent processes and the communication workload was distributed over 56 FIFO channels. We analyzed the network and concluded that the computational workload was very well balanced over the 10 concurrent processes. However, the distribution of the communication workload was not optimal. We found that the number of communication FIFO channels can be reduced from 56 to 30 FIFOs by merging some FIFOs without obstructing the exploited parallelism. The techniques presented in this paper support FIFO merging by grouping edges as discussed in Section 3.4. However, the selection of channels to be merged is currently still the designers choice.

5. CONCLUSIONS

In this paper, we presented a novel systematic approach that allows automatic derivation of executable Kahn Process Network (KPN) specifications from Weakly Dynamic Applications (WDA). By introducing new notions like Dynamic Single Assignment Code, Approximated Dependence Graph, and Linearly Bounded Sets in our approach, we extend the range of applications where KPNs can be derived automatically.

Our experiments with the MJPEG application show that the proposed approach, implemented in the COMPAANPRO tool, produces an important reduction of the time required to generate executable KPN specifications from real-life applications.

The presented approach includes only basic techniques that have to be used in order to derive automatically KPNs from WDAs. The results, we have obtained for the MJPEG application, indicated that some optimization techniques have to be added to the approach that will help with improving the quality of the generated KPNs in terms of optimal partitioning of the computation and communication workloads.

6. ACKNOWLEDGMENTS

This research is supported by PROGRESS, the embedded systems and software research program of the Dutch organization of Scientific Research NWO, the Dutch Ministry of Economic Affairs and the Dutch Technology Foundation STW.

7. REFERENCES

[1] A. Aho, R. Sethi, and J. Ullman. *Compilers: Principles, Techniques, and Tools*. Addison-Wesley Publishing Company, 1986.

[2] E. de Kock. Multiprocessor Mapping of Process Networks: A JPEG Decoding Case Study. In *Proc. 15th Int. Symposium on System Synthesis (ISSS'2002)*, pages 68–73, Kyoto, Japan, Oct. 2-4 2002.

[3] E. de Kock et al. YAPI: Application modeling for signal processing systems. In *Proc. 37th Design Automation Conference (DAC'2000)*, pages 402–405, Los Angeles, CA, June 5-9 2000.

[4] P. Feautrier. Parametric Integer Programming. Operations Research, 22(3):243-268, 1988.

[5] P. Feautrier. Dataflow Analysis of Scalar and Array References. *Int. Journal of Parallel Programming*, 20(1):23–53, 1991.

[6] P. Feautrier and J.-F. Collard. Fuzzy Array Dataflow Analysis. Technical report, Ecole Normale Superieure de Lyon, 1994. ENS-Lyon/LIP N° 94-21.

[7] G. Kahn. The semantics of a simple language for parallel programming. In *Proc. of the IFIP Congress 74*. North-Holland Publishing Co., 1974.

[8] B. Kienhuis, E. Rijpkema, and E. F. Deprettere. Compaan: Deriving Process Networks from Matlab for Embedded Signal Processing Architectures. In *Proc. 8th International Workshop on Hardware/Software Codesign (CODES'2000)*, San Diego, CA, USA, May 3-5 2000.

[9] E. Lee and A. Sangiovanni-Vincentelli. A Framework for Comparing Models of Computation. *IEEE Transactions on CAD of Integrated Circuits and Systems*, 17(12):1217–1229, 1998.

[10] E. Lee et al. PtolemyII: Heterogeneous Concurrent Modeling and Design in Java. Technical report, University of California at Berkeley, 1999. UCB/ERL M99/40.

[11] P. Lieverse, T. Stefanov, P. van der Wolf, and E. Deprettere. System Level Design with SPADE: an M-JPEG Case Study. In *Proc. Int. Conference on Computer Aided Design (ICCAD'01)*, pages 31–38, San Jose CA, USA, Nov. 4-8 2001.

[12] A. Mihal and K. Keutzer. *Mapping Concurrent Applications onto Architectural Platforms*. in Networks on Chip (Chapter 3), Editors Axel Jantsch and Hannu Tenhunen, Kluwer Academic Publishers, 2003.

[13] E. Rijpkema. Modeling Task Level Parallelism in Piece-wise Regular Programs, 2002. PhD thesis, Leiden University, The Netherlands.

[14] A. Turjan, B. Kienhuis, and E. Deprettere. *Realizations of the Extended Linearization Model*. in Domain-Specific Embedded Multiprocessors (Chapter 9), Marcel Dekker, Inc., 2003.

[15] A. Turjan, B. Kienhuis, and E. Deprettere. A Technique to Determine Inter-process Communication in the Polyhedral Model. In *Proc. Int. Workshop on Compilers for Parallel Computers (CPC'03)*, Amsterdam, The Netherlands, Jan. 8-10 2003.

[16] P. van der Wolf, P. Lieverse, M. Goel, D. La Hei, and K. Vissers. An MPEG-2 Decoder Case Study as a Driver for a System Level Design Methodology. In *Proc. 7th Int. Workshop on Hardware/Software Codesign (CODES'99)*, Rome, Italy, May 3-5 1999.

A Low-Cost and Low-Power Multi-Standard Video Encoder

R. Peset Llopis, R. Sethuraman, C. Alba Pinto, H. Peters, S. Maul and M. Oosterhuis
Philips Research Laboratories
Prof. Holstlaan 4, 5656 AA Eindhoven, The Netherlands
+31 40 2742422
[rafael.peset.llopis, ramanathan.sethuraman, carlos.alba.pinto, harm.peters, steffen.maul]@philips.com

ABSTRACT
Video encoders are an important IP block in mobile multimedia systems. In this paper, we describe a low-cost low-power multi-standard (MPEG4, JPEG, and H.263) video/image encoder. The low-cost and low-power aspects are achieved by the right choice of algorithms and architectures. In the algorithm front, an embedded compression technique for reducing the size of loop memory has enabled a single-chip low-cost realization of the encoder. In the architectural front, an efficient hardware-software partitioning has contributed to the design of a low-power encoder. Further, the hardware components that accelerate the kernels of encoding are implemented as application specific instruction-set processors (ASIPs) thereby providing flexibility to address multi-standard encoding. The power and area estimates for the encoder for QCIF@15fps in 0.18μm CMOS technology are 30mW and 20mm^2 respectively including the loop memory.

Categories and Subject Descriptors
C.3 [**Computer Systems Organization**]: Special-Purpose and Application-based Systems – *real-time and embedded systems, signal processing systems.*

General Terms
Algorithms, Performance, Design, Reliability, Verification.

Keywords
Video Encoder, Multi-Standard, Low-Power, Low-Cost, ASIPs, Hardware/Software Partitioning.

1. INTRODUCTION
Video compression [1] plays a pivotal role in enabling video processing on mobile multimedia systems (e.g. mobile videophone). We, in this paper, present a low-cost, low-power multi-standard video encoder for mobile applications. The low-power and low-cost constraints on the encoder design are met by using innovative algorithms and efficient architectures. Further, the multi-standard aspect (MPEG4 SP@L3, JPEG, and H.263) demonstrates the flexibility of this encoder. Furthermore, this design is more efficient and flexible compared to other solutions like the ones offered by Hitachi [2] or Fujitsu [3].

Traditional implementations of encoders have always resulted in expensive multi-chip solutions due to the presence of a large loop memory [3,4]. The encoder presented in this paper, which is intended to support up to VGA@30fps (3.5Mbits of loop memory), achieves a single chip implementation by compressing the picture stored in the loop memory. Further, in order to support VGA the use of compressed loop memory is a must to achieve a single-chip solution.

The hardware-software partitioning of the encoder design has been along the traditional path of mapping compute-intensive tasks onto hardware (minimal flexibility) and control-intensive tasks onto software (maximal flexibility). The encoder uses an architecture template C-HEAP (CPU-controlled Heterogeneous Embedded Architectures for signal Processing [5]), wherein the processors with different levels of flexibility run concurrent tasks. The communication between these heterogeneous processors is through the use of C-HEAP communication protocol. The encoder uses ASIPs based on a very large instruction word (VLIW) template [12] to accelerate compute-intensive parts of video encoding.

The paper is organized as follows. Section 2 describes the algorithmic space of the video compression domain. In Section 3, the hardware-software partitioning employed in the encoder design is described apart from the design flow itself. The implementation figures are presented in Section 4. Finally, we conclude in Section 5.

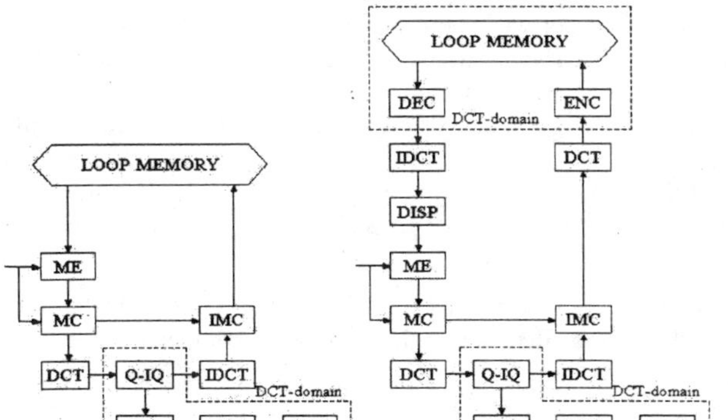

Figure 1. Video Encoders: (a) Conventional, (b) with Embedded Compression

2. ALGORITHM

Compression yields a compact representation of a signal by exploiting spatial and temporal correlation. Figure 1(a) shows a conventional encoder. It contains the following blocks: motion estimator (ME), motion compensator (MC), inverse motion compensator (IMC), (inverse) discrete cosine transform ((I)DCT), (inverse) quantizer ((I)Q), zigzag transform (ZZ), run length encoder (RLE), variable length encoder (VLE), and a loop memory.

The ME block determines the best match of the current macro-block (16 by 16 pixels) in the reconstructed image stored in the loop memory. The difference between the current macro-block and the best match in the reconstructed image is computed (MC), transformed (DCT), quantized (Q) and entropy encoded (ZZ, RLE, and VLE). The quantized data is inverse quantized (IQ), inverse transformed (IDCT), reconstructed (IMC) by adding the prediction, and stored in the loop memory to encode the next picture.

Implementations of this encoder have always resulted in two-chip solutions [3,4]. This is primarily due to large size of the loop memory (e.g. 3.5Mbits for a VGA). However, an efficient single-chip solution is possible if the picture stored in the loop memory can be compressed. This is achieved using the technique of embedded compression [7], wherein the loop memory is in the DCT domain and the DCT coefficients are stored using a scalable bit-plane based zonal coding approach. Figure 1(b) depicts a video encoder with embedded compression for the loop memory. The compression factor is fixed to 2.7 in order to avoid any quality degradation. Since the loop memory is organized in blocks (8x8 pixels), access to a macro-block from memory at a displaced position by the motion-estimator (ME) requires at most nine block-reads from the memory. This translates to few scalable decodes (DEC) and inverse-DCT (IDCT) operations. The displacement block (DISP) computes the displaced video block in spatial domain based on the blocks accessed from the loop memory. Note that without embedded compression, data read from e.g. SDRAM memories could be more than just the macro-blocks needed, this is because the addressing mechanism of the SDRAM which does not allow the access to single pixels but groups of them.

The motion estimator is responsible for determining the best match for the current macro-block with the picture stored in the loop memory. The motion estimator, based on the modified 3-dimensional recursive search (3DRS) algorithm [8], uses seven candidate vectors and performs full-, half- and quarter-pixel refinements. Since motion estimation is application dependent, flexibility is very important. This has been achieved by implementing the control parts in software and the compute intensive parts in hardware.

Loop filtering is employed to reduce noise content in the video data. This loop filter is based on a motion-compensated temporal filtering algorithm [4], and is implemented as part of the MC block.

The bit-rate control algorithm TMN8 [9] is used for setting the quantizer value in order to meet the bit-rate requirements. Since the bit-rate control algorithm is application dependent, it is completely done in software.

The above choice of algorithms, namely embedded compression to realize compress frame memory, 3DRS-based motion estimation and loop filtering, provide a low cost realization of video encoding.

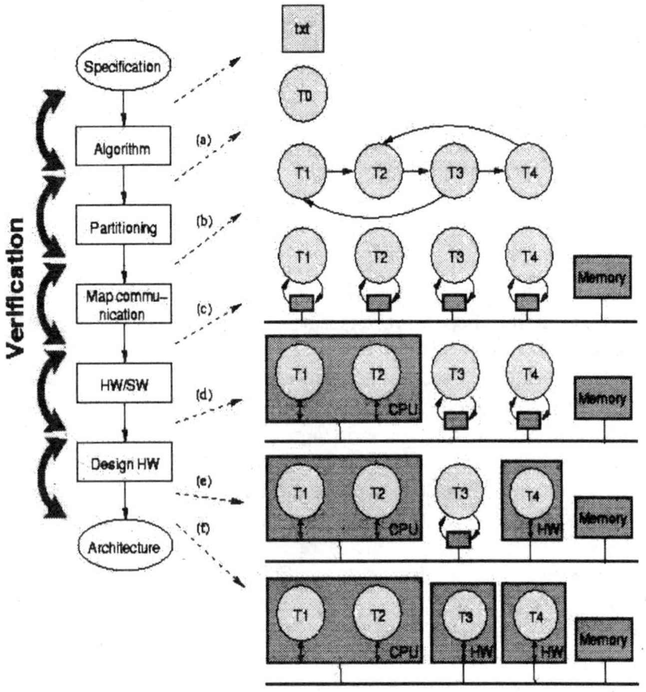

3. ARCHITECTURE

3.1 Design Flow

One of the important premises in the design of systems-on-a-chip (SoC) is to trade off efficiency for flexibility and time-to-market for cost. The design flow that abides by the premise above is to start from a high-level executable specification and converge towards a silicon implementation in several steps and iterations. One of the major tasks in this design flow is to ensure that hardware and software tasks communicate with each other correctly.

This can be accomplished by using a modular, flexible and scalable heterogeneous multi-processor architecture template based on distributed shared memory and an efficient and transparent protocol for communication. The protocol implementations have been incorporated in libraries that allow quick traversal of the various abstraction levels, hence enabling incremental design. Further, for ease of use, a well-defined set of primitives is required to hide the implementation of this protocol. The design decisions to be taken at each abstraction level are evaluated by either (co-) simulation or prototyping.

Following are the levels of abstraction used (Figure 2):

a) Algorithmic level (single-threaded C code), which is derived from the specification.

b) Partitioned algorithmic level (concurrent tasks).

c) Cycle-true communication level; bit- and cycle-true models for the communication and abstract functional models for the processing tasks.

d) Cycle-true embedded software level; bit- and cycle-true models for the communication, bit- and cycle-true functional models for software processing tasks, behavioral models for hardware processing tasks.

e) Partially implemented cycle-true hardware level; bit- and cycle-true models for the communication, bit- and cycle-true functional models for software and hardware processing tasks, combined with behavioral models for tasks still to be implemented in hardware.

f) Bit- and cycle-true level; bit- and cycle-true models for the communication, bit- and cycle-true functional models for hardware/software processing tasks.

The approach used for controlling the data-flow in heterogeneous multi-processor architectures is to have the processing devices synchronized autonomously [10]. This implies that each processing device should be able to initiate communication with any other device; hence the communication protocol must have a distributed implementation. With this approach, we can go to a smaller grain of synchronization, which allows smaller buffer sizes, and hence on-chip communication. For example, in a video context, we can synchronize on a block-line or block basis.

Our application specification is based on Kahn process Networks [6]. In this article, we refer to these processes as tasks. In this model, when a task wants to read from a channel and no data is available, the task will block. However, write actions are non-blocking. In our model, FIFOs are bounded in order to achieve an efficient implementation of the function. This means that a task will also block when it wants to write to a channel if the associated FIFO is full. In the remainder of this article we will refer to this model as a process network or task graph. The synchronization takes place on a per-token basis. While a token is the unit of synchronization, the amount of data associated with a token can vary. However, the size of a token is statically fixed per channel.

The communication protocol we describe involves the realization of the FIFO-based communication between the tasks, and does not refer to low-level protocols, e.g. bus protocols. Communication in our case is divided into 1) synchronization, and 2) data transportation. For efficiency reasons, all communication buffer memory is allocated at set-up and is reused during operation. Therefore, we need primitives to get and put buffer memory space. On the data producing side we want to get emptied token buffers and put full buffers. On the consuming side we want to get filled token buffers and put empty ones. Getting a token buffer is blocking, i.e. when no buffer is available the task blocks. Releasing (put) is non-blocking. The synchronization primitives are listed in Table 1.

Table 3.1. Synchronization Primitives

Primitive	Description
get_space	Claims empty token buffer (blocking)
put_data	Releases full token buffer (non-blocking)
get_data	Claims full token buffer (blocking)
put_space	Releases empty token buffer (non-blocking)

Two of the synchronization primitives, the "get_data" and the "get_space", return a pointer to the token on the input or output channel. Two additional primitives "load_data" and "store_data" are provided by C-HEAP to do the reading and writing from these pointers.

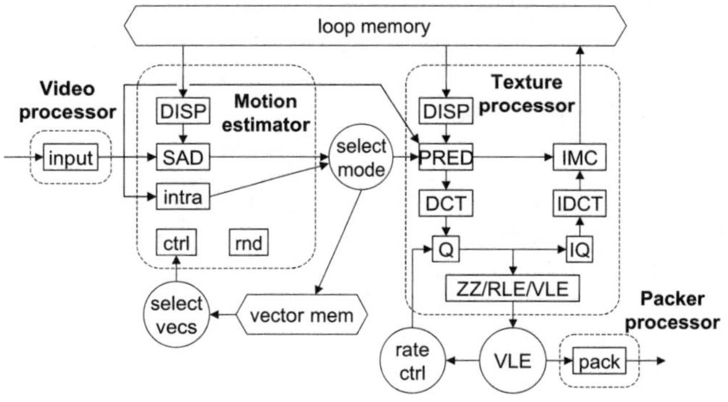

Figure 3. Hardware-Software Partitioning

3.2 Hardware-Software Co-Design

The first step consists of partitioning the video encoder application into hardware and software tasks. This step translates a single application task (task T0 in level 'a' of Figure 2) into multiple parallel tasks (T1 to T4 in level 'b'). This step can be divided into the following actions:

- A behavioral description in the C-language for the video encoder was used as the starting point. In order to obtain an estimate of the computational load, the C-code was profiled on an ARM processor. This provided the required clock frequency for a software-only solution and a breakdown of the computational load for different functional modules of the encoder. The latter was used as a starting point for determining the hardware-software partitioning. The main strategy was to implement the compute-intensive parts in hardware, while keeping the encoding standard and control related parts in software. This is illustrated in Figure 3, wherein the small rectangles represent hardware blocks, whereas circles represent software.
- The VLIW-based ASIPs used for implementing the hardware parts have the benefit that they offer the flexibility needed for the application domain (e.g. video coding) while achieving performance, area, and power numbers close to that of hard-wired solution. The hardware parts were clustered into processors, thus resulting in four processors for the video encoder: video input processor, motion estimation processor, texture processor and packer processor. The objective of this clustering is twofold. First, to reduce the synchronization overhead between hardware and software. Second, to hide all local communication inside the processors from global bus activity. The latter is crucial for low power. Figure 3 depicts the four hardware processors by dashed blocks. The communication between the processors is based on the previously described C-HEAP protocol. A behavioral version of the protocol was implemented on top of a multithreading package [11].

The four hardware processors perform the functions given below. The video input processor is responsible for doing a stripe to macro-block conversion. The motion estimation processor evaluates candidate motion vectors, and does motion vector refinements. The texture processor is responsible for encoding a macro-block. The packer processor interleaves the Huffman codes of the coefficients with those of the headers, in order to generate a compressed output video stream.

The partitioning resulted in a single software task. This partitioning maintains the necessary flexibility. Consider the motion estimation task as an example. The candidate motion vector selection is done in software. The motion estimation processor then determines the best motion vector, does a refinement, and transmits the results back to software. Further, in software, the encoding mode is selected, and the quantizer value is computed. The quantizer value and the choice of encoding mode are passed to the texture processor, which then encodes the macro-block. Furthermore, since the bit-rate control algorithm is application dependent, it is completely done in software.

The second step consists of mapping the communication backbone onto hardware, which corresponds to translation from level ‘b’ to ‘c’ in Figure 2. This is done as follows:

- The input variables of the hardware processors consist of two parts: initialization variables (e.g. number of pixels in horizontal and vertical direction of a picture), and run variables (e.g. the coordinates of the current macro-block being encoded). In the behavioral simulations, pointers to all the variables are passed to the processors, which use these pointers to access the variables. Once the communication backbone is mapped onto hardware, the processors will have to read the initialization variables for each macro-block from a shared memory. However, it is much more efficient to store the initialization variables locally during initialization. Therefore, an initialization mode was added to each processor, during which the initialization variables are read and stored locally. Only the run variables, which vary across macro-blocks, are communicated. This reduces the bandwidth on the bus considerably.
- The event-based C simulation framework (TSS simulator – Philips Internal Tool) was used for system simulations, wherein (bit- and cycle-true) TSS models of the AMBA bus and the memory were used. UNIX processes modeled the software and hardware tasks. A C-HEAP library using UNIX sockets implements the synchronization and communication of these processes with TSS. These simulations were used to obtain bus utilization figures, and to optimize the communication structure.

The third step focuses on improving the performance of the implementation. This can be seen as moving from level ‘c’ to ‘d’ in Figure 2. The result of the previous step consists of a system without concurrency. A software task starts a hardware task and awaits the completion of the hardware task (and vice versa), thus using the resources inefficiently. Concurrency can be implemented by pipelining the software and hardware tasks. However, some dependencies between software and hardware have to be broken. Since the breaking of the dependencies leads to a different behavior, extensive simulations were carried out in order to verify that the compression ratio and SNR are comparable to that of the original reference C description. Also the synchronization overhead has been optimized, by choosing the synchronization granularity as large as possible (given the flexibility constraints). This has resulted in two hardware processors (motion estimation and texture) synchronizing at macro-block granularity, and two other hardware processors (video input and packer) synchronizing at stripe granularity. Again the TSS simulator was used for the system simulations. TSS models for the ARM, the AMBA bus and the memory were used. UNIX processes, as in the previous step, modeled the hardware tasks. These simulations showed that the required number of clock cycles for the software tasks was smaller than the available cycle budget.

Figure 4 shows the pipelining of hardware and software tasks. The video input processor is one stripe ahead of motion estimation and texture processors. The motion estimation processor is two macro-blocks ahead of the texture processor, as required by the OBMC option of H.263. The header generation of a macro-block (VLE SW) is done one macro-block later than the encoding of the same macro-block. Last but not the least, the packer processor is one stripe delayed with respect to the texture processor. As stated before, only a single software task is required. Therefore, the scheduling of the hardware and software tasks is fixed (known at compile time).

For more details on the hardware-software co-design methodology, the reader is referred to [10].

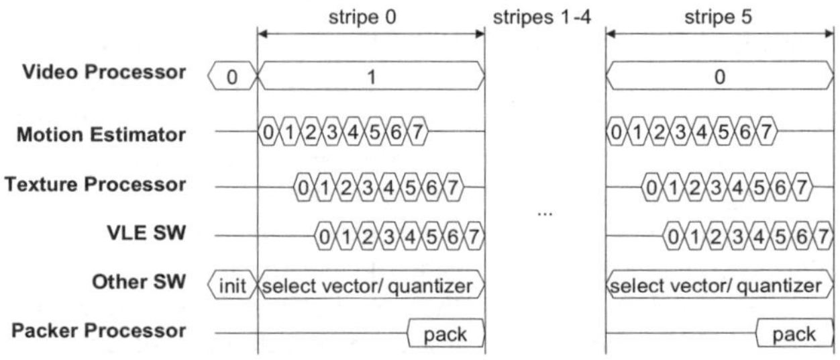

Figure 4. Pipelining of HW/SW Tasks

3.3 Hardware Processor Design

All hardware tasks are implemented as very-long- instruction-word (VLIW) processors. A|RT Designer [12] enables design of these VLIW processors. All application specific functional units (ASUs) used in the VLIW processors are designed using A|RT Builder [12], which translates a C-based functional specification of an algorithm into an RTL VHDL description. ASUs are used for performing dedicated compute-intensive kernels and hence are crucial for an efficient implementation of HW tasks. The choice and flexibility of those ASUs enable multi-standard encoder realization.

The following sections describe the design of hardware processors apart from the ASUs used in these designs (moving from level ‘d’ to ‘e’ and ‘f’ in Figure 2). The motion estimator and the texture processor have been implemented in two different configurations, namely, with and without embedded compression (EC).

3.3.1 Video Processor

The video processor is used for re-organizing the pixel format. This processor uses standard resources apart from an ASU for re-organizing pixels more efficiently.

The input format of pixels (namely, YYUYYV) is converted into four luminance and two chrominance 8x8 blocks in order to generate a macro-block output.

3.3.2 *Motion Estimator*

In the motion estimation hardware task, the current macro-block is motion estimated for all the candidate motion vectors in order to determine the best matching motion vector. Further, optionally, this best vector can be refined to half/quarter pixel accuracy. The 3DRS motion estimation uses sum-of-absolute-differences (SAD) as the matching criterion. The architecture of the motion estimator is shown in Figure 5. The granularity of the motion estimator processing is a macro-block.

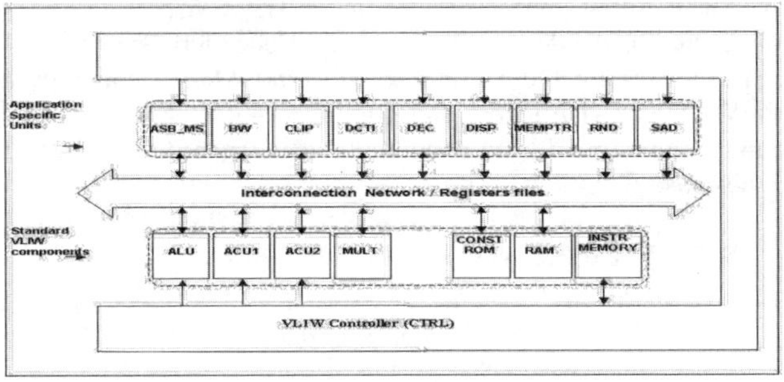

Figure 5. Motion Estimator Architecture

Table 3.2. Application Specific Units of ME

ASU	Purpose
BW	Byte/word conversions
CLIP	Clip engine (pixels, coordinates, vectors)
DCTI	(Inverse) discrete cosine transform (EC)
DEC	Embedded decompression (EC)
DISP	Displacer (cache/interpolator)
MEMPTR	Memory pointer address calculation
RND	Random number generator
SAD	Sum of absolute difference engine

For (every macro-block)
- Fetch a block from current frame
- Determine actions to be performed
- **For** every action:
  - → Initialization
  - → **For** every vector:
    - ▪ Initialization
    - ▪ **For** every component:
      - Displace DCT block
      - Calculate SAD
    - ▪ Update results
  - → Update and write results

Figure 6. Pseudo Code for Motion Estimator

The VLIW architecture of the motion estimator consists of standard resources like arithmetic-logic-units (ALUs), address computation units (ACUs), multipliers, constant-ROM, RAM, instruction memory, VLIW controller, apart from ASUs (refer to Table 2).

The first step in the motion estimator process is to determine the flow of actions, by analyzing software-controlled options. Subsequently all actions are executed as depicted in the pseudo code shown in Figure 6. The inner loop iterates over all luminance components of the macro-block. Within this loop the candidate vector block is displaced, delivered to SAD engine and SAD calculation is done. The middle loop iterates over the number of candidate vectors for this particular action.

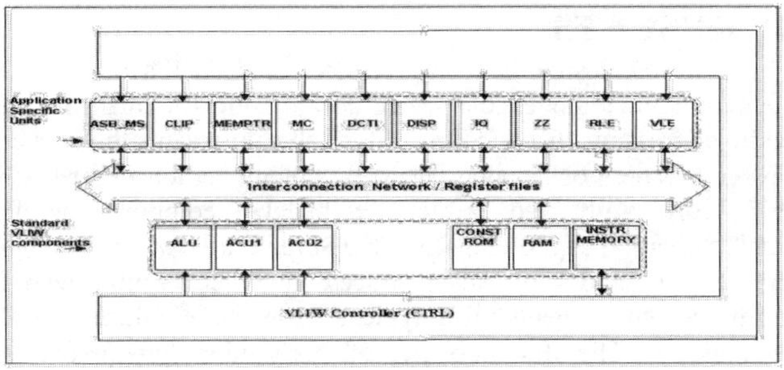

Figure 7. Texture Processor Architecture

Table 3.3. Application Specific Units of TC

ASU	Purpose
BW	Byte/word conversions
CLIP	Clip engine (pixels, coordinates, vectors)
MEMPTR	Memory pointer address calculation
MC	Motion compensator (predictor)
DCTI	(Inverse) discrete cosine transform (EC)
DISP	Displacer (cache/interpolator)
IQ	(Inverse) quantizor
ZZ	Zigzag transform
RLE	Run length encoder
VLE	Variable length encoder (Huffman table)

For (all blocks in macro-block)
- Fetch a block from current frame
- Fetch a block from the previous reconstructed frame (if not available in the cache)
  - → Perform displacement to get sub-pixel accurate block
- Motion compensate current block from the block fetched from the previous reconstructed frame
  - → Perform motion compensated loop filtering
  - → Perform overlapped block motion compensation (OBMC)
- Perform DCT and Quantization on the motion compensated block
- Perform IQ/IDCT/IMC and store the reconstructed block in the loop memory (loop memory holds the reconstructed frame)
- Perform loss less coding (ZZ/RLE/VLE) and store the Huffman encoded coefficients

Figure 8. Pseudo Code for Texture Processor

3.3.3 *Texture Processor*

The tasks of the texture processor are to calculate the difference between the current macro-block and the best match in the reconstructed image (prediction), transform, quantize, and entropy encode. The quantized data is inverse quantized, inverse transformed, reconstructed by adding the prediction, and stored in the loop memory to encode the next picture. The texture processor also has macro-block granularity. The architecture of the texture processor is shown in Figure 7. Again, the architecture contains standard resources apart from ASUs. An overview of ASUs is shown in Table 3 and the pseudo code is provided in Figure 8.

3.3.4 *Packer Processor*

The packer processor combines the Huffman coded video stream together with header information in order to generate compressed video stream of a given format. The packer processor uses one ASU for packing bit streams apart from standard resources. The ASU packs the Huffman codes into multiples of 32-bit words.

4. RESULTS

The C-based design flow and VLIW-based ASIPs used in the encoder realization enable faster design time (36 man-months) while addressing cost and flexibility. Table 4 presents the area and power numbers of a video encoder implementation described in this work with and without embedded compression. The implementation supports up to CIF@30fps. The motion estimator, the texture, and the packer processors where synthesized as hardware components for typical case in 0.18μm CMOS technology. The functionality of the video processor was implemented in software run by the CPU. The multi-standard video encoder was verified (bit-true and cycle-true) until the netlist.

Table 4.1. Area/Power Numbers of Encoder

Instance	Area (mm^2)	Power (mW)	Area with EC (mm^2)	Power with EC (mW)
ARM7TDMI-S	0.62	3.93	0.62	5.15
CPU memory	3.25	1.56	3.25	1.88
Loop memory	off-chip	off-chip	4.39	0.77
Motion estimator	1.62	6.03	2.74	8.70
Texture codec	4.24	4.30	5.39	6.21
Packer processor	0.50	0.08	0.50	0.08
Shells & busses	3.41 (*)	5.50 (*)	2.98	7.55
Total	13.64 (*)	21.40 (*)	19.86	30.34

(*) Off-chip loop memory data are not included

The CPU processor is an ARM7TDMI-S built in 0.18μm CMOS technology, with 0.39mW/MHz of power consumption. The frequency of the CPU clock is scaled down to just meet the performance requirements of the application. The memory instance includes only the CPU memory in the case without compression and the CPU- and loop memories in the case with embedded compression. While the loop memory has been embedded on-chip in the second case, the size of the motion estimation processor and texture processor have been increased due to the extra functional units needed for compression. The shells around the processors and busses support the communication among the components. Table 4 presents also the power dissipation numbers that are obtained under a typical simulation scenario (25ºC, 1.8V) for QCIF@15fps. QCIF@15fps has been chosen to facilitate benchmarking with existing solutions. The hardware processors run at 100MHz and are clock-gated when not in use.

Table 4.2. Benchmarking

Benchmark	Standard	Area (mm^2)	Power (mW)
Hitachi [2]	MPEG4	43	170
Our design	MPEG4, H.263, JPEG	19.9	30.3
Toshiba [13]	MPEG4	86	40
Fujitsu [3]	MPEG4	28	9

Table 5 shows the benchmarking of our design with three different encoder solutions [2,3,13]. The implementation in [2] is a complete SW solution using a fused RISC/DSP CPU and hence has higher area and power numbers. The implementation in [3] is an ASIC solution with off-chip SDRAM for loop memory, and the power indicated in the table does not consider the off-chip memory consumption. Compared to the ASIC solution, our design is more flexible and multi-standard. The implementation of [13] addresses flexibility similarly to our design while consuming more power for the same functionality.

5. CONCLUSIONS

In this work we presented the design of a low-cost, low-power and multi-standard video encoder. The right choice of algorithms and architectures had enabled an efficient solution for the video encoder. The use of embedded compression technique for reducing the size of the loop memory had enabled a single-chip low-cost solution. Further, the choice of HW/SW partitioning had contributed to the design of a low-power encoder. The power and area estimates for the encoder in 0.18μm CMOS technology are 30mW (for QCIF@15fps) and 20mm^2 respectively including the loop memory, and it is more competitive compared to state-of-the-art designs.

6. REFERENCES

[1] V. Bhaskaran, and K. Konstantinides. Image and Video Compression Standards. Algorithms and Architectures. 2nd Edition. Kluwer Academic Publishers. 1997.

[2] T. Yamada. A 133MHz, 170mW, 10μA Standby Application Processor for 3G Cellular Phones. In: *IEEE Solid-State Circuits Conference*. 2002.

[3] H. Nakayama. An MPEG-4 Video LSI with a 9mW Error-Resilient Codec based on a Fast Motion Estimation Algorithm. In: *IEEE Solid-State Circuits Conference*. 2002.

[4] A. van der Werf, et al. I.McIC: A Single-Chip MPEG-2 Video Encoder for Storage. In: *IEEE Journal of Solid-State Circuits*, vol. 32, no. 11. Nov. 1997.

[5] A. Nieuwland, et al. C-HEAP: A Heterogeneous Multi-Processor Architecture Template and Scalable and Flexible Protocol for the Design of Embedded Signal Processing Systems. In: *Kluwer Design Automation of Embedded Systems*, Oct. 2002.

[6] G. Kahn. The Semantics of a Simple Language for Parallel Programming. In: *Information Processing*. J. Rosenfeld, Ed. North-Holland Publishing Co. 1974.

[7] R. Kleihorst, et al. DCT-Domain Embedded Memory Compression for Hybrid Video Coders. In: *Journal of VLSI Signal Processing Systems*, vol. 24, pp. 31-41, 2000.

[8] G. de Haan, et al. True-Motion Estimation with 3-D Recursive Search Block Matching. In: *IEEE Transactions on Circuits and Systems for Video Technology*, vol. 3, no. 5. Oct. 1993.

[9] ITU-Telecommunication Standardization Sector. H.263 Version 2 (H.263+). Video Coding for Low Bit-Rate Communication. 1998.

[10] A. Nieuwland and P. Lippens. A Heterogeneous HW/SW Architecture for Hand-held Multi-media Terminals. In: *IEEE Workshop on Signal Processing Systems*. 1998.

[11] PAMELA. A Performance Modeling Language, ce-serv.et.tudelft.nl

[12] Adelante Technologies. A|RT Builder and A|RT Designer Manuals. www.adelante.com

[13] H. Arakida, et al. A 160mW, 80nA Standby, MPEG-4 Audiovisual LSI with 16Mb Embedded DRAM and a 5GOPS Adaptive Post Filter. In: *IEEE Solid-State Circuits Conference*. 2003.

A Case Study of Mapping a Software-Defined Radio (SDR) Application on a Reconfigurable DSP Core

Behzad Mohebbi, Eliseu Chavez Filho, Rafael Maestre, Mark Davies
Morpho Technologies Inc
19772 Mac Arthur Blvd, Irvine, CA 92612
{behzad, ecf, rafael, mdavies}@morphotech.com

Fadi J. Kurdahi
EECS Department,
University of California
Irvine, CA 92697
kurdahi@uci.edu

ABSTRACT
We present a case study involving the implementation of a complete Wideband CDMA (WCDMA) digital receiver part of an AMR channel onto a reconfigurable core. WCDMA is one of the two major standards for the third generation (3G) cellular systems. Traditionally most of the receiver components were confined to ASIC implementation for performance, size and power consumption reasons. The MS1 reconfigurable DSP core provides both a microprocessor and reconfigurable fabric as well as a variety of peripherals. The various functions of the receiver were mapped onto different core components. The complete system was tested both in simulation as well as on a hardware platform comprising a silicon implementation of the MS1 DSP core.

Categories: C3 Real-time Embedded systems

General Terms: Algorithms, Design, Experimentation

Keywords: Software-Defined Radio, Reconfigurable Computing

1. Introduction
Reconfigurable computing systems represent a hybrid approach between the paradigms of general-purpose and application-specific systems. They combine a software programmable processor and a reconfigurable hardware component that can be reused in different applications. This combination allows reconfigurable systems to achieve performance levels significantly higher than obtained with general-purpose systems and with wider flexibility than that offered by application-specific systems. This paper introduces the Morpho Technologies' MS1 reconfigurable DSP (rDSP) Core. The MS1 rDSP Core is primarily targeted for applications with inherent parallelism, word-level granularity and computation-intensive characteristics. Examples of key applications are baseband processing in digital wireless communication systems, and video compression and image processing in multimedia systems.

One of the key components in the case of mobile or airborne devices is the Software-Defined Radio (SDR). SDR promises to revolutionize the way such systems are implemented. SDR is the implementation of wireless network protocol whose operation modes can be changed after manufacturing. The relegation of more functions to programmable DSP or DSP-like hardware enables high performance, ubiquitous wireless terminals, infrastructure, equipment and services that allow seamlessness across diverse networks and integration of capabilities that encompass multiple standards and operational paradigms.

One of the key target standards that can benefit from an SDR approach is the third generation wireless system. Third-generation (3G) wireless standards such as WCDMA or CDMA2000 present computationally demanding tasks that until now have been dealt with only by application-specific cores. These ASICs typically perform chip-level baseband processing (e.g. the RAKE receiver) as well as encoding/decoding of source

information (e.g. voice and video). Conventional DSPs are usually employed for Forward Error Correction except in the case of Turbo decoding, which is implemented in ASIC logic due to its performance requirements. The Medium-Access Control (MAC) layer typically runs on an off-the-shelf microcontroller core.

ASICs present several disadvantages in this context: they have to be designed for the worst case processing scenario; they increase the time-to-market due to the long design cycle time; they increase cost as several ASIC cores have to be utilized in such multi-mode application; and finally they can not adapt to new standard releases, as it is impossible to do modifications after silicon tapeout.

We have proven in practice that a single MS1 rDSP Core is capable of performing all the chip-level baseband processing as well as source encoding/decoding (both voice and video) without the need for ASIC blocks. The results are simplification of design, cost reduction due to the simpler design, faster time to market, and smaller silicon area and flexibility for modifications after product delivery.

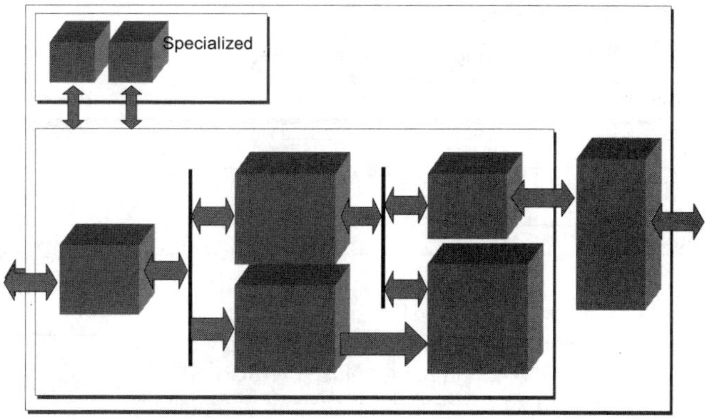

Figure 1: The MS1 Core Architecture

2. The MS1 rDSP Architecture

Morpho Technologies provides Reconfigurable DSP (rDSP) solutions based on a reconfigurable array processing paradigm, known as MS1 rDSP, which is briefly discussed here.

As in conventional reconfigurable systems [1], the MS1 Core contains a reconfigurable block, called the RC Array, and a 32-bit RISC processor, called the mRISC (Figure 1). The RC Array consists of Reconfigurable Cells (RCs) interconnected by a reconfigurable network. Both the functionality of the RCs and the network interconnections are determined by a configuration program, called Context. By writing the appropriate context, the developer can use the RC Array to exploit the parallelism available in the application. The mRISC Core Controller determines the application's control flow, executes the sequential tasks of the application, and starts transfers to/from the off-core memory. The instructions for the mRISC are stored in the Instruction Memory.

The MS1 Core also contains a Context Memory, a Data Buffer and an I/O Controller. The Context Memory stores the context words for the RC Array. The context words configure the operations performed by the RCs and their interconnectivity. The Data Buffer stores the input data to the RC Array as well as the produced results. The Data Buffer allows data input/output to be overlapped with data processing. The I/O Controller performs context loading from the off-core memory into the Context Memory and data transfers between the Data Buffer and the off-core memory. The I/O Controller receives transfer requests from the mRISC and generates an interrupt once the transfer is complete.

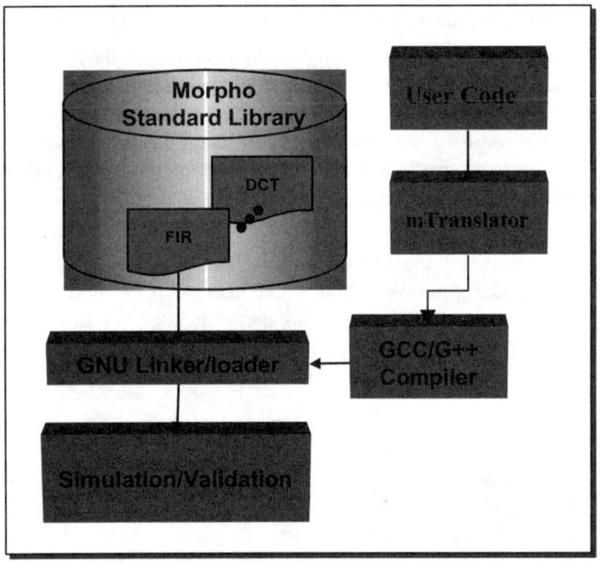

Figure 2: MS1 Programming Model

The Reconfigurable Cell is the programmable element in the RC Array. It performs general-purpose operations as well as word- and bit-level DSP functions. Input operands can be either internal to the RC, or from other RCs or from the Data Buffer. Due to the flexible interconnect structure and reconfiguration capabilities, the RC Array can operate in several modes whereby groups of cells can perform similar operations. The size and composition of these groups as well as the mode of operation can be changed dynamically, by switching contexts during runtime. The operation of the RC Array is coordinated by the mRISC Core Controller, which selects and switches contexts at runtime.

3. Development Tools for the MS1 Core

Programs for the MS1 Core consist of two parts: context code and mRISC Core Controller code. Both components are automatically generated from a single Morpho-C program, which is a C/C++ program (labeled "User Code" in Figure 2) with special mStatements. mStatements are high-level statements that the programmer embeds into regular C/C++ code in order to control the operation of the MS1 Core. In a Morpho-C program, the programmer can schedule tasks in order to overlap context loading, data input/output and processing, in many different ways. The Morpho-C code is preprocessed by the mTranslator. The output of mTranslator is a plain, pre-processed C program that is recognizable by the GNU gcc compiler. Both the mTranslator and the gcc compiler are part of the tool set provided with the MS1 Core. Therefore, the programming approach for the MS1 is similar to the paradigm employed by today's conventional DSP processors, with additional instructions for the rDSP fabric. It is important to note that no HDL code is generated at any point in this tool chain. This avoids the lengthy and unpredictable tasks of hardware design such as layout, timing closure and verification and validation.

4. The WCDMA AMR Receiver

The WCDMA AMR channel is defined in [2]. It is a channel that supports data rates from 4.75 to 12.2 kbits/s. However, due to algorithm availability, a GSM EFR is used as the speech codec. The GSM EFR vocoder has the same input and the encoded parameters as the AMR-NB vocoder in mode MR122 [3].

A top-level block diagram of the receiver chain is shown in Figure 3. The received IQ data (at 3.84 Mchips/sec x oversampling rate) is first filtered by a 49-tap RRC FIR filter. The baseband signal is then processed by the RAKE receiver, which performs the tasks of despreading and demodulation, along with the correction for channel and transmitter impairments. The output of the RAKE is then demultiplexed to remove the various physical layer control information such as pilot and power control bits, and passed trough the 2nd Interleaver. After the collection of two radio frames, the 1st

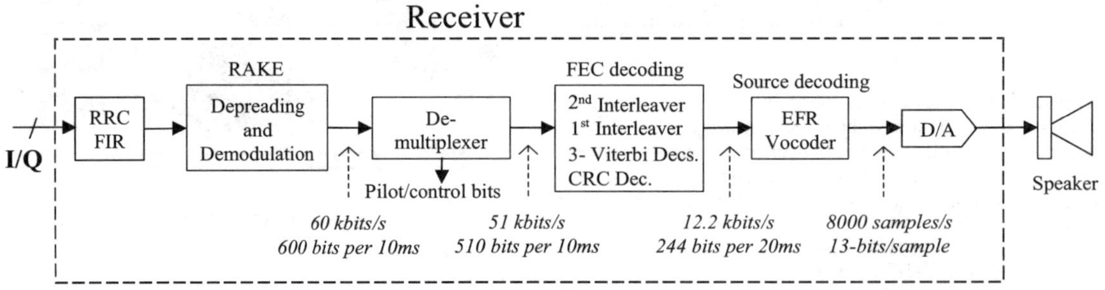

Figure 3: The WCDMA AMR Receiver

interleaver is performed on the received data, after which some control bits (DTX) are removed. The received encoded bits are then processed by the three Viterbi decoders to correct any possible errors caused by the channel. CRC parity decoding is performed on the decoded bits to detect any uncorrected errors on this class of data. The data stream is demultiplexed to its original state at 12.2 kbits/s. These bits are then processed by the GSM EFR decoder, to recover the original PCM speech frame. A Digital-to-Analogue Converter (DAC) processes the audio output signal, and the analog audio signal is played through a speaker. The above mentioned tasks are performed in a regular, time multiplexed schedule within one symbol duration (or Spreading Factor) of 256 "chips" on the RC array.

4.1 RAKE Receiver

The overall RAKE receiver architecture is shown in Figure 4. Each RAKE finger demodulates one signal path. The outputs of all the fingers are combined as a weighted sum in order to maximize the Signal-to-Noise Ratio (SNR).

The internal functions of each RAKE finger are shown in Figure 4. As shown, channel estimation, and clock and carrier synchronization are performed independently for each finger. An external path-searching algorithm provides the necessary timing information to select the optimum sampling instant prior to decimation. With input samples at 2x the chip rate, the Delay Locked Loop (DLL), used for clock synchronization, is capable of correct synchronization, in the presence of worst case expected noise and interference, with an initial acquisition error in excess of ½ chip period. After timing correction by interpolation, the received samples are decimated by a factor of 8, for subsequent chip rate processing by the correlation/despreader units. Soft output data are generated for the Dedication Physical CHannel (DPCH) and the Common PIlot CHannel (CPICH), at the corresponding symbol rates. Early and late correlation values are also generated for the CPICH channel at ±½ chip periods away from the current (punctual) sampling instant. These are used for timing synchronization purposes.

5. Mapping of the Receiver

Starting with a MATLAB simulation model, the receiver and transmitter were validated for functionality and performance. Following that, a fixed point C model was written and was used as the starting point for the mapping. The mapping consists of two major tasks: the first one is to partition the system onto code that runs on the mRISC controller and code that exercises the RC array. The second task is to map the latter code onto the RC array in order to maximize performance and/or reduce code size. The receiver was mapped using a meet-in-the-middle strategy. A first-cut partitioning

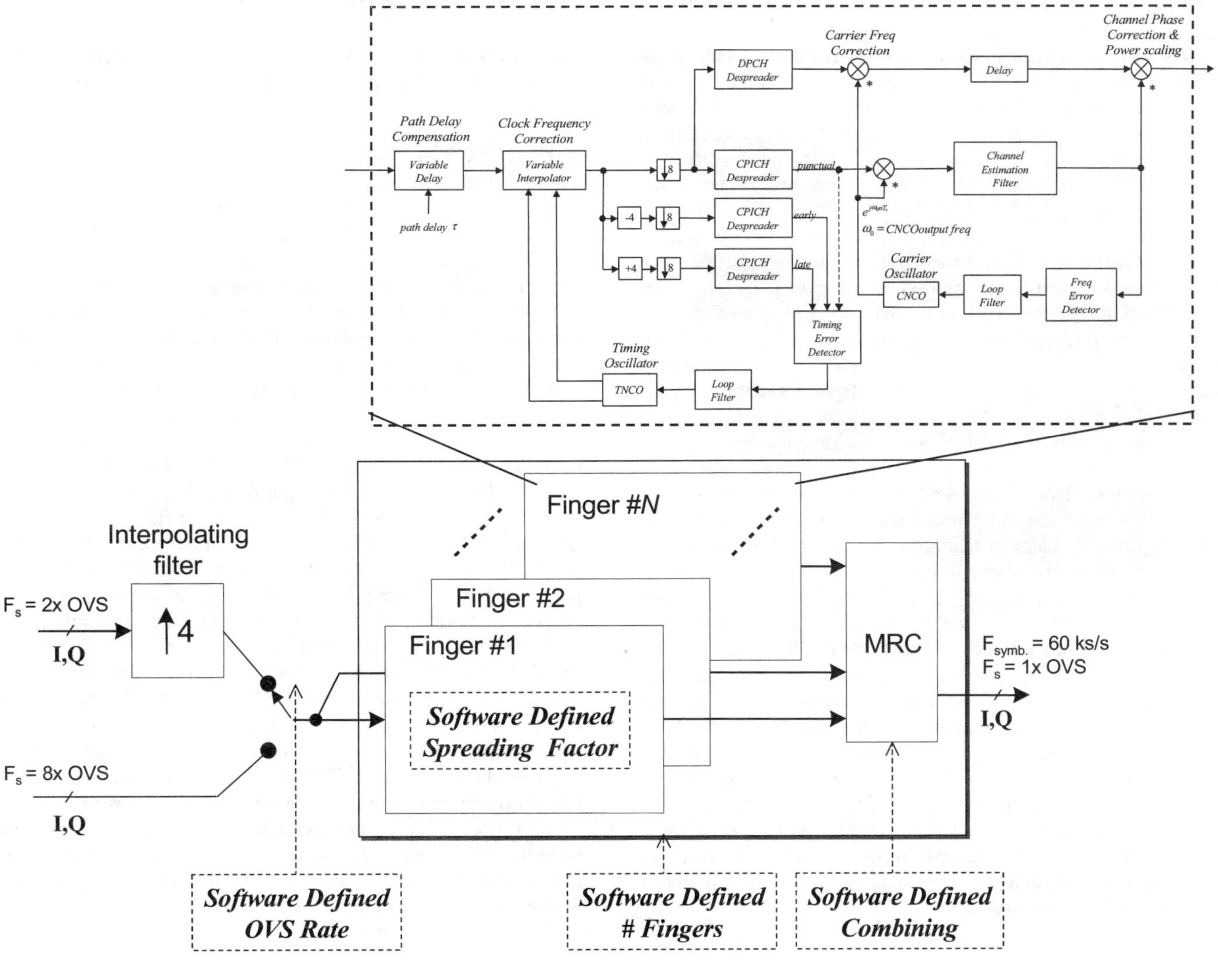

Figure 4: The RAKE receiver

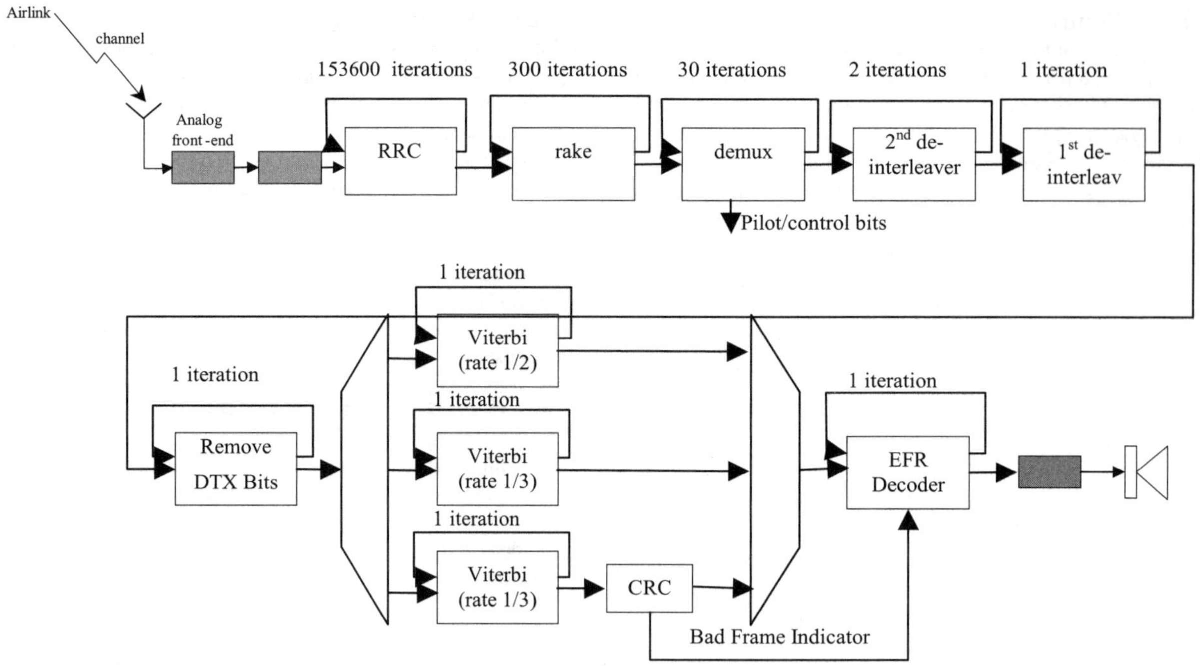

Figure 5: Process Diagram of the AMR Receiver

of tasks was performed manually and the major tasks identified as shown in Figure 5. Next, the tasks that are to run on the RC array were further partitioned onto components that were individually mapped as application kernels and encapsulated as parameterized function calls. Next, the system level C code was modified to incorporate the aforementioned kernels. Contrary to an ASIC solution, the receiver tasks are now executing on a single unit (the MS1 core) in a time-multiplexed mode. This necessitated a scheduling of the kernels in order to ensure that all the real-time requirements for each kernel as well as the overall receiver were met. Additionally, the scheduling has to be applied to the configurations (contexts) for each kernel that must be moved into the core at the right time prior to the execution of the target kernel. The system level scheduling of the overall process diagram of the receiver shown in Figure 5 was adjusted to accommodate the varying granularities of kernels. This necessitated the establishment of buffers between blocks. Recall that the RAKE fingers operate at symbol-rate (66.7μsec), the second interleaver at radio frame rate (10 msec), and all the other operations at speech frame rate (20 msec). In order to maintain real-time operation of the receiver, we chose the coarsest granularity of operation, which in this case is 20 msec as the outer loop iteration time. During that time, the RAKE receiver would output 300 symbols while the second interleaver would output two radio frames. Thus, all the iteration counts shown in Figure 5 were set to produce a speech frame. The code was fine-tuned to maximize the cycle performance. Some kernels or portions of kernels were moved between the mRISC controller and the rDSP fabric depending on the relative performance as well as the communication cost between the two. Conceptually as well as practically, the software-defined nature of the receiver made it quite easy to make code modifications, create buffers, or change scheduling at any time. By contrast, an ASIC implementation would have necessitated a respin of the silicon along with all the associated redesign and fabrication costs.

The following sections describe the receiver algorithms and the mapping strategies employed to optimize their performance on the MS1 core.

5.1 EFR Mapping

Consider the GSM Enhance Full Rate (GSM EFR) vocoder which has the same input and the encoded parameters as the AMR-NB vocoder in mode MR122 [3]. The EFR is the third defined vocoder for GSM systems, and belongs to the Code Excited Linear Prediction (CELP) speech compression family. The EFR with a bit rate of 12.2kbits/sec is an Algebraic CELP (ACELP) vocoder, where an excitation signal is built for each pulse, rather than the selection from a codebook as a codevector, as was the case with classical CELP vocoders. In the EFR vocoder, the codevector is defined as ten pulses of 1 or –1, out of 40 optional subframe locations, where the remaining 30 are set to zero. Thus, the search operation is based on finding the best ten locations for the pulses, and establishing whether each pulse is a 1 or a –1. This task is performed four times per 20msec. Prior to the search and determination of the codevector, two other speech analyses are performed. These are Linear Prediction Coding (LPC) analysis and pitch estimation. These are the fundamental components of the encoder that provide the decoder with the ability to reproduce the synthesized speech at the receiver [4]. There are more than 24 functions for the encoder and more than 12 functions for the decoder part provided by the standard C code [5]. Amongst the encoder functions, the search algorithm (search_10i40) by far consumes most of the encoder processing, which is more than 22% of the total required cycle count for the encoder. This function alone has considerable inherent parallelism, and speed-ups of more than 4x have been achieved in executing this function on a 16-element reconfigurable fabric. Other EFR sub-algorithms such as correlation and filtering also exhibit considerable parallelism, which is dealt with in the following discussions.

5.2 FEC Decoder

This algorithm is known as the Viterbi Algorithm (VA) [6]. With each received n-tuples, the decoder computes a metric or measure of likelihood for all paths that could have been taken during that interval and discards all but the most likely to terminate on each node. An arbitrary decision is made if the path metrics are equal. The metrics can be formed using either hard or soft decisions information with little differences in implementation complexity.

Before the VA is mapped onto the MS1 core, it is necessary to identify the possible strategies for optimal performance. One of the major steps in the Viterbi algorithm is to update the *path metrics* (*pm*), by the appropriate *branch metrics* (*bm*) which are executed in a process known as *Add-Compare-Select* (ACS). Executing a VA on a sequential machine would consume too many cycles and must be sped up for acceptable overall real-time performance. In general, additional parallelism can be introduced into the VA at the bit level, the word level and the algorithm level [7]. At the bit level, transformations allow introduction of bit level pipelining, such that the critical path for each implementation runs only through a few bit levels resulting in the possibility of significant increase in the clock rate [8]. At the word level, using algebraic transformations, the two operations of the ACS recursion may be identified to form an algebraic structure called semi-ring which can represent the VA as linear vector recursion [8]. Using this algebraic transformation, the bottleneck of VA (the non-linear feedback in ACS) is eliminated. At the word level, it is also possible to perform the operation of each of the states independently, in parallel. Finally, at the algorithm level, the asymptotic behavior of the VA can be exploited to derive parallel processing architectures [9]. The bit level parallelism can be incorporated into almost any arithmetic logic unit, regardless of the particular choice of parallel architecture. However, the utilization of word level parallelism is highly dependent on the computational fabric and resources. For a parallel processing engine, with a "modest" number of ACS units at each node (e.g. <10), the feasible word level parallel execution is the concurrent state implementations, ideally with one butterfly operation at each node. It is also possible to assign a single state to each processing node, which might lead to excessive intermediate data movement between the nodes. Algorithm level parallelism offers the highest rewards in extracting the maximum parallelism. The only two drawbacks associated with algorithm level parallelism are, first, the increase in processing latency and, second, the overhead associated with the block overlap. There is usually a tradeoff between the two, where the block overlap overhead can be reduced at the expense of greater throughput latency.

5.3 Interleaver/Deinterleaver

Interleaving is used after the FEC encoding, for randomizing the burst of channel errors caused by multipath fading, such that the errors appear as random as an AWGN channel at the input to the FEC decoder. The random appearance of errors is essential for effective operation of the decoder. The deinterleaving operation is required in the receiver to arrange the data into its original sequence, which is usually the opposite operation to that of interleaving.

The channel interleaving block or bit is usually defined by mathematical or operational algorithms (e.g. the WCDMA first and second interleaving algorithm defined in [10]). A parallel processing fabric, especially with reconfigurable interconnect, may be used for limited permutation changes and bit re-ordering operations. However, for long interleaving depths used in channel interleaving little or no advantage can be gained from such platforms.

5.4 RAKE Receiver

Recall the RAKE receiver functionality described in Figure 4 While current RAKE receiver implementations are done either completely or partially in ASIC logic, the MS1 core is capable of performing the complete RAKE functionality in software running on the MS1. As the chip-rate implementation (i.e. the front-end despreading in each finger) of the RAKE receiver is carried out in software, a number of parameters that were traditionally "hard-wired" in ASICs, can be defined by the operating condition and the required overall performance of the system (i.e. Software Defined). For example, as shown in Figure 4, at the expense of more processing, it is possible to reduce the memory requirement of the input sampled data, by operating at twice the chip rate (i.e. 2x OVS) and using an interpolation filter, to achieve the desired time resolution for fine timing adjustments. It is also possible to set, and change at run-time, the desired number of RAKE fingers and the spreading factor of each finger. Finally, Maximal Ratio Combining (MRC) is used for path combining. Alternatively, any other combining scheme can be integrated in the software, and selected "on-the-fly". The most computationally expensive portion (and fortunately, the most amenable to acceleration) is the despreading. The spreading and despreading of data, performed for spread spectrum modulation, exhibit the most regular form of parallelism, where the same operation is carried out on all the data samples, in parallel. For example, in a WCDMA terminal, the despreading operation of a symbol of an AMR channel requires 128 multiplications of the received data with the appropriate complex code and the accumulation of the multiplication results. This operation can efficiently be spatially mapped to a group of processors where the samples in each block are processed in parallel. The complex chips are moved into the processors, where they are multiplied by the despreading codes, and accumulated in each processing element. After the operation on the final block, a final summation is then performed of all the accumulators of the processors. Therefore, algorithms such as despreading, correlation and FIR filtering that can be implemented usinig a similar structure on the on a reconfigurable processor array, should asymptotically be implemented N times faster on N processors compared to conventional sequential DSP engines. The reconfigurable nature of the RC array plays a central role in the efficient execution of these operations whereby the processors may operate in an SIMD fashion when partial sums are accumulated on individual elements, and switching to an MIMD mode when sums are accumulated across elements. The above mapping example utilizes the word-level parallelism inherently present in the correlation algorithm. Due to the immense flexibility of the reconfigurable fabric, it is also possible to devise alternative spatial mappings that utilize the algorithm-level parallelism, where even higher computational gain should be possible.

The other computationally intensive part of the receiver is the interpolation filter. Almost all the above operations are based on a transversal tap-delay structure that exhibits similar word and algorithm level parallelism, as was discussed for FIR filters in the despreading section, resulting in nearly a N times processing advantage (N = the number of RC processors).

The other components of the RAKE receiver deal mainly with synchronization and recovery loops. These loops occur at different granularities and exhibit little parallelism at the word level. Our first implementation was using mostly sequential code which resulted in adequate but not highly optimized performance. But after closer examination, considerable parallelism can be extracted for each loop both at the word and, more importantly, at the algorithm level. For example, a WCDMA receiver may require up to eight RAKE fingers to run in parallel. Each of these eight fingers requires independent recovery loops that can be executed in parallel on a reconfigurable processing fabric. Further, at the expense of some data latency, each algorithm can be applied to several symbols in parallel.

The final component of the RAKE receiver is the channel estimation. Radio signals that are subject to multipath propagation suffer attenuation from *Multipath Fadings*. In CDMA based air-interfaces, a "path searcher" unit is used to estimate the delay component, while either the common pilot or dedicated pilot symbols are used for the estimation of the attenuation and phase associated with each significant resolvable propagation path. The path searcher of CDMA based systems uses correlation algorithms based on a transversal filter which is highly parallelizable and very similar to the despreading used in the RAKE receiver.

6. Test bed results

Recalling that the RAKE fingers operate at the symbol-rate (66.7μsec), the second interleaver at radio frame rate (10msec), and all the other operations at speech frame rate (20 msec), the test-bed demonstration showed that a unified time multiplexed approach of all the functions, based on the lowest time granularity, is a feasible processing approach for the implementation of real-time software defined systems. It also demonstrated that the rDSP reconfigurable platform is capable of providing the required processing capacity for the AMR receiver algorithms, including both the chip-rate and symbol-rate processing units. The processing requirement of the chip-rate algorithms (mainly the RAKE receiver) is around 70%, and the Symbol rate (the transport layer) is 30%, of the total processing load required by the these functions. Typically, traditional DSPs are only capable of performing the EFR decoding in real time (which is a very small portion of the overall receiver processing), while the rest of the receiver tasks are performed exclusively by ASIC blocks. Overall, a comfortable amount of headroom was left over to accommodate any additional processing needs, or alternatively to power down to conserve power.

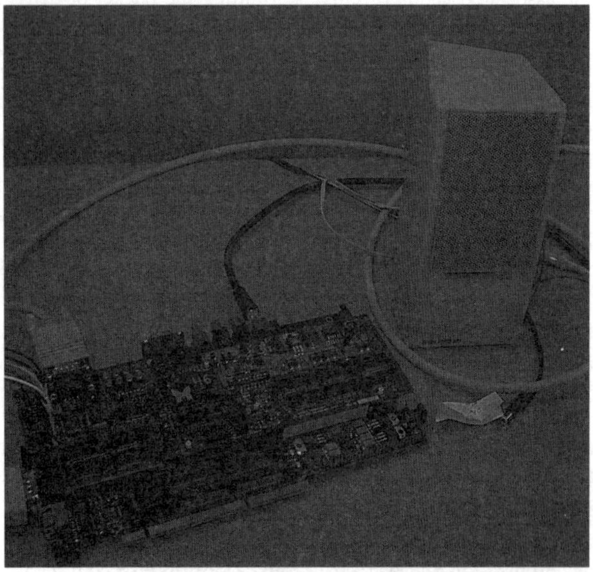

Figure 6: The Hardware Testbed

The AMR receiver was fully implemented using the compilation toolchain described in Section 3 and validated both on a cycle accurate simulator as well as a hardware development system shown in Figure 6. In fact, the test-bed results, and supporting cycle-accurate simulations indicate that all the transmit/receive baseband functions of a handset can be comfortably supported by a single rDSP core with 16 RC processing elements.

While the above discussion was based on a circuit-switched forward-link AMR channel, further benchmarking and cycle-accurate simulations of a 384 kbits/s (Spreading Factor=4) WCDMA channel, supporting packet transmission mode, showed that the same core can support all the transmitter/receiver functions of such channel. The 384 kbits/s channel requires a different RAKE receiver design, to work with relatively shorter transmission duration of packet mode, and supports Turbo encoding/decoding and MPEG codecs. This change is accomplished by simply running a different piece of software than for the previous channel.

7. REFERENCES

[1] W. H. Mangione-Smith *et al.*, "Seeking Solutions in Configurable Computing," *IEEE Computer*, Dec. 1997, pp. 38-43

[2] 3GPP TS 34.108, "Common Test Environments for User Equipment (UE) Conformance Testing", Release 4, Technical Specification Group Radio Access Network, 3rd Generation Partnership Project.

[3] 3GPP-AMR-NB With ETSI-EFR Implementation on the StarCore SC140 Core, (AN2280/D), Rev 0, 5/2002, Motorola application note.

[4] 3GPP TS 46.051, "Enhanced Full Rate (EFR) speech processing functions: General description" Release 4, Technical Specification Group Services and System Aspects, 3rd Generation Partnership Project.I

[5] GSM 06.53: "Digital cellular telecommunications system (Phase 2+); ANSI C code for the GSM Enhanced Full Rate (EFR) speech codec".

[6] A. J. Viterbi, "Error bounds for convolutional coding and an asymptotically optimum decoding algorithm," *IEEE Trans. Information Theory*, vol. IT-13, pp. 260-269, April 1967.

[7] G. Fettweis, H. Meyr, "A Modular Variable Speed Viterbi Decoding Implementation for High Data Rates," North-Holland Signal Processing IV, Proc. EUSIPCO '88, pp. 339-342, 1988

[8] G. Fettweis, H. Meyr, "High-Speed Parallel Viterbi Decoding: Algorithm and VLSI Architecture," IEEE Communication, pp. 46-55, May. 1991

[9] G. Fettweis, H. Meyr, "Feedforward Architectures for parallel Viterbi Decoding," Kluwer J. on VLSI signal processing, No. 3 pp. 105-119, 1991.

[10] 3GPP TS 25.212, "Multiplexing and channel coding (FDD)", Release 4, Technical Specification Group Radio Access Network, 3GPP.

A Codesigned On-Chip Logic Minimizer

Roman Lysecky, Frank Vahid*
Department of Computer Science and Engineering
University of California, Riverside
{rlysecky, vahid}@cs.ucr.edu
*Also with the Center for Embedded Computer Systems at UC Irvine

Abstract

Boolean logic minimization is traditionally used in logic synthesis tools running on powerful desktop computers. However, logic minimization has recently been proposed for dynamic use in embedded systems, including network route table reduction, network access control list table reduction, and dynamic hardware/software partitioning. These new uses require logic minimization to run dynamically as part of an embedded system's active operation. Performing such dynamic logic minimization on-chip greatly reduces system complexity and security versus an approach that involves communication with a desktop logic minimizer. An on-chip minimizer must be exceptionally lean yet yield good enough results. Previous software-only on-chip minimizer results have been good, but we show that a codesigned minimizer can be much better, executing nearly 8 times faster and consuming nearly 60% less energy, while yielding identical results.

Categories and Subject Descriptors

C.3 [**Special-Purpose and Application-Based Systems**]: Real-time and embedded systems

General Terms: Algorithms, Performance.

Keywords: Logic minimization, dynamic optimization, on-chip logic minimization, on-chip synthesis, system-on-a-chip, embedded systems, hardware/software codesign, embedded CAD.

1. Introduction

On-chip logic minimization is becoming increasingly important in applications requiring dynamic optimizations. Unfortunately, most logic minimization algorithms have been developed with the expectation the algorithms will be run on a desktop workstation. The use of these minimization algorithms for performing dynamic optimizations within an embedded system is limited. While the applications of on-chip logic minimization are just recently emerging, logic minimization is already useful in performing dynamic hardware/software partitioning, dynamically reducing network routing table size, and dynamically reducing network access control lists.

In [12], we presented a first approach to dynamic hardware/software partitioning. In this approach, the dynamic partitioning system monitors an executing application, determines the critical loops of the application, and executes these loops in hardware using on-chip configurable logic. Such an approach requires several tools to convert the software description of the loop to hardware, including decompilation, logic synthesis, technology mapping, and place and route. During the logic synthesis phase, the dynamic hardware/software partitioning system uses two-level logic minimization in an iterative process to optimize the hardware circuit, requiring an on-chip logic minimizer.

Logic minimization is also useful for performing optimization in other applications not related to synthesis of hardware circuits. Such applications include IP (Internet Protocol) routing table reduction and network access control list (ACL) reduction. Network routers route an incoming IP packet to its destination by determining the packet's next hop. The router compares the packet's destination IP with the router's routing table and uses the longest prefix match to select the packet's destination port. While simple lookup schemes work for small routers, large network routers with ten of thousands of routing table entries can require long lookup times. Longest prefix matching can be directly mapped to Ternary CAMs [9]. However, TCAMs require large hardware resources and tend to have high power consumption. Liu developed a method for reducing the routing table size using two-level logic minimization and hence reducing the cost of using TCAMs [7].

Logic minimization is also helpful in reducing the size of a network router's access control list. Most commercially available network routers have ACLs that allow the router to accept or deny incoming IP packets. The router uses information from the incoming IP packet to search the ACL for the first matching entry and takes the associated action of either permitting the packet or denying the packet. Large ACLs often have thousands of entries, making sequential lookup infeasible. Furthermore, hardware-based parallel lookup approaches are limited because the approach must preserve the ordering of the ACL entries. In [8], we developed an approach using TCAMs to efficiently search ACLs, involving an optimization

Figure 1: Comparison of off-chip and on-chip logic minimization methods.

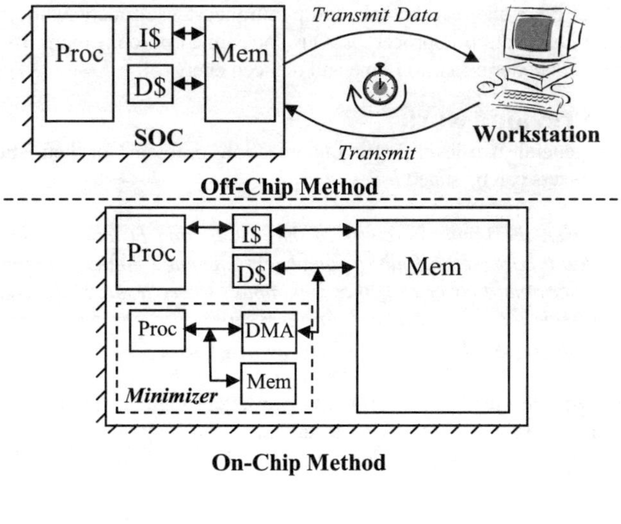

technique using two-level logic minimization to reduce the size of the ACL.

Dynamic hardware/software partitioning, IP routing table reduction, and ACL reduction require dynamic execution of logic minimization. Figure 1 highlights two possible methods for performing logic minimization dynamically. In the off-chip method, the application transfers the required data to a logic minimizer executing on a desktop workstation accessible through a communication link such as Ethernet. The workstation optimizes the data and transmits the results back to the application. While an off-chip method has the benefit of using a powerful workstation-based minimizer, the communication overhead can greatly slow the minimization process, especially when minimization is applied frequently. The method also has drawbacks related to ensuring the workstation is always available, and reducing security risks (ACL lists are heavily guarded by most companies, for example).

Alternatively, we can perform logic minimization on-chip by adding an on-chip minimizer to the chip itself. One approach to this method executes the optimizer as an additional task that shares the same processing resources as the application itself. Another approach to the on-chip method implements the minimizer using a separate embedded processor/memory system with direct access to the main processor's memory. Both on-chip approaches benefit from reducing or eliminating data transfers between the application and the logic minimizer, and they eliminate the complexity and security issues of the off-chip approach.

In either on-chip minimization approach, the logic minimizer will have limited processing resources, in terms of both processor speed and available instruction and data memory. These limitations require the need for a lean minimizer designed to execute on-chip. However, a lean minimizer must still provide "good enough" results within a reasonable time. We developed a lean software minimizer, ROCM (Riverside On-Chip Minimizer), designed to execute on an ARM7 processor [2], which is a low-cost lean 32-bit embedded processor. While the use of ROCM to perform IP routing table reduction, ACL reduction, and dynamic hardware/software partitioning provided good results with very low memory requirements, these benefits came at the cost of slower execution speed and additional energy consumption require by the minimizer.

In this paper, we present a codesigned on-chip minimizer that improves performance and reduces energy consumption. We started with customized versions of ROCM, called ROCM-32 and ROCM-128, customized for applications with fixed input sizes of 32 bits and 128 bits, respectively. In our approach, we first modified the data structures and algorithms used by ROCM to make ROCM more amenable to hardware/software partitioning. We then isolated the critical computational kernels and partitioned these functions/loops to a minimization coprocessor. Our codesigned on-chip minimizer results in better execution time and reduced energy.

2. Previous work

The general two-level logic minimization problem for heuristic minimizers can be stated as:

> *Given the inputs F (cover of the on-set) and D (cover of the don't care set) of an incompletely specified logic function, determine a cover of F that is minimal, where a minimal cover of F is a cover that is not a proper superset of any other cover of the function.*

We designed our original two-level logic minimization algorithm, ROCM, employing techniques used by both Espresso-II [3] and Presto [12], which form the heart of many popular commercial synthesizers today. The ROCM algorithm uses a simple heuristic approach with a single expand phase implemented with the main goal of very small memory usage. First, ROCM orders the implicants according to decreasing implicant size, under the assumption that larger implicants are more likely to cover other implicants and less likely to be covered by other cubes [3]. ROCM uses an iterative expansion process that attempts to expand each implicant and determines if each expansion is valid. While the use of the off-set for determining the validity of expanded implicants, as is done by Espresso-II, yields a very efficient algorithm, the size of the off-set can be very large. We therefore chose not to compute the off-set, and we instead employ a tautology-based approach similar to that used by Presto. Using this simplified methodology, ROCM required on average an order of magnitude less code size and only one third the data memory of Espresso-II. ROCM's low memory requirements came at the expense of a mere 2% decrease in minimization quality. ROCM's execution time (ignoring communication time) was 13% longer, but when applied incrementally (as typical for the network applications) was 10 times faster, and when executing on an ARM7 was still 2-5 times faster than Espresso-II on a 500 MHz Sun Ultra60 workstation.

In embedded systems, customizing an algorithm for a particular application is often beneficial. A customized version of our logic minimizer would require less memory and reduce dynamic memory allocation while improving performance. Therefore, in our original work, we created customized versions of ROCM, called ROCM-32 and ROCM-128, optimized for applications with known input size [8]. For example, ROCM-32 is optimized for routing table reduction applications where the input size is 32-bits. ROCM-32 required an average of 11% less data memory and 37% less execution time than the non-customized version.

Cong et al [4][5] sped up two-level logic minimization by utilizing an FPGA to speedup the tautology checking algorithm of Espresso-II. In their work, the hardware coprocessor performs tautology checking for functions of eight or fewer variables. Their implementation using an FPGA achieved an average speedup of 1.36, with a maximum speedup of 2.94. The main limitation of their approach is the use of a minterm evaluator for which 2^k terms must be evaluated, where k is the number of input variables. The hardware required for a larger number of variables quickly becomes infeasible using their coprocessor design.

In designing our codesign on-chip logic minimizer, we can exploit the customization of ROCM to the input size of the intended application. The known input size of the minimization algorithms allows for better partitioning and small hardware requirements. A small, embedded processor is still required as there is much dynamic memory allocation and control logic, which is more feasible to implement in software than hardware. We will design the hardware coprocessor to efficiently implement the critical computational kernels within our minimization algorithms.

3. Codesigned On-Chip Logic Minimizer

We performed an initial profiling of the customized ROCM-32 and ROCM-128 programs to determine the critical kernels of those logic minimizers. To profile the programs, we used a SimpleScalar [11] simulator, ported for the ARM family of processors, and extended to produce an instruction trace. We then used a loop analysis tool [15] to process the instruction trace along with the disassembled binary executable to determine the critical functions, loops, and sub-loops. Our initial profiling of the logic minimizers revealed good potential speedups. However, we noticed some initial limitations resulting from our algorithms' implementation and the organization of data structures. Our early investigation identified six critical kernels from

Table 2: ROCM-32 profiling results for IP router table reduction.

Function/ Loop	Total Instr.	Loop Instr.	Loop Time%	Loop Size%	Speedup Bound
DoesInter	15401	34	42.7%	0.22%	1.7
SetLit	15401	23	5.7%	0.15%	1.1
GetLit	15401	8	8.8%	0.05%	1.1
IsCov	15401	67	3.4%	0.44%	1.0
Tautology.1	15401	67	1.7%	0.37%	1.0
Cofactor.1	15401	57	28.5%	0.44%	1.4
Overall	**15401**	**256**	**90.7%**	**1.68%**	**10.8**

Table 1: ROCM-128 profiling results for ACL reduction.

Function/ Loop	Total Instr.	Loop Instr.	Loop Time%	Loop Size%	Speedup Bound
DoesInter	15518	51	21.3%	0.33%	1.3
SetLit	15518	27	21.3%	0.17%	1.3
GetLit	15518	12	25.9%	0.08%	1.4
IsCov	15518	83	0.5%	0.54%	1.0
Tautology.1	15518	204	11.0%	1.32%	1.1
Cofactor.1	15518	59	12.8%	0.38%	1.1
Overall	**15518**	**436**	**92.8%**	**2.81%**	**13.9**

within ROCM-32 and ROCM-128 that could be potentially implemented in hardware. However, we initially designed our algorithms using dynamic memory allocation within the critical software loops. We modified these algorithms to remove the dynamic memory allocation from within the critical loops. While we were able to rewrite the algorithms to eliminate the memory allocation from the loops, we added additional code before the critical loop to handle the memory allocation, resulting in 3% slower execution. Fortunately, the degradation in execution speed is easily overcome after partitioning our minimizer.

Additionally, we performed another simple modification to the logic minimization code to improve the potential speedup we could achieve using a hardware coprocessor. The basic underlying data structure used for storing implicants contains many different data items. While these data items are used for various purposes throughout the execution of our logic minimizer, many of these data items are not needed during the critical portions of code. However, in the original C code, the pertinent data items were interleaved with the non-essential data items throughout the data structure. Using a compiler that byte-aligns data structures, the data items that we are interested in will reside at multiple memory locations. Therefore, the original data structure organization would require more memory accesses by the hardware coprocessor during execution. Therefore, we reorganized the data structures to ensure the required data items were located in sequential memory locations as tightly packed as possible.

This necessary rewriting of the algorithms and data structures for more efficient hardware execution is something often overlooked in codesign research. The rewriting was quite fundamental and likely could not be automated easily using existing compiler or synthesis transformation methods. Vahid et al [6] observed this phenomenon in several other applications. The necessary rewriting has implications for top-down codesign approaches that seek to automatically partition a single specification among hardware and software.

After we modified our logic minimization tools, we again profiled ROCM-32 for IP routing table reduction and profiled ROCM-128 for network ACL reduction. Table 2 displays the profiling results for ROCM-32, and Table 1 displays the profiling results for ROCM-128, listing the six critical kernels that we identified. *Function/Loop* identifies the critical kernels. *TotalInstr* is the total number of instructions of the application. *LoopInstr* is the number of instructions within the critical kernel. *LoopTime%* is the percent of overall execution time spent within the critical kernel. *LoopSize%* is the percent of overall code size corresponding to the critical kernel. *SpeedupBound* is the maximum speedup possible assuming the critical kernel is executed in zero time. For ROCM-32, the six critical functions/loops account for over 90% of the execution time but less than 2% of the overall code. Similarly, ROCM-128 accounts for over 90% of the execution time and only 3% of the code. The six critical kernels include *DoesInter*, *SetLit*, *GetLit*, *IsCov*, *Tautology.1*, and *Cofactor.1*. *DoesInter* determines if two implicants intersect. *SetLit* sets a literal within an implicant to the specified value. *GetLit* retrieves a specific literal from within an implicant. *IsCov* determines if an implicant is covered by another implicant. *Tautology.1* is a loop that handles special cases for determining if the specified function is a tautology. Finally, *Cofactor.1* is the main loop that determines the cofactor with respect to a specified implicant.

Figure 2(a) shows the overall architecture of our codesigned minimizer, which consists of an ARM7 processor coupled with a small memory and the minimization coprocessor. Additionally, the coprocessor has direct access to memory. We implemented all six critical kernels within the coprocessor. We modified the minimization software running on the ARM7 to activate the coprocessor instead of executing the original code. During the coprocessor activation, the software transfers the required initialization information along with an encoded value indicating which of the six kernels is to be executed. After activating the coprocessor, we place the ARM7 in a low power mode until the coprocessor wakes up the processor using an interrupt, signaling completion.

Figure 2(b) shows a more detailed architecture of the minimization coprocessor. The *Proc/Mem Interface* is responsible for communication with the processor and internal hardware components. The *Proc/Mem Interface* also handles all memory accesses for *DoesInter*, *GetLit*, *SetLit*, and *IsCov*, as all four of these hardware components are implemented as combinational logic consisting of simple logic gates, 2-bit muxes, and shifters. On the other hand, *Tautology.1* and *Cofactor.1* perform many memory accesses, as both algorithms must traverse an array of implicants during execution. Therefore, we implemented *Tautology.1* and *Cofactor.1* as separate hardware components that receive the initialization data from the *Proc/Mem Interface* but during execution have direct access to memory. While we can implement the internal computation required by *Cofactor.1* using simple logic gates, adders, and shifters, *Tautlogy.1* also requires the use of a 32-bit multiplier.

We created two codesigned on-chip logic minimizers for the two distinct input sizes needed for our applications. The codesigned version of ROCM-32 will be referred to as CD-ROCM-32, and the codesigned version of ROCM-128 will be referred to as CD-ROCM-128.

Figure 2: Codesigned on-chip logic minimizer architecture: (a) overall codesigned minimizer architecture, (b) detailed co-processor architecture.

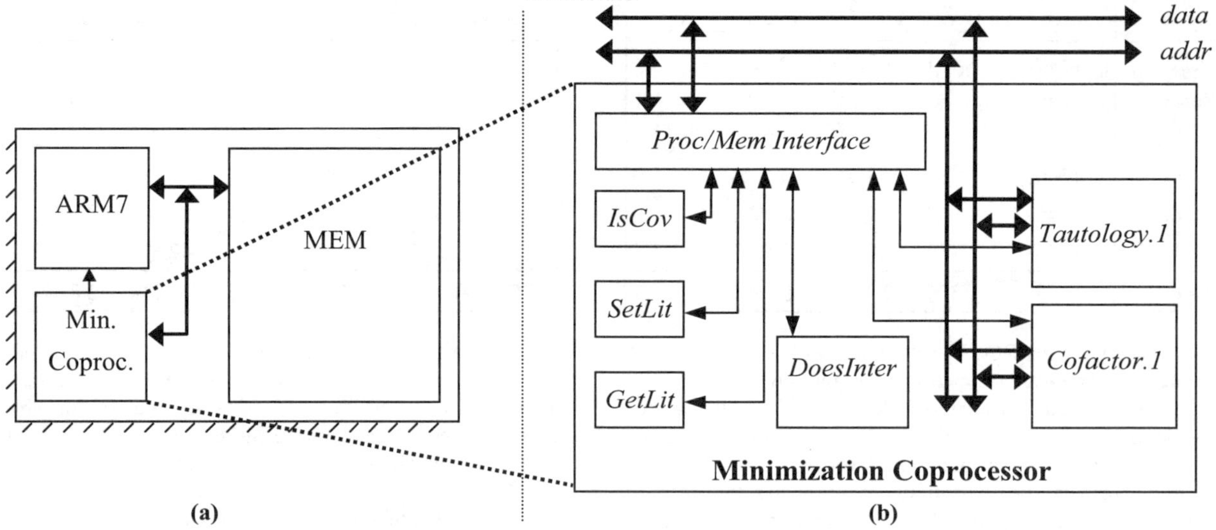

4. Results

While our main requirements for an on-chip logic minimizer is small instruction and data memory requirements, the execution time, required hardware area, and power consumption are also important. In our original approach, we only required a small ARM7 processor to execute our logic minimization software. The addition of an ARM7 dedicated to executing our software minimizer would require roughly 100,000 gates including caches and consume 49 mW of power executing at 75 MHz. Such an addition is small compared with current chip capacities of several million gates; we saw a router chip 3 years ago with 36 ARM processors. Nevertheless, we can eliminate the need for an additional processor by sharing a single processor with the main application, if the main application's time constraints allow for this sharing. However, our codesigned on-chip logic minimizer requires the use of dedicated hardware resources.

We implemented the coprocessor for CD-ROCM-32 and CD-ROCM-128 using VHDL to determine the required hardware area and power consumption. We synthesized both coprocessors using Synopsys Deign Compiler [14] using the UMC 0.18μm technology library provided by Artisan Components [1]. Furthermore, we determined the power consumption of both coprocessor using Design Compiler and gate-level simulations. The CD-ROCM-32 coprocessor required roughly 19,000 gates and has a power consumption of 100 mW when active. The CD-ROCM-128 minimizer required roughly 32,000 gates with a power consumption of 388 mW. Both coprocessors execute at 200 MHz.

Table 3 highlights the speedup of our codesigned minimizers for IP routing table reduction, ACL reduction, and logic synthesis optimization with dynamic hardware/software partitioning. For IP routing table reduction, we compared ROCM-32 with our codesigned CD-ROCM-32, and for ACL reduction and dynamic hardware/software partitioning, we compared ROCM-128 with our codesigned CD-ROCM-128. *Orig. SW Time* is the time required by our software only minimizer. *SW Loop Time* is the total time required by the six critical kernels when implemented in hardware. *HW Loop Time* is the time required for those critical kernels when executed using our hardware coprocessor. *HW/SW Time* is the total time for required by our codesigned minimizer. *Speedup* is the overall speedup of our codesigned minimizer compared to the all software version. Our overall speedup for CD-ROCM-32 over an all software approach is 7.6, and our overall speedup of CD-ROCM-128 is 7.9.

Table 3 also provides the energy reduction of our codesigned minimizers over the software based ROCM-32 and ROCM-128. *Orig. SW Energy* is the energy required by our original software minimization tools. *SW Energy* is the energy consumed by the ARM7 to execute the software for our codesigned logic minimizers. *HW Energy* is the energy required by our minimization

Table 3: Codesigned on-chip logic minimizer speedup and energy reduction for IP routing table reduction, ACL reduction, and dynamic HW/SW partitioning logic synthesis compared with ROCM-32 and ROCM-128.

Codesigned Minimizer	Performance (s)					Energy (mJ)				
	Orig. SW Time	SW Loop Time	HW Loop Time	HW/SW Time	Speedup	Orig. SW Energy	SW Energy	HW Energy	Total Energy	Energy Savings
CD-ROCM-32 (IP)	1.64	1.49	0.06	0.22	7.6	80.1	8.2	6.3	14.6	81.8%
CD-ROCM-128 (ACL)	1.53	1.42	0.08	0.19	7.9	74.7	6.4	32.3	38.8	48.1%
CD-ROCM-128 (LogSyn)	0.054	0.050	0.003	0.007	7.9	2.61	0.22	1.14	1.36	47.8%
				Average:	7.8				Average:	59.2%

Table 4: Execution time (*seconds*) of ROCM, ROCM-32, and CD-ROCM-32 for IP routing table reduction, and speedup of CD-ROCM-32 versus ROCM executing on a 75MHz ARM7.

Example	ROCM	ROCM-32	CD-ROCM-32	Speedup
MaeWest	2214	1328	175	12.7
AADS	2341	1419	187	12.5
Paix	271	199	26	10.4
PacBell	2666	1581	208	12.8
			Average:	**12.1**

coprocessors. *Total Energy* is the total energy required by our codesigned on-chip logic minimizer. Finally, *Energy Savings* is the percent energy reduction of our codesigned logic minimizers compared with ROCM-32 and ROCM-128. We calculated the energy required for ROCM-32, ROCM-128, and our codesigned minimizers we used the following set of equations:

Although the minimization coprocessors required up to an order of magnitude more power than the ARM7 processor, the overall energy reduction of our codesigned minimizers is on average 59.2%. Furthermore, CD-ROCM-32 requires over 81% less energy than ROCM-32, while CD-ROCM-128 requires roughly 48% less energy than ROCM-128.

We also analyzed the performance of our codesigned on-chip logic minimizers compared to our original on-chip minimizer, ROCM, and the customized version ROCM-32 and ROCM-128. Table 4 presents overall execution times of ROCM, ROCM-32, and CD-ROCM-32 in performing routing table reduction using data from for four large network routers, MaeWest, AADS, Paix, and PacBell, from data available at [10]. Furthermore, Table 5 presents overall execution time for performing ACL reduction of five access control lists ranging in size from 99 entries to over 3000 entries. For performing IP routing table reduction, our codesigned on-chip minimizer CD-ROCM-32 has a maximum speedup of 12.8 and an average speedup of 12.1 compared to ROCM. Furthermore, although logic minimization is executing on-chip using a 75 MHz ARM7 processor coupled with a 200 MHz coprocessor, CD-ROCM-32 is on average 1.2 times faster than Espresso-II executing on a 500 MHz Sun Ultra60 workstation for performing IP routing table reduction. For performing ACL reduction, CD-ROCM-128 has a maximum speedup of 18.5 and an average speedup of 15.3 compared to our initial on-chip logic minimizer.

5. Conclusions

On-chip logic minimization requires a fast and lean minimizer component producing “good enough” results. We have developed such a component through hardware/software partitioning, achieving speedups of nearly 8x compared to an earlier software-only minimizer component, while using a very reasonable number of extra gates. The codesigned component also reduces energy by more than half. During our codesign process, we needed to modify the underlying data structures and algorithms of ROCM, which may imply new directions of hardware/software partitioning research.

$$E_{total} = E_{ARM} + E_{HW}$$
$$E_{ARM} = P_{ARM(idle)} \times t_{idle(ARM)} + P_{ARM(active)} \times t_{active(ARM)}$$
$$E_{HW} = P_{HW} \times t_{active(ARM)} + P_{static} \times t_{total}$$

Table 5: Execution time (*seconds*) of ROCM, ROCM-128, and CD-ROCM-128 for ACL reduction, and speedup of CD-ROCM-128 versus ROCM executing on a 75MHz ARM7.

Example	ROCM	ROCM-128	CD-ROCM-128	Speedup
Bad	15.63	8.22	1.04	15.0
Typ1	6.87	5.89	0.72	9.5
Typ2	6.15	2.62	0.33	18.5
Long	1572.44	686.81	86.94	18.1
Univ	17.98	86.94	1.16	15.6
			Average:	**15.3**

The feasibility of fast and lean on-chip logic minimization may open up many new applications of logic minimization, beyond the networking and dynamic partitioning applications we described, that were previously not considered feasible due to the complexity of off-chip logic minimization.

6. Acknowledgements

This work was supported in part by the National Science Foundation (CCR-0203829), the Semiconductor Research Corporation, and a Department of Education GAANN fellowship.

7. References

[1] Artisan Components. http://www.artisan.com, 2003.

[2] Advanced RISC Machines Ltd. ARM7. http://www.arm.com/armtech/ARM7_Thumb/, 2002.

[3] Brayton, R., et al. Logic Minimization Algorithms for VLSI Synthesis. Kluwer Academic Publishers, Boston, MA, 1984.

[4] Cong, J., J. Peck. On Acceleration on the Check Tautology Logic Synthesis Algorithm using an FPGA-based Reconfigurable Coprocessor. Proc. Field-Programmable Custom Computing Machines (FCCM), 1997.

[5] Cong, J., J. Peck. On Acceleration on the Check Tautology Logic Synthesis Algorithm using an FPGA-based Reconfigurable Coprocessor. Technical Report TR-970010, University of California, Los Angeles, 1997.

[6] Grattan, B., G. Stitt and F. Vahid. Codesign Extended Applications. IEEE/ACM Int. Symposium on Hardware/Software Codesign, May 2002, pp. 1-6.

[7] Liu, H. Routing Table Compaction in Ternary-CAM. IEEE Micro, pp. 58-64, Jan/Feb 2002.

[8] Lysecky, R., F. Vahid. On-Chip Logic Minimization. Proc. 40th Design Automation Conference, 2003.

[9] McAuley, A. P. Francis. Fast Router Table Lookup Using CAMs. Proc. Infocom, Vol. 3, pp. 1382-91, 1993.

[10] Merit Network, Inc. Internet Routing Table Statistics, http://www.merit.edu/ipma/routing_table/, 2002.

[11] SimpleScalar LLC. http://www.simplescalar.com, 2003.

[12] Stitt, G., R. Lysecky, F. Vahid. Dynamic Hardware/Software Partitioning: A First Approach. Proc. 40th Design Automation Conference, 2003.

[13] Svoboda, A., D.E. White. Advanced Logical Circuit Design Techniques. Garland Press, New York, 1979.

[14] Synopsys, Inc. Design Compiler. http://www.synopsys.com, 2003.

[15] Villarreal, J., R. Lysecky, S. Cotterell, F. Vahid. Loop Analysis of Embedded Applications. UC Riverside Technical Report UCR-CSE-01-03, 2001.

Synthesis of Real-Time Embedded Software with Local and Global Deadlines[1]

Pao-Ann Hsiung and Cheng-Yi Lin
Department of Computer Science and Information Engineering
National Chung Cheng University, Chiayi–621, Taiwan, ROC
hpa@computer.org

ABSTRACT

Current methods cannot synthesize real-time embedded software applications when the global deadline of a task is shorter than the total of all local deadlines along a critical path in the task. This creates unnecessary modeling limitations which directly affect the types of systems synthesizable. We propose a *quasi-dynamic scheduling* algorithm for simultaneously guaranteeing both local and global deadlines, while satisfying all precedence constraints among subtasks and among tasks. Through this scheduling procedure, we are able to formally synthesize real-time embedded software from a network of *Real-Time Petri Nets* specification. Application examples, including a driver for the Master/Slave role switch in Bluetooth wireless communication devices, are given to illustrate the feasibility of the scheduling algorithm.

Categories and Subject Descriptors

C.3 [**Special Purpose and Application-Based Systems**]: Real-time and embedded systems; D.2.2 [**Software Engineering**]: Design tools and techniques—*Petri nets*

General Terms

Design, Algorithms

Keywords

real-time embedded software, Real-Time Petri Nets, quasi-dynamic scheduling, software synthesis, code generation

1. INTRODUCTION

A real-time embedded system task is composed of some constituent subtasks, each of which has its own *local deadline*, while the task itself has a *global deadline*. Current scheduling algorithms do not explicitly consider such multilevel deadlines leading to the necessity for work-around efforts. We propose a scheduling algorithm to resolve this issue and show how it can be used for synthesizing real-time embedded software specifications into actual program code.

[1]This work was supported by project grants NSC91-2213-E-194-008 and NSC92-2213-E-194-003 from the National Science Council, Taiwan.

CODES+ISSS'03, October 1–3, 2003, Newport Beach, California, USA.

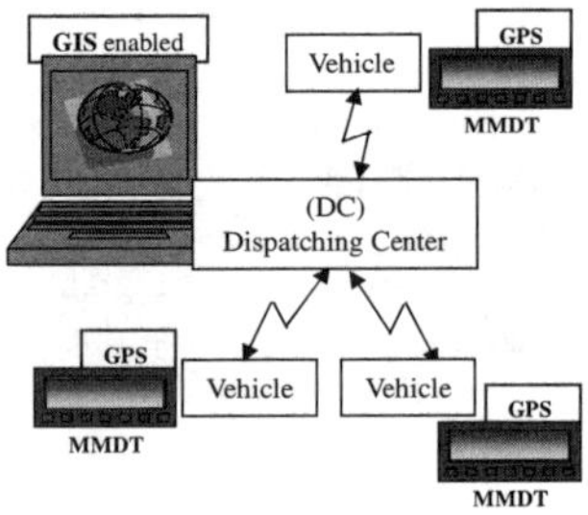

Figure 1: Modular Mobile Dispatching System

As a motivating example depicted in Fig. 1, consider the *Modular Mobile Dispatching System* (MMDS) [16], which consists of a GPS receiver, a GIS database, a GSM communication module, and other I/O peripherals for dispatching of vehicles through a call center. Besides the local deadlines on each GPS, GIS, and GSM task, there is also a global deadline on each scenario which is composed of several tasks with precedence and concurrency relationships. A typical scenario would be that of a vehicle driver encountering an emergency situation, in which the driver uses MMDS and expects to get help within 4 minutes from the time a call is made from the vehicle to the call center. Within this time span, MMDS must get GPS location information, transmit it to the call center through GSM communication, the call center must plot the driver's location on a digital map using GIS, locate the nearest help on the map, dispatch help (such as an ambulance) to the location by notifying the target help through GSM, while providing navigation guidelines through an active GIS database.

There are several issues involved in such a typical real-time scenario, as detailed in the following.

- How to determine which subtasks are concurrently enabled at any point of execution?
- How to check if each subtask completes execution within its local deadline, while satisfying all precedence constraints among the subtasks?
- How to check if each task completes execution within its global deadline?
- How to obtain an optimal schedule of all system tasks such that shortest execution time is guaranteed, if one exists?

- How to estimate the amount of memory space required for the execution of a real-time embedded software system?

Corresponding to each of the above issues, we propose a set of solutions in the form of a scheduling method called *Quasi-Dynamic Scheduling* (QDS), which incorporates the respective solutions as briefly described in the following.

- *Concurrently Enabled Group*: We maintain a group of concurrently enabled subtasks, while the system's behavior is statically simulated to satisfy all precedence relationships.
- *Tentative Schedulability Check*: Since the group of concurrently enabled subtasks changes dynamically with system execution, its schedulability can be checked only tentatively for the current group.
- *Global System Timer*: A global system timer is maintained that keeps count of the current total amount of processor time taken by the execution of all tasks.
- *Pruned Reachability Tree*: Because schedulability checks are only tentative for a group of subtasks, a reachability tree is created so that an optimal schedule can be found. The tree is pruned for efficiency without affecting optimality.
- *Maximum Memory Estimation*: Using various memory estimation techniques, both static and dynamic memory space allocations are statically counted, including memory spaces for both local and global variables.

Basically, quasi-dynamic scheduling is a combination of quasi-static scheduling and dynamic scheduling. Data dependent branch executions are statically decomposed into different behavior configurations and quasi-statically scheduled [17]. For each quasi-statically decomposed behavior configuration, dynamic scheduling is employed to satisfy all local deadlines of each subtask, all precedence constraints among subtasks, and all global deadlines of each task.

To illustrate the importance of this research result, consider how existing scheduling approaches must be applied to a system with both local and global deadlines. In this case, there is a need for work-around methods such as making global deadline the sum of all local deadlines in a critical path of the task. The user is burdened with the responsibility of analyzing a task and finding the critical path, a non-trivial task in some cases, apriori to scheduling. Further, this work-around method only works if the global deadline is not smaller than the sum of all local deadlines in a critical path of a task, because otherwise it would amount to restraining each local deadline, thus making an otherwise schedulable system unschedulable. In summary, the work presented here is not only a flexibility enhancement to current scheduling methods, but also a necessary effort in checking schedulability for real systems.

This article is organized as follows. In Section 2, we delve on some previous work in quasi-static scheduling and real-time scheduling related to the synthesis of real-time embedded software. In Section 3, we formulate our target problem to be solved, our system model, and give an illustrative example. In Section 4, we present our quasi-dynamic scheduling algorithm and how it is applied to the running example. Section 6 concludes the article giving some future work.

2. PREVIOUS WORK

Since our target is formally synthesizing real-time embedded software, we will only discuss scheduling algorithms that have been used for this purpose.

Due to the importance of ensuring the correctness of embedded software, *formal synthesis* has emerged as a precise and efficient method for designing software in control-dominated and real-time embedded systems [11, 9, 17, 18]. Partial software synthesis was mainly carried out for communication protocols [15], plant controllers [14], and real-time schedulers [1] because they generally exhibited regular behaviors. Only recently has there been some work on automatically generating software code for embedded systems [2, 13, 17], including commercial tools such as MetaH from Honeywell. In the following, we will briefly survey the existing works on the synthesis of real-time embedded software, on which our work is based.

Previous methods for the automatic synthesis of embedded software mostly do not consider temporal constraints [13, 17, 18], which results in temporally infeasible schedules and thus incorrect systems. Some recently proposed methods [9, 12] explicitly take time into consideration while scheduling, but have not solved the multilevel deadlines issue. Details of each method are given in the rest of this section.

Lin [13] proposed an algorithm that generates a software program from a concurrent process specification through intermediate Petri-Net representation. This approach is based on the assumption that the Petri-Nets are safe, *i.e.*, buffers can store at most one data unit, which implies that it is always schedulable. The proposed method applies *quasi-static scheduling* to a set of safe Petri-Nets to produce a set of corresponding state machines, which are then mapped syntactically to the final software code.

A software synthesis method was proposed for a more general Petri-Net framework by Sgroi et al. [17]. A quasi-static scheduling (QSS) algorithm was proposed for *Free-Choice Petri Nets* (FCPN) [17]. A necessary and sufficient condition was given for a FCPN to be schedulable. Schedulability was first tested for a FCPN and then a valid schedule generated by decomposing a FCPN into a set of *Conflict-Free* (CF) components which were then individually and statically scheduled. Code was finally generated from the valid schedule.

Later, Hsiung integrated quasi-static scheduling with real-time scheduling to synthesize real-time embedded software [9]. A synthesis method for soft real-time systems was also proposed by Hsiung [10]. The free-choice restriction was first removed by Su and Hsiung in their work [18] on extended quasi-static scheduling (EQSS). Recently, Gau and Hsiung proposed a more integrated approach called time-memory scheduling [11] based on reachability trees.

A recently proposed *timed quasi-static scheduling* (TQSS) method [12] extends two previous works: (1) the QSS [17] method by handling non-free choices (or complex choices) that appear in system models, and (2) the EQSS [18] by adding time constraints in the system model. Further, TQSS also ensures that limited embedded memory constraints and time constraints are also satisfied. For feasible schedules, real-time embedded software code is generated as a set of communicating POSIX threads, which may then be deployed for execution by a *real-time operating system.*

Balarin et al. [2] proposed a software synthesis procedure for reactive embedded systems in the *Codesign Finite State Machine* (CFSM) framework with the POLIS hardware-software codesign tool. This work cannot be easily extended to other more general frameworks.

Besides synthesis of software, there are also some recent work on the verification of software in an embedded system such as the *Schedule-Verify-Map* method [6], the linear hybrid automata techniques [5, 7], and the mapping strategy [4]. Recently, system parameters have also been taken into consideration for real-time software synthesis [8].

3. SOFTWARE SYNTHESIS

Our target is the formal synthesis of real-time embedded software, with local and global deadlines, using scheduling techniques. A system is specified as a set of concurrent tasks, where each task is composed of a set of subtasks, with precedence relationships. Time constraints are classified into two categories: *local* deadlines and *global* deadlines. A local deadline is imposed on the execution of a subtask, whereas a global deadline is imposed on the execution of a task in a system model [11].

Previous work on software synthesis were mainly based on a subclass of the Petri net model (introduced later in Section 3.1). We also adopt the Petri net model for software requirements specification, but we associate explicit semantics to the firing time intervals, which will be explained when the system model *Real-Time Petri Net* (RTPN) is defined. Just like *Time Complex-Choice Petri Nets* (TCCPN) used in [12], RTPN places no free-choice restriction on the model expressivity and adds timing constraints on each transition, which represents a subtask. Thus, a wider domain of applications can be precisely modeled by RTPN. Details on the RTPN system model, our target problem, and an illustrative example will be described in Sections 3.1, 3.2, and 3.3, respectively.

3.1 System Model

The requirements for real-time embedded software are modeled by a set of RTPNs. Graphically, an RTPN can be depicted as shown in Fig. 2, where circles represent places, vertical bars represent transitions, arrows represent arcs, black dots represent tokens, and integers labeled over arcs represent the weights as defined by F. A place with more than one outgoing transition is called a *choice* place and the transitions are said to be *conflicting*. For example, p_0 is a choice place and t_1 and t_2 are conflicting transitions in Fig. 2. We define RTPN as follows, where $\mathcal{N}$ is the set of positive integers.

DEFINITION 1. *Real-Time Petri Nets (RTPN)*
A Real-Time Petri Net *is a 5-tuple* (P,T,F,M_0,τ), *where:* P *is a finite set of places.* T *is a finite set of transitions,* $P \cup T \neq \emptyset$, $P \cap T = \emptyset$, *and some of the transitions are* source *transitions, which fire periodically.* $F : (P \times T) \cup (T \times P) \longrightarrow \mathcal{N}$ *is a weighted flow relation between places and transitions, represented by arcs, such that: (a) Synchronization at a transition is allowed between a branch arc from a choice place and another arc, and (b) A self-loop from a place back to itself is allowed only if there is an initial token in one of the places in the loop.* $M_0 : P \longrightarrow N$ *is the initial marking (assignment of tokens to places).* $\tau : T \longrightarrow N \times (N \cup \infty)$, *i.e.,* $\tau(t) = (\alpha, \beta)$, *where* $t \in T$, α *is the* worst case execution time *(WCET) of* t, *and* β *is the* deadline *for* t, *which will be denoted as* $\tau_\alpha(t)$ *and* $\tau_\beta(t)$, *respectively.* ||

3.2 Problem Formulation

A user specifies the requirements for a real-time embedded software by a set of RTPNs. The problem we are trying to solve here is to find a construction method by which a set of RTPNs can be made feasible to execute on a single processor as a piece of software code, running under given finite memory space and time constraints. The following is a formal definition of the real-time embedded software synthesis problem.

DEFINITION 2. *Real-Time Embedded Software Synthesis*
Given a set of RTPNs, an upper-bound on available memory space, and a set of real-time constraints such as periods and deadlines for each RTPN, a piece of real-time embedded software code is to be generated such that: (a) it can be executed on a single processor, (b) it satisfies all the RTPN requirements, including precedence constraints and local deadlines, (c) it satisfies all global real-time constraints, including RTPN (task) periods and deadlines, and (d) it uses memory no more than the user-given upper-bound. ||

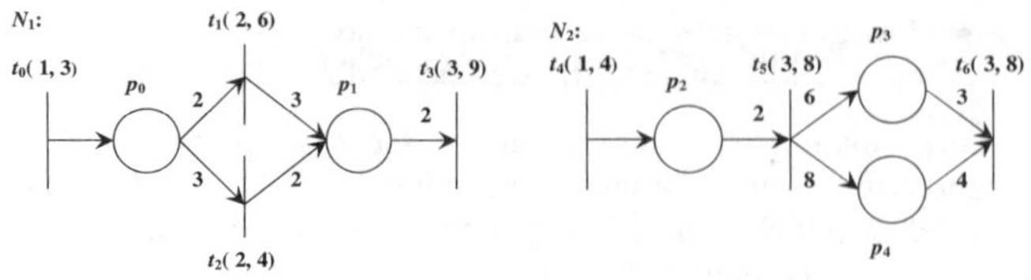

Figure 2: Illustration Example

As described in Section 1, there are five issues involved in solving this problem and the solutions to these issues are integrated into a quasi-dynamic scheduling method, which will be presented in Section 4. Due to page-limit, we leave out the code generation part of software synthesis, which has a multi-threaded architecture based on PThreads [18].

3.3 Illustration Example

This is a simple toy example to illustrate how our proposed scheduling method works. The RTPN model for this example is shown in Fig. 2, which consists of two nets $N_1 = (P_1, T_1, F_1, M_{01}, \tau_1)$ and $N_2 = (P_2, T_2, F_2, M_{02}, \tau_2)$, where $P_1 = \{p_0, p_1\}$, $P_2\{p_2, p_3, p_4\}$, $T_1 = \{t_0, t_1, t_2, t_3\}$, $T_2 = \{t_4, t_5, t_6\}$, the flow relations F_1, F_2, and the firing intervals τ_1, τ_2 are obvious from the numbers on the arcs and transitions, respectively. The initial markings M_{01}, M_{02} are all empty.

4. QUASI-DYNAMIC SCHEDULING

To solve the several issues raised in Section 1 for synthesizing real-time embedded software, a *Quasi-Dynamic Scheduling* (QDS) method is proposed. QDS employs both quasi-static and dynamic scheduling techniques. Details of the QDS algorithm are presented in Tables 1, 2, 3. Rather than going into the details of each step of the algorithms, we present the main ideas as follows.

- Data dependent branch executions are statically decomposed into different behavior configurations and quasi-statically scheduled using EQSS [17, 18]. (Step 1 of Table 1)
- For each quasi-statically decomposed behavior configuration, dynamic scheduling is employed to satisfy the local deadline of each subtask, all precedence constraints among subtasks, and the global deadline of each task as follows.
  - A *set G of concurrently enabled transitions* is used to represent the state of the system (corresponding to an RTPN marking in the model). A global system clock (*STime*) and a global memory usage (*SMem*) are used to record the absolute global time and memory for each group, respectively.
  - To find a feasible optimal schedule, a reachability tree is constructed in a depth-first search manner (Step 15 of Table 2), where each node represents a marking with a corresponding set of concurrently enabled transitions and each edge represents the firing of a selected transition. Exhaustive construction of the tree is avoided by pruning it under appropriate conditions as described in the following. It can be proved that optimality of the feasible solution is not affected by such pruning conditions.

Table 1: Quasi Dynamic Scheduling

QDS(S,μ,ψ)
$S = \{A_i \mid A_i = (P_i, T_i, F_i, M_{i0}, \tau_i), i = 1,2,\ldots,n\}$;
μ: integer; // maximum memory
ψ: global real-time constraints; // periods, deadlines, etc.
{
  $m =$ **EQSS**(S,μ,H); // $m = |H|$, H: EQSS schedules [18] (1)
  for($j = 0; j < m; j{+}{+}$) { (2)
    $G =$ **initial_group**(H, j); (3)
    if(**schedule_tree**(H,G,S,ψ,μ)) output(H, j); (4)
    else return Unschedulable_Error; (5)
  }
}

Table 2: Schedule Tree Construction in QDS

schedule_tree(H,G,S,ψ,μ)
H: set of EQSS schedules;
G: group of concurrently enabled transitions;
S: set of RTPN;
ψ: global real-time constraints; // periods, deadlines, etc.
μ: integer; // maximum memory
{
  if(**choose_schedulable**(G, G') == False) return False; (1)
  for each transition $t \in G'$ { (3)
    $STime = t \to exec + G \to STime$; (4)
    if ($STime > deadline(\psi)$) continue; (5)
    $SMem = t \to mem + G \to SMem$; (6)
    if ($SMem > \mu$) continue; (7)
    $G'' =$ **copy**(G); (8)
    $G'' \to STime = STime$; $G'' \to SMem = SMem$; (9)
    fire_trans(t); (10)
    if (**last_firing**(t)) $G'' = G'' \backslash \{t\}$; (11)
    for each transition $t' \in$ **successor**(t, S) (12)
      $G'' = G'' \cup \{t'\}$; // add newly enabled transitions (13)
    if($G'' == NULL$) return True; // end of schedule (14)
    if(**schedule_tree**(H, G'', S, ψ, μ)) return True; (15)
  }
  return False; (16)
}

  * *Negative Laxity*: There is not enough time left for at least one of the enabled transitions to execute until completion. (Steps 4, 5 of Table 3)
  * *Local Deadline Violation Forecast*: After a simulation-based analysis of the group of enabled transitions, if it is found that none of the transitions can be executed last in the group, then that group of transitions is not schedulable. (Steps 6–11 of Table 3)
  * *Global Deadline Violation*: The system clock has exceeded the global deadline of at least one of the RTPN. (Steps 4, 5 of Table 2)
  * *Memory Bound Violation*: The memory usage has exceeded a user-given upper bound. (Steps 6, 7 of Table 2)

- For each node in the tree, not all successor nodes are generated. Some nodes are not generated under various conditions as described in the following. (Steps 12–24 of Table 3)
  * If there is at most only one urgent transition, with execution time ($\tau_\alpha(t)$) same as its remaining time ($\rho(t)$) (i.e., $\tau_\alpha(t) = \rho(t)$: zero laxity), then only one successor node is generated.
  * All transitions whose execution can be deferred such that even if they are the last ones to execute among the currently enabled transitions, they will still satisfy their respective deadlines, then their corresponding nodes are not generated. This heuristic is applied provided there is some node to be generated.

Some advantageous features of QDS are as follows.

- *No need of system-wide WCET analysis*: After quasi-dynamic scheduling, we have total execution time for each system schedule, which may be smaller than the sum of worst-case execution times of all the transitions in that schedule.
- *Optimal schedules*: QDS always generates a set of optimal schedules because all feasible schedules are explored using the reachability tree. Due to page limits, the optimality of generated schedules and the time/space complexity of the QDS algorithm are given without proofs in this Section.
- *Efficient scheduling*: QDS uses several different heuristics to avoid searching exhaustively in the solution space and these heuristics are proven to be helpful, but harmless, that is, they do not eliminate any optimal schedule.
- *Multi-objective optimizations*: Since both time and memory constraints are considered during scheduling, QDS allows a user to easily optimize the resulting schedules in terms of either shortest schedule time or smallest memory usage. Trade-offs are inevitable between these two objectives, and QDS leaves such trade-off analysis to the user.
- *All issues solved*: All the issues presented in Section 1 are solved by QDS.

The following lemma and theorem show the correctness of the QDS algorithm.

LEMMA 1. *RTPN transitions that are eliminated from successor node generation by the* **choose_schedulable** *algorithm given in Table 3 cannot be in a feasible schedule.*

THEOREM 1. *The schedule generated by the QDS algorithm given in Table 1 is optimal in terms of shortest execution time.*

Instead of the exponential complexity in terms of the total number of transitions in a system configuration, the QDS algorithm induces a multiplicative factor reduction through the careful selection of successor nodes to generate (Table 3). Details are omitted.

Limitations of QDS are as follows.

- *Transition parameters*: Worst case execution time of each transition and local deadlines must be user given or derived from some analysis of the software code represented by a transition.
- *Interrupt handling*: QDS must be extended to handle interrupts. This part of the work is still ongoing and the basic idea is to include the set of allowable interrupts to the parameters of each transition and to consider the worst-case of interrupts arriving during the execution of each transition.
- *Periods and deadlines*: Currently, in QDS it is assumed that all RTPN have the same periods and deadlines. This restriction can be easily removed by scheduling a time slot that spans the least common multiple of all periods.

To illustrate how QDS works, we use the running illustration example given in Fig. 2. First of all, EQSS is applied to the two

Table 3: Selection of Schedulable Transitions in QDS

```
choose_schedulable(G, G')
G: set of concurrently enabled transitions
G': empty set of transitions
{
    G' = copy(G); G'_old = NULL;
    while(True) {
        G_last = G_tmp = NULL;
        for each transition t ∈ G' {
            if(t → remain < t → exec) return False;
            Gtime += t → exec; }
        for each transition t ∈ G' {
            if(t → remain >= Gtime) G_last = G_last ∪ {t};
            else G' = G'\{t};    }
        if (empty(G_last)) {
            if empty(G'_old) return False;
            else return True; }
        else if (empty(G')) {
            G' = G_last; return True; }
        else {
            Gtime = 0;
            for each transition t ∈ G' Gtime += t → exec;
            for each transition t ∈ G_last {
                Gtime' = Gtime + t → exec;
                for each transition t' ∈ G'
                    if (t' → remain >= Gtime') {
                        G_tmp = G_tmp ∪ {t}; break; }
            }
            G' = G' ∪ G_tmp;
            if (equal(G', G'_old)) return True;
            G'_old = G';    } // end else
    } // end of while
}
```

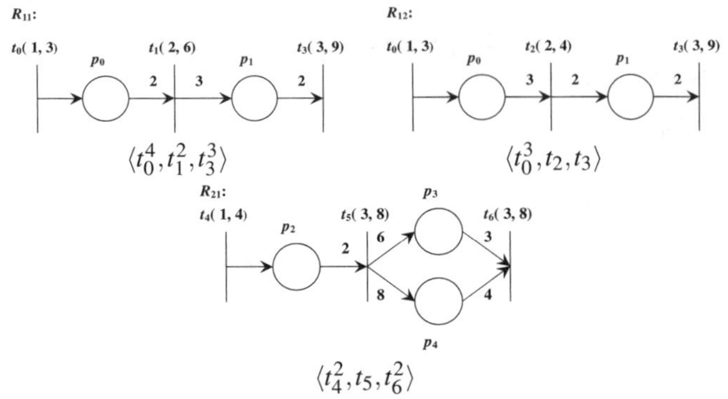

Figure 3: EQSS schedules for Illustration Example

RTPN. The resulting conflict-free components and corresponding schedule for each of those components are given in Fig. 3. There are totally three such components: R_{11} and R_{12} for N_1 and R_{21} for N_2. But, the EQSS schedule for each component has some degree of choices in the repeated firings, for example in the schedule for R_{11}, $\langle t_0^4, t_1^2, t_3^3 \rangle$, it can also be scheduled as $\langle t_0^2, t_1, t_3^2, t_0^2, t_1, t_3 \rangle$, where the exponents represent number of firings. QDS explores this degree of choices for satisfying the local deadlines and global deadlines of each system configuration, where a system configuration is a combination of one conflict-free component from each RTPN. Thus, there are totally two system configurations for this example, namely $\{R_{11}, R_{21}\}$ and $\{R_{12}, R_{21}\}$.

On applying QDS to this example, we found that it is indeed schedulable and satisfies all local and global deadlines. Though there are two reachability trees for the two system configurations, we present only one of them for illustration. The reachability tree for $\{R_{12}, R_{21}\}$ is presented in a tabular form in Table 4. The first column is the index of the nodes in the tree and the last column gives the child nodes of the corresponding node from the first column. G is the group of concurrently enabled transitions in the marking represented by that node. α is the execution time of each transition. ρ is the time left before the deadline β is reached and it is calculated from the time the transition was enabled. *STime* and *SMem* are the current global records of system time and memory, respectively. $G' \subseteq G$ is the subset transitions that are chosen in the generation of successor nodes. The 8th column consists of the actual transitions that are fired and thus also gives the schedule that is generated by QDS. At the end of Table 4, it is found that the system configuration is schedulable. The total time and memory used for the schedule $\langle t_0^3, t_4, t_2, t_4, t_3, t_5, t_6^2 \rangle$ are 19 time units and 14 memory units, respectively. Similarly, when QDS is applied to the other system configuration $\{R_{11}, R_{21}\}$, it is schedulable and the total time and memory used are 28 time units and 18 memory units, respectively, for the schedule $\langle t_0^3, t_4, t_0, t_1, t_4, t_1, t_3, t_5, (t_3, t_6)^2 \rangle$.

Table 4: QDS scheduling for R_{12} and R_{21}

n	G	α	ρ	*STime*	*SMem*	G'	fire	next
0	t_0	1	3	0	0	Y	t_0	1
	t_4	1	4			Y		
1	t_0	1	3	1	1	Y	t_0	2
	t_4	1	3			Y		
2	t_0	1	3	2	2	Y	t_0	3
	t_4	1	2			Y		
3	t_2	2	4	3	3	N		
	t_4	1	1			Y	t_4	4
4	t_2	2	3	4	4	Y	t_2	5
	t_4	1	4			Y		
5	t_3	3	9	6	3	N		
	t_4	1	2			Y	t_4	6
6	t_3	3	8	7	4	Y	t_3	7
	t_5	3	8			Y		
7	t_5	3	5	10	2	Y	t_5	8
8	t_6	3	8	13	14	Y	t_6	9
9	t_6	3	8	16	7	Y	t_6	Found!
Time & Memory				19	14	$\langle t_0^3, t_4, t_2, t_4, t_3, t_5, t_6^2 \rangle$		

n: node, ρ: time left before deadline, Y: Yes, $\in G'$, N: No, $\notin G'$

5. APPLICATION EXAMPLE

The QDS method for software synthesis was applied to several real-world applications such as ATM virtual private network scheduling, Bluetooth wireless communication protocol, motor speed control system, and medic-care system. For purpose of illustration, we describe one of the examples, which is a real-time embedded software driver for the master-slave role switch between two wireless Bluetooth devices. In the Bluetooth wireless communication protocol [3], a *piconet* is formed of one master device and seven active slave devices. There are three situations in which a master device and a slave device would attempt to perform a Master/Slave (M/S) role switch. Due to wireless device mobility, M/S role switches are quite frequent and are accomplished by exchanging some commands between the two devices at the host control and link manager layers and a time-division duplex switch.

In our RTPN model of an M/S switch between two devices A and B, there are totally four Petri nets [12]: 2 host devices and 2 Host Control / Link Manager (HC/LM) models. Timings for the transitions are allocated as follows. A Bluetooth device times out after 32 slots of $625 \mu s$ each, which is totally 0.02 second. Thus in our model, we take 0.01 second as one unit of time.

The proposed QDS algorithm (Table 1), was applied to the given

Table 5: EQSS Schedules for Bluetooth M/S Role Switch

RTPN	H: EQSS Schedules	Time
Host A,B	$A_{11} = \langle t_0,t_1,t_2,t_4,t_5,t_6 \rangle$,	[20,41]
	$A_{12} = \langle t_0,t_1,t_2,t_4,t_7 \rangle$	[8,40]
	$A_{13} = \langle t_0,t_1,t_3,t_5,t_6 \rangle$	[18,34]
	$A_{14} = \langle t_0,t_1,t_3,t_7 \rangle$	[6,33]
HC/LM A,B	$A_{21} = \langle t_0,t_1,t_2,t_4,t_6,t_7,t_{10},t_{11},t_{12},t_{14} \rangle$	[17,35]
	$A_{22} = \langle t_0,t_1,t_3,t_5,t_6,t_8,t_{10},t_{14} \rangle$	[15,29]
	$A_{23} = \langle t_0,t_1,t_2,t_4,t_6,t_7,t_{10},t_{11},t_{13},t_{15},t_{16},t_{18} \rangle$	[20,40]
	$A_{24} = \langle t_0,t_1,t_2,t_4,t_7,t_{11},t_{13},t_{15},t_{16},t_{18} \rangle$	[18,37]
	$A_{25} = \langle t_0,t_1,t_2,t_4,t_6,t_7,t_{10},t_{11},t_{13},t_{15},t_{17},t_{19},t_{20} \rangle$	[21,42]
	$A_{26} = \langle t_0,t_1,t_3,t_5,t_6,t_9,t_{15},t_{17},t_{19},t_{20} \rangle$	[18,35]

system of four RTPN. First, EQSS is applied. The results of EQSS scheduling are given in Table 5. The last column in Table 5 gives the best-case and worst-case execution times of each net EQSS schedule. Further, reachability trees were constructed for all the 24 different configurations. All deadlines and periods are given as 45 time units. For illustration purpose, the application QDS to one of the configurations $\{A_{11}, A_{25}\}$ is given partially in Table 6, which has a schedule time of 41 time units and memory usage of 2 memory units for the schedule $\langle t_{2,6}, t_{2,10}, t_{1,0}, t_{2,0}, t_{1,1}, t_{2,1}, t_{1,2}, t_{2,2}, t_{2,4}, t_{1,4}, t_{2,7}, t_{2,11}, t_{2,13}, t_{2,15}, t_{2,17}, t_{2,19}, t_{2,20}, t_{1,5}, t_{1,6} \rangle$. It is finally derived that the system is schedulable.

6. CONCLUSION

No more workarounds are needed when both local and global deadlines are to be satisfied because quasi-dynamic scheduling (QDS) has solved this problem in the context of real-time embedded software synthesis. QDS has integrated static and dynamic scheduling to efficiently derive an optimal schedule time or memory based on some simple heuristics. Application examples show that we can avoid the worst case analysis when QDS can used for scheduling. Through a real-world example on the master/slave role switch between two wireless Bluetooth devices, we have shown the feasibility of our approach. In the future, we plan to extend QDS in several ways: to handle dissimilar periods and deadlines, to handle interrupts during scheduling, and to estimate transition parameters.

7. REFERENCES

[1] K. Altisen, G. Gössler, A. Pneuli, J. Sifakis, S. Tripakis, and S. Yovine. A framework for scheduler synthesis. In *Real-Time System Symposium (RTSS'99)*. IEEE Computer Society Press, 1999.

Table 6: QDS scheduling for A_{11} and A_{25} (partial)

n	G	α	ρ	$STime$	$SMem$	G'	fire	next
0	$t_{1,0}$	2	4	0	0	N		
	$t_{2,0}$	2	6			N		
	$t_{2,6}$	1	2			Y	$t_{2,6}$	1
1	$t_{1,0}$	2	3	1	1	N		
	$t_{2,0}$	2	5			N		
	$t_{2,10}$	1	1			Y	$t_{2,10}$	2
2	$t_{1,0}$	2	2	2	0	Y	$t_{1,0}$	3
	$t_{2,0}$	2	4			N		
... (intermediate executions omitted)								
15	$t_{2,19}$	1	2	26	2	Y	$t_{2,19}$	16
	$t_{1,5}$	12	14			N		
16	$t_{1,5}$	12	13	27	2	N		
	$t_{2,20}$	1	1			Y	$t_{2,20}$	17
17	$t_{1,5}$	12	12	28	1	Y	$t_{1,5}$	18
18	$t_{1,6}$	1	1	40	1	Y	$t_{1,6}$	Found!
Time & Memory				41	2	$\langle t_{2,6}, t_{2,10}, \ldots, t_{1,5}, t_{1,6} \rangle$		

n: node, ρ: time left before deadline, Y: Yes, $\in G'$, N: No, $\notin G'$

[2] F. Balarin and M. Chiodo. Software synthesis for complex reactive embedded systems. In *Proc. of International Conference on Computer Design (ICCD'99)*, pages 634 – 639. IEEE CS Press, October 1999.

[3] J. Bray and C. F. Sturman. *Bluetooth: Connect Without Cables*. Prentice Hall, 2001.

[4] J.-M. Fu, T.-Y. Lee, P.-A. Hsiung, and S.-J. Chen. Hardware-software timing coverification of distributed embedded systems. *IEICE Trans. on Information and Systems*, E83-D(9):1731–1740, September 2000.

[5] P.-A. Hsiung. Timing coverification of concurrent embedded real-time systems. In *Proc. of the 7th IEEE/ACM International Workshop on Hardware Software Codesign (CODES'99)*, pages 110 – 114. ACM Press, May 1999.

[6] P.-A. Hsiung. Embedded software verification in hardware-software codesign. *Journal of Systems Architecture — the Euromicro Journal*, 46(15):1435–1450, December 2000.

[7] P.-A. Hsiung. Hardware-software timing coverification of concurrent embedded real-time systems. *IEE Proceedings — Computers and Digital Techniques*, 147(2):81–90, March 2000.

[8] P.-A. Hsiung. Synthesis of parametric embedded real-time systems. In *Proc. of the International Computer Symposium (ICS'00), Workshop on Computer Architecture (ISBN 957-02-7308-9)*, pages 144–151, December 2000.

[9] P.-A. Hsiung. Formal synthesis and code generation of embedded real-time software. In *Proc. of the 9th ACM/IEEE International Symposium on Hardware Software Codesign (CODES'01, Copenhagen, Denmark)*, pages 208 – 213. ACM Press, April 2001.

[10] P.-A. Hsiung. Formal synthesis and control of soft embedded real-time systems. In *Proc. of IFIP International Conference on Formal Techniques for Networked and Distributed Systems (FORTE'01)*, pages 35–50. Kluwer Academic Publishers, August 2001.

[11] P.-A. Hsiung and C.-H. Gau. Formal synthesis of real-time embedded software by time-memory scheduling of colored time Petri nets. In *Proc. of the Workshop on Theory and Practice of Timed Systems (TPTS'2002, Grenoble, France), Electronic Notes in Theoretical Computer Science (ENTCS)*, April 2002.

[12] P.-A. Hsiung, T.-Y. Lee, and F.-S. Su. Formal synthesis and code generation of real-time embedded software using timed quasi-static scheduling. In *Proc. of the 9th Asia-Pacific Software Engineering Conference (APSEC)*, pages 395–404. IEEE CS Press, December 2002.

[13] B. Lin. Software synthesis of process-based concurrent programs. In *Proc. of Design Automation Conference (DAC'98)*, pages 502 – 505. ACM Press, June 1998.

[14] O. Maler, A. Pnueli, and J. Sifakis. On the synthesis of discrete controllers for timed systems. In *22th Annual Symposium on Theoretical Aspects of Computer Scoence (STACS'95)*, volume 980, pages 229 – 242. Lecture Notes in Computer Science, Springer Verlag, March 1995.

[15] P. Merlin and G.V. Bochman. On the construction of submodule specifications and communication protocols. *ACM Trans. on Programming Languages and Systems*, 5(1):1 – 75, January 1983.

[16] W.-B. See, P.-A. Hsiung, T.-Y. Lee, and S.-J. Chen. Modular mobile dispatching system (MMDS) and logistics. In *Proc. of the 2002 Annual Conference on National Defense Integrated Logistics Support (ILS)*, pages 365–371, August 2002.

[17] M. Sgroi, L. Lavagno, Y. Watanabe, and A. Sangiovanni-Vincentelli. Synthesis of embedded software using free-choice Petri nets. In *Proc. Design Automation Conference (DAC'99)*. ACM Press, June 1999.

[18] F.-S. Su and P.-A. Hsiung. Extended quasi-static scheduling for formal synthesis and code generation of embedded software. In *Proc. of the 10th IEEE/ACM International Symposium on Hardware/Software Codesign (CODES'02, Colorado, USA)*, pages 211–216. ACM Press, May 2002.

Pareto-Optimization-Based Run-Time Task Scheduling for Embedded Systems *

Peng Yang†　Francky Catthoor‡

IMEC, Kapeldreef 75, B3001 Leuven, Belgium, {yangp, catthoor}@imec.be

ABSTRACT

Pareto-set-based optimization can be found in several different areas of embedded system design. One example is task scheduling, where different task mapping and ordering choices for a target platform will lead to different performance/cost tradeoffs. To explore this design space at run-time, a fast and effective heuristic is needed. We have modeled the problem as the well known Multiple Choice Knapsack Problem(MCKP) and have developed a fast greedy heuristic for the run-time task scheduling. To show the effectiveness of our algorithm, examples from randomly generated task graphs and realistic applications are studied. Compared to the optimal dynamic programming solver, the heuristic is more than ten times faster while the result is less than 5% away from the optimum. Moreover, due to its iterative feature, the algorithm is well suitable to be used as an on-line algorithm.

Categories and Subject Descriptors

D.4.7 [**Operating Systems**]: Organization and Design—*real-time systems a nd embedded systems*; D.4.1 [**Operating Systems**]: Processing Management

General Terms

Algorithms, Performance, Design

Keywords

Pareto optimization, scheduling, embedded system, low-power

1. INTRODUCTION

The merging of computers, consumer and communication disciplines gives rise to very fast growing markets for personal communication, multimedia and broadband networks. At the same time, technology advances lead to platforms with enormous processing capacity, which is however not matched with the current system design productivity. The future embedded system design should be based on platforms, which have sufficient computation and memory resources, consume extremely low energy and are flexible enough to cope with the dynamic behavior of future multimedia applications.

For this kind of design, one of the most critical bottlenecks is the very dynamic and concurrent behavior of many of these new applications, which are fully specified in software oriented languages (like Java, UML, SDL, C++) and still need to be executed in real-time cost/energy-sensitive way on the usually heterogeneous SoC platforms. An effective methodology is required to map this system specification onto an embedded multiprocessor platform, and normally this leads to a tradeoff among different system design objectives.

Pareto optimization is a good way to represent and explore these tradeoffs. The Pareto-optimal concept comes from multiobjective optimization problems, where more than two conflicting optimization objectives exist (e.g., for a given IC processing technology, one can not reduce the delay and power of a digital circuit simultaneously). A solution is said Pareto-optimal when it is optimal in at least one optimization objective direction. Such a set of Pareto-optimal solution is normally called a Pareto set and can be conveniently represented by a Pareto curve. In real-world applications, Pareto optimal set can be the result of many different factors, such as architecture (CPU and/or memory) mapping, quality of service control(QoS), as long as more than one optimization objective exists. A systematic way is presented on how to generate the Pareto curves [6] when the designer explores the design space. Traditional design methodology extract that Pareto optimal set and select one point from that set, both at design time. This approach can be used for static systems. However, for modern dynamic systems, we can explore the design space at design time but defer the selection step till run time, to better tune the system to the changing environment.

The Pareto optimal set can come from many design parameters[6]. In this paper we will focus on on-line task scheduling in the Dynamic Voltage Scaling(DVS) context[8] because it is well known to most of the embedded system design researchers. However, the methodology and algorithm are not limited to DVS and can be readily applied to any other similar problem where a multiobjective tradeoff exists.

The rest of the paper is structured as follows. Section 2 uses a motivational example to illustrate our task scheduling method. In Section 3, related work is discussed. Following the problem formulation and algorithm description in Sec-

*This work was partly supported by the Flemish government in the scope of the MEDEA and MESA projects.

†also Ph.D. student of K.U.Leuven-ESAT

‡also professor of K.U.Leuven-ESAT

CODES+ISSS'03, October 1–3, 2003, Newport Beach, California, USA.

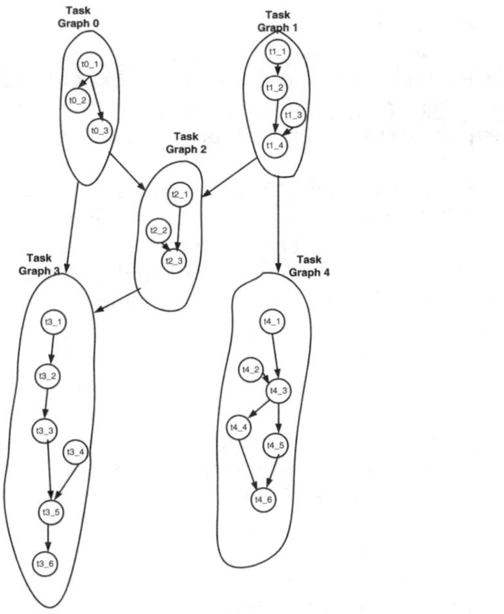

Figure 1: The task graph of the motivational example.

tion 4, Section 5 gives our experimental results on both randomly generated and real-life applications. Finally Section 6 concludes the paper.

2. MOTIVATIONAL EXAMPLE

The advantages of our novel approach can be shown by an example generated by Task Graph For Free (TGFF)[5]. Fig. 1 shows an application which requires the cooperation of five task graphs, denoted from 0 to 4. The details of those task graphs can be found in Tab. 1, in which the first

	TG0	TG1	TG2	TG3	TG4
Number of nodes	8	47	12	29	21
Number of arcs	9	59	13	35	26
Exec. time(us)	284	1258	371	826	661
En. consum.(uJ)	222	1211	331	814	671

Table 1: Task graphs generated by TGFF.

row shows the number of nodes in each task graph, the second row is the number of arcs, and the third and fourth rows give the execution time and energy consumption respectively when the task graph is executed completely on a 3.0V processor. We assume the application is frame based, i.e. every time frame the application will be executed once to process the current input data. This is a reasonable abstraction for the multimedia processing or communication (e.g. mp3 or image decoding). Depending on the content of the input data, not all 5 task graphs of the application will be needed for that specific time frame. In our motivational example we simply assume that every time frame each task graph is selected randomly. The last assumption is that the application has to finish before a deadline, which is normally the period of the time frame.

In this paper, we investigate the single-processor task scheduling. To handle the worst case, which happens when all 5 task graphs are selected, the CPU has to be powerful enough to complete the application before the deadline. On the other hand, most of the time only a few of the 5 task graphs are active and hence DVS can be applied to save energy. The online inter-task DVS algorithm[19], which is called so because the voltage scheduling is done dynamically at the boundary of task graphs, monitors the application execution. Whenever it sees some slack time available, it scales the working voltage accordingly. For instance, with a deadline of 3.4ms, a CPU working at 3.0V is just good enough to finish all the task graphs in time. Every task graph will take exactly the execution time and energy given in Tab. 1. Now suppose at the end of task graph 0, the inter-task DVS scheduler notices that task graph 3 will not be active for the current time frame. Therefore a slack of 0.826ms is available. We still have to run task graph 1, 2 and 4, which will normally take 2.29 ms and consume 2213uJ, while the time available is 3.4ms subtracted by 0.284ms, i.e. 3.12ms. Using the conventional equation[7], even if the inter-task DVS reduces the CPU working voltage by 2.29/3.12=0.73, the application can still be completed in time, but the energy consumption is now 2213*0.73*0.73=1179uJ, i.e. almost half of the original value.

The inter-task DVS can save much energy, but it assumes a continuous variable voltage. That requires special circuit design and processing technology and a DC-DC converter which is not very energy efficient(80-95%, depending on the output voltage[4]). Besides, inter-task DVS cannot see the internal contents of the task graph, and is not able to explore the slack time coming from that.

Our scheduler behaves quite differently from the inter-task DVS. Firstly, we use only a limited set of discrete voltages (two for the first example, namely 3.0V and 1.0V). Secondly, the internal content of the task graph is divided into scheduling nodes and scheduled at that granularity. Thirdly, we schedule it in two phases. At design time, the task graph is scheduled at the scheduling node granularity, i.e. each node is assigned to one of the discrete voltages and ordered in time, generating a set of Pareto points with different execution time and energy consumption. The Pareto curve we extract for task graph 2 is given as an example in Fig. 2. At run time, knowing the active task graphs of the current time frame and their Pareto curves, the run-time scheduler is able to select one Pareto point (which represents a specific voltage assignment and ordering for that task graph) from each active curve and can combine them together to get the complete scheduling, taking into account the time constraints.

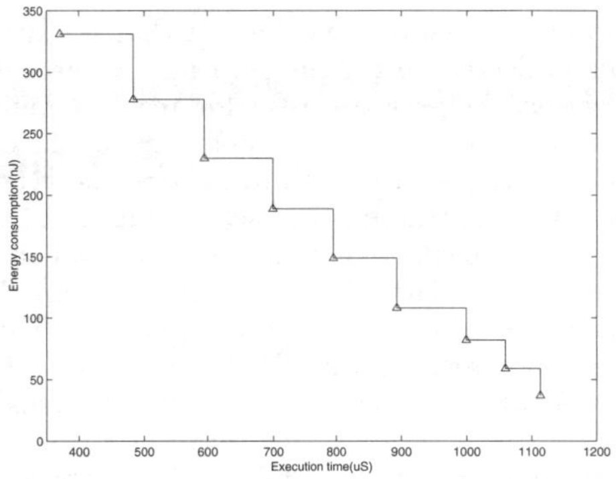

Figure 2: The Pareto curve of task graph 2.

Our approach benefits from the fact that we know which task graph is selected for the current frame when we schedule the application. This is realistic for real-life multi-media applications by inserting extra code to extract the necessary information, at the start of each frame (see e.g. [21]). If it is impossible to do so, the run-time scheduling decision should be re-evaluated as soon as that info becomes available during the task execution. But even then, our run-time heuristic is fast enough to accommodate that situation. This is also one of the major reasons why the heuristic should be fast, and preferably also scalable in terms of speed versus solution quality.

We have simulated the scheduling of the above problem for 1000 frames. In each frame the task graphs are selected randomly and the time constraint is always 3.4ms. The results are shown in Tab. 2, in which our two-Vdd scheduler is denoted as PC_2. For comparison, we also list the energy number for an "optimal" scheduler which uses a continuous optimal DVS strategy. This is not achievable in practice because it requires the full knowledge of the future run-time behavior of the tasks. In this simple example, compared to the state-of-the-art inter-task DVS schedulers (see related work section), our approach saves 7% more energy, which is quite good taking into account we have only two discrete voltages instead of a continuously changeable one. When a third voltage, 1.5V, is available (PC_3), 15% more energy can be saved compared to the inter-task case. This result also comes close (within 7%) to the theoretical (unachievable) optimal value.

	no DVS	inter.	PC_2	PC_3	optimal
en. cons.(uJ)	1620	1068	956	823	705
en. saving	0	34%	41%	49%	56%

Table 2: Energy consumption of the motivation example with different schedulers.

These results show clearly the potential advantage of our method. In section 4 we will present a run-time scheduling heuristic on how to achieve it.

3. RELATED WORK

Task scheduling has been investigated overwhelmingly in the last decades. When a set of concurrent tasks - i.e. tasks that can overlap in time - have to be executed on one or more processors, a predefined method, called scheduling algorithm, must be applied to decide the order in which those tasks are executed. For a multiprocessor system, another procedure, assignment, is also needed to determine on which processor one task will be executed. A good overview of scheduling algorithms can be found in [17]. In our paper, the terminology *task scheduling* is used for both the task ordering and the processor assignment.

Generally speaking the scheduling algorithms can be classified as off-line and on-line algorithms. We focus here only on the latter because it provides better opportunity for run-time optimization. These algorithms are usually priority-based and are derived from Liu and Layland's classical paper [11], in which the priority of a task is either set statically, e.g. the Rate Monotonic (RM), or dynamically, e.g. the Earliest Deadline First (EDF). Nowadays, RM and EDF are still the most used algorithms.

Recently, Dynamic Voltage Scaling(DVS) is getting popular ([8, 16] for a good survey). Traditionally, the CPU works at a fixed supply voltage, even for a light workload, when high CPU speed is unnecessary and can be traded for a lower energy/power consumption by a reduction of the supply voltage. This simple observation leads to many algorithms.

Shin and Choi [19] extended the normal fixed-priority scheduler to implement an on-line inter-task DVS for real-time application. They slow down the processor when there is only one eligible running task and completely shut it down when that last task ends earlier than expected. Their work is extended in [20] by adding a two-phase strategy: an off-line algorithm decides the basic voltage for a task set with a priority-based scheduler, while the on-line algorithm refines the off-line decision, using the approach in [19].

To fully utilize the slack time in the on-line DVS, some new approaches are proposed recently. They can be classified as intra-task DVS, because they benefit from looking inside the boundary of a task. Lee and Sakurai [9] partition a task into several pieces, called *time-slots*, then dynamically control the supply voltage on a "time-slot by time-slot" basis, with the feedback from the software. In [10], a combination of hierarchical Finite State Machine and Synchronous Data Flow (SDF) actors is used to model the system. Scheduling is done at the SDF actor level. Whenever one actor finishes, the scheduler is recalled to see whether the current execution path has more slack time available, either because the previous actor finishes earlier or because an execution path different from the worst case is selected. Other approaches include checking the current code execution against data generated at compile time to find the opportunity for voltage scaling[2, 18]. To take full advantage of DVS, some authors further suggest a handshake between the content or application and the OS[3, 15]. Our approach also has a compile-time stage. However, different to the above ones, it computes and stores a partial scheduling which is used in the run-time phase.

The Knapsack Problem and its generalization, Multiple Choice Knapsack Problem (MCKP), which forms the underlying base for our technique, have been studied for decades due to their importance in operation and optimization problems. Martello and Toth[12] discuss the knapsack-like problem in detail. A good exact algorithm is given in [14]. Good heuristics are being looked for in many different contexts[1]. Mejia-Alvarez *et al* applied it to DVS-like problems and a heuristic is constructed from the linear relaxation of the original MCKP[13].

4. RUN-TIME SCHEDULING ALGORITHM

Section 2 shows the effectiveness of our two-phase, Pareto-curve-based scheduling methodology. The key step of this method is the run-time scheduler. Given a set of Pareto curves and a deadline, the run-time scheduler has to select one and only one point from each active Pareto curve and combine them into the final scheduling. It has to be done fast because that will allow a more frequent (re)evaluation of the run-time scheduling decision or the handling of more tasks in a single shot. Both will result in still more energy saving. The quality of the solution is also important because it affects the amount of energy saved.

In this section, we will first formulate the problem in the MCKP model. Then a greedy heuristic is proposed for our specific problem.

4.1 Problem Specification

The run-time scheduling problem can be formulated as a constrained minimization problem:

$$minimize: \quad z = \sum_{i=1}^{k} \sum_{j=1}^{N_i} e_{ij} x_{ij} \qquad (1)$$

$$subject\ to \quad \sum_{i=1}^{k} \sum_{j=1}^{N_i} t_{ij} x_{ij} \leq D, \qquad (2)$$

$$\sum_{j=1}^{N_i} x_{ij} = 1, i = 1, \ldots, k, \qquad (3)$$

$$x_{ij}\ is\ 0\ or\ 1, i = 1, \ldots, k,\ j = 1, \ldots, N_i. \qquad (4)$$

where k is the number of Pareto curves, each of which has N_i Pareto points. e_{ij} and t_{ij} are the energy consumption and execution time of the jth point on the ith curve respectively. x_{ij} is 1 if the jth point on the ith curve is selected; otherwise it is 0. The total number of points is denoted by n, $n = \sum_{i=1}^{k} N_i$.

The minimization problem can be transformed into a different form[13]. Taking into account that each Pareto curve is an ordered set, we can substitute e_{ij} with s_{ij} as

$$s_{ij} = (e_{i0} - e_{ij}), s_{ij} \geq 0. \qquad (5)$$

Thus Eqn. 1 becomes a maximization problem:

$$maximize: z' = \sum_{i=1}^{k} \sum_{j=1}^{N_i} s_{ij} x_{ij} \qquad (6)$$

With the same set of constraints, this is a classical Multiple Choice Knapsack Problem (MCKP) and it is known as NP hard[12].

When of limited size, MCKP can be solved optimally in pseudo-polynomial time through dynamic programming. However, the worst case computation complexity of DP is still exponential, which is not acceptable as an on-line algorithm for big problem size.

Several approximate algorithms exist for MCKP but all have limitations or are not suitable for our problem. Current heuristics are designed for big problems, which can not be solved easily by an accurate algorithm due to its NP-hard feature. They rival each other in which can get a solution closer to the optimal value or which can handle a bigger (or more difficult) problem. Execution time is only the second or third concern to them, which makes them unsuitable to work as an on-line algorithm. In addition, most of the heuristics do not recognize that in our case, all points are already Pareto optimal and ordered. That can save quite extra computation effort.

The goal of our heuristic is to find a good enough solution in as short as possible time for a typical problem size. It is not our major interest to improve the solution by 1% if it means 2 times longer execution time. Moreover, the heuristic should be constructive, which improves the solution incrementally in every iteration so that it can be interrupted if the time slot assigned to the run-time scheduler expires. Then it returns its best solution at that moment.

4.2 The Greedy Heuristic

We have developed a fast and effective greedy heuristic with the above considerations. Alg. 1 consists of two stages, the initialization (line 2 to 16) and the iteration stage (line 18 to 41). Every point i of our Pareto curve m is denoted by two basic parameters, $t_{m,i}$ and $e_{m,i}$, standing for the execution time and energy consumption if that point is selected by the scheduler(the corresponding concepts in MCKP are weight and profit). D is the deadline. In the initialization stage, we compute the changes of t and e if we move to the right (from point i to $i+1$) or to the left (to point $i-1$) and the corresponding slopes (line 5 to 12). Here a superscript "+" means the rightward direction and "-" means the leftward direction. The initial solution is found at line 13 and 14: a portion of the deadline(s_m) is assigned to a curve proportional to the execution time of its left-most point. Therefore it guarantees a valid initial solution can always be found for that curve. When finding the initial solution we use an on-the-fly strategy. The difference between the time assigned to curve m and the actual execution time of its initial solution will be accumulated in the variable *slack* and added to the available time of the following curves.

Algorithm 1 The greedy heuristic algorithm.

1: **INITIALIZATION**
2: **step 0:**
3: slack=0;
4: **for all** curve m **do**
5:   **for all** point i on curve m **do**
6:     $\delta e^{+}_{m,i} = e_{m,i} - e_{m,i+1}$;
7:     $\delta e^{-}_{m,i} = e_{m,i-1} - e_{m,i}$;
8:     $\delta t^{+}_{m,i} = t_{m,i+1} - t_{m,i}$;
9:     $\delta t^{-}_{m,i} = t_{m,i} - t_{m,i-1}$;
10:     $slope^{+}_{m,i} = \delta e^{+}_{m,i} / \delta t^{+}_{m,i}$;
11:     $slope^{-}_{m,i} = \delta e^{-}_{m,i} / \delta t^{-}_{m,i}$;
12:   **end for**
13:   $s_m = t_{m,0} D / \sum_{l=0}^{k-1} t_{l,0}$;
14:   search for maximal j with $t_{m,j} \leq (s_m + slack)$;
15:   update slack;
16: **end for**
17: **ITERATIVE IMPROVEMENT**
18: **step 1:**
19: sort $slope^{+}$ descendingly and $slope^{-}$ ascendingly;
20: **for all** curve m in $slope^{+}$ **do**
21:   **for all** curve n in $slope^{-}$ and $m \neq n$ **do**
22:     **if** $slope^{+}_{m} \leq slope^{-}_{n}$ **then**
23:       goto step 2;
24:     **end if**
25:     **if** $\delta e^{+}_{m} > \delta e^{-}_{n} and \delta t^{+}_{m} < \delta t^{-}_{n} + slack$ **then**
26:       change solution of curve m from i to $i+1$;
27:       change solution of curve n from j to $j-1$;
28:       update slack;
29:       goto step 1;
30:     **end if**
31:   **end for**
32: **end for**
33: **step 2:**
34: sort $slope^{+}$ descendingly;
35: **for all** curve m in $slope^{+}$ **do**
36:   **if** $\delta t^{+}_{m} < slack$ **then**
37:     change solution of curve m from i to $i+1$;
38:     update slack;
39:     goto step 2;
40:   **end if**
41: **end for**

After the initialization, we explore the chances of finer tuning the solution in two steps, *step*1 and *step*2. *step*1 checks the possibility of moving the operating point on one curve to the right and the operating point on another curve to the left in pair. At line 19, all curves are sorted according to the slopes of their current solutions, $slope^+$ descendingly and $slope^-$ ascendingly. Then the algorithm will try to find two curves m and n, which satisfy the time constraint and reduce the energy consumption most, if the solution of m is changed from i to $i+1$ and the solution of n from j to $j-1$. When no such kind of tuning is possible, the algorithm will enter the next step. *step*2 does the final tuning by finding any curve m which can still satisfy the time constraint if we move its current solution form i to $i+1$.

Assuming k curves and l points are present on each curve, the complexity of the initialization step is $O(k \log l)$ because for every curve we have only to do an ordered search(line 14). The complexity of the iterative stage is also very low. In *step*1 every iteration takes maximally $O(k^2)$ operations, while in *step*2 $O(k)$ operations. The heuristic ends when no improvement is possible, but we can interrupt the iteration at any moment to finish the run-time scheduling in a predefined time slot. In that case the algorithm just returns the best available solution. This capability is very important for a real-time system where bounded and deterministic service is always desirable. The performance of our greedy heuristic is illustrated in Section 5.

5. EXPERIMENTAL RESULTS

We have implemented the greedy algorithm in C and tested it with both randomly generated and real-life applications.

The first test set we have used is the task graphs generated by TGFF. For each task graph, a Genetic Algorithm is used to extract the Pareto curve, on an architecture like the one we used in section 2. Finally the heuristic is applied to find the on-line task scheduling within a given deadline. A dynamic programming(DP) optimal algorithm[14] is used in this step to check the speed and quality of our heuristic.

We have generated three task sets with TGFF, containing 5, 10, and 20 task graphs respectively. For every task graph, we have extracted two Pareto curves, one with 5 points and the other with 9 points. The former is just a subset of the latter. The points are distributed almost uniformly, in the sense of execution time, between the lowest and highest possible values. Different deadlines are then tried on the same task set and same Pareto curves and the results are summed in Tab. 3 and Tab. 4.

no. of cv.	av. sp. up	max. sp. up	av. error	max. error	av. init. sp. up	max. init. sp. up	av. init. error	max. init. error
5	14.9	24.0	1.2%	5.2%	44.0	58.7	4.1%	9.1%
10	8.8	13.2	1.0%	2.9%	42.9	53.3	6.8%	13.4%
20	3.9	7.3	1.0%	2.0%	24.0	50.2	4.5%	8.7%

Table 3: The performance of the greedy algorithm compared to DP, 5 points per curve.

no. of cv.	av. sp. up	max. sp. up	av. error	max. error	av. init. sp. up	max. init. sp. up	av. init. error	max. init. error
5	15.4	24.9	0.6%	3.5%	46.0	65.1	3.4%	10.3%
10	8.4	14.5	0.8%	2.1%	34.5	55.6	4.1%	8.7%
20	4.3	7.7	0.9%	1.9%	26.2	43.4	3.5%	7.0%

Table 4: The performance of the greedy algorithm compared to DP, 9 points per curve.

The performance of our heuristic can be evaluated in two ways: the execution time and the quality of the result. Tab. 3 and Tab. 4 give the overview of the result. In the tables, the first column is the number of curves; the second column is the average speedup of execution time of the greedy heuristic against the DP solver; the third column is the maximum speedup; the fourth column gives the average error between the heuristic and DP solution and the fifth column is the maximum error. The next four columns are just the same but for the initial solution given by *step*0 of Alg. 1.

The results show that our heuristic has an up to 15 times average speedup against the optimal solver, while maintaining a very high solution quality (error within 1.2% on average). If the initial solution is considered, the average speedup is up to 46 times while the solution error is up to 6.8%, on average. This is quite acceptable for an on-line scheduling algorithm, because if the optimal solution means an energy reduction from 1000nJ to 500nJ, a 10% error just means the energy is reduced to 550nJ, which is already a big improvement compared to the original value, especially if we take into account the high speed to find the initial solution.

For the on-line scheduling stage, the time spent on the scheduler itself will not contribute to the application functionality execution. So it has to be minimized or bounded, even though we can have a separate CPU to run the scheduler in some architectures. Our heuristic provides the capability of improving the initial solution iteratively until the time slot assigned to the scheduler depletes. This is especially important for big problem sizes, when the scheduler could not run to its end and still has to find a solution in a short time slot. Tab. 5 shows the iterative improvement of our heuristic. The result is for the 9 points per curve, 20 curves case because it is the worst case in our experiment when the execution time is considered. The optimal result is 37836nJ and it takes the DP 232k processor cycles to find it. With the heuristic, to find the final solution 38443nJ, it takes 119k cycles, which may be too long. However, the final solution is only 1.6% from the optimal one and we are usually already satisfied with solutions which are not that good but can be found rather fast. If we assume we have 50k(100k) cycles available for the scheduler, which is 0.25ms(0.5ms) on a 200MHz processor, the result we can find is 38857nJ(38538nJ) and it is only 2.7%(1.9%) away from the optimal solution. Even the initial solution is acceptable in this case, which can be found in less than 12k cycles. Given the fact that the run-time scheduler is triggered by external events (e.g. user related) at the frequency of tens of ms, this result is quite good.

iter. no.	time(cycles)	solution(nJ)
0	11554	39366
1	36909	39102
2	48201	38857
3	59389	38695
4	70700	38640
5	81939	38556
6	93502	38538
7	103381	38526
8	113225	38463
9	119312	38443

Table 5: The iterative improvement of the heuristic for a 20 curves, 9 points case.

We have also tried our heuristic on some real-life applications. One example is the quality of service(QoS) adjustment algorithm of a 3D image rendering application. Every

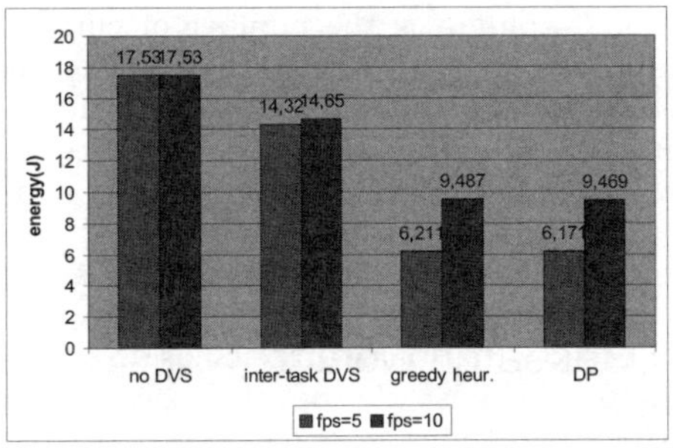

Figure 3: The energy consumption of QoS adjustment algorithm for 1000 frames.

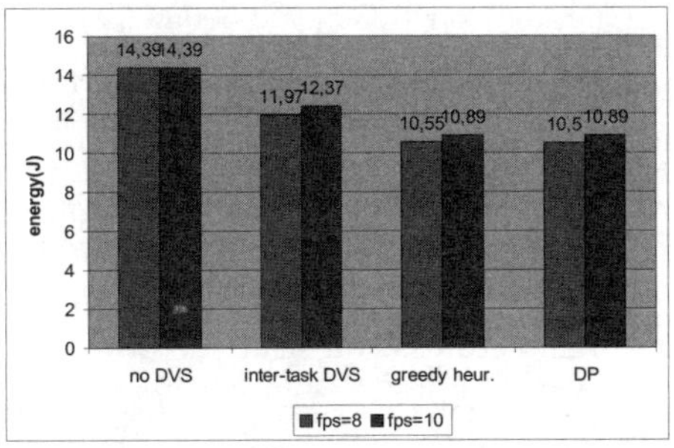

Figure 4: The energy consumption of the VTC decoder for 1365 frames.

time frame, depending on the number of visible objects and which kind of objects they are, the QoS controller will adjust the number of vertices assigned to each object, in order to provide the best quality at a fixed computation power. Fig. 3 illustrates the energy consumption of QoS adjustment algorithm for 1000 frames, with a frame rate of 5fps(frame per second) or 10fps. From this figure it is obvious that our run-time scheduler can achieve a very high energy saving (65% for 5fps and 46% for 10fps). The inter-task DVS does not work very well here because the number of task graphs and the execution time of each task graph varies dramatically in this application. Having to assume the worst case for the unscheduled task graphs, the inter-task DVS scheduler has a limited chance to scale the voltage. Another observation is that the difference between the greedy heuristic and the DP is very small. This is because most of the frames the heuristic and DP will give the same solution, due to the limited problem size.

Another real-life application we have experimented on is the Visual Texture Coding(VTC) decoder of the MPEG-4 standard. Similar to the QoS example, it is frame based. However, unlike the varying number of objects in QoS, the number of blocks to be decoded is fixed (3 in this experiment) for every frame, though the workload of each block varies from frame to frame. As shown in Fig. 4, this example gives less space for voltage scaling because of its relative high and less varying work load. In spite of that, our heuristic still outperforms the inter-task DVS and provides an energy saving of 27%. Again the results from the heuristic and DP are very close.

6. CONCLUSION

In this paper we have modeled the Pareto-optimization-based run-time task scheduling with Multiple Choice Knapsack Problem and have proposed a greedy heuristic for it. Results on randomly generated and real-life applications prove that our heuristic is fast (speedup of more than 10) and high quality (suboptimality less than 5%). The incremental and scalable feature makes the heuristic well suitable for on-line task scheduling. Further research is continuing to extend the heuristic to handle more than two optimization objectives and to integrate the run-time scheduler into Real-Time Operating Systems.

7. REFERENCES

[1] M. Akbar et al. Heuristic Solutions for the Multiple-Choice Multi-Dimension Knapsack Problem. In *Int. Conf. Computational Science*, pages 112–117, June 2001.

[2] A. Azevedo et al. Profile-based dynamic voltage scheduling using program checkpoints. In *Proc. Design Automation and Test in Europe*, pages 168–75, 2002.

[3] E.-Y. Chung, L. Benini, and G. De Micheli. Contents Provider-Assisted Dynamic Voltage Scaling for Low Energy Multimedia Applications. In *Proc. Int. Symp. on Low Power Electronic Device*, pages 42–7, Aug. 2002.

[4] A. P. Dancy, R. Amirtharajah, and A. P. Chandrakasan. High-Efficiency Multiple-Output DC-DC Conversion for Low-Voltage Systems. *IEEE Trans. VLSI Syst.*, 8(3):252–63, June 2000.

[5] R. P. Dick, D. L. Rhodes, and W. Wolf. TGFF: Task Graphs for Free. In *Proc. Int. Work. Hardware/Software Codesign(CODES)*, pages 97–101, 1998.

[6] T. Givargis, F. Vahid, and J. Henkel. System-level Exploration for Pareto-optimal Configurations in Parameterized System-on-a-Chip. *IEEE Trans. VLSI Syst.*, 10(4):579–592, Aug. 2002.

[7] I. Hong et al. Power Optimization of Variable Voltage Core-Based Systems. *IEEE Trans. Computer Aided Design*, 18(12):1702–14, Dec. 1999.

[8] N. K. Jha. Low Power System Scheduling and Synthesis. In *Int. Conf. Computer-Aided Design*, pages 259–63, 2001.

[9] S. Lee and T. Sakurai. Run-Time Voltage Hopping for Low Power Real-Time Systems. In *Proc. 38th Design Automation Conf.*, pages 806–9, 2000.

[10] S. Lee, S. Yoo, and K. Choi. An Intra-task Dynamic Voltage Scaling Method for SoC Design with Hierarchical FSM and Synchronous Dataflow Model. In *Proc. Int. Symp. on Low Power Electronic Device*, pages 84–7, Aug. 2002.

[11] C. L. Liu and J. W. Layland. Scheduling Algorithms for Multiprogramming in a Hard Real-Time Environment. *J. ACM*, 20(1):46–61, Jan. 1973.

[12] S. Martello and P. Toth. *Knapsack Problems: Algorithms and Computer Implementations.* John Wiley and Sons, 1990.

[13] P. Mejia-Alvarez, E. Levner, and D. Mosse. Power-Optimized Scheduling Server for Real-Time Tasks. In *Proc. the 8th IEEE Real-Time and Embedded Technology and Applications Symp.*, 2002.

[14] D. Pisinger. *Algorithms for Knapsack Problems.* PhD thesis, Dept. of Computer Science, University of Copenhagen, Denmark, 1995.

[15] J. Pouwelse, K. Langendoen, and H. Sips. Energy Priority Scheduling for Variable Voltage Processors. In *Proc. Int. Symp. on Low Power Electronic Device*, pages 28–33, 2001.

[16] G. Quan and X. Hu. Energy Efficient Fixed-Priority Scheduling for Real-Time Systems on Variable Voltage Processors. In *Proc. 38th Design Automation Conf.*, 2001.

[17] K. Ramamritham and J. A. Stankovic. Scheduling Algorithms and Operation Systems Support for Real-Time Systems. *Proc. IEEE*, 82(1):55–67, Jan. 1994.

[18] D. Shin, J. Kim, and S. Lee. Low-Energy Intra-Task Voltage Scheduling Using Static Timing Analysis. In *Proc. 38th Design Automation Conf.*, pages 438–43, 2001.

[19] Y. Shin and K. Choi. Power Conscious Fixed Priority Scheduling for Hard Real-Time Systems. In *Proc. 36th Design Automation Conf.*, pages 134–139, 1999.

[20] Y. Shin, K. Choi, and T. Sakurai. Power Optimization of Real-Time Embedded Systems on Variable Speed Processors. In *Int. Conf. Computer-Aided Design*, pages 365–8, 2000.

[21] P. Yang et al. Managing Dynamic Concurrent Tasks in Embedded Real-Time Multimedia Systems. In *Proc. Int. Symp. on System Synthesis*, pages 112–9, Oct. 2002.

A Low Power Scheduler Using Game Theory

N. Ranganathan and Ashok K. Murugavel
Dept. of Computer Science and Engineering
Nanomaterials and Nanomanufacturing Research Center
University of South Florida
Tampa, Florida 33620

ABSTRACT

In this paper, we describe a new methodology based on game theory for minimizing the average power of a circuit during scheduling in behavioral synthesis. The problem of scheduling in data-path synthesis is formulated as an auction based non-cooperative finite game, for which solutions are developed based on the Nash equilibrium function. Each operation in the data-path is modeled as a player bidding for executing an operation in the given control cycle, with the estimated power consumption as the bid. Also, a combined scheduling and binding algorithm is developed using a similar approach in which the two tasks are modeled together such that the Nash equilibrium function needs to be applied only once to accomplish both the scheduling and binding tasks together. The combined algorithm yields further power reduction due to additional savings during binding. The proposed algorithms yield better power reduction than ILP-based methods with comparable run times and no increase in area overhead.

Categories and Subject Descriptors

B.5.1 [**Design**]: Data-path design

General Terms

Algorithms, Low Power Design, High-level Synthesis, Game Theory, Auction Theory

1. INTRODUCTION

The advent of portable and wireless computing has increased the need for low power high performance compute intensive VLSI circuits. Increased power consumption, reduces the battery life in portable systems as well as the reliability and increases the packaging costs [12]. The various steps of behavioral synthesis are: scheduling, allocation and binding [12]. Scheduling is the process of determining when a resource is to be executed, allocation is the process of determining the number of instances of a required resource, and binding is the process of attaching a resource to an operation that needs to be performed [13]. A detailed treatment on low power behavioral synthesis can be found in [2]. Numerous algorithms have been proposed in the literature for low power scheduling. In [15], a force directed low power scheduling algorithm based on heuristics is described. Minimizing the number of times the input operands to a functional unit change reduces the power consumed by the functional units, which is explored in [7]. In [9], a module assignment algorithm for pipelined datapath's is formulated as a max-cost multi-commodity flow problem. A combined register and module assignment algorithm for low power data-path synthesis is presented in [18].

Power reduction through combined scheduling and binding has been investigated in the following works. A scheduling and binding algorithm that minimizes switching activity with simulated annealing is investigated in [1]. In [2], an iterative mechanism based on an initial solution with efficient pruning techniques is used for low power synthesis. A novel approach involving the use of constrained logic programming to minimize the switched capacitance, during scheduling and binding is described in [8]. A heuristics based algorithm under a resource constraint can be found in [13]. In [5], a stepwise approximation algorithm for combined scheduling and binding is described. In [3], a scheduling and binding algorithm, that reduces glitches through clock gating is investigated. Most recently, an integer linear programming (ILP) method for scheduling and a linear programming (LP) method for binding are given in [19].

In this work, we model the problems of low power scheduling and binding as auction based game theoretic problems and solve them using the Nash equilibrium function. The scheduling and binding algorithms achieve power reduction through the use of neighborhood operations, path balancing, functional unit sharing to reduce switched capacitance and glitch reduction. The proposed algorithms do not increase the area overhead, since there is no addition of modules or multiplexors. The application of economic models and game theory as well as the Nash equilibrium for power optimization for the scheduling task in high-level synthesis is being attempted for the first time in this work.

2. GAME THEORY

Game theory is a tool for analyzing the interaction of decision makers with conflicting objectives. Economists have used game theory as a tool to understand the action of economic agents. The basic building blocks of game theory are based on theories proposed by von Neumann in 1928 [10] and Nash in 1950 [11]. A game, in which the rules can be previously stated or agreed upon by the players for use in deducing common strategies, is called a cooperative game. A game in which such agreements cannot be made is called a non-cooperative game [11]. Non-cooperative games are played with fully rational players who know the complete details of the game, including each others preferences and outcomes. One of the first works in applying game theory to VLSI CAD problems was attempted in [17], a 2-person zero sum game theoretic formulation has been used to solve the system-level power management policy problem. A game theoretic solution to the problem of binding is described in [4].

The salient features of game theory that aid in the formulation of the behavioral synthesis problem are: *(i) Rationality:*Each player is always selfishly trying to optimize its gain. *(ii) Coalition:* Coalition formation is significant when a subset of players have the same agenda in terms of strategies for optimization can pool in their resources during resource allocation. *(iii) Competition:* In game theory, multiple decision makers who control a specified set of system variables and seek to optimize their conflicting objectives. *(iv) Equilibrium:* A solution is in an equilibrium state when all the players' objectives have been optimized with respect to one another.

The first step is to transform the behavioral synthesis problem into a performance model considering power, delay and area as resources. The second step is to transform the performance model into an economic optimization model based on auction theory, with a set of buyers and a seller, all selfishly trying to optimize their individual resources. The goal is to achieve a stable solution which is good for everyone including the seller and the buyers. The Nash equilibrium proposed in [11], is an elegant solution to achieve the stable point. Auction theory is the science of studying the selling of objects among different buyers, such that the seller and the buyers optimize their gain [6]. The cost that each buyer is willing to pay is called a bid. Among the different types of models available in auction theory, the first-bid sealed auction model is most suitable for modeling power optimization in behavioral synthesis. In the first bid sealed auction, the buyer places sealed bids to the seller that cannot be changed and the seller decides, to which buyer the seller is willing to sell his item based on the bids from the potential buyers.

A finite game can be generalized to consist of n players who can choose from a set of strategies S_i where, $i = 1, ..., n$, and a set of payoff functions p_i where, $i = 1, ..., n : S_1 \times ... \times S_n \rightarrow \Re$, where, $\Re$ is the set of all real numbers and a payoff value is assigned to each pair of strategies chosen by the players. The rationality or the equilibrium point is a set of strategies that maximizes the payoff of the player assuming that all other players strategies are held fixed. The game is played until each players strategy is optimal with respect to the strategies of others. The following example is useful in understanding the concepts.

	P2			
	3	−2	1	3
P1	2	1	0	−4
	−1	1	−2	2

The game consists of two players, **P1** and **P2**, and the matrix given above. The entries in the matrix are the possible outcomes of the game, corresponding to the selections made by the two players. The various possible alternatives for player **P1** are the rows of the matrix and for player **P2** are the columns of the matrix. The alternatives are the strategies that each of the players can choose from. In this game, for **P2**, column 1 is the best since at most he loses 1 and for **P1**, rows 2 and 3 are the best since at most he loses 2. These are the secure strategies of the two players. If **P2** plays the game first then his strategy will be to choose column 1, and the unique strategy of **P1** is row 3, with an outcome gain of 1 by **P1**. But, if **P1** plays first, he can choose either row 2 or row 3. If **P1** chooses row 2, then the best strategy for **P2** is column 1, but, if **P1** chooses row 3, then the best strategy for **P2** will be column 4. In this game, we could assume that the players do not make their decisions independently, and there is a predetermined ordering for the players. If **P1** decides first and passes the choice of his row to **P2** then **P2** has an advantage over **P1**. If the best choice for **P1** (i^*), and the optimal response of **P2** (j^*), is given as,

$$a_{i^*j^*} = \max_j a_{i^*j} = \bar{V} = \min_i\{\max_j a_{ij}\} \quad (1)$$

where, the $\min$ and $\max$ operations are specified in the order in which they are to be performed. The outcome of the game when **P1** follows **P2** is a gain of 1 by player **P1**. When **P2** follows **P1**, the outcome of the game is a gain of 2 by **P2**. If the two players choose independent of each other which is normally the case, player **P2** gains 2, which is the equilibrium solution for this game. Determining this equilibrium solution is complex for games with multiple players. Hence, we apply the rational Nash equilibrium to find such a solution.

Let S_i be the set of various possible strategies of player i, where, $i = 1, ..., N$, and p^i be the payoff for player i. Nash equilibrium can be stated as: a set of strategies $(n_1^* \in S_1), ..., (n_N^* \in S_N)$ such that $p^i_{(n_1^*,...,n_i^*,...,n_N^*)} \geq p^i_{(n_1^*,...,n_i,...,n_N^*)}$ for all i, $n_i \in S_i$. In words, this translates to, a player's payoff does not increase if any of the players unilaterally deviate from the Nash equilibrium strategy. The Nash equilibrium NE, defines the payoff function for all the players in the game. The result that we are interested in, is the global payoff $\bar{p}$ of all the players in the game, or the average payoff of each player due to the combined strategies, $NE = \{n_1^*, ..., n_N^*\}$. Mathematically, this can be given as,

$$\bar{p} = \sum_{i=1}^{N} p^i_{(n_1^*,...,n_N^*)} \quad (2)$$

The Nash equilibrium for an N-player finite game is a N-tuple set of strategies $\{n_1^*, n_2^*, ..., n_N^*\}$, given by N inequalities such that, no single player can gain by individually changing his strategy. The inputs needed to calculate the Nash equilibrium are: (i) the strategies available for each player, (ii) the number of players in the game, and (iii) the number of alternatives a_i that are available for each player i. The steps for calculating the Nash equilibrium are: (i) determine all possible outcomes for the given game were the number of possible outcomes for the given game is $(\sum_{i=1}^{N} a_i^N)$, where a_i denotes the number of alternatives for player i, (ii) determine the inequalities for each player i such that his departure from the Nash equilibrium will lead to no increase in his gain which is stated formally as $(p^{i^*} \triangleq p^i_{(n_1^*,...,n_i^*,...,n_N^*)} \geq p^i_{(n_1^*,...,n_i,...,n_N^*)})$, and (iii) the outcome that satisfies all the inequalities defined in step (ii) forms the Nash equilibrium solution of the game.

An elegant proof for the existence of equilibrium points for a finite game is given in [11]. An interesting fact about the Nash equilibrium is that, *there is a guaranteed existence of a solution* if we allow n_i to be of mixed strategies [11].

3. SCHEDULING

We model the scheduling problem as an auction based first-bid sealed auction and then describe a game theoretic solution.The auctioning of items by a seller through bidding can be extended to the auctioning of operations in the DFG, G_f, among the modules of the architecture, G_a as, with an operation being bought by only one module and the sale entity being power consumption. In the presence of multiple operations and modules, an equilibrium point needs to be achieved. An auction consists of a set of available resources M, and a set of interested buyers O, where M is not equal to O and a buyer can only buy a single item at a time. The buyer $(b \in O)$ may also have some preference for some resources over the others, and this can be specified in terms of a cost function

f_{sch}, These functions are mappings from the buyers domain to the resource domain. Let f_{sch}, be the cost function that maps buyer b in the buyers domain to the resources x, y in the resource domain. If the buyer prefers $x \succ y$, then, $f_{sch}(x,b) < f_{sch}(y,b)$.

input : Data flow graph (DFG) G_f, Architecture G_a
output : Scheduled data-flow graph (S-DFG) G_{sf}
$i \leftarrow 0$;
% initially level i is set to top level;
$CG \leftarrow DFG$;
**: Perform breadth first search of current data-flow graph CG;
$O_{cg} \leftarrow$ Operations in the top level of the CG;
for *each set of operations* $O_{ij} \in O_{cg}$ **do**
% O_{ij} is the set of operations of same type j at level i that can be assigned to the same module;
$CMP_{sch}, CMD_{sch} \leftarrow$ Payoff matrix (O_{ij}, M_{ij}, i);
$NE_{sch}(i) \leftarrow$Nash sol. $(CMP_{sch}, CMD_{sch}, M_{ij}, S)$;
% Nash equilibrium solution at control step i - see Alg 2;
$O_{sf} \leftarrow$ Set of operations that form the Nash equi.;
$CG \leftarrow \{CG - O_{sf}(i)\}$;
% Remove operations that are scheduled and their edges;
$O_{sf} \leftarrow O_{sf} \cup O_{sf}(i)$;
% Assign operations that form the Nash equilibrium to step i;
if CG != $EMPTY$ **then**
$i \leftarrow i + 1$;
goto **;
end
else
return;
end
end

Algorithm 1: Game theoretic scheduling algorithm

Formally, we can look at the preference mapping as: A buyer has a preference to an allocation, such that $x \succeq y$, i.e., resource x is preferred over resource y, where $x, y \in M$, where M is the set of all available resources at the time instant and $M \in \Re^b$. If a buyer has no preference between resources x and y, then it is denoted as $x \sim y$. We assume that the preferences are transitive, i.e., if $x \succeq y$ and $y \succeq z$, then it implies $x \succeq z$, where $x, y, z \in M$. The scheduling of the feasible resources under a given resource constraint for power optimization can be given as,

$$FS(\vec{m}) = \{x : \vec{m} \cdot x \leq w\} \tag{3}$$

where, $FS(\vec{m})$ is the *feasibility set* for all the operations and their resources and $\vec{m}$ is the cost vector corresponding to the resources. If there exists a preference for an operation towards a particular resource, the *preference set* for the operation is a set of allocations with that preferred module, operation pair. The preference set is a subset of the *feasibility set*. The preference set $PS(\vec{m})$, is defined mathematically as,

$$PS(\vec{m}) = \{x : x \in FS(\vec{m}), f_{sch}(x) \geq f_{sch}(x'), \forall x' \in FS(\vec{m})\} \tag{4}$$

The power cost function of a module m for operation o at control step i is mathematically given as,

$$CMP_{sch}[m, o] = P_{pow_i} + P_{com_i} + \sum_{k=0}^{i-1}(P_{pow_k} + P_{com_k}) \tag{5}$$

where, P_{pow_i} is the power consumed by module m for operation o at level i, P_{com_i} is power consumed by communication between the modules with m being the destination at level i and the last term

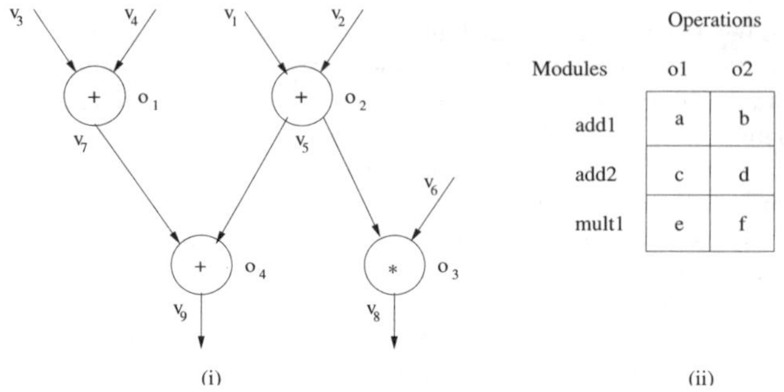

Figure 1: (i) Data-flow graph (ii) Cost matrix

is the average power consumed by the given module from level 0. The delay cost function of a module m for operation o at control step i is mathematically given as,

$$CMD_{sch}[m, o] = D_{pow_i} + D_{com_i} + \sum_{k=0}^{i-1}(D_{pow_k} + D_{com_k}) \tag{6}$$

input : Cost Matrix CM, Number of player N, Set of various possible strategies S
output : Nash equilibrium solution NE_{sch}
for *each player i, where i* $\leftarrow$ 1 *to* N **do**
for *each set of strategies* $(n_1 \in S_1)$*,...,*$(n_N \in S_N)$ **do**
Calculate $p^i_{(n_1,\ldots,n_N)} = CM[i, n_i]$;
end
% The payoff for strategy set $(n_1, ..., n_N)$ is calculated;
for *each strategy* $(n_i \in S_i)$ **do**
$n_i^* \leftarrow$ Nash equi. strategy for player i given by the inequality $p^i_{(n_1^*,\ldots,n_i^*,\ldots,n_N)} \geq p^i_{(n_1^*,\ldots,n_i,\ldots,n_N)}$;
end
$NE \leftarrow NE \cup n_i^*$;
end
% $NE = \{n_1^*, ..., n_i^*, ..., n_N^*\}$, set of optimized strategies for all N players;

Algorithm 2: Algorithm to calculate the Nash equilibrium

where, D_{pow_i} is the delay of module m for executing operation o at level i, D_{com_i} is communication delay between the modules m at level i and the modules to which it was connected in the previous cycles and the last term is the average delay for the given module from level 0. In our formulation, the two optimizing parameters, namely delay and power are considered as a single optimizing parameter. This helps to simplify the formulation and solve problem as a simple resource allocation game.

Consider an architecture with two adders and a multiplier for the data-flow graph given in Figure 1. From the example given in Figure 1-(1), operations *o1, o2* can be scheduled in control cycle 1. We will discuss the game for control cycle 1 to help in understanding the problem, Figure 1-(ii) gives the power cost matrix for cycle 1. Let, a, c, e be the cost associated with scheduling operation *o1* to the modules *add1, add2, mult* respectively and b, d, f the cost associated with scheduling operation *o2* to the modules *add1, add2, mult* respectively. Simply, $co(m, o)$ is the cost of scheduling operation o to module m. The bidding strategy, is the bids by the operation for the modules *add1, add2, mult*. The Nash Equilibrium is the set of bids for the modules, such that no operation can gain by deviating unilaterally (i.e. operations changing their bids).

The complete set of module and operation pairs that are possible for a given cycle is referred to as MO. In the examples, if adder 1 is combined with operation 1 and adder 2 with operation 2, the MO will be {(1,1),(2,2)}. For the set MO, the total cost $CO = co(1,1) + co(2,2)$. Another such combination is adder 1 with operation 2 and adder 2 with operation 1, the corresponding MO is {(1,2),(2,1)}. Now, for each control step, the problem is to find the minimum of all CO's (CO_{min}),

$$CO_{min} = min_{l,k=1,2,3l\neq k}[co(m_l,1) + co(m_k,2)] \quad (7)$$

This work is based on the assumption that Nash equilibrium strategies exist for the scheduling of operations such that the total power for the set MO is minimized. In other words the competition drives the operations to choose the modules such that power minimization is achieved. Normally, in a bid, the bidder has a profit but in the case of the modules, they don't have a profit of their own and so the bid is a value from the cost matrix. The bid by module 1 for operation 1 will be given as, $b(1,1) = co(1,1)$. The generalized cost matrix CM of size x_j x y_j is given as,

input : Nodes O_{ij}, modules M_{ij}, control step i
output : Power pay off matrix CMP_{sch}, delay pay off matrix CMD_{sch}

for *each module* $m \in M_{ij}$ **do**
  for *each operation* $o \in O_{ij}$ **do**
    P_{pow_i} ←power to execute oper. o on module m in i;
    D_{pow_i} ←delay for oper. o on module m at step i;
    P_{com_i} ←power to communicate data to module m at step i from a previous step;
    D_{com_i} ←communication delay for module m at step i from a previous step;
    $P_{sum} \leftarrow \sum_{k=0}^{i-1}(P_{pow_k} + P_{com_k})$;
    $D_{sum} \leftarrow \sum_{k=0}^{i-1}(D_{pow_k} + D_{com_k})$;
    $CMP_{sch}[m,o] \leftarrow P_{pow_i} + P_{com_i} + P_{sum}$;
    $CMD_{sch}[m,o] \leftarrow D_{pow_i} + D_{com_i} + D_{sum}$;
  end
end

Algorithm 3: Payoff matrix calculator for scheduling

$$CM = \begin{bmatrix} co(1,1) & \dots & co(1,y_j) \\ \dots & \dots & \dots \\ co(x_j,1) & \dots & co(x_j,y_j) \end{bmatrix}$$

The set of module-operation pairs $A \in S$ is given as $A = (m_1, o_1), ..., (m_{y_j}, o_{y_j})$, where $m_1, ..., m_{y_j} \in M_{ij}$ are the modules, $o_1, ..., o_{y_j} \in O_{ij}$ are the operations, and S is the set of all possible module-operation pairs. A is a feasible set of module-operation pairs, there could be several such possible "A" sets within S. The module set corresponding to A is, $MS_A = \{(m_A(1), ..., m_A(y_j)\}$. The Nash equilibrium solution A^*, represents the set of module-operation pairs satisfying the Nash equilibrium inequality. The total power (CO) due to all the modules in a given set A is,

$$CO(A) = \sum_{o=1,\dots,y_j} co(m_A(o), o) \quad (8)$$

The proposed algorithm is aimed at minimizing the above equation. Thus, the total power $CO(A^*)$ corresponding to the power optimal set A^* is,

$$CO(A^*) = CO_{min} = \min_{A\in S} CO(A) \quad (9)$$

where, $A^* = \{(m_{A^*}(o), o), o = 1, ..., y_j)\}$ is the Nash equilibrium set of module-operation pairs and MS_{A^*} is the set of modules for A^*. The pseudo-code for scheduling is given in Algorithm 1.

Notations and Definitions

G_f	directed data-flow graph
G_{sf}	scheduled data-flow graph
$O_{sf}(i)$	operations scheduled during control step i
G_a	architecture
x_j	number of modules of type j in the architecture
y_j	number of operations of type j in the architecture
M_{ij}	set of all modules of type j in control step i
O_{ij}	set of all operations of type j in control step i
$NE_{sch}(i)$	Nash equilibrium solution at control step i
CG	current data-flow graph
O_{cg}	operations in the top level of the levelized DFG
$co(m,o)$	power for executing operation o on module m
CMP_{sch}	power cost matrix, $CMP_{sch} = [co(m,o)]$
CMD_{sch}	delay cost matrix, $CMD_{sch} = [co(m,o)]$
S	set of all module-operation pairs available
A	$A \subset S$ is any feasible set of module-operation pairs
MS_A	module set of A, MS_A = {m}, where $m = 1, ..., y_j$
CO	total cost for a specific $A \subset S$
CO_{min}	the minimum total cost of any $A \subset S$

The inputs to the scheduling algorithm are the data-flow graph G_f and the architecture G_a, and the output from the algorithm is the scheduled data-flow graph G_{sf}. A breadth first search of the data-flow graph is performed and the input nodes to the DFG form the nodes in the top level of the DFG. For each set of compatible operations in the top level nodes of the DFG, the payoff matrixes CMP_{sch}, CMD_{sch} are compiled Nash equilibrium solution NE for the game is determined. The Nash equilibrium solution gives, the power optimal schedule for the given DFG at each control step. The payoff matrix equations 5 and 6 are used in Algorithm 3. The nodes that have been scheduled are removed from the data-flow graph. For the current data-flow graph the process is repeated. If all the nodes in the DFG are scheduled, the S-DFG is given as the union of all the Nash equilibrium solutions.

4. SCHEDULING AND BINDING

The algorithm for scheduling and binding can be applied in sequence to obtain a power optimal behavioral synthesis solution. However, this involves applying the Nash equilibrium twice. In this section, we propose a combined scheduling and binding algorithm that applies the Nash equilibrium only once and results in better power reduction than applying the separate algorithms in sequence. The most important step in the combined algorithm is the determination of the payoff matrix, such that the power optimization is maximized. The first-bid sealed auction discussed in the previous sections is used here and hence is not explained again. The algorithm to calculate the payoff matrix used in Algorithm 4 is given in Algorithm 5.

The cost function aims at reducing the delay and the switching activity of the circuit. The power consumption for a module operation pair is,

$$P_{sw} = P_{pow_i} + P_{com_i} + \sum_{k=0}^{i-1}(P_{pow_k} + P_{com_k}) \quad (10)$$

where, P_{pow_i}, is the power consumed by the module m for the operation o in cycle i, similarly P_{com_i} is the power consumed due to the communication between the modules with m as the destination at cycle i, the final term is the total average power of the module from level 0 to level $i-1$. For binding we identify neighborhood operations that can be grouped for the same module to reduce switching activity. If the power due to the neighborhood operations is P_{inp}, then the power cost equation is given as,

$$CMP[m,o] = P_{sw} - P_{inp} \quad (11)$$

The combined scheduling and binding problem is formulated as a resource allocation game with two inter-related parameters to be optimized among the N-players. The notations in Sections 3 are also applicable here.

The inputs to the algorithm are the data-flow graph G_f and the architecture G_a, and the output of the algorithm is the binding matrix B. A breadth first search of the data-flow graph is performed and the input nodes to the DFG form the nodes in the top level of the DFG. For each set of compatible operations in the top level nodes of the DFG, the payoff matrix CM is calculated. The payoff matrix is given in Algorithm 5. The Nash equilibrium for the game is calculated using Algorithm 2 to determine the optimal binding of the operations to the modules and also obtain the power optimal schedule. The register binding task determines the optimal binding for the variables to the registers in each control cycle. Each functional unit that was active in the current control cycle is determined if it was active in the previous control cycle. Then, the input variables to the functional unit in the current cycle are bound to the same registers as in the previous cycle. If the functional unit was inactive in the previous control cycle, then variables are assigned to registers that are equidistant from the functional unit in-terms of the interconnect length.

```
input  : Data flow graph (DFG) G_f, Architecture G_a
output : Binding matrix B
  i ← 0;
% initially level i is set to top level;
  CG ← DFG;
**: Perform breadth first search of current data-flow graph
  CG;
  O_cg ← Operations in the top level of the CG;
  for each set of operations O_ij ∈ O_cg do
      CMP, CMD ← Payoff matrix (O_ij, M_ij, i);
      NE ← Nash equi. solution (CMP, CMD, M_ij, S);
% Nash equilibrium solution at control step i - see Alg 2;
      Represent A* as a binary binding matrix B;
      CG ← {CG − O_sf};
% Remove edges and operations that have been scheduled;
    if CG != EMPTY then
        for each active functional unit m ∈ MS_A* in control step i do
            for each control step k, where k ← 1 to i − 1 do
                if Functional unit m was active in step k then
                    Assign the input variable to the same
                    registers as in step k;
                end
                else
                    Assign the variables to new registers
                    with balanced paths;
                end
            end
        end
        i ← i + 1;
        goto **;
    end
    else
        return;
    end
  end
```

Algorithm 4: Combined scheduling and binding algorithm

```
input  : Nodes O, modules M, level i
output : Power pay off matrix CMP, delay payoff matrix
         CMD
for each module m ∈ M do
    for each operation o ∈ O do
        P_pow_i ← power to execute oper. o on module m in i;
        D_pow_i ← delay for operation o in module m at step i;
        P_com_i ← power to communicate data to module m at
        step i from a previous step;
        D_com_i ← communication delay for module m at step
        i from a previous step;
        P_sum ← Σ_{k=0}^{i-1} (P_pow_k + P_com_k);
        D_sum ← Σ_{k=0}^{i-1} (D_pow_k + D_com_k);
        P_sw ← P_pow_i + P_com_i + P_sum for scheduling to
        module m at step i;
        Identify power reducing neighborhood operations;
        Determine the # of inputs to the oper. that change;
        P_inp ← power reduction due to neighborhood oper.;
        CMP[m, o] ← P_sw − P_inp;
        CMD[m, o] ← D_pow_i + D_com_i + D_sum;
    end
end
```

Algorithm 5: Payoff matrix calculator for the combined algorithm

5. RESULTS AND CONCLUSIONS

The experimental results on benchmark circuits for scheduling and their resource constraints are given in Table 1. The power values for the circuits and the individual modules were obtained by simulation with 100,000 input vectors using the Synopsys RTL power estimation tool "Power Arc". The input vectors are random, 16-bit, two's complement integers. A library for all the functional units and the registers has been developed based on the TSMC $0.25\mu m$ technology. This library is used by the algorithms to provide a realistic comparison of the various algorithms. The proposed scheduling algorithm (S_{GT}) is compared with an integer linear programming (ILP) based methodology (S_{ILP}) proposed in [19] and a latency based scheduler (S_L) [14]. It should be noted that the latency based scheduler is not optimized for power. Column 2 in Table 1 specifies the resource constraint for the algorithms as the # of adders (A) and the # of multipliers (M). The results for the combined scheduling and binding algorithm are tabulated in Table 2. The ILP-based methodology was obtained by applying in sequence the ILP-based scheduling algorithm and the LP-based binding algorithm proposed in [19]. The Nash equilibrium is computed using *Gambit: Software tools for game theory* [16]. The algorithm has a % power savings of about 11.8 % and 41.3 % on an average over the ILP-based methodology and the algorithm with a random binding and latency based schedule respectively.

Since, the Nash equilibrium algorithm is NP-complete, the proposed game theoretic algorithms are of exponential time complexity. However, it should be noted from the Tables 1 and 2, that the run-times are small, which is due to the fact that the time complexity of the algorithm is a function of the number of players in the game and the set of strategies for each player of the game. In our algorithm, we have restricted the number of players in each game to be less than 4, and there are multiple games for each control step in the behavioral synthesis process. Hence, the run-times are much smaller than one would expect if all the games in a single level are combined into a single game. The time complexity of the Nash equilibrium for an N player game with S strategies for each player is given as $O(N^S NS)$ [16]. Assuming this to be the

Table 1: Experimental results for scheduling

Benchmark Circuits	Resource constraint A, M	Sehwa scheduler [14] (S_L) Latency cycles	Power mW	ILP approach [19] (S_{ILP}) Latency cycles	Power mW	**% savings w.r.t. S_L**	Runtime s	Game-theoretic approach (S_{GT}) Latency cycles	Power mW	**% savings w.r.t. S_L**	Runtime s
Diff. eqn	2, 2	4	26.5	4	24.8	**6.4**	18	5	23.9	**9.8**	22
FIR	3, 3	9	99.7	9	82.8	**16.9**	113	10	78.7	**21.1**	107
IIR	2, 2	8	18.9	8	15.6	**17.4**	48	9	14.8	**21.7**	52
Lattice	3, 3	8	121.0	9	91.3	**24.5**	105	9	82.9	**31.5**	90
EWF	2, 2	16	386.6	17	262.8	**32.0**	182	19	251.0	**35.1**	153
WAVE	2, 2	25	352.1	26	258.2	**26.6**	254	27	232.8	**33.9**	215
NC filter	2, 2	27	507.2	27	389.7	**23.1**	295	27	363.4	**28.4**	256
Average						**20.9**				**25.9**	

Table 2: Experimental results for combined scheduling and binding

Bench-mark circuits	Latency scheduler & random binding ($S_L + B_R$) Latency cycles	Power mW (1)	ILP-based scheduling & LP-based binding [19] ($S_{ILP} + B_{LP}$) Latency cycles	Power mW	**% sav w.r.t. (1)**	Run-time (s)	Latency scheduler & Game-theoretic binding ($S_L + B_{GT}$) Latency cycles	Power mW	**% sav w.r.t. (1)**	Run-time (s)	Game-theoretic scheduling & binding ($S_{GT} + B_{GT}$) Latency cycles	Power mW	**% sav w.r.t. (1)**	Run-time (s)
Diff. eqn	4	26.6	4	22.9	**13.9**	35	4	20.1	**24.4**	59	5	16.0	**40.0**	37
FIR	9	95.7	10	61.7	**35.5**	221	9	57.7	**39.7**	216	10	50.4	**47.3**	165
IIR	8	18.3	8	12.8	**30.0**	100	8	12.3	**32.8**	110	9	11.2	**39.0**	96
Lattice	8	113.0	9	66.3	**41.3**	207	8	64.1	**43.2**	215	10	55.9	**50.5**	161
EWF	16	317.2	17	204.0	**35.6**	259	16	210.0	**33.8**	285	19	191.3	**39.6**	204
WAVE	25	291.9	26	201.2	**31.0**	427	25	196.3	**32.7**	427	27	179.2	**38.6**	332
NC filter	27	438.1	27	324.3	**25.9**	501	27	312.8	**28.6**	528	27	286.7	**34.6**	377
Average					**30.5**				**33.6**				**41.4**	

complexity of the Nash equilibrium, the complexity of the scheduling algorithm is given as, $O(lcN^S NS)$, where l is the number of levels for the given DFG and c is the number of sets of compatible operations at each level of the DFG. The space complexity of the algorithms is given as, $O(MO)$, where M is the number of modules and O the number of operations in the game. The algorithm can be further improved by incorporating voltage scaling and dynamic frequency clocking. We plan to incorporate interconnect binding in our game theoretic formulation since, interconnects will play a significant role in synthesis of data-path circuits as we move into deep sub-micron and nano regimes.

6. REFERENCES

[1] A. Dasgupta and R. Karri. Simultaneous scheduling and binding for power minimization during micro-architecture synthesis. In *Proc. Intl. Symp. on Low Power Electronics and Design*, pp 69-74, 1995.

[2] A. Raghunathan and N.K. Jha. SCALP: An iterative improvement based low-power data path synthesis system. *IEEE Trans. on CAD*, 16(11):1260-1277, Nov. 1997.

[3] A. Raghunathan, S. Dey and N.K. Jha. Register transfer level power optimization with emphasis on glitch analysis and reduction. *IEEE Trans. on CAD*, 18(8):1114-1131,Aug.1999.

[4] A.K. Murugavel and N. Ranganathan. A game-theoretic approach for binding in behavioral synthesis. In *Proc. Intl. Conf. on VLSI Design*, pp 452-458, 2003.

[5] C. Park, T. Kim and C.L. Liu. An efficient data path synthesis algorithm for behavioral-level power optimization. In *Proc. Intl. Symp. on Circuits and Systems*, v 1, pp 294-297, 1999.

[6] D.F. Ferguson, C. Nikolaou, J. Sairamesh and Y. Yemini. Economic models for allocating resources in computer systems. In Clearwater S., editor, *A Paradigm for Distributed Resource Allocation*. World Scientific, 1996.

[7] E. Musoll and J. Cortadella. Scheduling and resource binding for low power. In *Proc. Intl. Symp. on System Synthesis*, pp 104-109, 1995.

[8] F. Gruian and K. Kuchcinski. Operation binding and scheduling for low power using constraint logic programming. In *Proc. Euromicro Conf.*, v 1, pp 83-90, 1998.

[9] J.-M. Chang and M. Pedram. Module assignment for low power. In *Proc. European Design Automation Conf.*, pp 376-381, 1996.

[10] J. von Neumann. Zur Theorie der Gesellschaftsspiele. *Zur Theorie der Gesellschaftsspiele*, pp 295-320, 1928.

[11] J.F. Nash. Non-cooperative games. *Annals of Mathematics*, 54(2):286-295, Sep. 1951.

[12] L. Benini and G. Micheli. System-level power optimization: Techniques and tools. *ACM Trans. on Design Automation of Electronic Systems*, 5(2):115-192, Apr. 2000.

[13] L. Kruse, E. Schmidt, G. Jochens, A. Stammermann, A. Schulz, E. Macii and W. Nebel. Estimation of lower and upper bounds on the power consumption from scheduled data flow graphs. *IEEE Trans. on VLSI*, 9(1):3-14, Feb. 2001.

[14] N. Park and A.C. Parker. Sehwa: A software package for synthesis of pipelines from behavioral specifications. *IEEE Trans. on CAD*, 7(3):356-370, Mar. 1988.

[15] P.G. Paulin and J.P. Knight. Scheduling and binding algorithms for high-level synthesis. In *Proc. Design Automation Conf.*, 1989.

[16] R.D. McKelvey, A. McLennan and T. Turocy. *Gambit: Software tools for game theory*. California Inst. of Tech., Uni. of Minnesota and Texas A & M Uni., v 0.97, Sep. 2002.

[17] S.K. Shukla and R.K. Gupta. A model checking approach to evaluating system level dynamic power management policies for embedded systems. In *Proc. Intl. High-level validation and Test Workshop*, pp 53-57, 2001.

[18] V.K. Srikantam, N. Ranganathan and S. Srinivasan. CREAM: combined register and module assignment with floor-planning for low power data-path synthesis. In *Proc. Intl. Conf. on VLSI Design*, pp 228-223, 2000.

[19] W.T. Shiue and C. Chakrabarti. ILP-based scheme for low power scheduling and resource binding. In *Proc. Intl. Symp. on Circuits and Systems*, v 3, pp 279-282, 2000.

VL-CDRAM: Variable Line Sized Cached DRAMs

Ananth Hegde, N. Vijaykrishnan, Mahmut Kandemir and Mary Jane Irwin
Micro Systems Design Lab
The Pennsylvania State University, University Park
{hegdeank,vijay,kandemir,mji}@cse.psu.edu

ABSTRACT

Many of the current memory architectures embed a SRAM cache within the DRAM memory. These architectures exploit a wide internal data bus to transfer an entire DRAM row to the on-memory cache. However, applications exhibit a varying spatial locality across the different DRAM rows that are accessed and buffering the entire row may be wasteful. In order to adapt to the changing spatial locality, we propose a Variable Line size Cached DRAM (VL-CDRAM) that can buffer portions of an accessed DRAM row. Our evaluation shows that the proposed approach is effective in not only reducing the energy consumption but also in improving the performance across various memory configurations.

Categories and Subject Descriptors: B.3.1 [Memory Structures]: Dynamic Memory (DRAM)
General Terms: Measurement, Performance, Design
Keywords: Variable Line, VL-CDRAM, CDRAM, Energy

1. INTRODUCTION

The growing disparity in the performance of memory and the processor is an important concern for many data intensive embedded applications. The memory performance is influenced by both the limited bandwidth of data transfer between the processor and off-chip DRAMs [1] and the large DRAM access latency. While advances in bus technology have significantly mitigated the bandwidth problem [2], the DRAM access latency has not improved much. Many of the current memory architectures address the DRAM latency problem by embedding a SRAM cache within the memory [8]. These architectures rely on the fact that SRAM accesses are faster than DRAM accesses and also exploit the use of a wide internal data bus for data transfers from the DRAM to the on-memory cache. A key difference between on-memory caches and traditional on-processor L1 caches (that can also benefit from the faster SRAM accesses) is the width of the transfer.

There are different variants of the DRAM architectures that employ on-memory caches such as cached DRAMs [6, 7], enhanced DRAMs and VC-DRAMs. A main distinction between the different approaches is in the number of cache lines that they support. Case a in Figure 1 shows the DRAM organization where only a single cache line is used to buffer an entire row of DRAM. Subsequent memory accesses to the same row are then serviced directly by the SRAM without having to access the DRAM. However this configuration is inefficient if successive accesses are not confined to the same DRAM row and can cause thrashing of the cache line.

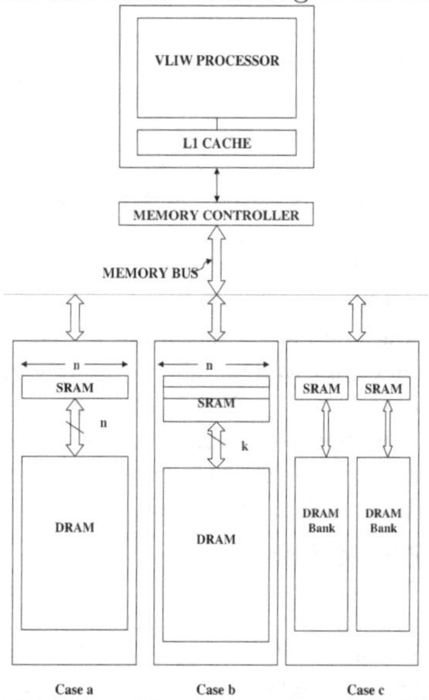

Figure 1: DRAMs with on-memory SRAM caches. (a) Single bank configuration with a single cache line SRAM, (b) Single bank configuration with multiple cache lines SRAM and (c) Multi-bank configuration with single cache line SRAM.

There are two approaches to handling this problem, one is the use of multiple banks of DRAM and associating a SRAM buffer with each bank(see Case c in Figure 1). The other approach is to use multiple cache lines with the DRAM memory (see Case b in Figure 1(b)). Prior approaches that have used multiple on-memory cache lines either use a small cache line as in traditional L1 caches [3] or use wide cache lines that are of the same size as a DRAM row [4, 5]. Further, the cache lines can either be fully-associative, direct-mapped or set-associative. Prior investigation shows that fully-associative configuration is preferable from a performance perspective [12].

The on-memory caching approaches are based on the premise that there is a significant spatial locality between the accesses in a DRAM row. Further, using fixed size cache lines assumes uniform spatial locality across different DRAM row accesses. However, applications may exhibit a varying ex-

CODES+ISSS'03, October 1–3, 2003, Newport Beach, California, USA.

tent of spatial locality across the different rows that are accessed.

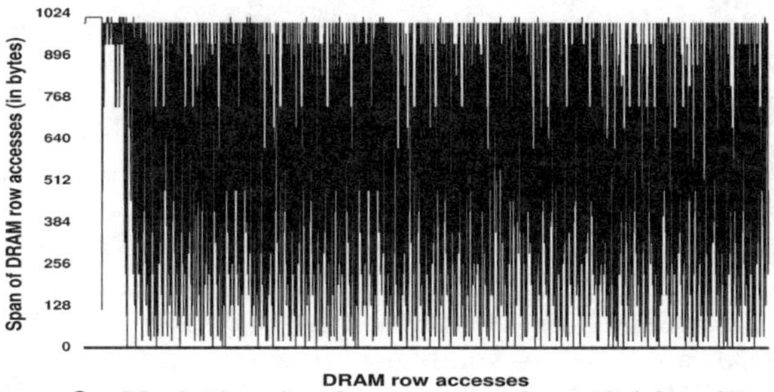

Figure 2: Variation in the extent of spatial locality in the different DRAM rows accessed during the execution of tomcatv benchmark. Here we use 1KB DRAM rows.

Figure 2 shows the variation in spatial locality in different DRAM rows that are accessed for the `tomcatv` application in our suite using a metric defined as the `span`. The `span` shown in this figure is measured by using an 8KB fully associative on-memory cache that caches the DRAM rows that are accessed. All DRAM rows are buffered in this on-memory cache and the difference between the maximum and minimum addresses accessed from this buffered row before it is evicted is defined as the `span`.

There are various reasons for the variation in spatial locality observed from this figure. Scalar variables and arrays have different spatial locality. Further, each array has a different size and this can influence the extent of locality. Another reason is that data reuse might occur in different loop levels. Let us consider the following code fragment as an example.

```
for j= 1 to 32
      for i = 1 to 1024
            a[i]
            b[1024*i]
            c[j]
      endfor
endfor
```

Here, we observe that arrays `a` and `b` have different strides in their accesses. While array `a` would benefit from caching the entire row of 1024 bytes, caching array `b` in contrast does not provide any performance benefits. In fact, since there is no spatial reuse of the cached line, caching the entire row of `b` wastes energy in the on-memory cache. Further, it can affect performance as the storage of array `b` will conflict with currently cached rows that exhibit more spatial locality. The conflicts are of a concern because of the limited number of cache lines typically available in on-memory caches. In this example, we also note that elements of array `c` have little spatial locality in the inner loop. Hence, caching an entire row of `c` can be wasteful as well. Further, we can see that only 32 elements of `c` are required and caching more elements from the DRAM row in which it is contained may not be useful. Since the amount of energy expended in the integrated DRAM ranged between 30-90% of the energy expended in the data memory hierarchy for the applications in our suite, optimizing the DRAM energy by reducing the wasted energy is significant.

In this paper, we propose a *Variable Line size Cached DRAM* (VL-CDRAM) that uses a variable line size buffering for the on-memory cache in order to adapt to the varying degrees of spatial locality. Dynamically varying cache line sizes has been used previously for L1 caches in [13] [14] to exploit varying spatial locality in applications. Our technique is different from [14], in that while [14] focuses on data-caches in an multiprocessor environment, our work focus is on the cache in the DRAM. [14] uses variable line sizes to reduce false sharing between different processors. For example, if a large line is cached in processor 1, there may be portions that it never uses actually that may required for processor 2. Thus, variable line sizing helps reduce coherence activity in this case. Due to this inherent difference, the scheme for choosing the line sizes is entirely different. Variable line caching in DRAMs have been explored before in [9] [10]. Our technique is different from them in that our approach relies on static profiling to associate the line size information with the load/store instructions while it uses dynamic information about the presence of adjacent lines to adjust the fetch/store width and associates line size information with the physical cache line (instead of the load/store instructions in our case). Due to the dynamic nature, their work incurs a learning time overhead to adapt to the appropriate cache size. Further, when the same load instruction accesses different cache lines (as in the case of array codes that access non adjacent entries), our technique is able to capture patterns of correlation in line sizes across cache lines. In contrast, the approach in [9] requires training across each cache line. While the underlying goal is the same in both the approaches, the solution for determining the line sizes are very different. Using a set of eight array-dominated applications that exhibit good spatial locality and a VLIW processor based system, we show that the VL-CDRAM can reduce the energy consumed in the DRAM by 31% as compared to using a scheme that always buffers the entire DRAM row (our default parameters explained later). We also show that our technique is effective across different memory configurations.

The rest of this paper is organized as follows. The next section describes the operation of the on-memory SRAM caches in our system. Section 3 shows the necessary architectural support for the VL-CDRAM. Section 4 explains our experimental framework and simulator. The evaluation of the VL-CDRAM with respect to energy is performed in Section 5. Section 6 provides the concluding remarks.

2. CACHED DRAM OPERATION

The target system is based on a VLIW processor that contains an on-chip cache and an off-chip cached DRAM (CDRAM). The CDRAM is an integrated memory unit consisting of an on-memory cache and a DRAM core and is accessed using a memory controller whenever there is a cache miss in the on-chip cache.

The memory controller maintains the tags corresponding to the cache lines of the on-memory cache. Whenever there is a read access to the memory unit, the tags in the memory controller are checked for a hit in the on-memory cache. If one of the tags matches, the cache line index of the matching cache line is transferred to the memory unit along with the column address. Then, the on-memory cache is accessed and the column address is used to address the appropriate portion of the indexed cache line. However, when none of the tags matches, it indicates a read miss for the on-memory cache. In addition,the index of the cache line selected for replacement is also sent to the CDRAM. The least recently used cache line is selected for replacement in our implementation. Next, the DRAM row is activated and the data is transfered to the on-memory cache. Then, the column address is used to find the appropriate offset of data from the replaced cache line to read. Note that a write hit is similar to a read hit except the additional operation of setting the dirty bit corresponding to the written cache line in the memory controller. This dirty bit is used to identify whether a write back is required when replacing a cache line or to perform write backs of the cache lines whenever DRAM core is idle. Figure 3 shows the variation in memory access latencies when a memory request hits in the on-memory cache and misses in the on-memory cache.

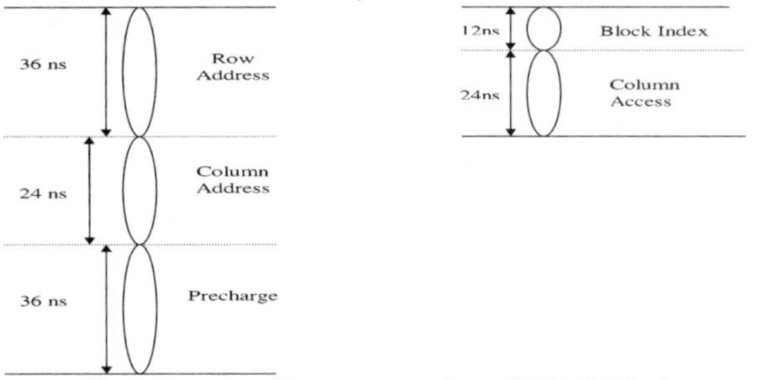

Figure 3: Access Sequences for CDRAM Accesses. On-memory cache miss (left) and on-memory cache hit (right).

3. VL-CDRAM ARCHITECTURE AND ITS OPERATION

The proposed VL-CDRAM operates similar to the CDRAM except that it does not buffer a fixed portion of the DRAM row. In the VL-CDRAM the size of the cache line is smaller than the DRAM row size. Based on the extent of spatial locality in a given DRAM row access, multiple adjacent cache lines are used to buffer the selected width of the DRAM row. The replacement policy identifies the least recently used cache line and also uses the lines adjacent to it if the buffering size is larger than a cache line. We consider the LRU policy at the cache line size level and not the replacement block size level since considering it at the replacement block size level requires more tag comparisons and additional hardware. This would not only complicate the design, but would also lead to an increase in energy consmption. In order to enable transfer of multiple cache lines in the same cycle, we enforce an alignment for the variable size blocks as shown in Figure 4 to select the adjacent cache lines.

The tag matching as usual takes place in the memory controller. Cache hit works similar to that of the CDRAM except that the row address and the column address are sent to the control unit of the memory irrespective of a hit or a miss. Since the address bus is multiplexed, the row address and column address are sent in consecutive cycles

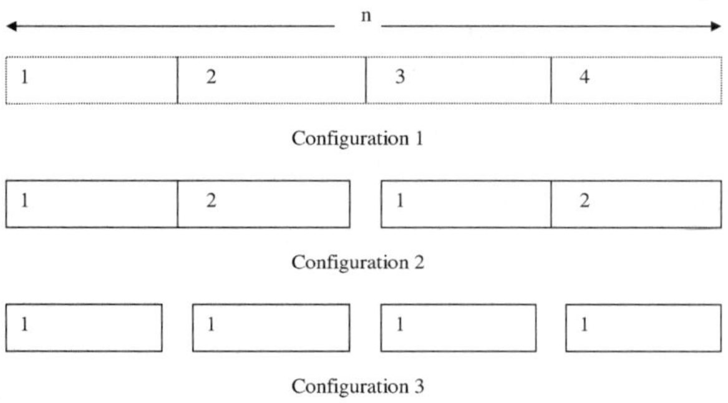

Figure 4: Valid alignments of DRAM row buffering in multiple cache lines. Here four cache lines equal the size of the DRAM row.

and get latched in the row address latch and column address latch. On a hit, the request is serviced directly by the on-memory cache. On the other hand a cache miss would signal a row address strobe which would decode the row address. The miss signal would also enable the sizing control logic which would read the `log n` input bits (Block size bits) being fed by the memory controller along with the `log n` most significant bits of the column address, where $n = size\ of\ DRAM\ row/size\ of\ cache\ line$. The column address bits are needed to decide on the offset of the block in the DRAM row. The sizing control logic is a combinational logic which generates `log n` signals which enable/disable the sense amplifiers that are divided into `log n` groups. When the row address gets decoded and a particular row gets activated, the sizing control logic would disable the appropriate sense amplifiers to support variable length DRAM row buffering. Figure 5 shows the timing diagram for a cache miss. The additional hardware to support VL-CDRAM shown in the Figure 6 was designed in verilog and synthesized using 0.13 micron technology and the energy consumed by it was calculated. We found that the energy consumed by this additional hardware is less then 0.01% of the total energy consumed by a DRAM access. Also the area impact of this additional hardware is negligible.

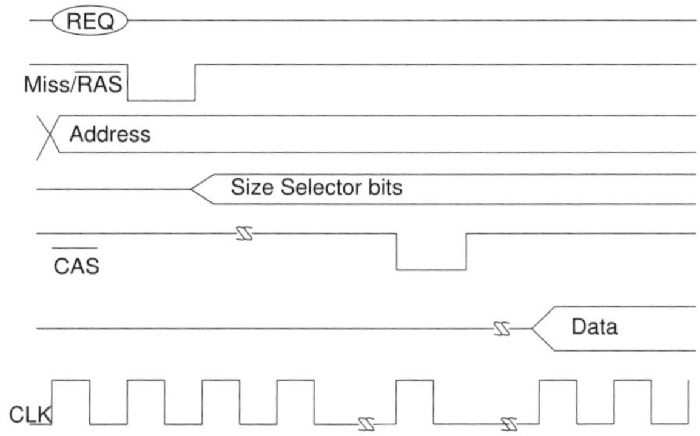

Figure 5: Timing diagram on a cache miss.

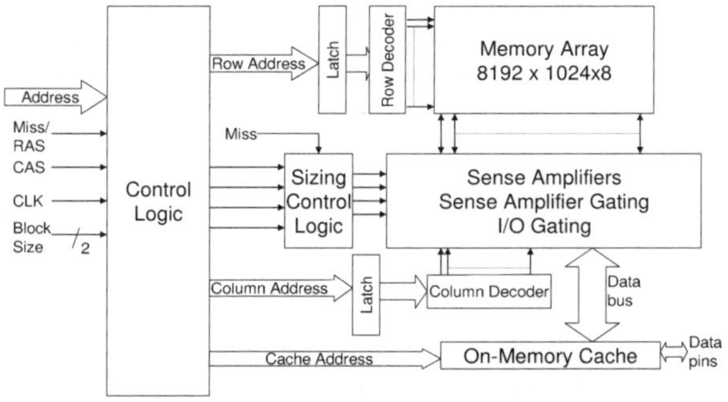

Figure 6: Modifications to the underlying hardware.

Variable block sizes impose two other constraints that need to be handled. First, if multiple cache lines chosen for replacement are dirty, the delay incurred is proportional to the number of cache lines that must be written back. However, the probability of encountering multiple dirty lines for replacement is small as write backs of the dirty blocks are performed in the background whenever the DRAM core is not busy. Second, due to the caching of multiple cache lines of variable length, we need to ensure that there is no duplication of the data in the on-memory cache. For example, consider the sequence shown in Figure 7. First, the on-memory cache buffers the entire DRAM row containing

A and B in two cache lines. Then, A is evicted later by a block C. The next load that accesses A observes that there is an on-memory cache miss and indicates the entire row consisting of two cache lines should be buffered. While the tag miss for A is the one that initiated an access to the DRAM row, the tag match for B is required to avoid duplicate buffering. Thus, in the variable line size buffering, we perform the tag check for each of the multiple cache lines that are buffered. After buffering, the valid bits of only the cache lines whose tag does not match with that of an existing cache line are marked as valid. Instead of increasing the number of tag ports to simultaneously check the tags of multiple cache lines, we perform this operation of marking tag bits valid sequentially for the adjacent cache lines in the memory controller. This operation can be overlapped with the column access in the CDRAM to mask any performance penalty. In our simulation tool we have incorporated this technique to avoid duplicates.

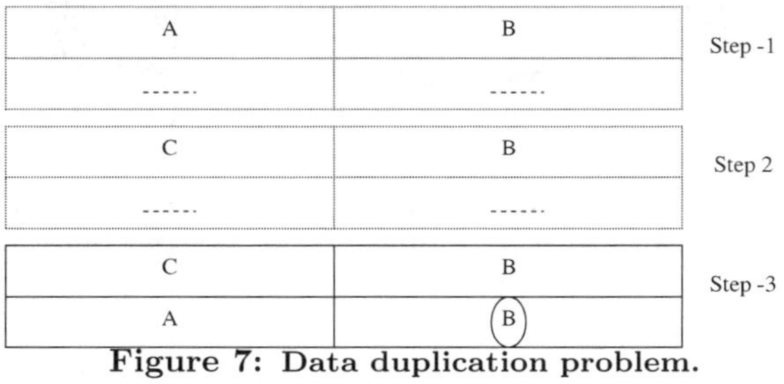

Figure 7: Data duplication problem.

Next, it is necessary to generate the `log n` bits which provide information on the extent of the DRAM row to buffer. Our approach is based on *profiling* which is widely used for optimizing embedded applications. We profiled the applications to identify the extent of spatial locality of load/stores. All the load/stores that incur an on-memory cache miss were tracked as they initiate the DRAM row buffering. To associate a single value with the static load/store instructions in the program , we average the extents observed at all dynamic instances of that static instruction. For example, Figure 8 shows average values and standard deviations of the `span` of buffered rows accessed by dynamic instances for a subset of static load/store instructions for the mxm application in our suite. We make use of `log n` bits to associate this value with each static instruction. This associated information indicates the number of cache lines that need to buffered when the DRAM row access was initiated by that static instruction. The additional `log n` bits with load/store instruction is accommodated using the unused bits in instruction format of the VLIW instruction set architecture ([11] provides more details of such opportunities in the load/store instruction format in the case of IA64). We call this technique, the Average Block Size(ABS) technique.

4. SIMULATION FRAMEWORK

In order to evaluate the VL-CDRAM approach, we used a set of applications executing on a VLIW processor architecture to generate the memory access behavior. The VLIW architecture was simulated using the Trimaran framework [15] while the VL-CDRAM simulator was custom designed. Only data cache trace was considered for the simulations. The default parameters used in our simulations are shown in Table 1. Table 2 shows the applications used in our evaluation and the last column shows the energy consumed in the CDRAM when using the base configuration with a fixed on-memory cache line size of 1024 bytes.

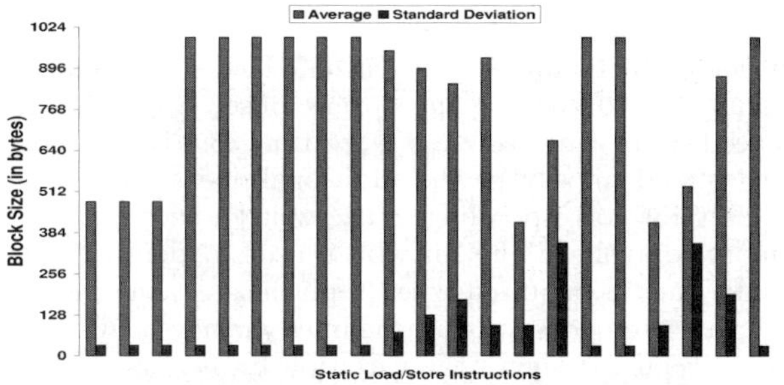

Figure 8: Average span for the blocks for each static load/store instance and their standard deviation for the mxm benchmark

Parameter	Value
Technology	0.13micron
VLIW Issue Width	9
Number of LD/ST units	2
L1 data cache size	32KB
L1 data cache associativity	2-way associative
L1 data cache line size	32 bytes
CDRAM Internal Bus Width	1024 bytes
On-Memory Cache Size	4KB
On-Memory Cache Line Size	256 bytes
DRAM core size	16MB
DRAM Banks	1
CPU Cycle Time	2ns
On-Memory Cache Hit Latency	12 cycles
DRAM Row Access Latency	18 cycles
DRAM Column Access Latency	12 cycles
DRAM Row Activation Energy	17 nJ
DRAM Read/Write Energy per byte	2.1 nJ
DRAM internal bus energy per byte	0.48 nJ
No. of address bits used by the size selection logic	2
No. of tag bits generated by the compiler with each load/store	2

Table 1: Default simulation parameters

We primarily focus on the reduction in the memory energy consumption because of the use of VL-CDRAM. Energy consumption in the VL-CDRAM is modeled as follows. A hit in the on-memory cache incurs energy consumed in accessing the associative cache. This energy was modeled for a 0.13 micron technology using CACTI [16]. A miss on the other hand requires a DRAM access. The energy consumed on a miss involves the DRAM access energy in addition to the on-memory cache access energy. A DRAM access activates the selected row and transfers that row's data to the sense amps. The energy consumed by this row activation is represented as $E(ACT)$. This is followed by a read (write) energy during which the column address selects certain number of cells for amplifying and latching into (from) the output buffers. Finally, energy is consumed in the internal buses based on the length of the DRAM row that is buffered and driven. Thus the DRAM access involves, a row activation energy ($E(ACT)$), read/write energy $E(RW)$, and the bus energy $E(DQ)$. These energy numbers were evaluated using average activation current (IDD0), active standby current (IDD3N), read/write current (IDD4(R/W)), the row activation cycles (Trc), supply voltage (VDD), output current (Iout) and the DRAM cycle time obtained from data sheets [17]. These energies are calculated as follows

$$E(ACT)=(IDD0-IDD3N)*Trc*VDD*clock\_period$$
$$E(RW)=(IDD4(R/W)-IDD3N)*VDD*clock\_period*buffering\_size$$
$$E(DQ)=VDD*Iout*clock\_period*8*buffering\_size$$

Note that using the optimal sizes for the buffering the DRAM row will reduce the read/write energy and the bus energy as only the portions that need to be buffered in the on-memory cache are read and transferred. Further, we also

Program	Source	Memory energy (nJ)
tsf	Perfect Club	1257189667
eflux	Perfect Club	1028302543
btrix	Specfp92	14746347130
tomcatv	Specfp95	1551753573
mxm	Specfp92	3051618425
bmcm	Perfect Club	365088561
vpenta	Specfp92	65165438853
adi	Livermore	107773748

Table 2: Benchmark characteristics.

save energy in the on-memory cache because the amount of data written into it is smaller. Thus, reading only the required data for buffering saves energy even if there is no improvement in the hit rate to the on-memory caches.

We already discussed the latency reduction that can be achieved when a read or write hits in the on-memory cache. Hence, any improvement in hit rates to the on-memory caches using the VL-CDRAM approach can reduce the memory access latency. Further, hits in the on-memory cache limits energy consumption to only the on-memory cache and no energy is consumed in the DRAM core. Finally, performance improvements due to reduced memory access latencies can also reduce energy consumed due to refresh and also in the rest of the system (these savings will improve the presented results but are not accounted for in this evaluation).

5. RESULTS

We used two techniques to simulate the VL-CDRAM.

1. Oracle Technique : This technique would know the exact size of the block that needs to be buffered for each dynamic instance of load/store instruction. We profiled the applications to identify the extent of spatial locality of loads/stores. All the load/store instructions that incur an on-memory cache miss were tracked as they initiate the DRAM row buffering. We measured the extent of the buffered DRAM row that was accessed before it was replaced from the on-memory cache for each load/store instructions.
2. Average Block Size (ABS) technique : In contrast to the Oracle technique, we associate the buffering size with each static load/store instruction in the ABS technique as discussed above in Section 4.

We show the results for the ABS technique while comparing it with the Oracle technique. While the Oracle technique would tell us the maximum savings that could be achieved, the ABS technique shows how well this could be practically achieved.

Figure 9 shows the variation of the spatial locality in the different applications. These results were obtained by monitoring the access behavior of the buffered DRAM row that was accessed before it was replaced using an 8K on-memory cache and other default parameters. We find buffering the entire DRAM row would have been unnecessary in at least 30% of the cases across all applications. We also find that using a finer granularity of buffering can potentially save a significant amount of energy expended in reading and buffering unused portion of the DRAM row.

Next, we investigate how well this characteristic translates into energy savings. Figure 10 shows the amount of energy savings that can be obtained when different sizes are chosen for the on-memory cache lines as compared to the currently used scheme of buffering the entire row. For example, an 128 byte cache line can support buffering of either 128, 256, 512 or 1024 bytes of a DRAM row that is accessed. An average energy savings when using 128, 256 and 512 bytes

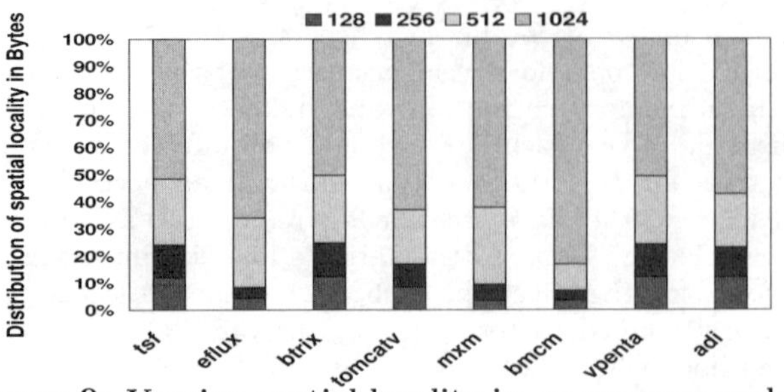

Figure 9: Varying spatial locality in on-memory cache.

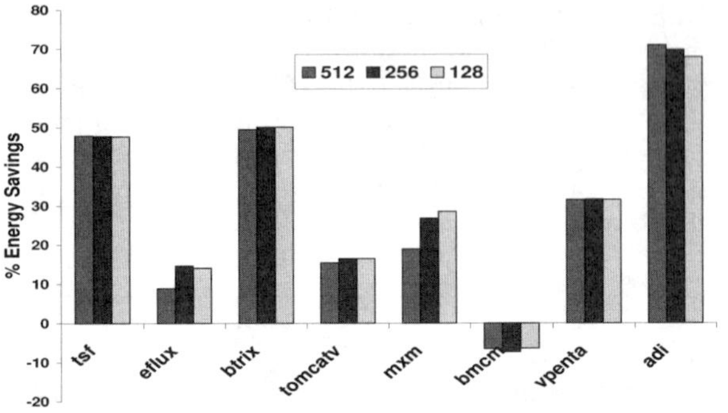

Figure 10: Percentage of DRAM energy reduction using VL-CDRAM with base configuration and varying cache line sizes over using fixed cache line size of 1024 bytes.

for cache line size provided on the average 31%, 31% and 30% energy savings for the ABS technique when compared to 38%, 36% and 29% of energy savings for the Oracle technique. While one might expect the energy savings to be higher when the block sizes are 128 and 256 when compared to using a block size of 512, we see a much more uniform behavior across different block sizes when using ABS from Figure 10. This is due to the fact that different instances of a static load/store instruction might require different block sizes and when we average the extents, we end up using one average block size value for each instruction. We also see that the energy consumption increases for one of the benchmarks bmcm, this occurs due to a very high irregularity in the block sizes for different dynamic instances of a static load/store instruction.

Next, we analyzed the sensitivity to the capacity of the on-memory cache sizes. While larger cache sizes can potentially capture more number of distinct cache lines, the complexity and area overheads need to be limited. Specifically, the complexity is of concern in the on-memory cache architecture as it is fully associative and the area overhead is an issue because we are embedding the SRAM within the DRAM which is preferred for its compactness. With these limitations in consideration, we varied the on-memory cache size with 2KB, 4KB and 8KB and analyzed the energy savings of the VL-CDRAM approach using a 256 bytes cache line. Figure 11 shows the results for the different cache sizes. We observe that the energy savings for the 2KB, 4KB and 8KB caches were 32%, 31% and 30% on the average respectively, across all the benchmarks using the ABS technique when compared to 36%, 36% and 33% of maximum energy savings that we could have achieved. This shows that our technique is quite effective across different configurations. We also observe that the energy savings achieved increases for smaller sized on-chip caches as there is a lesser place for contentions for replacements.

We also tried to study the impact of these energy opti-

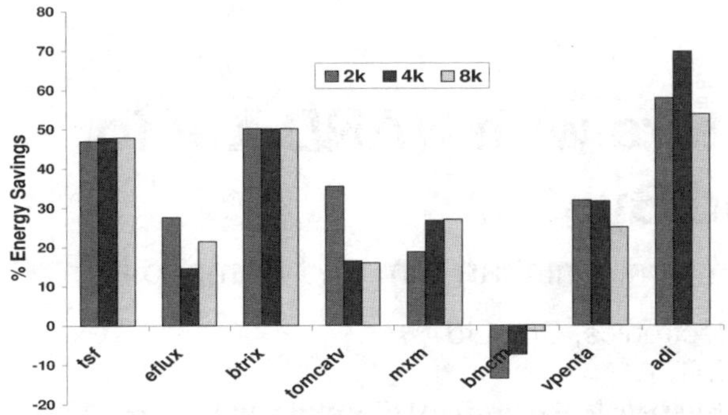

Figure 11: Percentage of DRAM energy reduction using VL-CDRAM with 256 bytes on-memory cache lines over fixed 1024 bytes on-memory cache lines for different on-memory cache sizes.

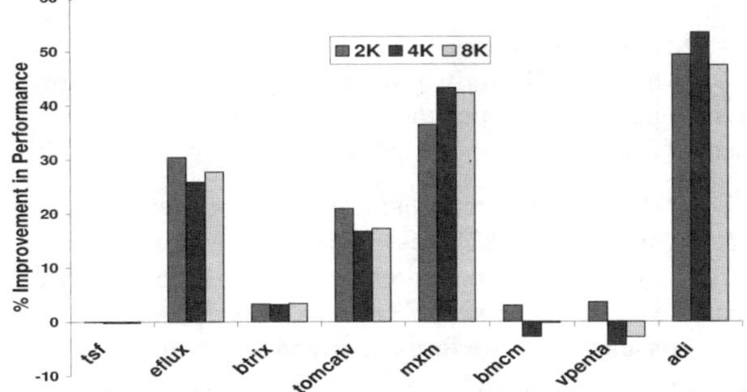

Figure 12: Percentage improvements in latency for different sizes of on-memory cache with cache line size of 256.

mizations over the latency. We observed that if the size of the cache is small, the latency will almost always improve. Figure 12 shows the percentage improvements in latency for different sizes of on-memory cache. We observed a percentage improvement in latency by 23%, 18% and 17% for 2KB, 4KB and 8KB using the ABS technique as compared to maximum achievable values of 21%, 15% and 13%. We see that certain benchmarks do not show any improvement in latency due to increase in miss rates since we consider the LRU policy at the cache line size level and not the replacement block size level.

The L1 cache sizes in the processor can influence the memory access pattern. Thus, we experimented by varying the L1 data cache size from 8KB to 32KB. Our results show that while larger L1 cache reduces the number of memory accesses and the overall energy expended in the CDRAM, it does not significantly impact the extent of spatial reuse in the on-memory cache. On the contrary, the average energy savings increase. The average energy savings when employing the VL-CDRAM with cache line size of 256 bytes and default parameters were 23%, 27% and 31% for L1 cache sizes of 8KB, 16KB and 32KB, respectively using the ABS technique, as compared to 33%, 34% and 36% for the Oracle technique.

6. CONCLUSIONS AND FUTURE WORK

On-memory caches are being employed in most commercial DRAM chips in order to reduce the effective memory access latency. However, most of the current approaches buffer a fixed size of an accessed DRAM row into the on-memory cache and waste a significant portion of the energy due to this inflexibility. In this work, we presented a VL-CDRAM that provides adaptivity to the size of DRAM row that can be buffered. Our analysis using various programs showed that there is a noticeable variation in spatial locality within different DRAM rows that are accessed. Specifically, we find that for at least 30% of the accessed DRAM rows, in all the eight applications that we used, caching the entire row wastes energy. Our approach focuses on eliminating this wastage by capturing the variability in the DRAM row spatial locality and associating this information with the load/store instructions in the application. This information is used to direct the amount of buffering to be used when the DRAM rows are accessed. We observe that our technique is effective in reducing energy across different configurations of the on-memory chip and the L1 data cache in the processor. Using 256 bytes cache line for the VL-CDRAM and other default parameters, on the average, 31% of the memory energy was saved as compared to using a fixed cache line size.

Our future effort will focus more on the impact of specific code optimizations on the effectiveness of our approach. Specifically, we will try to design better techniques which could achieve results much closer to the Oracle technique. We will also investigate techniques that transform the data layout to improve the locality in DRAM row accesses. Finally, our on-going work aims at analyzing in more detail the impact of the different bank interleaving strategies on the spatial locality of the DRAM row accesses.

7. ACKNOWLEDGEMENTS

This work was supported in part by NSF Grant 0103583, NSF CAREER Awards 0093082 & 0093085 and MARCO 98-DF-600 GSRC grant.

8. REFERENCES

[1] D. Burger, J. R. Goodman, and A. Kagi. Memory bandwidth limitations of future microprocessors. In *Proc. International Symposium on Computer Architecture*, 1996.

[2] V. Cuppu et al. A Performance comparison of contemporary DRAM architectures. In *Proc. International Symposium on Computer Architecture*, 1999.

[3] W. Hsu and J. E smith. Performance of cached DRAM organizations in vector supercomputers. In *Proc. International Symposium on Computer Architecture*, 1993.

[4] R. P. Koganti and G. Kedem. WCDRAM : a fully associative integrated cached-DRAM with wide cache lines. Technical Report CS-1997-03, Dept. of Computer Science, Duke Univ, Durham, N. C., 1997

[5] W. Wong and J. L. Baer. DRAM on-chip caching. Technical Report UW CSE 97-03-04, Dept. of Computer Science and Engineering, Univ. of Washington, 1997.

[6] H. Hidaka et al. The cache DRAM architecture with on-chip cache memory. *IEEE MICRO*, vol. 10, no. 2, Mar. 1990.

[7] C. A Hart. CDRAM in a unified memory architecture. In *Proc. International Computer conference (COMPCON 94)*, 1994.

[8] F. Jones. A new era of fast dynamic RAMs. *IEEE Spectrum*, Oct. 1992.

[9] K.Inoue, K. Kai, and K. Murakami. Dynamically Variable Line-Size Cache Architecture for Merged DRAM/Logic LSIs. *IEICE Transactions on Information and Systems*, May 2000.

[10] K.Inoue, K. Kai, and K. Murakami. Performance/Energy Efficiency of Variable Line-Size Caches on Intelligent Memory Systems A new era of fast dynamic RAMs. *Proc.2nd Workshop on Intelligent Memory SystemsIEEE Spectrum*, Nov. 2000.

[11] IA-64 Application developer's architecture guide, Intel corporation, 1999.

[12] Z. Zhang, Z. Zhu, and X. Zhang. Cached DRAM for ILP processor memory access latency reduction. *IEEE MICRO*, vol. 21, no. 4, July/Aug.. 2001.

[13] Weiyu Tang, Alexander V. Veidenbaum, Alexandru Nicolau, Rajesh Gupta. Adaptive Line Size Cache. *UC, Irvine, Technical Report ICS-TR-99-56*, Nov.1999.

[14] C.Dubnicki and T.J. LeBlanc. Adjustable Block Size Coherent Caches. In *Proceedings of the 19th International Symposium on Computer Architecture*, May 1992.

[15] Trimaran home page. http://www.trimaran.org.

[16] P. Shivkumar and N. Jouppi. CACTI 3.0: An Integrated Cache Timing, Power and Area Model. WRL Research Report, August 2001.

[17] Data Sheet for 16Mb SDRAM. http: download.micron.com/pdf/datasheets/dram/

A Low-cost Memory Architecture with NAND XIP for Mobile Embedded Systems

Chanik Park, Jaeyu Seo, Sunghwan Bae, Hyojun Kim, Shinhan Kim and Bumsoo Kim

Software Center, SAMSUNG Electronics, Co., Ltd.
Seoul 135-893, KOREA
{ci.park, pelican, sunghwan.bae, zartoven, shinhank, bumsoo}@samsung.com

ABSTRACT

NAND flash memory has become an indispensable component in mobile embedded systems because of its versatile features such as non-volatility, solid-state reliability, low cost and high density. Even though NAND flash memory is gaining popularity as data storage, it can be also exploited as code memory for XIP (execute-in-place). In this paper, we present a new memory architecture which incorporates NAND flash memory into an existing memory hierarchy for code execution. The usefulness of the proposed approach is demonstrated with real embedded workloads on a real prototyping board.

Categories and Subject Descriptors

B.3.2 [**Memory Structures**]: Design Styles – Cache memories; D.4.2 [**Operating Systems**]: Storage Management – Secondary storage; B.6.1 [**Logic Design**]: Design Styles – Memory control and access.

General Terms

Algorithms, Measurement, Performance, Design

Keywords

Memory architecture, NAND XIP, Priority-based caching

1. INTRODUCTION

A memory architecture design is a main concern to embedded system engineers since it dominates the cost, power and performance of mobile embedded systems. The typical memory architecture of mobile embedded systems consists of ROM for initial bootstrapping and code execution, RAM for working memory, and flash memory for permanent data storage. In particular, emerging memory technology, the flash memory, is becoming an indispensable component in mobile embedded systems due to its versatile features: non-volatility, solid-state reliability, low power consumption, etc.

CODES+ISSS'03, October 1-3, 2003, Newport Beach, California, USA

The most popular flash memory types are NOR and NAND. NOR flash is particularly well suited for code storage and execute-in-place (XIP) [1] applications, which require high-speed random access. While NAND flash provides high density and low-cost data storage, it is not applicable to XIP applications due to the sequential access architecture and long access latency

Table 1 shows different characteristics of various memory devices. Mobile SDRAM has advantages in performance but requires high power consumption over other memories. There is a tradeoff between low power SRAM and fast SRAM in terms of power consumption, performance and cost. In non-volatile memories, NOR flash provides fast random access speed and low power consumption, but the cost of NOR flash is high compared to NAND flash. Even though NAND flash shows long random read latency, it has advantages in power consumption, storage capacity, and erase/write performance in contrast to NOR flash.

Table 1. Characteristics of various memory devices. The values in the table were calculated based on SAMSUNG 2003 memory data sheets [1-2].

		Current (mA)		Random Access (16bit)		
Memory	$/Gb	idle	active	read	write	erase
Mobile SDRAM	48	0.5	75	90ns	90ns	N.A
Low power SRAM	320	0.005	3	55ns	55ns	N.A
Fast SRAM	614	5	65	10ns	10ns	N.A
NOR	96	0.03	32	200ns	210.5us	1.2 sec
NAND	21	0.01	10	10.1us	200.5us	2 ms

Even though NAND flash memory is widely used for data storage in mobile embedded systems, NAND flash memory researches for code storage are hardly found in industry or academia.

In this paper, we present a new memory architecture for NAND flash memory to provide XIP functionality. With XIP functionality in NAND flash, the cost of the memory system can be reduced since the NAND flash can be used not only as data storage but also as code storage for execution. As a result, we can obtain cost-efficient memory systems with reasonable performance and power consumption.

The basic idea of our approach is to exploit the locality of code access pattern and implement a cache controller for repeatedly accessed codes. The prefetching cache is used to hide memory latency resulting from NAND memory access. In this paper we concentrate on code execution even though data memory is also an important aspect of memory architecture. There are two major

[1] XIP is the execution of an application directly from the flash memory instead of having to download the code into the systems' RAM before executing it.

contributions in this paper. First, we demonstrate that the NAND XIP is feasible in real-life systems through a real hardware and commercial OS environment. Second, we apply highly optimized caching techniques geared toward the specific features of NAND Flash.

The rest of this paper is organized as follows. In the next section, we describe the trend of memory architecture in mobile embedded systems. Section 3 reviews related work in academia and industry. In Sections 4 and 5, we present our new memory architecture based on NAND XIP. In Section 6, we demonstrate the proposed architecture with real workloads on a hardware prototyping board and evaluate cost, performance and power consumption over existing memory architectures. Finally, our conclusions and future work are drawn in Section 7.

2. Motivational Systems: Mobile Systems

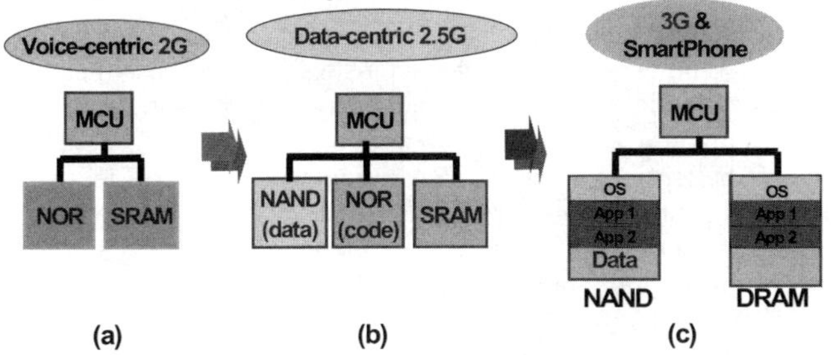

Figure 1. The memory architectures for mobile systems

Figure 1 shows the trend in memory architecture of mobile systems. The first approach is to use NOR for code storage and SRAM for working memory as shown in Figure 1(a). It is appropriate for low-end phones, which require medium performance and cost. However, as mobile systems evolve into data centric and multimedia-oriented applications, storage with high performance and huge capacity has become necessary. The second architecture (Figure 1(b)) seems to meet the requirements in terms of storage capacity through NAND flash memory, however its performance is not enough to accommodate 3G applications which consist of real-time multimedia applications. In addition, the increased number of components increases system cost. The third architecture (Figure 1(c)) eliminates NOR flash memory and uses only NAND flash memory by using a shadowing[2] technique. Copying all code into RAM offers the best performance possible, but contributes to the slow boot process. A large amount of DRAM is necessary to hold both the OS and the applications. The higher power consumption from power hungry DRAM memory is another problem for battery-operated systems. Thus, it is important to investigate an efficient memory system in terms of cost, performance and power consumption.

3. RELATED WORK

In the past, researchers have exploited NOR flash memory as caches for magnetic disks due to its low power consumption and high-speed characteristics. eNvy focused on developing a persistent storage architecture without magnetic disks [7]. Fred et al showed that NOR flash memory can reduce energy consumption by an order of magnitude, compared to magnetic disk, while providing good read performance and acceptable write performance [9]. B. Marsh et al examined the impact of using NOR flash memory as a second-level file system buffer cache to reduce power consumption and file access latency on a mobile computer [8].

Li-Pin et al investigated the performance issue of NAND flash memory storage subsystems with a striping architecture, which uses I/O parallelism [10].

In industry [5], NAND XIP is implemented using small size of buffer and I/O interface conversion, but the XIP area is limited to boot code. The OS and application codes should be copied to system memory at booting time.

In summary, even though several researches have been made to obtain the maximum performance and low power consumption from data storage, few efforts to support XIP in NAND flash are found in academia or industry.

4. NAND XIP ARCHITECTURE

In this section, we describe NAND XIP architecture. First, we look into the structure of NAND flash memory and illustrate the basic implementation of NAND XIP based on caching mechanism.

4.1 BACKGROUND

A NAND flash memory consists of a fixed number of blocks, where each block has 32 pages and each page consists of 512 bytes main data and 16 bytes spare data as shown in Figure 2. Read/write operation is performed on page basis. In order to read a page, command and address are inputted to NAND flash memory through I/O pins. After a fixed delay time, selected page is loaded into data and spare registers. Spare data can be used to store auxiliary information such as bad block identification and error correction code (ECC) for associated main data. NAND flash memories are subject to a condition called "bad block", in which a block cannot be completely erased or cannot be written due to partial or 2-bit errors. Bad blocks may exist in NAND flash memory when shipped or may occur during operation. The system design must be able to mask out the invalid blocks via address mapping. For example, as shown in Figure 3, if block 2 and 5 are initially bad, the bad block numbers and the replacement block numbers are recorded in a bad block map table. The bad block map table is managed by hardware or software.

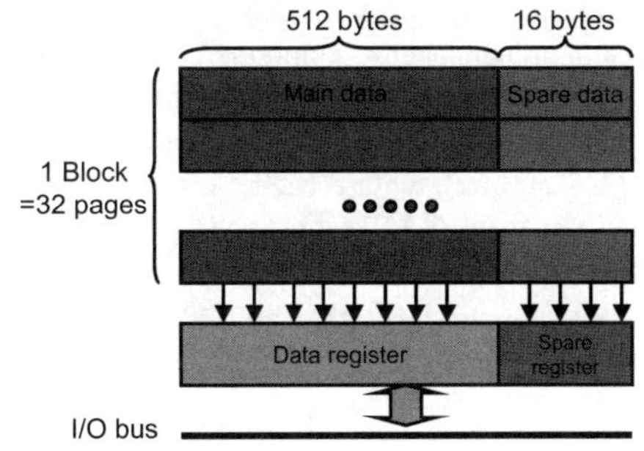

Figure 2. Structure of NAND flash memory

[2] During system booting time, entire code image is copied from permanent storage into systems' RAM for execution.

In order to implement the NAND XIP, we should consider the following points.

- Average memory access time
- Worst case handling
- Bad block management

The performance of memory system is measured by average access time [3]. In order to implement XIP functionality, the average access time of NAND flash memory should be comparable to that of other memories such as NOR, SRAM and SDRAM. Though average memory access time is a good metric for performance evaluation, worst-case handling, or cache miss handling is another problem in practical view since most mobile systems such as cellular phones include time-critical interrupt handling for call processing. For instance, if the time-critical interrupt occurs during cache miss handling, the system may not satisfy the given deadline and to make it worse, it may lose data or connection. Another consideration in NAND XIP is to manage bad blocks because bad blocks cause discontinuous memory space, which is intolerable for code execution.

4.2 BASIC IMPLEMENTATION

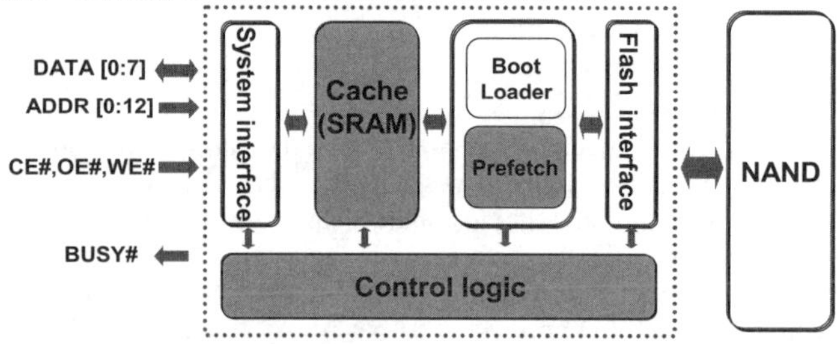

Figure 3. NAND XIP controller

The proposed architecture consists of a small amount of SRAM for cache, interface conversion logic, the control logic and NAND flash memory as shown in Figure 3. Interface conversion is necessary to connect the I/O interface of NAND flash memory to memory bus. For cache mechanism, direct map cache with victim cache is adopted based on Jouppi's work in [4] with optimization for NAND flash. In [4], the victim cache is accessed on a main cache miss; if the address hits the victim cache, the data returned to the CPU and at the same time it is promoted to the main cache; the replaced block in the main cache is moved to the victim cache, therefore performing a "swap". If the victim cache miss also occurs, NAND flash memory access is performed; the incoming data fills the main cache, and the replaced block will be moved to the victim cache. In next section, we modify the above "swap" algorithm using system memory and *page address translation table (PAT)*. The prefetching cache is used to hide memory latency resulting from NAND memory access. Several hardware prefetching techniques can be found in literature [13]. In our case, prefetching information is analyzed through profiling process and the prefetching information is stored in spare data at code image building time.

5. INTELLIGENT CACHING: PRIORITY-BASED CACHING

Though the basic implementation is suitable for application code which shows its spatial and temporal localities, it may be less effective in systems code which has a complex functionality, a large size, and interrupt-driven control transfers among its procedures [14]. Torrellas et al. presented that the operating system has the characteristics which large sections of its code are rarely accessed and suffers considerable interference within popular execution paths [14]. For example, periodic timer interrupt, rarely-executed special-case code and plenty of loop-less code disrupt the localities. On the other hand, real-time applications should be retained as long as possible to satisfy the timing constraints[3]. In this paper, we distinguish the different cache behavior between system and application codes, and adapt it to the page-based NAND architecture. We apply profile-guided static analysis of code access pattern.

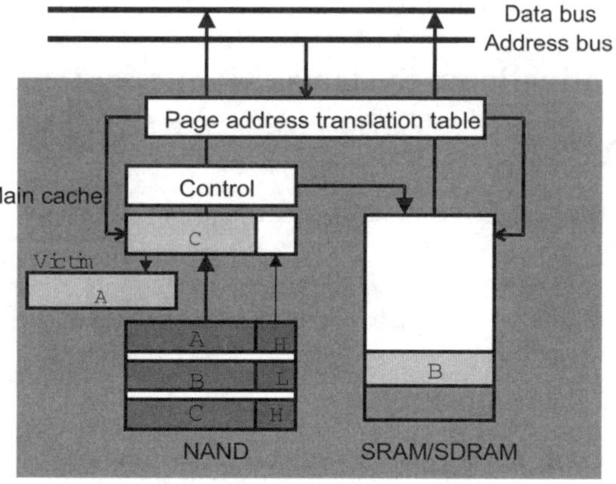

Figure 4. Priority-based cache architecture

We can divide code pages into three categories depending on their access cost: high priority, mid priority and low priority pages. Even though the priority can be determined by various objectives, we set the priority to pages based on the number of references to pages and their criticality. For example, if a specific page is referenced more frequently or has time critical codes, it is classified as a high-priority page and should be cached or retained in cache to reduce the later access cost in case that the page is in NAND flash memory. OS-related code, system libraries and real-time applications have high-priority pages. On the other hand, mid-priority page is defined to be normal application code which is handled by normal caching policy. Finally, low-priority page corresponds to sequential code such as initialization code, which is rarely executed. PAT is introduced to remap pages in bad blocks to pages in good blocks and to remap requested pages to swapped pages in system memory. We illustrate the caching mechanism in detail in Figure 4. First, when page *A* with high-priority is requested, it is cached from NAND flash to main cache. Next, when page B is requested from the CPU, it should be moved to main cache or system memory. Here assuming that page B is in conflict with page A, page B is moved to system memory (SRAM/SDRAM) since page B is low priority page ("*L*" in spare area of NAND flash memory means *low-priority*). At the same time, PAT is updated so that later access to page B is referred to system memory. Again, when page C is requested and in conflict with page A, page C replaces page A and page A is discarded from main cache since C's priority is high. The evicted page A is

[3] In this paper, real-time applications indicate multimedia applications with soft real-time constraints.

moved to victim cache. In summary, on NAND flash's page demand, the controller discards or swaps existing cache page according to the priority information stored in spare area data. The detail algorithm is explained in Figure 5. Another usage of spare area data is to store prefetching information based on profiling information gathered during code execution. This static prefetching technique improves memory latency hiding without miss penalty from miss-prediction at run-time.

```
Priority Caching (address)
{
   page = convert(address);
   if (isInPAT(page))
       main memory hit;
   else if(isInMainCache(page))
       Cache hit;
   else if(isInVictimCache(page))
       Victim hit;
   else { // miss, fetch a page from NAND flash memory

       page_priority = NAND[page].priority;
       if (cache[page%CACHE_SIZE].priority ==HIGH)
          NAND[page] → main memory;
       else if (cache[page%CACHE_SIZE].priority == MID)
       {
          cache[page%CACHE_SIZE] → victim;
          NAND[page] → cache[page%CACHE_SIZE];
       }
       else
          NAND[page] → cache[page%CACHE_SIZE];
   }
}
```

Figure 5. Priority-based cache algorithm

6. EXPERIMENTAL SETUP

This section presents our experimental environment. Our environment consists of a prototyping board, our in-house cache simulator with pattern analysis and a real workload, or PocketPC[6]. The prototyping board has ARM9-based micro-controller, SRAM, SDRAM, NOR flash and NAND memories as shown in Figure 6. It is used not only to implement a real cache configuration on FPGA but also to gather memory address trace from running applications for cache simulator. The specification of main processor and NAND flash memory is shown in Table 2. The cache simulator explores various parameters such as miss rate, replacement policy, associativity and cache size based on memory traces from the prototyping board. The real embedded workload, PocketPC supports XIP-enabled image based on the existing ROMFS file systems in which each application can be directly executed without being loaded into RAM.

Table 2. The specification of the prototyping board

Parameter	Configuration
CPU clock	200 MHz
L1 Icache	64 way, 32byte line, 8KB
Bus width	16 bit = 1 word
NAND read initial latency	10 us/512byte
NAND serial read time	50 ns/word
SRAM read time	10 ns/word
SDRAM read time	120 ns/4word
NOR read time	210 ns/4word

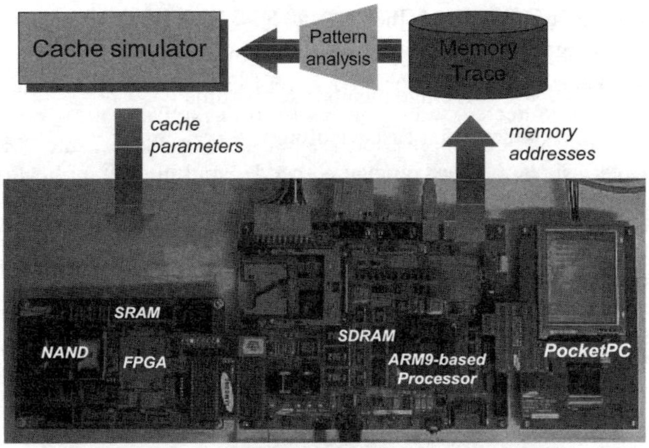

Figure 6. Prototyping board for NAND XIP

6.1 PERFORMANCE MODELING

In general, the memory system performance is evaluated by the average access time:

*Average memory access time = hit time + miss rate * miss penalty .* (1)

Hit time is the time to fill the L1 cache (32byte line) and the miss penalty is the time to fill the L2 cache from NAND flash memory.

The total energy consumed by the system is the sum of energies consumed by system components such as processor, bus, memory and the DC-DC converter. In this paper, we concentrate on the energy consumption of the processor and memory system:

$$E_{system} = E_{CPU} + E_{memory} \quad (2)$$

The energy consumption of CPU is divided into two parts:

$$E_{CPU} = P_{CPU\_active} \times T_{CPU\_active} + P_{CPU\_idle} \times T_{CPU\_idle} \quad (3)$$

T_{CPU_active} is assumed to be constant regardless of memory system since the number and execution time of instructions are fixed. Thus, we are concerned about T_{CPU_idle} which is proportional to off-chip memory access time.

In memory case, the number of accesses to the memory is directly proportional to energy consumption. The unit access energy consumption can be estimated from the active power specified in the data sheet [1-2]:

$$E_{memory} = E_{access} \times N_{access} \quad (4)$$

The cost of memory system is computed from parameters shown on Table 1:

$$Cost_{memory\_system} = \sum_{m}^{N} density_m \times unit\ cost_m + Cost_{controller} \quad (5)$$

The $Cost_{controller}$ is computed based on the synthesis result in Xilinx FPGA: totally 270,000 gates including 4KB and using off-chip SRAM for TAG and cache memory.

Finally, booting times are measured using real-time measurement tools.

6.2 EXPERIMENTAL RESULTS

In Figure 7, we compare the miss ratio over various configuration parameters such as associativity, replacement policy and cache size. We collected address traces from PocketPC while we were executing various applications such as "Media Player" and "MP3 player" since they are popular embedded multimedia applications which involve real-time requirements.

Note that the cache size is the most important factor to affect miss ratio as shown in Figure 7.

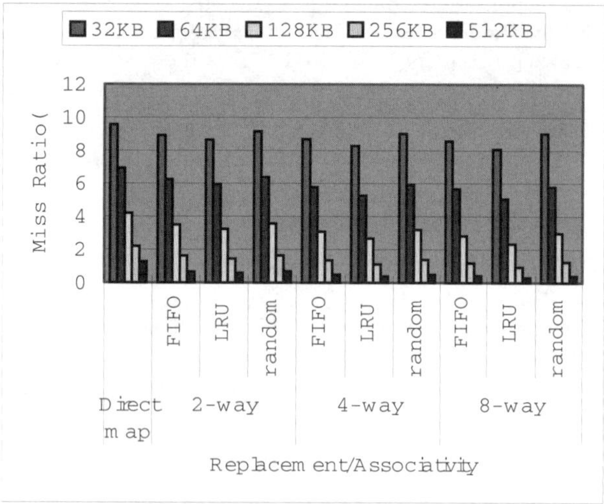

Figure 7. Associativity with different replacement policies and cache sizes versus miss ratio

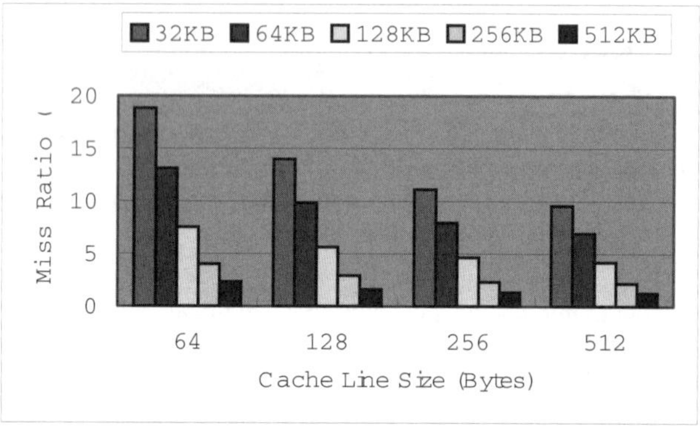

(a)

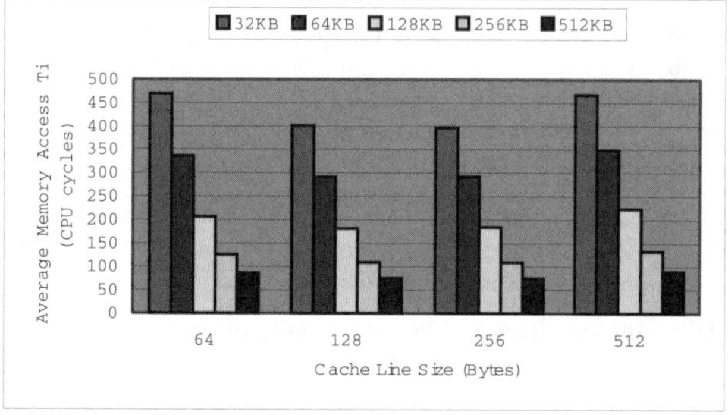

(b)

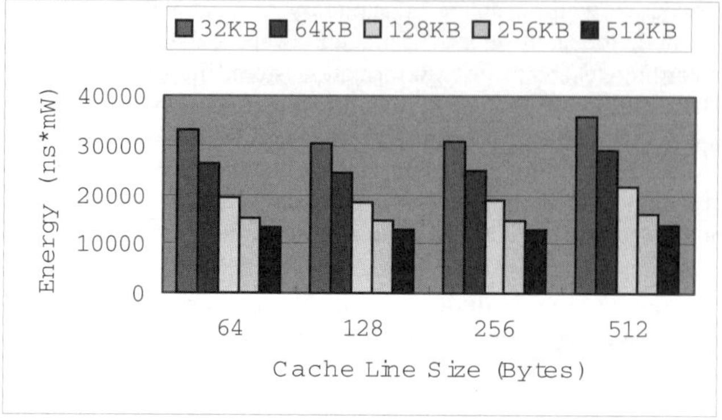

(c)

Figure 8. Cache line size versus (a) miss ratio, (b) access time per 32-byte and (c) energy consumption

To analyze the optimal cache line size in NAND XIP cache, simulation has been done with the memory trace which is gathered from the prototyping board. The line size of 256-byte shows better numbers in average memory access time and energy consumption over all other cache sizes as shown in Figure 8. Therefore, the line size of NAND XIP controller is determined to be 256-byte hereafter.

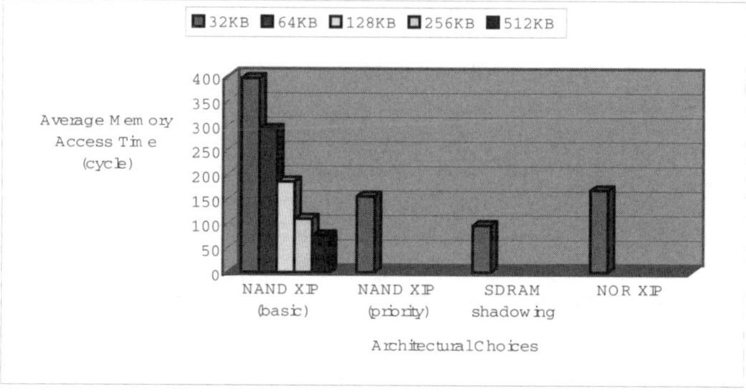

(a)

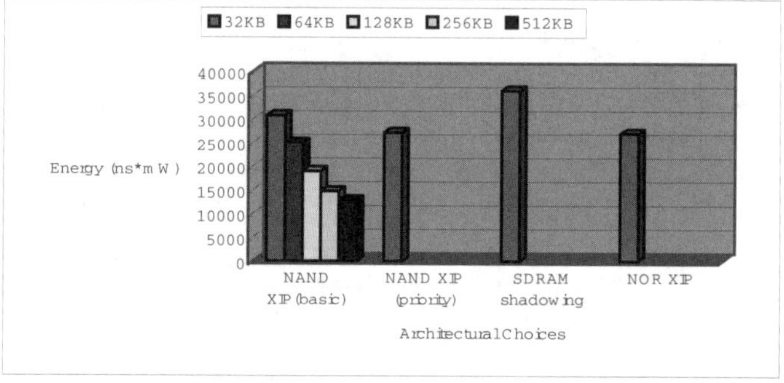

(b)

Figure 9. Overall performance comparison of different memory architectures: (a) average memory access time and (b) energy consumption.

Architectural Choices	Components	Booting Time (sec)	Cost ($)
NOR XIP	NOR(64MB)+SDRAM(32MB)	13	60
SDRAM Shadowing	NAND(64MB)+SDRAM(64MB)	15	35
NAND XIP (basic)	NAND XIP(64MB)+SRAM(256KB) Controller+SDRAM(32MB)	14	26
NAND XIP (priority)	NAND XIP(64MB)+SRAM(64KB) Controller+SDRAM(32MB)	14	24

Figure 10. Overall booting time and cost comparison of different memory architectures.

Figure 9 and 10 show overall performance comparison among different memory architectures based on our prototyping results. NOR XIP architecture (NOR+SDRAM) shows fast boot time and low power consumption at high cost. Even though SDRAM shadowing architecture (NAND + SDRAM) achieves high performance, it suffers from a relatively long booting time and inefficient memory utilization. Finally, our approach NAND XIP shows reasonable booting time, performance and power consumption with outstanding cost efficiency. Two implementations of NAND XIP (basic and priority) are also compared. The NAND XIP (basic) is composed of 256KB cache and 4KB victim cache. On the other hand, the NAND XIP (priority) has 64KB cache, 4KB victim and 2KB PAT. The NAND XIP (priority) has advantage of cache size reduction with the assistance of system memory and priority based caching.

6.3 Worst Case Handling

Even though NAND XIP offers an efficient memory system, it may suffer from worst-case handling, namely cache miss handling. A straightforward solution is to hold the CPU until the requested memory page arrives. This can be implemented using wait/ready signals' handshaking method. However, the miss penalty, 35us[4] is not trivial time especially in case that a fast processor is used. Besides CPU utilization problem, if the time-critical interrupt request occurs to the system, the interrupt may be lost because the processor is waiting for memory's response. In order to solve this problem, a system-wide approach is needed. First, OS should handle the cache miss as a page fault as in virtual memory management. The CPU also should supply "abort" function to restart the requested instruction after cache miss handling. In analytical approach view, task timing analysis and schedulability test will be helpful in the domain of real-time[12].

7. CONCLUSIONS

We presented the new low cost memory architecture with NAND XIP functionality which enables NAND flash memory to be used as code storage as well as data storage. In order to hide a long read access latency, we applied the priority-based caching mechanism geared for NAND specific features. As a result, we can accomplish cost and power efficient memory systems with reasonable performance and booting time. As future work, compiler's assistance will be helpful to improve NAND XIP in embedded memory architectures. Code packing and positioning will be achieved in near future.

[4] It is calculated as sum of NAND initial delay (10us) + page read (512 x 50ns).

REFERENCES

[1] Samsung Electronics Co., "NAND Flash Memory & SmartMedia Data Book", 2002.

[2] http://www.samsung.com/Products/Semiconductor/index.htm

[3] J.L. Hennessy and D.A. Patterson, "Computer Architecture: A Quantitative Approach", 2nd edition, Morgan Kaufman Publishers, 1996.

[4] N. Jouppi, "Improving Direct-Mapped Cache Performance by the Addition of a Small Fully-Associative Cache and Prefetch Buffers," ISCA-17:ACM/IEEE International Symposium on Computer Architecture, pp. 364-373, May 1990.

[5] http://www.m-sys.com/files/documentation/doc/Mobile_DOC_G3_DS_Rev1.0.pdf

[6] Microsoft Co., "Pocket PC 2002", http://www.microsoft.com/mobile/pocketpc

[7] M. Wu, Willy Zwaenepoel, "eNVy: A Non-Volatile, Main Memory Storage System", Proc. Sixth Int'l Conf. On Architectural Support for Programming Languages and Operating Sys. (ASPLOS VI), San Jose, CA, Oct. 1994, pp. 86-97.

[8] B. Marsh, F. Douglis, and P. Krishnan, "Flash memory file caching for mobile computers," Proc. 27th Hawaii Conf. On Sys. Sciences, Wailea, HI, Jan. 1993, pp. 451-460.

[9] F. Douglis et al., "Storage Alternatives for Mobile Computers", Proc. First USENIX Symp. On Operating Sys. Design and Implementation, Monterey, CA, pp 25-37, Nov. 1994.

[10] Li-Pin Chang, Tei-Wei Kuo, "An Adaptive Striping Architecture for Flash Memory Storage Systems of Embedded Systems," The 8th IEEE Real-Time and Embedded Technology and Applications Symposium (RTAS 2002) September, 2002. San Jose, California.

[11] J. R. Lorch and A. J. Smith, "Software Strategies for Portable Computer Energy Management", IEEE Personal Communications, June, 1998.

[12] C.-G. Lee, K.-P. Lee, J. Hahn, Y.-M. Seo, S.L. Min, R. Ha, S. Hong, C.Y. Park, M. Lee, and C.S. Kim, Bounding Cache-related Preemption Delay for Real-time Systems, IEEE Transaction on Software Engineering, vol 27, no 9, pp805-826, 2001.

[13] C. Young, E. Shekita, "An Intelligent I-Cache Prefetch Mechanism," in Proceedings of the International Conferences on Computer Design, pp. 44-49, Oct 1993.

[14] Josep Torrellas, Chun Xia, and Russell Daigle, "Optimizing Instruction Cache Performance for Operating System Intensive Workload", Proc. HPCA-1: 1st Intl. Symposium on High-Performance Computer Architecture, p.360, January 1995.

[15] Zhang Yi, Steve Haga and Rajeev Barua, "Execution History Guided Instruction Prefetching", Proceedings of the Sixteenth ACM Int'l Conference on Supercomputing (ICS), New York City, NY, June, 2002.

Design Space Minimization with Timing and Code Size Optimization for Embedded DSP

Qingfeng Zhuge, Zili Shao, Bin Xiao, Edwin H.-M. Sha
Department of Computer Science
University of Texas at Dallas
Richardson, Texas 75083
qfzhuge,zxs015000,bxiao,edsha@utdallas.edu

ABSTRACT

One of the most challenging problems in high-level synthesis is how to quickly explore a wide range of design options to achieve high-quality designs. This paper presents an Integrated Framework for Design Optimization and Space Minimization (IDOM) towards finding the minimum configuration satisfying timing and code size constraints. We show an effective way to reduce the design space to be explored through the study of the fundamental properties and relations among multiple design parameters, such as retiming value, unfolding factor, timing, and code size. Theoreies are presented to produce a small set of feasible design choices with provable quality. IDOM algorithm is proposed to generate high-quality design by integrating performance and code size optimization techniques. The experimental results on a set of DSP benchmarks show the efficiency and effectiveness of the IDOM algorithm. It constantly generates the minimal configuration for all the benchmarks. The cost of design space exploration using IDOM is only 3% of that using the standard method.

Categories and Subject Descriptors

C.3 [**Computer Systems Organization**]: Special-Purpose and Application-Based Systems—*signal processing systems*
; D.3.4 [**Programming Languages**]: Processors—*optimization*

General Terms

Algorithms, Design

Keywords

Retiming, unfolding, code size reduction, DSP processors

1. INTRODUCTION

Embedded systems usually have strict timing requirement and limited memory resources. Architectural-level synthesis with code generation is a critical stage toward generating embedded systems with stringent requirements. One of the most challenging problems in high-level synthesis is how to explore a wide range of design options to achieve high-quality designs within a short time [1, 4, 7]. In this context, the design space exploration problem is to find the minimum number of functional units (or processors) for executing an application with timing and code size requirements.

To achieve high performance, optimization techniques such as unfolding and software pipelining are commonly used to improve the execution time of loops. [2, 5, 8]. The proper unfolding factor and software pipelining degree need to be chosen in architectural-level synthesis to satisfy the performance constraint. On the other hand, these optimization techniques introduce large code size expansions [10], which is not desirable due to very limited memory resources. Therefore, a good design exploration method should be able to exploit both performance and code size optimization techniques, to produce a high-quality design solution. Without this capability, a design exploration method either easily fails for finding feasible solutions, even with exhaustive search, or cannot locate the superior solutions.

In order to find feasible design points in a large design space concerning multiple design parameters within a short time, design space minimization problem becomes a very important problem in high-level synthesis. A number of research results are published on optimization problems [8, 10] and design space exploration [1, 4, 7, 9]. However, we are unaware of any previous work that addresses the combination of various optimization techniques and their effects on the design space minimization. We strongly believe that an effective way to reduce the design space is through the study of the fundamental properties and relations among multiple design parameters, such as retiming value, unfolding factor, time, and code size.

When retiming and unfolding are applied to optimize the performance, a critical question is: What are the feasible unfolding factors that can achieve the timing requirement by combining with retiming. Then, based on this understanding, we can produce *the minimum set of unfolding factors* for achieving timing requirement. Many unfolding factors can be proved to be infeasible, and eliminated immediately *without performing real scheduling*. Thus, the design space and search cost are significantly reduced. Intuitively speaking, the obtained interrelation *reduces the points to be selected from a higher-dimensional volume to a small set of lower-dimensional planes.*

Since retiming and unfolding greatly expand the code size [8,10], it's possible that the generated code is too large to be fit into the on-chip memory. Thus, the relationship between schedule length and code size must be studied. As we found in our research, the relationship between code size and performance can be formulated by mathematical formula using retiming functions. It provides an efficient technique for reducing the code size of any software-pipelined loops.

In this paper, we propose an Integrated Framework for Design Optimization and Space Minimization (IDOM). It distinguishes itself from the traditional design exploration in the following ways: First, it greatly reduces the design space and the exploration cost by exploiting the fundamental properties of retimed unfolded data flow graph and the relationship between design parameters. Second, it

CODES+ISSS'03, October 1–3, 2003, Newport Beach, California, USA.

combines several optimization techniques, namely, unfolding [8], extended retiming [6] and code size reduction [10], to produce a superior solution satisfying schedule length and code size requirements.

Theories are presented to reveal the underlying relationship between unfolding, retiming, performance, and code size. IDOM algorithm is proposed and compared with the traditional approaches. Our experimental results on a set of DSP benchmarks show that the search space and search cost are greatly reduced. For example, the search space of 4-stage Lattice Filter is reduced from 909 design points to 55 points, and the search cost using IDOM is only 4% of that using the standard method. The average search cost using IDOM is only 3% of that using the standard method for our benchmarks. Our experiments also show that IDOM algorithm constantly generates the minimal configurations.

In the next section, we present the basic concepts and theorems of the integrated framework for design optimization and space minimization. Section 3 provides the algorithms and computation cost for several design space exploration algorithms. An example for design optimization and space exploration is demonstrated in Section 4 to compare the size of search space, the computation cost and the quality of design solutions among four different design space exploration algorithms. In Section 5, we present the experimental results on a set of DSP benchmarks. Finally, concluding remarks are provided in Section 6.

2. OPTIMIZATION TECHNIQUES AND DESIGN SPACE MINIMIZATION

In this section, we present the the theoretical foundation of the integrated framework for design optimization and space minimization. We provide an overview of the basic principles of retiming and unfolding in Section 2.1. An in-depth analysis for these optimization techniques based on data flow graph model reveals underlying relations between the design parameters. Section 2.2 presents the theorems of design space minimization. It shows that the search space and search cost of design space exploration can be greatly reduced based on the properties and relations between the design parameters considering unfolding factor, retiming function and iteration period. Section 2.3 presents an code size optimization technique that reduces the code size for retimed data flow graph.

2.1 Performance Optimizations

Many DSP applications can be modeled as **data flow graphs (DFG)**. Then, optimization problems, such as retiming and unfolding, can be regarded as graph transformation problems. A data flow graph $G = (V, E, d, t)$ is a node-weighted and edge-weighted directed graph, where V is a set of computation nodes, $E \subseteq V \times V$ is a set of edges, d is a function from E to $\mathbb{N}$ representing the number of delays on each edge, and $t(v)$ represents the computation time of each node.

Programs with loops can be represented by cyclic DFGs. An *iteration* is the execution of each node in V exactly once. Inter-iteration dependencies are represented by weighted edges. For any iteration j, an edge e from u to v with delay $d(e)$ conveys that the computation of node v at iteration j depends on the execution of node u at iteration $j - d(e)$. An edge with no delay represents a data dependency within the same iteration. An iteration is associated with a static schedule. A static schedule must obey the precedence relations defined by the DFG. The ***cycle period*** $c(G)$ of a data-flow graph G is the computation time of the longest zero-delay path, which corresponds to the schedule length without resource constraint. For example, $c(G)$ of the graph in Figure 1(a) is 2.

Given a DFG G which may contain cycles, retiming and unfolding can be used to minimize the execution time of all tasks in one iteration.

Retiming [5] is one of the most effective graph transformation techniques for optimization. It transforms a DFG to minimize its

(a) (b)

Figure 1: (a) A simple DFG. (b) The retimed DFG with $r(A) = 1$ and $r(B) = 0$.

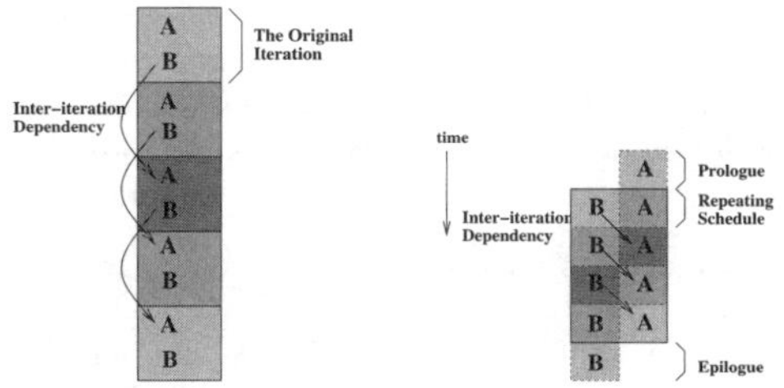

(a) (b)

Figure 2: (a) A static schedule of original loop. (b) The pipelined loops.

cycle period in polynomial time by redistributing delays in the DFG. The commonly used optimization technique for DSP applications, called *software pipelining*, can be correctly modeled as a retiming.

A *retiming* r is a function from V to $\mathbb{Z}^+$ that redistributes the delays in the original DFG G, resulting a new DFG $G_r = \langle V, E, d_r, t\rangle$ such that each iteration still has one execution of each node in G. The delay function changes accordingly to preserve dependencies, i.e., $r(v)$ represents delay units pushed into the edges $v \rightarrow w$, and subtracted from the edges $u \rightarrow v$, where $u, v, w \in G$. Therefore, we have $d_r(e) = d(e) + r(u) - r(v)$ for every edge $u \rightarrow v$ and $d_r(\ell) = d(\ell)$ for every cycle $\ell \in G$. Figure 1(b) shows the retimed DFG of Figure 1(a) with retiming functions $r(A) = 1, r(B) = 0$.

When a delay is pushed through node A to its outgoing edge as shown in Figure 1(b), the actual effect on the schedule of the new DFG is that the ith copy of A is shifted up and is executed with $(i-1)^{th}$ copy of node B. Because there is no dependency between node A and B in the new loop body, these two nodes can be executed in parallel. The schedule length of the new loop body is then reduced from two control steps to one control steps. This transformation is illustrated in Figure 2(a) and Figure 2(b).

In fact, every retiming operation corresponds to a software pipelining operation. When one delay is pushed forward through a node u, every copy of this node is moved up by one iteration, and the first copy of the node is shifted out of the first iteration into the prologue. With retiming function r, we can measure the size of prologue and epilogue. When $r(v)$ delays are pushed forward through node v, there are $r(v)$ copies of node v appeared in the prologue. The number of copies of a node in the epilogue can also be derived in a similar way. If the maximum retiming value in the data flow graph is $max_u r(u)$, there are $max_u r(u) - r(v)$ copies of node v in the epilogue. For example, the retiming value of node A is 1 in Figure 1(a). Then, there is one copy of node A in the pipelined schedule as shown in Figure 2(b).

The extended retiming allows the delays to cut the execution time of a multiple-cycle node to achieve optimal schedule length [6]. Due to the space limitation, we will not illustrate the extended retiming in details.

Unfolding [3,8] is another effective technique for improving the average cycle period of a static schedule. The original DFG G is unfolded f times, so the unfolded graph G_f consists of f copies of the original node set. Thus, a schedule with unfolding factor f contains f iterations of the original DFG.

For any DFG G, the average computation time of an iteration is called the ***iteration period*** of the graph. The instruction-level parallelism between the iterations in an unfolded loop helps to improve the iteration period $P = c(G_f)/f$. For a DFG containing a loop, the iteration period is bounded from below by the iteration bound of the graph which is defined as follows:

DEFINITION 2.1. *The* ***iteration bound*** *of a data-flow graph G, denoted by $B(G)$, is the maximum time to delay ratio of all cycles in G. This can be represented by the equation $B(G) = \max_{\forall \ell} T(\ell)/D(\ell)$, where $T(\ell)$ and $D(\ell)$ are the summation of all computation times and the summation of delays, respectively, in a cycle ℓ.*

It is clear that unfolding will increase code size by a factor of f. We want to find the minimum f with retiming r so the iteration period of the resultant loop schedule is optimal. But it is very likely that such an optimal f is too large for the program to fit into a small-size on-chip memory. Therefore, we need to explore what will be the good f, r for satisfying both iteration period and memory constraints.

Without retiming, the rate optimal unfolding factor is upper bounded by the least common multiple of the delay counts of all cycles in DFG. That is, if we unfolded the DFG G by $f = lcm(D(\ell))$, $\forall \ell \in G$, we can always get a DFG with the optimal execution rate $P(G_f) = T(\ell_{cr})/D(\ell_{cr})$. Consider the data flow graph G in Figure 3(a) with iteration bound $B(G) = 6/4 = 3/2$ and cycle period $c(G) = 7$. After unfolding by 4, the unfolded graph G_f in Figure 3(b) achieves the iteration period $P(G_f) = 6/4 = 3/2$ which is optimal.

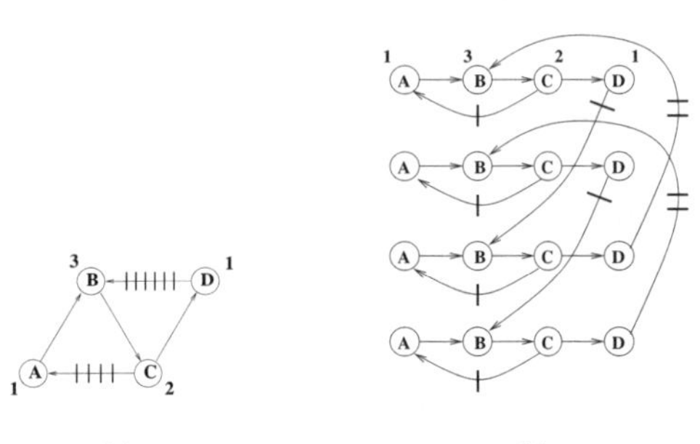

Figure 3: (a) A data flow graph. (b) The unfolded graph.

Since the unfolded graph is f times larger than the original DFG, we would like to find the minimum unfolding factor for achieving the optimal execution rate. By combining retiming and unfolding, the minimum unfolding factor can be reduced. For the example in Figure 3(a), the minimum unfolding factor is 2. In Figure 4(a), we show the retimed graph G_r. Note that traditional retiming can not achieve the optimal rate in this case, because the cycle period of G_r is bounded by the computation time of node B, which is 3. After unfolding G_r by 2, the unfolded retimed DFG G_{fr} shown in Figure 4(b) achieves the optimal iteration period $P(G_{fr}) = 3/2$. Therefore, retiming (software pipelining) and unfolding are usually combined in design optimization.

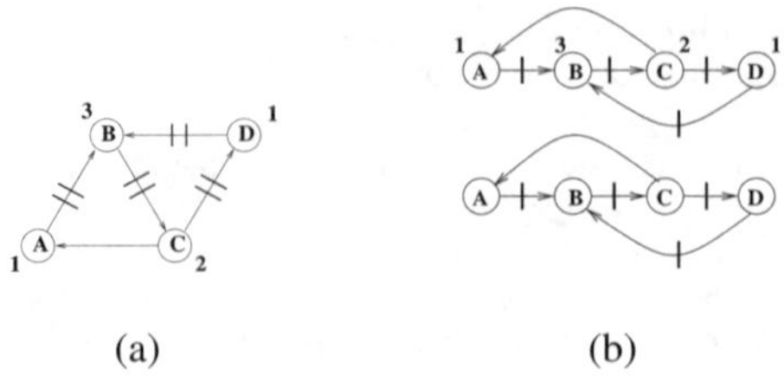

Figure 4: (a) The retimed graph. (b) The unfolded retimed graph.

2.2 Design Space Minimization

Design space is a n-dimensional space where each point represents a design solution and each dimension represents a design parameter. The design parameters we considered here are unfolding factor, retiming function, iteration period and code size. Let r be the retiming value, f the unfolding factor, S the number of points in design space. The design space considering various retiming value and unfolding factor is $r \times f \times S$. In this section, we present theorems for finding the minimum set of unfolding factors based on the fundamental relationships between the design parameters in a unfolded retimed graph, so that the search space and search cost can be greatly reduced.

Theorem 2.1 states the relationship between unfolding factor and corresponding minimum feasible cycle period. It shows the necessary and sufficient condition of finding a legal static schedule [2].

THEOREM 2.1. *Let $G = \langle V, E, d, t\rangle$ be a given data flow graph, $f \in Z^+$ an unfolding factor and $c \in R$ a cycle period, there exists a legal static schedule without resource constraints iff $c/f \geq B(G)$ and $c \geq max_v t(v)$, $\forall v \in V$. Thus, given unfolding factor f, the minimum cycle period $c_{min}(G_f) = max(max_v t(v), \lceil f \cdot B(G)\rceil)$.*

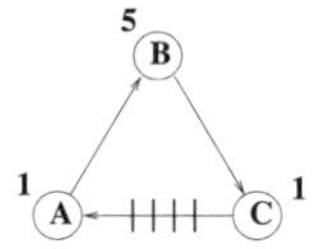

Figure 5: An exemplary DFG G with $B(G) = 7/4$.

Consider a simple DFG shown in Figure 5, the computation time of the circuit is $1 + 5 + 1 = 7$ time units. The delay count is 4. Thus, the iteration bound $B(G) = 7/4$. If the unfolding factor $f = 2$, we can directly find the minimum feasible cycle period as $c_{min}(G_f) = max(5, 4) = 5$. Thus, it proves that it is impossible to find a schedule with cycle period < 5 with $f = 2$.

On the other hand, given an iteration period constraint, we can quickly know the feasible unfolding factors that are possible to produce a schedule that satisfies the constraint as stated in the following theorem.

THEOREM 2.2. *Let $G = \langle V, E, d, t\rangle$ be a data flow graph, f an unfolding factor, P a given iteration period constraint. The following statements are equivalent:*

1. *There exists a legal static schedule of unfolded graph G_f with iteration period less than equal to P.*
2. $B(G) \cdot f \leq c_{min}(G, f) \leq P \cdot f$.

As to the previous example, assume that we want to achieve an average iteration period $P = 7/3$, and we would like to know what unfolding factor is possible for achieving this requirement. For instance, how about unfolding factor $f = 2$? Since the cycle period of the unfolded graph is $c_{min}(G_f) = 5$ from Theorem 2.1. We find that $c_{min}(G_f) > P \cdot f = 14/3$. Therefore, the iteration period constraint cannot be achieved with unfolding factor $f = 2$. By using Theorem 2.1 and Theorem 2.2, we can immediately eliminate many infeasible ones *without performing real scheduling*, and thus significantly reduce the search space and search cost.

Since unfolding multiples the code size, we would like to find the minimum possible unfolding factor that can achieve the iteration period constraint via retiming. We can use these two theorems to easily check (without real scheduling) if an unfolding factor is possible to satisfy timing requirement or not.

2.3 Code Size Optimization

Since retiming and unfolding greatly expand the code size, it's possible that the generated code is too large to be fit into the on-chip memory of embedded DSP processors. A simple *for* loop and its code after applying software pipelining are shown in Figure 6(a) and Figure 6(b). The loop schedule length is reduced from four control steps to one control step for software-pipelined loop. However, the code size of software-pipelined loop is three times larger than the original code size.

```
for i = 1 to n do
  A[i] = D[i-3] + 9;
  B[i] = A[i-1] * 5;
  C[i] = A[i] + B[i];
  D[i] = C[i] * 0.2;
end
```

(a)

```
A[1] = D[-2] + 9;
B[1] = A[0] * 5;
A[2] = D[-1] + 9;
B[2] = A[1] * 5;
C[1] = A[1] + B[1];
for i = 1 to n-2 do
  A[i+2] = D[i-1] + 9;
  B[i+2] = A[i+1] * 5;
  C[i+1] = A[i+1] + B[i+1];
  D[i] = C[i] * 0.2;
end
C[n] = A[n] + B[n];
D[n-1] = C[n-1] * 0.2;
D[n] = C[n] * 0.2;
```

(b)

Figure 6: (a) The original loop. (b) The loop after applying software pipelining.

In our research work, we study the underlying relationship between retiming and software pipelining, and found that the size of code expansion is closely related to the retiming function. As we found in Theorem 2.3, the relationship between code size and software pipeline degree can be formulated by mathematical formula using retiming functions.

THEOREM 2.3. *Let $G_r = \langle V, E, d_r, t \rangle$ be a retimed DFG with a given retiming function r. Let n be the number of iterations of the original loop. The prologue and epilogue can be correctly executed by conditionally executing the loop body.*

- *For prologue, executing node u whose $r(u) = k$ for k times starting from the $(max_u r(u) - k + 1)$-th iteration, $\forall u \in V$ and $k \geq 0$.*
- *For epilogue, executing node $u \in V$ with retiming value $r(u) = k$ for $(max_u r(u) - k)$ times in the last $max_u r(u)$ iterations starting from the $(n+1)^{th}$ iteration, $\forall u \in V$ and $k \geq 0$.*

Based on Theorem 2.3, the code size expansion introduced by prologue and epilogue of software-pipelined loops can be removed if the execution order of the retimed nodes can be controlled based on their retiming values. The code size reduction technique uses the retiming function to control the execution order of the computation nodes in a software-pipelined loop. The relative values are stored in a counter to set the "life-time" of the nodes with the same retiming value. For node v with retiming value $r(v)$, its counter is set as the maximum retiming value minus the retiming value of node v, i.e. $p = max_u r(u) - r(v)$. We also specify that the instruction is executed only when $0 \geq p > -n$. In other words, the instruction is disabled when $p > 0$ or $p \leq -n$, where n represents the original loop counter.

Based on this understanding, code size reduction technique can remove the code in prologue and epilogue by conditionally executing the loop body using either conditional branches or predicate registers. For a processor with predicate register, an instruction *guarded* by a predicate register is conditionally executed depending on the value of the predicate register. If it is "true", the instruction is executed. Otherwise, the instruction is disabled. Each register is initialized to a different value depending on its retiming value, and is decreased by one for each iteration. After applying code size reduction, each iteration executes only the static schedule of the loop body after applying CRED. Code size reduction can be generally applied to any processors with or without predicate registers, and achieves smaller code size. For the details, please refer to the work published in [10].

3. ALGORITHMS

In this section, we describe four different design optimization and space exploration algorithms assuming there are two types of functional units (or processors). Each algorithm employs different techniques to approach the design space exploration problem. We will also compare their computation costs.

Four algorithms are: STDu, STDur, IDOMe and IDOMeCR. Algorithm 3.1 (STDu) is a standard method which uses unfolding to optimize the schedule length and search the design space. Given a data flow graph G, the iteration period constraint P, and the memory constraint M. Algorithm STDu generates the unfolded graph G_f for each unfolding factor $1 \leq f \leq f_{max}$, where f_{max} is derived from the memory constraint. For each unfolded graph, the algorithm computes the upper bound for each type of functional units using As Soon As Possible scheduling. Then, the algorithm schedule the DFG with each possible configuration using list scheduling. Algorithm STDu exhaustively searches the space for f_{max} unfolded graphs. Note that using unfolding only may not be able to find a solution satisfying iteration period constraint even with unlimited functional units, because the unfolding factor is upper bounded by memory constraint.

Algorithm STDur is another standard method that applies retiming to optimize schedule length of the unfolded graphs. By using retiming, the cycle period of an unfolded graph is optimized before scheduling. Therefore, algorithm STDur is able to find more feasible solution than algorithm STDu. However, retiming extends the search space and increase the computation cost.

Algorithm 3.2 (IDOMeCR) shows the algorithm of IDOM. The algorithm computes the minimum feasible cycle period c_{min} using Theorem 2.1. Then, it eliminates the infeasible unfolding factors from a set of unfolding factors $1 \leq f \leq f_{max}$ using Theorem 2.2, which selects a minimum set of candidate unfolding factors $F = \{f : c_{min}/f \leq P\}$. It means that we do not need to generate and schedule all the unfolded graphs. Therefore, the computation cost of design space exploration is significantly reduced. In step 5, it performs extended retiming instead of the traditional one to find optimal cycle period for an unfolded graph. In addition to the computation of the upper bound of the functional units, the lower bound of each type of functional units is also computed using latency bound $\lfloor P \cdot f \rfloor$ in step 6. It further reduces the search space. Finally, the algorithm schedules the retimed unfolded graphs and performs code size reduction. A less powerful IDOM algorithm, called IDOMe, will not apply code size reduction as in IDOMeCR.

The computation cost of the design space exploration algorithms can be compared using the complexity of list scheduling as a unit of the computation cost. The complexity of list scheduling is $O(|V|+$

Algorithm 3.1 An Standard Approach (STDu)

Input: DFG $G = \langle V, E, d, t\rangle$, iteration period constraint P and code size constraint M.
Output: The minimum configuration $(fu1, fu2)$.
Step 1. Compute the upper bound on unfolding factor $f_{max} = \lfloor M/|V| \rfloor$.
Step 2. For each $f \in \{F : 1 \le f \le f_{max}\}$ in increasing order, compute the unfolded graph G_{f_i}.
Step 3. Compute the upper bound of functional units $(fu1_{max}, fu2_{max})$.
Step 4. Schedule G_{f_i} for each configuration in $S_i = \{(fu1, fu2) : 1 \le fu1 \le fu1_{max}, 1 \le fu2 \le fu2_{max}\}$ in increasing order, until a schedule satisfying P and M is found.

$|E|$). The complexity of unfolding is $O(f|V| + f|E|)$. Let F be a set of feasible unfolding factors, and S_T be the set of points in the design space to be searched by an algorithm. Here we compute the search cost of an algorithm in terms of the number of times list scheduling is applied to the original graph. The computation cost of STDu algorithm can be estimated as the summation of unfolding cost (C_{uf}) and scheduling cost (C_{sche}) for the unfolded graphs, i.e., $C_{uf} + C_{sche} = \sum_{f_i \in F} f_i + \sum_{f_i \in F} f_i |S_T|$.

The search cost of the other algorithms can be computed in the similar way. The computation cost of retiming an unfolded graph is $C_{tr} = \sum_{f_i \in F} {f_i}^2 |V| + \sum_{f_i \in F} {f_i}^2 |V| \log(f_i|V|)$. The search cost of STDur algorithm can be computed as $C_{uf} + C_{tr} + C_{sche}$.

The search cost of IDOM is the summation of the cost of unfolding, scheduling, and extended retiming (C_{er}), i.e., $C_{uf} + C_{er} + C_{sche}$. Since the size of unfolding factor set $|F|$ and the search space $|S_T|$ are significantly reduced in IDOM approach, the computation costs of unfolding and scheduling are also greatly reduced. The computation cost of extended retiming on an unfolded graph can be computed as $C_{er} = {f_i}^2|V|$, which is smaller than traditional retiming cost. The search cost of each algorithm will be computed and compared using a design space exploration example in the next section.

Algorithm 3.2 IDOMeCR Algorithm

Input: DFG $G = \langle V, E, d, t\rangle$, iteration period constraint P and code size constraint M.
Output: The minimum configuration $(fu1, fu2)$.
Step 1. Compute the upper bound on unfolding factor $f_{max} = \lfloor M/|V| \rfloor$.
Step 2. For each $1 \le f \le f_{max}$, compute the minimum feasible cycle period c_{min}. (Theorem 2.1)
Step 3. Select the feasible unfolding factor: $F = \{f : c_{min}/f \le P\}$. (Theorem 2.2)
Step 4. Generate unfolded graph for each $f \in F$.
Step 5. Apply extended retiming on G.
Step 6. Compute the lower bound of functional units $(fu1_{min}, fu2_{min})$ with latency bound $\lfloor P \cdot f \rfloor$.
Step 7. Compute the upper bound of functional units $(fu1_{max}, fu2_{max})$.
Step 8. Schedule G_{f_i, r_i} for each configuration in $S_i = \{(fu1, fu2) : fu1_{min} \le fu1 \le fu1_{max}, fu2_{min} \le fu2 \le fu2_{max}\}$ in increasing order, until a schedule satisfying P and M is found.
Step 9. Apply code size reduction. (Theorem 2.3)

4. EXAMPLE

In this section, we use a simple example to illustrate the design exploration process using the Integrated Framework of Design Optimization and Space Minimization, and compare the efficiency and quality of different algorithms. Figure 7 shows an exemplary DFG.

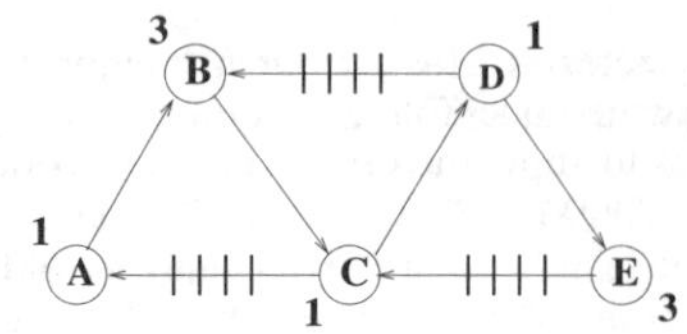

Figure 7: Data flow graph of an example.

The iteration bound of this DFG G is $B(G) = 5/4$. Given the iteration period constraint $P = 4/3$, and the code size constraint $M = 25$ instructions, the design task is to find the minimum configuration satisfying the requirements for an architecture with 2 different types of functional units (or processors).

Table 1 compares four algorithms in terms of the size of search space and the quality of outcomes. Column "Search Points" shows the number of points to be explored by the algorithms. Column "Search Cost" lists the computation costs of searching the design space and performing the optimization using the computation described in Section 3. Column "Solutions" shows the resulting design solutions. The parameters displayed in this column are: the iteration period ("Iter. Period"), unfolding factor ("uf"), number of various types of processors ("#fu2" and "#fu2"), and the resulting code size. Assuming that the code size reduction is performed on class 3 processors in the IDOMeCR algorithm. If an entry under column "Solutions" is marked by an "F", it indicates that the corresponding algorithm cannot find a feasible solution. In the following, we explain the various design approaches with the example.

Algorithms	**Search Points**	**Search Cost**	**Solutions**				
			uf	**#fu1**	**#fu2**	**iter. per.**	**code size**
STDu	55	230	F	F	F	F	F
STDur	117	660	4	8	8	5/4	F
IDOMe	1	51	3	3	5	4/3	F(90)
IDOMeCR	**1**	**51**	**3**	**3**	**5**	**4/3**	**21**

Table 1: The search costs and outcomes of four different design exploration methods.

For the STDu algorithm, the upper bound of unfolding factor imposed by code size constraint is $f_{max} = \lfloor M/|V| \rfloor = 5$. The upper bound on the number of functional units is obtained from ASAP schedule of an unfolded graph. It exhaustively searches all the possible configurations within the upper bound for all the unfolding graphs. The total number of design points is 55 in this case. Even after computing with all the design choices in the design space, this method cannot find a feasible solution satisfying the iteration period constraint. It shows that using unfolding hardly finds any solution for tight iteration period and code size constraints.

For the STDur algorithm, various retiming functions increases the number of search points to be 117. The algorithm find a feasible configuration of 8 fu1 and 8 fu2 with unfolding factor f=4. Although the schedule length is satisfied, the code size constraints is violated. Thus, no feasible solution can be produced.

The fourth and fifth rows of Table 1 show the features of IDOMe and IDOMeCR algorithms. The minimum cycle period, and thus iteration period, for each unfolding factor is computed using Theorem 2.1. Then, the iteration period is 2 for f=1. It is 3/2 for f=2, 4/3 for f=3 5/4 for f=4 and 7/5 for f=5. Since the iteration period constraint ($\le 4/3$) can be satisfied only for unfolding factors f=3 or f=4, we can eliminate the unfolding factors 1, 2, and 5 (Theorem 2.2). Furthermore, since the low bound and upper bound on the number of processors appear to be the same, the design space is further reduced to just 1 point. The minimum configuration found by IDOM is 3 fu1 and 5 fu2 with unfolding factor 3, which is better than that found by the STDur algorithm.

The code size generated by the IDOMe algorithm is 90 instructions. It exceeds the code size constraints. We list the code size in the parenthesis to show the effectiveness of code size optimization used in the IDOMeCR algorithm. The code size is reduced from 90 instructions to 21 instructions using IDOMeCR algorithm. Then, the memory constraint can be satisfied.

5. EXPERIMENTAL RESULTS

To demonstrate the performance and quality of IDOM algorithm, we conduct a series of experiments on a set of DSP benchmarks. Table 2 shows the experimental results. The experiments are conducted using two different design exploration algorithms, one is STDur, the other is IDOMeCR. To make the cases more complicated for design space exploration, we apply different slow down factors to the original circuits [5, 6], and choose the computation times for additions and multiplications arbitrarily. We also assume the code size constraint is $M = 5(|V| + 1)$ for all the cases. The measurement of code size is based on the number of instructions in the compiled code for a simulated processor with predicate register similar with TI's TMS320C6x. The experimental results show that IDOM can generate a better design solution with much less computation cost.

For Biquad Filter ("Biquad"), we assume that addition takes 1 time unit and multiplication 4 time units. The resulting circuit has an iteration bound $B(G) = 3/2$. Given an iteration period constraint $P = 5/3$. an configuration satisfying the iteration period constraint is found by STDur. It has 3 adders and 16 multipliers with unfolding factor f=4. The resulting iteration period is 3/2. However, the code size exceeds the memory constraint. For the illustration purpose, we still show the resulting code size generated by the STDur algorithm in the parenthesis. For the same case, IDOMeCR find a smaller configuration of 3 adders and 10 multipliers with unfolding factor f=3. The resulting schedule satisfies both iteration period and memory constraints. Furthermore, the search cost of IDOMeCR is only 4% of that using STDur, as shown in column "Ratio".

The experimental settings for the other cases are described in the following. For Partial Differential Equation ("DEQ"), assume that an addition operation takes 1 time unit, and a multiplication operation takes 3 time units. The resulting iteration bound is $B(G) = 8/5$. The iteration period constraint is $P = 7/4$. For Allpole Filter ("Allpole"), an addition operation takes 2 time units, and a multiplication operation takes 5 time units.the iteration bound is $B(G) = 18/5$, and the iteration period constraint is given as $P = 15/4$. For 5th Order Elliptic Filter ("Elliptic"), an addition takes 1 time unit, and a multiplication takes 5 time units, the iteration bound is $B(G) = 18/5$, and the iteration period constraint is $P = 15/4$. For 4-Stage Lattice Filter ("4-Stage"), an addition takes 1 time unit, and a multiplication 6 time units, the iteration bound is $B(G) = 7/4$, and the iteration period constraint is $P = 9/5$.

Applying the algorithms on all these experimental cases clearly yields the conclusion that IDOMeCR significantly reduces the search cost of design exploration process compared to the standard method. Its search cost is only 3% of that using STDur on average. Furthermore, IDOMeCR always find the minimal configurations for all the benchmarks.

6. CONCLUSION

In this paper, we presented an Integrated Framework of Design Optimization and Space Minimization (IDOM) to find the minimum configuration satisfying the schedule length and memory constraints. The properties of unfolded retimed data flow graph are studied to produce the minimum set of feasible unfolding factors without performing real scheduling. The relationships among unfolding factor, retiming function, iteration period and code size are stated in our theorems. We found that after we clearly understood the intrinsic relationships between the design parameters, a huge number of design points are immediately proved to be infeasible. Therefore, the design space to be explored is greatly reduced. We integrated several optimization techniques, i.e., retiming, unfolding and code size reduction to produce superior designs. The experimental results show that the search cost of IDOM is only 3% of the standard method on average. We believe that this fundamental study is essential to make the design space exploration to be more efficient.

Benchmarks	Search Points	Search Cost	Ratio	Solutions				
				uf	#add.	#mult.	iter. per.	code size
Biquad(std.)	228	2165		4	4	16	3/2	F(80)
Biquad(ours)	**4**	**87**	**4%**	**3**	**3**	**10**	**5/3**	**28**
DEQ(std.)	486	6017		5	10	18	8/5	F(110)
DEQ(ours)	**6**	**120**	**2%**	**3**	**5**	**15**	**5/3**	**37**
Allpole(std.)	510	7957		5	10	10	18/5	F(150)
Allpole(ours)	**6**	**156**	**2%**	**3**	**10**	**3**	**11/3**	**51**
Elliptic(std.)	694	19062		F	F	F	F	F
Elliptic(ours)	**2**	**142**	**0.7%**	**2**	**6**	**9**	**5**	**76**
4-Stage(std.)	909	15329		F	F	F	F	F
4-Stage(ours)	**55**	**640**	**4%**	**4**	**7**	**33**	**7/4**	**112**

Table 2: The design solutions generated by STDur and IDOMeCR algorithms.

7. REFERENCES

[1] C. Chantrapornchai, E. H.-M. Sha, and X. S. Hu. Efficient acceptable design exploration based on module utility selection. *IEEE Trans. on Computer-Aided Design of Integrated Circuits and Systems*, 19(1):19–29, Jan. 2000.

[2] L.-F. Chao and E. H.-M. Sha. Static scheduling for synthesis of DSP algorithms on various models. *Journal of VLSI Signal Processing*, 10:207–223, 1995.

[3] L.-F. Chao and E. H.-M. Sha. Scheduling data-flow graphs via retiming and unfolding. *IEEE Trans. on Parallel and Distributed Systems*, 8(12):1259–1267, Dec. 1997.

[4] S. Chaudhuri, S. A. Blythe, and R. A. Walker. A solution methodology for exact design space exploration in a three dimensional design space. *IEEE Trans. on VLSI Systems*, 5(1):69–81, Mar. 1997.

[5] C. E. Leiserson and J. B. Saxe. Retiming synchronous circuitry. *Algorithmica*, 6:5–35, Aug. 1991.

[6] T. O'Neil, S. Tongsima, and E. H.-M. Sha. Extended retiming: Optimal scheduling via a graph-theoretical approach. In *Proc. IEEE Int'l Conf. on Acoustics, Speech, and Signal Processing*, volume 4, pages 2001–2004, Mar. 1999.

[7] K. V. Palem, R. M. Rabbah, V. J. Mooney, P. Korkmaz, and K. Puttaswamy. Design space optimization of embedded memory systems via data remapping. In *Proc. the Joint Conf. on Languages, Compilers and Tools for Embedded Systems: Software and Compilers for Embedded Systems (LCTES'02-SCOPES'02)*, pages 28–37, Jun. 2002.

[8] K. K. Parhi. *VLSI Digital Signal Processing Systems: Design and Implementation*. John Wiley & Sons, 1999.

[9] R. S. Sambandam and X. Hu. Predicting timing behavior in architectural design exploration of real-time embedded systems. In *Proc. 34th ACM/IEEE Design Automation Conf. (DAC)*, pages 157–160, Jun. 1997.

[10] Q. Zhuge, E. H.-M. Sha, and C. Chantrapornchai. CRED: Code size reduction technique and implementation for software-pipelined applications. In *Proc. IEEE Workshop of Embedded System Codesign (ESCODES)*, pages 50–56, Sept. 2002.

SEAS: A System for Early Analysis of SoCs

Reinaldo A. Bergamaschi[1], Youngsoo Shin[1], Nagu Dhanwada[2], Subhrajit Bhattacharya[1], William E. Dougherty[2], Indira Nair[1], John Darringer[1], Sarala Paliwal[2]

[1] IBM T.J. Watson Research Center, Yorktown Heights, NY, USA

[2] IBM EDA Laboratory, Fishkill, NY, USA

ABSTRACT

Systems-on-chip (SoC) continue to be very complex to design and verify, despite extensive component reuse. Although reusable components are pre-designed and pre-verified, when they are assembled in an SoC there is no guarantee that the whole system will behave as expected from a performance, cost and integration point of view. In many cases this is because of faulty early design decisions regarding the architecture, core selection, floorplanning, etc. This paper presents a system for early analysis of SoCs which helps designers make early design decisions regarding performance, area, timing and power; and allows them to quickly evaluate cross-domain effects, such as the effect that an architectural decision may have on the performance and chip area.

Categories and Subject Descriptors

J.6 [**Computer-aided design**]; B7.2 [**Integrated circuits**]:Design aids

General Terms

Algorithms

Keywords

Design analysis, design space exploration, performance, power, floorplanning

1. INTRODUCTION

Systems-on-chip (SoC) built from pre-designed and pre-verified intellectual property blocks (IPs, or cores) have been hailed as the most effective means of bridging the design productivity gap [1]. However, even with extensive IP reuse, SoC design remains complex and still hampered by many of the same design problems confronting traditional large application-specific integrated circuit (ASIC) design.

These common problems are usually related to decisions made early in the design process which turned out to be either innacurate or impossible to fulfill later in the design. Such mistakes include, for example, (1) pessimistic die-size estimation which resulted in a more expensive chip, (2) architectural modifications needed for performance, which complicated the final placement, routing and timing closure of the design, (3) inaccurate early floorplanning which precluded timing problems from being detected early and later incurred in lengthy timing closure. These problems are not new and many different solutions have been attempted for ASIC designs. Nevertheless, the reuse of IP cores in SoC designs opens up new algorithmic possibilities for early analysis tools which can address the above problems. In an IP-based SOC the cores are pre-designed and pre-characterized, as opposed to a custom ASIC where many of the logic blocks are yet to be designed. The characterization of the cores provides reliable data regarding number of gates, layout size, performance parameters, timing constraints, etc. This data is reliable since it is extracted from pre-designed cores, but it is not necessarily accurate for a specific design because cores may accept parameters which can change the internal logic and its values (e.g., performance, timing) may depend on its context (e.g., external loads). The accuracy of this data also depends on whether the core is provided as a soft core (VHDL, Verilog) or a hard core (GDS-II).

This paper presents a System for Early Analysis of SoCs (SEAS) comprising a set of algorithms and a methodology for front-end design and analysis of SoCs. SEAS uses IP characterization data in conjunction with tools for performance, floorplan, timing and power analyses and is able to analyze the results in an integrated manner. The ability to analyze the cross-effects among architecture, floorplan, timing and power is crucial in preventing problems later in the design cycle.

This paper is organized as follows. Section 2 gives and overview of the tool; section 3 describes the individual algorithmic components of the tool; section 4 presents the experimental results, followed by conclusions in section 5.

2. OVERVIEW

SEAS allows users to easily specify a design in a block-diagram-like description and run types of analyses that would normally be impossible to do early in the design process with acceptable accuracy. These analyses include performance, floorplanning, timing and power. SEAS can handle core-based SoC designs, where the cores are available in a library, together with characterization data and models. The types of models needed will be described in the following sections.

A typical flow through the tool could be as follows. The designer builds the block diagram for a design (for example, an Ethernet router) and runs performance analysis, which returns values below targets, i.e., the Ethernet subsystem is not able to handle the flow of packets coming in. He/she then changes the architecture by adding another core, another Ethernet controller to double the number of channels, and as a result the performance numbers become acceptable. The modified design is then fed to the floorplanner which estimates a chip die size and global routing. It is possible that as a result of the extra added core the new chip dimensions require a larger die size which makes the chip more

CODES+ISSS'03, October 1–3, 2003, Newport Beach, California, USA.

costly; or require longer interconnections which may create critical timing paths.

The main advantage of SEAS from a user point of view is the ability to describe, measure and change the specification at a very high-level of abstraction and quickly evaluate the effects in performance, area, timing and power. If the results are not satisfactory, the designer can quickly change the architecture, the floorplan, or the cores being used and run the analyses again. Figure 1 illustrates SEAS overall organization. The individual analysis algorithms are not necessarily novel, however they had to be adapted and tuned to the design representation being used (block-diagram). This tuning is critical to the accuracy of the results.

Several previous works focused on early system-level estimation of performance, area and power [2][3][4][5]. These works are different from SEAS in many ways, but primarily in the level of input description which determines how early the estimations can be obtained. In [2] and [3], the system performance is estimated, based on the estimations of its software and hardware components. Both works assume that the system specification is available and give algorithms for estimating the various system processes as implemented in hardware or software. In [4] the system power is estimated also based on the power of its hardware and software components, again assuming that a system specification is available. In [5] the system architecture and instruction set are generated automatically, and the area and timing are derived from its RTL-based hardware specification. In all these systems, the detailed system specification is required for any meaningful analysis. In SEAS this is not the case, the "early" analysis can be done before any detailed system specification is available.

3. SEAS COMPONENTS

As illustrated in Figure 1, SEAS comprises an input description similar to a block diagram and four analyses engines. Each engine has its own set of algorithms and internal model derived from the initial block diagram, and uses characterization data and models for the cores available from a core library. The following sections explain these components in detail.

3.1 SoC Representation

For an early analysis system, it is vital that the input specification be at an abstraction level easily captured by the designer in a few hours at most, and using familiar methods (e.g., schematic capture or hardware-description language). Moreover, this description should be easily modified. This immediately precludes any functional description at the register-transfer or behavioral levels,

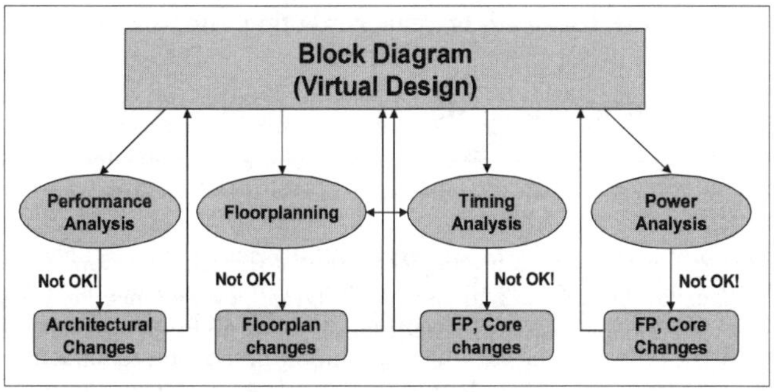

Figure 1: SEAS Overview

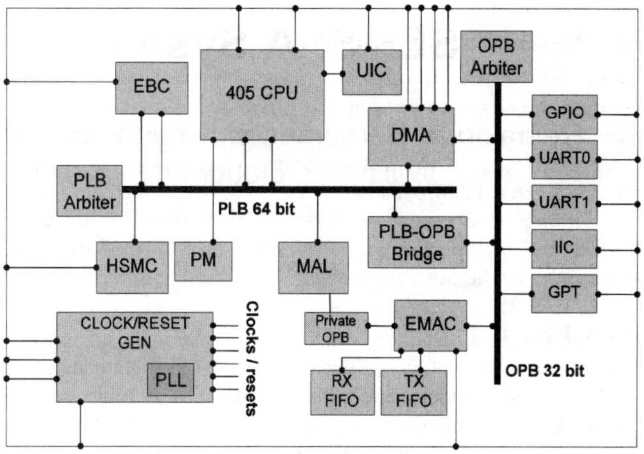

Figure 2: PowerPC 405 PBD Virtual Design

as they would take days to write up and modify. In addition, in core-based SoCs, the designer has to be familiar with the functionality and pins of the cores in order to connect and configure them properly. This again is time consuming, error-prone and inadequate for an early analysis system.

The simplest specification format that is already very familiar to designers is the *block diagram*, or a schematic-like description with blocks representing the cores and a few lines representing the major interconnections, such as clocks, buses, etc. We have developed a system called CORAL [6] for automating the design of SoCs using cores in which we have defined a synthesizable block diagram-like specification called the *Virtual Design*. In order to make this paper self-contained we add here a brief description of the Virtual Design and its properties.

The Virtual Design is a netlist specification consisting of virtual components, virtual nets and virtual pins, and it can be created using a standard schematic editor or hardware-description languages. Virtual components are abstract representations of the actual cores in a library (called real components). For example, there is a single virtual component for a family of microprocessors (e.g., the virtual PowerPC represents an abstraction of all real PowerPC cores). The virtual component contains virtual pins, and each virtual pin is an encapsulation of a subset of the real pins in the real component. For example, the PowerPC405 core has two master interfaces to the Processor Local Bus (PLB) [7], each comprising a total of 18 pins and 188 bits. In contrast, each master interface in the virtual component is represented as a single virtual pin. Virtual pins are connected using virtual nets.

Figure 2 illustrates the virtual design for the PowerPC 405 platform-based design (PBD) [8]. As the figure shows, the virtual design resembles a block diagram. Each virtual component has a small number of pins, and each pin is marked with the type of interface it belongs to. Coral [6] understands these interface types and can automatically create a virtual design based on a set of selected virtual components and some configuration parameters set by the designer.

In SEAS each virtual component is associated with 3 other models besides a real component, namely, a performance model, an area image for floorplanning and a power state-machine model. These models are stored in a library and retrieved by SEAS during analysis.

3.2 Performance Analysis

System performance is often the most important factor used for deciding the architecture of an SoC. The overall performance of a system is dependent on the raw performance of individual components and on the interaction between them. SEAS uses a simulation-based approach in order to account for dynamic effects such as bus contention, buffer overflows, etc. These effects depend on the performance of individual components, the architecture of the SoC, the software application and the workload being run on the system.

The performance behavior of a core is captured in a high-level abstract model as a set of communicating finite state machines (FSMs). The models are created by abstracting out the functionality of the core and by considering only its performance impact. Actual data computation is not modeled, just the delay aspects of it, namely, number of cycles and latency. The FSM models for the cores communicate via token passing. The arrival of a token may trigger state transitions, or events, which in turn generate new tokens.

The performance models developed in this work can achieve very high simulation speed at the expense of some accuracy. At this early analysis stage, speed is more important than accuracy, provided that results are still meaningful and useful. The core models capture the typical behavior of the core; exceptions and corner-case behaviors are ignored. Some data-dependent delays are not accurately modeled.

The effects of the software running on the system and its interactions with the architecture have to be considered as well. In SEAS, a model for the behavior of the software is created, which generates delays and bus traffic without actually performing any function. The delay values associated with software running on the processor are obtained using profiling techniques off-line. The environment is modeled in terms of data rates or traces. For example, an Ethernet channel port would be modeled by the network speed, packet rate (number of packets/sec) and the size of each packet arriving from the network.

An important factor that affects simulation speed is the granularity of atomic operations. An atomic operation is executed in a single simulation step in the performance model but may take several clock cycles in the actual hardware. A burst transfer over a bus is an example of a single atomic operation in the performance model. The actual number of cycles of such a transfer is computed by the bus performance model depending on the number of bytes being transferred and certain core parameters (e.g., allowed burst sizes).

We have developed SystemC 2.0 [9] performance model for several of the IBM CoreConnect cores, including those used by the design in Figure 2. The virtual design is automatically converted to a SystemC program which has constructor calls for all modules representing the components and interconnections in the virtual design. To enhance reusability, the models are fully parameterized with respect to speed, width, etc. More details on performance modeling can be found in [10].

3.3 Floorplanning

In order to create a virtual design floorplan which is representative of the final real design floorplan, the virtual components need to be characterized for size and shape (a process called *Area Planning*). Each virtual component has a corresponding real component core in a library. This core is available either as a hardware description (in case of soft cores) or directly as a piece of layout (for hard cores). Hard cores have their shapes and sizes fixed by the layout. For soft cores, area planning is a one time step (performed as part of library generation) that involves:

- Running logic synthesis to generate a fully technology mapped netlist
- Setting appropriate image, power terminal related blockages and generating an initial outline for the component based on an area estimation method. This method uses netlist connectivity, blockage information and wiring estimates for computing an initial area and shape for the virtual component.
- Placement and global routing
- Refining initial area and shape estimates based on actual placement and global wiring information.

The area planning step sizes the components to achieve an area utilization of 65 – 70%. This is done to account for any potential increase in area that might happen later in the design process due to chip level gate sizing and buffering for timing correction. As a result of area planning all virtual components are associated with a size and shape for a given technology image, which can then be used in the floorplan of the whole virtual design.

Pin locations also need to be considered as they are important during global routing. A pin assignment algorithm is used to fix the pin locations in the virtual components based on the locations of the real pins in the corresponding hard core (if available) or based on an initial placement of the virtual components and their interconnections (for soft cores).

The inputs to the floorplanner are: the virtual design netlist, area planning characterizations of all virtual components used in the design, and the expected number of total real IO pins. An initial chip image is selected based on the total area of the virtual components and number of real IO pins. The task of floorplanning is part automatic and part manual. Designers usually know which cores contain more critical connections, such as high-speed IOs, processors, and clock generation cores, and will manually place those cores on the chip image. Given a set of such preplaced components, an automatic simulated-annealing-based floorplanning algorithm [11] is used to place the rest of the components and produce a legal non-overlapping floorplan for the virtual design.

Based on the generated floorplan, the previously fixed image is retained or is switched to an image that is a better fit to the virtual design floorplan. The result is a die size that satisfies the area and IO requirements with acceptable levels of wire congestion. This die size and the locations of the virtual components on the floorplan are later passed to the real design as a very good starting point for the back-end placement, routing and timing closure steps.

3.4 Timing Analysis

Timing closure is a critical part of any design process and cannot be ignored even during the initial architectural analysis and performance modeling stage. In current deep submicron technologies the delay of signals traveling across the chip already approaches or exceeds the cycle time, forcing designers to pay close attention to the chip floorplan and the architectural options available. New techniques like pipelining global interconnections are becoming more prevalent as means to deal with the inability to transmit a signal across the length of a chip. This makes timing closure decisions tightly intertwined with architecture decisions and floorplanning. The challenge lies in being able to analyze timing early in the design process, at the virtual design abstraction level.

The problem in measuring timing at the virtual design level is that the virtual pins are not associated with drivers and there are no buffers inserted in the virtual design floorplan. Although we can assign average drivers for the virtual pins, the absence of real drivers and buffers make any timing measurement less reliable.

In practice the designer has a good understanding of where the major timing problems may lie, based on the real cores assertions available from the library and on his/her own experience. Hence, the main unknowns with respect to early timing are the delays of the main global interconnections (or indirectly wire length). In SEAS, as part of floorplanning the virtual design, there is a global routing step which creates global interconnections for all virtual nets and reports the wire lengths. The wire lengths and capacitances of global interconnections are reported to the designer. Timing analysis, integrated with the floorplanner, is then run using average drivers, mainly to give the designer an approximate value for the worst case delay through the wire. Virtual wires correspond to virtual nets and not to the real nets in the real design, however the system can estimate the number of real wires per virtual net and estimate routing congestion. Moreover the virtual wire lengths and delays do represent an approximation of the real wire lengths and delays, which can be very useful for flagging critical wire delays early in the design.

3.5 Power Analysis

Power analysis at the early stage of design is also an important component of SEAS. At this early stage, the typical way to estimate power consumption uses spreadsheets based on conventional or empirical power formulas. These formulas return average power consumption values for the cores, given parameters, such as the size and type of the logic block, capacitances, switching activity, frequency and power supply. In order to explore the power design space, designers have to run these spreadsheets multiple times with different values of parameters, which is very time consuming and does not provide representative coverage of the possible execution scenarios.

In SEAS we have implemented a simulation-based approach intended to compute power for specific performance simulation scenarios. The power for each core is still computed based on spreadsheet formulas which were expanded to account for different power modes. Each core is associated with a power state machine (PSM) [12] which defines its power states and transitions and the transition delays (or how many cycles it takes to change power states).

The performance models described in section 3.2 were extended to capture the power state machine for the cores. During the performance analysis, the simulation records the active cores, i.e., involved in the execution of the transaction, as well as cores in idle or sleep states. By adding up the power values for the states which the cores transition to during simulation, we can compute the average power for the whole system for a given simulation scenario. A power management unit (PMU), which manages the power consumption of a system by controlling each core, is also modeled with parameters that can be controlled during simulation.

By combining the performance analysis simulation with power computation, SEAS can evaluate dynamic effects such as the overhead of delay and power when cores change their power states, and the effects of power management policy on performance.

3.6 Real Design

SEAS is dedicated to early analysis of SoCs. However, for the design process to complete successfully, the early analysis estimates and parameters have to be honored by the rest of the design process.

SEAS operates on the virtual design. The Coral tool [6] is capable of understanding this block-diagram-like description and automatically maps it to an RTL description for the complete SoC. This description, along with the RTL for all the actual cores used in the design, is loaded into synthesis for optimization and technology mapping. The mapped netlist is fed to a floorplanner which uses the die size and core locations estimated by SEAS. The floorplanner has to deal with all real interconnections and may adapt the floorplan accordingly. This is followed by detailed placement and routing and timing closure.

4. EXPERIMENTAL RESULTS

In order to validate the SEAS approach we devised an experiment to evaluate the following: (1) how easy is it to create and change a design using the virtual design representation, (2) how useful are the early analyses proposed, (3) can the effects of architectural changes be estimated across multiple domains, (4) can the lower-level tools effectively honor the early analysis decisions, and (5) can the early analyses results be correlated with post-physical design results.

The design used in this experiment is shown in Figure 2. It is a platform-based design developed around the PowerPC 405 CPU, the CoreConnect Bus architecture and IBM's Blue Logic core library. It contains an Ethernet subsystem represented by the Ethernet controller (EMAC), the Media Access Layer (MAL) core, and receive and transmit FIFOs. It also contains a high-speed memory controller (HSMC), an external bus controller (EBC), DMA controller, interrupt controller and various peripherals including 2 UARTs, 1 IIC and 1 timer. The cores are all connected to either the high-speed Processor Local Bus (PLB), or the On-chip Peripheral Bus (OPB). The experiment consists of evaluating this design for Ethernet packet processing purposes. Performance analysis will be used for measuring the system throughput and CPU utilization, after which the architecture will be changed by adding a second Ethernet controller and the performance analysis repeated. The floorplan for both designs will be generated and die sizes estimated, along with wire length and power information.

The first part of the experiment consisted of creating the virtual design representation and running performance analysis, floorplanning, timing and power analysis. Since all virtual components are available in a component library, creating a virtual design is a matter of selecting the desired components and interconnecting the pins, which can be done very quickly (e.g., a couple of hours) using a schematic editor, a Tcl script, or directly using VHDL or Verilog [6].

The cores involved in packet processing are the EMAC, MAL, PLB Arbiter, CPU, and HSMC. The packets arrive from the network to the EMAC input and are received into its receive buffer. The MAL works as a dedicated DMA and transfers the packet through the PLB, to the memory controller and finally into

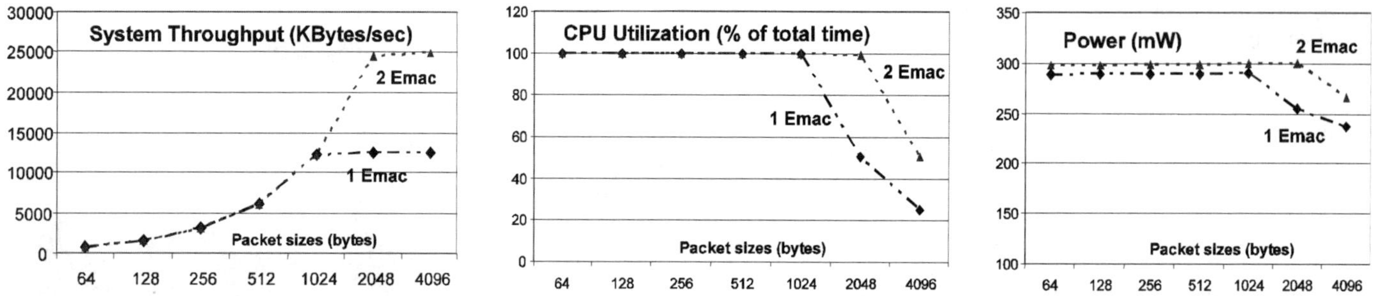

Figure 3: Performance and power analysis results for 1-EMAC and 2-EMAC designs

an external memory. The time it takes for receiving a packet into memory depends on the data rate, the size of the packet, the capacity of the MAL (size of burst transfer, number of bursts needed per packet) and some constant delays associated with the EMAC and HSMC. After the packet is received in memory, the CPU processes it by reading the header, computing a new address and writing back a new header. In this example, it is assumed that this CPU header processing is constant and does not depend on the size of the packet. This CPU time is measured off-line by profiling techniques. The packet is then read by the MAL and transmitted, through the EMAC, back to the network.

The system throughput and CPU utilization are shown in Figure 4 for various packet sizes. Throughput is defined as the number of Kbytes per second transmitted by the system. This depends on the number of packets, size of the packet, processing capacity, and it is limited by the maximum channel capacity, that is, the maximum number of bits/sec that the EMAC can transmit. CPU utilization is a measure of how much time the CPU is busy vs. idle. With small packets and 1 EMAC, the CPU is 100% busy and throughput increases with packet size, up to the maximum allowed by the channel. In this example the EMAC is limited to 100 Mbits/sec. Above a certain packet size, throughput remains capped at 100Mbits/sec, and the CPU starts becoming idle as the time to receive a packet becomes larger than the CPU processing time.

In order to increase throughput beyond 100Mbits/sec, the only alternative is to add one or more extra EMACs to the design. Adding one extra EMAC doubles the maximum throughput to 200Mbits/sec which allows for higher packet rates and bigger packets to be processed.

A new version of the design was created by adding an extra EMAC to the first virtual design. Both EMACs are connected to the MAL, which arbitrates (in a simple round-robin scheme) and alternates between the two EMACs for transferring their packets to memory. As soon as a first packet P1 is received (through EMAC-1 and MAL), the CPU can start processing it. The two emacs operate concurrently, hence depending on the packet size, a second packet P2 will be received and available to the CPU after P1 is received, but before the CPU completes processing P1. Therefore, once the CPU is done with P1, it is readily available to process P2 and there will be no CPU idle time, or 100% utilization. As the packet size increases, it will take longer to receive a packet, and P2 may not be available when the CPU completes processing P1, thus the CPU may be underutilized even in the 2 EMAC design. Throughput and utilization for the 2 EMAC design are shown in Figure 4.

In practice, the system may be doing something else besides packet processing (e.g., computing statistics and printing a report through the UART), which requires some CPU utilization. In this case the goal will not be to keep the CPU 100% busy with packet processing, but perhaps make sure that the target throughput is achieved with 80% CPU utilization, thus leaving some CPU capacity for other processing. This example demonstrates the ability in SEAS to change the architecture to meet the requirements and quickly verify it using performance analysis.

Power analysis is run with the performance simulation. Figure 4 shows the power consumed by the system during packet processing for the two virtual designs. It can be seen that power does not increase significantly in the 2-EMAC case, which is expected since most of the power is dissipated by the CPU when active. It also shows that when the CPU becomes partly idle the power decreases accordingly. This simulation assumes that the EMAC, MAL and CPU will be active when in use, and idle otherwise, and all other cores are in sleep mode.

Given these two architectural design points, they now need to be evaluated for size and timing. We generated the floorplan for both virtual designs and estimated their required die sizes. Based on floorplan area alone, the 1 EMAC version fit into a 5.57x5.57mm image, whereas the 2 EMAC version needed the next larger size, a 6.05x6.05mm image. However, this design was actually pin-limited, that is, the required number of pins (437) for the 1-EMAC version exceed the maximum number of pins in the 5.57mm image, hence the 6.05x6.05mm image had to be used, also for the 1-EMAC version. Both floorplans are shown in Figure 5. SEAS benefit in this case was to show that the higher performance design (2 EMACs) could fit in the same die size, with the same silicon cost.

In order to complete the design process we submitted the first design (1 EMAC) through the rest of the design flow, that is, RTL generation, logic synthesis, floorplan, detailed placement and routing and timing closure (repowering, buffer insertion). The core locations and areas in the virtual design floorplan were fixed in the final floorplan. Detailed placement was not allowed to modify core locations, but it could alter the aspect ratio of the area for each core in order to suit specific layout requirements for hard macros. The final layout, shown in Figure 5, was able to meet the timing constraints. As expected the final layout is very similar to the virtual design floorplan since the locations of the cores were fixed. The fact that the timing constraints could be met indicates that the early virtual design floorplan was indeed realistic enough to be used in the real design.

Comparing the timing of individual paths between the virtual design and the real design proved less accurate, mainly because the virtual design has no concept of driver strength and buffers, which are essential for accurate timing. Instead of comparing

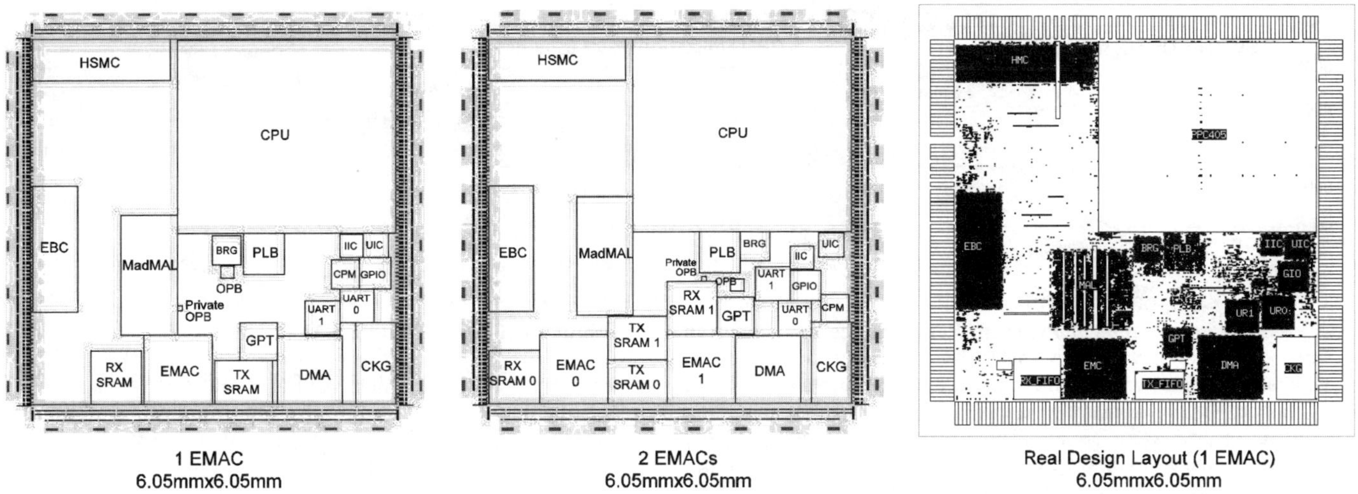

Figure 4: Virtual design floorplans and corresponding real layout

timings on individual paths, we compared the wire length of a virtual net (in the virtual floorplan, after global routing) and the average wire length for all corresponding real nets in the final real layout. The results, given in Table 1, show a good correlation between wire lengths estimated on the virtual design and the actual wire lengths in the final layout, in most cases. The two cases were the differences are over 40% are due to differences in pin locations between the virtual design layout and the final layout. Designers can look at the wire lengths for the major interconnections in the virtual design and determine if they may be too long for timing purposes.

We also compared this final design with an independently generated version of the same design produced using a traditional RTL-based design methodology: the die-size was the same and the timing constraints were met in both designs, although the actual most critical paths were different due to different layouts.

Table 1: Wire lengths of global interconnections in the virtual floorplan and in the real detailed layout (um)

Nets	Virtual FP	Detailed Layout	% Diff
PLB to DMA	1131	1420	20.4%
DMA to PLB	1131	1994	43.3%
PLB to ICU/CPU	1852	2115	12.4%
ICU/CPU to PLB	1852	2151	13.9%
PLB to DCU/CPU	1244	1459	14.7%
DCU/CPU to PLB	1244	1547	19.6%
PLB to EBC	2448	2727	10.2%
EBC to PLB	2448	2939	16.7%
PLB to MAL	1102	763	-44.4%
MAL to PLB	1102	1169	5.8%

5. CONCLUSIONS

Early design decisions, if misguided, can have a significant impact on the ability to meet performance, area, timing and power constraints on SoCs. This paper presented a system which helps designers make these early decisions. The advantages of the approach include: (1) a simple block-diagram-like notation for design specification which allows the designer to create and modify the design quickly, (2) integrated analyses algorithms for performance, floorplan, timing and power, which allow the designer to change the architecture, the core selection or the floorplan of the design and quickly evaluate the effect on other domains. Results have shown that estimations based on our approach are accurate enough to guide early design decisions as well as used by lower-level tools.

6. REFERENCES

[1] "International Roadmap for Semiconductors, 2001 Edition", available from http://public.itrs.net.

[2] J. Grode and J. Madsen, "A Unified Component Modeling Approach for Performance Estimation in Hardware/Software Codesign", *Proceedings of the 24th Euromicro Conference,* August 1998, pp.65 -69.

[3] A. Allara, C. Brandolese, W. Forniciari, F. Salice, D. Sciuto, "System-level Performance Estimation Strategy for Sw and Hw", *Proceedigns of the International Conference on Computer Design (ICCD '98)*, Oct. 1998, pp.48 -53.

[4] M. Lajolo, A. Raghunathan, S. Dey, and L. Lavagno, "Cosimulation-Based Power Estimation for System-on-Chip Design", *IEEE Transactions on Very Large Scale Integration Systems*, v. 10, no.3, June 2002, pp.253-266.

[5] G. Hadjiyiannis, P. Russo, S. Devadas, "A methodology for accurate performance evaluation in architecture exploration", *Proceedings of the 36th Design Automation Conference*, June 1999, pp.927 -932.

[6] R. Bergamaschi, S. Bhattacharya, R. Wagner, C. Fellenz, W. R. Lee, F. White, M. Muhlada and J-M. Daveau, "Automating the Design of SoCs Using Cores", *IEEE Design & Test of Computers*, v.18, no.5, Sept/Oct. 2001, p.32-45.

[7] "The CoreConnect™ Bus Architecture", white paper, available from http://www.ibm.com/chips/products/coreconnect/.

[8] "IBM Platform-Based Design Kit", described in http://www.ibm.com/chips/products/asics/methodology/design_kit.html.

[9] T. Grotker, S. Liao, G. Martin, and S. Swan , "System Design with SystemC", Kluwer Academic Publishers, 2002.

[10] J. Darringer, R. Bergamaschi, S. Bhattacharya, D. Brand, A. Herkersdorf, J. Morrell, I. Nair, P. Sagmeister, Y. Shin, "Early Analysis Tools for System-on-a-Chip Design", *IBM Journal of Research and Development*, v.46, no.6, November 2001, 691-707.

[11] J. Sayah et. al., "Design Planning for High-Performance ASICs", *IBM Journal of Research and Development*, v.40, no.3, 1996, 431-452.

[12] L. Benini, R. Hodgson, and P. Siege, "System-level power estimation and optimization"', in *Proceedings of the* International *Symposium on Low Power Electronics and Design (ISLPD)*, 173-178, ACM, August 1998.

Programmers' Views of SoCs

JoAnn M. Paul
Electrical and Computer Engineering Department
Carnegie Mellon University
Pittsburgh, PA 15213 USA
jpaul@ece.cmu.edu

Abstract

System-on-chip (SoC) designs have the potential to change the way we organize computation. This potential has gone unrealized. Future SoCs will have multiple heterogeneous processing elements, most likely organized around an on-chip network. Thus, SoCs are increasingly modeled as systems in the large. But a chip also has a fixed set of programmable hardware elements that are much more closely coupled than for systems in the large. New application types will require the chip to be considered programmable along with the individual processing elements on the chip. New programmers' views of SoCs are required to capture this new design space. A set of primitives for next generation design languages that support the development of new programmers' views of SoCs is motivated.

Categories and Subject Descriptors

C.0 [Computer Systems Organization]: General – *hardware/ software interfaces.*

General Terms

Performance, Design, Languages.

Keywords

Design Languages, Heterogeneous Multiprocessing, Networks on Chip, Programmers' Views, Systems-on-Chips (SoCs).

1. Introduction

Soon it will be possible to integrate a billion transistors on a single chip. Currently, two points of view dominate how they will be utilized. The first is that they will be applied to single processors that preserve existing programming abstractions with increasingly sophisticated hardware that is hidden from the programmer. The second is that Systems-on-a-Chip (SoCs) will result.

SoCs have been likened to other system types including system on a board that happens to be on a single chip, heterogeneous multiprocessors on single chips [1], and more recently, networks on chips (NoC) [2][3]. All of these views are borrowed from systems in the large. Systems in the large are systems that can be built across many chips. This includes virtually all computer systems other than single chip systems. Similarly networks in the large may even be wide area networks (WANs) which can describe systems with elements that may be literally a world apart from each other.

Virtually all current SoC design and modeling approaches can be applied to other kinds of custom systems, such as the traditional, embedded functionality in automobiles [4]. A separation of computation and communication [5][6] leads to the need to partition and design the system around explicit communications interfaces. Individual processing elements (PEs) have separately compiled programs and memories for which all interactions are static and determined at design time, much like low-level hardware design. Many are left wondering if there is anything really new about SoCs that will impact single chip computer organization.

Future technology will provide the opportunity to consider a single chip as a network of heterogeneous processors, with the potential for hundreds of ARM equivalent processors to be integrated onto single chips within the next 5 years. The application space of next generation computers will pose new challenges beyond the present day focus on network processors, multimedia and embedded applications as primary SoC design challenges. Size and power constraints will result in a need to tune ever more sophisticated software to the machine upon which it executes. These systems will exhibit heterogeneous parallelism at the system level, prompting an entirely new type of system design.

Approaches to SoC design that are limited to dataflow are organized only around computation and communication, limiting the view of the SoC as an embedded, reactive system. Without a system-wide view of control, these approaches do not capture the rich set of possibilities when an SoC is considered a programmable entity. SoCs design languages such as SystemC are really only extensions of hardware description languages, focusing only on the net physical behavior of a reactive style of design.

Single chip hardware design has long permitted performance-optimization of control flow for a custom application. For SoCs the challenge will be in preserving the ability to optimize control flow for a semi-custom set of applications when design elements are parallel processors. The opportunity over that of systems in the large is the optimization of control flow across a *fixed* set of PEs tuned to a set of applications. New forms of programmable control flow in SoCs can result in new programmers' views.

A programmers' view (PV) is to a heterogeneous multiprocessor SoC what an Instruction Set Architecture (ISA) is to a single PE. The SoC may contain many individual ISAs for the many individual PEs it contains. However, the PV of the SoC captures the programmable nature of the chip as a distinct design artifact.

The set of instructions in an ISA includes three classes: that of computation, communication, and control of the underlying machine. The class of control instructions is what permits the machine to be considered programmable; this is so in single PEs because control instructions permit the program counter to be dynamically changed. A program counter is a pointer to a program which may, itself, be updated as a result of the program execution.

New PVs for SoCs must be defined and developed, organized around fixed sets of heterogeneous PEs and memories, ultimately permitting SoCs to be new, programmable devices that are not just mere extensions of hardware design. The PVs must include computation, communication and control as in Figure 1. We define system state for heterogeneous multiprocessing systems as the

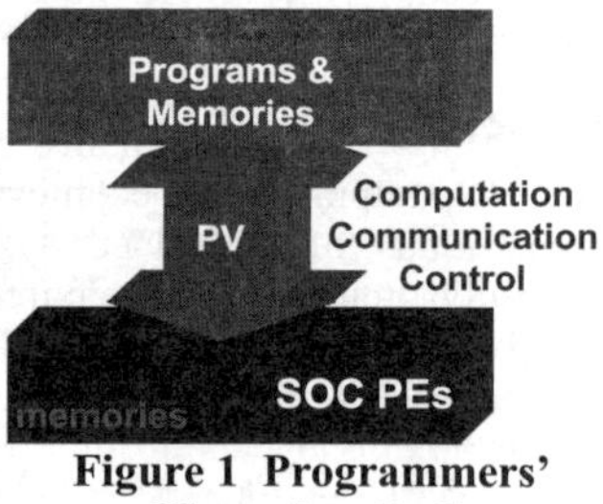

Figure 1 Programmers' View of an SoC

equivalent of a program counter in a single PE; it is finite state that can be used as the basis for dynamic, data-dependent decision making. An SoC can respond to situations programmatically, with data-dependent control flow optimized to a fixed set of PEs.

We start by considering the future application space of SoCs, motivating a need for effective implementation of sophisticated software on parallel processors. Then, we consider how control flow has been fundamental to both software and hardware computer organization by comparing and contrasting it to dataflow. We then consider how PEs might be organized on NoCs, again comparing control and data flow organization at the highest levels of design. By considering an SoC to have a fixed set of PEs, we contrast it with systems in the large, ultimately motivating the need to explicitly include coordination of PEs in support of system level control flow in PVs of next generation SoC design.

2. Future Applications

Probably the most competitive arena for computer design is in consumer electronics — where design time, size, speed, power, and innovation come together to make for competitive advantage. Most consumer-oriented future computing devices will be portable. A subset of applications that might appear on these devices includes that of current cell phones, current personal digital assistant (PDA) applications, global positioning system (GPS) sensing, Bluetooth, motion sensing, ad hoc networking, 3-D image processing, compression/decompression, security, and a broad set of human computer interaction (HCI) software.

Research in ubiquitous and pervasive computing results in new scenarios for even more complex functionality with possibilities only limited by the ability to design and technically realize these scenarios in the individual computing devices [7]. No longer will it be possible to consider computer systems as falling into traditionally separate categories of embedded, general purpose, multimedia or network processors; future systems will have aspects of each. Novel applications will result from the interactions of previously separate types of functionality as computers simultaneously interact with the physical world, other computers, and humans.

The term "embedded computing" resulted from thinking of a computer system as being embedded in a non-computer system. Embedded system design is often thought of in terms of designing "hardware in the loop," which resulted in thinking of a computer system as reacting to the physical world with guaranteed response times. A reactive style of design naturally captures the need to communicate and compute in a fixed relationship with the non-computer system. However, most computers already interact with other computers in a networked sense.

HCI will become an increasingly important application area in its own right as traditional means of interacting with the computer (keyboard, mouse, display) will be replaced with multi-modal forms of interaction that include various forms of human "recognition" such as speech, handwriting and face recognition. Advanced forms of HCI are like real time simulations; they execute sophisticated models of humans in real time. Other kinds of simulations have been a successful application of parallel processing. HCI functionality that lies between the SoC's input and output pins will become increasingly sophisticated. While some kinds of embedded systems have functionality that is naturally limited by the requirements of the physical world, it is almost impossible to conceive of limits to the benefits of additional compute power applied to HCI.

The mix of new application types on these systems will result in a variety of performance demands. Some tasks may continuously execute while others may be event driven, and still others may be considered appropriate for best effort models. Different operating modes for the system may result in different performance demands for entire sets of tasks, as when different applications execute on today's desktop computers.

The important point is that the anticipation of what is possible in these systems must clearly utilize design principles that are at least as powerful of those of the past. While there will be increased ability to design for parallel execution of tasks, it will also be necessary to design the chip as a programmable entity.

3. Control Flow and Data Flow

Hardware Design Languages (HDLs) remain organized largely around the design of single FSMs. A significant feature of the FSM is that computation decisions are made around global machine state. The coordination of incoming data with the machine state permits a control flow style of design, in which the next state of the machine is computed as an interaction of incoming data with current state. This is depicted in Figure 2.

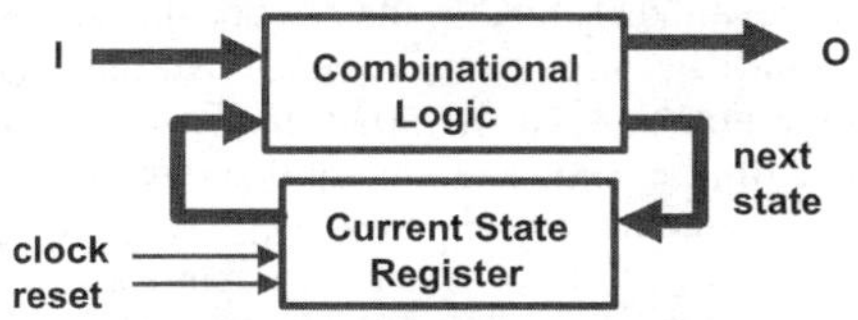

Figure 2 Finite State Machine

The positive aspects of the FSM include the ability to sequence operations in a programmatic style of design while the drawbacks largely center upon the serialization of execution. This serialization extends to individual processors. A processor is an FSM where machine inputs are separately categorized as program and data. The interleaving of programmatic and data inputs at runtime allows for processors to execute more complex forms of control flow than FSMs, such as permitting design for conceptually unbounded amounts of state.

Figure 3 shows a single PE as a relationship between a program, its data, an ISA and an FSM. The figure shows that there are really two kinds of state that contribute to the overall performance of a conventional processor, that of the data and program stored in external memory and that of the underlying FSM. The state in the FSM is thought of as the state in the registers, including not only the data registers, but also the instruction pointer and program counter. This permits the finite state of the processor to control the conceptually unbounded state of the program it executes.

Figure 3 Single PE

Unlike the state in an FSM, a processor memory location can mean different things at different times during the execution of a given program; this permits conceptually unbounded execution as memory resources are allocated and deallocated at runtime either explicitly by the program or implicitly by the context of the local variables in nested function calls. The conceptually unbounded execution allows a processor to approximate a Turing Machine; a software program is fundamentally different from a hardware description. System-level models that distill software and hardware to single models over-restrict the design space [8].

The state relationships in a processor may be considered layered; the memory external to the processor is in a layered relationship to the state of the FSM in the underlying processor [9][10]. This layered relationship permits software programs to rely on only a few features in the underlying FSM in order to execute on the FSM. However, one of the key features is the ability to dynamically load the program counter.

A processor not only loads and stores instructions and data (communication) and does arithmetic and logical operations on them (computation), but it also can load the program counter in response to specific situations, thus changing its execution sequence in response to system data (control).

Note the similarities between Figure 3 and Figure 1. While Figure 3 is a classic view of a PE, Figure 1 is what we propose for future SoCs where the hardware is a collection of heterogeneous, programmable processors. In section 5, we propose system state as the equivalent of the program counter in the analogy. It is finite state which can be updated dynamically as a result of computation and around which data-dependent decisions can be made. However its coordination across a fixed set of PEs must be explicitly supported. The point is that PVs that permit designers to define and effectively manipulate control flow across a collection of programmable resources on an SoC are required.

In recognizing the parallel nature of computation on SoCs, many have proposed that SoC system-level design should be organized around dataflow style graphs such as shown in Figure 4. The figure shows a dataflow graph in which sequencing is unidirectional (no feedback). In such graph-based approaches, computation is presumed to be triggered by tokens [4][5][6]. Static analysis is required so that response times are predictable and queues need not be considered unbounded. The concept is not unlike that of gate-level design where the execution of individual gates is triggered by events.

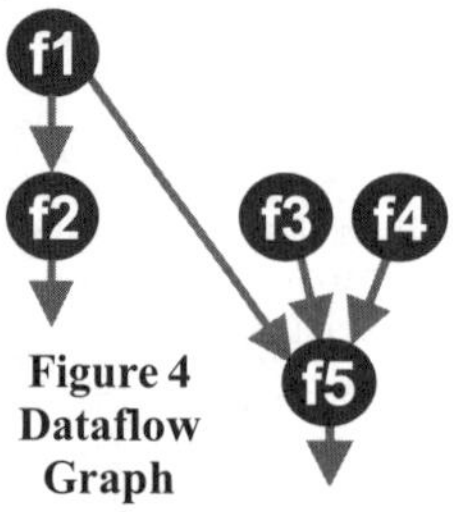

Figure 4 Dataflow Graph

Dataflow tends to result in a graph-based style of design with static execution schedules; this is evidenced by the observation that dataflow tends to be described by graphs with vertices and edges while control flow often results in program-like descriptions. Dataflow graphs are poorly suited to describe arbitrary, complex software programs. Programmatic data dependencies resolved at runtime permit the system to respond to a wider range of situations. Programs can have conceptually unbounded loops on single processors and multithreaded descriptions where M tasks can be mapped to N resources on multiprocessors.

For the past several decades, the synchronous finite state machine (FSM) and the programmed processor have been the dominant design abstractions for digital computation. They have conveniently captured the underlying hardware abstractions as well as provided a basis for effective specification of system functionality in no small part because it is easier to design computer system functionality in terms of a control flow sequence.

Sequential specification of functionality requires some context for global state. For single processor systems and FSMs, the global state is not problematic, it is a natural part of the specification of the behavior of the machine. But for parallel computer machines, such as future SoCs, architecting global state so that dynamic decision making across a set of parallel processors can be effective has been challenging [11].

Heterogeneous multiprocessing on single chips and the increasingly sophisticated applications that mobile computers will execute are each virtual certainties. Some state will be private and local to resources. Overall performance for many applications will benefit from utilizing private state and the establishment of dataflow across a number of PEs. However, the need to maintain some forms of global control flow across a number of PEs will also be important for many of these applications.

This leads us to the first of a set of modeling primitives. We propose that future design languages that support the development of PVs for SoCs must include:

PV-P1) trade-offs of control flow vs. data flow implemented across a number of PEs.

We will number our proposed set of modeling primitives throughout the paper as PV-Pn, for design primitive number n.

By considering SoCs as being organized around NoCs while at the same time pointing out the differences between NoCs and networks in the large, we next motivate possibilities for effectively preserving control flow in high-level PVs of SoCs.

4. Networks on Chips

Networks on Chip (NoC) have been proposed to support modular design while enabling high-performance circuits to reduce latency and increase bandwidth. They also support the globally asynchronous, locally synchronous (GALS) nature of design as single clock domain systems will no longer scale to future device densities and chip sizes. [2][3]

While NoC may be suitable for solving problems related to on-chip communications it does not address how state will be advanced across the chip. Concerns that single chip systems conceived as networks of processors will suffer from the same kinds of obstacles that made it difficult to achieve performance benefits from parallel systems in the large seem valid. Yet, while there are many similarities between NoC and networking in the large, there are differences between even the most fundamental objectives of the two. By taking advantage of the fixed and finite set of PEs on a chip in conjunction with the programmable nature of a network, new PVs for SoCs become apparent.

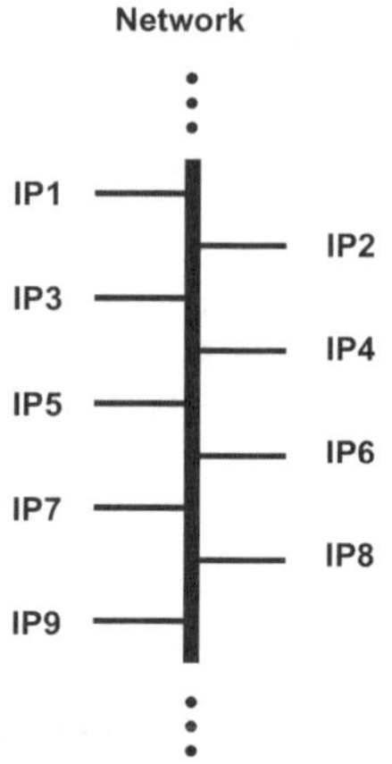

Figure 5 9 nodes on an Extensible Network

4.1 Finite, Programmable Networks

Networking in the large had a primary goal of robust communications. The network protocol was designed so that communications would take place despite the disabling of a large portion of the infrastructure. Large portions of the network can be disabled and communications will still work between remaining portions of the network. Accordingly, networking in the large is designed to support a conceptually infinite number of network nodes; the network protocol was designed to support a system for which the exact number of nodes on the network at any one time need never be known, which is clearly the current reality!

By contrast, a chip has finite extent. Consider a general purpose network, as in Figure 5. The figure shows nine nodes, labeled as nine Intellectual Property (IP) elements. While a simple diagram, Figure 5 contains several implications. First, all of the nodes in the network are considered peers. There is no dominant network node unless one is established with some higher level of programming that sets up the cooperation of the nodes. Second, the figure implies that there is no preferred direction of information exchange between any two nodes on the

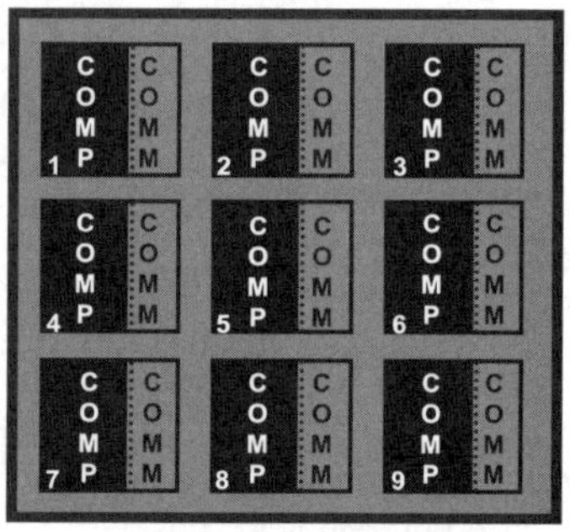

Figure 6 9 IP blocks with NoC interfaces

network. Again, if one node is preferred to another, this must be set up in a programming context. Third, the diagram implies that the network is extensible; nodes may be added to (or subtracted from) the network and the network abstraction will be preserved. The number of nodes is conceptually unbounded. Finally, the state in the system is presumed to be perfectly distributed. Each node in the system may contain state, but the state of the system is the aggregate state of all nodes in the system at any point in time.

While the network of Figure 5 is the inspiration for NoC, Figure 6 illustrates how nine intellectual property (IP) blocks with common network interfaces might be placed on an SoC. For most network models, each PE on a network includes support for network communication. Figure 6 shows this for the single chip where the nine IP blocks are divided into computation and communication parts. The similarities between Figure 5 and Figure 6 are that each of the IP blocks have equal access to a global network that allows the blocks to communicate in a GALS manner. Further, packets will be used for information exchange between the IP Blocks.

However, there are significant differences between the networks of Figure 5 and Figure 6. While the number of IP Blocks shown in Figure 6 is conservative at only nine, the important point is that it is a fixed set. While it will be possible to conceive of hundreds of PEs in the next several years the actual number and types of PEs on a single chip will be known at design time. Packet exchange can take place in a pre-programmed manner; the state upon which dynamic decision making is based can be finite.

Note that acknowledging the finite nature of an SoC does not diminish the scalable properties of communications organization around a network. It remains useful to have a communications standard that applies for ever-larger systems. However, the scalable abstraction must not constrain designers from taking advantage of optimizing software and hardware around a fixed set of programmable resources.

Because the chip has a fixed set of PEs, it is possible to explicitly define and coordinate a level of global state around which dynamic, control flow decisions can be made. This leads us to our second modeling primitive:

PV-P2) selection of a fixed set of PEs to be considered a programmable collection.

The fixed set of PEs can then be optimized to the applications for which the chip is being architected.

4.2 Local vs. Global State

At the heart of the issue of SoC design is what state on the chip should be local (private) vs. global (shared). Current design languages and methodologies do not permit designers to reason about trade-offs between the two. Clearly not all state should be global to the chip. However, design paradigms that consider all state to be privatized in individual PEs or IP blocks from the start fail to capture the singular strength of single chip designs — that large collections of PEs can be more closely coupled than ever before with sets of PEs and the method of communication between them more tuned to applications than ever before.

With advances in the ability to integrate multiple computers onto single boards and then chips, shared memory gains advantages [12]. On single chips, busses that support shared memory can become major bottlenecks. However, the use NoCs need not result in the abandonment of global state.

NoCs can create a new class of network, with more specificity of than the prioritization of packets for Quality of Service (QoS) for networks in the large, and less specificity than networks on FPGAs where the network is intended to mimic static routing.

NoCs can be programmed to dynamically make routing decisions for different types of packets. Some packets can be exchanged with greater efficiency than others. Some state can appear shared among resources because it can be exchanged far more efficiently, while other state appears distributed — even though all state is exchanged across the network. This can be based solely on how the network is programmed. This leads us to two additional modeling primitives:

PV-P3) trade-offs of global vs. local state.

PV-P4) customization of the on-chip network protocol.

These provide a basis for distinguishing system level state around which decisions are made across multiple programmable resources [13], and state which supports other computation.

5. System State

While some problems are designed to scale with the number of resources in a system, others require the optimization of a fixed set of processing resources to a problem of fixed size. Applications that have near perfect scalability are rare. Thus, explicitly tuning a set of heterogeneous, interacting resources to specific portions of computation can provide a vast performance improvement over that of a purely scalable or extensible solution. Design optimization for this class of problems must be achieved by optimizing the coordination of a fixed set of elements to carry out the behavior of one or more computational problems. This can be considered analogous to the design of an application specific processor (ASIP) for a class of applications, except that the processor is now a collection of individually programmable, networked PEs.

We define *system state* as state which supports the coordination of information flow among a set of PEs. Like a program counter, system state is finite but may be dynamically updated at runtime. System state can support programmatic, data-dependent decision making across a set of PEs. *Computation state* is all other state in the system, such as that of individual PEs that compute the net system functionality.

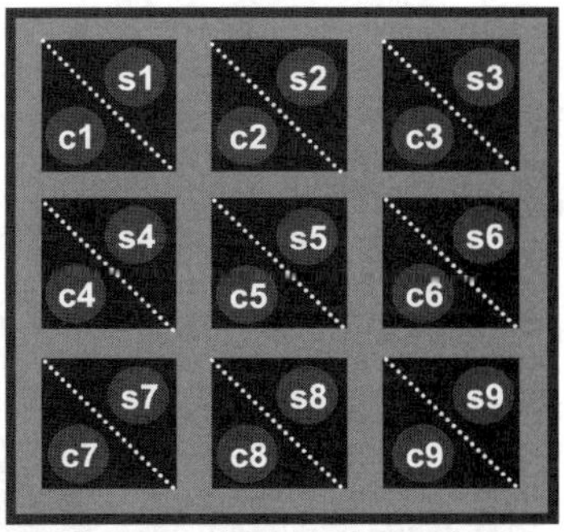

Figure 7 System State (s) & Computation State (c)

Figure 7 shows the same nine IP blocks on a single chip. The state in each block has been divided into computation state (ci) and system state (si). System state can be used as a basis for coordinating information flow among a set of processing resources in a variety of ways.

The mechanisms for coordination of system state can be architected at design time. But it can also support run-time decision making. Thus, system state is more like a chip-level program counter than a schedule synthesized at design time. System state directly supports chip-level programming of SoCs. As such, it is more of an architectural feature which is a by-product of the fact that the design elements of the SoC are heterogeneous multiprocessors. This leads us to our next modeling primitive:

PV-P5) chip-level architectural infrastructure, such as finite system state, distinguished from computation state, around which runtime decisions concerning the coordination of collections of PEs are made.

5.1 Two Forms of System State

Network interfaces coordinate network routing decisions according to a common protocol. While it may be the goal of system designers to keep the amount of packets stored in network queues to a minimum, only in a purely statically scheduled system will there be no information stored in the network. When decision making is made in the presence of state, programming is possible.

Thus, the programming of a network can be a primary factor in coordinating state advancement across the elements of the chip. In addition to state in individual processor resources, the state of the network can also contribute to the system state. This situation is shown in Figure 8, where the system state is shown to have two parts. At each node, i, where i=1...9 for the SoC, there is a contribution to system state from the network as routing state, ri, as well as from the computation at each IP block, the bi. In general, system state at each node, i, is si=(ri,bi), while the overall system state, S, on the SoC, is the set of all system state contributed by each node, or S={s1,...s9}={(r1,b1),...(r9,b9)}.

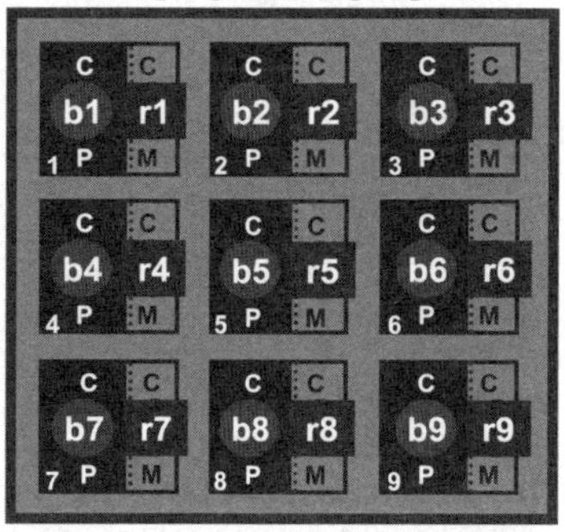

Figure 8 Routing (r) and IP Block (b) Forms of System State

While the non-ideal properties of a network may be thought of as a liability, the possibility to program the network to make decisions about which packets are routed next can be an asset. For instance, system state may be routed at a much higher priority than computation state so that control flow constructs may be set up across collections of PEs. Unlike quality of service (QoS) for networking in the large, which must be based largely upon statistical and analytical techniques because of the lack of a priori knowledge about applications and underlying resources, a chip with a fixed set of PEs permits a network to be considered programmable, setting up a richer set of possibilities for the coordination of PEs than pure dataflow or pure control flow.

5.2 Coordinating System State

Currently approaches simplify the problem of multi-element coordination on SoCs by considering the chip to fall into one of two broad categories, that of control flow based upon a central controller and that of data flow where static forms of scheduling route information between elements. In each case, system state, S, is greatly simplified. We illustrate each of these on our simple SoC diagrams, thus motivating why they are overly simplistic for the rich design space of next generation SoCs.

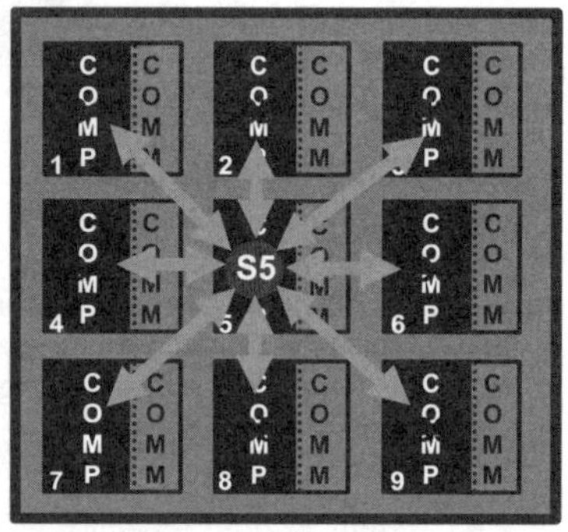

Figure 9 Central Controller

5.2.1 Control Flow Central Controller

Control flow is easiest to realize when a central controller coordinates all system resources as master-slaves; this is shown for the nine node SoC in Figure 9 where block 5 is a central controller. In this case the network might be designed with a naive protocol. All system state resides in the central controller, i.e., S=s5. The main advantage of coordinating system state in this way is in the preservation of a sequential control flow scheme for programming the chip; this is largely a programmatic solution in which distinct blocks of software may be accelerated by execution on custom hardware or on many blocks in parallel, if not both. Many current SoCs fall into this category of design, where a general purpose processor serves as the central controller.

The main disadvantage of this approach is that the central controller can be a bottleneck The system can only execute as fast as the sequential fractions of software [14] can execute on block 5. In general, the software executing on the central controller must be as simple as possible or the central controller must have sophisticated scheduling that tunes the application to the slave processors so that throughput can be maintained.

For certain applications with highly independent parallel threads, this can be a valid solution. However, most of these applications fall into two categories which differ from that anticipated for future SoCs: highly regular computations such as matrix product or server applications in which multiple users access the same set of resources. However, new PVs that permit tuning the application to a heterogeneous set of processors on a programmable network can reveal how control flow can be effectively supported.

5.2.2 Dataflow

Many designs can benefit from optimizations when information flows through a fixed number of hardware resources in a fixed pattern. This dataflow style of design is suited to algorithms for which computation can be effectively pipelined. This situation is depicted in Figure 10 for the nine node SoC.

In the figure, the data is routed from node to node in a statically scheduled manner that allows the nodes to be thought of as interconnected as in a graph. Information is shown entering the system on node 1, then pipelined to exit the system via nodes 6 and 8. The first pipeline is nodes 1, 2, 3, 5, 9, 8, 7, and the second pipeline is nodes 1, 2, 4, 6. All of the system state can be thought of as being in the network where packets act as tokens that trigger computation elements in a static manner, i.e., S={r1,...r9}.

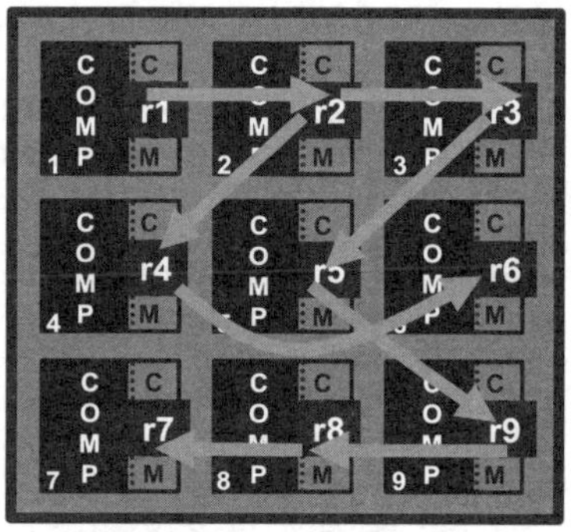

Figure 10 Dataflow on Chip

A significant amount of information about both the application and the processing capabilities of each node needs to be known in advance of designing a statically scheduled system. For data-independent functionality, static scheduling can give the greatest performance; it is much like the pipelining of a processor. For an SoC, with many computation units, the possibility that certain pipeline stages can take advantage of parallel computation units can further enhance system performance. However, the limitations of data flow all focus on the need to consider the system statically scheduled with no data dependencies. Thus, the next primitive:

PV-P6) system state as residing in both the programmable network and the programmable IP blocks.

Beyond either of these two categories, better techniques for coordinating sets of PEs are needed for future SoC designs.

6. The Need for New Programmers' Views

We assert that in the absence of new PVs for SoCs, the demands that future computer system applications place on designers will not be met. Optimal SoC designs will most likely lie between that of a central controller residing on a single PE (Figure 9) and pure dataflow designs (Figure 10) with no central controller to dynamically direct resource cooperation. More complex models of

S will appear in new forms of control flow coordinated across multiple PEs. Designers must be able to effectively consider trade-offs between system state and local state in next generation SoCs.

A PV for an SoC is distinguished from an ISA because it must represent not only the available set of computation, communication and control primitives, but must also include a *means* by which control flow is coordinated around system state. For example, when system-level control flow does not reside in a single processor accessing a single memory (i.e. unlike Figure 9), system infrastructure must be defined and coordinated in new PVs.

6.1 Finite, Distributed Control Flow

Consider the central controller of Figure 9. While many programming models include the controller as a PE, SoCs afford the possibility that the state and functionality upon which control flow decisions are made does not reside on a central PE. This situation can be likened to the way a single scheduler can be formed by the cooperation of schedulers on individual PEs. In distributed system design in the large, the coordination of separately cached copies of data must be explicitly considered. Currently this problem is solved by various operating systems and middle-ware. However, the problem of achieving performance enhancement over a collection of resources is difficult for systems in the large, where extensibility is prioritized. The overall philosophy is one of hiding the properties of the underlying hardware platform from the distributed software applications so that net performance is relative to the available resources. This is an extension of the philosophy that software design should be considered independent of as many properties of the underlying machine upon which it executes as possible. Mechanisms for state coordination across multiple resources in the form of middleware provide the means of thinking in terms of distribution primitives without the need to think in terms of the actual size and capacity of the underlying machine.

However, once a chip is designed, nodes will not be added or subtracted. Control flow can be optimized over a fixed set of PEs by explicit coordination of finite system state if explicit support is provided for design of system infrastructure as a part of the PV of the chip. Finite, distributed control flow is one optimization possible when support is provided for viewing the chip as a programmable set of heterogeneous PEs.

6.2 Multi-path Control

Dynamically scheduled datapaths may be established across sets of PEs on an SoC. Either a central controller or distributed, finite control may dynamically set up patterns of cooperation among PEs where the patterns are tuned to specific programming situations. We refer to this property as *multi-path control.*

Consider PE 1 of Figure 10 to be a central controller, which implements all of the functionality of a present-day personal digital assistant (PDA), plus enhanced HCI and computer-computer networking, as discussed in section 2. Figure 10 shows one way the central controller (PE 1) might set up the cooperation of the remaining PEs in the system when the PDA is acting as a cell phone in the middle of a call. However, when the PDA is not actively processing a call, PE 1 might well set up a different pattern of dataflow among the PEs in the system. In multi-path control, multiple data paths are set up by a scope of control flow, either a single processor or a cooperative collection of processors; PE 1 need not be considered a single processor when control decisions are made using distributed, finite control. This leads us to our final proposed modeling primitive:

PV-P7) novel architectural views for coordinating system state and control flow across a finite number of PEs such as finite, distributed control flow and multi-path control.

7. Conclusions and Future Directions

The set of proposed primitives that new design languages must support as discussed throughout this paper might seem straightforward. However, the important point is that existing system design approaches and languages such as SystemC do not directly include them.

Current languages do not permit designers to think in terms of systems in which not only will individual PEs be programmable, but the chip, as a whole, is considered programmable, including the network that supports information exchange across the chip. SoC hardware is a fixed set of PEs; its PVs can significantly differ from past forms of system organization.

Next generation design languages must enable the architecting of novel SoC designs, focusing on explicit support for the design and programming of system infrastructure that coordinates information flow across a fixed set PEs. The modeling primitives of such languages must capture the performance cost-benefit of a rich middle ground, between pure dataflow, pure control flow, pure global state, and pure distributed state. Design languages must also support the design of custom networks and the selection of the PEs that are programmed as a collection, forming the basis of new programmers' views of SoCs.

8. Acknowledgements

This work was supported in part by ST Microelectronics, General Motors, and the National Science Foundation under Grant 0103706. Any opinions, findings, and conclusions or recommendations expressed in this material are those of the authors and do not necessarily reflect the views of the NSF.

I would like to thank Alex Bobrek, Jeffrey E. Nelson, and Joshua J. Pieper for their valuable comments on this paper. Much appreciation to Donald E. Thomas for his feedback on this paper and his incomparable support.

9. References

[1] "Are Single-Chip Multiprocessors in Reach?" *IEEE Design & Test*, Jan - Feb 2001.

[2] W. Dally, B. Towles. "Route Packets, Not Wires: On-Chip Interconnection Networks," *DAC* 2001.

[3] L. Benini, G. De Micheli, "Networks on chips: A New SoC Paradigm," *IEEE Computer*, January 2002.

[4] F. Balarin, et al. *Hardware-Software Co-design of Embedded Systems. The Polis Approach.* Boston: Kluwer. 1997.

[5] W. Cesario, G.. Nicolescu, et al. "Colif: A Design Representation for Application-Specific Multiprocessor SOCs," *IEEE Design & Test of Computers*, Sept. - Oct. 2001.

[6] K. Keutzer, et al. "System-Level Design: Orthogonalization of Concerns and Platform-Based Design," *IEEE T. CAD*. '00.

[7] Special Issue on Ubiquitous Computing, *Communications of the ACM,* December 2002.

[8] B. Grattan, G. Stitt, F. Vahid. "Codesign-extended applications." *CODES 2002*.

[9] J. Paul, D.Thomas. "A Layered, Codesign Virtual Machine Approach to Modeling Computer Systems," *DATE* 2002.

[10] A. Cassidy, J. Paul, D. Thomas. "Layered, Multi-Threaded, High-Level Performance Design," *DATE* 2003.

[11] D. Skillcorn, D. Talia. "Models and Languages for Parallel Computation," *ACM Computing Surveys*. 1998.

[12] D. Culler, J. Singh. *Parallel Computer Architecture, A Hardware/Software Approach.* S.F.: Morgan Kaufman. 1999.

[13] J.Paul, A.Bobrek, J. Nelson, J. Pieper, D. Thomas. "Schedulers as Model-Based Design Elements in Programmable Heterogeneous Multiprocessors," *DAC* 2003.

[14] G. Amdhal. "Validity of the Single Processor Approach to Achieving Large Scale Computing Capabilities," *AFIPS 1967 Spring Joint Computer Conference*. pp. 483-485.

Security Wrappers and Power Analysis for SoC Technologies

C.H. Gebotys, Y. Zhang
Dept of Electrical and Computer Engineering
University of Waterloo
(519)885-1211
cgebotys@uwaterloo.ca

ABSTRACT

Future wireless internet enabled devices will be increasingly powerful supporting many more applications including one of the most crucial, security. Although SoCs offer more resistance to bus probing attacks, power/EM attacks on cores and network snooping attacks by malicious code are relevant. This paper presents a methodology for security on NoC at both the network level (or transport layer) and at the core level (or application layer) is proposed. For the first time a low cost security wrapper design is presented, which prevents unencrypted keys from leaving the cores and NoC. This is crucial to prevent untrusted software on or off the NoC from gaining access to keys. At the core level (application layer) power analysis attacks are examined for the first time for parallel and adiabatic architectural cores. With the emergence of secure IP cores in the market, a security methodology for designing NoCs is crucial for supporting future wireless internet enabled devices.

Categories and Subject Descriptors

C.3 [**Special Purpose and Application Based Systems**].

General Terms: Security

Keywords: Design, Security, Performance, VLIW, Adiabatic.

1. INTRODUCTION

Future nanometer technologies will support large SoC or 3D ICs with a mix of architectures and technologies. A large number of heterogeneous cores on the SoC may be application specific. For example security cores already exist on the market and will be crucial in future wireless SoCs. Also cores may have varying degrees of parallelism or may be implemented in various technologies including adiabatic circuitry to significantly decrease core energy dissipation. Design methodologies must be developed for security on SoCs.

As networks move to the chip level, increasing the complexity of the system on a chip (SoC), security increases in importance. Architectures must be designed which protect the user's private key from attackers (in particular untrusted software resident from invasive computing or untrusted external devices such as EM reading devices or hostile IP hosts). In general it will be of primary importance to additionally protect the secure IP cores from untrusted software and prevent exposure of keys outside of the SoC and even within the SoC communication network. Although there is new research studying networks on chips (NoC) [2], there is a lack of research studying how security would be integrated into these SoCs. Furthermore outside of smartcard research[6,7] (which typically is limited to cheaper 8-16 bit processors) few researchers have examined secure implementations of cryptographic software under the threat of power attacks on highly parallel or adiabatic cores. Design for security involves secure design of hardware cores, secure algorithm design, and secure network protocols, all important for NoCs of the future.

This paper illustrates a general security methodology for NoCs. At the processor core level, security cores must be resistant to power/EM attacks. At the network level, a security wrapper supporting symmetric key cryptography is implemented for communication between IP cores on the NoC which are involved in security applications. A security wrapper for each core and a central key-keeper core are proposed to ensure that unencrypted keys do not leave any core and the NoC itself. Security for NoCs has not previously been studied, however this approach has advantages for IP core vendors providing further protection of not only their hardware IP but also software which will run on their IP core. At the core level the impact of parallelism and adiabatic circuits on power/EM analysis is illustrated for the first time. This paper presents a security methodology for NoCs at both the network and core level which is crucial for future nanometer technologies.

NoC research has emerged as an important and growing area of interest. Researchers are developing tools to customize or reprogram the communication network design[2] as well as investigating reliability issues. Network layers for NoCs have been suggested in [2], specifically: the physical layer, architecture and control layer (data link, network and transport) , and software layer (application and system). NoCs in general will be highly constrained by reliability in addition to power dissipation and error correcting codes will be a necessity[2]. However security or security protocols have not been researched for NoCs.

Researchers have examined ASIC implementations of various encryption algorithms, system architectures for wireless security[5], and recently a number of secure IP cores have emerged such as AES cores, SHA-1, 3DES cores and others. IP

CODES+ISSS'03, October 1–3, 2003, Newport Beach, California, USA.

core protection includes both hardware protection such as watermarking techniques and simulation with software module IP protection in a CAD design environment such as [8]. In the later case public key cryptography is used to support simulation of chips which include software IP modules as well as hardware IP cores. A JavaCAD environment is described for designers which protects IP yet simulates designs which include hardware IP cores running third party IP software modules for example.

Power or electromagnetic (EM) attacks of NoCs may be relevant since cores may have separate power pins and EM radiation from the communication network may be significant. Researched power attacks of smart cards, have utilized general purpose processors with low clock frequencies [1,6,7] and more sophisticated processors with parallel instruction execution have only recently been reported in the literature[11]. Researchers have suggested security against power attacks be achieved through 70% increase in computational cost[3]. However in portable devices, energy dissipation is very important hence a general purpose processor not optimized for power dissipation will not be suitable for running encryption in wireless communication[5].

Thus a methodology for security is crucial for future NoC designs and a necessity for designing with secure IP cores available on the market today. This research presents a security methodology at the network level (or transport layer) and at the core level (or application layer). At the network level the security design utilizes a special key-keeper core and a network key on the NoC. This security architecture is independent of the type of communication network on the chip in general. The security methodology ensures no unencrypted keys leave cores or the NoC and additionally supports IP secure cores running only trusted software. At the core level (or application layer) differential power analysis is demonstrated and the impact of parallelism and adiabatic circuits on security is analyzed. The next section will describe the security methodology for NoCs at the communication network level, followed by security methodology at the core level in section 3, specifically for software running on a VLIW core and an adiabatic circuit.

2. SECURITY FOR NoC

In NoCs the communication network may vary significantly from packet based communication to global bus communication[2]. The NoC will be required to support security for several reasons such as: 1) wireless communication or IP enabled applications requiring user authentication, encryption; 2) product authentication

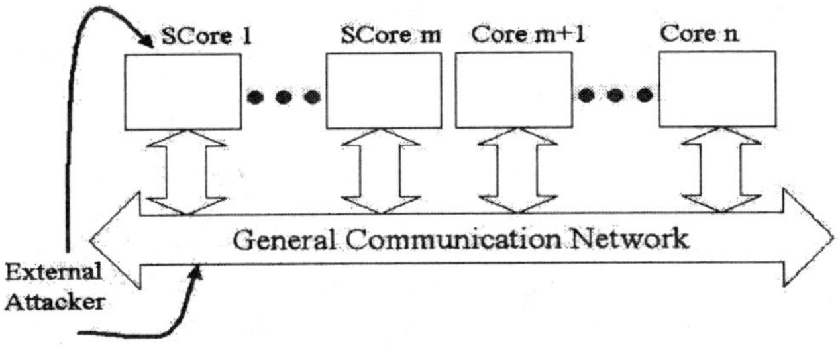

Figure 1. An example of a general NoC and security attacks.

(preventing counterfeit products); 3) NoC chip authentication; 4) even IP-core authentication on the NoC itself. We will assume NoCs have *m* secure cores (or SCores in figure 1) and another *n-m* other cores, where $m \geq 1$. A secure core is defined as a hardware IP core which can execute one or more security applications (such as encryption, authentication, key exchange, etc) and it may also be able to execute other general non-security application as well. This NoC scenario suits current secure IP cores on the market today as well where authentication and encryption requires several secure cores such as an AES core, a SHA-1 core, etc. The NoC should in either case be resistant to external attacks which can obtain data from the communication network (through external I/O pins attached to the communication network or EM radiation from it), shown as bottom arrow in figure 1 or through power analysis attacks on individual core power pins (see top arrow figure1). Key distribution is important, since keys are updated from time to time, the NoC will require a mechanism to allow downloading of the key onto the chip and into the memory of the secure IP core. Furthermore malicious software running on a regular core (Core) could attempt to acquire keys or send false keys to security cores. Protection against malicious software and untrusted cores must be supported in the NoC. The proposed security methodology at the network level will be described next. It supports key protection, and secure transmission on the communication network.

The network level methodology for security is based on symmetric key cryptography. A secure core can be a AES core, SHA-1 core, a prime field operation elliptic curve core, etc... Each secure core (*i*) has its own security wrapper, see shaded (*Kn*) boxes in figure 2. The security wrapper is located between the secure core and the network wrapper (see figure 2).

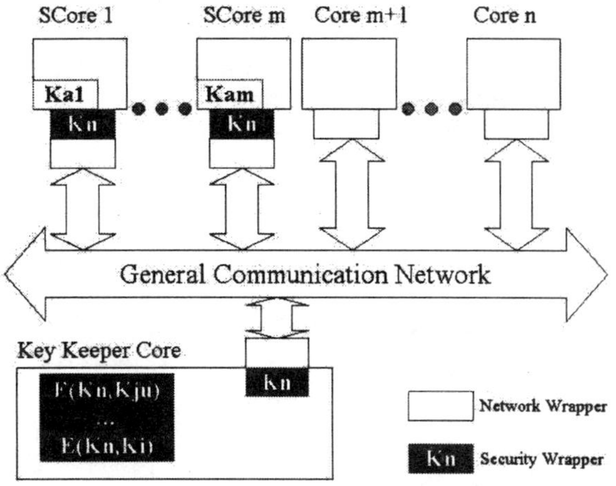

Figure 2. Security methodology at network level protecting keys.

The keys stored in the security wrapper are 1) the network master key, *Kn*, and 2) the working key *Kn'* (generated from the master key *Kn*), both stored in non-volatile memory within the security wrapper and 3) message authentication code (MAC) keys, *Kmac i* and *Kmac k* (key keepers mac key), are also stored. Since SCores may often receive keys from the key keeper (ie. user keys for encryption, or authentication), the key keeper's mac key (*Kmac k*) is stored for convenience in the security wrapper for quick authentication. If sufficient memory is available and security requirements are high it is possible that mac keys of other SCores could be also stored in the security wrapper. Inside the secure core an authentication key (*Kai* in figure 2) is stored in non-volatile memory, for use in core authentication and core software authentication. The security wrapper performs a number of functions including 1) encryption of messages from the secure core to the network E(.), 2) decryption of messages from the network to the secure core D(.), 3) create a hash of a message h(.), and 4) create a MAC mac(.). The hardware of the security wrapper will be described later.

A key-keeper core in the NoC (see figure 2) is responsible for secure key distribution on the NoC. This core is also a secure core (and therefore has its own security wrapper). It stores encrypted keys, such as encrypted keys for individual applications, encrypted user private keys (*Kju*) (ie. authentication or encryption keys to be used for decryption of audio, video, email, ebanking or signature generation or authentication of outgoing messages, etc), other users public keys (*Ki*) (ie. for encryption of outgoing audio, video, email, signature verification, etc) and SCore MAC keys (*Kmac i*). The key keeper is also responsible for updating the master network key (*Kn*) at random times using a symmetric key exchange protocol.

The following terminology will be used to describe the functionality of the security in the security wrapper: E(a,m) represents encryption of *m* using key *a*; D(b,c) is decryption of *c* using key *b*; h(m) is a *x*-bit hash of a message *m*; and MAC(k,m) is a *n*-bit MAC of message *m* using key *k*. Also for SCore i, let $tcnt_j$ represent the count of how many messages were sent to SCore j, $rcnt_j$ represent how many message were received from SCore j and || represent concatenation. Consider sending a message from SCore i to SCore j. The following three steps are involved 1) generate a working key (since it is well known that one should not use the same key to transmit different messages), 2) Encrypt the message, and 3) provide authentication (step 3 below) or integrity (step 4 below) by attaching a tag to the encrypted message. These three steps are performed within the security wrapper of SCore i and are illustrated below:

1. $Kn' = h(Kn \,\|\, tcnt_j)$
   $tcnt_j$ ++
2. $c = E(Kn', m)$
3. $t = mac(Kmac\ i, c)$
   Send $c \,\|\, t$
4. or
   $i = h(c)$
   Send $c \,\|\, i$

Only SCore's have access to the mac keys of SCores. Hence an untrusted core cannot obtain the mac keys. It is assumed that the SCores only run trusted software (and do not have any malicious codes). The security methodology tries to minimize the chance that the untrusted cores may be able to obtain the network master key, through changing it at random times. However even if the master network key is obtained, the working keys and mac keys would be difficult to obtain. SCore j will receive the message ({*c* || i} or {*c* || t}) by performing the following steps inside the security wrapper.

5. $Kn' = h(Kn \,\|\, rcnt_i)$
   $rcnt_i$ ++
6. $m = D(Kn', c)$
7. $t1 = mac(Kmac\ i, c)$
   If t1 == t accept else request retransmission
8. or
   $i1 = h(c)$
   if i1 == i accept else request retransmission

This basic protocol, for exchanging messages, supports key transfer from the key keeper to SCores, the updating of new authenticated keys which have been sent to the portable device, and others. For example using this basic protocol new authenticated user keys can be authenticated using authentication SCores, decrypted using AES SCores, and reencrypted with working network keys and sent back to the key keeper for storage. Each transmission on the network ensures unencrypted keys or messages are never sent between SCores. Hash tags ensure that the data has not changed during transmission. MACs attached to encrypted mesasge are used to verify that the encrypted message came from a trusted source.

One possible suggestion for hardware of the security wrapper will be presented next. The hardware to be described is a very low cost approach to supporting encryption, hashing and mac generation. The security wrapper will contain LFSRs (linear feedback shift registers), general shift registers, counters, XOR gates and small amount of non-volatile memory for storage of the working key, and the mac keys. The following terminology will be used to describe the hardware: LFSR(s) represents a 1 bit output from a LFSR with seed *s* (or it is clocked for *y* cycles if a *y*-bit output is implied in the formula); $\{\}_{m-x\,..\,m}$ represent the last *x* bits of a *m*-bit quantity in brackets; let + represent exclusive or operation; and let m_i represent bit i of M. Now the hardware defining the functions of the security wrapper will be given:

$$E(k, m) = C \mid c_i = m_i + [\,LFSR(k) + c_{i-m}\,]$$

$$D(k, c) = M \mid m_i = c_i + [\,LFSR(k) + c_{i-m}\,]$$

$$mac(k, m) = E(k, m)_{m-n\,..\,m}$$

$$h(m) = LFSR(m)_{m-x\,..\,m}$$

The LFSR is used as the low cost key stream generator. The mac() or h() will identify if the message was modified in transit (due to noise or reliability problems on NoC). The LFSR streaming cipher is used in cipher feedback mode which is ideal for NoC's since synchronization errors are recoverable. Furthermore cipher text errors affect only the corresponding bits in the plaintext in the design above, hence minimal retransmission is required for correcting errors.

The internal SCore authentication key (key located in SCore, not in security wrapper) which has not been used so far is important for a number of security purposes. For example secure cores could receive new software upgrades (wirelessly) from their IP core vendors. Since only trusted software is assumed to be running on security cores, this new software would have to be authenticated. This is performed by sending to the NoC executables authenticated with the internal private authentication key of the secure core, *Kai* in figure 2, which only the vendor of the IP core can do since they are the only ones who know the secure core's private key, *Kai*. Again this upgrade can be performed remotely or wirelessly. Authentication (for example with crypto checksums to ensure all security code executables are authenticated) could occur within the SCore (not the security wrapper) to safeguard the private SCore authentication key.

Additionally the vendor of the IP core can use the core's private authentication key to prevent illegal use of the core in unauthorized NoCs (which have not paid license fees etc for use of the core). The core vendors would create an activation key *(K_activation)* for their core to be used in the NoC from the cores Kai and the IDs of the other cores in the network. Legal uses of the core would receive this activation key from the core vendor and store it encrypted in the key keeper core. For example on reset of the NoC the secure core would receive an activation key (*K_activation*) from the key keeper and verify this key by calculating its own security function (F(), which would be encryption for an encryption core, etc) with its private key (*Kai*) and the concatenation of all other core IDs (obtained from polling all other cores) on the NoC. For example if *K_activation* = = F(*Kai*, core ID 1|| core ID 2 ||…core ID n), then the secure core will function properly else it will not operate and shut down permanently. Standards would have to exist so that each core would have a core ID number. Ensuring confidentiality of communications on the on-chip network, and authenticity of executables which utilize private keys, a secure SoC environment for security applications is possible. Next the core level security will be addressed illustrating how different architectures within a core can affect the security (specifically susceptibility to differential power attacks).

3. SECURITY FOR CORES

3.1 Application Layer

The previous section provided a methodology for ensuring that key's are safe within the communication network. Security within the secure IP cores is also important. Since cores will typically have their own power pins on SoC chips, differential power analysis (DPA) attacks on cores will be relevant. The cores typically may be application specific and vary significantly with respect to architecture. Cores may also be optimized for power. For example application-specific cores which dissipate large amounts of energy may have to use adiabatic architectues to avoid hotspots on the NoC chip. Specifically adiabatic circuits will be briefly introduced in section 3.1 followed by an introduction to differential power analysis in section 3.2. Finally results of DPA applied to both parallel architectures and adiabatic architectures are presented in section 3.3.

3.2 Introduction to Adiabatic Circuits

Adiabatic CMOS logic circuits have been reported for their potentials for low-power VLSI applications. Early adiabatic logic circuits used diodes or diode-like devices for the purpose of precharge, which caused the unavoidable energy loss due to the threshold voltage of the diodes. Later on, the cascode voltage switch logic concept was adopted to get rid of the diode from the circuit. An efficient charge recovery logic was proposed based on this concept in which the diodes are eliminated. But the outputs were still not full-swing due to the existance of the threshold voltage of two switching PMOS devices, resulting in non-adiabatic dissipation. After that, a full swing energy efficient logic (eel) [9] circuit was reported to give out a better performance, but the clock system was very complex (it needed eight clocks: four ramp-like power clocks and four pulse clocks) and therefore not practical. A novel adiabatic differential switch logic (adsl) with bootstrap technique introduced in [10] achieved better noise immunity, higher operation frequency and less energy dissipation. The conventional dynamic logic (con), full swing energy efficient logic (eel) and adiabatic differential swing switch logic (adsl) will be power analyzed for security purposes in section 3.3. To illustrate how secure these varying architectures may be, differential power analysis, DPA, is used. The next section will introduce DPA.

3.3 Introduction to DPA

The DPA attack which correlates power to data placed on the bus utilizes the following variables: $C_i(t)$ represents the instantaneous power at time t of the ith power trace, where $i=1,\dots,n$; and j is the bit of the data placed on the bus being attacked in the ith execution of the algorithm. The attack makes a guess on how the data was transformed (for example in DES the attacker guesses the 6bit key). Since the attacker knows the input data used to generate each power trace (the plaintext in DES), the attacker can determine the data value computed resulting from the guessed computation. With the guess the attacker partitions the power traces into two groups according to bit j of the guessed data value (or data being attacked in DES which is output of Sbox). One group contains all power traces where bit j, or b_j, of the guessed data value on the bus is equal to 0 and the other group contains all power traces whose bit j of the guessed data value is equal to 1. Let $x_1(t) = \{C_i(t) \mid \forall i = 1,..n, b_j = 0\}$

$x_2(t) = \{C_i(t) \mid \forall i = 1,..n, b_j = 1\}$ be the two groups of power traces. Then the difference of means or differential power trace is :

$$\overline{x_1(t)} - \overline{x_2(t)}$$

The standard deviation of the difference of means is defined as :

$$\sqrt{\frac{\sigma_1(t)^2}{n1} + \frac{\sigma_2(t)^2}{n2}}$$

If the guess made was correct there would be a DPA characteristic or "peak" in the differential trace, otherwise the guess would be wrong. The DPA characteristic (or peak) is significant if it is much greater than the standard deviation of the difference of means. In this paper we use 2 standard deviations to test the significance as given below:

$$\overline{x_1(t)} - \overline{x_2(t)} > 2\sqrt{\frac{\sigma_1(t)^2}{n1} + \frac{\sigma_2(t)^2}{n2}}$$

In DPA attacks on DES applications, the largest DPA characteristic from 64 differential traces is chosen to determine which of the 6 bits of the key were the correct guess. However in other public key cryptographic attacks since only one differential trace is used to guess the first key bit, the above formula is important in helping to determine if the guess was correct or not.

3.4 DPA Results: parallelism, adiabatic

DPA results using real power measurements and HSPICE power measurements are analyzed in this section. Real power measurements of a VLIW processor core[4] is utilized for analysis of the impact of parallelism on DPA. Three adiabatic circuits are analyzed with HSPICE to study their DPA characteristics. For the adiabatic circuits, a 4-bit pipelined carry lookahead adder (CLA) is used along with a bus and small memory to analyze susceptibility to power attacks. Matlab was used to analyze the power traces and perform the DPA calculations. The DPA peaks are treated as significant if their height exceeds two times the standard deviation of difference of means presented in section 3.2.

A program (ILP 1) was created with single instruction execution sets (no parallelism) using only load data instructions. The program was executed 56 times (each time recording the power trace) and only one data word loaded by 3 pairs of load instructions was changed. Each of the 56 power traces was an average of 50 power traces (for a total of 2800 power traces). The first two instructions were executed near 2.4us, the next two were executed near 2.9us and the last two instructions were executed near 3.5us. The power trace is shown at the top of figure 3. All three DPA peaks are significant as illustrated in figure 4 by taking the differential trace and subtracting the two standard deviations (data above x-axis indicates significance).

The parallel program (ILP 5) utilized all parallel execution sets with 4 ALU (logic and arithmetic) instructions and 1 load instruction per cycle. The program was executed 62 times (and power was recorded) each time with different data being loaded in 2 pairs of load instructions. Each power trace was an average of 50 power traces. One power trace, the differential trace of a correct guess of data bit 0 and the differential trace for an incorrect guess of data bit 0 are shown at the bottom of figure 3. The first pair of load instructions occurs near 1.6us and the next pair near 2.2us. The DPA characteristics were 0.0287mA and 0.025mA, lower than the ILP 1 characteristics at the top of figure 3. However both DPA characteristics were also significant as seen in figure 5, where again the differential minus the two standard deviations are plotted.

The DPA of the three adiabatic circuits (adsl, eel, con) are illustrated in figure 6, all shown with same y-axis range (0.06 to -0.02mA). The adsl and eel adiabatic circuits clearly showed a lower DPA characteristic than the same circuit using conventional dynamic logic. Also the adsl dissipates 35% less energy than eel and 68% less energy than con. In the adiabatic circuits the DPA peaks are significant with respect to two standard deviations.

Table 1 compares the DPA characteristics and circuits with previous research. The supply voltage (V), frequency (f in MHz), maximum standard deviation of all power traces together (σ), DPA characteristic (pk), and maximum amplitude of incorrect differential (inc) are listed in the table. The adiabatic circuit characteristics are also listed in this table, however no direct comparison with previous research smartcard processor [6,7] or the parallel processor core (ILP 1, ILP 5) would be applicable since the DPA was only performed on the 4bit ALU circuit. Nevertheless comparisons between adsl, eel and con, the two adiabatic circuits versus conventional logic can clearly be made since all circuits were identical except for the circuit technology. Clearly, as supported by figure 6 the adiabatic circuits have smaller DPA peaks than conventional logic (con) which is advantageous for security.

4. DISCUSSION/CONCLUSIONS

This paper presented for the first time a methodology for security on NoCs. It presented a symmetric-key based cryptography design for securing the communication network within the NoC. Authentication, encryption, key exchange, new user keys, public key storage, etc are supported in this methodology. Additionally there are benefits to the IP core vendor for this setup including more protection of software running on their hardware IP core (a solution to untrusted or invasive software). Another advantage of this new methodology is that copying IP cores without the activation keys (provided by vendors) will prevent their illegal use in SoCs. The symmetric key system simplifies the NoC design

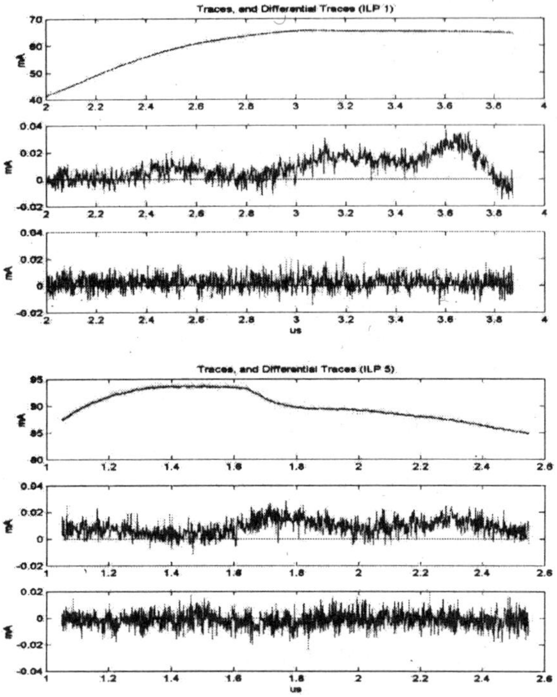

Figure 3 Power traces, differential and incorrect guess for ILP of 1 (top) and 5 (bottom).

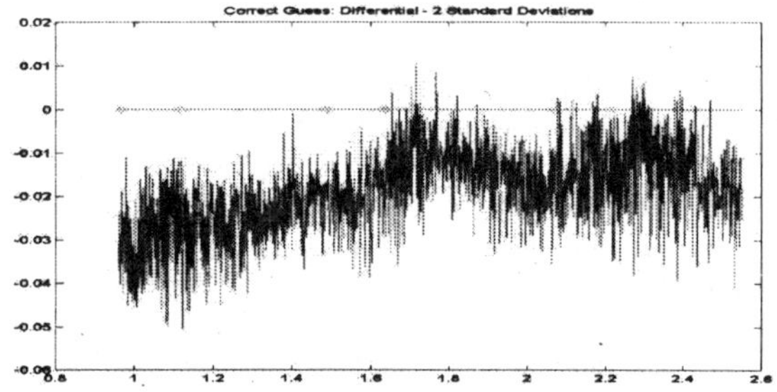

Figure 4. Differential minus two standard deviations for ILP=1.

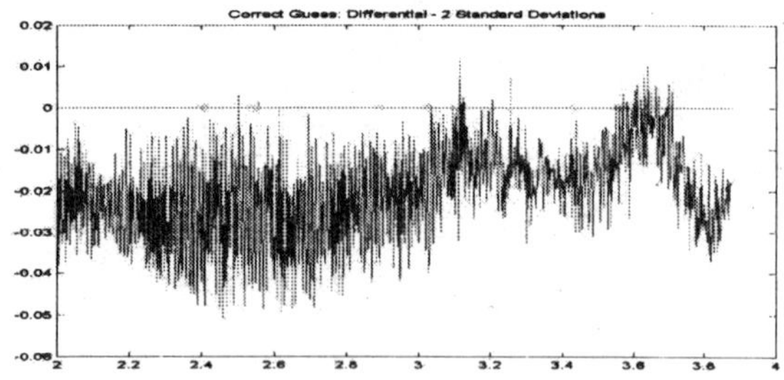

Figure 5. Differential minus two standard deviations for ILP=5.

Table 1. Comparison of DPA results.

	[6]	[7]	ILP 1	ILP 5	con	eel	adsl
V	-	5	2	2	0.8	0.8	0.8
f	3.57	4	100	100	200	200	200
σ	0.3	-	0.1	0.1	9.8E-4	6E-5	3E-5
pk	0.04	0.46	0.03	0.02	.05	.003	.003
inc	0.005	0.20	0.02	0.01	71E-4	3E-4	2E-4

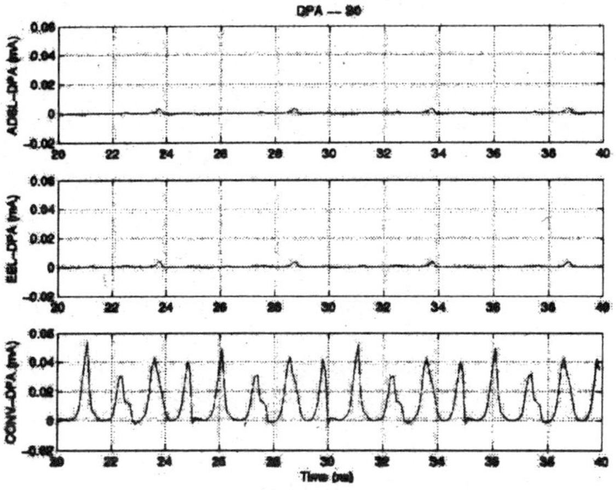

Figure 6. Spice Generated Differentials for adsl, eel, con (top to bottom).

process and key management for security in SoCs. It also helps to protect hardware IP (ie. preventing unauthorized access to it) as well as software IP (ie. preventing modification of software IP through authentication). If user keys were not expected to change, each secure core could also have copies of these keys in local non-shared nonvolatile memory (however this situation is very restrictive and costly, and future NoCs should support new user keys). Key management is still necessary since public keys would still be distributed and sent to secure cores. For added security multiple LFSRs could be used however since the network master key will be changed at random times, the attacks on the LFSR are limited.

The security wrapper could be standardized and implemented by the NoC designer or core vendor. Specific encryption and authentication algorithms and very low cost hardware (with low performance and power overheads) for the security wrapper have been described, however other designs such as RC4 could be used as well depending upon the NoC requirements (where all secure cores in the NoC would have the same secure wrapper). Since reliability is crucial in NoCs of the future its possible that combined decryption and error correcting would be highly advantageous (similar to the cipher feedback mode chosen in this paper). The security methodology could also be extended to support dynamic nature of NoCs where depending upon current battery energy levels and QoS of messages, secure cores could run at different clock frequencies, power levels, etc and operate different encryption algorithms (varying from weak to strong security). Additionally during reset, a new NoC key could also be generated using a pseudo random number generator with a key exchange algorithm to ensure further security.

This study presents for the first time a methodology for security of NoCs by providing network level symmetric-key cryptography for key distribution and at the core level by illustrating the impact of parallelism and adiabatic technology on DPA. Unlike previous research, which has not studied security on NoCs, this scheme has added advantages for protection of software and hardware IP. For core-level security, it is shown that architecture can have an important impact on security, making DPA more difficult (as illustrated by smaller DPA characteristics for parallelism and adiabatic technology). This research is crucial for supporting a methodology for designing security for NoCs which will be prevalent in wireless IP-enabled devices designed with nanometer technologies of the future. The authors would like to thank RIM, CITO, NSERC and Motorola for their support.

5. REFERENCES

[1] P.Kocher, "Timing attacks on implementations of Diffie-Hellman, RSA, DSS, and other systems", LNCS, 1998.

[2] L.Benini, G.DeMicheli, "Networks on Chips: A New SOC Paradigm" Computer, Vol.35, No.1, Jan 2002, pp.70-78

[3] P.Liardet, N.Smart "Preventing SPA/DPA in ECC systems using the Jacobi Form", LNCS 2162, May 2001, pp391-401

[4] "Star*Core 140 DSP Core Reference Manual", Motorola/Lucent, Sept 1999.

[5] S.Ravi, A.Raghunathan, N.Potlapally "Securing Wireless Data: System architecture challenges", ISSS, 2002, pp.195-200.

[6] P.Kocher, J.Jaffe, B.Jun "Differential Power Analysis" Crypto'99, LNCS 1666, 1999

[7] T.Messerges, E.Dabbish, R.Sloan "Investigations of Power analysis attacks on Smartcards" USENIX workshop on Smartcard Technology, 1999.

[8] M.Dalpasso, A.Bogliolo, L.Benini "Hardware /Software IP Protection", Proceedings of DAC, 2000.

[9] C.Yeh, J.Lou and J.Kuo, "1.5 V CMOS full-swingenergy efficient logic (EEL) circuit suitable for low-voltage andlow-power VLSI", Electronics Letters, 33(16), 1997, pp. 1375-1376

[10] Y.Zhang, H.Chen, J.Kuo, "0.8 V CMOS adiabatic differential switch logic circuit using bootstrap technique for low-voltage low-power VLSI", Electronics Letters, 38(24), 2002, pp. 1497 –1499

[11] C.Gebotys, R.Gebotys, "Secure Elliptic Curve Implementations: An analysis of resistance to power-attacks in a DSP processor", CHES 2002, LNCS 2523, pp114-128.

First Results with eBlocks: Embedded Systems Building Blocks

Susan Cotterell, Frank Vahid, Walid Najjar, Harry Hsieh
Department of Computer Science and Engineering
University of California, Riverside
{susanc, vahid, najjar, harry}@cs.ucr.edu
*Also with the Center for Embedded Computer Systems at UC Irvine

Abstract

We describe our first efforts to develop a set of off-the-shelf hardware components that ordinary people could connect to build a simple but useful class of embedded systems. The class of systems, which we call monitor/control systems, is composed primarily of sensors – light, motion, sound, contact, and other types – and output devices – light-emitting diodes, beeping speakers, or even electric relays that control electric appliances like lamps. For example, one monitor/control system would detect if a house's garage door was open at night, and would blink an LED inside the house to alert the homeowner of this normally undesirable situation. Today, configuring even the most basic monitor/control system requires knowledge of electronics and programming. We seek to create a set of building blocks, which we call eBlocks, that would enable someone with no knowledge of electronics or programming to be able to build simple but useful monitor/control systems. We are creating eBlocks largely by incorporating intelligence into previously dumb sensors and output devices, and by developing a set of standards and methods that enable eBlocks to work together seamlessly when connected. eBlocks have only recently become possible due to the extremely low cost, low power, and small size of embedded microprocessors. We describe our first results of creating a basic class of eBlocks, Boolean eBlocks, that from a user's perspective transmit or receive only "yes" or "no" signals. We discuss the internal eBlock design, eBlock system design issues and decisions, and several eBlock-based systems designed by ourselves and by undergraduate students.

Categories and Subject Descriptors

C.3 **[Special-Purpose and Application-Based Systems]**

General Terms

Design, experimentation, human factors.

Keywords

Embedded systems, intelligent homes, networks.

1. Introduction

Home and office environments today typically include numerous embedded computing systems, such as burglar alarm, temperature control, and remote appliance control systems. Those systems are designed by engineers. However, there is a class of useful embedded systems that ordinary people with no engineering training could build themselves if only the right building blocks existed.

We refer to that class of systems as simple *monitor/control systems*. A monitor/control system senses events, such as a person walking across a room, a door being opened, or a button being pressed. Such a system then responds by generating outputs, such as blinking a light-emitting diode (LED), sounding a beep, or turning on an electric relay that controls an electric appliance like a lamp. We focus on human-scale monitor/control systems, referring to events and outputs that a person could observe or generate, as distinguished from other scales of events or outputs, like detecting or generating radio signals.

Human-scale monitor/control systems are grossly under-represented in existing commercial embedded system products. Some applications are available as products, like motion-sensing lights or timer-controlled relays, but these products are very limited in their function and cannot easily be extended or customized. The main reason for the under representation is cost: most applications are too specialized to be cost effective when one considers the many real costs (packaging, marketing, store placement, etc.) of introducing a new consumer product into the market.

Consider the following potential application. New homeowners often forget to close their garage door at night. A useful application would blink an LED inside the house if this condition occurs. Such an application could be built using a light sensor, a magnetic contact switch, a microcontroller that computes a logic function of those two inputs, a wireless transmitter, a wireless receiver, another microcontroller, and an LED. While seemingly simple, building a working system from these components is beyond the skills of ordinary people, and even a challenge for most engineers who haven't been specifically trained in embedded system design. Yet, companies generally could not profit from such a product, since most people are not willing to spend more than perhaps $20-$40 on such a product. People willing to spend much more than that would instead purchase a home alarm system.

Similar applications are plentiful. A storeowner may want to detect a customer at the front counter and sound a beep in the storeroom. A dog owner may want to display if the backyard gate is left open. A cafeteria manager may want a simple way for service line workers to indicate to kitchen staff which food items need replenishing. A hard-of-hearing person may want a small vibrating device that indicates noise (perhaps from a crying baby). A classroom teacher may want students to be able to anonymously vote on various subjects by pressing buttons at their desks. A farm owner may want to detect if there is mail in his remotely located mailbox. A carpool driver may want a way other than honking the horn to inform a passenger that the car is outside the passenger's apartment. All of these applications are useful, but none by itself is in high enough demand to warrant a stand-alone product, and the aforementioned applications have enough differences that prevent a single product from covering all the applications.

We are developing a set of building blocks from which ordinary people could easily implement these and many other applications, without any training in electronics or programming. We refer to these blocks as *eBlocks*, or embedded system building blocks. In this paper, we first discuss related work in Section 2. In Section 3, we describe the subset of eBlocks that we have addressed so far, known as Boolean eBlocks. Section 4 highlights numerous challenges and solutions in designing Boolean eBlocks. Section 5 describes several useful monitor/control systems that we and undergraduate students have designed using Boolean eBlocks. Section 6 discusses eBlock prototypes and the feasibility of battery based eBlocks. Section 7 describes experiences testing eBlocks on various users. Section 8 provides conclusions and points to numerous future directions.

2. Related Work

Much work has been done to simplify and make computing devices more accessible. MIT's Beyond Black Boxes project [6] focuses on providing tools and materials for science education. MIT Crickets, evolved from the Programmable Bricks project [14][15] and Thinking Tag project [2]. A cricket is a tiny computer, powered by a 9-volt battery, that can receive information from two sensors and can control two motors. Crickets are programmed utilizing the Logo language [17][20] – a simple, graphical, highly intuitive language. In fact, Crickets provided the foundation for the Lego Mindstorms [25], which include numerous sensors and actuator Lego blocks that are connected to a central microprocessor block to build a variety of small robots. The central microprocessor block is programmed using a simple graphical language included with the kit. While the Beyond Black Boxes projects seek to motivate people to program crickets, eBlocks seek to enable people to build systems. However, we can of course introduce eBlocks that could be programmed by "advanced" users, and we suspect such programming would build upon the Logo language.

Home automation is another area in which much work on ubiquitous computing has been done. In home automation, an emphasis is placed on interoperability between higher-end consumer electronics, such as audio, video, and other media content, and the PC. However, many problems still exist. A consumer will encounter systems that are complex to set up and maintain. There are a myriad of issues facing consumers discussed in [9] including knowledge of networking, media management, security, and content protection. Such issues quickly overwhelm the majority of the population.

To address some of these problems, a framework to support home interoperability is presented in [19]. A network exists in which devices have the ability to discover, configure, and control other devices on that network. Network devices range from a PC, television, stereo, or a variety of consumer electronics. This type of system eliminates the need for a user to configure and control each device independently on the network. The setup, configuration, and control aspects of the system are transparent to the user and make the system more feasible. There is no need for a professional to setup a device every time a new device is added to the system.

Figure 1: Smart Dust

Courtesy of Joe Kahn

To guarantee interoperability between devices on the network a common protocol is required. The Universal Plug and Play Forum (UPnP) [22][24] is an emerging industry initiative that is trying to make connectivity between stand-alone devices and PCs simple and consistent. They are currently working on defining standards and templates for classes of devices so that when an individual device is added to the network it can easily be integrated, regardless of how the individual devices are implemented because a common interface exists. Home interoperability and UPnP devices are typically complete applications, not building blocks, yet we expect to eventually develop an eBlock that interfaces to a UPnP device.

X10 [26] is another emerging protocol for compatible devices throughout the home to communicate via existing 110V wiring in the house. X10 superimposes a (digital) signal onto the power signal, without interfering with the power signal. X10 devices detect the superimposed signal and look for their ID number, and then react to commands to turn on or off. A common application of X10 is to control all the lights or power appliances of a home from a single master device.

Smart sensors [13][18][23] embed a sensor's data sheet information directly in the sensor device, typically in a non-volatile memory like EEPROM. This embedded information is known as a Transducer Electronic Data Sheet, or TED and includes information such as the manufacturer ID, model number, sensor's use, calibration information, voltage levels, and temperature ranges. The embedded information relieves a system designer from having to manually enter the information into their software and enables some automatic configuration. IEEE has developed several standards related to such basic smart sensors, known as IEEE P1451 [12]. In addition, advanced smart sensors seek to perform processing in sensors themselves, primarily to reduce the amount of network data traffic [3]. Sensors which have added intelligence, are able to perform tasks such as conversions, monitor machinery for wear, perform image compression, monitor neighborhoods for real-time pollen count, or even spy plane applications, as discussed in [1][11][21].

There has also been work done in miniature wireless sensing devices [4][7][8], referred to as the Mica wireless platform. These devices have sensing, communication, and I/O capabilities and are intended to last years in the field utilizing only a pair of AA batteries. Each Mica node consists of processor/radio circuits that are sandwiched together with sensor circuits. A variety of sensor circuits such as temperature, magnetic field, light, acceleration, vibration, and acoustics are available. A system designer would customize the Mica node to their particular application by selecting which sensors are incorporated. A collection of Mica nodes are capable of self-configuring a multi-hop network, utilizing RF communication, and support dynamic reprogramming within the network. The nodes also contain the TinyOS operating system and allow designers to customize communication protocols to suite their networks. The newest generation of these wireless platforms is Smart Dust [5][26], which are on the millimeter scale in size as shown in Figure 1 – illustrating just how small devices like eBlocks could eventually become. Smart Dust utilizes thick film batteries, a solar cell, or both for power, providing roughly 1-2 Joules per day. These devices share many of the characteristics of the Mica nodes but utilize optical communication and have more restrictive power utilization limits.

The field of sensor networks in general focuses on coarse-grained network-level applications. In addition, the Mica and Smart Dust platforms require knowledge of the underlying architecture and communication, programming, operating systems, networking, etc. Unfortunately, ordinary people do not have such expertise. While some of the sensing capabilities of Mica and Smart Dust are similar to eBlocks, the internal design and communication interface requirements for eBlocks are vastly different, as eBlocks are intended for a different audience, namely people with no engineering experience. While designing a low-power, self-configuring device is useful in developing eBlocks, we must incorporate such features without requiring any additional effort by the user.

3. Defining Basic eBlocks

We initially defined a basic set of eBlocks from which a variety of monitor/control systems could be built. A principle guiding the definition task was that eBlocks should be intuitive and easy to understand by nearly anybody old enough to want to build such a system. In particular, we assumed no engineering or technical training from the users, and no training in logic. We sought for eBlocks to be usable almost immediately with little training, and to be usable in remote locations without access to a centralized computer. Based on these requirements, we early on determined that eBlocks should be decentralized and should work just by connecting them together.

3.1 eBlocks that Operate on Boolean Values

We sub-divided the basic set of eBlocks into three categories:

1. Sensor blocks – These blocks detect environmental events of interest, such as motion, light, sound, or contact.
2. Output blocks – These blocks generate events for observation or control, such as lighting an LED, sounding a tone, or controlling an electric relay.
3. Communication/logic blocks – These blocks assist with communication among sensor blocks, supporting wireless transmission, wireless reception, boosting of signals over long wires, storing of signals for certain durations, and logically combining multiple signals into a new signal.

After initially exploring potential definitions of eBlocks and creating hypothetical eBlock-based systems, we realized that the challenge was enormous. We thus decided to first focus on a restricted but still very useful subset of eBlocks that transmit and receive Boolean values only, as opposed to also including integer values or other types of values. We refer to such blocks as *Boolean eBlocks.*

Boolean eBlocks presented an initial challenge of choosing the most intuitive representation of "true" and "false." We found that ordinary people are not particularly comfortable with the notions of "true" and "false" in the context of monitor/control systems. (In contrast, to a reader of this paper, true and false are likely obvious concepts, as the reader likely has some experience using Boolean logic). After considering numerous possible representations, such as true and false, 1 and 0, high and low, on and off, etc., and presenting different possibilities to non-engineers of various ages, we settled upon *yes* and *no* as the most intuitive for eBlocks. For example, we describe a motion sensor by asking the question: "Is motion detected? *yes* means motion is detected, *no* means motion is not detected."

3.2 A Basic Boolean eBlock Catalog

We sought to develop a catalog of Boolean eBlocks that balanced the conflicting goals of having the fewest possible eBlocks, of having eBlocks that were intuitive, and of having eBlocks that required minimal configuration expertise. At one extreme, we could have a single eBlock that could do anything, but that eBlock would likely be big, power-hungry, and require extensive programming. At the other extreme, we could build a unique eBlock for every possible component, but that would result in an intimidating large catalog too big for a user to readily comprehend, and systems that required too many basic components for users to reasonably build.

We developed our eBlock catalog by considering a dozen applications, many of which we listed in the introduction. We started with a minimal set of eBlocks, and introduced new eBlocks, or added features to an existing eBlock, only when building an application with the minimal set seemed to be too difficult for an ordinary user.

Below are the eBlocks we defined.

- Sensor eBlocks:
    - Magnetic Contact Switch - detects when contact between two sensors is made
    - Light-Beam Switch - composed of a light source and light sink, this device detects when the light beam is broken
    - Motion Sensor - detects the presence of motion
    - Light Sensor - detects the presence of light
    - Sound Sensor - detects the presence of sound
    - 3-Key Entry - detects if a predetermined sequence of keys is pressed correctly
    - 10-Key Entry - detects if a predetermined sequence of keys is pressed correctly
    - Button - detects when a button is pressed
- Output eBlocks:
    - Green/Red LED - blinks a green light when input is *yes*, blinks a red light when input is *no*
    - Blinking LED - blinks a light when input is *yes*
    - Beeper - emits a beeping sound when input is *yes*
    - Electric Relay - transmits electricity when input is *yes*
- Communication/Logic eBlocks:
    - Pulse Generator - outputs *yes* and *no* pulse where the *yes* time and *no* time is user defined
    - Clock Timer - user sets pins to indicate at which times to toggle the output over a 24-hour period
    - Splitter - receives a signal and replicates that signal on each output
    - Toggle - input of *yes* toggles the current value outputted by the device
    - Prolonger - input of *yes* causes output to become *yes*, output resets to *no* when the device times out

- Wireless Transmitter - wirelessly transmits a signal to another eBlock
- Wireless Receiver - wirelessly receives a signal from another eBlock
- 2-Input Logic Block - configurable logic block programmed by the user via DIP switch
- 3-Input Logic Block - configurable logic block programmed by the user via DIP switch
- Yes/No Block - outputs a constant *yes* or *no* depending on user defined setting

Table 1 includes a more detailed description for a subset of eBlocks used in later examples.

4. Design Issues

We now describe several challenges and solutions during the design of eBlocks.

4.1 Logic Blocks

A key challenge was finding a way to create an eBlock that would generate an output that is a logical expression of the block's input values. The challenge lied not in technical issues, but rather user interface issues. In the garage door example in the introduction, we want to blink an LED when the garage door is open and outside is dark. Our sensors would be a magnetic contact switch that outputs *yes* when the door is closed (let's call this signal *A*) and an outdoor light sensor that outputs *yes* when light is detected (signal *B*). The correct logical expression would be *A'B'*, or the door is not closed and light is not detected. However, this simple exercise of creating the correct Boolean logic expression is well beyond the skills of ordinary people. For example, when we began to explain the logical expression approach to a group of potential users, one of the users interrupted to say "I have *no clue* what you are talking about." Again, the reader of this paper is likely *not* an ordinary person in the context of comfort with Boolean logic. The task becomes even more difficult if the user wants to detect multiple conditions, e.g. *AB + A'B'*. Thus, creating a logic eBlock that requires the user to enter a Boolean expression is undesirable. Some studies show that most people can't form basic logical expressions, and this largely explains why such expressions are almost completely unused in common applications like Internet search queries [10].

We observed potential users naturally trying to figure out the function of a logic eBlock by enumerating the input possibilities and deciding the appropriate output for each possibility – in other words, creating a truth table. After considering numerous options and observing potential users, we developed the following initial solution to the challenge. We provide two and three input logic eBlocks. For a two-input logic eBlock, we provide a four-switch DIP (dual-inline package) switch. Each switch can be moved to a *yes* or *no* position. The eBlock has two inputs *A* and *B*. Each of the four switches correspond to a particular combination of input values, as follows:

A	B	Output
no	no	
no	yes	
yes	no	
yes	yes	

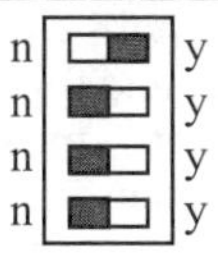

This simple table can be printed directly on the eBlock package next to the DIP switch. Likewise, an eight-pin DIP switch would be used for a 3-input logic eBlock. This solution has the benefit of minimizing the translation of the input values to output values and avoids "encoding" the logic expression in a Boolean function. The solution involves having the user simply provide the appropriate output for each possible input, something users tended to try to do anyways.

A limitation of the above solution is that the user must still translate sensor outputs into variables *A* and *B*. Furthermore, the solution does not extend well to more than 3 inputs – we currently require the user to manually use multiple logic blocks for more inputs.

Table 1: Partial Boolean eBlock Catalog

	eBlock	Diagram	Description	Interface
Sensor	Magnetic Contact Switch	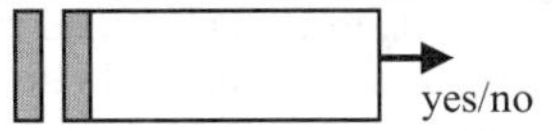	Determines when contact between two sensors is made.	yes = contact between sensors no = no contact between sensors
Sensor	Light Sensor	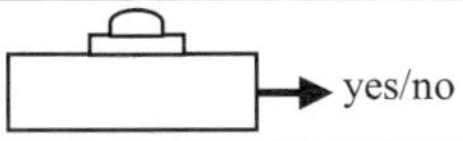	Sensor detects presence of light.	yes = light detected no = no light detected
Sensor	Button	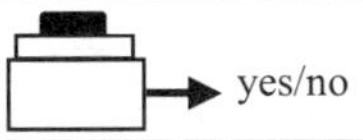	Indicates whether button is pressed or not.	yes = button pressed no = button not pressed
Output	LED	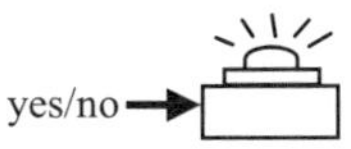	Device blinks a light when input is a yes. Device emits no light when input is no.	yes = blink LED no = turn LED off
Communication/logic	Splitter	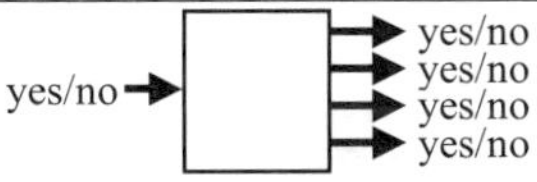	Device receives a signal and replicates that signal on each output.	yes = output yes signal no = output no signal
Communication/logic	Toggle	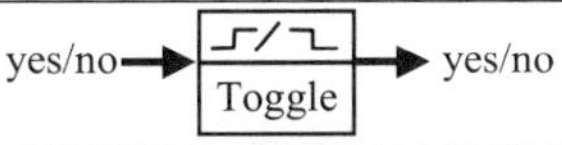	An input of yes toggles (inverts) the current value outputted by the device.	yes = toggle previous output value no = do nothing
Communication/logic	2-Input Logic Block	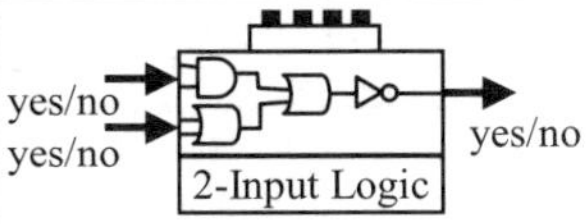	Configurable logic block programmed by the user via DIP switch.	For each of the possible outcomes of a and b, there is a corresponding switch which can be set so the resulting output is a yes or no for that particular combination.

Figure 2: eBlock Internals (a) Sensor Block – Light Sensor eBlock (b) Communication/Logic Block – 2-Input Logic eBlock (c) Output Block – Green/Red LED eBlock

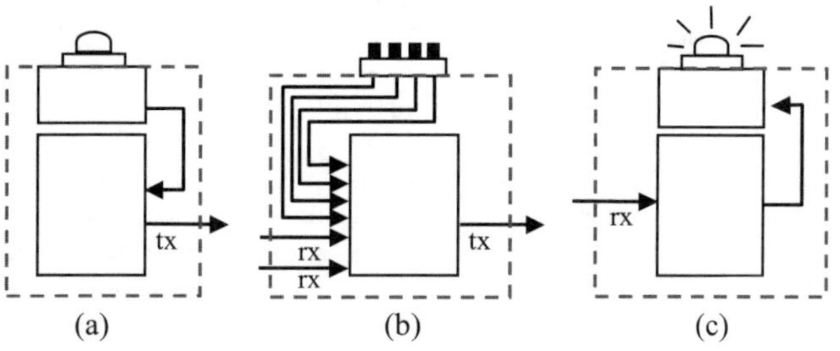

4.2 Computers in Every Block

We quickly determined that communication of logic values among eBlocks could not be implemented directly as a physical wire carrying 1 for *yes* and 0 for *no*, for several reasons. First, for low power, we did not want to transmit a signal at all times. Transmission of the output signal is one of the most power-costly operations of a block. Yet, we want eBlocks to potentially be powered by small batteries like a watch battery. Thus, we want to transmit as infrequently as possible. Second, glitches are common among sensors, yet we do not want to trigger outputs unless real events are detected. Third, we may want to transmit a message indicating an *error* rather than *yes* or *no*. Fourth, we may in the future want to transmit information about the sensors to assist the user in configuring logic blocks. Fifth, we want to support the option of wireless transmission.

Thus, we determined that blocks should communicate packets, not just 1 and 0 for *yes* and *no*. Physically, the blocks are connected via a single serial line. That single line carries serially transmitted packets. A packet consists of a start bit, followed by two bits indicating *yes/no/error*, followed by several stop bits. In the future, we will incorporate identification information into the packet. A block can also transmit no signal at all. Blocks with inputs from other blocks can use a pull-up resistor circuit to convert a situation in which these is no input signal into a stop bit.

To support packets, every block must contain a simple computer, as shown in Figure 2. A sensor block converts its physical input signal into a packet that the block sends over the serial output. An output block receives packets and decodes them into a physical output. A communication block receives an input packet and either changes the block's internal state, or sends out an identical output packet. A logic block receives input packets, computes the logic output, and transmits a new output packet.

Clearly, the compute requirements are modest. We therefore have chosen to use a PIC microcontroller, which is a popular 8-bit microcontroller distinguished for very low costs of less than a dollar (in quantity), very low power measured in microwatts (whereas milliwatts is more typical of other microcontrollers), and small size. The microcontroller typically includes on-chip non-volatile program memory and several peripherals, like analog-digital converters and serial transmitters/receivers (UARTs). Such microcontrollers are found in a myriad of common low-cost low-power items, such as sneakers with blinking LEDs.

The computer in every block and standard communication features are what distinguishes eBlocks from existing off-the-shelf sensor, output, and communication blocks.

4.3 Event Granularity

The rate at which eBlocks send packets must be selected carefully. The rate should be variable so eBlocks can reduce the rate to reduce power. Yet the fastest rate must be known to all eBlocks so that one eBlock does not send packets faster than another can process those packets. The slowest rate should not be so slow as to create annoying time lag in the system, and should be known to all eBlocks so a failed eBlock can be detected. We examined rates in light of their impact on power and found that rates faster than around 50 milliseconds yielded too short of battery lifetimes while rates slower than a few seconds yielded unacceptable delays in some systems. Thus, we have presently set the fastest rate at 50 milliseconds and the slowest at 3 seconds. We found 50 milliseconds to be plenty fast for nearly all sensing activities -- in fact, such speed is hardly ever really necessary. We found 3 seconds to introduce a slightly annoying lag in some systems having chains of about 6 eBlocks (chains typically don't get much longer), resulting in a 15-20 second delay from input to output. That could be annoying for systems where a user pushes a button that should generate an output, but is no problem for systems that monitor slower events (like the Garage Door Open at Night Detector).

We anticipate adding a simple adjustment screw to eBlocks to allow a user to vary the rate from a default rate of about 1.5 seconds, to accommodate the need for longer battery or faster system response (note: precision is not important in selecting the rate). Such screw-based adjustment is already commonplace in certain sensors, like motion and light sensors.

Note that the packet send rate is independent of the baud rate. We require all eBlocks to communicate their packets at 1200 baud.

5. eBlock-Based Systems

Utilizing the eBlocks shown in Table 1, we can build a variety of systems. For example, Figure 3(a) illustrates how the Garage

Figure 3: eBlock Systems: (a) Garage Door Open at Night Detector (b) Cafeteria Food Alert.

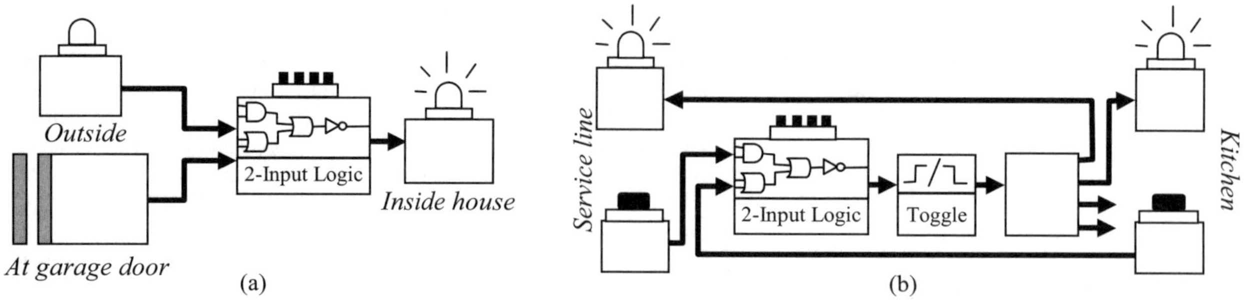

Figure 4: eBlock prototypes

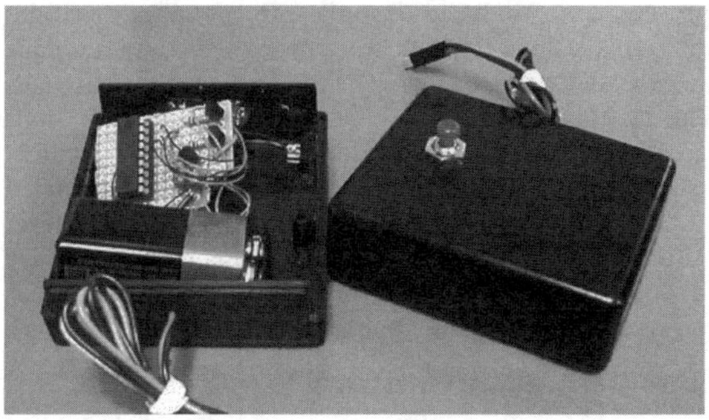

Door Open at Night Detector application, described earlier, could be built. A light sensor is utilized to determine when it is dark outside and a contact sensor is used to determine if the garage door is open. The outputs of these sensors are fed into a 2-input logic block. Because we are interested only when it is dark and the door is open, we want to output a *yes* from the 2-input logic block when the light sensor emits a *no* and the magnetic contact switch emits a *no*. We accomplish this functionality by setting dip switch 0 to the *yes* position.

Furthermore, using the same eBlocks shown in Table 1, a cafeteria manager can design a simple system for service line workers to indicate to kitchen staff which food items need replenishing. As shown in Figure 3(b), we start by placing an LED and button pair by the service line workers. When a food item runs low, the service line worker can simply press the button. The LED will start to blink indicating to the service line worker a request has successfully been made. A second LED and button pair is also located in the kitchen. When the service line worker presses the button, the LED in the kitchen will also blink, indicating that a food item is running low. When the food item has been replenished, either button can be pressed to turn both LEDs off. However, if there are numerous food items in the service line then workers in the kitchen do not know which item needs to be replenished. Thus, we can extend the design so that each food item has a LED/button pair associated with it. The kitchen could then have labels with LED/button pairs corresponding to each food item.

6. Simulation and Prototypes

6.1 VHDL

We have simulated sixteen eBlocks including the eBlocks used in the aforementioned examples in VHDL. We then built the systems shown in Figure 3 as well as ten others by combining the corresponding eBlock components in VHDL. We simulated those systems using Synopsys and verified them for correctness.

6.2 Prototypes

We next built physical prototypes, shown in Figure 4, using a PIC microcontroller, the corresponding circuitry for each of the various eBlocks, and a 9V battery. Currently we have the following eBlock prototypes implemented: Button, Light Sensor, Motion Sensor, 2-Input Logic, Toggle, Prolonger, LED, Green/Red LED, Buzzer, Electric Relay, and Magnetic Sensor eBlocks. On average, we implemented each of the various eBlock prototypes using 275 lines of C code. Communication between eBlocks was implemented using the internal UART of the PIC microcontroller at a transfer rate of 1200 baud. Furthermore, we successfully tested how far eBlock communication was effective by connecting a button eBlock to an LED eBlock and testing various lengths of wire. Currently, we have exceeded a distance of 1 mile (approximately 6000 feet) using standard twisted pair wire. We plan to keep increasing the length of wire to determine at which point communication fails, however at such lengths we would expect a user to use wireless receiver and transmitter eBlocks. Using the aforementioned eBlocks prototypes, we implemented the Garage Door Open At Night and Cafeteria Food Alert system, discussed in Figure 3, as well as others.

Table 2: eBlock Prototype Estimated Battery Lifetimes with PIC Constantly Running (battery capacity = 19278 Joules).

eBlocks	Energy/day (J/day)		Lifetime
	PIC	HW	
Button	8.684	0	6 years
Light Sensor	8.684	1339.2	0.5 months
LED	8.640	64.8	9 months
Green/Red LED	8.640	129.6	5 months
Beeper	8.640	180.0	3 months
2-Input Logic Block	8.728	0	6 years
Toggle	8.684	0	6 years
Prolonger	8.684	0	6 years

6.3 Battery Lifetime

We want most eBlocks to be battery powered, to avoid the complexity of connecting every component to a wall power source. In addition, we must ensure that battery life is sufficient such that a user is not constantly changing batteries. We used an off-the-shelf 9V battery with a capacity of 19,278 Joules, which correlates with the goal of trying to keep eBlocks to be as small as possible. Table 2 shows the expected battery life for several of the various eBlock prototypes implemented. For each of the eBlocks we list the Joules consumed per day required by the PIC microcontroller in the *PIC* column, the Joules consumed per day for the corresponding circuitry in the *HW* column, and finally the expected lifetime of the prototype denoted in months or years in the *Lifetime* column.

We determined the energy consumption of the PIC microcontroller using the corresponding datasheet [16]. The PIC microcontroller consumes 20 μA when active and 0.20 μA when in power down mode. Furthermore, driving a PIC port high consumes 3 mA, and driving a PIC port low consumes 8.5 mA. We also consider the power of driving a wire up to 100 feet long, based on physical measurements of a standard low-cost wire. The PIC energy consumption, listed in the *PIC* column, assumes that the PIC sends a packet every 2.5 seconds and considers driving the output port and 100 feet of wire. Normally the PIC will send a packet every 3 seconds; however, we also wanted to consider packets sent upon a change of the eBlock's input.

Furthermore, we considered the energy consumed by the sensors and corresponding circuitry of each of the various eBlocks. To obtain the energy consumed by the circuitry of each of the various eBlocks we physically measured the current when the device was active. For example, we connected a multimeter to the LED eBlock, and measured the current when the LED was on. We found that the LED consumes 8.9 mA at 5 volts when on. Recall however that our LED eBlocks blink rather than being constantly illuminated, since a constantly on LED would drain a battery very quickly. We then took into consideration that the

Table 3: eBlock Prototype Estimated Battery Lifetimes with PIC Power Down Mode Activated and Low Power Components (battery capacity = 19278 Joules).

eBlocks	Energy/day (J/day)		Lifetime
	PIC	HW	
Button	2.722	0	20 years
Light Sensor	2.722	44.5	1 year
LED	2.678	14.4	3 years
Green/Red LED	2.678	28.8	2 years
Beeper	2.678	27	2 years
2-Input Logic Block	2.766	0	19 years
Toggle	2.722	0	20 years
Prolonger	2.722	0	20 years

LED eBlock blinks roughly every 3 seconds for about a tenth of a second and estimated that the status of the block would be *yes* half of the time. Thus, on average, the LED is illuminated a tenth of a second roughly every 6 seconds. We estimated the energy of each of the eBlocks that require additional hardware in a similar manner and listed the corresponding energy consumption in Table 2.

As shown in Table 2, for most eBlocks the 9V battery will provide enough energy to last several years. However, some eBlocks have a short battery life expectancy. For example, the light sensor eBlock is estimated to last less than a month and thus does not have a reasonable battery life. Currently, this eBlock will require a different power source.

In the future, we must either develop a different implementation using lower power components or consider a sampling approach in which we sample the light inputs at some specific interval. Table 3 show the estimated battery lifetimes for each of the corresponding eBlocks if we use power saving strategies such as powering down the PIC microcontroller when the PIC is idle, using lower power components, and sampling inputs. For example, lower power components were not available for the light sensor. Thus, we considered a sampling approach that monitors the light level at an interval of every 3 seconds. Instead of constantly powering the light sensing circuitry, we only need to power the circuit for a short duration while sampling. Otherwise, we can shutdown the circuitry, thereby significantly increasing battery life from less than one month to slightly longer than 1 year. Furthermore, we can add configurability to the light sensor, which allows the user to customize the sampling rate to their specific application. If a user is only interested in sampling the light level once every hour, the lifetime of the light sensor eBlock would be further increased to over 6 years.

7. Experiences with eBlocks

For several years, we have required a three-week project in an upper-division embedded systems university course. The project was similar in complexity to the garage door open at night project. The students already had several months of experience in programming microcontrollers, assembling basic electronic systems, implementing serial communication, and interfacing with some sensors and display devices. The project involved new sensors and display devices, and hence students had to find components in electronics catalogs and read datasheets to learn how to interface with those components. Of about 50 students who have attempted the project, only 20 were able to successfully complete the project in the three weeks. Most problems encountered related to misunderstanding certain data sheets, errors during interfacing, and difficulty in debugging.

This year, we introduced a similar project but allowed the 22 students to use eBlocks, which were described using a simple 3-page catalog that included basic examples. The students needed less than 30 minutes to comprehend that material. All students successfully designed the garage door open at night system using eBlocks, in less than one hour (designs could be simulated in VHDL, but at the time we did not yet have a complete set of physical prototype blocks). Furthermore, students were given two hours more to create new designs, and they came up with numerous creative and useful applications.

8. Conclusions and Future Work

eBlocks greatly reduce the time needed to build basic monitor/control embedded systems and eliminate the need for programming or electronics expertise. eBlocks will not replace existing engineer-designed embedded systems, but will enable ordinary people, as well as a wider variety of engineers and programmers, to quickly realize a large range of new and useful applications.

We built physical eBlock prototypes and will use those in future courses as well as in local high schools (to observe truly non-experienced users). Immediate future work will include support to make logic configuration even simpler and extension to eBlocks that communicate integers rather than just Boolean values. As we discuss eBlocks with people in various fields, new applications that could be straightforwardly implemented with eBlocks continue to surface, such as detecting the speed of vehicles on a local street (requiring integer eBlocks), detecting if a child or hospital patient gets down out of a bed, detecting a water leak in a second home and calling the homeowner with a prerecorded message, and controlling a heat lamp and fan in a temperature-sensitive chemistry experiment. The potential list of applications is likely enormous.

9. Acknowledgments

This work is being supported by the National Science Foundation (CCR-0311026), and by a Department of Education GAANN fellowship. We also thank Daniel Tan and Shawn Nematbakhsh for their contributions in developing a set of prototype eBlocks.

10. References

[1] K. Aizawa. On Sensor Image Compression. IEEE Transactions on Circuits and Systems for Video Technology, Vol. 7, No. 3, June 1997.

[2] R. Borovoy, M. McDonald, F. Martin, and M. Resnick. Things that blink: Computationally augmented name tags. IBM Systems Journal, Vol. 35, No. 3&4, 1996.

[3] M. Clarkson. Smart Sensors. Sensors Magazine, May 1997.

[4] Crossbow Technology Inc., http://www.xbow.com

[5] Dust, Inc. http://www.dust-inc.com

[6] Epistemology and Learning Group, MIT Media Laboratories. Beyond Black Boxes. http://llk.media.mit.edu/projects/bbb/

[7] J. Hill, D. Culler. MICA: A Wireless Platform For Deeply Embedded Networks. IEEE Micro, Vol. 22. No. 6, November/December 2002.

[8] M. Horton, D. Culler, K. Pister, J. Hill, R. Szewczyk, A. Woo. MICA The Commercialization of Microsensor Motes. Sensors, April 2002.

[9] Interoperable Home Infrastructure. Intel Technology Journal Vol. 6, Issue 4, 2002.

[10] B.J. Jansen, and U. Pooch. Web user studies: A review and framework for future work. Journal of the American Society of Information Science and Technology. 52(3), 2000, 235 – 246.

[11] C. Johnson. Smart Sensors Extend Web Scale. EE Times, April 2001.

[12] K. Lee. A Synopsis of the IEEE P1451 – Standards for Smart Transducer Communication. National Institute of Standards and Technology, 1999.

[13] T. R. Licht. The IEEE 1451.4 Proposed Standard And Emerging Compatible Smart Transducers and Systems. National Institute of Standards and Technology, 2000.

[14] F. Martin, et. al. The MIT Programmable Brick. http://lcs.www.media.mit.edu/groups/el/projects/programmable-brick/

[15] F. Martin, et. al. Crickets: Tiny Computers for Big Ideas. http://lcs.www.media.mit.edu/people/fredm/projects/cricket

[16] Micochip, http://www.microchip.com

[17] S. Papert. Mindstorms: Children, Computers, and Powerful Ideas. Basic Books, New York, 1980.

[18] D. Potter. IEEE P1451.4's Plug-and-Play Sensors. Sensors Magazine, December 2002.

[19] Y. Rasheed, J. Edwards, C. Tai. Home Interoperability Framework for the Digital Home. Intel Technology Journal, Vol. 6, Issue 4, 2002.

[20] M. Resnick, S. Ocko, and S. Papert, LEGO, Logo, and Design, Children's Environments Quarterly 5, No. 4, pg. 14-18, 1988.

[21] P. Saffo. Smart Sensors Focus on the Future. CIO Insight, April 2002.

[22] E. Steinfeld, Devices that play together, work together. EDN Magazine, September 13, 2001.

[23] B. Travis. Sensors Smarten Up. EDN, March 1999.

[24] Universal Plug and Play Forum. http://upnp.org/

[25] P. Wallich. Mindstorms Not Just a Kid's Toy. IEEE Spectrum, Vol. 38, No. 9, September 2001.

[26] B. Warneke, M. Last, B. Liebowitz, and K. Pister. Smart Dust: Communicating with a Cubic-Millimeter Computer. Computer Magazine, pg. 44-51, January 2001.

[27] X10 protocol, http://www.x10.org/.

Verification of Design Decisions in ForSyDe*

Tarvo Raudvere, Ingo Sander, Ashish Kumar Singh, Axel Jantsch
Royal Institute of Technology
Stockholm, Sweden
tarvo,ingo,ashish,axel@imit.kth.se

ABSTRACT

The ForSyDe methodology has been developed for system level design. Starting with a formal specification model that captures the functionality of the system at a high abstraction level, it provides formal design transformation methods for a transparent refinement process of the specification model into an implementation model that is optimized for synthesis. A transformation may be semantic preserving or a design decision. The latter modifies the semantics of the system level description and changes the meaning of the model. The main contribution of this paper is the incorporation of model checking to verify that refined system blocks satisfy the design specification. We illustrate the translation of the ForSyDe code to the SMV language and the verification of local design decisions with a case study of a ForSyDe equalizer model.

Categories and Subject Descriptors

B.6.3 [**Logic Design**]: Design Aids—*Verification*; C [**Computer Systems Organization**]: Systems specification methodology

General Terms

Design, Verification

Keywords

System Design, Design Refinement, Verification

1. INTRODUCTION

Future applications and architectures with extreme complexity can be implemented on a single chip since the capacity of integrated circuits is continually growing. In order to develop these applications we believe that a system design methodology has to start at a high abstraction level, where (1) functions should be separated from architecture and (2) computation should be separated from communication. Also the methodology has to make it possible to incorporate formal methods to verify systems at different levels of abstraction, since simulation alone is not sufficient.

These arguments have been a basis for the development of the ForSyDe (Formal System Design) methodology which addresses the transformational design of embedded systems. A series of transformations is applied to an initial abstract formal and functional specification model to refine the model into a final implementation model. In [14, 15] we have introduced transformations for ForSyDe.

The objective of this paper is to verify that blocks of the system model satisfy system specific properties after design decision transformations. Simulation techniques can not guarantee the correct behavior for all input stimuli. For complex designs producing a mathematical proof in order to prove the effect of design decisions on the system behavior requires high level of expertise and may be impossible in practice. An alternative approach to validate a system is to apply formal verification techniques to prove that the system satisfies the specification. We intend to use model checking in cooperation with abstraction to validate that after each design decision the refined system block locally satisfies system specific properties.

2. RELATED WORK

According to the tagged signal model developed by Lee and Sangiovanni-Vincentelli [10] the ForSyDe system model can be classified as a synchronous computational model. It is based on the synchrony hypothesis, that also forms the base for the synchronous languages. According to Benveniste and Berry "the synchronous approach is based on a relatively small variety of concepts and methods based on deep, elegant, but simple mathematical principles" [3]. The synchronous assumption implies a total order of events and leads to a clean separation between computation and communication and gives a solid base for formal methods.

Two of the well known formal techniques for verification of the design correctness are theorem proving [7, 8] and model checking [6]. In the former case the correctness of a system is determined through mathematical proof composed by the designer which demands good knowledge and ingenuity. The latter method applies state exploration techniques to decide over the correctness of a system. The state space of a system must be finite for this approach. In order to have a finite state space abstraction techniques can be applied.

A good overview about program transformation in general is given in [12] and for transformation of functional and logical programs in [13]. One of the most well known transformation systems is the CIP (computer-aided, intuition-guided programming) project [2]. Inside CIP, program development is viewed as an evolutionary

*This research was supported by the Swedish Foundation for Strategic Research within the INTELECT program.

CODES+ISSS'03, October 1–3, 2003, Newport Beach, California, USA.
Copyright 2003 ACM 1-58113-742-7/03/0010 ...$5.00.

process that usually starts with a formal problem specification and ends with an executable program for the intended target machine. The individual transformations are done by semantic preserving transformation rules, which guarantees that the final version of the program still satisfies the initial specification.

Transformational approaches have been used mostly for development of software programs [13] but software transformational approaches do not deal with synchronous sub-domains and resource sharing which are required in ForSyDe. There are also a number of other transformational approaches targeting hardware design, e.g. [16], but none of them explicitly develops the concept of design decisions or addresses the refinement of a synchronous model into multiple synchronous sub-domains.

Lava [5] is a hardware description language based on Haskell. Theorem proving is used for the verification of Lava programs. An abstract circuit should be constructed containing both a system and a property for a theorem proving method. In our approach we are performing a direct mapping of ForSyDe into a state machine description in SMV from which properties can be verified by automatic tools. Hence, little expertise is needed for constructing a proof and this makes it easier for transformations verification. Esterel [4] is a synchronous language for programming reactive systems. Both an Esterel and a ForSyDe model can be translated into a form of a finite state machine as an input for automata verification systems to perform behavior analysis and proofs. However the ForSyDe model may include more complex data-flow descriptions compared with Esterel which is mostly control oriented. Therefore the task of verification is more involved. Lustre [9] is a synchronous data-flow language for programming critical real-time systems. The advantage of the ForSyDe methodology is that a system model may have control and data-flow behaviors at the same time. The Lustre program includes a system description as a set of input/output relations, assumption about the behavior of the environment as a set of assertions and finally a set of properties which will be checked by a verification tool. The verification will be done similar to the symbolic model checking by using binary decision diagrams for state space exploration. In the ForSyDe methodology we are using a step-wise transformational approach where we need to verify each of these transformations against a design specification.

3. THE FORSYDE METHODOLOGY

3.1 The Design Process

The ForSyDe design process starts with the development of a formal, abstract, functional *specification model* that can be executed using the functional language Haskell [17]. This model is then refined inside the *functional domain* by a stepwise application of well defined design transformations into an *implementation model*. As the implementation model is a refined version of the specification model, the same validation and verification methods can be applied to both models. In the partitioning phase, the implementation model is partitioned into hardware and software blocks, which are mapped on architectural components. Only now, in the code generation phase, we leave the functional domain and enter the *implementation domain* to produce VHDL or C/C++ for the hardware and software parts as discussed in [11].

3.2 The Specification Model

The specification model is based on a synchronous computational model and uses ideal data types such as real numbers and infinite buffers. It abstracts from implementation details, such as low-level communication mechanisms and enables the designer to focus on the functional behavior of the system rather than structure and architecture. The specification model leaves a wide design space for further design exploration and design refinement, which is supported by our transformational refinement techniques (Section 4).

We describe our computational model in the sense of signals and processes where processes are executed concurrently and synchronous communication between them is modeled by signals. A signal is defined as a set of events where each event e_i has a value and a tag i. As we use the perfect synchrony hypothesis [3], all signals have the same set of tags. In order to model the absence of a value at a certain tag, a data type D can be extended into a data type $D_\perp$ by adding the special value $\perp$. Absent values are used to establish a total order of events when dealing with signals with different or aperiodic event rates. A system can be constructed as a network of processes and modeled as a set of equations.

We implement the synchronous computational model with the concept of *process constructors*. A process constructor is a higher-order function that takes *combinational functions* and *values* as input and produces a process as output. The ForSyDe methodology obliges the designer to use process constructors for the modeling of processes. This leads to a well defined specification model with a clean separation between *synchronization* (process constructors) and *computation* (combinational function). In addition each process constructor has a structural *hardware and software semantics* which is used to translate the implementation model into a hardware/software implementation [11].

The process constructor *mapSY* (Figure 1) takes a combinational function f and constructs a process with one input and output signal, where f is applied on all values of the input signal.

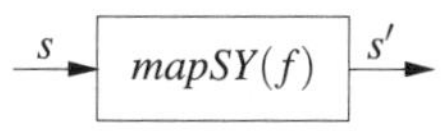

$$
\begin{aligned}
mapSY(f) &= P \\
\text{where} \quad P(s) &= s' \\
f(e_i) &= e'_i
\end{aligned}
$$

Figure 1: The Combinational Process Constructor ***mapSY***

Figure 2 illustrates a $mooreSY_n$ process which models a n-input Moore state machine. The process constructor $mooreSY_n$ takes two combinational functions f and g as next state function and output function and m_0 as initial state. The process constructor $zipWithSY_n$ is similar to *mapSY* and applies a n-variable combinational function f to all events of the input signals. The process constructor $delaySY_1$ models one-cycle delay and emits m_0 as the first value of the output signal.

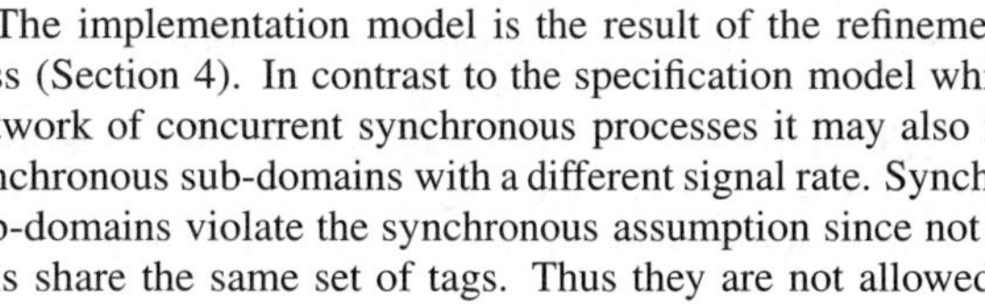

Figure 2: The $mooreSY_n$ **Process Constructor**

3.3 Implementation Model

The implementation model is the result of the refinement process (Section 4). In contrast to the specification model which is a network of concurrent synchronous processes it may also include synchronous sub-domains with a different signal rate. Synchronous sub-domains violate the synchronous assumption since not all signals share the same set of tags. Thus they are not allowed in the specification model, but are introduced by well-defined transformations during the refinement process. Inside a synchronous subdomain the synchronous assumption is still valid and the same formal techniques can be used as for the specification model.

4. REFINEMENT OF THE SYSTEM MODEL

The initial specification model is stepwise refined through the use of well defined design transformations into a final implementation model.

There are two classes of transformation techniques:

Semantic Preserving Transformations do not change the meaning and the behavior of the model, rather these are mainly used to optimize the model for synthesis.

Design Decisions change the meaning of a model. A typical design decision is the refinement of an infinite buffer into a fixed-size buffer with n elements. While such a design decision clearly modifies the semantics, the transformed model may still behave in the same way as the original model. For instance, if it is possible to verify that a certain buffer will never contain more than n elements, the ideal buffer can be replaced by a finite one of size n.

The designer applies transformations to a system model by choosing transformation rules from the transformation library. The transformation rules are characterized by a name, the required format and constraints of the original process network, the format of the transformed process network and the implication for the design, i.e. the relation between original and transformed process network is expressed by the characteristic function. For a more elaborate discussion see [15].

Since the system properties are preserved by semantic preserving transformations the verification is needed only for design decisions. Design decisions can be put into various categories, for instance *a clock domain refinement* which introduces multiple clock domains in the original synchronous model or *communication refinement* which can be used to partition the system into hardware and software parts and the communication interface between them [14]. We will take up an example of communication refinement of a synchronous channel into an asynchronous protocol which is suitable to model hardware-software interfaces (Figure 3). For this transformation the channel is required to be type of $V_\perp$. First an identity process is introduced, and then this process is refined into the handshaking protocol by introducing the processes *FIFO*, *Send* and *Receive*. When *Send* is idle it tries to read data from *FIFO*. If the reading was successful then *Send* emits the message DataReady to *Receive* and after receiving the message Ready, it sends the data. After the data is received the *Receive* sends a message Ack to *Send*.

The timing behavior of the refined interface is different from the original interface since the handshake protocol implies a delay of several cycles for each event, as *Send* and *Receive* are synchronous processes. Also the sub-system in the *Receive* side of the channel will not process exactly the same combination of values in each event cycle as in the specification model. These consequences have to be taken into account, when interfaces are refined. In order to validate that the refined system block satisfies the design specification for given assumptions about the input characteristics of the channel and size of the FIFO buffer, we need to incorporate verification.

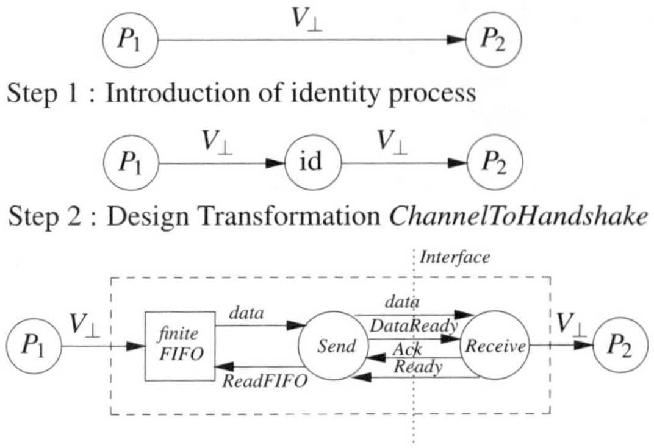

Figure 3: Refinement into a Handshake Protocol

5. VERIFICATION IN FORSYDE

The design flow starting from the development of a specification model M_0 to an implementation model M_n through transformations T_i is shown in Figure 4. A transformation $T(M,R,PN) \rightarrow M[R(PN)/PN]$ refines the process network PN, which is a part of the entire process network inside the model M, according to the transformation rule R. The result of the transformation is an intermediate system model M' where in contrast to the model M the process network PN is replaced with $R(PN)$. In order to verify the correctness of system blocks after design decisions we incorporate model checking techniques.

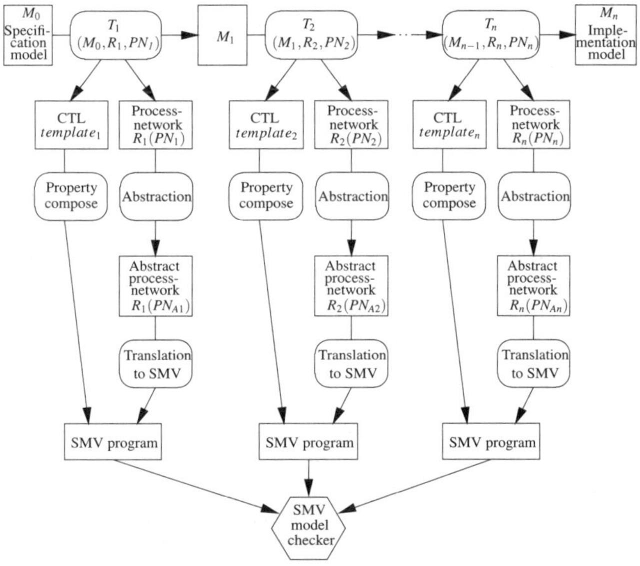

Figure 4: Verification of Design Transformations

For every design transformation we have a set of predefined specification templates which helps the designer to construct a CTL specification. For example a decision may be taken based on assumptions about system environment. We can assume some certain data rate in the input of a FIFO buffer and according to the rate to set the size of the buffer. To verify that the size of the FIFO buffer will not be exceeded we offer a configurable input pattern generator and a template for a CTL specification.

In contrast to theorem proving techniques model checking can be applied only to systems with a finite state space. Since a ForSyDe specification model is allowed to describe a system with an infinite state space the designer has to determine the finite state space through abstraction. The design flow continues with the translation of the refined part of the system model with the abstract state space into the input language of a model checking tool. We use the Cadence version of SMV (Symbolic Model Verifier) since the tool has been used successfully for model checking and there is a straightforward mapping from the ForSyDe language to the SMV language as described in Section 5.2.

The translation from ForSyDe into SMV can be fully automated and we give the guideline of properties which should to be verified. Based on the latter we estimate that the verification flow without abstraction takes much less time than the designer needs for selecting proper design decisions.

5.1 The SMV Tool

SMV [1] is a tool for the formal verification of finite state systems. The tool is based on a technique called symbolic model checking and can be used to check whether a system satisfies a specification given in the temporal logic CTL. CTL makes it possible to define various properties composing liveness, fairness, safety and deadlock freedom which can describe very complex relations of signals in terms of timing and values. If the system does not satisfy the given specification then the tool gives a counter example. The counter example is a trace from the system initial state to a state where the verified property does not hold. Systems can be expressed in the SMV language which offers modular hierarchical descriptions and reusable components of a system.

5.2 Translation from ForSyDe to SMV

The system mapping from ForSyDe to SMV entails datatype definitions, translation of function and process definitions, and specification of connections between processes. Each of these steps is described in further detail in the following subsections.

The translation is illustrated with a receiver which is a part of the refined equalizer model (Section 6). The equalizer specific ForSyDe code of a part of the receiver is given in Figure 5. The state of the receiver is modeled as a tuple of two elements, the first element tells if the receiver is waiting for data or has received the data and the second element is used to keep the values of events received from the sender. The first component of the state may have values *WaitDataReady*, *WaitData* or *OutputData* which are defined through the scalar datatype *RecState*. The receiver is constructed with the process constructor *moore2SY* which has the state function *recState*, the output function *recOutput* and the initial state value (*WaitDataReady*, 0) as arguments. The state transition function and the output function are defined using pattern matching. The last three lines in Figure 5 defines the output function *recOutput*. If the first element of the current state is *WaitDataReady* then the first output has value *Prst Ack* and the second has value *Abst*.

```
data RecState = WaitDataReady | WaitData | OutputData

receiver = moore2SY recState recOutput (WaitDataReady,0)

recOutput (WaitDataReady,_) = (Prst Ack     ,Abst)
recOutput (WaitData     ,_) = (Prst Ready   ,Abst)
recOutput (OutputData   ,v) = (Abst         ,Prst v)
```

Figure 5: Receiver in ForSyDe

5.3 Datatypes

The datatypes offered by the SMV language are Boolean, Scalar, Struct and Array. This is a proper base to construct datatype definitions for all the ForSyDe datatypes with some minor restriction.

- Integers are defined as Scalars which demands the user to specify the range of all reachable values. The SMV tool treats them as Integers and provides arithmetic and logic operation on them. In the following we give an example of datatype definition of *Int_0_7* which covers Integers values from 0 to 7:

```
typedef Int_0_7 0..7;
```

- A definition of a Scalar datatype contains the name of the new datatype and a set of all possible values. An example of the RecState type definition is the following:

```
typedef RecState = {WaitDataReady ,
          WaitData , OutputData};
```

- Constructor based datatypes will be translated to structural datatypes. For example an absent extended Integer with possible values *Abst* and *Prst Int_0_7* has the following definition:

```
typedef AbstExt {Prst,Abst};
typedef Abst_Int_0_7 struct {
    Con : AbstExt ; Val : Int_0_7};
```

- A list is defined as a pair of an Array and an Integer value where the Integer value is employed to store the count of elements in the list. We assume that lists have a finite size defined by the user.

- Each element of a tuple will be defined as an independent variable with its own datatype.

5.4 Functions

Functions which are arguments for process constructors in ForSyDe will be expressed as modules in SMV. In ForSyDe a function has the following shape:

```
function_name::input1_type->...->inputN_type->output_type
function_name  condition1 = expression1
...
function_name  conditionM = expressionM
```

The first line of a function definition express input and output datatypes. Each of the following lines consists of one condition and one expression. If the condition is satisfied then the corresponding expression evaluates the function output. The SMV module generated according to the upper function has the following style:

```
MODULE function_name(input1,...,inputN){
   out : datatype;
   out := case {
            condition1 : expression1;
            ...
            conditionM : expressionM;}}
```

The line *out* : *datatype*; defines a new variable *out* and the next line assigns a value to the variable through a conditional case expression. To address the variable one has to write *function_name.out*.

5.5 Processes

Process constructors in the ForSyDe library are classified as constructors for predefined processes and constructors for user defined processes. For the former we have predefined SMV modules since their functionality is fixed for example memories. The latter process constructors are higher order functions which take a set of user defined functions as arguments. The definition of a process P which has behavior of a Moore state machine is $P = mooreSY_n(f, g, m0)$ where f is a next state function, g is an output function and $m0$ is an initial state value of the state machine. The process has the following translation into SMV:

```
MODULE Pmoore(inp1,...,inpN){
   state        : datatype;
   output       : datatype;
   stateFunc    : f(state,inp1,...,inpN);
   outputFunc   : g(state);
   init(state)  := m0;
   next(state)  := stateFunc.out;
   output       := outputFunc.out;}
```

In the SMV language *init* denotes the initial value of a variable and *next* denotes its value in the next state.

5.6 Netlists

A system is modeled as a network of processes in ForSyDe where signals are used to connect processes with each other. The network is expressed as a netlist. In SMV we construct a similar netlist in the main module. For example the process network in Figure 6 is expressed in ForSyDe as the following:

```
system s1 = s5
  where
  (s2,s3) = P1 s1
  s4      = P3 s3
  s5      = P2 s2 s4
```

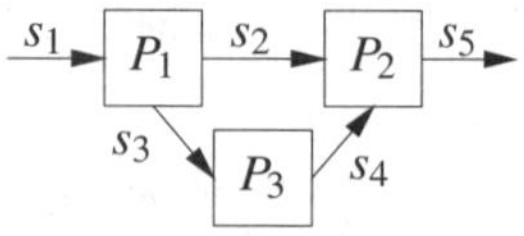

Figure 6: A Network of Processes

and the corresponding definition in SMV is the following:

```
s23  : P1(s1);
s4   : P3(s23.out2);
s5   : P2(s23.out1,s4.out);
```

In the SMV code the signals *s23.out1* and *s23.out2* correspond to the ForSyDe signals *s2* and *s3* respectively.

6. VERIFICATION OF DESIGN TRANSFORMATIONS

We illustrate refinement and verification in ForSyDe by means of the system model of an equalizer (Figure 7). The main task of the equalizer is to adjust the audio signal according to the *Button Control*.

The *Button Control* subsystem monitors the button inputs and the override signal from the subsystem *Distortion Control* and adjusts the current bass and treble levels. Since the aperiodic data rate of the *Button Control* and the *Distortion Control* subsystem is much lower than the data rate of the *Audio Filter* and *Audio Analyzer*, the *Button Control* and *Distribution Control* are implemented in software and the *Audio Filter* and *Audio Analyzer* in hardware. We use the design transformation *ChannelToHandshake* (Figure 3)

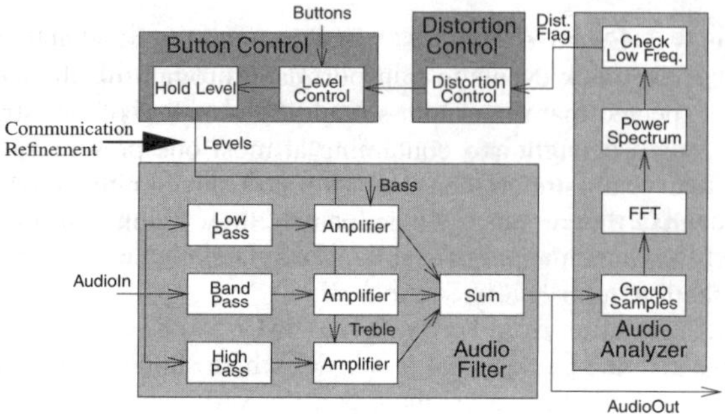

Figure 7: Subsystems of the Equalizer

[15] to refine the communication between the *Button Control* and the *Audio Filter* in Figure 7.

We translated the refined handshake protocol into SMV. In order to verify the correctness of the refined system block and to estimate the size of the FIFO buffer we checked the following properties:

Property 1 The implementation of the handshake protocol includes a finite size FIFO buffer. It is obvious that any higher data rate of input values than the buffer size was dimensioned for, will cause buffer overflow and the loss of data. We can verify that any data entering the channel when there was at least one empty slot in the FIFO buffer will be transmitted into the channel output. If this property holds we can say that there is no data lost other than caused by overflow. The specification of this property expressed in CTL is the following:

```
SPEC AG ((input_stream.Con=Prst &
        input_stream.Val = 0  &
        fifoOutput.st2 < SIZE-1) ->
        AF (recOutput.out2.Con = Prst
          & recOutput.out2.Val = 0));
```

The signal *input_stream* is the input of the channel and may have any value type of *AbstExt_Int_0_7*. The state variable *fifoOutput.st2* represents the current number of elements in the FIFO buffer. The constant SIZE is defined as maximum number of elements the FIFO buffer can store. *recOutput.out2* is the output signal of the channel. The given specification defines the following property: Always if the FIFO buffer has at least one empty slot and the channel input holds an event *Prst* 0 then the channel always in the future emits value *Prst* 0. In a similar way we can verify the property for any other value instead of 0.

Property 2 We specified the handshake protocol so that it takes seven clock cycles to transport a data from the channel input to the output if the sender process is in the initial state when the data enters into the channel. The CTL specification of this property is the following:

```
SPEC AG ((input_stream.Con = Prst &
          fifoOutput.st_2 = 0 &
          sender.st1 = ReadFifo) ->
         (AX AX AX AX AX AX AX
          recOutput.out2.Con = Prst));
```

The variable *sender.st1* represents the state of the sender process and initial value of the sender according to the system model is *ReadFifo*.

Property 3 Based on the last property which says that it takes seven clock events to transport data through the channel we expected that if an input stream is composed of sub-streams length of eight and containing at most one present value in every sub-stream then the buffer size stays finite. In order to verify this property we defined in SMV a non-deterministic FSM which generates these sub-streams and we checked the following property:

```
SPEC AG (fifoOutput.st2 < SIZE);
```

The SMV tool reported that the given specification is incorrect and gave a trace which lead to the state where the property was not satisfied. Later we increased the length of sub-streams from eight to nine and the proposed specification was true. The first specification did not hold because it takes two event cycles for the receiver to ask for the next data after it has delivered the last data.

The designer can in a similar way estimate the required buffer size according to any other input stream by defining a corresponding FSM to generate input sub-streams.

The wrong presumption about the safe input data rate is a typical mistake which shows that in order to validate a system we need to incorporate formal techniques instead of using only the designer intuition or simulation techniques.

Property 4 Finally we checked that present values in the output preserves the same order they have in the input.

The CPU time of a Sun Ultra 5 (192 MB RAM) required to verify the properties and the number of BDD nodes created by the SMV tool are given in Table 1.

Property	CPU time (sec.)	BDD nodes
Property 1	2.54	61961
Property 2	0.28	0
Property 3	0.44	3739
Property 4	9.05	127040

Table 1: Verification Time and Number of BDD Nodes

We have shown that the design transformation *ChannelToHandshake* can be used for the communication refinement from a synchronous channel into an asynchronous protocol.

7. CONCLUSION

In the ForSyDe methodology the design flow starts from the development of a specification model to an implementation model through design transformations. The contribution of this paper is the integration of a model checker for verification of refined system blocks by introduction of mapping rules from ForSyDe to state machine descriptions in SMV. For the transformations presented in the transformation library we offer a set of specification templates that helps the designer to construct a CTL specification.

At present we have not incorporated a methodology to reduce the state space of SMV specifications and thus the abstraction has to be done by the user. Therefore we plan to incorporate state space abstraction techniques in order to elaborate a methodology which helps the user to create an abstract system model with finite and reduced number of states.

8. REFERENCES

[1] The SMV model checker. http://www-cad.eecs.berkeley.edu/~kenmcmil/smv/.

[2] Friedrich Ludwig Bauer, Bernhrad Möller, Helmut Partsch, and Peter Pepper. Formal program construction by transformations – computer-aided, intuition guided programming. *IEEE Transactions on Software Engineering*, 15(2), February 1989.

[3] Albert Benveniste and Gérard Berry. The synchronous approach to reactive and real-time systems. *Proceedings of the IEEE*, 79(9):1270–1282, September 1991.

[4] Gerard Berry and Georges Gonthier. The esterel synchronous programming language: Design, semantics, implementation. *Science of Computer Programming*, 19(2):87–152, 1992.

[5] Per Bjesse, Koen Claessen, Mary Sheeran, and Satnam Singh. Lava: Hardware design in Haskell. In *International Conference on Functional Programming*, 1998.

[6] Edmund M. Clarke, Orna Grumberg, and David E. Long. Model checking and abstraction. In *Proceedings of the 19th ACM SIGPLAN-SIGACT symposium on Principles of programming languages*, pages 343 – 354. ACM Press, 1992.

[7] David Cyrluk, S. Rajan, Natarajan Shankar, and Mandayam K. Srivas. Effective theorem proving for hardware verification. In *Theorem Provers in Circuit Design (TPCD '94)*, volume 901 of *Lecture Notes in Computer Science*, pages 203–222, Bad Herrenalb, Germany, September 1994. Springer-Verlag.

[8] Michael J.C. Gordon and Tom F. Melham. *Introduction to HOL: A Theorem Proving Environment for Higher-Order Logic*. Cambridge University Press, 1993.

[9] Nicolas Halbwachs, Fabienne Lagnier, and Christophe Ratel. Programming and verifying real-time systems by means of the synchronous data-flow language LUSTRE. *Software Engineering*, 18(9):785–793, 1992.

[10] Edward A. Lee and Alberto Sangiovanni-Vincentelli. A framework for comparing models of computation. *IEEE Transactions on Computer-Aided Design of Integrated Circuits and Systems*, 17(12):1217–1229, December 1998.

[11] Zhonghai Lu, Ingo Sander, and Axel Jantsch. A case study of hardware and software synthesis in ForSyDe. In *Proceedings of the 15th International Symposium on System Synthesis*, Kyoto, Japan, October 2002.

[12] Helmut A. Partsch. *Specification and Transformation of Programs*. Springer-Verlag, 1990.

[13] Alberto Pettorossi and Maurizio Proietti. Rules and strategies for transforming functional and logic programs. *ACM Computing Surveys*, 28(2):361–414, June 1996.

[14] Ingo Sander and Axel Jantsch. Transformation based communication and clock domain refinement for system design. In *39th Design Automation Conference (DAC 2002)*, New Orleans, USA, June 2002.

[15] Ingo Sander, Axel Jantsch, and Zhonghai Lu. Development and application of design transformations in ForSyDe. In *Design, Automation and Test in Europe Conference (DATE 2003)*, Munich, Germany, March 2003.

[16] Tiberiu Seceleanu. *Systematic Design of Synchronous Digital Circuits*. PhD thesis, University of Turku, Finland, 2001.

[17] Simon Thompson. *Haskell The Craft of Functional Programming Second Edition*. Addison-Wesley, 1999.

A Multiobjective Optimization Model for Exploring Multiprocessor Mappings of Process Networks

Cagkan Erbas
Dept. of Computer Science
University of Amsterdam
Kruislaan 403, 1098 SJ
Amsterdam, The Netherlands
cagkan@science.uva.nl

Selin C. Erbas
Dept. of Stochastics
Aachen Univ. of Technology
Wüllnerstrasse 3, 52056
Aachen, Germany

Andy D. Pimentel
Dept. of Computer Science
University of Amsterdam
Kruislaan 403, 1098 SJ
Amsterdam, The Netherlands

ABSTRACT

In the Sesame framework, we develop a modeling and simulation environment for the efficient design space exploration of heterogeneous embedded systems. Since Sesame recognizes separate application and architecture models within a single system simulation, it needs an explicit mapping step to relate these models for co-simulation. So far in Sesame, the mapping decision has been assumed to be made by an experienced designer, intuitively. However, this assumption is increasingly becoming inappropriate for the following reasons: already the realistic systems are far too complex for making intuitive decisions at an early design stage where the design space is very large. Likely, these systems will even get more complex in the near future. Besides, there exist multiple criteria to consider, like processing times, power consumption and cost of the architecture, which make the decision problem even harder.

In this paper, the mapping decision problem is formulated as a multiobjective combinatorial optimization problem. For a solution approach, an optimization software tool, implementing an evolutionary algorithm from the literature, has been developed to achieve a set of best alternative mapping decisions under multiple criteria. In a case study, we have used our optimization tool to obtain a set of mapping decisions, some of which were further evaluated by the Sesame simulation framework.

Categories and Subject Descriptors

C.4 [**Performance of Systems**]: Design studies, Modeling techniques; C.3 [**Special-Purpose and Application-Based Systems**]: Real-time and embedded systems, Signal processing systems; G.1.6 [**Optimization**]: Integer programming

General Terms

Performance, Design

Keywords

Design space exploration, Performance estimation with simulation, Evolutionary multiobjective optimization

1. INTRODUCTION

In the context of the Artemis project [6], we are developing the Sesame [1], [7] framework which provides modeling and simulation methods and tools for the efficient design space exploration of heterogeneous embedded multimedia systems. This framework should allow for rapid performance evaluation of different architecture designs, application to architecture mappings, and hardware/software partitionings. In addition, it should do so at multiple levels of abstraction *and* for a wide range of multimedia applications. To achieve this flexibility, the Sesame environment recognizes separate application and architecture models within a single system simulation. The application model defines the functional behavior of an application, including both computation and communication behavior. The architecture model defines architecture resources and captures their performance constraints. An explicit mapping step maps an application model onto an architecture model for co-simulation.

So far in Sesame, the mapping step is assumed to be performed by an experienced designer, intuitively. However, this assumption is increasingly becoming inappropriate for efficient design space exploration. First of all, the Sesame environment targets exploration at an early design stage where the design space is very large. At this stage, it is very hard to make critical decisions such as *mapping* without using any analytical method or a design tool, since these decisions seriously affect the rest of the design process, and in turn, the success of the final design. Besides, modern embedded systems are already quite complicated, generally having a heterogeneous combination of hardware and software parts possibly with dynamic behavior. It is also very likely that these embedded systems will become even more complex in the near future, and intuitive mapping decisions will eventually become obsolete for future designs. Moreover, coping with the design constraints of embedded systems, there exist multiple criteria to consider, like the processing times, power consumption and cost of the architecture, all of which further complicate the mapping decision.

In this paper, we develop a mathematical model to capture the trade-offs faced during the mapping stage in Sesame. In our model, these trade-offs, namely the maximum processing time, power consumption and total cost of the architecture, are formulated as the multiple conflicting objectives of the mapping decision problem. Then using our optimization software tool, which is based on a widely-known evolutionary algorithm, we solve the mapping decision problem for a multimedia application. Finally, choosing two conflicting solutions from our optimization results, we simulate their performance consequences for validation using the Sesame simulation framework.

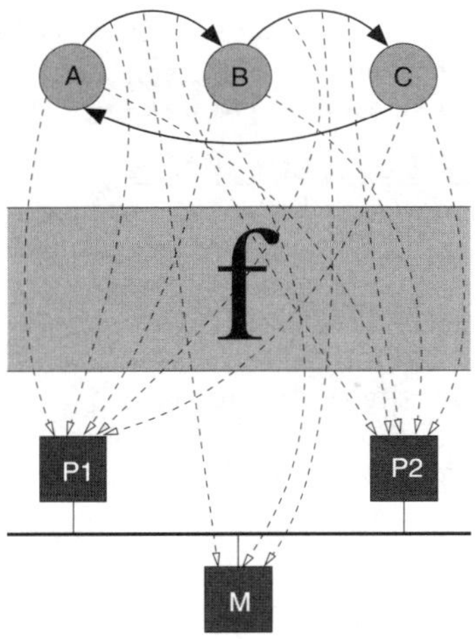

Figure 1: The mapping problem on a simple example.

The rest of the paper is organized as follows: we model the mapping decision in Sesame as a multiobjective combinatorial optimization problem in the next section. Section 3 introduces the multiobjective optimization theory and presents our solution approach. In Section 4, we study an M-JPEG encoder application and explore its design space. Section 5 discusses related work. Finally, Section 6 concludes the paper.

2. PROBLEM AND MODEL DEFINITION

In the Sesame framework, applications are modeled using the Kahn Process Network (KPN) [4] model of computation in which parallel processes – implemented in a high level language – communicate with each other via unbounded FIFO channels. By executing the application model, each process records its actions in order to generate its own trace of application events which is necessary for driving an architecture model. There are three types of application events in two groups: *execute* for computation events and *read* and *write* for communication events.

The architecture models in Sesame, simulate the performance consequences of the computation and communication events generated by an application model. They solely account for performance constraints and only model timing behavior, since the functional behavior is already captured in the application model. An architecture model is constructed from generic building blocks provided by a library which contains template models for processing cores and various types of memory.

Since Sesame makes a distinction between application and architecture models, it needs an explicit mapping step to relate these models for co-simulation. In this step, the designer decides for each application process and FIFO channel a destination architecture model component to simulate its workload. Thus, this step is one of the most important stages in the design process, since the final success of the design is highly dependent on these mapping choices. In Figure 1, we illustrate this mapping step on a very simple example. In this example, the application model consists of three Kahn processes and FIFO channels. The architecture model contains two processors and one shared memory. To decide on an optimum mapping, there exist multiple criteria to consider: maximum processing time in the system, power consumption and the total cost. This section aims at defining a mapping function, shown with **f** in Figure 1, to supply the designer with a set of best alternative mappings under the mentioned system criteria.

2.1 Application Modeling

The application models in Sesame are represented by a graph $KPN = (V_K, E_K)$ where the set V_K and E_K refer to the Kahn nodes and the directed FIFO channels between these nodes, respectively. For each node $a \in V_K$, we define $B_a \subseteq E_K$ to be the set of FIFO channels connected to node a, $B_a = \{b_{a1}, \dots, b_{an}\}$. For each Kahn node, we define a computation requirement, shown with α_a, representing the computational workload imposed by that Kahn node onto a particular component in the architecture model. The communication requirement of a Kahn node is not defined explicitly, rather it is derived from the channels attached to it. We have chosen this type of definition for the following reason: if the Kahn node and one of its channels are mapped onto the same architecture component, the communication overhead experienced by the Kahn node due to that specific channel is simply neglected. For the communication workload imposed by the Kahn node, only those channels that are mapped onto different architecture components are taken into account. So our model neglects internal communications and only considers external communications. Formally, we denote the communication requirement of the channel b with β_b. To include memory[1] latencies into our model, we require that mapping a channel onto a specific memory asks computation tasks from the memory. To express this, we define the computational requirement of the channel b from the memory as α_b. The formulation of our model ensures that the parameters β_b and α_b are only taken into account, when the channel b is mapped onto an external memory.

2.2 Architecture Modeling

Similarly to the application model, the architecture model is also represented by a graph $ARC = (V_A, E_A)$ where the sets V_A and E_A denote the architecture components and the connections between the architecture components, respectively. In our model, the set of architecture components consists of two disjoint subsets: the set of processors (P) and the set of memories (M), $V_A = P \cup M$ and $P \cap M = \emptyset$. For each processor $p \in P$, the set $M_p = \{m_{p1}, \dots, m_{pj}\}$ represents the memories which are reachable from the processor p. We define processing capacities for both the processors and the memories as c_p and c_m, respectively. These parameters are set such that they reflect processing capabilities for processors, and memory access latencies for memories.

One of the key considerations in the design of embedded systems is the power consumption. In our model, we consider two types of power consumption for the processors. We represent the power dissipation of the processor p during *execution* with w_{pe}, while w_{pc} represents its power dissipation during *communication* with the external memories. For the memories, we only define w_{me}, the power dissipation during *execution*. For both processors and memories, we neglect the power dissipation during idle times. In our model, we also consider the fixed costs associated with the architecture model components. Using an architecture component in the system adds a fixed amount to the total cost. We represent the fixed costs as u_p and u_m for the processors and the memories, respectively.

2.3 The Mapping Problem

We have the following decision variables in the model: $x_{ap} = 1$ if Kahn node a is mapped onto processor p, $x_{bm} = 1$ if channel b is mapped onto memory m, $x_{bp} = 1$ if channel b is mapped onto processor p, $y_p = 1$ if processor p is used in the system, $y_m = 1$ if memory m is used in the system. All the decision variables get a value of zero in all other cases. The constraints in the model are:

[1] In this paper, *memory* refers to any kind of hardware that can be used for data transfer. Buses, FIFOs, RAMs, etc. are all memories.

- Each Kahn node has to be mapped onto a single processor,

$$\sum_{p \in P} x_{ap} = 1 \qquad \text{for all } a \in V_K. \tag{1}$$

- Each channel in the application model has to be mapped onto a processor or a memory,

$$\sum_{p \in P} x_{bp} + \sum_{m \in M} x_{bm} = 1 \qquad \text{for all } b \in E_K. \tag{2}$$

- If two communicating Kahn nodes are mapped onto the same processor, then the communication channel(s) between these nodes have to be mapped onto the same processor.

$$\text{If } \exists\, b = (a_i, a_j) \in E_K \text{ with } x_{a_i p} = 1 \text{ and } x_{a_j p} = 1, \text{ then } x_{bp} = 1. \tag{3}$$

- The constraint given below ensures that when two communicating Kahn nodes are mapped onto two separate processors, the channel(s) between these nodes are to be mapped onto an external memory.

$$\text{Let } p_k \neq p_l \in P, a_i, a_j \in V_K \text{ and } b \in B_{a_i} \cap B_{a_j}. \text{ If } x_{a_i p_k} = 1 \text{ and } x_{a_j p_l} = 1 \text{ then } x_{bm} = 1 \text{ for an } m \in M_{p_k} \cap M_{p_l}. \tag{4}$$

- The following constraints are used to settle the values of y_p and y_m's in the model. We multiply the right-hand side of the first equation series by the total number of Kahn nodes and FIFO channels, since this gives an upper bound on the number of application model components that can be mapped to any processor. Similar logic is applied to the equations related with memory.

$$\sum_{a \in V_K} x_{ap} + \sum_{b \in E_K} x_{bp} \leq (\mid V_K \mid + \mid E_K \mid) y_p \qquad \text{for all } p \in P, \tag{5}$$

$$\sum_{b \in E_K} x_{bm} \leq \mid E_K \mid y_m \qquad \text{for all } m \in M. \tag{6}$$

Three conflicting objective functions exist in the optimization problem:

- The first objective function tries to minimize the maximum processing time in the system. For each processor and memory, f_p and f_m represent the total processing time in the processor and memory, respectively. We also show the total time spent by the processor for the execution events as f_p^e and for the communication events as f_p^c.

$$f_p = f_p^e + f_p^c, \tag{7}$$

$$f_p^e = \frac{1}{c_p} \sum_{a \in V_K} \alpha_a x_{ap}, \tag{8}$$

$$f_p^c = \frac{1}{c_p} \sum_{a \in V_K} x_{ap} \sum_{b \in B_a, m \in M_p} \beta_b x_{bm}, \tag{9}$$

$$f_m = \frac{1}{c_m} \sum_{b \in E_K} \alpha_b x_{bm}. \tag{10}$$

So the objective function is expressed as

$$\min \max_{i \in V_A} f_i. \tag{11}$$

- The second objective function tries to minimize the power consumption of the whole system. Similarly, g_p and g_m denote the total power consumption of processor p and memory m.

$$g_p = f_p^e w_{pe} + f_p^c w_{pc}, \tag{12}$$

$$g_m = f_m w_{me}. \tag{13}$$

$$\min \sum_{i \in V_A} g_i. \tag{14}$$

- The last objective function aims at minimizing the total cost of the architecture model.

$$\min \sum_{p \in P} u_p y_p + \sum_{m \in M} u_m y_m. \tag{15}$$

DEFINITION 1. *The Multiprocessor Mappings of KPNs Problem is the following multiobjective integer optimization problem:*

$$\textit{minimize} \quad f = (\max_{i \in V_A} f_i, \sum_{i \in V_A} g_i, \sum_{p \in P} u_p y_p + \sum_{m \in M} u_m y_m),$$
$$\textit{subject to} \quad (1) - (10), (12) \text{ and } (13).$$

3. MULTIOBJECTIVE OPTIMIZATION

DEFINITION 2. *A general multiobjective optimization problem is defined as:*

$$\textit{minimize} \quad \mathbf{f}(\mathbf{x}) = (f_1(\mathbf{x}), \ldots, f_k(\mathbf{x}))$$
$$\textit{subject to} \quad \mathbf{x} \in X$$

where $\mathbf{x}$ *represents a solution and* X *is a set of feasible solutions. The objective function vector* $\mathbf{f}(\mathbf{x})$ *maps a solution vector* $\mathbf{x}$ *in decision space to a point in objective space.*

In general, in a multiobjective optimization problem, it is not possible to find a single solution that minimizes all objectives, simultaneously. Therefore, one is interested to explore a set of solutions, called the *Pareto optimal* set, which are not *dominated* by any other solution in the feasible set. The corresponding objective vectors of these Pareto optimal points, named *efficient points*, form the *Pareto front* on the objective space.

DEFINITION 3. *We say* $\mathbf{x}$ *dominates* $\mathbf{x}^*$ *iff* $\forall i \in \{1, \ldots, k\}$ $f_i(\mathbf{x}) \leq f_i(\mathbf{x}^*)$ *and there exists at least one* $i \in \{1, \ldots, k\}$ *such that* $f_i(\mathbf{x}) < f_i(\mathbf{x}^*)$.

The most traditional approach to solve a multiobjective optimization problem is to aggregate the objectives into a single objective by using a *weighting mean*. However this approach has major drawbacks. It is not possible to locate the non-convex parts of the Pareto front [3] and it requires several consecutive runs of the optimization program with different weights. Recently, there has been an increasing interest in evolutionary multiobjective optimization. This is because of the fact that evolutionary algorithms (EAs) seem well-suited for this type of problems, as they deal simultaneously with a set of possible solutions called *population*. This allows us to find several members of the Pareto optimal set in a single run of the algorithm.

To solve the mapping problem given by Definition 1 in Section 2.3, we use the Strength Pareto Evolutionary Algorithm (SPEA) [11] which maintains an external set to preserve the nondominated solutions encountered so far besides the original population. It uses the concept of dominance in order to assign fitness values to individuals. Distinct fitness assignment schemes are defined for the

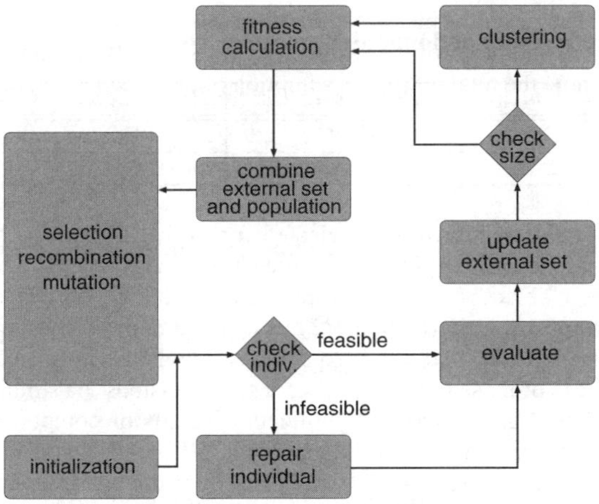

Figure 2: Overview of SPEA.

population and the external set to always ensure that better fitness values are assigned to individuals in the latter. Additionally, SPEA performs *clustering* to limit the number of individuals in the external set while also maintaining diversity among them. For selection, it uses binary tournament with replacement. Finally, both population and the external nondominated set take part in selection. In our SPEA implementation, we have introduced a repair mechanism to handle infeasibility. The repair takes place before the individuals enter evaluation to make sure that only valid individuals are evaluated. The details of our repair mechanism will be explained later. Figure 2 gives an overview of SPEA which also includes the repair mechanism. The big loop in the figure is performed for a certain number of generations.

3.1 Individual Coding

Each genotype consists of two main parts: a part for Kahn process nodes and a part for FIFO channels. Each gene in the chromosome has its own allele set which is determined by the type of the gene and the constraints of the problem. For genes representing Kahn process nodes, only the set of processors at the architecture model form the allele set, while for genes representing the FIFO channels, both the set of processors and the set of memories constitute the allele set. The constraints of the problem may include

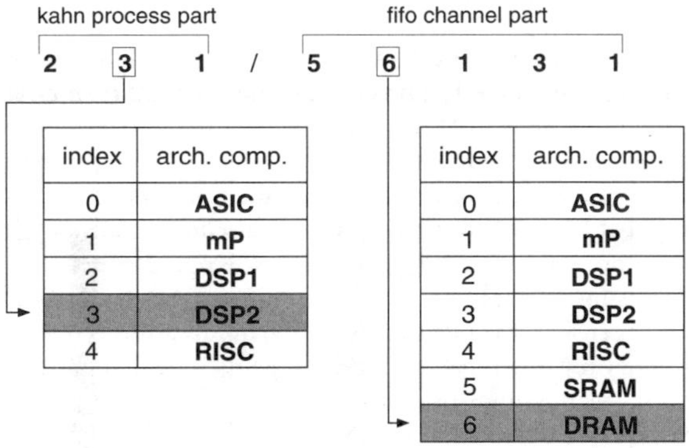

Figure 3: An example individual coding.

some limitations which should be considered in individual coding. For example, if there exists a dedicated architecture component for a specific Kahn process, then this architecture component has to be included only in the allele set of this Kahn process.

In Figure 3, an example chromosome is given. The first three genes are those for Kahn process nodes, and the rest are those for FIFO channels. For this gene, the second Kahn process is mapped onto DSP2 while the second FIFO channel is mapped onto DRAM. We also see that the allele sets for these two genes are different.

3.2 Constraint Violation

We have developed a repair mechanism to deal with the constraint violations. The encoding of the individual ensures that the constraints (1) and (2) are never violated. However, due to randomness in SPEA (in initialization, crossover and mutation steps), the constraints (3) and (4) are prone to violation. The repair mechanism given in Algorithm 1 only considers the FIFO channel part of the individuals, since constraints (3) and (4) ensure correct mapping of the FIFO channels. Our repair algorithm simply checks for each FIFO channel whether the Kahn processes it is connected to are mapped onto the same processor. If this condition holds, then it ensures that the FIFO channel is also mapped onto that processor. If the condition does not hold, which means that the Kahn processes are mapped onto different processors (say, P_1 and P_2), it finds the set of memories reachable from both P_1 and P_2 (mathematically, $M_{P_1} \cap M_{P_2}$). Then it selects a memory from this set randomly and maps the FIFO channel onto that memory. However, if $M_{P_1} \cap M_{P_2} = \emptyset$, then it maps the Kahn processes and the FIFO channel between them onto the processor P_1. We have adapted our repair algorithm in SPEA such that it is applied before the evaluation step to make sure that only valid individuals are evaluated.

Algorithm 1 Individual Repair Algorithm

input: I (individual)
output: I (individual)

```
for all FIFO channel genes do
  get Kahn nodes connected by this FIFO channel: K1 and K2.
  if K1 and K2 are mapped onto the same processor then
    repair: map FIFO channel onto the same processor.
  else if FIFO channel is mapped onto a processor then
    get processors K1 and K2 are mapped onto: P1 and P2.
    if M_P1 ∩ M_P2 ≠ ∅ then
      choose randomly a memory from M_P1 ∩ M_P2: M.
      repair: map FIFO channel on M.
    else
      repair: map FIFO channel and K2 on P1.
    end if
  end if
end for
```

4. CASE STUDY

We have chosen a modified M-JPEG encoder application, referred as M-JPEG*, to explore its design space. It differs from traditional M-JPEG encoders in three main ways: M-JPEG* only supports lossy encoding while M-JPEG supports both lossless and lossy encodings, M-JPEG* can operate on YUV and RGB video data whereas M-JPEG usually operates on YUV format, and finally M-JPEG* can change quantization and Huffman tables dynamically while M-JPEG has no such behavior. In Figure 4, we give the Kahn process network model of our M-JPEG* application. In our simulations, the frame size is 128x128 with 8 bits/pixel. The frame format is RGB. A more detailed discussion of the M-JPEG* application can be found in [7].

In Figure 5, we present a target platform architecture for the M-JPEG* application. The architecture model consists of a general purpose microprocessor (mP), two DSPs, two ASICs (VIP and

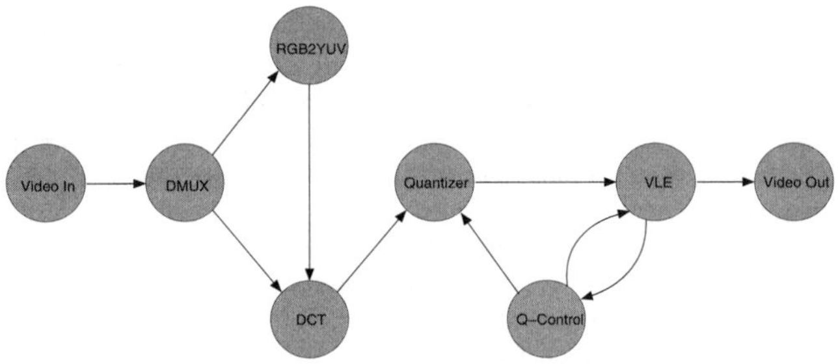

Figure 4: M-JPEG* encoder application model.

VOP), an SRAM and a DRAM. For these architecture components, realistic latency values from [7] have been used to calculate their processing capacities: c_p and c_m. Similarly, for the Kahn processes and FIFO channels in Figure 4, computational and communicational requirements (namely the parameters α_a for the nodes and the parameters α_b and β_b for the FIFO channels) have been calculated using statistics obtained from the C++ implementation code of this Kahn process network.

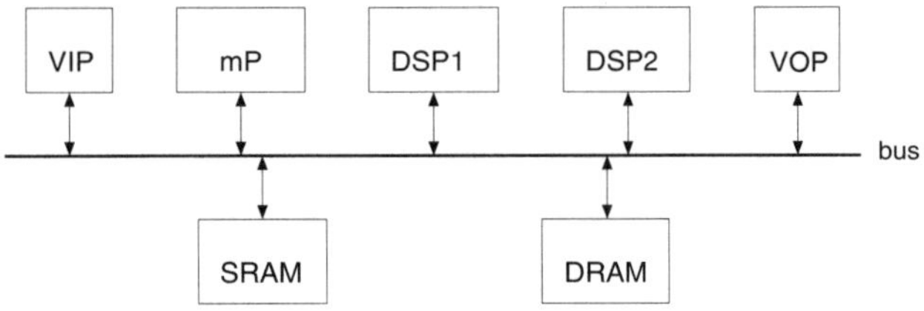

Figure 5: M-JPEG* encoder platform architecture model.

We have implemented the SPEA algorithm in C++ to solve our mapping problem given by Definition 1 in Section 2.3. Our software is based on GAlib[2] [10], a C++ library of genetic algorithm components. We have chosen a population size of 100, crossover probability of 0.5 and a mutation rate[3] of 0.056. The size of the external set is chosen as 20. In Figure 6, we show the nondominated front (approximated Pareto front) obtained by our optimization software after 300 generations in a single run. In the figure, there exist two distinct points where the maximum processing time attains its peak values. When we compare these two extreme points, we observe that with a slight increase of cost from 160 to 180, we obtain a big gain in power consumption (drops from 1003 to 919). On the other hand, one can also see that the compromise points are around the middle of the nondominated front.

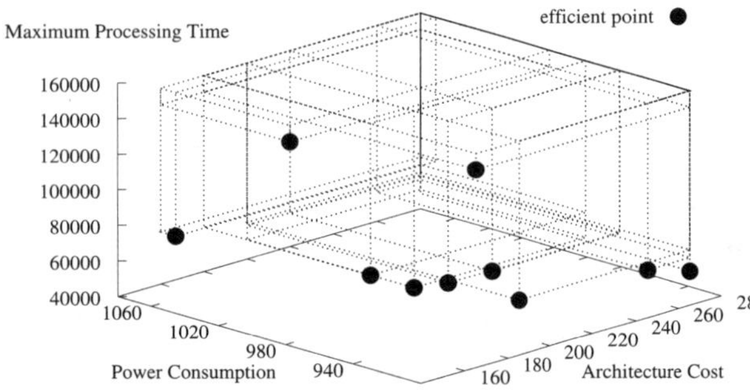

Figure 6: Nondominated front for the M-JPEG* case study.

[2]Originally, GAlib solves optimization problems with a single objective. We modified it to solve problems with multiple objectives.
[3]We calculated this with $1/(\text{chromosome length}) = 0.056$.

Table 1: Two nondominated solutions chosen for simulation.

Solution	*Max. Processing Time*	*Power Cons.*	*Cost*
$P1$	50762	981	200
$P2$	140808	1003	160

Two solutions have been selected for further evaluation by the `Sesame` framework. In Table 1, the chosen solutions $P1$ and $P2$, and their objective function values are given. $P1$ is one of the compromise solutions while $P2$ has its maximum processing time close to maxima. Our aim is to demonstrate the performance consequences of these two conflicting design decisions via simulation.

Figures 7 and 8 show the utilization details of components in the architecture models of the mappings $P1$ and $P2$, respectively. In both architecture models, only a subset of the available components are used, so actually these mappings are different instances of the platform architecture. For example, for storing data $P1$ utilizes SRAM while $P2$ uses DRAM. When we compare the architecture models of $P1$ and $P2$, we observe a dramatic difference between systems throughput. The former one has a video throughput of 154.2 frames/sec while the latter is only at 82.9 frames/sec. We can explain the reason behind this as follows: when we examine both Figures 7 and 8, we observe that the M-JPEG* application is quite sensitive to communication between the components. This is demonstrated by the large I/O times of mP and DSP1 in Figure 7 and DSP2 in Figure 8. This makes choosing a fast memory very critical for good system performance, so using an SRAM instead of a DRAM in the first architecture dramatically improves the overall performance. This fact is also noticed by the large busy times of the

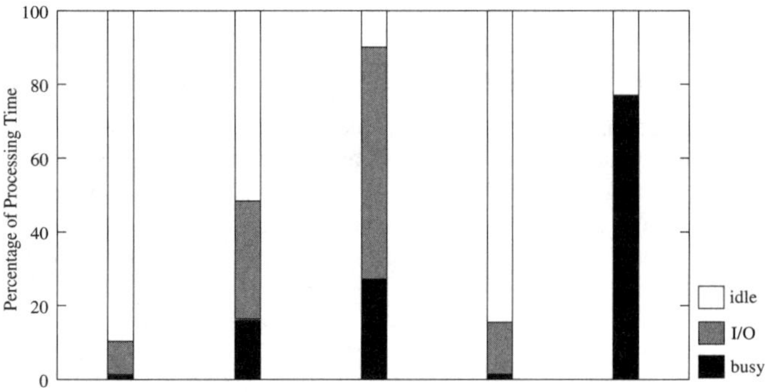

Figure 7: Simulation results showing the utilization of architecture components in $P1$. The throughput is 154.2 frames/sec.

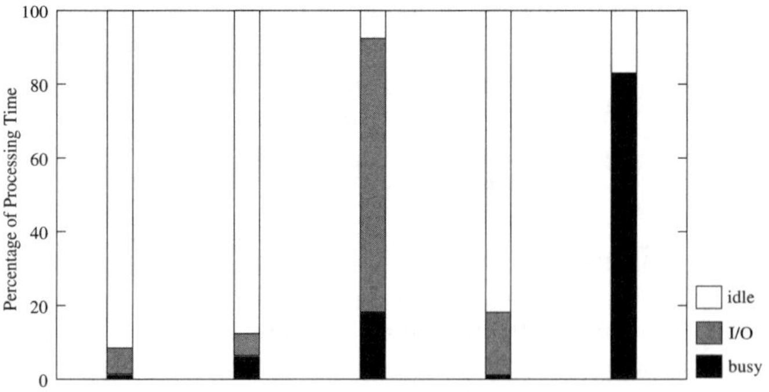

Figure 8: Simulation results showing the utilization of architecture components in $P2$. The throughput is 82.9 frames/sec.

SRAM and DRAM components in the figures. The second architecture also has an additional drawback that it is not well-balanced. When we compare the utilizations of DSP1 and DSP2 in Figure 8, we see that DSP1 is idle more than 80% of its execution time while DSP2 is only idle for less than 10%.

5. RELATED WORK

In the domain of embedded systems and hardware/software codesign, multiobjective optimization studies have been performed extensively for *system-level synthesis* [2], [8], [9]. The latter means the problem of optimally mapping a task-level specification onto a heterogeneous hardware/software architecture. Teich et al. [8] partition this problem into two steps: the selection of the architecture (allocation), and the mapping of the algorithm onto the selected architecture in space (binding) and time (scheduling). In their framework, they only consider cost and speed of the architecture, power consumption is ignored. Besides, they use penalty functions to cope with infeasibility. This technique reduces the number of infeasible individuals to an acceptable degree [8], while our repair mechanism replaces all infeasible individuals. In [9], a similar synthesis approach is applied to evaluate the design tradeoffs in packet processor architectures. But additionally, this model includes a real-time calculus to reason about packet streams and their processing.

In the MOGAC framework [2], starting from a task graph specification, the synthesis problem is solved for three objectives: cost, speed and power consumption of the target architecture. To accomplish this, an adaptive genetic algorithm which can escape local minima is utilized. However, this framework lacks the management of possible infeasibility as it treats all non-dominated solutions equally even if they violate hard constraints. The invalid individuals are only removed at the end of evolution. As a consequence of this, the MOGAC framework may confront convergence problems, i.e. convergence to a set of infeasible solutions.

In [5], configuration space of a parameterized system-on-chip (SoC) architecture is explored using an exploration algorithm which combines genetic algorithm and exhaustive search techniques. The approximated Pareto-optimal set obtained by the exploration algorithm is afterwards compared to the actual Pareto-optimal set using a distance function for fitness calculations.

In the `Sesame` framework, we do not target at the problem of system synthesis. Therefore, a schedule is not constructed at the end of the design process. Our aim is to develop a methodology which will quickly evaluate a large design space and provide us a number of approximated Pareto-optimal solutions. These solutions are then input to our simulation framework for further evaluation. After simulation, figures about system-level trade-offs (utilization of components, data throughput, communication media contention, etc.) are provided to the designer. Thus, our goal is efficient design space exploration in terms of simulation. As a final remark, we should also note that our framework differs from the mentioned frameworks in the sense that it uses process networks for algorithm specification rather than task graphs.

6. CONCLUSION

In this paper, we have developed a novel analytical method to optimally map application models, defined as Kahn process networks, onto multiprocessor target architectures. This methodology is specifically designed and developed for the `Sesame` modeling and simulation framework to be used prior to simulation. In many cases, simulation environments have to cope with large design spaces, where the simulation of all alternatives is too expensive or even impossible. Although finding the optimal mapping is an intractable problem, this study tackles the mapping problem by providing the designer a set of approximated Pareto-optimal solutions to be further evaluated in terms of simulation. To illustrate the practical aspects of our theoretical results, we have taken a modified M-JPEG encoder application and explored its design space in a case study. We could quickly evaluate two conflicting design choices for this multimedia application using `Sesame`'s efficient simulation methodology.

The current research in `Sesame` is to extend this work in two distinct tracks. One track is to formulate a new evolutionary algorithm and compare it against SPEA and probably also against other candidates from the literature. Another track is to refine the model introduced in this study. Some of the assumptions in this study can be further refined for getting better optimization results, but this should be done with special care as one should avoid adding details that may hamper the efficiency in terms of optimization time.

7. ACKNOWLEDGEMENTS

We thank Marco Laumanns and Eckart Zitzler for their help in plotting the nondominated front.

8. REFERENCES

[1] J. E. Coffland and A. D. Pimentel. A software framework for efficient system-level performance evaluation of embedded systems. In *Proc. of the ACM Symposium on Applied Computing*, Mar. 2003.

[2] R. P. Dick and N. K. Jha. MOGAC: A multiobjective genetic algorithm for hardware-software co-synthesis of distributed embedded systems. *IEEE Transactions on Computer-Aided Design of Integrated Circuits and Systems*, Oct. 1998.

[3] M. Ehrgott. *Multicriteria Optimization*. Lecture Notes in Economics and Mathematical Systems. Springer-Verlag, 2000.

[4] G. Kahn. The semantics of a simple language for parallel programming. In *Proc. of the IFIP Congress*, 1974.

[5] M. Palesi and T. Givargis. Multi-objective design space exploration using genetic algorithms. In *Proc. of the 10th Int. Symposium on Hardware/Software Codesign*, May 2002.

[6] A. D. Pimentel, P. Lieverse, P. van der Wolf, L. O. Hertzberger, and E. F. Deprettere. Exploring embedded-systems architectures with Artemis. *IEEE Computer*, Nov. 2001.

[7] A. D. Pimentel, S. Polstra, F. Terpstra, A. W. van Halderen, J. E. Coffland, and L. O. Hertzberger. Towards efficient design space exploration of heterogeneous embedded media systems. In *Embedded Processor Design Challenges: Systems, Architectures, Modeling, and Simulation*. Springer, 2002.

[8] J. Teich, T. Blickle, and L. Thiele. An evolutionary approach to system-level synthesis. In *Proc. of the 5th Int. Symposium on Hardware/Software Codesign*, Mar. 1997.

[9] L. Thiele, S. Chakraborty, M. Gries, and S. Künzli. A framework for evaluating design tradeoffs in packet processing architectures. In *Proc. of the ACM/IEEE Design Automation Conference*, June 2002.

[10] M. Wall. *GAlib: A C++ Library of Genetic Algorithm Components*. Massachusetts Institute of Technology, 1996.

[11] E. Zitzler. *Evolutionary Algorithms for Multiobjective Optimization: Methods and Applications*. PhD thesis, Swiss Federal Institute of Technology Zurich, 1999.

A Fault Model Notation and Error-Control Scheme for Switch-to-Switch Buses in a Network-on-Chip

Heiko Zimmer
Darmstadt University of Technology
Darmstadt, Germany
heiko@mes.tu-darmstadt.de

Axel Jantsch
Royal Institute of Technology (KTH)
Stockholm, Sweden
axel@imit.kth.se

ABSTRACT

The reliability of a Network-on-Chip will be significantly influenced by the reliability of the switch-to-switch connections. Faults on these buses may cause disturbances on multiple adjacent wires, so that errors on these wires can no longer be considered as statistically independent from one another, as it is expected due to deep submicron effects. A new fault model notation for buses is proposed which can represent multiple-wire, multiple-cycle faults. An estimation method based on this notation is presented which can accurately predict error probabilities. This method is used to examine bus encoding schemes. Finally, an encoding scheme for four Quality-of-Service classes is proposed which can be dynamically selected for each packet.

Categories and Subject Descriptors

B.4.3 [**Input/Output and Data Communications**]: Interconnections (Subsystems); B.8.1 [**Performance and Reliability**]: Reliability, Testing, and Fault-Tolerance

General Terms

Design, Reliability

Keywords

Network-on-Chip, Fault Tolerance, Bus Encoding

1. INTRODUCTION

To efficiently use the billions of transistors that will soon be available on a single chip, new design methods will be necessary. While the reuse of components in building Systems-on-Chip (SoC) will continue, their interconnection becomes a major concern. Currently used shared buses and dedicated wires exhibit limited scalability.

A new approach to overcome these limitations is to implement a *Network-on-Chip* (NoC) to handle the on-chip communication [2, 7, 8]. In such an architecture, communication can be decoupled from computation: The computational blocks called *resources* (which can be anything from processors or DSPs over FPGA, mixed signal or ASIC blocks to any kind of memory) are connected to an inter-resource communication network.

We assume a NoC-architecture that employs packet switching in a $n \times m$ mesh of switches. Adjacent switches are connected by wide buses so that a complete packet can be transmitted in parallel. By a *network interface*, one resource is connected to every switch. These switches must be as small and efficient as possible [10] in order to limit the overhead (in terms of area, power and delay) introduced by the NoC.

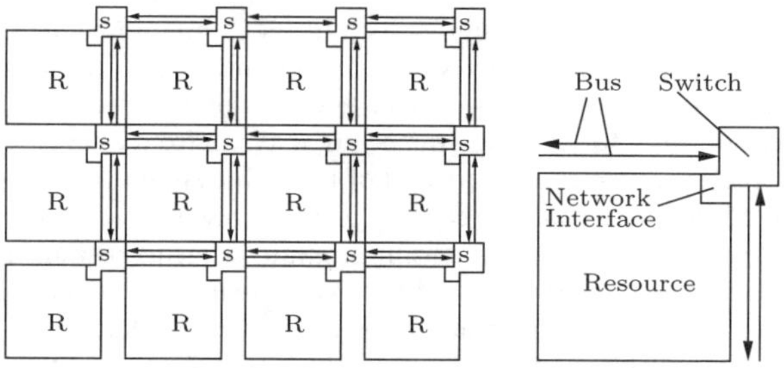

Figure 1: Complete NoC and detailed view of one resource/switch block

QoS Levels

The Network-on-Chip becomes the communication backbone to handle all data transmitted between components of a SoC. Due to the varying requirements of communication streams, it must implement transmission at multiple Quality-of-Service (QoS) levels (classified by parameters like bandwidth, reliability, latency etc.) [7]. The transport of multimedia data may require maximum bandwidth whereas data integrity must be guaranteed for transfers from and to memories. We propose four QoS levels offering different characteristics to applications:

Maximum Bandwidth: Since the amount of wires available for routing the inter-switch buses is limited, the redundancy introduced by bus encoding will directly influence the application payload that can be transported with every packet. Consequently, maximum bandwidth is available to the application when no encoding is applied.

Guaranteed Integrity: To ensure data integrity as far as possible, error detection methods can be used. Data correction is not attempted since it might result in miscorrection. If erroneous data is detected, a flag can be set, a retransmission can be initiated or the whole packet can be dropped.

Minimum Latency: To achieve minimum latency, packets are always forwarded. Error correction is performed, the underlying assumption is that all errors can be corrected by the code used. This mode is well suited for applications that can tolerate rare errors (due to miscorrection) but depend on receiving data at a constant rate.

High Reliability: Using codes capable of correcting errors and detecting uncorrectable errors at the same time combines the characteristics of the two previously described modes at the expense of lower bandwidth and higher latency.

Faults on DSM buses

During the next decade, deep submicron (DSM) technology will have to cope with more transient faults than ever before. The number of single-event-upsets (SEU) due to various reasons (charge injection by neutrons or α-particles, process variations, electro-magnetic interference) will increase along with crosstalk, mainly affecting long interconnects [1]. Technology scaling also gives rise to new error sources: For instance can the effects of neutrons (which have formerly only been a concern with memories) now cause upsets in logic elements and low power/low capacitance buses as well [9]. However, the main source for errors on buses will be crosstalk, which can lead to increased delay or cause voltage glitches on wires [4]. Furthermore, crosstalk can inherently cause multi-bit and bidirectional errors [6] (i.e., disturbing multiple wires, causing both $0 \rightarrow 1$ and $1 \rightarrow 0$ errors). Since faults on the massively parallel buses between adjacent switches will mainly be transient and not necessarily confined to one wire, conventional fault models are not sufficient to accurately describe them. We have developed a new fault model notation for faults on on-chip buses. It is capable of describing a wide range of faults and as a significant feature, it supports the modeling of faults that affect multiple wires and last multiple bus cycles. Furthermore, arbitrary effects of faults can be represented.

We show that accurate prediction of error probabilities can be achieved by an estimation method based on this notation which includes structural information (effect, duration and affected wires) about the faults. Evaluating various bus encoding schemes, we derive some general design guidelines to achieve higher reliability of transmissions over on-chip buses in the presence of multiple-wire faults. Eventually, a case study combines all aspects of this work and shows how to select encoding schemes for a fault-tolerant NoC supporting network traffic with non-uniform QoS requirements.

System-wide energy management is not considered. When a NoC is operated in different power-saving modes, we expect different fault scenarios. Our approach is compatible and complementary to power-saving techniques such as [12].

2. RELATED WORK

The importance of crosstalk faults for bus reliability has lead to the development of a crosstalk fault model which can be used to generate test vectors [4]. To evaluate the dependability of interconnects, a hardware-software co-design methodology has been used to compare bus encodings [9]. Also, a combination of error detection and retransmission was identified as very energy efficient [3]. This was extended to an adaptive low-power transmission scheme for NoCs [12].

All these approaches lack a comprehensive fault model notation that is complete or can at least represent all expected fault types. Such a model must explicitly support faults spanning multiple wires and it must not be limited to one fault type. In the presence of crosstalk effects, statistical independence of errors on adjacent bus lines cannot be assumed. However, the effect of this on bus encoding schemes has not been discussed previously.

The main contribution of this paper is a high-level fault model notation for buses which can represent multiple-wire, multiple-cycle faults on single- or multi-layer on-chip bus architectures. Furthermore, we present an approach to adaptive encoding of on-chip buses with QoS-support.

3. MODELING FAULTS ON NOC-INTERCONNECTS

On a bus, arbitrary faults may occur. Of these, all faults that are caused by the same physical effect belong to one *fault type* f_i. For instance, crosstalk faults and faults caused by neutrons form two fault types. Faults of different types are statistically independent.

3.1 Fault Model Notation

The *fault model* $\mathcal{FM}(f_i)$ describes faults of type f_i in a given bus architecture. It is based on the faults' probability of occurrence (α_i), their characteristics (expressed in the matrix $\boldsymbol{P}_i$) and a distance metric DM_i influenced by the physical bus layout.

$$\mathcal{FM}\colon f_i \rightarrow (\alpha_i, \boldsymbol{P}_i, DM_i)$$

Probability of Occurrence

We define α_i as the probability of occurrence of a fault of type f_i per wire and cycle. Thus, $\alpha_i = \frac{1}{128}$ leads to one fault of type f_i occurring on a 128 bit wide bus every cycle or every 8 cycles on a 16 bit bus.

Fault Characteristics

When a fault of type f_i occurs, it has a probability $p_i(w, d, e)$ to affect w wires for a duration of d time units (typically clock or transfer cycles) with the effect e. The *effect* of a fault is selected from a list of all possible effects. See table 1 for an incomplete list including symbolic names.

Effect e		Description
1	`Inv`	logic value on wires inverted
2	`Set0`	wires forced to logic 0
3	`Set1`	wires forced to logic 1
4	`SetRand`	wires forced to random logic value
5	`Bridge`	wire w_i forced to value of wire w_{i-1}
6	`Del`	delay: wire set to previous value
7	...	...

Table 1: (Numerical) representation of faults' effects

All possible combinations of $p_i(w, d, e)$ are represented in the normalized matrix $\boldsymbol{P}_i$ of the dimensions $w_{max_i} \times (d_{max_i} + 1) \times e_{max}$. w_{max_i} and d_{max_i} are the maximum values for the number of wires affected and the fault's duration respectively. These maximum values can be different for every fault type f_i. While d_{max_i} can take any positive value, w_{max_i} must not exceed the bus width w_{max} of the interconnects between the switches: $w_{max_i} \leq w_{max}$. e_{max} is the number of different effects which can be described.

E.g., when setting $e_{max} = 1$ and thus restricting the model to the effect Inv, the normalized matrix $\boldsymbol{P}_i$ is written as

$$\boldsymbol{P}_i = \begin{pmatrix} p_i(1, 0, \texttt{Inv}) & \cdots & p_i(1, d_{max_i}, \texttt{Inv}) \\ p_i(2, 0, \texttt{Inv}) & \cdots & p_i(2, d_{max_i}, \texttt{Inv}) \\ \vdots & \ddots & \vdots \\ p_i(w_{max_i}, 0, \texttt{Inv}) & \cdots & p_i(w_{max_i}, d_{max_i}, \texttt{Inv}) \end{pmatrix} \Big\downarrow \text{no. of wires}$$

$$\xrightarrow{\textit{fault duration}}$$

A fault generally lasts at least one clock cycle ($d \geq 1$). The elements of $\boldsymbol{P}_i$ with the index $d = 0$ are used to indicate the probability of permanent faults.

Since the matrix elements describe the probabilities of different characteristics of one fault occurrence, their values must satisfy the following condition:

$$\sum_{a=1}^{w_{max_i}} \sum_{b=0}^{d_{max_i}} \sum_{c=1}^{e_{max}} p_i(a, b, c) = 1$$

The manifestation of a fault of type f_i affecting w wires for d cycles with effect e is determined by the probability of occurrence and the normalized value $p_i(w, d, e)$ to a probability of $\alpha_i \cdot p_i(w, d, e)$.

EXAMPLE 1 (FAULT TYPE f_1). *The characteristics of a single-event-upset that is always confined to one wire, lasts only one cycle and has the effect* Inv *are represented by matrix element* $p_1(1, 1, \texttt{Inv}) = 1$. *Since for this fault type* $d_{max_1} = w_{max_1} = 1$, *the resulting matrix is*

$$\boldsymbol{P}_1 = \begin{pmatrix} p_1(1, 0, \texttt{Inv}) & p_1(1, 1, \texttt{Inv}) \end{pmatrix} = \begin{pmatrix} 0 & 1 \end{pmatrix}$$

meaning that if a fault of type f_1 *occurs, it will always have the characteristics* $w = 1$, $d = 1$ *and* $e =$ Inv. *The probability that a fault of this type occurs is determined by its occurrence probability* α_1.

EXAMPLE 2 (FAULT TYPE f_2). $\boldsymbol{P}_2$ *characterizes a fault that can affect multiple wires* ($e =$ Inv) *for multiple cycles.*

$$\boldsymbol{P}_2 = \begin{pmatrix} 0 & 0.65 & 0.1 \\ 0 & 0.2 & 0.05 \end{pmatrix}$$

meaning that a fault of type f_2 *will be confined to one wire and one clock (or transfer) cycle in 65% of all occurrences. Another 20% of these faults will disturb two wires for one clock cycle. Only in 15% can the effects be noted for two cycles (on one (10%) or two wires (5%) respectively).*
Note that in both examples the elements of the first column are zero, indicating that faults of type f_1 *or* f_2 *will never lead to permanent errors.*

EXAMPLE 3 (PERMANENT FAULT). *A fault that causes a permanent defect on one wire whenever it occurs, can be described by a* $\boldsymbol{P}$*-matrix whose only non-zero elements are:*

$$p_{permanent}(1, 0, \texttt{Set0}) = 0.5 \qquad p_{permanent}(1, 0, \texttt{Set1}) = 0.5$$

meaning that faults of this type will cause a permanent error on one wire; stuck-at-0 and stuck-at-1 are equally probable.

Distance Metric

One parameter of the fault characteristics is the number of wires that are affected by a fault. This does not include the information which wires these are. Without loss of generality, we say that a fault affects w *adjacent* wires and describe the relative distance between wires in a *distance metric* DM_i. This distance metric may be different for every fault type and bus layout. We use a weighted, directed acyclic graph (DAG), examples are given in figure 2.

The w wires affected by a fault will be those with the lowest distance from the wire where the fault occurs. If multiple wires have the same distance, the choice among them is random.

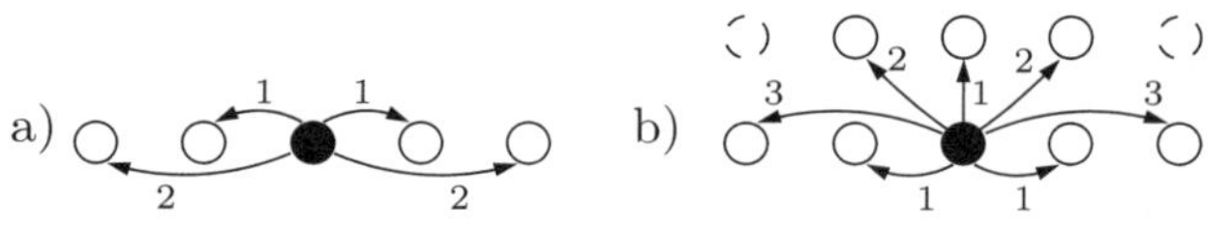

Figure 2: Example for distance relation between wires of a bus running on one or two layers

3.2 Fault Scenario

For a complete representation of all faults that occur in a given environment, a set of fault models is necessary. This set is referred to as a *fault scenario* and is defined as:

$$\mathcal{S} = \left\{\mathcal{FM}(f_1), \mathcal{FM}(f_2), \ldots, \mathcal{FM}(f_n)\right\}$$

When using a *fault scenario* in simulation, at every time step it will be checked for each wire if one or multiple faults have occurred (based on the probability of occurrence). If a fault of type f_i has occurred, $\boldsymbol{P}_i$ and DM_i are evaluated to determine the fault's duration, effect and the affected wires.

Used Fault Scenario

The fault scenario used throughout this paper is a set of three fault models:

$$\begin{aligned} \mathcal{S} &= \left\{\mathcal{FM}(f_1), \mathcal{FM}(f_2), \mathcal{FM}(f_3)\right\} \\ &= \left\{(\alpha_1, \boldsymbol{P}_1, DM_1), (\alpha_2, \boldsymbol{P}_2, DM_2), (\alpha_3, \boldsymbol{P}_3, DM_3)\right\} \end{aligned}$$

All three fault models were assigned the same probability of occurrence $\alpha_1 = \alpha_2 = \alpha_3 = \alpha = 10^{-9}$ and a distance metric equivalent to that from figure 2a was used. While the first two fault models are those from examples 1 and 2, the third one was extracted from a more detailed experiment:

Since the inter-wire capacitance C_I between adjacent wires of a bus has a significant influence on the total capacity which has to be charged during a bus transition, the signal delay depends strongly on the bus transition pattern.

Type	Transitions
4C	$v_1\overline{v_1}v_1 \longrightarrow \overline{v_1}v_1\overline{v_1}$
3C	$v_1\overline{v_1}v_2 \longrightarrow \overline{v_1}v_1v_2$
	$v_2v_1\overline{v_1} \longrightarrow v_2\overline{v_1}v_1$

Type	Transitions
2C	$v_1v_2v_3 \longrightarrow v_1\overline{v_2}v_3$
1C	$v_1v_2v_2 \longrightarrow v_1\overline{v_2v_2}$
	$v_2v_2v_1 \longrightarrow \overline{v_2v_2}v_1$

Table 2: Classification of crosstalk sequences

Considering three adjacent wires, transition patterns can be classified in 1C…4C sequences (table 2) depending on how much they slow down the transition of the middle signal [5]. Out of a large number of random data, we identified all 4C sequences (causing maximum signal delay) and marked the middle wire as fault location. Translating the resulting error patterns into our fault model using $e = \texttt{Inv}$, we derived

$$P_3 = \begin{pmatrix} 0 & 0.6768 & 0.0836 & 0.0102 & 0.0013 \\ 0 & 0.1521 & 0.0195 & 0.0028 & 0.0003 \\ 0 & 0.0353 & 0.0047 & 0.0007 & 0 \\ 0 & 0.0090 & 0.0009 & 0.0002 & 0 \\ 0 & 0.0019 & 0.0002 & 0 & 0 \\ 0 & 0.0003 & 0.0001 & 0 & 0 \\ 0 & 0.0001 & 0 & 0 & 0 \end{pmatrix}.$$

Due to the lack of a more realistic fault scenario for future DSM technology, all further discussion and results are based on the described fault scenario. I.e., transmission over a planar bus in presence of the three fault types is considered.

4. ERROR-CONTROL CODING FOR NOC COMMUNICATION BUSES

In this section, possibilities are explored how error-control coding can be used on the switch-to-switch buses of a NoC to implement a network supporting different QoS levels.

Knowing that errors on adjacent wires of these buses are not always statistically independent, coding techniques to enhance the bus reliability are discussed. In a NoC running with gigahertz clock frequency, consisting of 100 switches and about 20.000 switch-to-switch wires, we have to take faults with a probability of 10^{-20} (one every 10^7 sec.) into account to assess reliability over four months. Since simulation cannot be used and to efficiently compare different coding schemes, a method for the estimation of error probabilities is presented. This method is finally used to compare coding schemes providing different QoS-characteristics.

4.1 Coding Techniques for NoC-Buses

A code protecting data on the switch-to-switch buses must allow for fast decoding because decoding has to be completed before the switch can make a routing decision. Additionally, area constraints motivate a switch design with as little buffers as possible. We assume a NoC architecture that requires very low area overhead and high performance from the switches. Thus, we consider only codes that can process 100-200 bit wide buses in a single clock cycle and that can be implemented in a few gates of hardware for each bit. The requirement of fast decoding can be fulfilled by combinatorial logic circuits of low logic depth. Therefore, parity-based codes (e.g., Hamming or Hsiao codes [11]) are considered. These can be employed at various coding schemes: A single-error correcting (SEC) code can correct all single errors. All other errors lead to miscorrection. A double-error detecting (DED) code, on the other hand, detects all single and double errors. In fact, a DED code detects even more errors: If there are 2^k valid codewords of length n, $2^n - 2^k$ error patterns are detected. The properties of these two operating modes are combined in SEC-DED codes which require one more bit of redundancy to encode the same amount of information. Using codes with the ability to detect/correct more than two random errors usually makes decoding slower because arithmetic decoding is necessary [11].

Therefore, we focus on SEC, DED and SEC-DED codes and propose methods that help to enhance the capabilities of these codes in the presence of multiple-bit errors.

One possibility is to divide the network packet into several smaller blocks encoded separately. This *parallel coding* increases the redundancy, but enhances the overall error detection/correction capabilities and reduces the length of the critical path in the decoder. This approach also enables using different codes for different parts of the packet.

If the data is split into multiple blocks encoded separately, the n bits of a data block can be assigned to n adjacent wires of the bus or they can be interleaved, so that they will be assigned to the wires $x, x+\delta, x+2\delta, \ldots, x+(n-1)\delta$. The distance δ between two wires that belong to the same block is called *interleaving degree*.

To compare the capabilities of different coding schemes, we use the probability of uncorrected and undetected errors in a packet, $P_{err,UC}$ and $P_{err,UD}$ respectively.

It can be seen from figure 5 that in the presence of multi-bit errors, interleaving can lead to the reduction of those probabilities by several orders of magnitude. At small interleaving degrees, multi-wire faults may easily affect multiple bits of one block. With increasing interleaving degree, the probability that a fault affects multiple wires of one block decreases. In the fault scenario used, faults can affect up to 7 adjacent wires. This is why in figure 5, $P_{err,UC}$ and $P_{err,UD}$ constantly decrease with increasing interleaving degree. For interleaving degrees greater than 7, no further improvement can be achieved for the fault scenario used.

4.2 Estimation of Error Probabilities

To assess coding schemes, simulation is not feasible for faults with occurrence probabilities as low as 10^{-20}.

We have therefore developed an estimation method to predict error probabilities which is based on the proposed fault model notation. Thereby, errors spanning multiple adjacent wires are taken into account. In order to be able to assess block codes, we compute error probabilities for each block. For instance, a single error in a block of 4 wires of a bus occurs if exactly one wire is erroneous. Single errors are caused by faults affecting only one of the wires within the block or if a wire at the block's border is affected by multiple-bit errors. Thus, the probability that a single error is caused by an erroneous value of a border wire is higher compared to a wire in the middle of the block. Figure 3 shows errors due to two different faults, both leading to a single error within the considered block.

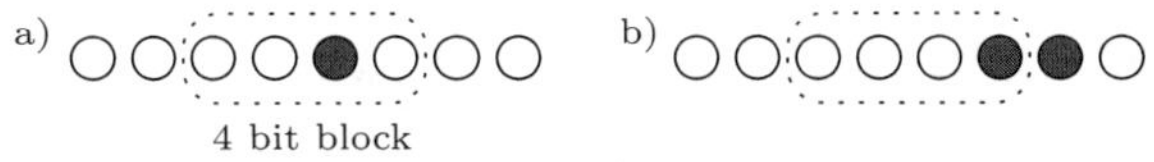

Figure 3: Faults affecting one and two adjacent wires, both leading to single errors in the 4 bit block

Figure 4 shows the probability of single and double errors when transferring data words of different width over a bus on adjacent wires or with interleaving. In these figures, estimations derived by the method proposed below are compared with simulation results and a second estimation based only on the fault occurrence probability. The simulation results were generated using a SystemC model for a bus which introduced errors according to the fault scenario from section 3.2. While results for a fault occurrence probability $\alpha = 10^{-4}$ are shown, other magnitudes of α yielded comparable accuracy for both interleaved and adjacent alignment.

The algorithm to estimate the probability of x-bit errors for blocks of n bits with an interleaving degree of δ is:

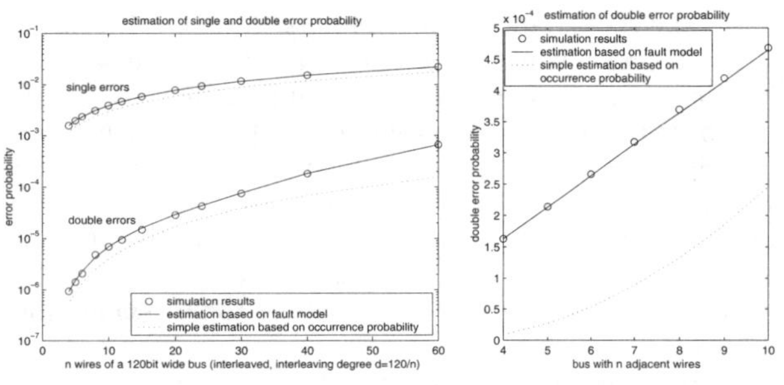

Figure 4: Estimation and simulation results

1. Compute the average probability that a wire is not affected by any fault: P_{ok}
2. Compute the probabilities $P_{b1}, \ldots, P_{bx}$ that $1 \ldots x$ adjacent bits on the border of the considered block are erroneous due to one fault. Combinations of different faults leading to erroneous bits are not counted.
3. In a similar way, compute the probabilities that $1 \ldots x$ adjacent bits in the middle of the considered block are erroneous. ($P_{m1}, \ldots, P_{mx}$)
4. From all possible error combinations leading to a x-bit error in the considered block (e.g., x single errors or one double error and $x-1$ single errors), the overall probability of x-bit errors is computed using P_{ok}, $P_{b1}, \ldots, P_{bx}$ and $P_{m1}, \ldots, P_{mx}$.
   Using this approach, the probability P_{de} of double errors in a block of n bits is for instance computed as

$$P_{de} = P_{ok}^{(n-2)} \cdot (2 \cdot P_{b2} + P_{b1}^2 + 2 \cdot P_{b1} \cdot P_{m1} \cdot (n-2) + (n-2-1) \cdot P_{m2} + P_{m1}^2 \cdot \binom{n-2}{2})$$

   The influence of the interleaving degree δ is contained in the values computed in the steps 1.–3.

The current implementation accurately predicts error probabilities for faults on a planar bus whose effect is to invert the logic value. It seems feasible to extend it to incorporate faults with different effects and other bus layouts.

4.3 Multiple QoS-levels in a NoC

The NoC must provide reliable communication services to resources. To guarantee packet delivery, the header (including destination address) of a packet must be particularly strong protected. On the other hand, the protection level of the payload should be tunable by the application.

Given a fixed number of physical wires, we propose to select the encoding scheme for the header first, so that the minimum reliability constraint is met. The number of wires required for header encoding limits those remaining for payload transmission. Payload encoding schemes for the desired service levels have to be selected so that the remaining wires are used efficiently. The selection is guided by trading off reliability versus bandwidth. We show this approach in the following example where we assume that 128 wires are available and that a 16 bits wide header is used.

Header Protection

Since the header protection should correct as many errors as possible while at the same time leaving as little errors as possible undetected, the obvious choice is a SEC-DED code. The header (16 bits) can be encoded as one block (1×16 SEC-DED), or as 2 blocks of 8 bits each (2×8 SEC-DED) or as 4 blocks (4×4 SEC-DED). The notation $b \times k$ means b blocks with k useful information bits each.

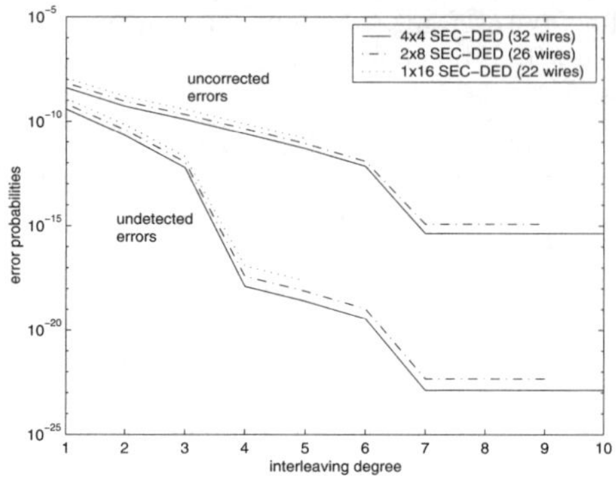

Figure 5: Reduction of error probabilities by interleaving blocks on a 128 bit bus

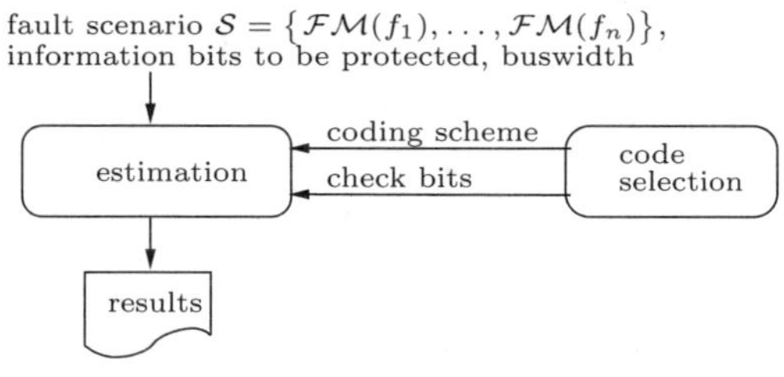

Figure 6: Code quality assessment

The estimation method we presented above was used to compare the properties of different encoding schemes. Figure 6 illustrates how this method was used to derive table 3 which shows the amount of wires required for the different encoding schemes along with information about the expected decoder logic depth and the probabilities of uncorrected and undetected errors ($P_{err,UC}$ and $P_{err,UD}$). As a comparison: When transmitting 16 bits over adjacent wires without encoding, the error probability is $5.33 \cdot 10^{-8}$.

Code	Wires	Max. interl.	Crit. path	$P_{err,UC}$	$P_{err,UD}$
1x16	22	5	9	$1.47 \cdot 10^{-11}$	$2.37 \cdot 10^{-18}$
2x8	26	9	8	$1.21 \cdot 10^{-15}$	$4.63 \cdot 10^{-23}$
4x4	32	16	6	$4.33 \cdot 10^{-16}$	$1.32 \cdot 10^{-23}$

Table 3: Comparison of header protection with different SEC-DED codes

Based on the information from table 3 and complementing experiments, the 2×8 SEC-DED code was chosen as header encoding scheme for this example. It is a reasonable trade-off between error probability and decoder speed, leaving 102 of the 128 wires to transmit the payload.

Payload Protection

Regarding the services discussed at the beginning of this paper, the *Maximum Bandwidth (MB)* mode is inherent in every implementation. In this example, the bandwidth of this mode is 102 bits/packet and the probability of an erroneous transfer is $3.36 \cdot 10^{-7}$.

Both the *Guaranteed Integrity (GI)* and *Minimum Latency (ML)* modes can be implemented with one code, using the property that every SEC code can also work as DED code: The same codewords are used for transmission, the encoder is identical and the DED code just uses the first part of the decoder block. Thus, these two services offer the same bandwidth to the application, but different protection characteristics. The possibility of this efficient implementation has influenced the selection of examined codes.

The selection of an appropriate coding scheme is guided by reliability and bandwidth constraints. Parameters are the number of parallel encoded blocks and their interleaving degree. This trade-off is shown in table 4. Out of these coding schemes, the appropriate one can be chosen.

Code	Max. interl.	Avail. bandw.	used as SEC $P_{err,UC}$	used as DED $P_{err,UD}$
1x95	1	95	$5.68 \cdot 10^{-8}$	$6.13 \cdot 10^{-9}$
2x45	2	90	$3.77 \cdot 10^{-9}$	$1.71 \cdot 10^{-10}$
3x28	3	84	$5.88 \cdot 10^{-10}$	$3.20 \cdot 10^{-12}$

Table 4: Error probabilities for different operation modes of SEC (or DED) codes, 102 physical wires

Since the *High Reliability (HR)* mode is based on a SEC-DED code, it will require different encoder/decoder logic in parallel to that used for the other modes. Note that SEC-DED codes offer one information bit less per block compared to SEC codes occupying the same amount of wires.

For the 128 bit bus of our example, we have selected the coding schemes from table 5. The selection of services and coding schemes a NoC supports is a design-time decision which depends on the intended application and environment, whereas each packet can be encoded with one of these codes during run-time. Since subsequent packets can be encoded differently, the information about the payload encoding scheme is transmitted as part of the header information.

Mode	Header protect.	Payload protect.	Payload
MB	2x8 SEC-DED	none	102
GI	2x8 SEC-DED	2x45 DED	90
ML	2x8 SEC-DED	2x45 SEC	90
HR	2x8 SEC-DED	3x27 SEC-DED	81

Table 5: Selected coding schemes

5. CONCLUSIONS

We have presented a fault model notation for faults occurring on on-chip buses that can represent a wide range of faults due to deep submicron effects, among them multiple-wire faults. We showed that error probabilities can be accurately predicted by this model in situations where the statistical independence of errors on bus lines cannot be assumed. This is important because crosstalk faults in future technology generations will most likely affect multiple wires.

Based on simulation and estimation results, we derived design guidelines for bus encoding schemes, namely splitting the data into multiple, separately encoded blocks and interleaving them. Using these simple methods, the probability of erroneous transfers can be reduced significantly.

The tradeoff between required reliability and the necessary overhead to achieve it was explored for different application requirements, leading to a proposal of a NoC that supports network traffic at four QoS levels. From these, each application can dynamically select the most appropriate one for its communication. An application can even adapt its policy during run-time when too many errors are encountered.

The specific constraints assumed for NoC-switches influenced the selection of considered codes which we belive is a good compromise when the critical path in the decoder should be kept as short as possible. With different requirements or when pipelining is possible, alternatives should be considered.

6. REFERENCES

[1] International Technology Roadmap for Semiconductors, 2001.

[2] L. Benini and G. De Micheli. Networks on chips: A new SoC paradigm. *IEEE Computer*, pages 70–78, January 2002.

[3] D. Bertozzi, L. Benini, and G. De Micheli. Low power error resilient encoding for on-chip data buses. In *Proc. Design, Automation and Test in Europe*, pages 102–109, March 2002.

[4] M. Cuviello, S. Dey, X. Bai, and Y. Zhao. Fault modeling and simulation for crosstalk in system-on-chip interconnects. *IEEE/ACM Int. Conf. on Computer-Aided Design*, pages 297–303, 1999.

[5] C. Duan, A. Tirumala, and S. P. Khatri. Analysis and avoidance of cross-talk in on-chip buses. *Hot Interconnects 9, 2001*, pages 133–138, 2001.

[6] M. Favalli and C. Metra. Bus crosstalk fault-detection capabilities of error-detecting codes for on-line testing. *IEEE Transactions on Very Large Scale Integration (VLSI) Systems*, pages 392–396, September 1999.

[7] K. Goossens, J. van Meerbergen, A. Peeters, and P. Wielage. Networks on silicon: Combining best-effort and guaranteed services. In *Proc. Design, Automation and Test in Europe*, March 2002.

[8] S. Kumar, A. Jantsch, J.-P. Soininen, M. Forsell, M. Millberg, J. Öberg, K. Tiensyrjä, and A. Hemani. A network on chip architecture and design methodology. In *Proc. of IEEE Computer Society Annual Symposium on VLSI*, April 2002.

[9] M. Lajolo, M. S. Reorda, and M. Violante. Early evaluation of bus interconnects dependability for system-on-chip designs. 14th *Int. Conf. on VLSI Design*, pages 371–376, January 2001.

[10] E. Nilsson, M. Millberg, J. Öberg, and A. Jantsch. Load distribution with the proximity congestion awareness in a network on chip. In *Proc. Design, Automation and Test in Europe*, pages 1126–1127, March 2003.

[11] T. Rao and E. Fujiwara. *Error-Control Coding for Computer Systems*. Prentice-Hall International, 1989.

[12] F. Worm, P. Thiran, P. Ienne, and G. De Micheli. An adaptive low-power transmission scheme for on-chip networks. In *Proc. of the 15th International Symposium on System Synthesis*, October 2002.

Invited Talk

Design Technology Challenges for System and Chip Level Designs in Very Deep Submicron Technologies

James Lin
National Semiconductor

Abstract

With very deep submicron process technologies, previously ignorable phenomena now have great impact on the robustness of IC designs. At the same time, the smaller feature sizes also enable an exponential increase in number of functions (or transistor count) available on chip. Complexity in process technology and design is widening the Design Technology gap, which, if not addressed properly, will threaten the continuation of process scaling and the industry's ability to benefit from it. The complexity of process and design technology, its impact on new designs, new products development and future solutions will be discussed in this presentation.

Biography

J. Lin

Mr. James Lin has been working in the semiconductor industry for more than 22 years. He has been working in various areas ranging from circuit and logic designs to test and product engineering. Currently, James is the Vice President of Technology Infrastructure Group of National Semiconductor Corporation, Santa Clara, California, where he is responsible for the research and development activities in Design Tools integration and development, Design flow, Design libraries and methodology.

Mr. Lin received MSEE from the Pennsylvania State University and is a member of IEEE and Chinese American Semiconductor Professional Association.

CODES+ISSS'03, October 1-3, 2003, Newport Beach, California, USA.
ACM 1-58113-742-7/03/0010.

Schedule-Aware Performance Estimation of Communication Architecture for Efficient Design Space Exploration

Sungchan Kim Chaeseok Im Soonhoi Ha

The School of Electrical Engineering and Computer Science

Seoul National University

Seoul 151-744, Korea

{ynwie, csim, sha}@iris.snu.ac.kr

ABSTRACT

In this paper, we are concerned about the performance estimation of bus-based architectures assuming that the task partitioning on the processing components is already determined. Since the communication behavior is usually unpredictable due to dynamic bus requests of processing components, bus contention, and so on, simulation based approach seems inevitable for accurate performance estimation. But it is too time consuming to explore the wide design space. To overcome this serious drawback, we propose a static performance estimation method that is based on the queuing model and makes use of memory traces and task execution schedule information. We propose to use this static estimation approach to prune the design space drastically before applying a simulation-based approach. Comparison with trace-driven simulation results proves the validity of our static estimation technique.

Categories and Subject Descriptors

B.8.2 [**Hardware**]: Performance and Reliability – *Performance Analysis and Design Aids.*

General Terms

Design, Performance

Keywords

Performance estimation, design space exploration, communication architecture, queuing theory

1. INTRODUCTION

In system level design, selection of appropriate communication architecture is a critical design step. In this paper we assume that the system behavior is modeled as a composition of function blocks. Differentiation between functions and communication allows the system designer to explore the communication architecture independently of component selection. Then, communication architecture selection is performed after a decision is made on which processing components are used and which function blocks are mapped on which processing components. And a task is defined as a group of function blocks sequentially scheduled on a processing component.

The key tool for exploring the design space of communication architecture is to estimate the performance of communication architectures, which is the main theme of this paper. In particular, we are concerned about the bus-based architectures since the bus-based architecture is most widely adopted due to its simplicity and popularity. From the mapping result of function blocks to the processing elements, we obtain the bus requests from the processing elements and those bus requests are input data to the performance estimation tool. Unlike the previous work similar to ours [8], we take into account the bus requests for the local memory accesses as well as for the shared memory access of inter-component communication.

Since the communication behavior is usually unpredictable due to dynamic trace of memory accesses, bus contention, and so on, simulation based approach seems inevitable for accurate performance estimation. However, since the memory traces of processing elements are enormous, trace driven simulation needs a huge data storage for simulating only a few seconds of execution of application. Some commercial tools and research tools use execution-driven simulation where the simulator executes the tasks to produce the bus requests on-line which are passed to the module that accurately models the communication architecture. But the main drawback of a simulation-based approach is that it is too slow to be used for exploring the wide design space of architectures.

Even after a specific bus standard is chosen to be used, the design space can still be huge if a single bus segment cannot accommodate all memory requests within a given time budget. For example, we need to determine how many bus segments are used with what topology and which processing elements and memory banks are mapped to which bus segments. We also have to decide the memory types and memory system configurations. If we include the selection of bus operation frequency and arbitration policy, the design space explodes.

To explore the wide design space, we need a fast and accurate performance estimation method while the simulation-based approach is too slow. To overcome this difficulty, we propose a two-step communication architecture exploration scheme. We propose a static performance estimation method that is based on the queuing model and makes use of memory traces and task execution schedule information. We use this static estimation approach to prune the design space before applying a simulation-based estimation. As the static estimation gets more accurate, the design space to be explored by simulation would be narrower. The key contribution of this paper is to propose an accurate static estimation method taking into account of all dynamic behaviors due to bus contention and dynamic memory traces. We show the effectiveness of our method in terms of estimated time accuracy of entire execution compared with the results of trace-driven simulation.

The remainder of this paper is organized as follows. In section 2 we state our proposed design space exploration framework and outline the performance estimation techniques. Section 3 reviews some related works. In section 4 the queuing model for a priority-based single bus is explained. Section 5 contains the detailed discussion on the estimation method considering a task schedule and memory traces and on the extension to multiple bus systems. In section 6 we give some experimental results and draw conclusions in section 7.

2. PROPOSED DESIGN SPACE EXPLORATION FRAMEWORK

The proposed design space exploration procedure, depicted in Figure 1(a), assumes that a system behavior is modeled as a composition of function blocks. We do not assume any specific computing model for block composition as long as the system behavior is defined by a non-preemptive execution sequence of function blocks. The only restriction is that the execution order of function blocks is known a priori. Dataflow specification for digital signal processing (DSP) application is a well-known example that meets the restriction.

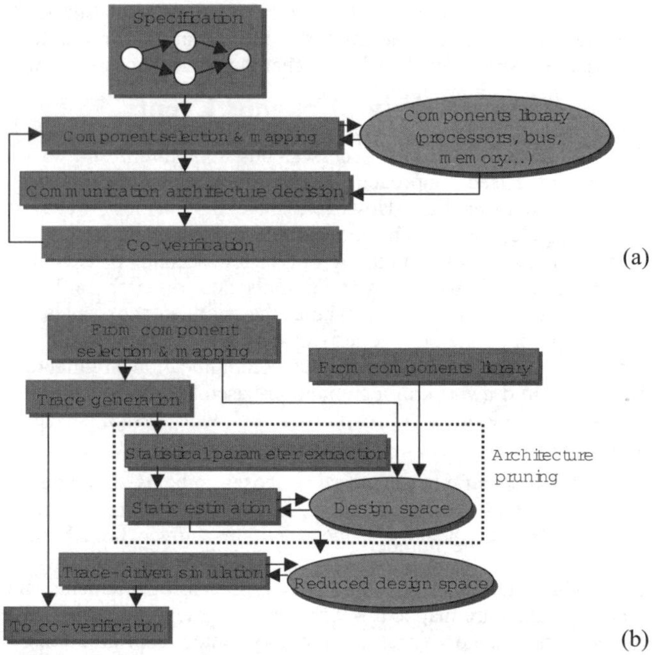

Figure 1. (a) The proposed design space exploration procedure and (b) the procedure of communication architecture exploration

From the functional specification of system behavior, we first perform platform and component selection and mapping of the function blocks to the processing components. Next, the design space of communication architectures is explored as shown in Figure 1(b). After mapping is completed, we obtain the memory access traces from all processing elements using component simulators: an instruction set simulator for a processor core, HDL simulator for ASIC parts, or IP simulators. In the trace information, we distinguish three different memory access types: code memory, local data memory, and shared memory accesses. We assume that the design space of communication architecture includes memory configurations and memory assignments. Therefore, we include the local memory accesses in the trace information. A memory trace consists of three fields: (processing component, memory access types, time stamp). When we obtain the time stamp, we assume that there is no resource contention, and all memory accesses are finished in a clock cycle.

From the traces, we extract some statistical parameter values to be used in the proposed static estimation method based on the queuing model. Using those parameter values, the static performance estimation of communication architectures is performed to prune the design space. How to prune the design space is beyond the scope of this paper. In the static estimation step, we utilize the task execution schedule on the processing components. The schedule information is used to determine which processing components participate in bus contention at a given instance of time. Finally, trace driven simulation is performed with a reduced set of candidate communication architecture.

3. RELATED WORK

Some researchers have considered communication architecture selection simultaneously during the synthesis of computation parts of system and mapping step. Since the communication overhead is needed for the mapping decision, static estimation of communication architecture has been investigated. A technique was proposed to estimate the communication delay using the worst-case response analysis of real-time scheduling [6]. Knudsen and Madsen estimated the communication overhead taking into account the data transfer rate variation depending on the protocol, configuration, and different operating frequencies of components [4][5]. However these techniques do not model the dynamic effects such as bus contention and explore only a limited configuration space.

While simulation-based performance estimation is proposed [2][3] and also widely adopted in the commercial tools at the transaction level [9][10] or at the pin-level [11], there have been proposed only a few static estimation techniques. One is to synthesize the bus architecture with a given and fixed bus request information [7]. But this approach is not applicable in the general case where memory request times are non-deterministic and bus contention exists. A hybrid approach between a static estimation and a simulation approach has been developed by Lahiri et. al. [8]. In their work, communication and computation segments are grouped to make the BSE(Bus and Synchronization Event) graph from the trace data obtained after system cosimulation. They focused on inter-component communication activities that are usually localized in time at the boundary of computation segment. The trace groups are scheduled on the communication media, being shifted by the estimated delays considering the resource contention. They use some static analysis to group the traces and apply a trace-driven simulation with the trace groups. Their approach is similar to ours in that they apply some static analysis to the memory traces to reduce the time complexity of trace-driven simulation. But the overall approach is different from ours. Moreover they do not consider the local memory accesses. If they consider the local memory accesses, the BSE graph size becomes prohibitively huge.

Our work is inspired by the work in [1] where a simple queuing model of SCSI bus is proposed and the model produces remarkable results comparing with the simulation results. Since the communication behavior of a processor-memory bus is quite different from an I/O bus, their approach can not be directly applicable. Instead, we made several extensions and improved the estimation accuracy significantly.

4. SIMPLE MODEL OF A SINGLE BUS

4.1 Base Queuing Model For A Single Bus

A base estimation technique using a queuing model for a single bus is explained in this section. The basic idea and notations used here are borrowed from [1]. There are N components, numbered 0 though N-1, competing for the use of the bus. It is assumed that the bus arbitration is based on the fixed priorities of components. Device 0 has the highest priority. The bus access is assumed non-preemptive. Figure 2 shows the queuing model of a single bus architecture. λ_i denotes the rate at which component i issues memory request. It is computed as the ratio between the memory access counts and the scheduled length of execution. If the execution time is lengthened due to bus contention, the effective arrival rate of request becomes smaller than λ_i. We denote the actual memory access rate by θ_i that is actually seen on the bus. The mean service time of a server for the request of component i is denoted by $1/\mu_i$. Let $\bar{k}_i$ be the expected number of requests from component i waiting for the bus. It is within the range of [0,1] if the component does not issue the next memory request until the current request is served. And we denote $\bar{w}_i$ as the expected waiting time of the stalled request. Then, we can obtain the following equation:

$$\theta_i = (1 - \bar{k}_i - u_i)\lambda_i\,, \tag{1}$$

where $u_i = \theta_i / \mu_i$ is the bus utilization factor by device i. Little's law shows

$$\bar{w}_i = \bar{k}_i / \theta_i\,. \tag{2}$$

From this equation, we want to obtain θ_i which indicates the delays incurred from contention on the bus. We can extract the parameters λ_i and μ_i from the memory traces. There is an unknown parameter $\bar{k}_i$. To obtain this parameter, we use the state transition diagram and steady-state probability.

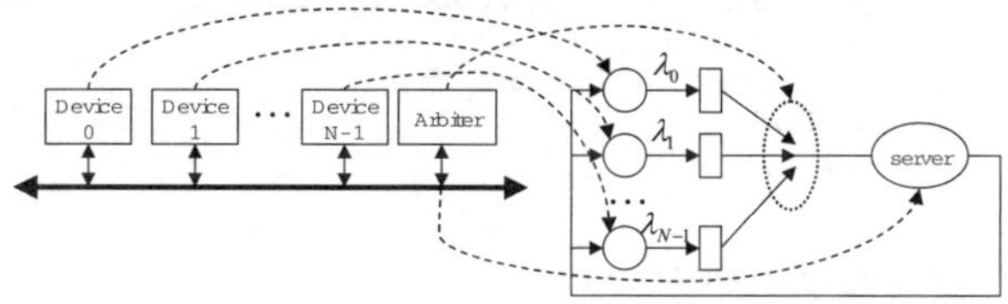

Figure 2. Queuing modeling of a single bus

We draw a state transition diagram from the viewpoint of component i (i=1,…,N-2). We define the system state as a quadruple and its steady state probability by $p(n_i,n_h,n_l,s)$, where n_i is the number of requests from device i (n_i=0,1), n_h(n_h=0,...,i-1) the number of requests from components of higher priority than i, n_l (n_l=i+1,…,N-1) the number of requests from components of lower priority than i, and s is the priority of component that is using the bus currently.

State (n_i,n_h,n_l,s) moves to (n_i,n_h+1,n_l,s) if another request arrives from a component of higher priority and its transition rate is approximated by α_h, $\alpha_h \approx (N_h - n_h)\gamma_h$, where $N_h = i$ is the total number of higher priority components and γ_h is the average rate of arrivals for higher priority requests. γ_h can be computed as follows by summing up the equation (1) from component 0 to component i-1.

$$\sum_{j=0}^{i-1}\theta_j = \left\{N_h - \sum_{j=0}^{i-1}(\bar{k}_j + u_j)\right\}\gamma_h\,. \tag{3}$$

The approximate transition rate β_h to state (n_i,n_h-1,n_l,s) is approximated as follows:

$$\beta_h \approx \sum_{j=0}^{i-1}\left(\mu_j \cdot u_j \Big/ \sum_{k=0}^{i-1} u_k\right), \tag{4}$$

The similar formulations can be given to the lower priority requests. The readers are referred to [1] for more details about derivation of α_h, β_h, α_l, and β_l respectively. From the state transition diagram and the transition rates, we can compute the steady-state probability $p(n_i,n_h,n_l,s)$ using an additional requirement of $\sum_{n_l=0}^{l}\sum_{n_h=0}^{N_h}\sum_{n_l=0}^{N_l}\sum_{S} p(n_i,n_h,n_l,s) = 1$. After all steady-state probabilities are computed, we can compute the expected number of waiting requests $\bar{k}_i$ by summing up the probabilities of a certain set of states as follows:

$$\sum_{n_h=0}^{N_h}\sum_{n_l=0}^{N_l}\sum_{S} p(1,n_h,n_l,s) = u_i + \bar{k}_i\,. \tag{5}$$

Note that evaluation of $p(n_i,n_h,n_l,s)$ needs $\bar{k}_i$ by (3) and (4). Therefore, these equations can be solved by an iterative method until $\bar{k}_i$ becomes stable. And, this iterative procedure to get $\bar{k}_i$ is repeated for each priority level i (i=1,…,N-2). We used an ILP package to solve the equations and found that the solutions are converged within less than 10 iterations in all cases, which takes much less than trace-driven simulation.

4.2 Extension To Simultaneous Events

The base queuing model of the previous section models a continuous system where the bus request can be served at any instance of time. In reality, however, bus arbitration is performed at discrete sampling points (i.e. clock edges) among all bus requests accumulated so far. If we assume that there occurs only one event, either request arrival or service completion, in each clock period, the base queuing model may be used as an approximate model. This assumption is suitable for the I/O bus case where bus requests are infrequent and service time is relatively large. But in our case, several events are very likely to occur during a single clock period. Thus we modify the model to allow simultaneous events. And, the state transition rate of a transition arc should be replaced by the state transition probability within a clock period.

The number of possible transitions from a state grows exponentially as the number of simultaneous events increases. Thus, we make a compromise between the modeling complexity and the modeling accuracy. The compromised model allows up to two simultaneous events. And an event is defined by a single increment or decrement of a coordinate of a state (n_i,n_h,n_l,s). Table 1 shows all possible state transitions whose total number is 15. Type 1 transition indicates the case that only one event occurs while type 2 transition indicates that two events arrive during the next clock cycle. For the computation of the transition probabilities, we introduce two new parameters d_h and d_l as the probabilities that at least one component issues a new request among high priority components and low priority components respectively:

$$d_h = 1-(1-\gamma_h)^{N_h-n_h},\; d_l = 1-(1-\gamma_l)^{N_l-n_l}. \quad (6)$$

And let S the service rate of component that is using the bus currently. For instance, the transition probability from state (n_i,n_h,n_l,s) to (n_i,n_h+1,n_l+1,s) becomes $(1-\lambda_i)d_h d_l(1-S)$. Note that this is a rough approximation of the state transition probability. Even though more than two requests may arrive from the higher-priority components, we only increase the number n_k by 1.

We performed a preliminary experiment to compare the accuracy of the base model and that of the modified model. In this experiment, the number of processing components is set to 10 and burst size of memory access is selected randomly. Memory access cycle is assumed one. About 36% of entire execution time is contributed by memory accesses when arrival rate λ is 0.1 and 67% when λ is 0.2. As shown in Table 2, the proposed modification improves the accuracy by 25.5% on average for maximum estimation error and 29.1% on average for average estimation error. We guess that more complicated modeling of state transitions would result in more accurate estimation.

Table 1. State transitions from state (n_i,n_h,n_l,s) to other states.

Type 1		Type 2	
Next state	Transition rate	Next state	Transition rate
(n_i+1,n_h,n_l,s)	$\lambda_i(1-d_h)(1-d_l)(1-S)$	(n_i+1,n_h+1,n_l,s)	$\lambda_i d_h(1-d_l)(1-S)$
(n_i,n_h+1,n_l,s)	$(1-\lambda_i)d_h(1-d_l)(1-S)$	(n_i,n_h+1,n_l+1,s)	$(1-\lambda_i)d_h d_l(1-S)$
(n_i,n_h,n_l+1,s)	$(1-\lambda_i)(1-d_h)d_l(1-S)$	(n_i+1,n_h,n_l+1,s)	$\lambda_i(1-d_h)d_l(1-S)$
(n_i-1,n_h,n_l,s)	$\mu_i(1-d_h)(1-d_l)$	(n_i-1,n_h+1,n_l,s)	$\mu_i d_h(1-d_l)$
(n_i,n_h-1,n_l,s)	$(1-\lambda_i)\beta_h(1-d_l)$	(n_i-1,n_h,n_l+1,s)	$\mu_i(1-d_h)d_l$
(n_i,n_h,n_l-1,s)	$(1-\lambda_i)(1-d_h)\beta_l$	(n_i+1,n_h-1,n_l,s)	$\lambda_i\beta_h(1-d_l)$
		(n_i,n_h-1,n_l+1,s)	$(1-\lambda_i)\beta_h d_l$
		(n_i+1,n_h,n_l-1,s)	$\lambda_i(1-d_h)\beta_l$
		(n_i,n_h+1,n_l-1,s)	$(1-\lambda_i)d_h\beta_l$

Table 2. Performance comparison of the base queuing model and the proposed queuing model

Arrival rate λ	0.1			0.2		
Error (%)	Base	Proposed	Improved	Base	Proposed	Improved
Minimum	0.73	0.21	71.22	2.40	2.41	-0.18
Maximum	16.02	12.14	24.19	16.73	12.25	26.75
Average	7.01	4.20	40.05	6.90	5.65	18.19

5. STATIC ESTIMATION USING SCHEDULE INFORMATION

5.1 Estimation Of A Single Bus

This section explains how task schedule information is used in our estimation method. A simple statistical modeling of bus requests from a processing component assumes that the bus requests are distributed throughout the whole execution duration of application. This assumption is one of the main sources of inaccuracy of simple static statistical modeling. The schedule information, on the other hand, discloses the active durations of bus requests as shown in Figure 3 (a): for example, it shows that during time 2 and 4, PE2 does not generate any bus request.

Therefore, we divide the time slots in such a way that all processing components maintain their bus request patterns during the time slot. And we apply the proposed queuing model analysis in each time slot starting from the beginning of the schedule. Figure 3 displays how the proposed scheme progresses. The shaded region indicates the remaining sections for static estimation. First, we perform the proposed queuing analysis during time 0 to 2 until PE2 finishes its execution (Figure 3(a)). Note that the schedule of Figure 3(b) is different from Figure 3(a) since the schedule of the first time slot is updated taking into account the bus contention. In the next time slot, we have to re-compute the statistical parameters for all processing components involved in bus contention.

The overall algorithm of the estimation technique for a single bus is described in Figure 4. The procedure ***Estimate_single_bus*** has 5 inputs. **B** represents a data structure of the single bus. **MT** and **ORI_SCHED** are the memory traces of all processing elements and the original schedule. **PL** is the set of processing components and **FL** is the set of tasks to be used for static estimation. The output, **EVAL_SCHED**, of this procedure is the updated schedule after considering all bus conflicts and other overheads if any.

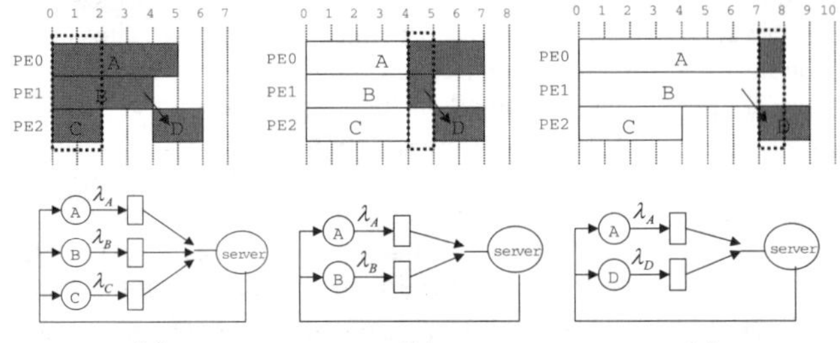

(a) (b) (c)

Figure 3. (a) Initial schedule of PE0, PE1, and PE2, and corresponding queuing system, (b) new queuing system of PE0 and PE1 after c finished, and (c) another queuing system of PE0 and PE2 in the last time slot

```
Estimate_single_bus
inputs: B, MT, ORI_SCHED, PL, FL
outputs: SCHEDULE EVAL_SCHED
begin
  EVAL_SCHED = ORI_SCHED;
  cur_time = 0;
  foreach pe ∈ PL
    pe.cur_fb=NULL;
    pe.cur_fb_done=FALSE;
  end for
  while (FL not empty)
    foreach pe ∈ PL
      if (pe.cur_fb_done==TRUE or pe.cur_fb==NULL)
        pe.cur_fb = get_current_fb(EVAL_SCHED, PL, FL);
        stat_params = get_stat_params(ORI_SCHED, PL, FL, MT);
        if (pe.fb_start_time < cur_time)
          cur_time = pe.fb_start_time;
        end if
      end if
    end for
    cur_time = estimate_end_time(B,PL,EVAL_SCHED,stat_params);
    update_schedule(EVAL_SCHED, cur_time);
  end while
end
```

Figure 4. Schedule-aware performance estimation algorithm for a single bus

The main procedure of queuing analysis is ***estimate_end_time.*** Before the queuing analysis, we first determine which processing components request the bus by calling the ***get_current_fb*** procedure and compute the statistical parameters by calling the ***get_stat_params*** procedure. We compute two statistical parameters of each task from the **MT** memory trace: they are the memory access rate, θ, and the mean service time, $\overline{S}$. The memory access rate $\theta_{FB,PE}$ is computed by the following formula:

$$\theta_{FB,PE} = M_{FB,PE} / EXE_{FB,PE}, \tag{7}$$

where $M_{FB,PE}$ is a total memory access count during the execution of task FB and $EXE_{FB,PE}$ is the task execution time on PE. When computing the mean service time, we consider the different burst transfer size according to the memory access type. For example, code memory access is usually a burst access of which the size equals to the cache line size, whereas data memory access may have various burst lengths for write operation and the cache line size for read. Then the mean service time $\overline{S}_{FB,PE}$ is computed as

$$\overline{S}_{FB,PE} = \sum_{i \in \{all\_access\_type\}} \left(\sum_{j \in \{all\_burst\_type\}} S_{i,j,PE} \cdot \frac{M_{i,j,FB,PE}}{M_{FB,PE}} \right), \tag{8}$$

where $S_{i,j,PE}$, $M_{i,j,FB,PE}$ are the service time (including the bus overhead as well as the memory access time) and the number of access counts of burst type *j* which belongs to memory access type *i* when task FB runs on processing component PE.

Final procedure ***update_schedule*** modifies the original schedule to obtain the updated schedule, **EVAL_SCHED,** after the current time slot. From the updated schedule, we define the next time slot and go back to the main iteration body until all tasks are considered.

5.2 Extension to Multiple Bus System

Communications across buses are achieved via bus bridge in a multiple bus system. A bus bridge plays both roles of a processing component and a memory system as displayed in Figure 5. We assume for simple analysis that no communication passes through more than 3 buses. Figure 5 shows how the bridge is modeled when a processing component on the *src* bus accesses a memory on the *dest* bus. The request rate of the component λ_{src} is reflected to the *dest* bus by the request rate λ_{dest} of the bridge. To compute λ_{dest} we have to know the mean waiting time, w_{src}, of the processing component on the *src* bus. At the same time, the bus bridge looks like a memory from the *src* bus point of view. The service rate μ_{src} of the bus bridge should be computed. Let w_{dest} be the mean waiting time of the bridge on the *dest* bus. Then, λ_{dest} and μ_{src} are computed as follows:

$$\frac{1}{\lambda_{dest}} = \frac{1}{\lambda_{src}} + w_{src} + O_{bridge}, \quad \frac{1}{\mu_{src}} = w_{dest} + O_{bridge} + \frac{1}{\mu_{dest}}, \tag{9}$$

where O_{bridge} is overhead time at bus bridge. On the other hand, w_{src} and w_{dest} are obtained from our static estimation technique after λ_{dest} and μ_{src} computation. Therefore the static estimation and bridge modeling are performed iteratively until all parameters become stable.

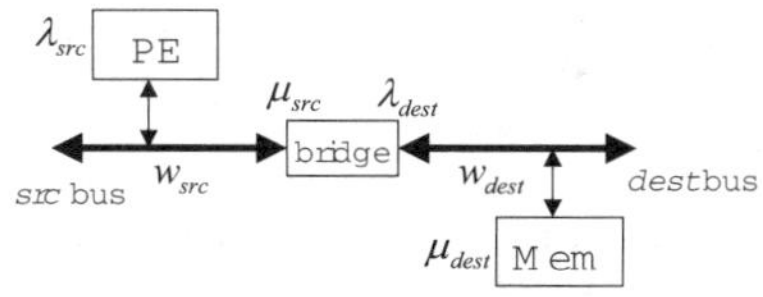

Figure 5. The modeling of communication via bus bridge

6. EXPREIMENTS

To investigate the accuracy of the proposed static estimation method over a wide variety of working conditions, we first perform the experiments on a single bus varying the number of processors, bus request rates, bus service rates (or memory access times), and burst lengths. We generate the memory traces from each processing component following a Poisson distribution (i.e. exponentially distributed inter-arrival times between bus requests).

We compare the estimation results with those obtained from trace driven simulation. Our trace driven simulator adjusts the time stamps of trace data by accurately modeling the communication architecture that includes buses and memories. More precisely, in these experiments, our bus model consists of 4 phases: bus-arbitration, start-address-drive, sequential-burst-transfer, last-data-drive.

Figure 6 shows the accuracy results on the varying number of processing elements (PEs=2,4,6,10) according to the various bus request rates (λ) and the various memory access times. We display the range of estimation error with a bar graph, which indicates the minimum and the maximum errors of completion times of processing components. The scheduled execution time without bus contention is set to 10,000 cycles.

The burst size is randomly selected. In case that λ is 0.1 and memory access time is 1 cycle, the portion of the total memory access time over the entire execution time is about 0.36. This is similar to the case when we run an H.263 encoding algorithm, which we will discuss later.

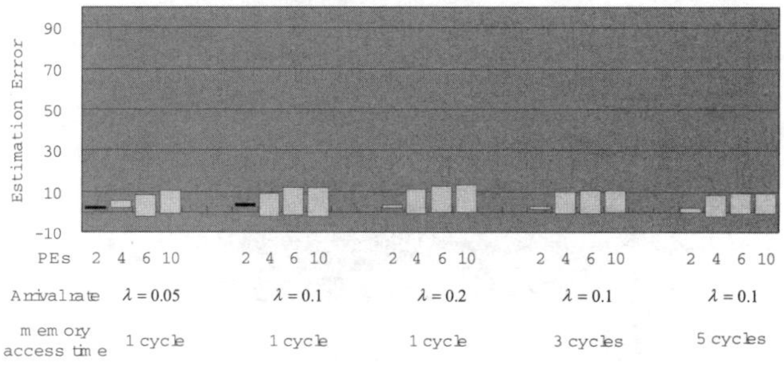

Figure 6. Estimation accuracy according to the various request rates and the various memory access times

In all cases, the estimation error of the proposed method does not exceed 13%. We also notice that the estimation results are greater than the simulation results: underestimation errors are below at most –3.0%. Three experiments show the robust performance of our estimation technique on various architecture configurations.

It is questionable whether there is a simpler static estimation method that is reasonably accurate. So, we devised an intuitive estimation method on the waiting time of processing elements *i*, w_i, by bus contention, for a single bus that has *N* processing elements, as shown in formula (10).

$$w_i = \frac{\sum_{j=0}^{i-1} m_j}{exe_i} \cdot \frac{ts_i}{2} \cdot (i-1) + \frac{\sum_{j=i+1}^{N-1} m_j}{exe_i} \cdot \frac{ts_i}{2}, \tag{10}$$

where m_j, exe_j, and ts_j are the total memory access times, the total execution time, and the mean service time of component *j* respectively. At the right side of equation (10), the first term is the expected waiting time due to the bus requests from higher priority components and the second term is the waiting time due to the current outstanding request of a low priority component. Table 3 shows the accuracy comparison between this intuitive method and the proposed method assuming that λ is 0.2, the memory access time is 3 cycles, and the burst size is 4. The results of intuitive method get worse rapidly according to the increase of PEs whereas the proposed method keeps its error range of estimation within 10%.

Table 4 shows the run time of the proposed static estimation and the maximum and the minimum number of states varying the number of PEs on Xeon 1.8GHz. We used a commercial ILP package to solve the linear equations of the proposed method [12]. For each processing component i, the number of states $\{(n_i, n_h, n_p, s)\}$ is $O(N^2)$ where N is the total number of components. The number of states depends on the priority of the component of interest. Since the time complexity of the LP(linear program) solver is pseudo-polynomial, the overall time complexity is also pseudo-polynomial. Table 4 confirms this fact that the proposed technique has acceptable complexity for design space exploration.

Table 3. Comparison with intuitive estimation method

PEs	2		4		6		10	
Method	int	pro	int	pro	int	Pro	int	pro
Min. Error(%)	16.72	2.06	9.78	1.32	5.15	0.00	46.63	0.31
Max. Error(%)	17.32	2.66	18.91	9.79	84.31	9.90	232.98	9.95
Avg. Error(%)	17.02	2.36	15.16	4.86	43.75	4.07	121.71	3.47

Table 4. Complexity of the proposed estimation technique

PEs	CPU time (sec)	Min. Number of states	Max. Number of states
2	0.03	5	5
4	0.07	21	21
6	0.33	37	47
10	2.94	69	129

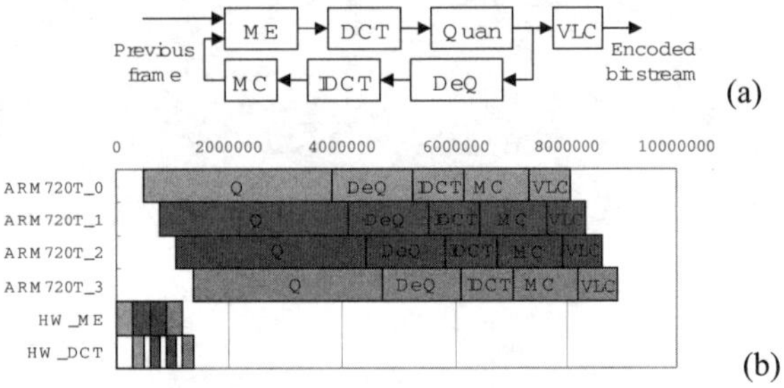

Figure 7. (a) Specification of an H.263 encoding algorithm, (b) the initial schedule of 4-channel digital video recorder (DVR)

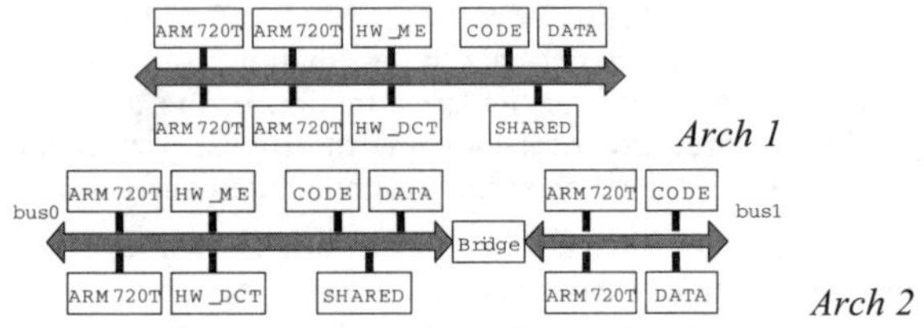

Figure 8. Alternative communication architectures

Finally, we validate our proposed technique by applying it to a practical example, 4-channel digital video recorder (DVR). DVR receives the raw bit streams from external 4 sources and encodes each stream separately using H.263 encoding algorithm. Figure 7(a) shows the specification of H.263 encoding algorithm. All function blocks of the H.263 encoder except ME and DCT blocks are mapped to one ARM720T. And all MEs and DCTs are mapped to a motion estimation (ME) hardware block and a discrete cosine transform (DCT) hardware block respectively so that four H.263 encoders share two hardware blocks. Therefore we construct the initial schedule of each function block like Figure 7(b). Also two communication architectures are chosen: a single bus architecture *Arch 1* and two bus, one bridge architecture *Arch 2* in Figure 8. In *Arch 2*, two ARM720Ts in bus1 access shared memory in bus0 to communicate with HW_ME and HW_DCT. A comparison of estimation results for two communication architectures with trace-driven simulation are shown in Table 5. Errors of overall execution time estimation are still within 10% in both of two architectures. Ideal execution time of *Arch 2* is larger than *Arch 1* due to bus bridge overhead. The real execution time gets larger in *Arch 2* by just 14% due to the concurrency of memory accesses in two buses whereas *Arch 1* extends its real execution time by 85% due to serious bus contentions. Consequently *Arch 2* is faster than *Arch 1* by about 30%.

Table 5. Experimental results about DVR

Architecture candidates	Arch 1	Arch 2
Schedule	8949897	8949897
Ideal	13427568	13541616
Simulation	24871433	15402311
Estimation	23559707	16473155
Error (%)	-5.27	6.95

7. CONCLUSION

In this paper, we presented an efficient static estimation technique of fixed-priority based communication architecture. It is based on the queuing model and makes use of the schedule information and memory traces. Since the estimation time is polynomial to the number of processing components, the number of tasks, and the number of bus segments, the proposed technique can be used to prune the large design space before trace-driven simulation. Experimental results show our proposed technique performs well providing suitable estimation error, at most 10% to 15%, compared with trace driven simulation in various communication architecture configurations.

Future researches will be focused on the development of design space exploration algorithm and the modeling of other bus arbitration schemes such as round robin and TDMA.

8. ACKNOLWEDGMENT

This work was supported by National Research Laboratory Program(number M1-0104-00-0015) and Brain Korea 21 Project. The RIACT at Seoul National University provided research facilities for this study.

9. REFERENCES

[1] A. Brandwajn, "A note on SCSI bus waits", ACM SIGMETRICS Performance Evaluation Review Vol.30, Issue 2, pp.41-47, Sept. 2002.

[2] P. Lieverse, P. V. Wolf, E. Deprettere and K. Vissers, "A methodology for architecture exploration of heterogeneous signal processing systems", IEEE Workshop on Signal Processing Systems, pp.181-190, 1999.

[3] J. A. Rowson and A. Sangiovanni-Vincentelli, "Interface based design", Design Automation Conf., pp.178-183, June. 1997.

[4] P. V. Knudsen and J. Madsen, "Communication estimation for hardware/software codesign", Int. Symp. on Hardware/Software Codesign, pp.55-59, 1998.

[5] P. Knudsen and J. Madsen, "Integrating communication protocol selection with partitioning in hardware/software codesign", Int. Symp. on System Level Synthesis, pp.150-155, Sept.1998.

[6] T. Yen and W. Wolf, "Communication synthesis for distributed embedded systems", Int. Conf. on Computer-Aided Design, pp.437-444, Nov.1995.

[7] M. Gasteier and M. Glesner, "Bus-based communication synthesis on system level", ACM Tran. on Design Automation Electronic Systems, pp.1-11, Jan.1999.

[8] K. Lahiri, A. Raghunathan, and S. Dey, "Fast performance analysis of bus-based system-on-chip communication architectures", Int. Conf. on Computer Aided Design, pp.590-597, Nov. 1999.

[9] Synopsys CoCentric System Studio, http://www.synopsys.com/products/ cocentric_studio/cocentric_studio.html

[10] CoWare N2C Design System, http://www.coware.com/cowareN2C.html

[11] Mentor Graphics SeamlessCVE, http://www.mentorg.com/seamless/

[12] ILOG CPLEX, http://www.ilog.com/products/cplex/

Accurate Estimation of Cache-Related Preemption Delay

Hemendra Singh Negi Tulika Mitra Abhik Roychoudhury

School of Computing
National University of Singapore
Republic of Singapore 117543.
[hemendra,tulika,abhik]@comp.nus.edu.sg

ABSTRACT

Multitasked real-time systems often employ caches to boost performance. However the unpredictable dynamic behavior of caches makes schedulability analysis of such systems difficult. In particular, the effect of caches needs to be considered for estimating the inter-task interference. As the memory blocks of different tasks can map to the same cache blocks, preemption of a task may introduce additional cache misses. The time penalty introduced by these misses is called the Cache-Related Preemption Delay (CRPD).

In this paper, we provide a program path analysis technique to estimate CRPD. Our technique performs path analysis of both the preempted and the preempting tasks. Furthermore, we improve the accuracy of the analysis by estimating the possible states of the entire cache at each possible preemption point rather than estimating the states of each cache block independently. To avoid incurring high space requirements, the cache states can be maintained symbolically as a Binary Decision Diagram. Experimental results indicate that we obtain tight CRPD estimates for realistic benchmarks.

Categories and Subject Descriptors

C.3 [**Computer Systems Organization**]: Special-Purpose and Application-Based Systems—*Real-time and Embedded Systems*

General Terms

Measurement, Performance, Reliability.

Keywords

Caches, Multitasking, Preemption, Formal Analysis.

1. INTRODUCTION

Real-time embedded systems involve tasks operating under deadlines which need to be met. Consequently schedulability analysis of such tasks has been a topic of active research. For each task, schedulability analysis needs to know the worst case execution time (WCET), that is, an upper bound on the task execution time. For preemptive task scheduling, we also need to estimate the inter-task interference (the additional execution time introduced when a high priority task preempts a low priority task). However, performance enhancing micro-architectural features of modern processors make such estimation difficult.

Ideally, the WCET of a program should be the cost of its longest path. However, this assumes that the execution time of each instruction is constant. In reality, the execution time of a memory access instruction depends on the past instructions executed (which decides whether it is a cache hit/miss). Thus, path analysis of the program cannot be done at the level of assembly code; it also needs to take into account the effect of micro-architectural features such as caches [5, 9, 11, 14]. This explains the importance of cache behavior modeling for WCET analysis.

Caches have a role to play in inter-task interference estimation as well. Consider a low priority task τ which is preempted by a higher priority task τ'. Let the set of cache blocks to which the memory blocks of τ (τ') get mapped be C_τ ($C_{\tau'}$). If $C_\tau \cap C_{\tau'} \neq \emptyset$ then τ' may displace some memory blocks of τ from the cache, resulting in additional cache misses when τ resumes. This effect of task preemption on cache performance is known in the literature as *Cache-Related Preemption Delay* (CRPD).

CRPD estimation is important from the point of view of schedulability analysis. In particular, [7, 8] reports how CRPD can be used to derive accurate response times of multiple periodic tasks running on a single processor for fixed-priority preemptive scheduling. We can avoid CRPD estimation by ignoring arbitrary preemption (as in [10] which only studies the interference at the beginning of a periodic task's execution). Alternatively, we can employ cache partitioning [6], where each task is allowed to use only a portion of the cache. However, this leads to severe degradation of performance. Thus, for multitasked preemptive real-time systems with caches, CRPD estimation is necessary.

When a task τ is preempted by a higher priority task τ' what are the additional cache misses introduced? To answer this question, we need to consider the following factors. First, all the memory blocks of τ which are in the cache when τ is preempted may not be re-referenced after resumption. Secondly, all the memory blocks of τ which are in the cache when τ is preempted may not be replaced by τ'. Thirdly, there are several possible cache contents when

τ is preempted (resulting from the different paths of τ), and when τ resumes execution (resulting from the different paths of τ'.) Last but not the least, there are several possible memory reference patterns after τ resumes execution (due to different paths of τ).

The importance of some of these factors on CRPD is mentioned in [4]. However, *no estimation technique is given* and only simulation results are presented. The work of Lee et. al. [7] performs set based analysis of the cache blocks used by the preempted task τ before and after preemption. This is extended in [8] to also consider the set of cache blocks used by the high-priority task τ'. Tomiyama and Dutt perform implicit path analysis of the preempting task τ' but ignore the effects of the preempted task τ [13].

In this paper, we propose methods to improve the accuracy of CRPD estimation. As per existing works [7, 8, 13], we only consider the effects of the instruction cache (and not data cache). Our technique performs path analysis of both τ and τ'. Furthermore, we compute the possible states of the cache when the lower priority task τ is preempted and when the higher priority task τ' is completed. This is more accurate than existing set-based analysis techniques which estimate the cache states by inferring the set of memory blocks which may exist in each cache block. Suppose that the cache has two blocks and the possible states of the cache when τ is preempted are as follows

$$\{\langle m_0, m_1\rangle, \langle m_2, m_3\rangle\}$$

In the above m_0, m_1, m_2, m_3 are memory blocks with m_0, m_2 mapping to the first cache block and m_1, m_3 mapping to the second cache block. Existing path analysis techniques such as [7, 8] will report the possible states as follows.

Content of first cache block $\in \{m_0, m_2\}$
Content of second cache block $\in \{m_1, m_3\}$

This actually denotes the four cache states

$$\{\langle m_0, m_1\rangle, \langle m_0, m_3\rangle, \langle m_2, m_1\rangle, \langle m_2, m_3\rangle\}$$

clearly leading to an over-approximation.

Note that we represent the cache states at a program point in a task as a set of tuples (where each tuple denotes an assignment of memory blocks to the cache blocks). This is more expensive than representing the possible contents of each cache block as a set of memory blocks. To avoid an exponential blow-up in the space consumption we can represent the possible cache states at any program point implicitly as a Binary Decision Diagram (BDD) [1]. A BDD is an efficient data structure for representing a propositional logic formula.

We now describe the core CRPD estimation technique. Section 3 explains the technique with a concrete example. Section 4 gives experimental results regarding accuracy of our estimation technique as well as its time and space consumption. Concluding remarks and discussions on space reduction appear in Section 5.

2. CRPD ESTIMATION

Recall from Section 1 that when a task τ is preempted by a higher priority task τ', the additional cache misses introduced depend on (a) cache content when τ is preempted, (b) cache content after τ' completes execution, and (c) cache reference pattern after τ resumes execution. Clearly, (a) and (c) require analysis of τ – the low priority task that gets preempted and (b) requires analysis of τ' – the high priority preempting task. Our analysis considers both τ and τ'.

Cache States. We use the terminology "cache state" to denote the contents of all the cache blocks. For simplicity of exposition, we assume a direct-mapped cache. However, the technique can be easily generalized to set-associative caches. For a direct mapped cache with n blocks, a **cache state** is a vector of n elements $c[0 \ldots n-1]$ where $c[i] = m$ if cache block i holds memory block m. Otherwise, if the ith cache block does not hold any memory block we denote this as $c[i] = \perp$. Thus, a cache state is a vector of length n where each element of the vector belongs to $M \cup \{\perp\}$ (M is the set of all memory blocks). In an abuse of notation, we assume that any operation $\odot$ over $M \cup \{\perp\}$ can be applied to cache states (by applying the operation pointwise to its elements). For example, if $\odot$ is a binary operation over $M \cup \{\perp\}$ and c, c' are cache states then $c \odot c' = c''$ where $c''[i] = c[i] \odot c'[i]$.

DEFINITION 1 (RCS). *The Reaching Cache States at a basic block B of a program, denoted as RCS_B, is the set of possible cache states when B is reached via any incoming program path.*

This notion helps us capture the cache content when the low-priority task is preempted.

DEFINITION 2 (LCS). *Given a program, we define the Live Cache States at a basic block B, denoted as LCS_B, as the possible first memory references to cache blocks via any outgoing program path from B.*

This notion helps us capture the cache reference pattern when the low-priority task resumes after preemption.

2.1 Computing Cache States

We consider the end of any basic block as a possible preemption point. [7] shows why it is sufficient to consider only these program points as candidate preemption points for CRPD estimation. The same reasoning can be extended to our analysis technique as well.

We now show how RCS_B and LCS_B are computed for each basic block B. This involves a modification of the work in [7, 8] since our notion of cache states is more elaborate. To compute RCS_B, we compute the quantities RCS_B^{IN} and RCS_B^{OUT} as a least fixed point. Once the fixed point is reached, we set $RCS_B = RCS_B^{OUT}$. Initially,

$$RCS_B^{IN} = \emptyset \qquad\qquad RCS_B^{OUT} = gen_B$$

For a basic block B, we define $gen_B = [m_0, \ldots, m_{n-1}]$ where $m_i = m$ if m is the *last* memory block in B that maps to cache block i and $\perp$ if no memory block in B maps to cache block i. Thus gen_B records all the memory blocks introduced into the cache by basic block B. The iterative equations are as follows:

$$RCS_B^{IN} = \bigcup_{p \in predecessor(B)} RCS_p^{OUT}$$

$$RCS_B^{OUT} = \{r \odot gen_B \mid r \in RCS_B^{IN}\}$$

The operation $\odot$ is defined over memory blocks as

$$m \odot m' = \begin{cases} m' & \text{if } m' \neq \perp \\ m & \text{otherwise} \end{cases}$$

It is extended to cache states by applying the operation to its individual elements in the usual way.

The computation of LCS_B is similar. Again we compute LCS_B^{OUT} and LCS_B^{IN} as a least fixed point and we set $LCS_B = LCS_B^{OUT}$ once fixed point is reached. Initially:

$$LCS_B^{OUT} = \emptyset \qquad\qquad LCS_B^{IN} = gen_B$$

Here for a basic block B, we define $gen_B = [m_0, \ldots, m_{n-1}]$ where $m_i = m$ if m is the *first* memory block in B that maps to cache block i and $\perp$ if no memory block in B maps to cache block i. The iterative equations are as follows:

$$LCS_B^{OUT} = \bigcup_{s \in successor(B)} LCS_s^{IN}$$

$$LCS_B^{IN} = \{l \odot gen_B \mid l \in LCS_B^{OUT}\}$$

The operation $\odot$ is as defined in the computation of RCS_B.

2.2 Computing Utility Vectors

Suppose the low-priority task τ is preempted at basic block B. Then RCS_B captures the possible cache states when τ is preempted and LCS_B captures the possible cache usages when τ resumes execution. This brings us to the notion of "useful cache blocks". These are cache blocks containing memory blocks at the point B which are referenced after B (before being replaced from the cache). To formally capture this notion in our representation of cache states we define the **Cache Utility Vector** CUV_B at basic block B. The following section discusses why this notion is more fine-grained than the "set of useful cache blocks" defined in [7].

$$CUV_B = \{l \approx r \mid l \in LCS_B, r \in RCS_B\}$$

The operator $\approx$ is the equality predicate over memory blocks, that is $m \approx m' = 1$ iff $m = m'$. It is extended to cache states by applying $\approx$ pointwise to its elements. For a cache with n blocks, CUV_B is a set of boolean vectors of length n. Each member of CUV_B records the useful cache blocks for some possible incoming and outgoing path of B.

Determining the useful cache blocks at the preemption point of the low-priority task τ is not enough. We also need to compute the possible cache states after the completion of the high priority task τ'. This will provide the usages of the n cache blocks along the different program paths of τ'. To formally capture this notion, we define the **Final Usage Vector** $FUV_{\tau'}$ of the high-priority task τ'. Let *end* be the last basic block of task τ' (the one that is executed just before completion of the task). Then

$$FUV_{\tau'} = \{used(r) \mid r \in RCS_{end}\}$$

Note that RCS_{end} is computed as a fixed point as described before. The function *used* is defined over cache states as $used(r) = r'$ where r' is the following bit-vector:

$$r'[i] = \begin{cases} 1 & \text{if } r[i] \neq \perp \\ 0 & \text{otherwise} \end{cases}$$

2.3 Computing CRPD

Given CUV_B at each basic block B of the preempted task τ and $FUV_{\tau'}$ of the preempting task τ', we compute the CRPD as follows. First, we define the intersection of $FUV_{\tau'}$ with CUV_B of task τ at all possible preemption points.

$$Delay(\tau, \tau') = \bigcup_{B \in BasicBlks(\tau)} \{c \wedge f \mid c \in CUV_B, f \in FUV_{\tau'}\}$$

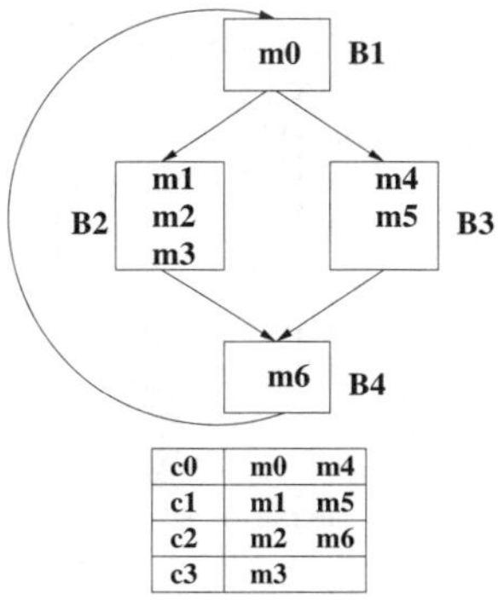

Figure 1: An example control flow graph.

where $\wedge$ is the AND operation applied to boolean vectors and $BasicBlks(\tau)$ is the set of all basic blocks of τ. Thus, if a cache block contains a useful memory block of τ and it is used by the memory blocks of τ' then it causes an additional cache miss. Finally

$$CRPD(\tau, \tau') = max\{cnt\_ones(v) \mid v \in Delay(\tau, \tau')\}$$

where $cnt\_ones(v)$ returns the number of 1's in bit vector v. Of course, to calculate the actual delay in terms of number of processor clock cycles $CRPD(\tau, \tau')$ should be multiplied by the cache miss penalty.

3. AN EXAMPLE

In this section, we illustrate our technique with a simple control flow graph (CFG) shown in Figure 1. The CFG consists of four basic blocks (B1 - B4) and seven memory blocks ($m0 - m6$) within a loop with a single if-then-else statement. We assume a direct mapped instruction cache with four cache blocks ($c0 - c3$). The mapping of memory blocks to cache blocks is shown in the figure.

The fixed point iterations to compute RCS_B are shown in detail in Table 1. Note that we set $RCS_B := RCS_B^{OUT}$ after fixed point is reached. We set gen_B as follows.

$$\begin{aligned} gen_{B1} &= [m0, \perp, \perp, \perp] \\ gen_{B2} &= [\perp, m1, m2, m3] \\ gen_{B3} &= [m4, m5, \perp, \perp] \\ gen_{B4} &= [\perp, \perp, m6, \perp] \end{aligned}$$

We should also mention that if there are two cache states c and c' in a set of cache states C such that c' is *subsumed* by c, then c' is removed from C. A cache state c' is subsumed by another cache state c if $\forall i \;\; c'[i] = c[i] \;\; or \;\; c'[i] = \perp$. Thus, in iteration 4 for basic block B3,

$$RCS_{B3}^{IN} = \{[m0, m1, m6, m3], [m0, m5, m6, \perp]\}$$

and $gen_{B3} = [m4, m5, \perp, \perp]$. Therefore,

$$RCS_{B3}^{OUT} = \{[m4, m5, m6, m3], [m4, m5, m6, \perp]\}$$

However, $[m4, m5, m6, \perp]$ is subsumed by $[m4, m5, m6, m3]$ and hence $RCS_{B3}^{OUT} = \{[m4, m5, m6, m3]\}$.

Iteration	Basic Block	RCS^{IN}	RCS^{OUT}
1	B1	$\emptyset$	$[m0, \perp, \perp, \perp]$
	B2	$\emptyset$	$[\perp, m1, m2, m3]$
	B3	$\emptyset$	$[m4, m5, \perp, \perp]$
	B4	$\emptyset$	$[\perp, \perp, m6, \perp]$
2	B1	$[\perp, \perp, m6, \perp]$	$[m0, \perp, m6, \perp]$
	B2	$[m0, \perp, \perp, \perp]$	$[m0, m1, m2, m3]$
	B3	$[m0, \perp, \perp, \perp]$	$[m4, m5, \perp, \perp]$
	B4	$[\perp, m1, m2, m3], [m4, m5, \perp, \perp]$	$[\perp, m1, m6, m3], [m4, m5, m6, \perp]$
3	B1	$[\perp, m1, m6, m3], [m4, m5, m6, \perp]$	$[m0, m1, m6, m3], [m0, m5, m6, \perp]$
	B2	$[m0, \perp, m6, \perp]$	$[m0, m1, m2, m3]$
	B3	$[m0, \perp, m6, \perp]$	$[m4, m5, m6, \perp]$
	B4	$[m0, m1, m2, m3], [m4, m5, \perp, \perp]$	$[m0, m1, m6, m3], [m4, m5, m6, \perp]$
4	B1	$[m0, m1, m6, m3], [m4, m5, m6, \perp]$	$[m0, m1, m6, m3], [m0, m5, m6, \perp]$
	B2	$[m0, m1, m6, m3], [m0, m5, m6, \perp]$	$[m0, m1, m2, m3]$
	B3	$[m0, m1, m6, m3], [m0, m5, m6, \perp]$	$[m4, m5, m6, m3]$
	B4	$[m0, m1, m2, m3], [m4, m5, m6, \perp]$	$[m0, m1, m6, m3], [m4, m5, m6, \perp]$
7	B1	$[m0, m1, m6, m3], [m4, m5, m6, m3]$	$[m0, m1, m6, m3], [m0, m5, m6, m3]$
	B2	$[m0, m1, m6, m3], [m0, m5, m6, m3]$	$[m0, m1, m2, m3]$
	B3	$[m0, m1, m6, m3], [m0, m5, m6, m3]$	$[m4, m5, m6, m3]$
	B4	$[m0, m1, m2, m3], [m4, m5, m6, m3]$	$[m0, m1, m6, m3], [m4, m5, m6, m3]$

Table 1: Computation of RCS_B for the CFG in Figure 1. Iteration steps 5 and 6 are not shown.

We can also compute LCS_B in a similar fashion

$$LCS_{B1} = \{[m0, m1, m2, m3], [m4, m5, m6, m3]\}$$
$$LCS_{B2} = \{[m0, m1, m6, m3], [m0, m5, m6, m3]\}$$
$$LCS_{B3} = \{[m0, m1, m6, m3], [m0, m5, m6, m3]\}$$
$$LCS_{B4} = \{[m0, m1, m2, m3], [m0, m5, m6, m3]\}$$

Given LCS and RCS for each basic block, we can compute

$$CUV_{B1} = \{[1,1,0,1], [0,0,1,1], [0,1,1,1], [1,0,0,1]\}$$
$$CUV_{B2} = \{[1,1,0,1], [1,0,0,1]\}$$
$$CUV_{B3} = \{[0,1,1,1], [0,0,1,1]\}$$
$$CUV_{B4} = \{[1,1,0,1], [1,0,1,1], [0,1,1,1], [0,0,0,1]\}$$

There are at most 3 useful cache blocks for B1 and B4.

Now let us illustrate the advantage of our technique over separate analysis of each cache block [7, 8]. In that case, RCS_B and LCS_B have a set of reaching memory blocks for each cache block as shown in the following.

$$RCS_{B1} = [\{m0\}, \{m1, m5\}, \{m6\}, \{m3\}]$$
$$RCS_{B2} = [\{m0\}, \{m1\}, \{m2\}, \{m3\}]$$
$$RCS_{B3} = [\{m4\}, \{m5\}, \{m6\}, \{m3\}]$$
$$RCS_{B4} = [\{m0, m4\}, \{m1, m5\}, \{m6\}, \{m3\}]$$

$$LCS_{B1} = [\{m0, m4\}, \{m1, m5\}, \{m2, m6\}, \{m3\}]$$
$$LCS_{B2} = [\{m0\}, \{m1, m5\}, \{m6\}, \{m3\}]$$
$$LCS_{B3} = [\{m0\}, \{m1, m5\}, \{m6\}, \{m3\}]$$
$$LCS_{B4} = [\{m0\}, \{m1, m5\}, \{m2, m6\}, \{m3\}]$$

Let us consider RCS_{B4}. From separate analysis of cache blocks, we infer that RCS_{B4} has four possible cache states: $[m0, m1, m6, m3]$, $[m0, m5, m6, m3]$, $[m4, m1, m6, m3]$, and $[m4, m5, m6, m3]$. However, our combined analysis of cache blocks infers that only two of these cache states are feasible. The identification of these infeasible cache states leads to decrease in the number of useful cache blocks (computed via intersection of RCS_B and LCS_B) at each program point. For example, our analysis infers at most 3 useful cache blocks for both B1 and B4 (Even though each of the cache blocks is useful along some path, all 4 of them are not useful along any path). Whereas, with separate analysis of cache blocks, we get 4 useful cache blocks for B1 and B4.

Note that we also maintain the Final Usage Vector (FUV) of the high priority task as a set of boolean vectors. This leads to further accuracy in CRPD analysis. For example, suppose we compute $FUV = \{[1,0,1,0], [1,1,0,0]\}$. This will allow our analysis to estimate the number of useful cache blocks to be 2 leading to even tighter CRPD estimation. In case of separate analysis of each cache block, the above FUV will be approximated as $FUV = [1,1,1,0]$. This only allows the separated analysis to tighten the CRPD estimate to 3 cache misses (as compared to the 4 cache misses estimated earlier based on the low-priority task).

Program	Description
`matsum`	Summation of two 100 × 100 matrices
`qsort`	Non-recursive quick sort algorithm
`crc`	Cyclic redundancy check program
`sqrt`	Square root calculation
`eqntott`	Drawn from SPEC'92 integer benchmarks
`des`	Data Encryption Standard
`whet`	Whetstone benchmark
`ssearch`	Pratt-Boyer-Moore string search
`math`	Basic math within nested loop

Table 2: Description of benchmark programs.

4. EXPERIMENTAL RESULTS

In this section, we present the accuracy and performance of our CRPD estimation technique.

4.1 Methodology

We select nine different benchmarks for our experiments (refer Table 2). Most of these benchmarks are from [12] and [11]. We use the Simplescalar architectural simulation platform [2] in the experiments. All the benchmarks are compiled to Simplescalar assembly language with modified gcc. A prototype analyzer written by us accepts assembly language code, disassembles it, identifies the basic blocks and constructs the control flow graph (CFG). Given the CFG of the low-priority and the high-priority task as well as the instruction cache configuration, our analyzer computes

LP Task	HP Task								
	matsum			eqntott			sqrt		
	A	C	S	A	C	S	A	C	S
qsort	19	20	24	16	22	28	18	19	26
crc	17	17	18	17	21	22	18	19	20
ssearch	19	22	23	19	25	27	21	22	25
des	22	23	24	21	24	26	22	22	25
whet	20	21	22	20	25	25	23	23	24
math	18	22	23	20	25	27	20	22	25

Table 3: Accuracy of CRPD analysis for a 32-block cache. A stands for actual number of misses in CRPD (found by exhaustive simulation), C stands for our combined analysis of all cache blocks and S stands for separate analysis of each cache block.

Task	Combined	Separate
matsum	23	24
eqntott	26	28
sqrt	23	26

Table 4: Maximum number of cache blocks used by high priority task for a 32-block cache.

the CRPD of the tasks. Our analyzer is parameterizable with respect to cache block size and number of cache blocks.

4.2 Accuracy

First we present the accuracy of our analysis method in computing CRPD. We choose `matsum`, `eqntott`, and `sqrt` as high priority tasks and others as low priority tasks. For each pair of low-priority and high-priority tasks, Table 3 presents CPRD in terms of number of useful cache blocks that may get replaced by the high-priority task. We assume a direct mapped instruction cache with 32 cache blocks and block size of 8 bytes. The results show that our analysis yields estimates which is are very close to the actual CRPD. Furthermore, as compared to the separated analysis of [8], our analysis obtains much tighter bound on CRPD with improvements as high as 37% for some benchmarks. Let us now analyze the factors working behind this improvement.

Table 4 shows the maximum number of cache blocks used by the high-priority task for a direct mapped cache with 32 blocks. For combined analysis, this is $max\{cnt\_ones(v) \mid v \in FUV_{\tau'}\}$ where τ' is the high-priority task; $cnt\_ones(v)$ returns the number of 1s in the bit vector v. Separate analysis per cache block results in higher value as it marks a cache block as useful if that block is used along any path in the task. However, cache block c and c' may never be used together along any program path, even though they may be used in different program paths. Our method captures that scenario and therefore results in lesser cache block usage by high priority task. Note that [13] also made the above observation. However, their analysis is based on integer linear programming (ILP) and is limited to only the high-priority task. Similarly, Table 5 shows the maximum number of useful cache blocks of the low-priority task at any program point. For combined analysis, this is equal to $max\{cnt\_ones(v) \mid v \in CUV_B, B \in BasicBlks(\tau)\}$ where τ is the low-priority task. Again separate analysis per cache block results in higher value as was explained earlier.

Table 5 shows that the maximum number of useful cache blocks in the low-priority task are quite close in our combined analysis and the separated per cache-block analysis.

Task	# of Cache Blocks							
	8		16		32		64	
	C	S	C	S	C	S	C	S
qsort	1	1	14	14	28	32	62	63
crc	2	2	12	12	26	26	48	48
ssearch	6	6	15	16	31	31	59	59
des	0	0	12	12	30	30	60	64
whet	1	2	11	14	29	29	59	59
math	4	5	14	16	30	31	63	64

Table 5: Maximum number of useful cache blocks of the low-priority task at any program point. C stands for combined analysis of all cache blocks and S stands for separate analysis of each cache block.

Task	# of Cache Blocks							
	8		16		32		64	
	#B	D	#B	D	#B	D	#B	D
qsort	0	0	1	1	2	4	1	1
crc	2	1	0	0	0	0	0	0
ssearch	0	0	2	2	0	0	0	0
des	0	0	0	0	9	2	47	15
whet	7	1	11	4	0	0	0	0
math	2	1	4	5	2	3	1	1

Table 6: Comparison of combined and separate analysis for low-priority task. #B denotes the number of basic blocks at which useful cache block count differs and D denotes the maximum of these differences.

However, this does not indicate that the CRPD values produced by the two techniques are equally close (Table 3). Recall that the CRPD of tasks τ, τ' is defined as:

$$max\{cnt\_ones(c \wedge f) \mid c \in CUV_B, B \in BasicBlks(\tau), f \in FUV_{\tau'}\}$$

Thus, apart from the effects of the high-priority task, the CRPD depends on the estimated number of useful cache blocks at each preemption point of τ. In other words, even though the maximum number of useful cache blocks over all preemption points of τ (shown in Table 5) might be the same in both analysis techniques, the estimated number of useful cache blocks in individual preemption points of τ may be different. Table 6 shows the number of preemption points (basic blocks) at which useful cache block count differs in the two analysis as well as the maximum of these differences. Such differences in the useful cache block estimates for individual preemption points of τ produces a difference in CRPD when these estimates are combined with the cache block usage estimates from τ'.

4.3 Time and Space Overheads

Table 7 shows the time taken by our analyzer to compute CUV_B for all basic blocks in the low-priority task. The time taken to compute FUV of high-priority task is negligible and is not shown here. For all the benchmarks, it takes less than 1.5 minute on a Pentium IV 1.7GHz CPU with 1GB memory. One concern with our approach is that the number of cache states may increase exponentially while computing RCS_B and LCS_B. Assuming a task with B basic blocks, M memory blocks and a cache with C blocks, M/C memory blocks map to one cache block. Therefore, in the worst case, we can have total of $(M/C)^C \times B$ cache states. However, our experimental results indicate that the number of cache states is much smaller in practice. For example, for `qsort`

Task	# of Cache Blocks			
	8	16	32	64
qsort	0.003	0.004	0.022	0.082
crc	0.016	0.015	0.164	65.663
ssearch	0.007	0.025	1.613	16.168
des	0.010	0.022	0.525	55.329
whet	0.005	0.023	4.189	89.858
math	0.013	0.059	1.061	8.414

Table 7: Time to compute useful cache blocks for low-priority task in sec.

with $B = 40$, $M = 490$ and $C = 8$, we only get 68 cache states for LCS_B and 69 for RCS_B. When we set $C = 64$, number of cache states in LCS_B and RCS_B increase to only 425 and 600 respectively.

5. DISCUSSION

In this paper, we have studied the problem of estimating *Cache-Related Preemption Delay* (CRPD) in preemptive multitasked real-time systems. CRPD is the delay introduced in a low-priority task owing to additional cache misses caused via preemption (by a higher priority task). To enable accurate analysis, our approach maintains possible cache contents (1) at each preemption point of the low-priority task and (2) at the end of high-priority task. Our experimental results show that our approach leads to tighter estimates than existing approaches which estimate the possible contents of each cache block separately (for the low-priority as well as the high-priority task). Note that in our analysis, we have throughout assumed only two tasks. Extending the technique to m tasks is straightforward: we need to consider all possible preemption sequences.

One possible concern regarding our analysis technique is a blow-up in space consumption. As observed in the previous section, none of our benchmarks suffered from an exponential space blow-up due to our decision to represent cache states (instead of the content of each cache block separately).

Furthermore, we can handle possible blow-up in the representation of reaching/live cache states by adopting a symbolic representation of LCS_B and RCS_B. In particular, we can represent LCS_B and RCS_B (for any basic block B) as a Binary Decision Diagram (BDD). A BDD is a compact representation for a boolean function [1]. Consider a direct mapped cache with n cache blocks and at most k memory blocks mapping to each cache block. The content of any cache block in a cache state can then be captured with $\lceil log_2(k+1) \rceil$ boolean variables. For example if two memory blocks m and m' can map to a cache block, then the cache block can have three possible contents: m, m' and $\perp$ (that is, it does not hold any memory block). These three possibilities can be captured with $\lceil log_2(3) \rceil = 2$ boolean variables. A cache state simply denotes the content of all the n cache blocks. Therefore, a cache state can be represented via truth assignment of $n * \lceil log_2(k+1) \rceil$ boolean variables. A set of cache states S simply denotes a set of truth assignments of these $n * \lceil log_2(k+1) \rceil$ boolean variables, call it V_S. Thus, a set of cache states S can be represented as a propositional logic formula (or a BDD) f_S over the $n*\lceil log_2(k+1) \rceil$ boolean variables (s.t. f_S is true for only the truth assignments in V_S). We use this BDD representation for LCS_B and RCS_B (for any basic block B) since they are simply sets of cache states. The variable ordering in the BDD representation is obtained from a total ordering of the cache blocks. Given the BDD representation for LCS_B and RCS_B, the fixed point equations for computing these quantities (given in Section 2.1) are modified in a standard fashion.

We have used the Colorado University Decision Diagrams (CUDD) package [3] for computing the quantities LCS_B, RCS_B as BDDs. However, none of our benchmarks suffered from an exponential space blow-up in the number of cache states appearing in LCS or RCS. Therefore, the space gains obtained from the symbolic BDD representation (as compared to our enumerative set based representation) were modest in all our benchmarks. In future, we will conduct further experiments to evaluate the need for symbolic representation of cache states in our analysis technique.

6. ACKNOWLEDGMENTS

This work was partially supported by NUS research grants R252-000-088-112 and R252-000-150-112.

7. REFERENCES

[1] R.E. Bryant. Graph-based algorithms for boolean function manipulation. *IEEE Transactions on Computers*, C-35(8), 1986.

[2] D. Burger, T. Austin, and S. Bennett. Evaluating Future Microprocessors: The SimpleScalar Toolset. Technical Report CS-TR96-1308, Univ. of Wisconsin - Madison, 1996.

[3] CUDD. Colorado University Decision Diagram Package Version 2.3.1, 2001. Free software, `http://vlsi.colorado.edu/~fabio/CUDD/`.

[4] H. Dwyer and J. Fernando. Establishing a tight bound on task interference in embedded system instruction caches. In *International Conference on Compilers, Architecture and Synthesis of Embedded Systems (CASES)*, 2001.

[5] C. Ferdinand, F. Martin, and R. Wilhelm. Applying compiler techniques to cache behavior prediction. In *ACM Intl. Workshop on Languages, Compilers and Tools for Real-Time Sys. (LCTRTS)*, 1997.

[6] D.B. Kirk. SMART (strategic memory allocation for real-time) cache design. In *IEEE Real-Time Systems Symposium (RTSS)*, 1990.

[7] C-G. Lee et al. Analysis of cache-related preemption delay in fixed-priority preemptive scheduling. *IEEE Transactions on Computers*, 47(6), 1998.

[8] C-G. Lee et al. Bounding cache-related preemption delay for real-time systems. *IEEE Transactions on Software Engineering*, 27(9), 2001.

[9] X. Li, T. Mitra, and A. Roychoudhury. Accurate timing analysis by modeling caches, speculation and their interaction. In *ACM Design Automation Conf. (DAC)*, 2003.

[10] Y. Li and W. Wolf. Hardware/Software Co-Synthesis with Memory Hierarchies. *IEEE Transaction on Computer-aided Design of Integrated Circuit and Systems*, 1999.

[11] Y-T. S. Li, S. Malik, and A. Wolfe. Performance estimation of embedded software with instruction cache modeling. *ACM Transactions on Design Automation of Electronic Systems*, 4(3), 1999.

[12] Seoul National University Real-Time Research Groups. SNU real-time benchmarks. `http://archi.snu.ac.kr/realtime/benchmark/`.

[13] H. Tomiyama and N. Dutt. Program path analysis to bound cache-related preemption delay in preemptive real-time systems. In *ACM International Symposium on Hardware Software Codesign (CODES)*, 2000.

[14] F. Wolf, J. Staschulat, and R. Ernst. Associative caches in formal software timing analysis. In *ACM Design Automation Conf. (DAC)*, 2002.

Early Estimation of the Size of VHDL Projects

William Fornaciari, Fabio Salice, Daniele Paolo Scarpazza,
Politecnico di Milano - DEI
Piazza Leonardo da Vinci, 32, Milano, Italy
{fornacia, salice, scarpazz}@elet.polimi.it

ABSTRACT

The analysis of the amount of human resources required to complete a project is felt as a critical issue in any company of the electronics industry. In particular, early estimating the effort involved in a development process is a key requirement for any cost-driven system-level design decision.

In this paper, we present a methodology to predict the final size of a VHDL project on the basis of a high-level description, obtaining a significant indication about the development effort. The methodology is the composition of a number of specialized models, tailored to estimate the size of specific component types. Models were trained and tested on two disjoint and large sets of real VHDL projects. Quality-of-result indicators show that the methodology is both accurate and robust.

Categories and Subject Descriptors

B.6.3 [**Hardware**]: Design Aids—*Hardware description languages*; D.2.8 [**Software Engineering**]: Metrics—*complexity measures*

General Terms

Management, Design, Languages

Keywords

VHDL analysis, embedded systems, design metrics, cost estimation, system-level design

1. INTRODUCTION

In the last years we assisted to the growth of design reuse initiatives, such as the VSIA [1], and to the spread of third-party suppliers of intellectual property cells. There is a consistent number of cost models, which pay particular attention both to the advanced concept study phase (like in [5] for the automotive market) and to the management of the design cycle (like in [3]).

Technical managers face new scenarios, where the driving forces are *time to market* and flexibility, together with the capability of controlling costs. The success of a strategy often depends strongly on coarse-grained decisions taken during the early phases. For example, solving the *make or buy* problem requires such an accurate estimate of resource consumption and reuse cost-effectiveness.

There exist accurate estimation techniques and flows for performance, area and power consumption, some working at high level of abstraction too, but when it comes to human time (currently the most valuable and scarcest resource), a well-assessed theory to development effort estimation is still a long way to come.

In this paper we present a method for estimating the number of lines of VHDL code in which an embedded system design project will evolve, given its specification, which is recognized to be one of the factors affecting its development effort, e.g. through CoCoMo-style models [2] like $E = a \cdot S^b$, where E is the effort, S is the code size and a and b are parameters accounting for multiplicative and scale phenomena (see [7] for more details). In our methodology, without loss of generality, specifications are not provided in a distinct language but in VHDL itself: in fact any incomplete VHDL project can be considered as an intermediate step towards the final product. Our methodology can be applied at any stage of a development-by-refinement design process, and as the draft approaches the completed project, size estimates will converge to the actual final value.

The paper structure is as follows: section 2 provides the conceptual framework of the methodology, while section 3 introduces a convenient formal representation of VHDL designs on which the entire methodology is based. The core of the methodology is presented in section 4, where models for each of the basic elements composing the designs are presented, together with a constructive strategy to provide estimates for the entire design.

To apply our methodology, we implemented a complete evaluation flow (including a VHDL-93 compliant parser), able to perform model training, test and application. Details are described in section 5. Section 6 discusses the achievements of the methodology and possible improvements.

2. GENERAL APPROACH

Designing systems in VHDL consists in designing an appropriate set of interconnected entities, each accompanied by one or more implementations (called architectures) and their respective internals (processes, signals, variables, functions and procedures; see [8] and [4]). Usually, these entities are not developed concurrently at the same time, instead the whole project is first defined as a top-level entity with no internal details, then decomposed in more subsystems, developed as independent entities, and so on, in a top-down fashion.

When a project is complete, all of its components and relationships can be hierarchically represented with a graph, on which the calculation of the total project size from each part's size is trivial.

In incomplete projects (that is, projects considered at an arbitrary

CODES+ISSS'03, October 1–3, 2003, Newport Beach, California, USA.

intermediate development stage), parts are not all known equally: some parts are finished (*completely known*), for some only their external interface is known, typically because they were identified in a top-down decomposition but not yet decomposed in further subsystems (*externally known*), some are *completely unknown*, typically because they will be identified in the next decomposition steps of externally known parts.

For incomplete projects, we also found a formal and convenient way to represent the information available on completed parts, their completion status and the remaining of the project, still in the form of a graph. We will provide a set of models and application rules, that allow to estimate the overall resulting size of the finished project (expressed in lines of code, LOC) on the basis of the above graph.

Since a specification is nothing more than an incomplete project, considered at an arbitrary (usually early) stage of a top-down, development-by-refinement design process, it is correct to say that our method is capable of estimating the final size of a VHDL project on the basis of its specifications. Then, the development effort cost from the project size can be estimated, by following the strategy proposed in (as shown in [7]).

3. FORMAL ASPECTS

In this section we introduce some definitions required to describe the method in a formal and concise way. Intuitive explanations are reported in place of formalisms whenever the second would be unnecessarily tedious; for all the formalities, see [10].

3.1 Syntax objects and graphs

A *syntax object* (SO, for short) is any of the following: a project, an entity, an architecture, a process, a subprogram, a component declaration or instantiation. As anticipated, all the SOs of a complete project can be hierarchically arranged in a graph, called *syntax object graph* (*SOG* for short), which depicts their relationships. A SOG is a graph containing nodes of 7 types (one for each SO type) and edges of 2 types: *contains*-type and *references*-type edges. Given a project, building its SOG means:

- creating a node for each SO appearing in the project;
- connecting node A to node B with a *contains*-type edge ($A \supset B$) whenever the SO named A contains the SO named B (that is, B is defined inside the A, like a process can be defined inside an architecture);
- connecting node A to node B with a *references*-type edge ($A \longrightarrow B$) when SO A references SO B (informally, inside A there is a call or an instantiation to B).

A sample SOG, generated by our tools and depicting the structure of a Xilinx ADS7870 8-channel voltmeter Springboard module, implemented on a CoolRunner XPLA3 CPLD, is reported in fig. 1. Dashed lines represent $\supset$-type edges and solid lines represent $\longrightarrow$-type edges.

In incomplete projects, SO are usually known partially. To handle these cases, we introduce the KSOG, which is a decorated SOG, where a tag is added to each node, indicating its knowledge condition; in detail, a SO is marked with:

- (C) *completely known*, if it is complete and finished in all its constituents;
- (E) *externally known*, if its external interface is known (ports for an architecture, signature for a function, etc.); no internals need to be provided;

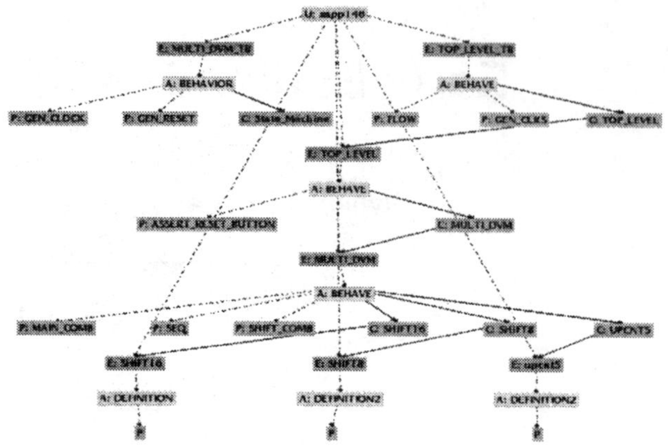

Figure 1: The SOG for a real VHDL project.

- (I) *internally known*, if it is externally known and all its directly contained element are at least externally known;
- (V) *virtually completely known*, when its cost is already known (e.g. it was reused, or bought externally), even though its details are not provided; dealing with these SO's is trivial, since they are treated as an additive cost constant;
- (U) *completely unknown*, when it is not declared at all: size estimates cannot be generated; instead, estimates for container objects must take into account the possible existence of unknown objects.

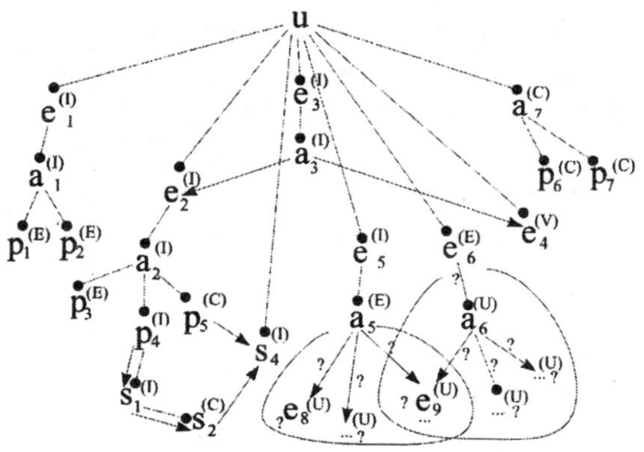

Figure 2: A sample KSOG.

Figure 2 shows a sample KSOG and illustrates some of the possible combinations of nodes and edges.

If we regard a project specification as an incomplete project (thus a KSOG), we can reduce the estimation of its development cost starting from its specifications to the evaluation of the cost of its KSOG.

3.2 Bunches

Most KSOGs have much higher complexity than samples in figures 1 and 2, possibly containing thousands of nodes and edges. Therefore, designing an appropriate evaluation algorithm running on KSOGs could be impractical. Instead, we introduce an object of intermediate granularity, the bunch, that simplifies the task of KSOG evaluation.

Roughly speaking, a bunch is a structure composed by a VHDL entity and whatever belongs to it. More formally, a bunch is a tree rooted at an entity E, containing all those nodes reached by the

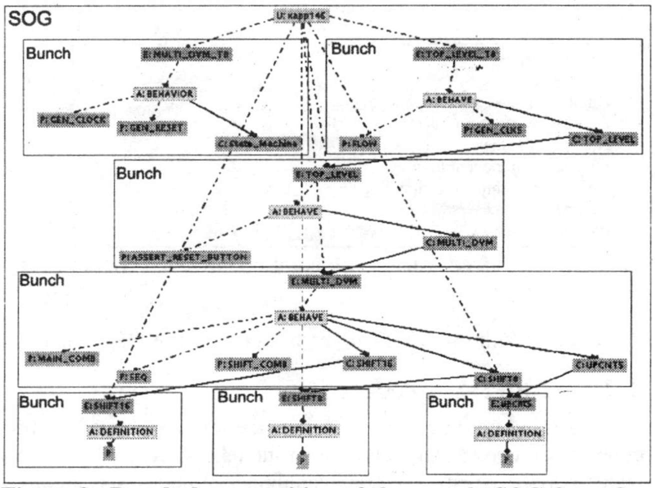

Figure 3: Bunch decomposition of the sample SOG from figure 1.

transitive closure of $\supset$ starting from node E. Bunches exhibit the following useful properties:

1. all the information required to evaluate the size of a bunch is associated to its nodes, therefore each bunch size can be evaluated independently;

2. any SOG and KSOG can be exactly partitioned into one or more bunches[1], as in figure 3, therefore the size of a SOG is given by the sum of its bunches' size. For KSOGs things are more complicated, since some bunches could be completely unknown and their size will be estimated (details in the next section).

3.3 Levels

It is convenient to arrange bunches in levels, thus obtaining a structure that matches the top-down decomposition process; the usefulness of this operation will become clear in the next section. To do that, we observe $\rightarrow$-type edges that cross bunch boundaries. Starting with all the bunches at the top level, and moving bunch R one level beneath Q's level whenever a $Q \rightarrow R$ cross-bunch edge is found, the desired arrangement is obtained.

As we did for partially known SOs, we introduce the additional hypothesis that specifications are not unbalanced, in the sense that either all bunches in a level are at least externally known, or all are completely unknown. Our methodology is not able to deal effectively with promiscuous levels, containing known and unknown bunches at the same time. Good sense suggests that incomplete projects can be unbalanced in the above sense, but specifications (a strict subset of incomplete projects) cannot, therefore the above condition is not really restrictive.

4. THE CORE OF THE METHODOLOGY

The application of our methodology consists of the following steps:

1. a KSOG is built starting from specifications;

2. the KSOG is decomposed into bunches;

3. bunches are split among levels according to their mutual structural $\rightarrow$-type edges;

4. for each bunch, its size is calculated by applying the most appropriate model aggregate;

5. for each known level, its size is calculated as the sum of sizes of all bunches belonging to that level;

6. the estimated cost of the KSOG (comprising unknown parts) is obtained from the sum of the size of the first n^{th} levels by applying an appropriate SOG model.

Our methodology works at different granularities, obtaining the size of a KSOG as a sum of the sizes of its levels, the size of each level as the sum of the sizes of its bunches, the size of each bunch as the sum of the sizes of its syntax objects. Since, at each granularity, one or more constituents can be incompletely known, the above summations would be impossible without a number of specialized models that allow to estimate the size of unknown parts from their available information.

4.1 Models

Accordingly with the methodology so far defined, we introduce three categories of models: SOG models, Bunch models and SO models.

SO models estimate the final size of a SO given the set of available information on it, not counting contained objects (which are subject to respective SO models, if at least externally known). For completely unknown SOs, their number and size are estimated at bunch level, thanks to bunch models. Through bunch models, an estimate of the final size of each at-least-externally-known bunch is obtained; then, SOG models are applied to obtain the size of the whole project as a function of the size of the at-least-externally-known levels.

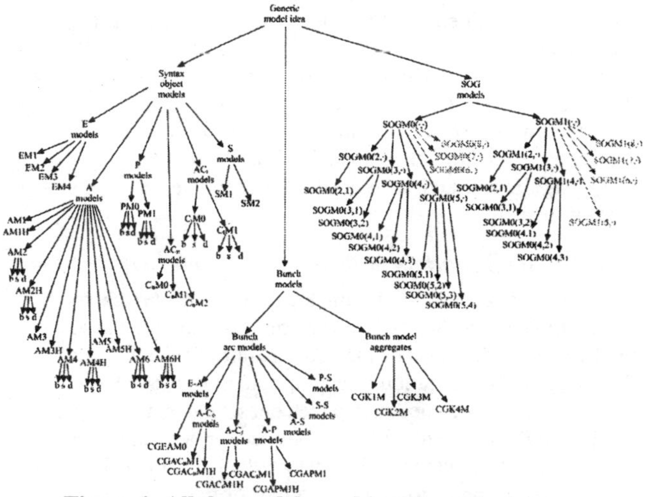

Figure 4: All the models used in this methodology.

The whole set of models used in our methodology is illustrated in figure 4; it is possible to classify them in a tree view.

4.1.1 *Syntax object models*

SO models return an estimate of the core size of a object for which some information is given; they are specialized on the basis of object type (entity, architecture, process, ...), object *mode* (behavioral, structural, data-flow) if applicable, and amount of information required. A list containing the most interesting variables and quantities subject to estimation is reported in table 1.

Similar models were developed for the other SO types; their full details and statistical performance evaluation can be found in [10].

[1]with negligible exceptions, shown in [10].

Quantity	Symbol
Total number of ports	n_p
Number of in, out, inout, other ports	$n_{ip}, n_{op}, n_{iop}, n_{xp}$
Total number of generics	n_g
Total number of internal signals	n_s, h_s
Number of component declarations, instantiations	n_{cd}, n_{ci}
Number of processes in an architecture	n_{pr}
Number of sensitivity signals in the i-th process	n_{ps_i}
Number of variables in the i-th process	n_{pv_i}
Length of entity declaration in LOC	L_e
Length of architecture core in LOC	L_{ac}
Length of the i-th component declaration in LOC	L_{cd_i}
Length of the i-th component instantiation in LOC	L_{ci_i}
Length of the i-th process in lines of code	L_{pr_i}

Table 1: Variables and estimates used in models.

	Last known-size level							
n	L1	L2	L3	L4	L5	L6	L7	L8
1	1	·	·	·	·	·	·	·
2	0.486	1	·	·	·	·	·	·
3	0.128	0.505	1	·	·	·	·	·
4	0.141	0.294	0.721	1	·	·	·	·
5	0.083	0.149	0.425	0.658	1	·	·	·
6	0.053	0.214	0.808	0.972	0.985	1	·	·
7	0.023	0.070	0.308	0.415	0.505	0.925	1	·
8	0.113	0.167	0.408	0.706	0.860	0.921	0.979	1

Table 2: Size of the first i levels as a fraction of the whole project.

4.1.2 Bunch models

Bunch models estimate the cardinality of a set of SOs, directly contained in a given SO, all of which are completely unknown and of the same type. For example, there are models to estimate the number of processes inside a given architecture, or the number of subprograms directly declared inside a process, and so on. Bunch models are classified on the basis of the type of nodes involved in the $\supset$-type edge.

In [10], we conducted an extensive study in order to identify all the possible combinations of node types involved in a $\supset$ relationship, then we counted the number occurrence for each type in our project base, realizing that only a small amount of them were statistically significant, and developed an appropriate set of models for each of them.

4.1.3 SOG models

Once the size of the not-completely-unknown bunch levels has been estimated, the last task to perform is to estimate the size of all the KSOG, on the basis of the above result. This is the purpose of SOG models. The creation of appropriate SOG models was a difficult task, since it was not clear which ones, among all the properties of the KSOG representing the incomplete project and other possible available data, were significant in order to estimate the full final KSOG size. In order to understand that, we designed a rich set of different hypotheses and tested them against our project base. The hypothesis with the highest predictive power turned out to be the following: given a KSOG of depth n, where the size of all levels from 1 to k is known, it should be possible to find an appropriate value, representing the following ratio:

$$\frac{L}{\sum_{i\leqslant k} L_i} = \frac{\sum_{i\leqslant n} L_i}{\sum_{i\leqslant k} L_i}$$

This ratio expresses how many times the whole project is larger than levels $1..k$. In each cell (row i, column j) of table 2 we reported the average values of such ratios collected on our project base. For example in projects with exactly 6 levels (row 6), the number of lines of code belonging to levels 3 and above (column L3) represents the 80.8% of all the lines of code of the project.

	K1	K2	K3	K4
Entity interface	✓	✓	✓	✓
Entity mode	✓	✓	✓	✓
Number of declared components	✓	✓	✓	·
Declared component interface	✓	✓	·	·
Number of instanced components	✓	✓	✓	·
Instanced component interface	✓	✓	·	·
Number of architecture signals	✓	·	·	·
Number of processes	✓	✓	·	·
Process variables	✓	·	·	·

Table 3: Required known information for each model aggregate.

4.2 Model Aggregates

As said before, in order to estimate the size of a bunch, a strict cooperation between SO and bunch models is required. Given a bunch populated with a reasonable number of nodes (one architecture, several processes and components, several signals and variables), the number of possible different knowledge conditions that could occur is remarkable. It is therefore impractical (and of dubious usefulness) to validate models in any possible condition; Instead, we established four discrete conditions, associated with respective model sets, ready to be applied to assess whether a bunch in a given refinement state qualifies or not for a given knowledge state. Such states, called K1, K2, K3 and K4, and the associated rules are illustrated in table 3. For each cell, the presence of a tick mark (✓) means that variables indicated in that row must be known in order to qualify for the knowledge state indicated in that column.

The corresponding model aggregate for condition K2 is reported below as an example.

$$\begin{aligned}(K2)\ \hat{L} &= \hat{L}_e(n_p, n_g) && \text{(EM3)}\\ &+ \hat{L}_{ac}(h_{ip}, h_{op}, h_{iop}, h_{xp}) && \text{(AM2H)}\\ &+ \textstyle\sum_{i=1}^{n_{cd}} \hat{L}_{cd_i}(n_{p_i}, n_{g_i}) && \text{(C}_\text{D}\text{M2)}\\ &+ \textstyle\sum_{i=1}^{n_{ci}} \hat{L}_{ci_i} && \text{(C}_\text{I}\text{M1)}\\ &+ n_{pr}\cdot \hat{L}_{pr} && \text{(PM0)}\end{aligned}$$

5. EXPERIMENTAL RESULTS

To assess the accuracy of our statistical modeling, we performed a number of experiments. First, to constitute a suitable database of projects, we collected 60 publicly-available fully-developed VHDL projects[2]. Their application scope covers general purpose processors, digital signal processors, basic building blocks like FFTs, microcontrollers, neural networks and so on. This base of project was split in two sets: one used to tune the methodology and the other used for validation purpose. Relevant statistical data characterizing of such projects are summarized in the following table:

	Tuning	Validation
Number of projects:	41	19
Number of VHDL files:	573	469
Number of VHDL code lines:	388,790	222,188
Cumulative size:	16.5M	12.0M
Number of entities:	945	571
Number of architectures:	967	570
Number of component declarations:	952	634
Number of component instantiations:	46,653	35,478
Number of subprogram declarations:	587	298
Number of ports:	9,276	4,984
Number of signals:	58,836	39,017
Number of variables in processes:	1,747	2,449
Number of variables in subprograms:	387	299

[2]the full contents of this archive is available at our website [9]

To automatically collect and process project base data, and to tune, validate and apply models, we developed a set of tools comprising a lexical filter to remove comments, a dedicated VHDL parser to read source files, extract syntax-related information and store it in a specifically-designed SQL database, a set of Tcl scripts to apply all the models and a rich, Tcl/Tk-based, graphical front-end to the above tools. The tool stack is represented in figure 5.

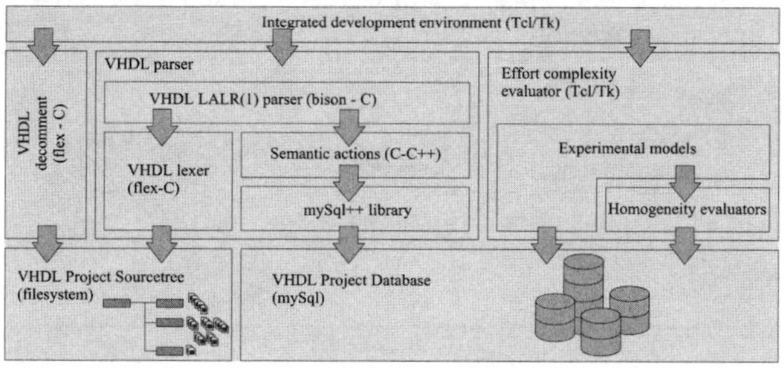

Figure 5: Automatic tools developed for this research.

An exhaustive evaluation of our methodology would consider any possible subset of each project SOG of our project base, thus obtaining a KSOG, then submitting it to the models and comparing the result with the real size of the SOG. But since the number of all possible partial knowledge conditions in a project is extremely high, a test like the one described above is impractical.

Instead, for each of our projects, we set as unknown all information apart those required by model aggregate K2. Then, for all possible k, we used as input the first k^{th} levels of the KSOG obtained at the previous step. Results follow:

Internal validation (based on tuning projects):

	L	$\hat{L}$	$\hat{L} - L$
Average value	2582.071	1826.582	427.492
Standard deviation	3868.919	2950.914	1400.412
Correlation coefficient between L and $\hat{L}$			0.8627

External validation (based on validation projects) :

	L	$\hat{L}$	$\hat{L} - L$
Average value	4016.750	2029.705	-489.674
Standard deviation	5514.420	3121.928	3034.134
Correlation coefficient between L and $\hat{L}$			0.8713

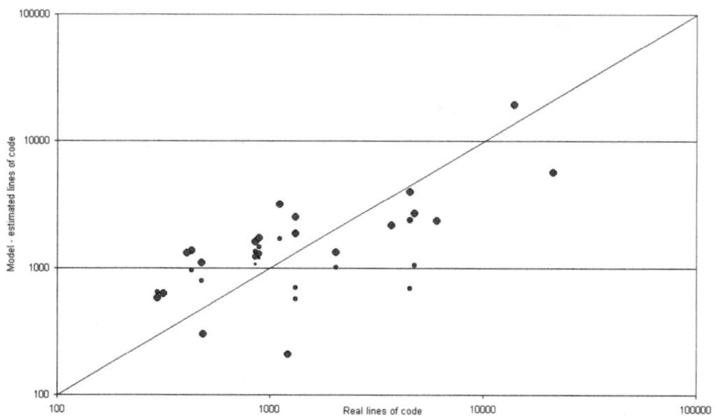

Figure 6: Test set: actual vs. estimated lines of code

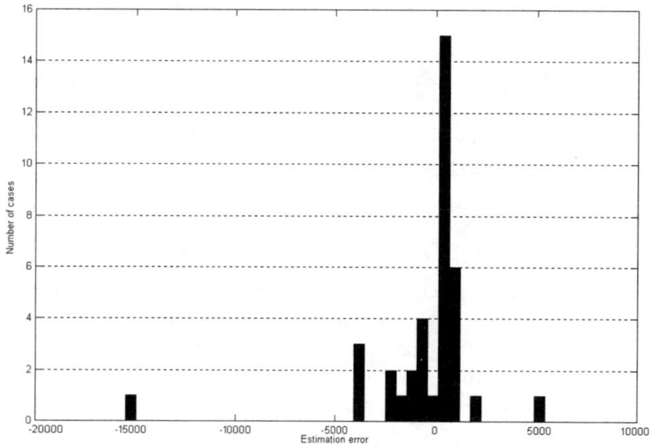

Figure 7: Test set: error density distribution.

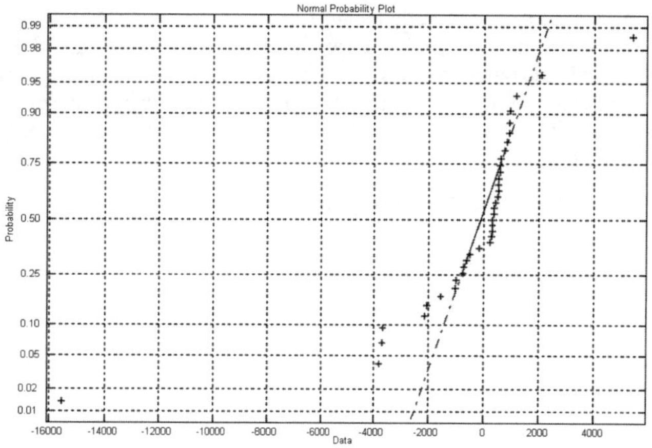

Figure 8: Test set: error cumulative distribution.

6. CONCLUSIONS

After collecting a relevant amount of code ($\geq$ 28 MB), belonging to real industry projects, and implementing automatic analysis and modeling tools, we delivered a methodology, able to estimate the size of each project, with a degree of accuracy depending on the amount of available knowledge. The methodology proves to be both accurate and robust.

Accuracy is proved by a high ρ between real and estimated data (0.8627 and 0.8713 respectively, for internal and external validation) and by acceptable σ_e (1400.412 and 3034.134 lines of code respectively; int more than 80% of the cases, estimation error falls in $\pm\sigma_e$; as represented in fig. 6, 7 and 8). Robustness is confirmed by null degradation of ρ and a tolerable degradation of σ_e when validation is switched from training to test set.

Error compensation occurred whenever models were aggregated: models resulting from composition of finer granularity sub-models exhibit better performances than their constituents (e.g. when syntax object models were integrated to form bunch models, and bunch models coalesced to constitute SOG models).

Our project base contains the vast majority of the public VHDL models on the Internet and is superabundant for SO model tuning, sufficient for bunch models, but scarce when it comes to SOG models. The current effort is to achieve better results with SOG models, by increasing the project base size, and to refine the back-end strategy to derive development effort from project sizes (as anticipated in [7]).

$\rho(\cdot, L)$	n_p	n_{ip}	n_{op}	n_{iop}	n_{xp}	n_g	n_{ps}
Entities	0.7875 (0.6536)	0.4277 (0.5544)	0.5687 (0.5670)	0.8740 (0.2495)	0.1509 (0.3066)	0.9059 (0.5737)	
Architectures	0.4622 (0.1625)	0.2535 (0.1090)	0.3174 (0.1615)	0.6192 (0.0932)	0.0844 (0.0923)	0.5640 (0.0127)	
Processes	0.2291 (-0.0372)					0.2867 (0.0771)	0.3239 (0.0849)

Table 4: Impact of reformatting on $\rho(\cdot, L)$.

7. CURRENT DEVELOPMENTS

Our research group is currently committed to enhancing the methodology in a number of ways: extending the number of projects in the training and test sets, removing the influence of different coding styles, and moving towards more complex models with higher contents in semantics.

7.1 Influence of coding-style

The next version of our estimation flow includes a VHDL reformatter (see [6]), which proved to be dramatically effective in reducing the source code length variability due to different coding styles. Preliminary studies show that the coefficients of correlation between the length of a given syntax object and each of its available variables exhibit significant increases after the code reformatting is performed, as shown in table 4 (values before reformatting are in related in paretheses).

7.2 Risks of overfitting

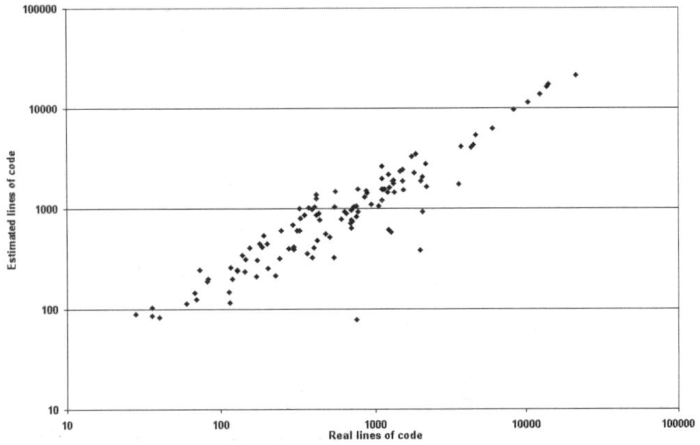

Figure 9: Training set: actual vs. estimated lines of code

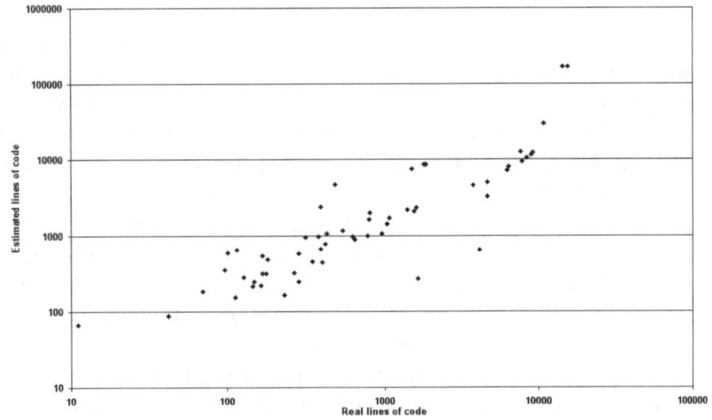

Figure 10: Test set: actual vs. estimated lines of code

The vast majority of the models introduced in section 4.1.1 are simple linear models, using only variables with high correlation coefficients with the length. In several cases, the influence of a given variable (e.g. number of ports) over an object's length is known to be linear, thus, a linear model is known to be correct *a priori*. For all the other cases, we are currently evaluating the use of higher-order models, using all the available variables.

In Figure 9 and 10 we report the results the internal and external validation respectively of an estimation flow in which most linear models have been replaced with second order models.

Internal validation:

	L	$\hat{L}$	$\hat{L} - L$
Average value	1543.269	1843.131	299.861
Standard deviation	3096.056	3375.566	622.811
Correlation coefficient between L and $\hat{L}$			0.9852

External validation:

	L	$\hat{L}$	$\hat{L} - L$
Average value	2376.034	8848.160	6472.126
Standard deviation	3659.174	30521.040	27922.626
Correlation coefficient between L and $\hat{L}$			0.7398

We believe that an improper use of high-order models using also low-correlation variables could lead to overfitting, as above, with very good accuracy in the internal validation and decreased accuracy in the external. These considerations deserve a deeper study and are currently our work goals.

8. REFERENCES

[1] Virtual Socket Interface Alliance, `www.vsia.org`.

[2] *COCOMO 2.0, Model definition manual, v.1.2.* 1997.

[3] Numetrics, *Measuring IC and ASIC design productivity*, white paper, `www.numetrics.com`, May 2002.

[4] P. J. Ashenden, *The Designer's Guide to VHDL*. Morgan Kauffmann Publishers, San Francisco, 1995.

[5] J. Axelsson, Cost model for electronic architecture trade studies. In *Proc. 6th Intl. Conf. on Engineering of Complex Computer Systems*, 2000.

[6] P. S. Elliot and M. Gumm, *MVP v1.1*, Institute for Parallel and Distributed Systems, Stuttgart, Germany, 1994.

[7] William Fornaciari et al., Development cost and size estimation starting from high-level specifications. In *Proc. 9th Intl. Symposium on Hw/sw Codesign*, pages 86–91, ACM Press, 2001.

[8] IEEE Standards Board, *ANSI/IEEE Std 1076-1993, IEEE Standard VHDL Language Reference Manual.*

[9] D. P. Scarpazza, VHDL effort estimation on-line resources at CEFRIEL, `www.cefriel.it/vhdl-estimate`.

[10] D. P. Scarpazza, Development effort and size estimation for partially specified VHDL projects. CEFRIEL Internal report, 2002.

Tracking Object Life Cycle for Leakage Energy Optimization *

G. Chen, N. Vijaykrishnan, M. Kandemir, M. J. Irwin
Department of Computer Science and Engineering
The Pennsylvania State University
University Park, PA 16802
{gchen, vijay, kandemir, mji}@cse.psu.edu

M. Wolczko
Sun Microsystems, Inc.
2600 Casey Ave
Mountain View, CA 94043
mario@eng.sun.com

ABSTRACT

The focus of this work is on utilizing the state of objects during their lifespan in optimizing the leakage energy consumed in the data caches when executing embedded Java applications. Our analysis reveals that a major portion of the leakage energy is actually wasted in retaining the objects beyond their last use. In order to eliminate this wastage, we investigate three approaches that use the garbage collector, escape analysis and last use analysis for reducing leakage energy. Finally, we track the access gap between successive object accesses to reduce leakage energy of live objects. A combination of these schemes is shown to provide 21% data cache leakage energy reduction in our default configuration.

Categories and Subject Descriptors

B.3.m [**Hardware**]: B.3 Memory Structures—*Miscellaneous*

General Terms

Algorithms, Experimentation

Keywords

Java, cache, leakage energy

1. INTRODUCTION

Optimizing power consumption has become important for a variety of systems ranging from high-performance systems to low end battery-operated devices. While optimizing dynamic power consumption has been the focus of most of the previous work, static power consumption due to leakage current is an important concern in future technologies [1]. Unlike dynamic energy consumption, static power is consumed independent of whether the component is accessed or not. Specifically, leakage power consumption is primarily dependent on the technology used and the number of transistors used for the design. As on-chip caches account for a major portion of the processor's transistor budget, they constitute a major portion of the energy budget of the processor. Leakage energy is projected to account for 70% of the cache power budget in 70nm technology [2].

We can reduce leakage by completely gating the supply voltage of cache lines. However, when the supply voltage is gated, the data stored in the cache line is lost (state-destroying leakage control) [3]. Hence, if another access is required to the same data, it should be fetched from lower levels of memory hierarchy, and this incurs a large performance penalty than using state-preserving leakage control. We refer to placing a cache line in low leakage mode as "turning off the cache line" and restoring the normal supply voltage as "turning on the cache line" in the rest of this paper. We use this term for both state-preserving and state-destroying modes and distinguish between them when relevant.

The effectiveness of the leakage reduction depends on how precisely the behavior of cache line can be tracked. While turning off a cache line later than the last use can waste energy consumption, prematurely turning off a cache line can incur energy/performance penalties when it needs to be accessed. Thus, deciding when to turn off a cache line is very important. In this work, we utilize the knowledge about the state of an object in its lifespan to direct the turning off cache lines. In particular, we identify different states in the lifetime of an object, when it is created, last-used, becomes garbage, and is collected by the garbage collector. It must be observed that the cache lines containing only objects beyond their last use waste leakage energy. Our analysis in this paper reveals that this wasted leakage energy contributes to a significant portion of data cache energy consumption. In order to control the turning off cache lines more precisely, we propose a series of object in its lifespan. Almost none of prior approaches (e.g., [4, 5]) utilizes the object lifetime information in optimizing leakage energy with the exception of [6] that manages the leakage in on-chip memory using the garbage collector. In this paper, in addition to the garbage collector, we further exploit object lifetime information by applying escape and last use analyses to find more leakage reduction chances. Further, as compared to the work in [6], we focus on the data cache rather than leakage control in memory where caching influences the potential of the scheme.

This work explores three different approaches that save cache leakage energy. In our first approach, the garbage collector is used to turn off the cache line(s) containing the collected objects. Note

*This research is supported in part by NSF Awards 0103583, 0130143; NSF CAREER Awards 0093082, 0093085; MARCO 98-DF-600 GSRC.

CODES+ISSS'03, October 1–3, 2003, Newport Beach, California, USA.

that in this case it is preferable to employ state-destroying leakage control as the object will never be accessed again. Our second technique exploits the observation that, for many objects, their lifetime is contained within the lifetime of a particular methods execution. We refer to such objects as "method local objects". Using a trace-based escape analysis technique, we identify the method local objects and turn the corresponding cache lines off when the method to which it is local completes its execution. Thus, this scheme can turn off cache lines much earlier than the garbage collector. However, only method local objects can benefit from this scheme. Our third technique attempts to be even more precise. We identify the last-use of the object by identifying the instruction that last uses it. We turn off the cache line containing the object immediately after executing this instruction. After these three optimization strategies, we focus our attention on object access times and show that it is beneficial to turn-off cache lines containing objects which have a large gap between their successive accesses.

In exploring these schemes, we focus on objects in embedded Java applications. Our choice is influenced by the wide adoption of Java in the energy-constrained mobile devices [7, 8]. The results of our evaluation of using ten embedded Java applications shows that the three proposed approaches provide significant savings in leakage energy consumption.

The remainder of this paper is organized as follows. In the next section, we introduce our experimental setup and the benchmark suite used. In Section 3, we show the energy consumption profile in the data cache based on object lifespan. Next, we evaluate our energy optimization schemes that use garbage collection, escape analysis and last-use analysis in Sections 4 through 6. In Section 7, we present how to optimize energy consumed by live objects. Finally, we provide conclusions in Section 8.

2. EXPERIMENTAL SETUP AND BENCHMARKS

We use ten applications that target embedded Java-based environments (Table 1). We believe these applications represent a good mix for typical Java-enabled personal devices. For obtaining detailed energy profiles, we have customized an energy simulator and analyzer using the Shade [9] (microSPARC instruction set simulator) tool-set and simulated the entire KVM (a small-footprint Java virtual machine designed for resource-constrained environments [10]) executing a Java code. As many of our optimization techniques are profile-based, we used a different training set to get the profiles and a different input set for evaluating the energy benefits. Shade is used to capture the cache access pattern of the application while the KVM was augmented with instrumentation code to track the lifespan of the objects. Figure 1 shows our experimental setup.

Once the cache access patterns are captured and the state of the cache lines is determined after applying the optimizations, we can evaluate the energy consumption. In our experiments, we assume that the processor has 32KB ICache and 32KB DCache. The dynamic energy for each cache access is 0.302nJ. When a cache line is in the active mode, it consumes 0.147pJ energy each cycle; while in the sleep mode, it does not consume leakage energy. These energy parameters are based on future 70nm CMOS technology. The cache data energy is obtained by using CACTI 3.0 [11]. Each cache line is either in *active* or *leakage control (sleep)* mode. A cache line needs to be in active mode to serve a cache access and consumes the maximum leakage energy. When a cache line is in the sleep mode, we assume state-destroying leakage control and assume zero leakage energy. Accessing a sleep cache line involves loading the data

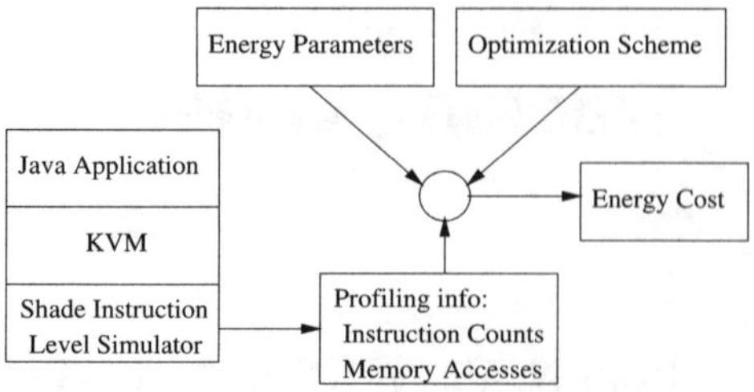

Figure 1: Experimental setup.

Benchmark	Brief Description	Heap Energy (mJ)		Cache Leakage Contribution
		Memory	Cache	
calculator	Arithmetic calculator for MIDP	0.84	4.21	84.9%
chess	User vs. computer chess game	16.26	87.38	80.4%
emailviewer	Light-weighted POP3 Client	2.65	16.29	86.3%
manyballs	Drawing bouncing balls	0.60	3.26	84.9%
mdoom	3D Shooting game	8.29	44.27	84.9%
mpg	Movie player for MIDP	7.16	35.64	80.9%
pushpuzzle	A conventional puzzle game	1.28	7.18	83.1%
scheduler	Personal monthly scheduler	0.67	8.08	94.3%
sfmap	Digital map for MIDP	3.47	17.03	85.9%
webviewer	WWW browser for MIDP	5.18	28.25	84.5%

Table 1: Our benchmarks.

from main memory, which is similar to a cache miss. The wakeup delay of the sleep cache line is overlapped with the delay due to the main memory access.

In order to control the leakage state, we support a special instruction, *deactivate(address, length)*, that can turn off cache lines and place them in sleep mode. This instruction takes two parameters, the starting address and the number of bytes (length) from the starting address to place in sleep mode. The deactivate instruction compares the tag of each cache line for addresses in this region sequentially and turns off cache lines whenever the tags match. Note that the tag match is necessary as only a part of the object may be present in the cache. A *deactivate* instruction may take several cycles to execute based on the size of the region being turned off. In order not to create conflicts in address port with other data cache accesses, the *deactivate* instruction needs an extra address decoder to control the supply voltage to cache lines. It should be noted that the *deactivate* instruction does not need to access the data itself.

3. OBJECT LIFETIMES AND CACHE ENERGY CONSUMPTION PROFILE

Table 1 shows the energy consumed in the data cache and memory due to the heap accesses for the applications in our suite. The last column of the table indicates the contribution of leakage energy to the cache energy. We can observe that it is a major contributor to overall cache energy.

Figure 2 illustrates the lifetime of a Java object. An object is created, used a number of times, and then reaches its last use. Following this, it becomes garbage, and after some time, it is collected (by the garbage collector). It should be pointed out that this object can be in the cache during these different phases of its lifetime. In fact, even after it is garbage collected, it can still be in the cache. Obviously, energy spent on a cache line that keeps an object which has passed its last-use is wasted, and should be reduced as much as possible.

Since the leakage current can be reduced only at the granularity of cache lines and not at the granularity of objects, it is important to identify how objects are mapped to cache lines. For an object whose size is larger than one cache line, all the cache lines occupied by it are called *relevant cache lines (RCLs)* (Figure 3). Since the

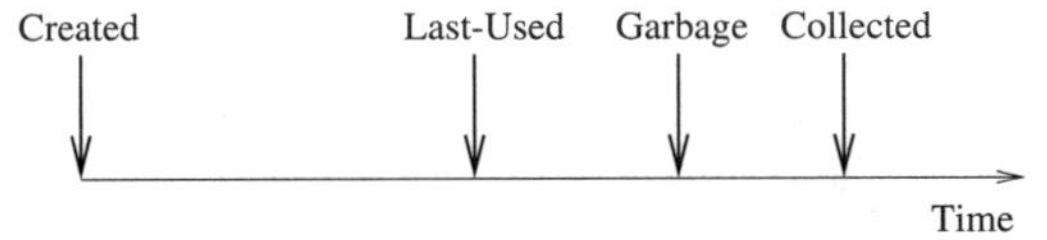

Figure 2: Lifetime of an object.

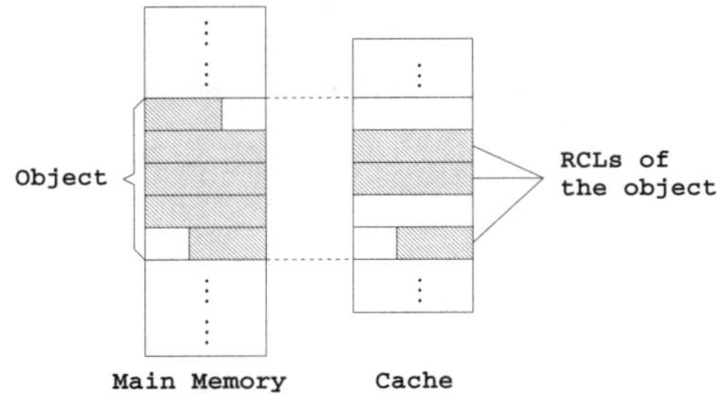

Figure 3: Relevant Cache lines of an object

objects are not necessarily aligned to the beginning of cache lines, it is possible for multiple objects to be contained in the same cache line. Further, these multiple objects can be in different phases of their lives. For example, two objects can share a cache line, and one of them might be live (i.e., its last use has not been reached yet), whereas the other one can be garbage. To capture these cases, we classify cache lines into the groups given in Table 2 according to their *states*. As an example, the state of a cache line is tagged as 'Last-Used' if it does not have a live object and has parts of (at least) one last-used object. It can also have objects that are garbage or collected. In this table, 'Not-Used' refers to a state where the cache line is not used by the application being executed.

Based on the discussion above, one can see that a cache line can be in one of the five states: live, last-used, garbage, collected, and not-used. Figure 4 shows the percentage data cache energy consumption breakdown as dynamic energy and static energy components. The static energy part is further divided into energies expended in different cache line states. This graph clearly shows that a large percentage of the cache energy is static energy consumed for maintaining cache lines that do not keep any useful data. In fact, a major portion of the leakage energy consumed in the caches is actually wasted because cache lines are not turned off when holding objects beyond their last use. Eliminating this energy consumption through object lifetime analysis can be very beneficial in practice.

Figure 4 also indicates the upper bounds on energy savings that can be achieved using optimal algorithms that target different phases of object lifetimes. For example, an optimization strategy that turns off cache lines holding collected objects can reduce overall cache energy by 10% for `emailviewer`. It should be noted that such a strategy can be implemented within the garbage collector itself. On the other hand, a different optimization strategy that turns off cache lines immediately after such lines transition to the garbage state can eliminate energies due to both cache lines in "garbage" and "collected" states. Finally, a strategy that turns off cache lines immediately after they transition to the last-used state can eliminate all wasted energy due to storing objects beyond their last use (saving 47% cache energy on the average). Up to this point, we have

	Objects that may be contained			
Status	Live	Last-Used	Garbage (Dead)	Collected
Live	Yes	Maybe	Maybe	Maybe
Last-Used	No	Yes	Maybe	Maybe
Garbage	No	No	Yes	Maybe
Collected	No	No	No	Yes
Not-Used	No	No	No	No

Table 2: Classification of cache lines into different states.

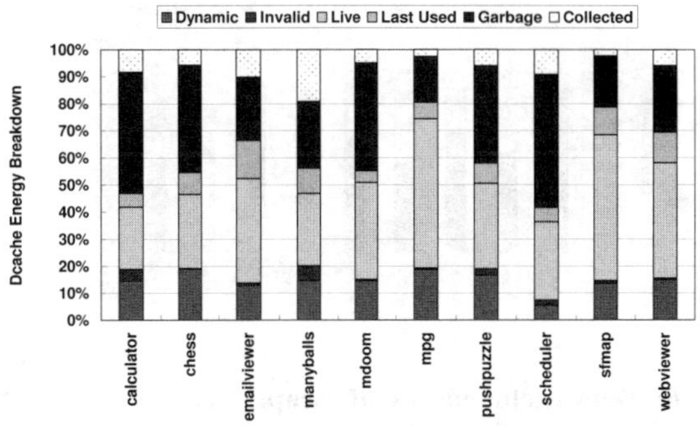

Figure 4: Energy breakdown in base case in data cache.

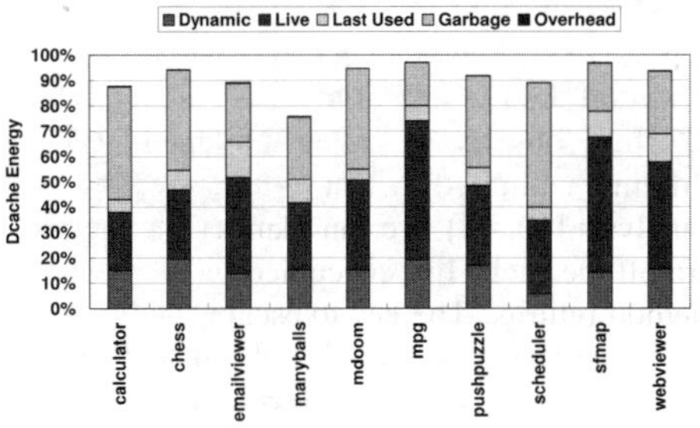

Figure 5: Data cache energy results for GC controlled cache line turnoff optimization (do this for other similar figures, too).

focused only on the wasted energy that is consumed after an object reaches its last use. However, objects that are live also cause their RCLs to consume leakage energy. If the gap between successive object accesses is large, it would be more beneficial to turn-off the cache lines rather than expend leakage energy during that interval. The focus of the rest of the paper is to implement schemes that can achieve close to the maximum energy savings possible while minimizing the overheads due to the implementation of the schemes themselves.

4. GARBAGE COLLECTION CONTROLLED CACHE LINE TURNOFF

KVM invokes the garbage collector(GC) when it runs out of heap memory. The collection is performed in two phases. In the mark phase, the collector traverses the reference graph from the roots to mark all the objects that are reachable from the roots. In the sweep phase, the collector collects all the objects that are not marked in the mark phase and merges them into free blocks. These free blocks are returned to the free memory pool for future allocation. Since the collected objects have been merged, we can turnoff the RCLs of several collected objects with contiguous addresses using one deactivate instruction. It should be noted that, during garbage collection, the header of each object (either live or dead) is accessed.

Figure 5 shows the impact of this garbage collector controlled cache line turnoff. All the energy values are normalized to the energy consumption of the cache without any optimization, as is shown in Table 1. The energy results for the optimized strategy also include the overhead energies consumed due to the execution of the deactivate instructions and for turning on the cache lines that are in sleep mode. Note that sleep cache lines need to turn-on when the next object maps onto the same cache line. On an average, this GC controlled cache line turnoff saves the overall data cache energy consumption by 9%. All the other schemes discussed in the rest of the paper use the GC controlled scheme.

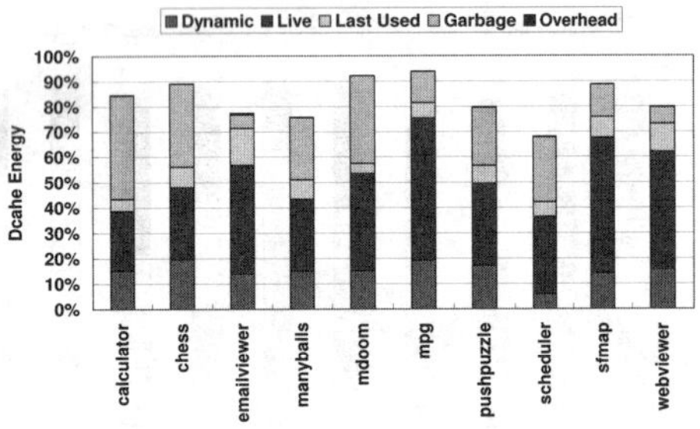

Figure 6: Data cache energy of escape analysis optimization. Also uses GC controlled leakage.

5. ESCAPE ANALYSIS

Prior research [12, 13] has shown that a big portion of objects do not survive beyond the lifetime of the method where these objects are created. These objects are called the "method local objects" since their lifetime is limited by that of their creating method. Using escape analysis [12, 13], we can identify the method local objects and turn off the cache lines occupied by them when the corresponding method returns. The key to escape analysis is to identify the local allocation sites, i.e., the bytecodes that allocate only local objects. In contrast to static analysis techniques employed in [12] and [13], we use a trace-based approach to identify method local objects. Specifically, we run each application with the training input sets using an instrumented virtual machine, which records the allocation site of each object. When a method returns, the instrumented virtual machine scans the heap to find out which objects that have been created within this method are still accessible. If an object created within the method is still alive, the allocation site of this object is marked as "global". When we are done with the training input sets, the instrumented virtual machine outputs the location of each global allocation site of each method. This information on the global allocation sites is then added to the corresponding class files using our class file annotation tool. During run time, when a class file is loaded, the virtual machine checks the annotations and marks each global allocation site. The unmarked allocation sites are regarded as local allocation sites.

We allocate all the objects created at the local allocation sites during the same invocation of each method together in a contiguous address space. When a method returns, all RCLs corresponding to its local objects can be turned off. The use of a contiguous address space helps to turn off all the cache lines containing the local objects of this method using only a single deactivate instruction. Note that since cache line turn-off using state-destroying leakage mode only evicts the copy in the data cache, even an accidental eviction of a non method local object is not a correctness issue (it may only hurt performance). Note that dirty (dirty indicates that the cache line was modified since it was brought into the cache) cache lines are always written back to the next level when they are turned off to maintain cache coherence. Figure 6 shows the effectiveness of escape analysis in conserving the energy consumption of the data cache when used along with garbage collector based turn off. Comparing Figure 6 with Figure 5, we can observe that the percentage of the leakage energy that is consumed by the cache lines containing garbage objects is reduced. On the average, we achieve 17% overall data cache energy savings in our 10 benchmarks by turning-off method local objects immediately after the corresponding method returns.

6. LAST USE ANALYSIS

Last use analysis is used to turn off the RCLs of objects more aggressively immediately after their last accesses. In the program

```
int f(int n) {
    Object o = new Object();
    int i = 0;
    int s = 0;
    while(++i < N) {
        access(o);
    }
    for(i=0; i<1000; i++) {
        s += g();
    }
    return s;
}
```

Figure 7: An example code fragment.

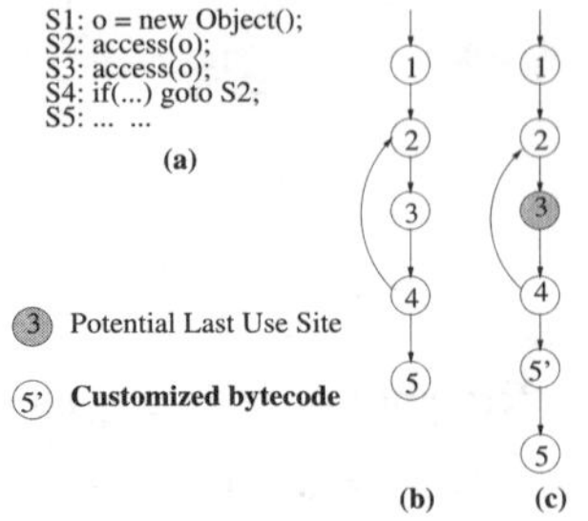

Figure 8: Last use analysis.

shown in Figure 7, we observe that object *o* will never be accessed after the while loop. Consequently, we can turn off the object *o* immediately after the exit of the while loop (i.e., much earlier than the exit of the method or before a garbage collector can collect it). It should be noted that, although the application does not access those last used objects, their headers and reference fields (for last used but still live objects) are still accessed in the garbage collection. This may cause extra cache misses and energy overhead (this overhead is also captured in our results). Fortunately, for most applications, garbage collection is not invoked very frequently.

In order to perform the last use analysis, we utilize a "last-reference register" that indicates the address of the object that has been last used. This can then be used by a deactivate instruction that is inserted into the bytecode sequence to turn-off the RCLs of the object pointed to by the last-reference register. The key here is to identify the last use sites (i.e., the bytecodes that will update the last-reference register) and where the deactivate instruction should be inserted. In some cases, it may not be possible to turn off the cache line at the last use site since the same static site can access the object multiple times. Hence, it is necessary to distinguish between the last use site and where the cache lines that hold the object can be turned-off.

Figure 8 shows an example of how our last use analysis works. Figure 8 (a) is a code fragment and (b) is its Control Flow Graph (CFG). From this CFG, we can identify a loop which consists of nodes 2, 3 and 4. Let us assume that object *o* is not accessed outside the loop. Both S2 and S3 access object *o* many times in the loop. However, none of the accesses made by S2 is a last access. Therefore, S2 is not a potential last use site. On the other hand, at the last iteration of the loop, S3 makes a last access to object *o*. Therefore, we mark S3 as a potential last use site. At S5, we observe that all the objects accessed by the previous potential last use site (S3) have become last used. Therefore, we insert a deactivate instruction (S5') right before S5 to turn off the RCLs of the objects that are last-used by S3.

Our current implementation uses training sets and profiling traces to find the addresses of bytecodes that make last uses and the addresses for inserting the *deactivate* instructions. Specifically, we first run each application with training input sets using our instrumented virtual machine, which keeps track of each bytecode and generates a detailed trace file. After this, we analyze the trace file using the following three steps to identify last use sites and the

	Code Fragment	Step 1	Step 2 A	Step 2 B	Step 3 A	Step 3 B
#1	i = 0		0	1	0	1
#2	j = 0		99	1	0	100
#3	o = new Object		99	1	0	100
#4	access o		99	401	0	100
#5	access o	mark	99	401	0	100
#6	j = j + 1		100	400	100	400
#7	if(j<5) goto 4		100	400	100	400
#8	i = i + 1		100	0	100	0
#9	if(i<100) goto 2		100	0	0	100
#10	return		1	0	0	1

Figure 9: Example: finding the locations to insert deactivate instructions.

addresses to insert deactivate instructions. An example is shown in Figure 9. The results of this analysis are added to the corresponding class files as annotations using our annotation tool. These annotations are used by the virtual machine at runtime to optimize data cache energy consumption (the details will be explained later).

Step 1: We scan the trace in the reverse order of execution to find: (1) when each object is last used; and (2) which bytecodes have ever made last accesses. The bytecodes that have ever made last accesses are marked as potential last use sites (see the "mark" in the third column of Figure 9).

Step 2: We scan the trace in the order of execution. In this scan, we update the last-reference register right after each execution of the bytecode that has been marked as potential last use site in step 1. Note that this register is shared by all potential last use sites. Further, associated with each static bytecode in the program are two counters: A and B. Before the execution of each bytecode, if the last-reference-register is not null and it refers to an object that has become last used (by comparing the object's death time against the execution time of current bytecode), we increase the counter A of the current bytecode by one. Otherwise, the counter B of this bytecode is increased by one. Obviously, $A + B$ is equal to the number of times that this bytecode has been executed. The fourth column in Figure 9 shows the contents of counters A and B for each bytecode after the code fragment (in the second column) returns. From this column, we observe that bytecode #6 is executed 500 times, for 100 of which the last-reference-register refers to the last used objects. Note that the initial value of the last-reference-register is null, and that the reference that is stored in the last-reference-register by bytecode #5 remains unchanged until next loop iteration. Therefore, we observe that A counters of bytecodes #2, #3, #4 and #5 are all set to 99. After the scan, all the bytecodes with $A/(A+B) > T$ (T is a given threshold, T=95% in this work) are marked as candidates for inserting the deactivate instruction.

Step 3: We scan the trace once more in the order of execution. The scan in this step is similar to that in step 2 except that, after the execution of each bytecode that has been marked as candidates for inserting in step 2, the last-reference-register is set to null. Our purpose here is to filter out the redundant insertion candidates. After this scan, the bytecodes whose A and B counters still satisfy $A/(A + B) > T$ are marked as inserting points. Their addresses, as well as the addresses of the last use sites that have been found in step 1, are fed into a class file annotation tool, which adds a notation to each Java method indicating which bytecodes in the method are inserting points and which are last use sites. The last column of Figure 9 gives the contents of counters A and B for each bytecode after the code fragment returns. In this example, only bytecode #8 is determined to be an inserting point.

During execution, when the notated Java class files are loaded, the virtual machine marks the bytecode at each last use site and inserts a deactivate instruction right before each bytecode that is notated as an inserting point. Right after each marked bytecode is executed, the virtual machine updates the last-reference-register. The inserted deactivate instruction uses the address in the last-reference register to identify the object and relevant RCLs to turn-off. Note that our approach is not always accurate in determining last use and sometimes may cause some of the objects to be turned off prematurely. This premature turn off may incur additional performance penalties for fetching the data again from memory (or L2 cache); however, this does not affect the correctness of execution. Our experiments (see Table 3) demonstrate that the impact of such extra cache misses is marginal. Another problem is that executing the inserted deactivate instructions incurs overhead. Table 4 shows the actual number of deactivate instructions inserted in the selected applications. Compared to the total number of bytecodes of the corresponding benchmarks, the numbers of inserted instructions are very small. The third/fourth column in Table 3 shows the cache miss rate/execution time increase of our ten benchmarks with the last use analysis optimization. Note that in some cases the miss rate is reduced and the performance is improved. This is because our optimization prevents the last-used data from competing for the cache lines with live data. Figure 10 shows the impact of last use analysis on the data cache energy consumption when used in conjunction with the GC-controlled leakage management. Last use analysis can also be combined with escape analysis to further conserve the leakage energy (denoted as "Escape + Last Use" in Figure 12). On the average, we achieved 11% data cache energy savings through last use analysis optimization. When it is combined with escape analysis, it saves 6% (on average) more energy as compared to using escape analysis without last use analysis. It should be noted that, in both cases, we use the GC-controlled leakage management as well.

Benchmark	Baseline Cache Miss Rate (%)	Last Use Cache Miss Rate (%)	Last Use Exec Time Increase (%)	Access Gap Cache Miss Rate (%)	Access Gap Exec Time Increase (%)
calculator	1.67	1.99	0.54	3.86	3.69
chess	1.83	1.85	0.04	2.66	1.89
emailviewer	4.50	4.54	0.07	5.65	1.61
manyballs	1.57	1.62	0.09	3.69	3.61
mdoom	1.44	1.41	-0.04	2.96	2.61
mpg	0.88	0.89	0.03	2.67	4.10
pushpuzzle	1.14	1.12	-0.04	1.65	1.01
scheduler	2.45	2.56	0.06	5.03	1.47
sfmap	2.15	2.19	0.07	3.22	1.67
webviewer	2.03	2.05	0.03	3.81	3.06

Table 3: Performance degradation due to last use and access gap analysis optimization

Benchmark	Last Use Inserted	Access Gap Marked
calculator	149	469
chess	130	818
emailviewer	206	1594
manyballs	98	394
mdoom	110	603
mpg	129	866
pushpuzzle	128	718
scheduler	133	566
sfmap	116	578
webviewer	196	1399

Table 4: The number of inserted deactivate instructions in last use analysis and the number of marked instructions in access gap analysis.

7. ACCESS GAP ANALYSIS

The optimization schemes that we have presented so far focus on the the RCLs of the objects that are no longer used by an application. The merit of these schemes is that they do not increase cache miss rate (except the last use analysis). Access gap analysis scheme analyzes the intervals between two consecutive accesses to each objects and turns off RCLs when the intervals are long enough. The

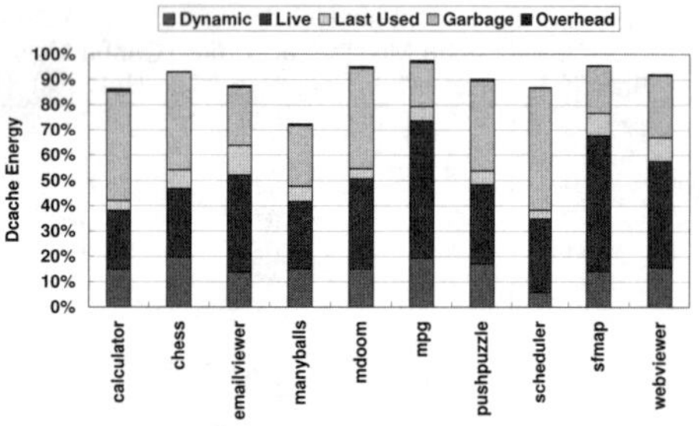

Figure 10: Data cache energy of last use analysis optimization. (The GC controlled scheme is also used.)

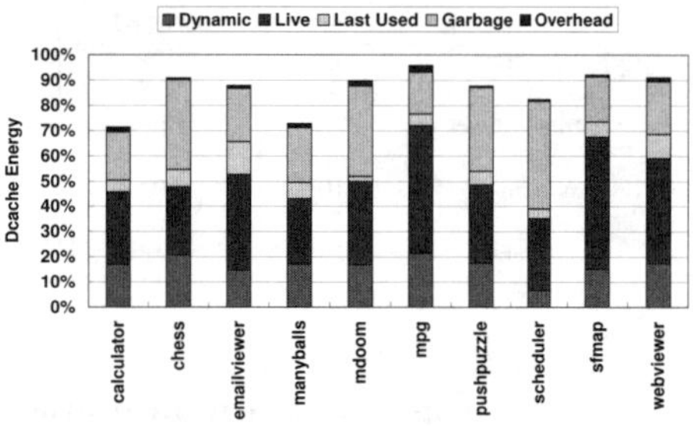

Figure 11: Data Cache energy of access gap analysis optimization. (The GC controlled scheme is also used.)

advantage of this scheme is that it has more chances to turn off cache lines. However, it also introduces extra cache misses since we may turn off the RCLs of some of objects that may be used in the near future. The cache miss rates of our benchmarks with access gap analysis optimization and the increase of execution time due to the extra misses are shown in the fifth and sixth columns of Table 3.

Our access gap analysis is also trace-based. Let us assume that bytecode $b1$ accesses object o at time t_1. Assume further that the next access to o is made by bytecode $b2$ at t_2. We define "the access gap associated with $b1$ " as $\Delta t = t_2 - t_1$. Note that if the access made by $b1$ is the last access to o, then $\Delta t = T - t_1$ where T is the overall execution time of the application. Based on the traces, we calculate the average length of access gaps associated with each bytecode. And then, we use our class file annotation tool to annotate each bytecode with the average length of the access gaps larger than the threshold G. The threshold G we used is based on the minimum duration required for leakage energy savings to amortize the penalties for the deactivate instruction and turn-on when the next access to the same object happens. During the course of execution, KVM marks the annotated bytecodes when the class file is loaded. Right after the execution of each marked bytecode, KVM immediately turns off the RCLs of the recently accessed object. The last column of Figure 4 gives the number of instructions that were marked in different applications.

Figure 11 shows the impact of this access gap analysis optimization when used in conjunction with the GC-control scheme. We achieve an average of 14% saving in the overall data cache energy consumption. Similar to the last use analysis, the access gap analysis may also be combined with the escape analysis and the GC-control scheme (denoted as "Escape + Access Gap" in Figure 12). With such a combination, the average saving of data cache overall energy is 21%.

Figure 12 shows how the different schemes compare with each other and how a combination of schemes can achieve significant energy savings.

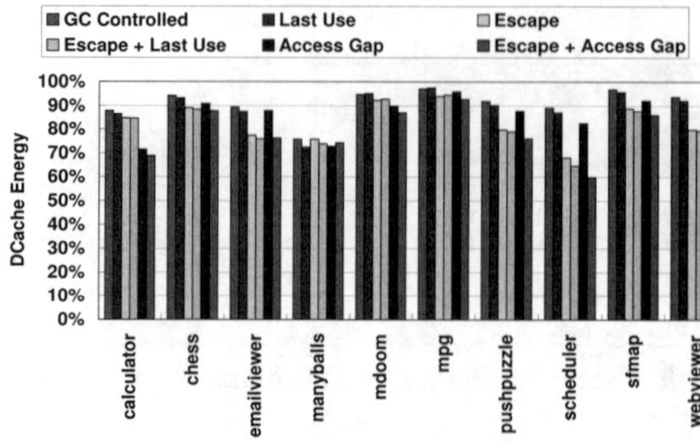

Figure 12: Comparison of optimization schemes. (All schemes use GC controlled approach as well.)

8. CONCLUSION

Leakage energy consumption is becoming an important concern for designers for future processors. This work specifically focuses on reducing the leakage energy in the data caches by exploiting the state of the object during its life span. Our analysis reveals that a major portion of leakage energy is wasted in retaining objects beyond their last use. Based on this observation, we explore the use of three different approaches that use the garbage collector, escape analysis and last-use analysis to reduce leakage energy. Finally, we also try to optimize the leakage energy consumed by the live objects by tracking their access interval. A combination of our schemes can reduce the data cache leakage energy by 21.3% on the average across different applications in our default configuration.

9. REFERENCES

[1] J. A. Butts and G. Sohi, "A static power model for architects," in *the 33th Annual International Symposium on Microarchitecture*, Dec. 2000.

[2] K. Flautner, N. Kim, S. Martin, D. Blaauw, and T. Mudge, "Drowsy caches: Simple techniques for reducing leakage power," in *the 29th International Symposium on Computer Architecture*, (Anchorage, AK, USA), May 2002.

[3] S. Kaxiras, Z. Hu, and M. Martonosi, "Cache decay: Exploiting generational behavior to reduce cache leakage power," in *the 28th International Symposium on Computer Architecture*, (Sweden), June 2001.

[4] N. S. Kim, K. Flautner, D. Blaauw, and T. Mudge, "Drowsy instruction caches: Leakage power reduction using dynamic voltage scaling and cache sub-bank prediction," in *the 35th Annual International Symposium on Microarchitecture (MICRO-35)*, (Istanbul, Turkey), 2002.

[5] H. Zhou, M. C. Toburen, E. Rotenberg, and T. M. Conte, "Adaptive mode control: A static-power-efficient cache design," in *International Conference on Parallel Architectures and Compilation Techniques (PACT'01)*, (Barcelona, Spain), Sept. 2001.

[6] G. Chen, R. Shetty, M. Kandemir, N. Vijaykrishnan, M. J. Irwin, and M. Wolczko, "Tuning garbage collection in an embedded java environment," in *the 8th International Symposium on High-Performance Computer Architecture (HPCA'02)*, (Cambridge, MA, USA), Feb. 2002.

[7] R. Riggs, A. Taivalsaari, and M. VandenBrink, *Programming Wireless Devices with the Java 2 Platform*. Addison Wesley, 2001.

[8] J. Lyman, "Java's surprising comeback." http://www.newsfactor.com/perl/story/18365.html.

[9] B. Cmelik and D. Keppel, "Shade: A fast instruction-set simulator for execution profiling," in *the 1994 ACM SIGMETRICS Conference on the Measurement and Modeling of Computer Systems*, pp. 128–137, May 1994.

[10] "CLDC and the K Virtual Machine (KVM)." http://java.sun.com/product/cldc.

[11] P. Shivakumar and N. P. Jouppi, "CACTI 3.0: An integrated cache timing, power, and area model," tech. rep., Compaq Computer Corporation Western Research Laboratory, 2001.

[12] J. Whaley and M. Rinard, "Compositional pointer and escape analysis for Java programs," in *ACM SIGPLAN Conference on Object-Oriented Programming Systems, Languages, and Applications (OOPSLA'99)*, (Denver, CO, USA), Nov. 1999.

[13] J.-D. Choi, M. Gupta, M. J. Serrano, V. C. Sreedhar, and S. P. Midkiff, "Escape analysis for java," in *the Conference on Object-Oriented Programming Systems, Languages, and Applications (OOPSLA)*, pp. 1–19, 1999.

Compiler Parallelization of C Programs for Multi-Core DSPs with Multiple Address Spaces

Björn Franke
Institute for Computing Systems Architecture (ICSA)
School of Informatics
University of Edinburgh
B.Franke@sms.ed.ac.uk

M.F.P. O'Boyle
Institute for Computing Systems Architecture (ICSA)
School of Informatics
University of Edinburgh
mob@inf.ed.ac.uk

ABSTRACT

This paper develops a new approach to compiling C programs for multiple address space, multi-processor DSPs. It integrates a novel data transformation technique that exposes the processor location of partitioned data into a parallelization strategy. When this is combined with a new address resolution mechanism, it generates efficient programs that run on multiple address spaces without using message passing. This approach is applied to the UTDSP benchmark suite and evaluated on a four processor TigerSHARC board, where it is shown to outperform existing approaches and gives an average speedup of 3.25 on the parallel benchmarks.

Categories and Subject Descriptors

D.3.4 [**Programming Languages**]: Processors—*Compilers, Optimization*

General Terms

Algorithms, Experimentation, Measurement, Performance

Keywords

DSPs, Data Partitioning, Address Resolution, Multiple Address Space Compilation

1. INTRODUCTION.

Although multi-core DSPs offer a cost-effective method of achieving high performance, porting existing uni-processor applications to such parallel architectures is currently complex and time-consuming. There are no commercially available compilers that will take existing sequential DSP programs and map them automatically onto a multi-processor machine [17]. Instead, users are typically required to rewrite their code as a process network or a set of communicating sequential processes [12]. Such an approach is well known to be highly non-trivial and error-prone, possibly introducing deadlock.

Rewriting an application in a parallel manner is a highly specialized skill. What is needed is a tool that takes existing programs and maps them automatically onto the new multiprocessor architecture efficiently. Although there has been over 20 years of research into auto-parallelizing compilation in scientific computing [5, 6, 7, 2], this has not taken place in the embedded domain. This is due to two main reasons: (i) DSP programs are written in C rather than Fortran [7] and make extensive use of pointer arithmetic and (ii) the multiple address spaces of multi-processor DSPs is difficult to compile for. We overcome the first problem by using an array recovery technique developed in our earlier work [3]. The second problem is solved by combining a novel data transformation scheme, that exposes the processor ID of remote data with a new address resolution technique that uses local pointer arrays to track remote data. This low overhead technique greatly simplifies code generation producing code similar to that produced for single-address space parallelization [5] without introducing complex (and potentially deadlocking) message passing code. By embedding these two techniques into an overall parallelization strategy, we have developed an auto-parallelizing C compiler for DSP applications that outperforms existing approaches on multiple address space embedded processors.

The paper is structured as follows. Section 2 provides a motivating example and is followed in section 3 by a detailed description of our auto-parallelization scheme. Section 4 empirically evaluates our approach and is followed by a short review of related work and some concluding remarks.

2. MOTIVATION & EXAMPLE

Our approach exploits the fact that although multi-processor DSP machines typically have multiple address spaces, part of each processor's memory space is visible from other processors, unlike pure message-passing machines. However, unlike single address space machines, such as the SGI Origin 3000, a processor must know both the identity of the remote processor and the location in memory of the required data value. For example, figure 1 (from [1]) shows the global memory map of a multi-processor system comprising the Analog Devices TigerSHARC processor. Each processor typically has its internal address space for accesses to local data. These accesses are purely local and not reflected on the external bus. In addition, the processors' memories form a global address space where each processor is assigned a certain range of addresses. This global address space is used for bus-based accesses to remote data where the global address (or equivalently the remote processor's identity and the data's local address) must be known.

We have developed a novel technique which combines single-address space parallelization approaches with a novel address resolution mechanism, based on a simple descriptor data structure, which, at runtime, determines the processor and memory location of all items.

2.1 Example

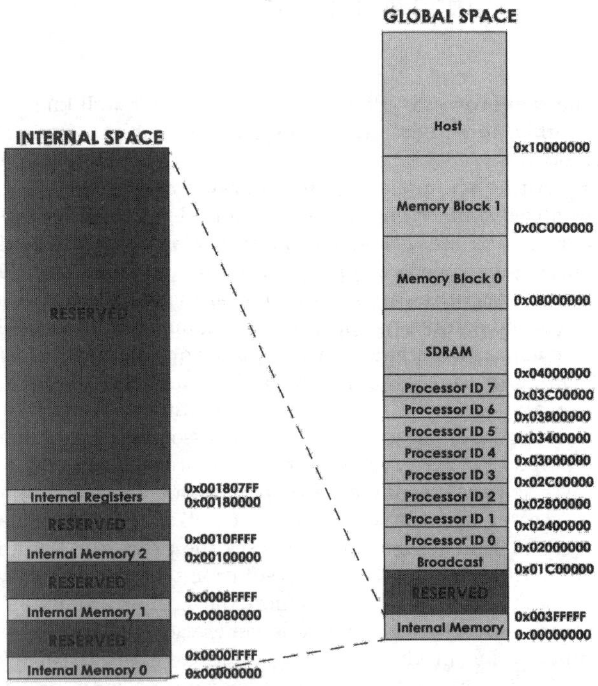

Figure 1: Global Memory Map [1]

The example in figures 2 and 3 illustrates the main points of this paper. The code in figure 2, box (1) is typical of C programs written for DSP processors; it is hybrid of two programs `n_real_updates` and `convolution` from the DSP-stone benchmark suite. The use of post-increment pointer traversal is a well know idiom [19]. This form, however, will prevent many optimizing compilers from performing aggressive optimization and will prevent attempts at parallelization. The second box (2) in figure 2 shows the program after array recovery [3].

The pointers are replaced with array references based on the loop iterator. SPMD owner-computes parallelization by partitioning the data and computation across the processor nodes is straightforward here. There is just one array dimension and one loop, both of which are partitioned by the number of processors. In this example we assume there are four processors. Standard partitioning [5] would generate the program in box (3) and, for single address space machines, this would be sufficient. To access remote data in multi-address space machines, however, the processor location of partitioned data needs to be explicitly available. Our scheme, achieves this by data strip-mining [14] each array to form a two dimensional array whose inner index corresponds to the four processors. This allows the processor location of partitioned data to be explicitly available. For instance, the array `D` is now partitioned such that `D[0][0...7]` resides on processor 0 and `D[1][0...7]` resides on processor 1 etc. Similarly for arrays `C`,`A` and `B`. The iterator is similarly partitioned to iterate over the work allocated to it, 0...7. The resulting code is shown in figure 2, box (4). Only the declarations of `D` and `B` are shown to simplify presentation of the later transformation stages.

We now need to generate a separate program for each processor. The partitioned code for processor 0 (as specified by `z`) is shown in figure 2, box (5). The code for processors 1,2,3 are identical except for `#define z 1,2` or 3. Multiple address space machines require remote, globally-accessible data to have a distinct name to local data[1]. Thus, each of the globally-accessible sub-arrays are renamed as follows: `D[0][0...7]` becomes `D0[0...7]` and `D[1][0...7]` becomes `D1[0...7]` etc. Similarly for arrays `C`, `A` and `B`. On processor 0 `D0` is declared as a variable residing on that processor while `D1, D2,D3` are declared `extern` (see the second and third lines of box (6) figure 2) . For processor 1, `D1` is declared local and the remainder are declared `extern` etc.

To access both local and remote data, a local pointer array is set up on each processor. This simple descriptor data structure is an array containing four pointer elements, which are assigned to the start address of the local arrays on the four processors. We use the original name of the array `D[][]` as the pointer array `*D[]` and then initialize the pointer array to point to the four distributed arrays `int *D[4] = {D0,D1,D2,D3}` (see box (6), figure 2) . This is shown diagrammatically in figure 3 for arrays `B` and `D`. The bold lines represent the data accessed by processor 0. Thus, there is local access to array `D0` but remote access to array `B3` by processor 0. Using the original name means that we have exactly the same array access form in all uses of the arrays `D`,`C`,`A`,`B` as in box(4). This has been achieved by using the fact that multi-dimensional arrays in C are arrays of arrays and that higher dimensions arrays are defined as containing an array of pointers to sub-arrays[2]. From a code generation point of view this greatly simplifies implementation and avoids complex and difficult to automate message passing.

3. OVERALL PARALLELIZATION ALGORITHM

Our overall parallelization algorithm is shown in figure 4. Pointer to array conversion is first applied to enable data dependence analysis (for further details see [3]). Once the program is in a pointer free form, standard data dependence analysis is applied to determine if the program is parallel and if so, we check to see if the amount available justifies parallelization[3].

3.1 Partitioning and Mapping

[1]Otherwise they are assumed to be private copies
[2]As defined in section 6.5.2.1 of the ANSI C standard paragraphs 3 and 4
[3]Currently we multiply the parallelized loop trip count by the number of operations and check it is above a certain threshold before continuing

Original code (1)

```
int *p_d,p_c,p_a,p_b;

for (i = 0 ; i <=31 ; i++)
   *p_d++  = *p_c++ + *p_a++ * *p_b-- ;
```

Array Recovery (2)

```
int D[32], C[32], A[32], B[32];

for (i = 0 ; i <=31 ; i++)
   D[i]  = C[i] + A[i] * B[32-i] ;
```

Standard Partitioning (3)

```
int D[32], C[32], A[32], B[32];

lo = (myid *32/numprocs);
hi = ((myid + 1) *32/numprocs) -1;

for (i = lo ; i <=hi ; i++)
   D[i]  = C[i] + A[i] * B[32-i] ;
```

Data transformation exposing processor ID (4)

```
int D[4][8], B[4][8];

for (z = 0; i<=3; i++)
 for (i = 0; i<=7; i++)

 D[z][i]  = C[z][i] + A[z][i] * B[4-z][7-i];
```

One program per processor (5)

```
#define z 0

int D[4][8], B[4][8];

for (i = 0; i<=7; i++)

 D[z][i]  = C[z][i] + A[z][i] * B[4-z][7-i];
```

Address resolution: local pointer arrays(6)

```
#define z 0

int D0[8];                          /* local  */
extern int D1[8], D2[8], D3[8]; /* remote */

int B0[8];                          /* local  */
extern int B1[8], B2[8], B3[8]; /* remote */


int *D[4] ={D0,D1,D2,D3}; /* pointer array */
int *B[4] ={B0,B1,B2,B3}; /* pointer array */

for (i = 0; i<=7; i++)

 D[z][i]  = C[z][i] + A[z][i] * B[4-z][7-i];
```

Figure 2: Example showing data transformation and address resolution scheme.

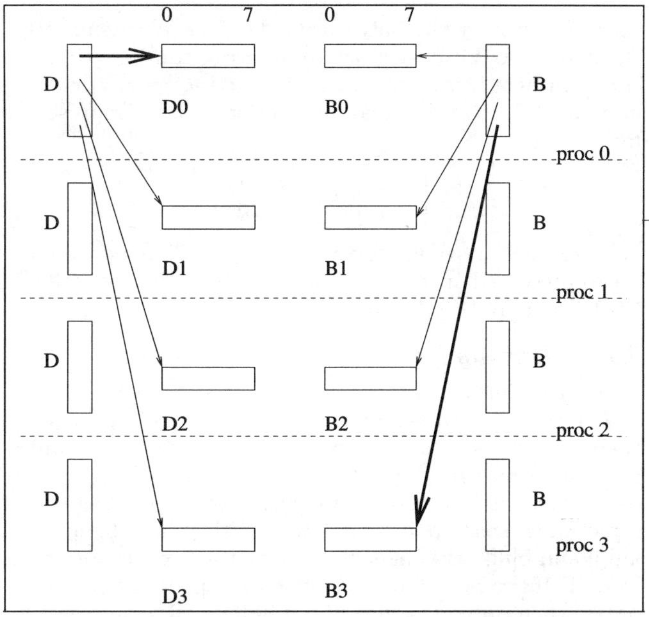

Figure 3: Data layout of arrays B, D for figure 2 box (5). Each processor has a local pointer array. The contents of the pointer arrays on processor 0 are illustrated. The bold lines represent the data accessed by the program in figure 2 box (6)

1. Convert pointers to arrays
2. IF pointer free THEN perform data dependence analysis
   (a) IF parallelizable and worthwhile
      i. Determine data partition
      ii. Partition + transform data and code
      iii. Perform address resolution

Figure 4: Overall parallelization algorithm

We exploit data parallelism within DSP programs by partitioning the data and computation across the processors. Choosing the best data partition has been studied for many years and is NP-complete [5]. In this paper we use a simple method based on exploiting parallelism and reducing communication [16]; later work will use more sophisticated analysis. The key point is that our partitioning approach using data strip-mining makes the processor identifier explicit, which is exactly what is needed to statically determine whether data is local or remote.

3.1.1 Notation

The loop *iterators* can be represented by a column vector $J = [j_1, j_2, \ldots, j_M]^T$ where M is the number of enclosing loops. Note the loops do not need to be perfectly nested and occur arbitrarily in the program. The loop ranges are described by a system of inequalities defining the *polyhedron* or *iteration space* $BJ \leq b$. The data storage of an array can also be viewed as a polyhedron. We introduce array *indices* $\mathcal{I} = [i_1, i_2, \ldots, i_N]^T$, to describe the *array index space*. This space is given by the polyhedron $A\mathcal{I} \leq a$. We assume that the subscripts in a reference to an array can be written as $\mathcal{U}J+u$, where $\mathcal{U}$ is an integer matrix and u is a vector. Thus in figure 2, box(2) the array declaration `D[32]` is represented by

$$\begin{bmatrix} -1 \\ 1 \end{bmatrix} [i_1] \leq \begin{bmatrix} 0 \\ 31 \end{bmatrix} \tag{1}$$

i.e. the index i_1 ranges over $0 \leq i_1 \leq 31$ The loop bounds are represented in a similar manner and the subscript of `D[i]` is simply $[1][j_1] + [0]$.

3.1.2 Partitioning

Determining those index dimensions that may be evaluated in parallel, in general, gives a number of options and therefore we use a simple technique to reduce communication based on data alignment. If two array references have every element in a certain dimension corresponding to the same index space points then we say they are aligned. i.e. a[i][j] and b[i][k] are aligned on the first index but not on the second. If two arrays are aligned with respect to a particular index, then no matter how those individual array elements are partitioned, any reference with respect to this index will always be local. Partitioning based on alignment tries to maximize the rows that are equal in a subscript matrix.

Let $\delta(x, y)$ be defined as follows:

$$\delta(x, y) = \begin{cases} 1 & x = y \wedge x \neq 0 \\ 0 & otherwise \end{cases} \tag{2}$$

This function determines whether two subscripts are non-zero and equal. The function $H(i)$ defined as:

$$H(i) = \sum_t \delta(\mathcal{U}_i^1, \mathcal{U}_i^t) \tag{3}$$

which measures how well a particular index i of an array read in assignment, $\mathcal{U}^t$, is aligned with the assigned array, $\mathcal{U}^1$. For each index the value of H is calculated, the index with the highest value being the one to partition along.

This technique is applied across all statements and in general there will be conflicting partition requirements. Currently, we consider only those statements in the deepest nested loops as they dominate execution time and calculate the value of H across all these statements for different parallel indices i. The highest value, $MaxH$, determines the index to partition along. We construct a partition matrix $\mathcal{P}$ defined:

$$\mathcal{P}_i = \begin{cases} e_i^T & i = MaxH \\ 0 & otherwize \end{cases} \tag{4}$$

where e_i^T is the ith row of the identity matrix. We also construct a sequential matrix $\mathbf{S}$ containing those indices not partitioned such that $\mathcal{P} + \mathbf{S} = I$. In the example in figure 2 there is only one index to partition along therefore

$$\mathcal{P} = [\ 1\ ]\ \mathbf{S} = [\ 0\ ] \tag{5}$$

3.1.3 Mapping

Once the array indices to partition have been decided, we data strip-mine the indices $\mathcal{I}$ based on the partition matrix $\mathcal{P}$ and strip-mine matrix S to give the new array indices $\mathcal{I}'$.

The data strip-mining matrix S is defined:

$$S = \begin{bmatrix} (.)\%p \\ (.)/p \end{bmatrix} \tag{6}$$

where p is the number of processors. In our example in figure 2, $p = 4$ For further details of the transformation framework see [14]. Here, the transformation is used to expose the processor ID of all array references and is critical to our scheme. To show this, let T be the mapping transformation

$$T = \mathcal{P}S + \mathbf{S} \tag{7}$$

thus the partitioned indices are strip-mined and the sequential indices left alone. In our example

$$T = [1]S + [0] = S \tag{8}$$

and the new array indices, $\mathcal{I}'$, are given by

$$\mathcal{I}' = T\mathcal{I} \tag{9}$$

The new array bounds, $A'\mathcal{I}' \leq a'$ are then found using

$$\begin{bmatrix} T & O \\ O & T \end{bmatrix} AT^{-1}\mathcal{I}' \leq \begin{bmatrix} T & O \\ O & T \end{bmatrix} a \tag{10}$$

which transforms the bounds in equation (1) to:

$$\begin{bmatrix} -1 & 0 \\ 0 & -1 \\ 1 & 0 \\ 0 & 1 \end{bmatrix} \begin{bmatrix} i_1 \\ i_2 \end{bmatrix} \leq \begin{bmatrix} 0 \\ 0 \\ 3 \\ 7 \end{bmatrix} \tag{11}$$

i.e `int D[4][8]` The new array subscripts are also found: $\mathcal{U}' = T\mathcal{U}$. In general, without any further loop transformations, this will introduce `mods` and `divs` into the array accesses. In our example in figure 2 we would have `D[i%4,i/4] = C[i%4,i/4] + A[i%4,i/4] * B[(32-i)%4,(32-i)/4]`

However, this framework [14] always generates a suitable recovery loop transformation, in this case the same transformation T. The original loop bounds, $BJ \leq b$ in figure 2, box(2) are given by

$$\begin{bmatrix} -1 \\ 1 \end{bmatrix} [j_1] \leq \begin{bmatrix} 0 \\ 31 \end{bmatrix} \tag{12}$$

i.e. the iterator `i` ranges over $0 \leq$ `i` ≤ 31. Applying T to the enclosing loop iterators gives the new iterators

$$J' = TJ \tag{13}$$

The new iterator bounds, $B'J' \leq b'$ are then found using

$$\begin{bmatrix} T & O \\ O & T \end{bmatrix} BT^{-1}J' \leq \begin{bmatrix} T & O \\ O & T \end{bmatrix} b \tag{14}$$

which transforms the bounds in equation (12) to:

$$\begin{bmatrix} -1 & 0 \\ 0 & -1 \\ 1 & 0 \\ 0 & 1 \end{bmatrix} \begin{bmatrix} j_1 \\ j_2 \end{bmatrix} \leq \begin{bmatrix} 0 \\ 0 \\ 3 \\ 7 \end{bmatrix} \tag{15}$$

i.e $0 \leq$ `z` $\leq 3, 0 \leq$ `i` ≤ 7 as shown in box (4) of figure 2. Updating the access matrices we have, for array `D`:

$$\mathcal{U}'' = T\mathcal{U}T^{-1} = \begin{bmatrix} 1 & 0 \\ 0 & 1 \end{bmatrix} \begin{bmatrix} j_1 \\ j_2 \end{bmatrix} \tag{16}$$

i.e.`D[z][i]`. The resulting code is shown in figure 2 box(4) where we have exposed the processor ID of each reference without any expensive subscript expressions.

1. For each program $q_i \in 1, \ldots p$
    (a) For each arrayName
        i. For $j \in 1, \ldots, p$
            A. IF $(j \neq i)$ THEN insert (`extern`)
            B. insert(TYPE arrayName$j$`[`N/p`];`)
        ii. insert (TYPE `*`arrayName`[`p`] = (`)
        iii. For $j \in 1, \ldots, p-1$
            A. insert (arrayName$j$ `,`)
        iv. insert (arrayName$p$ `,);`)

Figure 5: Address Resolution

3.2 Address Resolution

Once the array is partitioned across several processors, each local partition has to be given a new name as there is no single address space supported. Furthermore, the names must be distinct as two variables having the same name on distinct processors are assumed to be private variables. We therefore introduce a new name equal to the old name followed by the processor identify number. Thus, in a four processor system, X will be replaced by four local arrays $X0, X1, X2, X3$. We wish one of these arrays to reside and be allocated on the local processor and the remainder be declared `extern` allowing remote references, the address of which will be resolved by the linker.

In order to minimize the impact on code generation, a pointer array of size p is introduced which points to the start address of each of the p sub-arrays. Unlike the sub-arrays, this pointer array is replicated across the p processors and is initialized by an array initialization statement at the beginning of the program. The complete algorithm is given in figure 5 where the function insert, inserts the declarations. Figure 2, box (6), shows the declarations inserted for two of the arrays, `D` and `B`. The declarations for the remaining arrays are omitted due to lack of space.

The only further change is the type declaration whenever the arrays are passed into function. The type declaration is changed from `int [] []` to `*int[]` and this must be propagated interprocedurely. Once this has been applied, no further transformation or code modification is required.

3.2.1 Synchronization

It is beyond the scope of this paper to describe synchronization placement, though this is essential for correct execution. We mark all cross-processor dependences and use a graph based algorithm to insert the minimal number of barrier synchronizations [15].

4. EXPERIMENTAL FRAMEWORK

The best publicly available, auto-parallelizing, C compiler SUIF produces shared-memory data parallel C codes from sequential C input files and required the porting of the SUIF parallel runtime library to our target architecture. We prototyped our algorithm in the SUIF 1.3 compiler and evaluated it against the well-known DSP benchmark suite, UTDSP [11]. UTDSP contains both DSP kernels and applications. The programs were executed on a Transtech TS-P36N board with a cluster of four cross-connected 250MHz TigerSHARC TS-101 DSPs, all sharing the same external bus and 128MB of external SDRAM. The programs were compiled with the Analog Devices VisualDSP++ Compiler (version 6.1.18) with full optimization; all timings are cycle accurate. In addition to the partitioning and address resolution scheme described in the paper, further locality optimisations to exploit DMA transfers were also applied. This is beyond the scope of this paper. For further details see [4].

4.1 Performance

4.1.1 Parallelism and Scalability

While 19 of the 30 UTDSP programs are parallel, only 9 of the 19 are determined profitably parallelizable by our technique. The others are either sequential or exhibit too little work to parallelize and are rejected at stage 2(a) in our overall algorithm (see figure 4). Figure 6 shows how our approach scales with the number of processors for three selected programs, the *Compress, FIR 256/64* and *Mult_10_10* benchmarks. *Mult_10_10* only contains a 10 by 10 array yet after distributing the data across the processors, some speedup is available. In the other cases, with larger data sizes, the full potential of parallel execution can be exploited giving linear speedup with the number of processors.

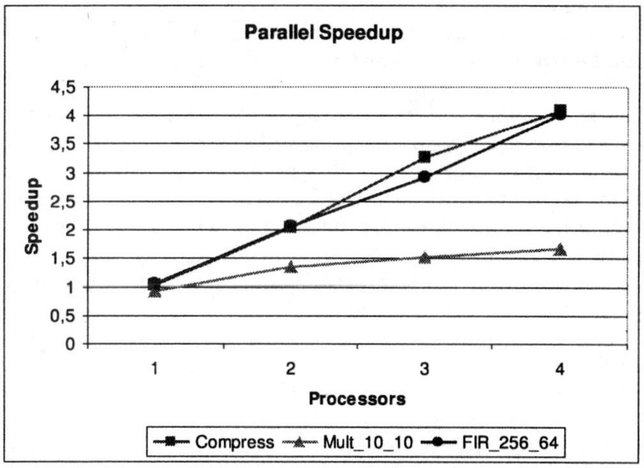

Figure 6: Speedup for different numbers of processors

4.1.2 Speedup due to Parallelization

An overview of the speedup of the selected UTDSP programs over their sequential versions is shown in figure 7. All programs benefit from our approach and show a substantial speedup in the range of 1.54 to 5.69. Linear or close to linear speedup is achieved for four programs (*FIR256/64, IIR4/64, Compress, Edge Detect*), whereas one program (*JPEG filter*) experiences super-linear speedup due to better sequential code generation after parallelization. The remaining three programs do not scale that well with the number of processors, still the speedup due to parallelization is at least 1.5. On average, we have a speedup of 3.25 across the four processors.

5. RELATED WORK

A good overview of existing parallelization techniques is given by Gupta et al. [6]. Cache-coherent multiprocessors with distributed shared memory are the subject of Chandra et al. [5]. Although compilers for such machines must

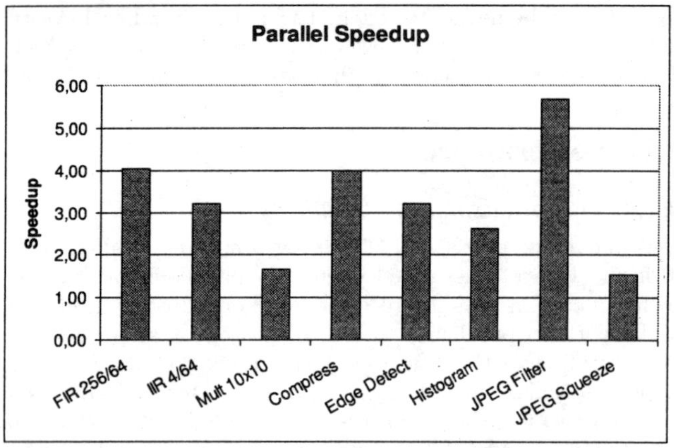

Figure 7: Speedup: UTDSP benchmarks on 4 processors

incorporate data distribution and data locality increasing techniques [2], they are not faced with the problem of multiple, but globally-addressable address spaces. Compiler-Implemented Shared Memory (CISM) as described by Larus [10] and Hiranandani et al. [7] is a method to establish shared memory on message-passing computers. However, these approaches assume separate distributed address spaces and require complex run-time bookkeeping. In [2], data tiling is used to improve spatial locality but the representation does not allow easy integration with other loop and data transformations.

An early paper [18] described how DSP programs may be parallelized but gave no details or experimental results. Similarly, in [8] an interesting overall parallelization framework is described but no mechanism or details of how parallelization might take place is provided. In [13] the impact of different parallelization techniques is considered, however, this was user-directed and no automatic approach provided. In [9] a semi-automatic parallelization method to enable design-space exploration of different multi-processor configurations based on the MOVE architecture is presented. However, no integrated data partitioning strategy was available and a single address space was assumed in the example codes. Furthermore, in the experiments, communication was modelled in their simulator and thus the issue of mapping parallelism combined with distributed address spaces was not addressed.

6. CONCLUSION

In this paper we have developed a new compiler parallelization approach that maps C programs onto multiple address space multi-DSPs. By using a novel data transformation and address resolution mechanism, we have achieved an average 3.25 speedup on four processors for those UTDSP program's containing sufficient parallelism.

The code generated is easy to read and amenable to further sequential optimization. Future work will consider the integration of multi-processor and uni-processor optimizations and consider the integration of task and pipeline parallelism.

7. REFERENCES

[1] Analog Devices, Inc. TigerSHARC DSP Hardware Specification Norwood, Mass., 2001.

[2] J. Anderson, S. Amarasinghe and M. Lam, Data and computation transformations for multiprocessors *ACM PPoPP*, 1995.

[3] B. Franke , M. F.P. O'Boyle, Array recovery and high-level transformations for DSP applications, *ACM Transactions on Embedded Computing Systems (TECS) 2 (2)*,2003.

[4] B. Franke , M. F.P. O'Boyle, Combining Program Recovery, Auto-parallelisation and Locality Analysis for C programs on Multi-processor Embedded Systems (to appear) *IEEE PACT* 2003.

[5] R. Chandra, D.-K. Chen, R. Cox, D.E. Maydan, N. Nedeljkovic, J.M. Anderson, Data Distribution Support on Distributed Shared Memory Multiprocessors. *ACM PLDI*, Las Vegas, 1997.

[6] R. Gupta, S. Pande, K. Psarris, V. Sakar, Compilation Techniques for Parallel Systems. *Parallel Computing*, 25(13), 1999.

[7] S. Hiranandani, K. Kennedy, C.-W-. Tseng, Compiling Fortran D for MIMD Distributed-Memory Machines. *CACM,35,(8)*, 1992.

[8] A. Kalavade, J. Othmer, B. Ackland, K.J. Singh, Software Environment for a Multiprocessor DSP. *ACM/IEEE Design Automation Conference*, 1999.

[9] I. Karkowski, H. Corporaal, Exploiting Fine- and Coarse-grain Parallelism in Embedded Programs. *IEEE PACT*, , 1998.

[10] J.R. Larus. Compiling for Shared-Memory and Message-Passing Computers. ACM LOPLAS 2, (1-4), 1993.

[11] C.G. Lee, UTDSP Benchmark Suite. *http://www.eecg.toronto.edu/ corinna/DSP*

[12] E.A. Lee, Dataflow process networks. *Proceedings of the IEEE*, 83(5), May 1995.

[13] D.M. Lorts, Combining Parallelization Techniques to Increase Adaptability and Efficiency of Multiprocessing DSP Systems. *DSP-2000*, Hunt, Texas, 2000.

[14] O'Boyle M.F.P and Knijnenberg P.M.W., Integrating Loop and Data Transformations for Global Optimisation, *JPDC*, 62, April 2002.

[15] O'Boyle M.F.P. and Stohr E.A., Compile Time Barrier Synchronisation Minimisation, *IEEE TPDS*, 13(6), June 2002.

[16] O'Boyle M.F.P. and Hedayat G.A., Data Alignment: Transformation to Reduce Communication on Distributed Memory Architectures, *IEEE Scalable High Performance Computing Conference*, 1992.

[17] E. Rypkema, E.F. Deprettere, B. Kienhuis, Compilation from Matlab to Process Networks. *CASES*, 1999.

[18] J. Teich, L. Thiele, Uniform Design of Parallel Programs for DSP. *IEEE Int. Symp. Circuits and Systems*, Singapore, June 1991.

[19] V. Zivojnovic, J.M. Velarde, C. Schlager, H. Meyr, DSPstone: A DSP-Oriented Benchmarking Methodology. *Proc. Signal Processing Applications & Technology*, Dallas, 1994.

Architectural Analysis and Instruction-Set Optimization for Design of Network Protocol Processors*

Haiyong Xie†, Li Zhao, and Laxmi Bhuyan
Computer Science & Engineering Department
University of California, Riverside
Riverside, CA 92521
{zhao, bhuyan}@cs.ucr.edu

ABSTRACT

TCP/IP protocol processing latency has been an important issue in high-speed networks. In this paper, we present an architectural study of TCP/IP protocol. We port the TCP/IP protocol stack from the 4.4 FreeBSD to the SimpleScalar simulation environment. The architectural characteristics, such as instruction level parallelism and cache behavior, are studied through simulation. We also compare the characteristics of TCP/IP protocol to that of SPECint benchmark programs. It turns out that the former is quite different from the latter due to the unique processing structure. Furthermore, in order to improve the effectiveness of instruction cache, frequent instruction pairs are analyzed, and corresponding architectural optimizations are made to the instruction set architecture. The performance is evaluated in the simulator. We find that a 23% improvement can be achieved by taking advantage of the optimization. The instruction set optimizations proposed in this paper will be helpful for the design of new programmable protocol processors in future.

Categories and Subject Descriptors

C.3 [**Special-Purpose and Application-Based Systems**]: Realtime and Embedded Systems

General Terms

Measurement, Design, Performance

Keywords

Network processing, Architecture simulation, Instruction optimization, TCP/IP protocol

*The research was supported in part by NSF grants CCR-0220096 and ACI-0233858.

†Haiyong Xie is currently with Computer Science Department at Yale University, New Haven, CT 06520. His current email address is yong@cs.yale.edu.

CODES+ISSS'03, October 1–3, 2003, Newport Beach, California, USA.

1. INTRODUCTION

The gaps between the available network bandwidth, CPU computation power, and the speed of memory system are expanding day by day. In the past decade, the speed of the physical layer has increased exponentially due to break-through advances in technology. The bandwidth of the Internet's trunk lines has increased over the years to 10 Gbps and will continue to grow at a rate of 4 times per year. This growth is much faster than that of the CPU performance and has led to a growing gap between the transmission bandwidth and processor speed [4][18].

The demands on needed computation power of CPUs and speed of memory systems to sustain higher network bandwidth are greater than ever before. For instance, in order to process a typical 64-byte TCP control packet, the CPU has to complete TCP/IP protocol processing and deliver the packet to the network interface card in 512 ns to sustain the 1Gbps bandwidth. However, as revealed by our study, the TCP/IP protocol stack executes more than 1600 instructions to process such a packet on a RISC machine (similar results in [15]). This means that for a CPU running at 1GHz with 1 instruction per cycle, it will take more than 1600 CPU cycles, or equivalently more than 1600 ns, to process such a packet. This time is for critical path processing, and does not include time on the connection establishment and tear-down, nor does it take into consideration factors such as memory access latency, the overhead introduced by the operating system, and the capability of upper layer applications. We conclude, therefore, that with special optimizations current computer systems do not have enough capability to fully sustain networks operating at 1Gbps bandwidth or higher.

TCP/IP protocol processing latency is vital to the overall performance of special network devices such as web switches [5][7], which perform not only transport-layer but also application-layer functions. With increasing demand on highly secure transmissions over network, future routers will have to look into both layer 4 and 5 information. Currently, network processors with hardware accelerators, multi-threading and multiprocessing are being designed and marketed aggressively. However, implementing protocol processing in network processors is a major concern, and poses several challenges.

TCP/IP processing latency can be attributed to two aspects: data-touching operations and non-data-touching operations [11][12]. Data-touching operations such as checksum computations dominate the processing latencies of large packets, and consume approximately 70% of the total processing overhead. However, non-data-touching operations, such as protocol data structure manipulation and protocol specific operations, are dominant in case of small- and medium-payload packets. Extensive research has been conducted to maximize the throughput by improving data-touching operations [1][8].

However, when a realistic distribution of message size is considered, non-data-touching operations introduce 84% of total protocol processing latency for TCP and 60% for UDP [11][12], which indicates that it is more important to improve processing of non-data-touching operations. Hence, we primarily focus on reducing the latencies for non-data-touching operations.

In this paper, we take TCP/IP protocol processing as an independent workload and study its various architectural characteristics by means of simulation. We measure the impact of architectural parameters like ILP and cache behavior on the TCP performance. Comparisons between TCP/IP and SPECint2000 [19] benchmark programs are also made in order to highlight the different characteristics.

We port the reference implementation of TCP/IP protocol stack in 4.4 FreeBSD [14] to the SimpleScalar simulation environment [17]. To the best of our knowledge, we are the first to run the complete standard TCP/IP protocol stack from Berkeley UNIX implementation in an execution-driven simulator. We extend the SimpleScalar simulation tool-set to break down the execution time into three categories: CPU execution time, data access time and instruction access time. This extended simulator is used to study architectural characteristics of, and evaluate the optimization for, TCP/IP protocol processing.

It is observed that the instruction cache has a greater impact on TCP/IP performance. In order to improve effectiveness of an instruction cache, we identify the frequently used instruction pairs by extending the simulator and profiling the protocol stack. We design and implement some new instructions for the simulated CPU so that the frequently used instruction pairs can be replaced with corresponding new instructions. By doing so, we expect to not only reduce the total number of instructions needed to process each packet, but also improve instruction cache performance and reduce the execution time. We make only minor modification to the instruction set architecture and evaluate the overall performance of this new ISA in the simulator. We find that 23% improvement can be achieved by taking advantage of the minor extensions to the instruction set architecture. This observation can be used to help design new programmable protocol processors in the future.

The rest of this paper is organized as follows. Section 2 describes the methodology employed in our work and the parameters of the simulation environment. The synthetic network traffic trace is described as well. Section 3 presents various results of performance evaluation with SimpleScalar. We also make comparisons between TCP/IP workload and SPECint benchmark programs. Section 4 analyzes the patterns of frequent instruction pairs and makes architectural optimizations to the instruction set architecture in order to improve the latency of non-data-touch operations. Section 5 presents background and related work. Section 6 concludes the paper.

2. METHODOLOGY

This section describes the methodologies used to evaluate the performance of TCP/IP protocol processing, including execution-driven simulation and synthetic network traces.

2.1 Execution-driven simulation

We use SimpleScalar Tool Set 3.0 to study the architectural characteristics of protocol processing. The default processor architecture we simulate has 16K 4-way set-associative L1 instruction and data caches. Both have block sizes of 32 bytes and LRU as the replacement strategy. The data cache is write-back, write-allocate, and non-blocking with 2 ports. There is a 256K 4-way set associative unified L2 cache with 64-byte blocks and a 6-cycle hit latency. The processor has an instruction level parallelism of 4, and bimodal as the default branch predictor. The bimodal branch predictor used in our reference processor is not state of the art, however, for TCP/IP protocol workload, it is almost as good as the perfect predictor, which is not shown in this paper due to space limitations.

We extend the detailed timing simulator, *sim-outorder*, to further break down the total execution time into three categories: CPU execution time when there are instructions being executed without stalling for data or instruction access, data access time when CPU stalls due to data cache misses, and instruction access time when CPU stalls due to instruction cache misses. The overlapped access time when CPU stalls waiting for both data and instruction access is taken as data access time.

2.2 Network traffic trace

TCP/IP protocol processing latency depends directly on the packet size. The packet sizes of both local area networks and wide area networks conform to bimodal distribution [20]. We analyze traffic traces available from NLANR for both local area networks (LAN) and wide area networks (WAN). The results in Figure 1 are similar to those in early studies. Approximately 52% of the packets in local area networks are smaller than 200 bytes in size. In the WAN traces, most of the packets (approximately 99%) are smaller than 1500 bytes, and the size distribution of these packets is similar to that of LAN traces.

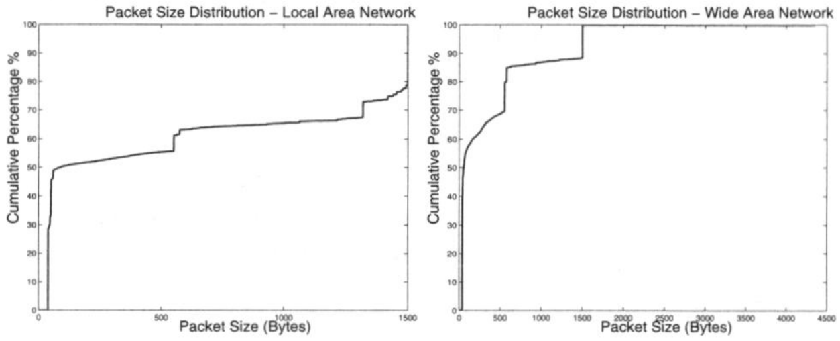

Figure 1: Packet size distribution of LAN and WAN

It is important to study the characteristics of TCP/IP protocol stack with realistic network traffic traces in execution-driven simulators. We instrument a client program with knowledge of the distribution of realistic network traffic. The program establishes TCP connections and transmits data, using predefined packet sizes, the distribution of which conforms to that in Figure 1. By doing so, we generate a synthetic trace of 10K packets. We call this trace as realistic or synthetic network trace throughout this paper. We evaluate the TCP/IP protocol stack in SimpleScalar using this synthetic trace.

3. PERFORMANCE EVALUATION THROUGH SIMULATION

In this section, we present the impact of various architectural parameters on TCP/IP. The results are obtained by running the protocol stack in the simulation environment with the synthetic network trace.

3.1 Instruction mix and ILP

We study the instruction mix and the impact of ILP on execution time by varying the instruction fetch, decode, and issue width and the number of functional units. The results are compared with that of SPECint benchmarks as well, as shown in Figure 2. Note that the execution time has been normalized to that of SPECint programs with ILP being 1. Both the benchmarks and TCP/IP run in the simulation environment with default configuration described in Section 2.

The TCP/IP protocol stack has an unexpected high percentage of unconditional branch instructions. This leads to not-so-good program structures that introduce higher instruction cache miss ratio. The TCP/IP protocol stack has a lower percentage of conditional branch instructions compared to SPECint benchmark. The reason is that the protocol processing is more like a streamlined processing with only a small number of loops. These program properties require different cache configurations compared to SPECint benchmark programs.

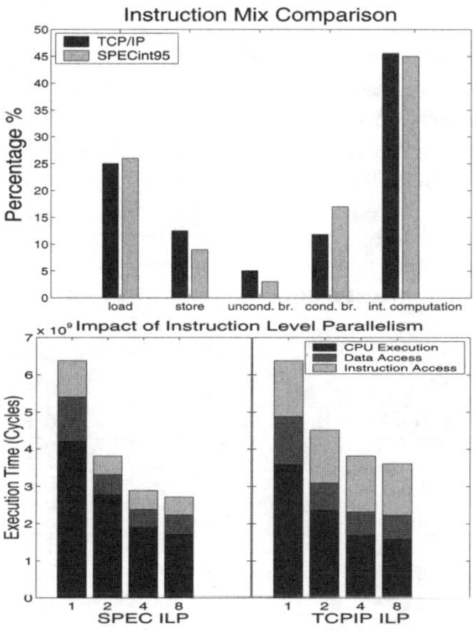

Figure 2: Instruction mix and ILP (top: instruction mix, bottom: ILP)

It is observed that TCP/IP protocol processing is less sensitive to instruction level parallelism, compared to SPECint programs. SPECint programs obtain improvement on both CPU execution time and instruction cache when ILP increases. However, for TCP/IP protocol processing, it does not improve data or instruction access time very much. For instance, the total execution time of SPECint programs improves 40% and 24%, while that of TCP/IP processing improves 29% and 15%, respectively, when the instruction level parallelism increases from 1 to 2 and 2 to 4. However, the execution time improves little (5%) with ILP greater than 4 for both SPECint and TCP/IP programs. The instruction level parallelism in TCP/IP is limited, and other techniques such as multi-threading are needed to go beyond this speed-up. The major problem with TCP/IP lies in the long instruction access time, which is unaffected by increasing ILP. Instruction cache plays a more important role in improving TCP/IP processing latency, as can be seen in later sections.

3.2 Cache behavior

We study both the L1 instruction and data cache behavior by varying such parameters as cache size, line size, and set associativity. Data cache behavior is similar to that of SPECint programs, which is not presented here due to space limitations. The results of instruction cache are presented in Figure 3, and those of SPECint benchmark are also shown in these figures for comparison purpose.

Figure 3 shows the different impact of cache size on L1 instruction cache (the figure on the upper-left). The miss ratio of instruction cache decreases as cache size increases. There is a 60% improvement as the cache size increases from 16KB to 32KB and 74% from 32KB to 64KB. From 64KB and beyond, the improvement is not so much as that from 8KB to 16KB and 64KB, which indicates that capacity misses become dominant. Due to the program structure of the TCP/IP protocol stack, which is a monolithic program with a small number of loops, the requirements on cache size are higher compared to that of SPECint benchmark programs, as can be seen in the figure. Instruction cache is very sensitive to cache size. It is because that TCP/IP has a very large kernel code size and has a large capacity miss. Additionally, data cache does not benefit from larger cache size than 8K and beyond (not shown here). On the contrary, a much smaller cache is enough to bound the miss ratio to a sufficiently low level for SPECint programs.

Similar behavior with varied associativity and line size is shown in Figure 3 as well. Higher associativity and larger line size both have greater impact on instruction cache. From Figure 3 we can see that there exists a great difference between TCP/IP and SPECint programs in terms of instruction cache performance. It is observed that TCP/IP processing almost always performs much worse than SPECint benchmark given the same cache parameters. For instance, a 16KB cache size is nearly enough for most of the programs in the benchmark to reduce instruction cache miss ratio to less than 1%, however, it is not the case with TCP/IP processing, which needs 4 times more cache size to obtain miss ratio less than 1%. It can also be seen that cache associativity and line size have much greater impact on TCP/IP performance than SPECint benchmark programs. For instance, cache miss ratio improves by 51% for TCP/IP processing compared to 25% when line size increases from 16 to 64 bytes. Instruction cache miss ratio continuously improves even when line size is larger than 64 bytes, while SPEC benchmark programs perform worse due to increased miss penalty.

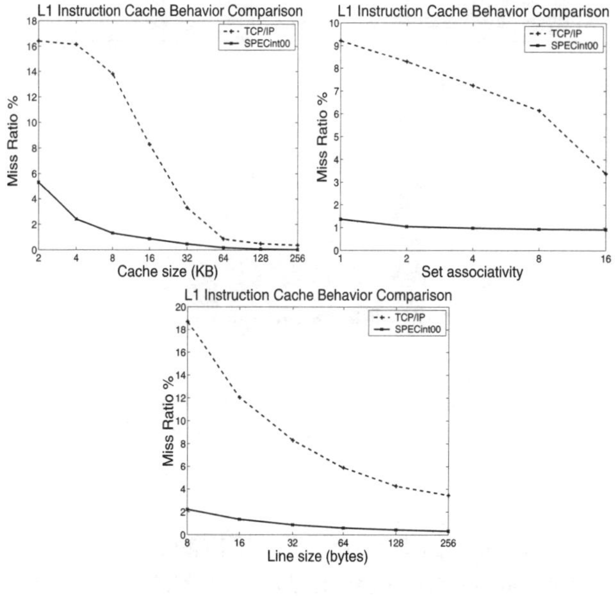

Figure 3: Impact of cache parameters (upper left and right: size, associativity; bottom: line size)

TCP/IP protocol stack benefits more from a instruction cache with larger size, higher associativity, or larger line size, compared to SPECint benchmark programs. The above observation leads to the conclusion that given a total L1 cache size on the chip, more area should be devoted to I-Cache and less to D-Cache. Compiling techniques aimed at minimizing the code size will help as well. In addition, there is a greater need to replace some of the code using hardware units. A detailed hardware/software co-design of the TCP/IP protocol processing is an interesting research direction.

3.3 Execution time analysis of cache behavior

The previous subsection presents the behavior of L1 instruction cache as a function of various architectural parameters. However, we are more concerned with the impact of these parameters on the categorized execution time, the results of which are shown in Figure 4.

It can be seen that CPU execution time accounts for less than a half of the total time in the baseline cases, where the configuration has 16KB 4-way set associative L1 instruction cache with 32-byte line size. In these baseline cases, more than half of the total execution time is spent in waiting for completion of data or instruction accesses. Instruction access time is at least 3 to 4 times longer than data access time when instruction cache performs worse than the baseline cases. It can also be seen that the total execution time is more sensitive to instruction cache performance. For instance, the reduction in execution time is 26% by increasing the cache size from 16KB to 32KB or 32KB to 64KB. Improving instruction cache performance has the greatest impact on overall performance. Data cache has almost negligible impact (around 1% improvement at best) on the overall performance compared to its counterpart.

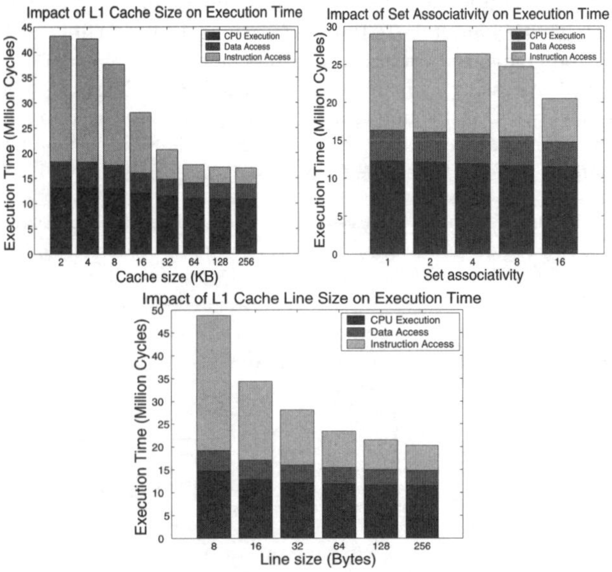

Figure 4: Impact of cache parameters on execution time (upper left and right: size, associativity; bottom: line size)

4. INSTRUCTION-SET OPTIMIZATION FOR NON-DATA-TOUCHING OPERATIONS

Non-data-touching operations dominate the protocol processing latency of the synthetic workload. Based on results in previous sections, instruction cache plays a more important role and therefore should be improved first. In this section, We will extend the ISA with some new instructions so that the frequently used instruction pairs can be replaced with corresponding new instructions. By eliminating frequently used instruction pairs, we expect to not only reduce the total number of instructions executed to process each packet, more importantly, but also improve instruction cache performance and decrease the execution time. The overall performance with this new ISA is evaluated using SimpleScalar.

4.1 Frequent instruction pairs

Frequent instruction pairs are also present in a lot of other network-related programs, e.g., ADD-SUBCC is the most frequent instruction pair occurring in CommBench benchmark programs [21]. The idea of replacing conventional frequent instruction pairs with single instructions has been brought forth by many researchers. The destination register of the first instruction has to be one of source registers of the second instruction. This dependence makes it possible to combine the instruction pair into a single new instruction that performs the same functionality. We extend the simulator to obtain profiling of instruction pairs with such dependence. We get the most frequent instruction pairs as shown in Table 1 with the extended simulator. To concentrate on the behavior of non-data-touching operations, we turn off data-touching operations such as checksum computation.

Table 1: Most frequent pairs with dependence

1st Instruction	2nd Instruction	Occurrence
ADDIU	BNE	4.91%
ANDI	BEQ	4.80%
ADDU	ADDU	3.56%
SLL	OR	3.38%
LUI	ADDU	2.50%
SLTUI	BNE	2.47%
ANDI	SRL	2.47%
SRL	ANDI	2.45%
ADDU	LW	2.29%
ADDIU	BEQ	2.26%

Table 1 shows that the first instruction of most frequent instruction pairs is mostly integer computation instruction. Non-data-touching operations such as header validation and packet classification need to first compute the values and then decide to continue processing or not. That is why such instruction pairs as compute-branch and comparison-branch occur so frequently in protocol processing.

4.2 ISA extension

We elect not to make radical changes to the original ISA. The instruction format and encoding are not changed. Only some new instructions, having the same format as old ones, are introduced.

Note that some of the instruction pairs cannot be combined in a single instruction, e.g., ADDU-ADDU, which may have 5 different register operands and it is impossible to put all of them in a single instruction. We elect to optimize those pairs that have either integer or logic operations followed by branch instructions, which are chosen from Table 1.

The first instruction of the selected pairs has to be either R-type or I-type instruction[1]. By taking advantage of unused bits in an instruction word, all the new instructions have either three register operands and one immediate operand for target address, or two register operands and two immediate operands (one for immediate number, the other for target address). Due to this limitation, only

[1]The format of R-type instructions is opcode rd, rs, rt; the format of I-type instructions is opcode rd, rs, imm. Details can be found in [17].

two types of instruction pairs are considered suitable for replacement, as shown in Table 2. Each type of instruction pairs can be further divided into R-type and I-type.

Table 2: Types of candidate instruction pairs

Type	Conditions	R-type example	I-type example
1	*rd1 == rs1 and*	*addu $2,$2,$3*	*addiu $2,$2,5*
	rd1 == rs2	*beq $2,$5,$L1*	*beq $2,$5,$L1*
2	*rt2 == $0 and*	*addu $2,$3,$4*	*addiu $2,$3,5*
	rd1 == rs2	*beq $2,$0,$L1*	*beq $2,$0,$L1*

In type one instructions, the source register *rs* of the first instruction, denoted as *rs1*, is the same as the destination register *rd1*; in type two, register *rt* of the second instruction, *rt2*, is $0. In both types, the destination register of the first instruction (*rd1*) is the same as one of the source registers of the second instruction (*rs2*). These two types are divided in such a way that the total number of operands can only be 4, either three different register operands and one target address, or two different registers, one immediate number, and one target address (register $0 in type 2 instructions can be safely omitted since it always holds 0).

Since we combine two operations in one, which means that the integer operation (integer computation or logic operation) and the branch operation must be done in one cycle, we need a simpler ALU to do the comparison and branch. The additional simpler ALU won't introduce significant delays to the data path, therefore the ISA with this minor modification will have nearly the same CPU cycle time as the original one.

4.3 Performance evaluation

We have sixteen alternatives to implement the above ISA extension. We can optimize I-type, R-type, or both for either type 1, type 2, or both instruction pairs. We name these alternatives using two letters, which represent the type of optimization for the first and second instruction, respectively. For instance, `rb` stands for optimizing R-type pairs of type 1 and both R- and I-type of type 2 pairs, while `--` stands for no optimizations, which can be taken as the baseline case for comparisons; `i-` stands for optimizing I-type pairs of type 1 only and no optimization for type 2 pairs.

We apply the ISA extension to the simulator, compile TCP/IP protocol using new instructions to replace corresponding pairs for each alternative optimization, and run the protocol stack with synthetic network traffic trace in the simulation environment. Results of performance improvement due to this optimized ISA and the corresponding execution time break-down are shown in Figure 5.

It is found that the number of instructions reduced is not necessarily proportional to the execution time improvement. Therefore, performance improvement of optimizing both type 1 and 2 pairs will not necessarily be the sum of them. I-type and R-type optimizations have different impacts on instruction cache behaviors. Optimizing I-type pairs of both type 1 and 2 has the highest improvement, which is 23% in total and twice as much as the second highest one. We further break down the improvement into 3 major sources: CPU execution, data access, and instruction access, as we did in previous sections. The result is shown in the bottom figure in Figure 5. The improvement comes mainly from improvement of instruction cache accesses. For the case with highest improvement, the CPU stall time due to instruction cache misses improves 47%. On the contrary, CPU execution time and data access time improve 3% and 14% respectively.

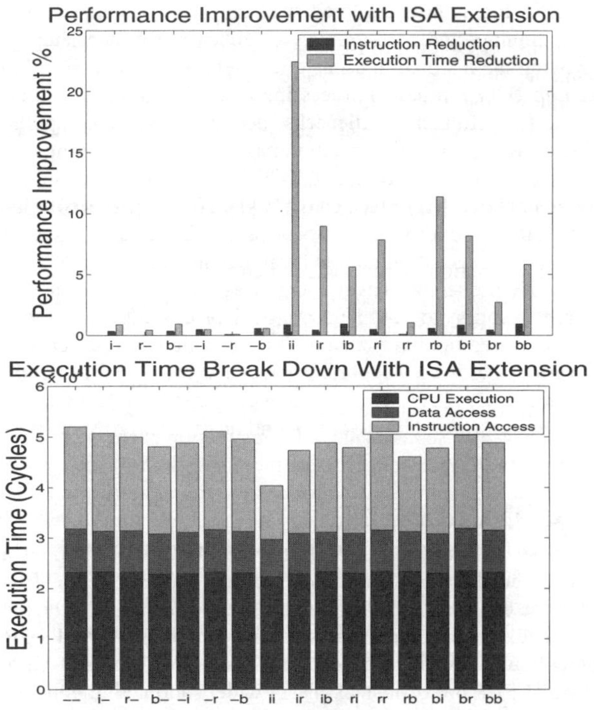

Figure 5: Performance of extended ISA (top: improvement of all configurations, bottom: execution time break-down; --=no optimization, i=I-type, r=R-type, b=both I- and R-type)

5. RELATED WORK

Many researchers have addressed issues of network protocol performance in the past few years. A lot of techniques have been devised to speed up the protocol processing. The research can be broadly divided into two categories. The first is to design and implement low-latency and high-throughput protocols, or to optimize current TCP/IP protocol stack with either the help of compilers to improve the protocol processing latency[15][16] or hardware units to eliminate the data-touching operations such as checksum computation [1][2]. The second is to design new architectures such as network processors to optimize protocol processing [9][13].

Most of the researchers focus on improving the performance of TCP/IP protocols by designing new mechanisms or optimizations. A relatively small number of researchers have studied various architectural characteristics of network protocols.

Some researchers found that the memory system is a key factor in dominating protocol latency and throughput, and the instruction cache has a greater impact on latency [3][15][16]. Erich Nahum *et al.* analyzed the cache behavior of network protocol in *x-kernel* [10]. They found that larger caches and increased associativity improve the performance. However, *x-kernel* is designed as a platform for quickly developing efficient network protocol software and is not implemented in the protocol stacks of real operating systems. We choose the implementation from FreeBSD because it is widely used in the variants of BSD systems and its derivatives exist in a lot of other commercial operating systems. The software structures have not been radically changed in the derivative protocol implementations in various commercial operating systems, although they have been improved over time. We also identified the peculiarity of TCP/IP protocol processing and compared its performance with SPECint benchmark programs.

In [15], the authors explored such compiler techniques as outlining, cloning, and path-inlining to reduce processing latency by improving the instruction cache effectiveness. Another solution to speed up TCP/IP protocol processing is the design of special hardware units to eliminate bottlenecks such as checksum computation and data movement. This solution has been explored in much detail. One example is offloading TCP/IP protocol processing onto intelligent network interface cards [2][1]. However, this solution is not effective in improving protocol processing latency, especially for small messages dominant in local area networks.

Network processors have emerged as another totally new and different solution to speed up protocol processing. Most of the network processors have been optimized with new instruction sets and various hardware supports (such as hardware multi-threading) to reduce processing latencies. However, network processors are not general-purpose processors for end hosts to improve the performance.

6. CONCLUSION

In order to evaluate the performance of TCP/IP protocol and study the headroom of improving protocol processing latency, we ported the complete TCP/IP protocol stack from FreeBSD operating system, which contains the standard implementation of TCP/IP protocol suite, to SimpleScalar simulation environment. Choosing the TCP/IP protocol stack that is widely adopted in both BSD-variant or BSD-derivative operating systems is more meaningful to capture the characteristics of the real systems.

We evaluated the performance of TCP/IP protocol stack and studied such architectural characteristics as ILP and cache behavior. We also identified the peculiarity of TCP/IP protocol processing and compared it with SPECint benchmark programs. They turn out to be quite different due to the unique processing structure and data sets of TCP/IP.

We also extended SimpleScalar simulation environment by dividing execution time into CPU execution time, data access time, and instruction access time. Thus, we could see clearly how the architectural parameters affect the overall performance of protocol processing.

Finally, in order to improve instruction cache which has greater impact on processing latency, frequent instruction pairs were analyzed. To optimize non-data-touching operations, we incorporated new instructions into the SimpleScalar ISA to replace the frequently used instruction pairs. The extension to the original ISA will not introduce much delay into the data path. The reduction in the number of total instruction improves effectiveness of instruction cache. The overall improvement is 23% with only 1% percent of instructions being eliminated when I-type pairs of both type 1 and type 2 are replaced. These results can be used to help design new programmable protocol processors in the future.

7. REFERENCES

[1] Boon S. Ang. An Evaluation of an Attempt at Offloading TCP/IP Protocol Processing onto an i960RN-based iNIC. *HP Labs Technical Report HPL-2001-8*, January 2001

[2] M. Benz. An Architecture and Prototype Implementation for TCP/IP Hardware Support. *TERENA Networking Conference 2001*, Turkey, May 2001

[3] Trevor Blackwell. Speeding Up Protocols for Small Messages. *ACM SIGCOMM Symposium on Communications Architectures and Protocols*, 1996

[4] Ross Callon. Predictions for the Core of the Network. *IEEE Internet Computing*, 4(1), February 2000

[5] Cisco CSS 11000 series content services switches, http://www.cisco.com/warp/public/cc/pd/si/11000/

[6] Ethereal Network Analyzer, http://www.ethereal.com

[7] Foundry Networks, Inc. BigIron, http://www.foundrynet.com/products/l3backbone/bigiron/

[8] A. Gallatin, J. Chase, K. Yocum. Trapeze/IP: TCP/IP at Near-Gigabit Speeds. *USENIX Technical Conference*, June 1999

[9] T. Halfhill. Intel Network Processor Targets Routers. *Microprocessor Report*, September 1999

[10] Norman Hutchingson, and Larry Peterson. The *x*-kernel: An Architecture for implementing network protocols. *IEEE Transactions on Software Engineering*, 17(1):64-76, January 1991

[11] J. Kay and J. Pasquale. The Importance of Non-Data Touching Processing Overheads in TCP/IP. *Proceedings of the SIGCOMM '93 Symposium on Communications Architectures and Protocols*, September 1993.

[12] J. Kay and J. Pasquale. Profiling and reducing processing overheads in TCP/IP. *IEEE/ACM Transactions on Networking*, Vol. 4, No. 6, December 1996

[13] K. Krewell. Rainier Leads PowerNP Family. *Microprocessor Report*, January 2001

[14] M.K. McKusick, K. Bostic, M.J. Karels, and J.S. Quarterman. *The Design and Implementation of the 4.4BSD Unix Operating System*. Adison-Wesley Publishing Company, MA, 1996

[15] D. Mosberger, L.L. Peterson, P.G. Bridges, and S. O'Malley. Analysis of Techniques to Improve Protocol Processing Latency. *Proceedings of SIGCOMM '91 Symposium on Communication Architectures and Protocols*, 1996

[16] E. Nahum, D. Yates, J. Kurose, and D. Towsley. Cache Behavior of Network Protocols. *SIGMETRICS*, 1997

[17] SimpleScalar LLC, http://www.simplescalar.com

[18] Jonathan M. Smith. Seleted Challenges in Computer Networking. *IEEE Computer*, 32(1), Jan 1999

[19] Standard Performance Evaluation Corporation, SPEC CPU 2000 Version 1.2, December 7, 2001

[20] K. Thompson, G. Miller, and R. Wilder. Wide Area Internet Traffic Patterns and Characteristics. *IEEE Network*, 11(6):10-23, November 1997

[21] T. Wolf and M. Franklin. Commbench: A Telecommunications Benchmark for Network Processors. *IEEE International Symposium on Performance Analysis of Systems and Software*, April 2000

Panel

The Future of System-Level Design: Can We Find the Right Solutions to the Right Problems at the Right Time?

Organizer:
Reinaldo Bergamaschi
IBM Research, NY, USA

Organizer & Moderator:
Grant Martin
Cadence Labs,
Berkeley, CA, USA

Panelists:

Wayne Wolf
Princeton University,
NJ, USA

Rolf Ernst
TU Braunschweig, Germany

Jack Kouloheris
IBM Research, NY, USA

Kees Vissers
UC Berkeley, CA, USA

Over the last 15 years we have seen and helped the evolution of design from behavioral modeling to hardware/software co-design, to today's system-level design. Arguably, many of the research efforts on behavioral synthesis, hardware / software co-design, co-simulation etc. have made their way into successful commercial tools, while others went no further than a conference paper. As we continue and expand system-level research with new approaches opening exciting new research avenues, we have an obligation to look back at our successes and failures. Then looking towards the future, we must answer the question: are we solving the right problems with the right solutions at the right time, or should we go back to the drawing board and think of brand new research approaches?

This panel will bring together panelists experienced in various aspects of system-level design who will present different views on what this community has achieved over the last 15 years and draw a roadmap for future research.

CODES+ISSS '03, October 1-3, 2003, Newport Beach, California, USA.
ACM 1-58113-742-7/03/0010.

CODES+ISSS 2004

PRELIMINARY CALL FOR PAPERS

http://www.ida.liu.se/codes/

Submission deadline: Monday, April 12, 2004

Stockholm, Sweden
Sept. 8-10, 2004

PREMIER EVENT IN SYSTEM LEVEL DESIGN

CODES+ISSS 2004 is the Second IEEE/ACM International Conference on Hardware/Software Codesign and System Synthesis. It is the premier event in design of embedded systems hardware, software, and tools. We are proud to contiue the tradition of upholding high quality in an open forum for promoting active discussion on innovative topics. The program actively seeks industry participation. High-quality original papers will be accepted for oral presentation followed by interactive poster sessions. Proceedings are published by ACM SIGDA, and select papers from the conference proceedings will be targeted for journal publication in a special issue.

AREAS OF INTEREST

The CODES-ISSS Conference invites papers on all aspects of the design and architecture of semi-custom heterogeneous embedded computing systems – such as medical devices, cell phones, network processors, handheld computers, automotive and multimedia systems, systems-on-a-chip (SoCs). Topics of interest include, but are not limited to:

1) High-level, architectural and system-level synthesis
Specification and modeling, design representation, synthesis, partitioning, estimation, design space exploration, codesign for reliable systems.

2) Hardware/software codesign
Codesign methodologies, test and debug strategies, interaction between architecture and software design, design space exploration beyond traditional hw/sw boundary, theory and algorithms.

3) Specification languages
System level models and semantics, timing, power, formal properties, heterogeneous systems and components

4) Embedded systems software
Compilers, memory management, virtual machines, scheduling, concurrent software for SoCs, distributed/resource aware OS, OS and middleware support for application specific processors.

5) Embedded systems architecture
Heterogeneous multiprocessors, reconfigurable platforms, memory management support, communication, protocols, network-on-chip.

6) Application-specific processor architectures and synthesis
Network processors, media processors, app-specific HW accelerators, reconfigurable processors, low power embedded processors, bio/fluidic processors.

7) Synthesis, modeling, and analysis
Low power, power-aware, testable, reliable, verifiable systems, performance modeling, validation and cosimulation, security issues.

8) Industrial practices and benchmark suites
System design, processor design, software, tools, case studies, trends, emerging technologies, experience maintaining benchmark suites, representation, interchange format, tools, copyrights, maintenance, reference implementations, and metrics.

9) New topics
New challenges for next generation semi-custom heterogeneous computing systems, arising from new technologies (e.g., nanotechnology) or new applications (e.g., ubiquitous computing). Studies of how technology and applications interact to motivate new solutions and design approaches, e.g., on-chip heterogeneous multiprocessing and user-friendly HCI leading to new programmer's views in system-level design and resulting in new benchmarks, models, architectures, design tools and methodologies.

New for 2004!

10) Design track: new solutions for the design of embedded systems
This track will be devoted to contributions that highlight design experiences of great interest to the community, by demonstrating the application of new theoretical approaches as well as state-of-the-art methodologies and tools to real-life problems

PAPER SUBMISSION

Papers should represent original work not published or submitted for publication in other forums. Formal proceedings will be published by ACM SIGDA in hardcopy, web page, and a CD-ROM forms. Papers should be submitted electronically over the web. By Mar.15 the CODES-ISSS website will open its paper submission page that will guide the authors through the submission process. The paper must be in PDF and should not exceed 6 pages. It should follow the ACM two-column proceedings format at a minimum of 9pt on 8.5"x11", letter-sized page (no A4 please). For the purpose of anonymous review, DO NOT REVEAL AUTHORSHIP DIRECTLY OR INDIRECTLY THROUGH REFERENCES. LaTeX users: please make sure your PDF uses vectored fonts, not bitmapped fonts.

By submitting a paper, the authors agree to prepare the final camera ready version and to present the paper in person at the symposium, if the paper is accepted.

Proposals for group discussions and special sessions are also invited. These should be single page proposals succinctly outlining the topic, problem(s) addressed, positioning and likely participants. Attention must be paid to audience participation in such discussions. While all technical topics within the areas of interest are welcome, we are especially interested in emerging technical areas.

IMPORTANT DATES

Deadline for submission:	**Monday, April 12, 2004**
Notification of acceptance:	**Friday, June 11, 2004**
Deadline for final version:	**Monday, July 5, 2004**

Papers submitted after the deadline, exceeding the page limit, or unveiling the authorship will automatically be rejected.

General Co-Chairs:

Alex Orailoglu
CSE, Univ. of California, San Diego
alex@cs.ucsd.edu

Pai H. Chou
EECS, Univ. of California, Irvine
chou@ece.uci.edu

Program Co-Chairs:

Petru Eles
Linköping University, Sweden
petel@ida.liu.se

Axel Jantsch
Royal Institute of Technology, Sweden
axel@mit.kth.se

Past General Co-Chairs:

Rajesh Gupta
CSE, Univ. of California, San Diego
gupta@cs.ucsd.edu

Yukihiro Nakamura
Kyoto University, Japan
nakamura@i.kyoto-u.ac.jp

Co-sponsored by (pending)

IEEE | CIRCUITS AND SYSTEMS SOCIETY | IEEE COMPUTER SOCIETY | acm | SIGda | SIGSOFT | SIGBED

Author Index